"This work fills a great need in dealing  people raise to challenge the credibility (despite its apparent size), and systematically read but to be used as a constant resource
—Darrell L. Bock, executive direct Howard G. Hendricks Center for Christian Leadership and Cultural Engagement, and senior research professor of New Testament studies, Dallas Theological Seminary

"At the core of the Christian gospel are the historical figure of Jesus of Nazareth and the historical events of his death and resurrection. The question of whether the Bible bears accurate testimony to the Messiah and his saving cross-work is therefore literally a matter of life and death. In this far-ranging compendium, Craig Blomberg painstakingly defends the historical reliability of Scripture and helpfully equips those who want to do the same. Highly recommended!"
—Andreas J. Köstenberger, senior research professor of New Testament and biblical theology, Southeastern Baptist Theological Seminary, and founder of Biblical Foundations™

"Thirty years ago (1987), Blomberg's *Historical Reliability of the Gospels* catapulted the author to prominence by demonstrating the weakness of many arguments against the reliability of the Synoptic Gospels. Blomberg would later write similar defenses of the reliability of John (2001) and of the entire Bible (2014). In this helpful volume, Blomberg shows the compelling evidence that supports the historical reliability of the New Testament as a whole. Exemplary scholarship, cogent argumentation, clear and interesting prose, and constant demonstration of the relevance of the topic all combine to make this an outstanding tool for Christians seeking to answer contemporary arguments against the reliability of the New Testament. Highly recommended!"
—Charles L. Quarles, director of PhD studies and professor of New Testament and biblical theology, Southeastern Baptist Theological Seminary

"I cannot think of a better person to write a book on the reliability of the New Testament than Craig Blomberg. We do not have the reflections of a novice here but of a seasoned and veteran scholar, one whose work has stood the test of time. All the virtues of Blomberg's scholarship are on display here: he is well versed in secondary sources, he is unfailingly fair to those who hold different views, and his own judgments reflect careful assessment of the evidence. Blomberg demonstrates that trust in the reliability of the New Testament is reasonable; one doesn't have to put one's head in the sand to find in the New Testament writings words that are true and accurate."

—Thomas R. Schreiner, associate dean of the School of Theology and James Buchanan Harrison Professor of New Testament Interpretation, The Southern Baptist Theological Seminary

"When it comes to a fair, accurate, and balanced defense of the historical reliability of the New Testament, no one does it better today than Craig Blomberg. This far-ranging volume summarizes much of Blomberg's previous work and brings together a wealth of evangelical scholarship in a clear and accessible format. It is another masterpiece from one of the leading voices in New Testament studies."

—Mark L. Strauss, University Professor of New Testament, Bethel Seminary

The Historical
Reliability of the
New Testament

B&H STUDIES in Christian Apologetics

Robert B. Stewart, *General Editor*

The Historical Reliability of the New Testament

Countering the Challenges to Evangelical Christian Beliefs

CRAIG L. BLOMBERG

ACADEMIC

NASHVILLE, TENNESSEE

für Eckhard Schnabel
Freund, Modell, und Inspiration

CONTENTS

PART TWO: THE GOSPEL OF JOHN

PART THREE: ACTS AND PAUL

PART FIVE: CANONICITY AND TRANSMISSION

PART SIX: THE PROBLEM OF MIRACLES

FOREWORD

Sometime in the latter part of the first decade of the 2000s, Dr. Eckhard Schnabel, the Mary French Rockefeller Distinguished Professor of New Testament Studies at Gordon-Conwell Seminary, asked me when I was going to write a book on the historical reliability of Acts. I chuckled because I thought he was teasing me for my seemingly one-track mind. I had already written several books that impinged on the topic of the historical reliability of the Gospels and imagined him to be showing mock surprise that I hadn't written yet one more on the one other major narrative portion of the New Testament. As it turned out, he was completely serious, so my next reply was to point out that *he* was the one at the time writing a major commentary on Acts (for the Zondervan Exegetical Commentary on the New Testament),[1] and I was sure he would have plenty on questions of the historicity of the passages as he made his comments.

Eckhard replied that he had already had to axe substantial amounts of text to reduce the commentary to the parameters the series and the

---

[1] Now available as Eckhard J. Schnabel, *Acts* (Grand Rapids: Zondervan, 2012).

publisher required, and he had often decided to considerably abbreviate his treatments of historicity. Moreover, I had shown in my other writings the ability to capture a semipopular level of contents and writing style while still being thoroughly abreast of all the requisite scholarship, interacting with a fair amount of it and footnoting other key resources. That kind of book on Acts, he decided, was just what was needed.

The Historical Reliability of the New Testament is not the book Eckhard wanted me to write. But it is a substantial work with two reasonably thorough chapters on Acts tucked inside twelve other chapters that together make the case for the overall reliability of the New Testament under all the major topical headings being discussed in the scholarly world today. Perhaps when he sees the end product, he will forgive me for not quite doing what he wanted me to do, even while giving me the inspiration for writing yet one more work on this particular topic.

I am grateful to many people for making this book a reality. Dr. Robert Stewart was enthusiastic about it fitting into a larger series of philosophical and apologetics books he was commissioning and planning to help edit. B&H Academic was glad to offer me a contract; I can only apologize for how late in coming the manuscript was, compared with the first contract submission date I received. Two research assistants over a three-year period, Emily Gill (now Emily Manuel) and Sara Bibb (now Sara Evans) read various chapters and made excellent suggestions for improving the document's clarity, as well as helping me track down the occasional book, article, quote, or reference to aid me in the writing process. The Carey S. Thomas library of the Denver Seminary where I teach, led by the expert guidance of its director, Dr. Keith Wells, continues to purchase a large number of the databases, books, and journals I need for my research, even if not quite as high a percentage as we used to be able to afford. What is not available on-site or online is often readily accessible at the Ira J. Taylor Library of the Iliff School of Theology in town, while almost everything else can be ordered and arrives remarkably promptly via our interlibrary loan service. Despite ever-increasing challenges to free up writing time for its faculty, my seminary's administration and board of trustees remain committed to encouraging those of us with the passion and abilities to research and publish to keep trying to do so. For all these provisions I am most thankful.

But I must return to talking about Dr. Schnabel. We first met at the beginning of my last and his first year of PhD studies in New Testament at the University of Aberdeen. It was the fall of 1981. When I asked him what he wanted to write his thesis on, he replied, "Law and Wisdom from ben Sira to Paul." I understood what each of the four major components of his title meant on its own but had no idea what the issue was that he would be investigating! In barely two years' time he had his degree completed, and in less than four years his revised thesis was published in the renowned series, *Wissenschaftliche Untersuchungen zum Neuen Testament*.[2] The title remained verbatim what he had told me four years earlier!

During the year that we overlapped in our studies, Eckhard and his wife, Barbara, attended the church we had joined, so between that context and the university I got to know him reasonably well. Despite his brilliance, which included fluency in both English and German as well as facility with several other modern and ancient languages, he was a down-to-earth person who loved God and cared deeply about the local church and his friends. Instead of looking immediately for a prestigious university post, he became a missionary professor at the Asian Theological Seminary in Manila, later returning to his German homeland to teach at small, evangelical Bible colleges in Wiedenest and Giessen. He finally agreed to emigrate to the U.S. to teach in the

---

[2] Eckhard J. Schnabel, *Law and Wisdom from ben Sira to Paul* (Tübingen: J. C. B. Mohr, 1985; Eugene, OR: Wipf & Stock, 2011).

evangelical seminary world where he would have considerably more time for research and writing, one of his major gifts and contributions to the larger world. Two consecutive seminaries, Trinity Evangelical Divinity School and Gordon-Conwell Theological Seminary, have indeed afforded him more opportunity to research and write than he ever had either on the mission field or back home in Germany. Meanwhile, he had to cope with some long-term health challenges for his wife, helping her raise two delightful children, all the while at times teaching noticeably more than he was required to, both in North America and around the world. Throughout, Eckhard has remained committed to publishing a fair amount of his scholarship with small evangelical German publishing houses so that his voice can continue to impact his homeland as well as other parts of the world, especially because Germany today has so few fully evangelical and academic publications. Meanwhile, the magnitude and meticulousness of his scholarship never fails to impress me.[3]

Eckhard has always looked forward to seeing me at our annual ETS, IBR, and SBL conferences around the country and sitting down, when possible, to catch each other up a little on our lives and our families' doings. He has faithfully modeled that elusive "long obedience in the same direction" that many admire or discuss but few emulate. I count it a privilege to have met him and become his friend, and I dedicate this book to him. And may God's kingdom be advanced in whatever ways God sees fit to use it.

Craig L. Blomberg
Cinco de Mayo, 2015

---

[3] Especially prodigious *and* useful is his *Early Christian Mission*, 2 vols. (Downers Grove: IVP, 2004).

INTRODUCTION

The reliability of the Bible continues to be a topic of great interest to many people. For more than two centuries, modern biblical critics have pored over almost every corner of the Scriptures in minute detail. Up through the late 1960s, a general trajectory of increasing skepticism could be traced. Since then the tide has been turning. Although the novel and avant-garde almost by definition are what receive the most attention in the media and interest on the Internet, the amount of solid scholarship that has been produced in the last forty-five years internationally that supports the historical trustworthiness of this or that portion of the Bible has grown exponentially. While we continue to need patient, painstaking analysis of key issues at the highest levels of scholarship, we need even more good, up-to-date overviews, conversant with a broad cross-section of this research, which can be understood by a wider audience. I hope to fill this niche.

Quite a few books today do a good job canvassing the evidence for the historical reliability of the New Testament Gospels, the canonical accounts of the life of Jesus. Some of these are detailed and technical,[1] others mid-range,[2] and still others introductory.[3] Readers who want a special focus on just the Synoptic Gospels (Matthew, Mark, and Luke) or on just the Gospel of John can choose from a variety of offerings that concentrate on those portions of the New Testament alone.[4] The Acts of the Apostles is not as well served at the introductory or popular levels but has outstanding detailed studies corroborating or rendering plausible a huge swath of its material.[5] There is also a small cottage industry of studies in the historical issues raised by the Epistles, especially the letters of Paul, both in terms of questions of authorship[6] and in terms of fitting their information together with the data of Acts.[7]

When one looks, however, for a reasonably detailed treatment of the historical issues surrounding the entire New Testament, almost nothing emerges. One can find good volumes on the transmission of the text,[8] the process of canonization,[9] and the identification and significance of

---

[1] See esp. James H. Charlesworth and Petr Pokorný, eds., *Jesus Research*, 2 vols. (Grand Rapids: Eerdmans, 2009–2014).

[2] See esp. Craig L. Blomberg, *The Historical Reliability of the Gospels*, 2nd ed. (Nottingham: Apollos; Downers Grove: IVP, 2007).

[3] See esp. Mark D. Roberts, *Can We Trust the Gospels: Investigating the Reliability of Matthew, Mark, Luke, and John* (Wheaton: Crossway, 2007).

[4] E.g., Paul R. Eddy and Greg A. Boyd, *The Jesus Legend: A Case for the Historical Reliability of the Synoptic Tradition* (Grand Rapids: Baker, 2007); and Craig L. Blomberg, *The Historical Reliability of John's Gospel: Issues and Commentary* (Downers Grove: IVP; Leicester: Apollos, 2001), respectively.

[5] See esp. Colin J. Hemer, *The Book of Acts in the Setting of Hellenistic History*, ed. Conrad H. Gempf (Tübingen: J. C. B. Mohr, 1989; Winona Lake, IN: Eisenbrauns, 1990).

[6] See esp. Terry L. Wilder, *Pseudonymity, the New Testament and Deception: An Inquiry into Intention and Reception* (Lanham, MD and London: University Press of America, 2004).

[7] E.g., John B. Polhill, *Paul and His Letters* (Nashville: B&H, 1999).

[8] See esp. Stanley E. Porter, *How We Got the New Testament: Text, Transmission, Translation* (Grand Rapids: Baker, 2013).

[9] See esp. Michael J. Kruger, *The Question of Canon: Challenging the Status Quo in the New Testament Debate* (Downers Grove: IVP, 2013).

the genres of the New Testament narratives.[10] There are even excellent treatments of the problem of miracles.[11] But no current works gather all these topics together under one cover, except for various New Testament introductions that by necessity supply only cursory treatments of each topic because of everything else they must cover as well.

This work tries to fill that gap. Fourteen detailed chapters subdivide into six major parts, discussing in turn the Synoptics, the Gospel of John, Acts and Paul, the remaining New Testament books, issues of canonicity and transmission of the text, and the unique problem of miracles. We look at issues of the formation of the literature, external corroboration of its contents, apparent internal contradictions, as well as points of commonality from Paul to Acts. We assess the so-called Gnostic Gospels (and other Gnostic literature) and the New Testament Apocrypha. We discuss the transmission of the text and the canonization of the books. And we do all this in enough detail to make each survey much more than superficial, yet without the technical language that makes these topics beyond the reach of many readers and without creating an encyclopedic-sized work that would make it accessible only to experts.

Because I have previously written several books that impinge on this topic, it is important for me to explain how this one differs from those. In *The Historical Reliability of the Gospels*,[12] I focused primarily on the Synoptic Gospels, addressing six major topics surrounding the formation and contents of their narratives. Only one additional chapter looked primarily at the Gospel of John. In *Jesus and the Gospels: An Introduction and Survey*,[13] I was creating a textbook designed to cover the waterfront of issues theological students

[10] See esp. Richard A. Burridge, *What Are the Gospels? A Comparison with Graeco-Roman Biography*, 2nd ed. (Grand Rapids: Eerdmans, 2004).

[11] See esp. Sean A. Adams, *The Genre of Acts and Collected Biography* (Cambridge: Cambridge University Press, 2013).

[12] See note 2 above.

[13] 2nd ed. (Nashville: B&H; Nottingham: Apollos, 2009).

typically address in courses on the Gospels or the life of Christ, so that every topic received only brief treatment. Issues of historicity were largely limited to short sections of a paragraph or two at the end of each main section within the specific chapters that surveyed the life of Christ and to one entire chapter that summarized the main line of evidence overall. *The Historical Reliability of John's Gospel: Issues and Commentary*[14] gave me an opportunity to proceed in far more detail, passage by passage through the Fourth Gospel in commentary format, while focusing exclusively on issues that bear on the question of historical trustworthiness. Finally, in *Can We Still Believe the Bible? An Evangelical Engagement with Contemporary Questions*,[15] I focused on six specific topics that span both Testaments about which a lot of skepticism had recently been expressed, even though the majority of scholarly developments in each area over the past generation had actually increased many scholars' confidence in the reliability of the Christian Scriptures.

This present work, *The Historical Reliability of the New Testament*, gathers most of the major threads of these works together, in a completely new topical arrangement, but also moves on to numerous additional issues that the scope of my previous works prevented me from addressing at all. While not nearly as erudite or prodigious as Kenneth A. Kitchen's magnificent *On the Reliability of the Old Testament*,[16] it does share with Kitchen's tome a desire to cover the major concerns spanning an entire Testament of the Bible with plentiful footnotes to just about every topic raised, in order to enable interested readers to dig more deeply wherever they might wish to do so.

I adopt an approach I have taken in my previous work, which, although widely practiced elsewhere, is not universally understood or

---

[14] See note 4 above.
[15] (Grand Rapids: Brazos, 2014).
[16] (Grand Rapids: Eerdmans, 2003).

represented accurately. I am a Christian believer of an evangelical persuasion with a high regard for the accuracy and authority of Scripture. But I did not begin my church or Christian life that way. It was a view I came to in large part as a result of my study and research. I was raised in a fairly liberal wing of a mainline Protestant denomination. I mark my true coming to faith as the result of a parachurch organization in my high school that was broadly evangelical and highly interdenominational. While it maintained a high view of Scripture, it did not burden its teens with debates about inerrancy versus infallibility, inspiration, authority, and the like. In my undergraduate education at a private liberal arts college historically attached to the denomination in which I was raised, I was taught that it was impossible to be an evangelical and maintain my intellectual integrity. I was taught that the Bible was replete with errors, that it was a collection of books authored by Jews and Christians articulating their beliefs about God and his ways with humanity, but no more uniquely inspired than any other inspiring religious literature that had been penned throughout the ages, and sometimes less so.

Over and over again I heard the mantra repeated that something was theological and therefore it was not historical. Almost as common was the scornful dismissal of someone's scholarship as just "apologetics"—defending the faith—and therefore worthy of no serious attention. I tried as hard as I could to make sense of these dichotomies and failed. I understood how something in service of an ideology might choose to distort the truth but recognized also how sometimes the nature of the ideology required its proponents to engage in as careful a recovery of historical facts as possible. I recognized that someone highly devoted to a cause that did not really merit their allegiance could exaggerate the evidence in its favor, but I also realized that people discovering truth through historical investigation might become passionately committed to a cause their research genuinely supported. Finally, I discovered I. Howard Marshall's *Luke: Historian and Theologian,*[17] just a few years after its first edition had appeared, and my hunches were confirmed. Something could be theological *and* historical. A work could exhibit high quality scholarship and be useful for defending the faith.

As a result, the first sparks of what would become a major pre-occupation of my scholarly career were kindled. I attended a major evangelical seminary and then a state-sponsored, largely secular university overseas (where Marshall taught) to round out my formal education for my master's and doctor's degrees. My first published book was the one on the reliability of the Gospels, and I find myself continually coming back to the question of the Bible's trustworthiness. It is the topic on which I have been asked to speak on college and university campuses and in local churches and community contexts more than any other, even though my book-length publications have ranged from topics as diverse as interpreting and preaching the parables,[18] hermeneutics and exegesis,[19] introductions to the New Testament,[20] commentaries on several of its specific books,[21] matters of material possessions and stewardship,[22]

---

[17] (Grand Rapids: Zondervan, 1970). Last revised in a 3rd ed. (Downers Grove and Leicester: IVP, 1998).

[18] *Interpreting the Parables,* 2nd ed. (Downers Grove: IVP; Nottingham: Apollos, 2012); *Preaching the Parables: From Responsible Interpretation to Powerful Proclamation* (Grand Rapids: Baker, 2004).

[19] William W. Klein, Craig L. Blomberg, and Robert L. Hubbard Jr., *Introduction to Biblical Interpretation,* 3rd ed. (Grand Rapids: Zondervan, 2017); Craig L. Blomberg with Jennifer Foutz Markley, *Handbook of New Testament Exegesis* (Grand Rapids: Baker, 2010).

[20] In addition to my *Jesus and the Gospels,* I wrote *From Pentecost to Patmos: An Introduction to Acts Through Revelation* (Nashville: B&H; Nottingham: Apollos, 2006).

[21] *Matthew* (Nashville: Broadman, 1992); *1 Corinthians* (Grand Rapids: Zondervan, 1994); *James,* with Mariam J. Kamell (Grand Rapids: Zondervan, 2008).

[22] *Neither Poverty nor Riches: A Biblical Theology of Possessions* (Grand Rapids: Eerdmans, and Leicester: IVP, 1999; Downers Grove: IVP, 2001); *Heart, Soul, and Money: A Christian View of Possessions* (Joplin, MO: College Press, 2000); *Christians in an Age of Wealth: A Biblical Theology of Stewardship* (Grand Rapids: Zondervan, 2013).

Evangelical-Mormon dialogues,[23] gender roles,[24] Jesus's meals with sinners,[25] biblical eschatology,[26] and effective generational ministry.[27]

Although I tailor and tweak my presentations to fit each setting, for the most part I do my best not to presuppose my Christian faith when I am speaking in pluralistic settings and often even when I am speaking in exclusively Christian contexts attempting to better educate fellow believers for interaction in the public square. I do not attempt to *prove* every last word of Scripture; the data are not available inductively for us to do that anyway. I attempt to limit myself to arguments and the presentation of evidence that does not depend on being a Christian. At the same time, I am aware that the extent to which a given person will find various arguments more plausible than not has a lot to do with whether they are inclined toward Christianity at all. My critics on the far right who allege that in fact I *don't* believe those things in the Bible, which I may say we cannot demonstrate, are simply wrong. It always amazes me how anyone else can think they know better what a person believes on a topic than that person himself or herself![28] And when they say they know of no one who has become more persuaded of the reliability of the Bible through

---

[23] *How Wide the Divide? A Mormon and an Evangelical in Conversation*, with Stephen E. Robinson (Downers Grove: IVP, 1997).

[24] *Two Views of Women in Ministry*, coedited with James R. Beck (Grand Rapids: Zondervan, 2001). In the 2nd ed. of 2005, I am a contributor rather than a coeditor.

[25] *Contagious Holiness: Jesus' Meals with Sinners* (Nottingham: Apollos; Downers Grove: IVP, 2005).

[26] *A Case for Historic Premillennialism*, coedited with Sung Wook Chung (Grand Rapids: Baker, 2009).

[27] *Effective Generational Ministry*, with Elisabeth A. Nesbit Spanotto (Grand Rapids: Baker, 2015).

[28] Most egregious of all have been Norman Geisler and F. David Farnell in numerous online writings and conference remarks. In *Can We Still Believe the Bible?* 262–63 n. 113, I itemize their twelve most serious errors and misrepresentations of my published works. Neither author has responded to any of them as of this writing, but they continue to disseminate their false reports about me.

this approach, I can offer them testimonies from countless students, readers, and people in audiences to whom I have spoken over the past thirty-five years. To my critics on the far left who can write off an entire work without reading it (or without reading much of it) simply because it is "apologetics," I would just say that I find it interesting how often they will read, immerse themselves in, and rely heavily on works that are equally passionate in supporting viewpoints they actually hold. Indeed, many of their books could equally legitimately be termed apologetics for skepticism.[29] A work is no better or worse in its scholarship because its author tries passionately to defend a viewpoint. It is better or worse depending on the accuracy of the information it includes and the cogency of its argumentation.

There was a time in the early 1990s when I thought interest was starting to wane in issues of biblical trustworthiness. Then the Jesus Seminar published their two books, color-coding every passage in Matthew, Mark, Luke, John, and the later Gospel of Thomas red, pink, gray, or black, according to the likelihood they thought Jesus really said or did what was attributed to him.[30] Public interest began to return, especially since the seminar found so tiny a percentage of the texts to be anything close to representing what the real Jesus of history was actually like.[31] Dan Brown's *Da Vinci Code* in 2003 took the

---

[29] The most extreme example I have encountered here are the works of Hector Avalos, a professor of religious studies at Iowa State University, whose repeatedly announced goal in teaching about the Bible is to so discredit it that subsequent generations need pay no attention to it! Would someone please explain to me how that does not violate the separation of church and state in public education at least as much as, and probably far more than, the hopes of a different professor that students might *adopt* a certain religious viewpoint?

[30] Robert W. Funk, Roy W. Hoover, and the Jesus Seminar, *The Five Gospels: The Search for the Authentic Words of Jesus* (New York and Toronto: Macmillan, 1993); Robert W. Funk and the Jesus Seminar, *The Acts of Jesus: The Search for the Authentic Deeds of Jesus* (New York and London: HarperCollins, 1998).

[31] Only 18 percent of his words and 16 percent of his deeds were either exactly or close to what Jesus actually said or did, according to their voting.

world by storm, despite all of its fiction about early Christian history that was packaged as if it were fact.[32] Suddenly believers and skeptics alike were discussing what the real facts were about the origins of Christianity with a flurry of interest that the world had not seen in almost three decades. Closely on the heels of Brown's blockbuster came the rediscovery of the so-called Gospel of Judas,[33] then claims about a discovery of "Jesus' family tomb" in Jerusalem,[34] and in this decade allegations about a scrap of ancient parchment purporting to be a "Gospel of Jesus'Wife"![35] Needless to say, interest in the topic has scarcely waned at all during this period.

The explosion of information and misinformation available on the Internet has created a brave new world as well. Millennials have grown up never knowing what it was like for people to try unsuccessfully to publish lies, half-truths, unresearched opinions, boring drivel, meaningless trivia, and so on, given the constant opportunities during their lifetimes for self-publishing or the creation of blogsites and websites online. Baby boomers can easily remember when it was hard for even some high-quality scholarship to get published because of the limited number of outlets for producing something in hard copy. All that has changed. The Internet has made amazing resources available, and information once scattered about the major libraries of the world

---

[32] Dan Brown, *The Da Vinci Code: A Novel* (New York: Random House, 2003). See esp. the frontispiece on p. 1 that claims, "All descriptions of artwork, architecture, documents, and secret rituals in this novel are accurate," when, in reality, there are multiple errors on all of these fronts, with the greatest number surrounding descriptions of early Christian documents!

[33] Rodolphe Kasser, Marvin Meyer, and Gregor Wurst, *The Gospel of Judas* (Washington, DC: National Geographic Society, 2006).

[34] Simcha Jacobovici and Charles Pellegrino, *The Jesus Family Tomb: The Discovery, the Investigation, and the Evidence That Could Change History* (New York: HarperOne, 2008).

[35] Anthony Le Donne, *The Wife of Jesus: Ancient Texts and Modern Scandals* (London: Oneworld Publications, 2013).

is now accessible with a few clicks of a mouse or taps on a screen if one knows how to search the web properly. But with all the new technology has also come the so-called democratization of information, which in its worst moments means anybody can make up anything they want and pass it off as sober truth and find willing followers from around the world who want to believe it. Of course private printing presses made that possible in a previous era, too, just not nearly as easily or to the phenomenal extent to which we see it happening today.

All this increases the need for this present book. By design this is not a volume which lays out the skeptical claims, point by point, in excruciating detail, only to then respond *ad seriatim* with equal detail in defense of the New Testament. That would have required a volume more than twice the size of the present one. It is easy enough to find books or websites that list as many problems with the Bible as their authors can find but that do not interact with the most cogent scholarly responses (or with *any* scholarly responses).[36] It is harder to find works that come from more conservative specialists who have immersed themselves in as much diverse scholarship (and, at times, pseudo-scholarship) as I have in the composition of this work, while at the same time packaging the material in what I hope are reasonably bite-size pieces that a wide range of the reading public can digest.[37] Readers will have to decide for themselves, however, to what degree the case I make is persuasive.

---

[36] One thinks for example of the various books of Earl Doherty alleging that Christ never existed or trying to respond to popular-level Christian apologists. For online materials all one has to do is google "contradictions in the Bible" for a sampling. When I did it, the top hit was Jim Merrit, "A List of Biblical Contradictions" (1992), *The Secular Web*, accessed @ http://infidels.org/library/modern/ jim_meritt /bible-contradictions.html.

[37] Exemplary models can be found, however, in a variety of the works of New Testament scholars such as Darrell Bock, Craig Evans, and Ben Witherington, among others.

The stage is thus set. We begin with the Synoptic Gospels, both because they form the first three books of the New Testament and because they are widely agreed to be our best sources for accessing the historical Jesus, the founder of Christianity. Then we proceed in canonical order through the rest of the New Testament. Finally, we append topics that are relevant to assessing the reliability of *all* portions of the distinctively Christian Scriptures. So now let the discussions begin.

Part One

The Synoptic Gospels

Chapter 1

The Formation of the Synoptic Gospels

I magine the Internet buzzing with some latest discovery of an ancient document dug up in Israel. It is written in Hebrew and appears to shed startling new light on the Jewish religion of its day. But is it authentic? Are its contents true? How would reputable archaeologists, historians, and linguists proceed? Early in their analysis would be the attempts to answer a variety of questions. Can we determine the author of the document and its original setting? Are we able to estimate a date for the manuscript and dates for any events or activities described in the manuscript? May we discern anything about its composition, that is, how it was written? Do its contents parallel those of any other documents from the ancient Mediterranean world? If so, how similar or different are they? These and related questions usually take time to answer, even though ours is a world that demands instant information. One thing, therefore, we can almost certainly know when new discoveries like this hit the press is that every immediate opinion expressed by someone is tentative and provisional. Scholarly

consensus, if it is achieved, will come much later, usually after all the
initial publicity has died down. Unless one deliberately follows developments for a few months or even years, one risks believing the exact
opposite or at least a considerable distortion of what is ultimately
decided about the new find!

The New Testament Gospels, of course, have been known for
nearly twenty centuries. Modern biblical scholarship has investigated
virtually every subject one could think to ask about them from almost
every conceivable angle for more than 200 years. Almost by definition
what counts as news is that which is new, novel, or arresting. Virtually
by definition what is utterly unprecedented in New Testament scholarship is almost guaranteed to be false because of the amount of investigation that has already gone into the discipline! It is *almost* guaranteed
but not *always*.[1] Still the proper response to any news item portraying
Christian origins in some sensational new light is skepticism. Proceed
cautiously, consult the sources, determine their credibility, look for dissenting views, and give the matter some time to see what, if anything
is resolved. Many new theories are old ones recycled and tweaked,
even though previously debunked. But a new generation that fails to
study history carefully doesn't know this and so can fall prey to the
new appearance of the theory. Even the theorist may not be aware how
well-worn his or her ideas actually are.[2]

---

[1] The most talked-about new discoveries over the last decade relating to the
New Testament were much of Dan Brown's supposedly historical facts about
ancient Christian history in *The Da Vinci Code*; the discovery of the so-called
Gospel of Judas; the discovery of the so-called Jesus family tomb in Talpiot, South
Jerusalem; and the discovery of tiny fragments from the so-called Gospel of Jesus's
wife. Virtually all of Brown's claims are sheer fiction, the tomb has nothing to do
with Jesus's family, and the fragments are a modern forgery. The Gospel of Judas,
however, is a genuine, ancient document we knew about but never had any actual
text of. See further below.

[2] A sizable body of popular and pseudo-academic literature recently has tried
to revive the notion that significant portions of the Gospels' portraits of Jesus were

In assessing the reliability of the Gospels of Matthew, Mark, and Luke, some issues must be addressed that recur for all New Testament documents. Others are unique to the literary genre of a Gospel. And because the contents of Matthew, Mark, and Luke overlap to a great extent in ways not true of other Gospels, inside or outside the canon, still other concerns affect the analysis of the three Synoptics alone. In this chapter we will address the issues of authorship, date, and circumstances of their composition, as is necessary for all biblical documents. We will look at the question of the nature of a Gospel and its author's intentions, an issue unique to Gospels' scholarship. Finally, distinctive to the study of Matthew, Mark, and Luke, we will address the "Synoptic Problem"—the question of the literary relationship of the first three Gospels—along with related subjects that such study raises. These will include the nature of the oral tradition that preceded the writing of the Synoptics. Assessing the credibility of the Gospels of Matthew, Mark, and Luke represents the ultimate goal of our investigation in all three of these categories.

The Settings of the Synoptics

What can we know about the writers of these three documents, along with the time and circumstances of their writing? Answers to a large degree depend on how much we value external evidence as over against

---

invented based on ancient Greco-Roman mythology. This view, associated with the "history of religions" school of thought of the late nineteenth and early twentieth centuries, was debunked a hundred years ago. Responsible historical Jesus scholarship from at least 1980 to the present is united in its affirmation of the thoroughly Jewish origins of the Gospels and the Jewishness of the historical Jesus, whatever else they may disagree on. See the comprehensive collection of essays and perspectives in Tom Holmén and Stanley E. Porter, eds., *Handbook for the Study of the Historical Jesus*, 4 vols. (Leiden: Brill, 2010). While elements of first-century Judaism were Hellenized, others were not, and the Jewishness of Jesus includes a number that were not.

internal evidence. External evidence refers to what information we have about the composition of a document apart from the contents of that document. Internal evidence refers to what we may deduce from the document itself. The external evidence for the formation of the Gospels begins to appear early in the second century. The standard New Testament introductions along with all the major commentaries on individual Gospels typically reproduce this information in detail;[3] we need highlight only the most important claims here. Which internal evidence is considered significant varies widely from one scholar to the next; again we will note only the most commonly observed phenomena.

Authorship and Audiences

The Christian writer, Papias, early in the second century, offers the oldest known testimony concerning the Gospel of Matthew. His testimony is preserved in quotations by the early fourth-century church historian Eusebius. Several of the Greek words in his statement can be translated in more than one way, as indicated by the bracketed words that suggest alternate but probably less likely renderings: "Matthew composed [compiled] his *logia* in the Hebrew [Aramaic] language [dialect, style], and everyone translated [interpreted] it as they were able" (*Hist. eccl.* 3.39.16). The most ambiguous part of Papias's statement is the meaning in this context of the Greek word *logia*, a plural noun I have left untranslated. A *logion* (the singular form) essentially means "a saying," referring to spoken words.[4] Some scholars have

---

[3] From varying theological perspectives, see, e.g., Andreas Köstenberger, L. Scott Kellum, and Charles W. Quarles, *The Cradle, the Cross, and the Crown: An Introduction to the New Testament* (Nashville: B&H, 2009), 178–327; Raymond E. Brown, *An Introduction to the New Testament* (New York and London: Doubleday, 1997), 126–278; and M. Eugene Boring, *An Introduction to the New Testament: History, Literature, Theology* (Louisville: Westminster John Knox, 2012), 520–637.

[4] BDAG, 598. In the NT and the early Christian literature canvassed by this standard lexicon, the word appears only in the plural. It also notes that in pre-Christian Greek literature the word refers mostly to "short divine sayings."

nevertheless assumed that here it refers to the entire Gospel because Eusebius has just cited what Papias taught about the whole Gospel of Mark, referring to it by means of the same word *logia*.[5] Papias, who in turn is citing an elder named John, whom we will discuss later, says:

> Mark was the translator [interpreter] of Peter; whatever he remembered, he wrote accurately, however not in order, of the things having been spoken or done by the Lord. For [Mark] neither heard the Lord nor followed him, but finally, as I said, was with Peter, who gave him the teachings as there was need (but not as making a systematic arrangement of the Lord's *logia*), so that Mark erred in no way (*Hist. eccl.* 3.39.15).

Despite those who would take *logia* to refer to a whole Gospel, it seems clear that the word here cannot refer to Mark's entire narrative because Papias is citing John the elder as describing constituent elements of that Gospel. He has just spoken of "the things . . . spoken or done by the Lord," so he could be referring to some portion of the Gospel that contains both kinds of material. Or, a bit more naturally, in light of the root meaning of a *logion*, he could now be referring simply to teachings or discourses of Jesus, which makes it probable that he is doing the same thing a few sentences later when he speaks about Matthew writing the *logia* of Jesus.[6]

What do we learn from all this testimony, if we accept it? At the very least we discover that Mark's Gospel relied largely on information from Peter, who in the Synoptics is one of the three apostles closest to Jesus. Mark's Gospel may not always be in chronological order, especially with respect to Jesus's teachings, but it is completely accurate in what it affirms. Matthew wrote something, probably as a precursor

---

[5] E.g., R. T. France, *Matthew: Evangelist and Teacher* (Exeter: Paternoster, 1989; Eugene, OR: Wipf & Stock, 2004), 58.

[6] E.g., John Nolland, *The Gospel of Matthew* (Bletchley: Paternoster; Grand Rapids: Eerdmans, 2005), 2–3.

to what we call the Gospel of Matthew, in Hebrew or Aramaic, per-haps a collection of Jesus's teachings. There may have been multiple translations of this document, including into Greek, which could have resulted in any or all of what we know as Matthew's Gospel.

From other early church fathers, we may add the testimony of the late-second century bishop of Lyons, Irenaeus, who declared that Matthew wrote his Gospel "while Peter and Paul were preaching the gospel and founding the church in Rome" (*Adv. haer.* 3.1.1), a refer-ence that fits most naturally into the 60s of the first century. Because Eusebius quotes Irenaeus also (*Hist. eccl.* 5.8.2), and does so accurately here where we can check him, we can be more confident than we otherwise would be that he quoted Papias accurately where we cannot check him. Justin Martyr, in the mid-second century, declared that Mark's Gospel was based on Peter's *apomnēmoneumata*, that is, his "remembrances" or possibly "memoirs" (*Dial.* 106.3).[7]

The only person we know of named Matthew from first-century Christianity was the converted tax collector, also known as Levi, who was one of Jesus's twelve closest followers (cf. Matt 9:9 with Mark 2:14). Mark was John Mark, a companion of both Peter and Paul, best known for deserting Paul midway through his first missionary journey (Acts 13:13; cf. 15:38) but later reconciled to him (2 Tim 4:11; cf. Col 4:10). The early church in Jerusalem also met for a time at the home of John Mark's mother (Acts 12:12). Luke was Paul's "beloved physi-cian" (Col 4:14 KJV)[8] and travel companion off and on throughout his missionary travels. He was believed to have written the book of Acts as a sequel to his Gospel, so that the periodic shift from third-person to first-person-plural narrative ("*we* did such and such") can then be

---

[7] Justin is also the first writer we know of to liken the Gospels to biography (on which see further, below). See Michael F. Bird, *The Gospel of the Lord: How the Early Church Wrote the Story of Jesus* (Grand Rapids: Eerdmans, 2014), 249–54.

[8] All biblical quotations in this book come from the 2011 NIV, unless other-wise indicated (as here).

explained as the places where Luke was actually present with Paul (Acts 16:10–17; 20:5–21:18; 27:1–28:16).

External evidence additionally claims that Matthew wrote in the province of Judea and, more specifically, from the city of Jerusalem (Monarchian Prologue, Jerome, Dorotheus, colophons of mss. K, 126, 174). Consistently, the patristic testimony insists that he wrote to Jewish Christians. Clement of Alexandria in the late second century declared that Mark wrote to Christians in Rome at their request (*Frag.* 9.4–20). One tradition notes that when Mark told Peter of his writing plan, "[Peter] neither actively prevented nor encouraged the undertaking" (Eusebius, *Hist. eccl.* 6.14.6–7)—a fairly halfhearted approval that would not likely be invented if it were fictitious![9] Of the Synoptics the least is said about Luke, but we do read that he was "incited by the Holy Spirit in the regions around Achaia" (the southern half of the Greek peninsula) and wrote particularly for Gentile believers, probably also in Achaia (anti-Marcionite Prologue; Gregory of Nazianzus). We are also told that Luke was originally from Antioch in Syria (Eusebius, *Hist. eccl.* 3.4).

What are we to make of these various claims? Each early Christian writer we have cited had a vested interest in linking the Gospels with apostolic tradition. Most of them elsewhere occasionally report information that appears to be distorted about some aspect of early Christianity.[10] But it is hard to believe that the oldest traditions would uniformly associate the first two Gospels with Mark and Luke without some good historical reason, because neither was otherwise viewed as a significant character in first-century Christianity.[11] First Peter 5:13

---

[9] Mark L. Strauss, *Mark* (Grand Rapids: Zondervan, 2014), 29.

[10] For a thorough survey see Margaret M. Mitchell, "Patristic Counter-Evidence to the Claim That 'The Gospels Were Written for All Christians,'" *New Testament Studies* 51 (2005): 36–79.

[11] For a robust defense of Markan authorship of the Gospel that bears his name, see Robert H. Gundry, *Mark: A Commentary on His Apology for the Cross*

confirms that Mark and Peter were together in Rome (using the code word "Babylon") in the early 60s, but otherwise Mark is best known for deserting Paul and Barnabas! Luke, as we have seen, appears by name only in two lists of those from whom Paul sends greetings at the end of his epistles. The apocryphal and Gnostic Gospels by comparison, not written until the mid-second century at the earliest, choose much better known figures from the first generation of Christianity as pseudo-authors of their more fictitious documents to try to gain them a hearing—Mary (probably Magdalene but maybe the mother of Jesus), the apostles Philip, Thomas, Bartholomew, Peter, James, and even Nicodemus.[12] Since we know of apocryphal works falsely ascribed to Peter, if the Gospel of Mark were just another such document, granted that the church fathers attributed much of its contents to Peter already, why not just simplify things and say Peter wrote it himself? Those who would believe that claim would then accept the book's authority that much more readily![13] Matthew, of course, *was* an apostle but, next only to Judas who betrayed Jesus, probably the least respected figure of the Twelve in Jewish circles because he had worked for the occupying enemy forces by collecting customs tolls for Rome. Judas *did* have a Gospel attributed to him but precisely because it turned him into a hero rather than a villain and most likely emanated from a thoroughly unorthodox Gnostic sect.[14] No one trying

(Grand Rapids: Eerdmans, 1993), 1026–45; for Lukan authorship of Luke, see Colin J. Hemer, *The Book of Acts in the Setting of Hellenistic History*, ed. Conrad H. Gempf (Tübingen: J. C. B. Mohr, 1989; Winona Lake, IN: Eisenbrauns, 1990), 308–64.

[12] See Edgar Hennecke, *New Testament Apocrypha*, vol. 1, *The Gospels and Related Writings*, rev. ed., ed. Wilhelm Schneemelcher and R. McL. Wilson (London: James Clarke; Louisville: Westminster John Knox, 1990).

[13] Cf. Darrell L. Bock, *Mark* (Cambridge: Cambridge University Press, 2015), 16–22.

[14] A good introduction to this work is Stanley E. Porter and Gordon L. Heath, *The Lost Gospel of Judas: Separating Fact from Fiction* (Grand Rapids: Eerdmans, 2007).

to promote orthodox Christianity would have ascribed a document they held sacred to Judas! The same logic may well have applied to Matthew.[15]

Turning to the internal evidence of the Gospels themselves, we discover no explicit claims for authorship. All known ancient Greek manuscripts containing the beginning of one of the Gospels include the titles "According to Matthew," "According to Mark," and so on. Yet it seems improbable that all of the Gospel writers would have independently chosen to call their works "According to [so-and-so]." The first communities to which each was written would have known the origin of the documents sent to them from the Christian courier who was assigned to deliver them and, according to the custom of the day, who probably read them aloud to the assembled congregation, possibly even adding interpretive explanations and/or fielding questions afterwards. Only when more than one Gospel began to circulate together, and especially when the fourfold collection of first-century Gospels was complete, would the need to distinguish one from another via written titles become essential.[16] Strictly speaking then, the Gospels are anonymous. No text within them states who wrote them, the way a majority of the New Testament *letters* begin with a greeting from their apparent authors.[17]

It therefore shows no necessary disrespect for the authority or accuracy of Scripture to suggest that someone other than Matthew, Mark, or Luke wrote the first three Gospels. Questions, for example, have

---

[15] Craig A. Evans, *Matthew* (Cambridge: Cambridge University Press, 2011), 3–4; Michael J. Wilkins, *Matthew* (Grand Rapids: Zondervan, 2004), 22–23.

[16] Martin Hengel (*The Four Gospels and the One Gospel of Jesus Christ* [London: SCM; Harrisburg: Trinity Press International, 2000], 48–56) argues somewhat plausibly, however, that Mark himself applied the title "according to Mark" to his original Gospel and that the other Gospel writers followed suit with their names. Similarly, Bird, *Gospel of the Lord*, 258.

[17] For debates surrounding the claims of epistolary authorship, see chaps. 8 and 10.

been raised about Matthew concerning its apparent anti-Semitism, whether any of it reads like translation from Hebrew, and if an apostolic writer would have relied heavily on a Gospel from a nonapostolic author like Mark (as we will see most likely happened). The Gospel of Mark is sometimes charged with having too many "Latinisms," too much confusion of geographical details in Israel, or too little respect in its portrayal of Peter to have come from a Jewish Christian from Jerusalem. Luke's Gospel especially is accused of promoting too different a theology from the main themes of the letters of Paul to have been written by one of his close companions.[18]

None of these charges carries all that much weight. Scholarship increasingly recognizes the sharp language about various Jews in the Gospel of Matthew (including on the lips of Jesus!) to reflect the intramural disputes within Judaism as to who were really the chosen people of God.[19] Latinisms in Mark would be appropriate for a Roman audience, geographical confusion comes only when we assume Jesus traveled in linear rather than peripatetic fashion, and it is arguable that only a Gospel authorized by Peter would have allowed as much disparagement of him (and of the apostles in general) as we find.[20] The theological differences between Luke and Paul undoubtedly prove that Paul did not write the Gospel (or Acts) but not that a companion of his couldn't have done so.[21]

---

[18] For these and other allegations, along with my responses to them, see Craig L. Blomberg, *Jesus and the Gospels: An Introduction and Survey*, 2nd ed. (Nashville: B & H; Nottingham: IVP, 2009), 138–40, 153–56, 173–74.

[19] See esp. John Nolland, "Matthew and Anti-Semitism," in *Built upon the Rock: Studies in the Gospel of Matthew*, ed. Daniel M. Gurtner and John Nolland (Grand Rapids: Eerdmans, 2008), 154–69.

[20] Cf. D. A. Carson and Douglas J. Moo, *An Introduction to the New Testament*, 2nd ed. (Grand Rapids: Zondervan, 2005), 176.

[21] David Wenham, "Acts and the Pauline Corpus II.: The Evidence of Parallels," in *The Book of Acts in Its Ancient Literary Setting*, ed. Bruce W. Winter and Andrew D. Clarke (Carlisle: Paternoster; Grand Rapids: Eerdmans, 1993), 215–58.

At the same time the credibility of the Gospels is not automatically called into question if the liberal consensus within New Testament scholarship turned out to be true—that anonymous first-century Christians, perhaps younger followers of the apostles or the traditional authors, were the actual writers in question.

Dating

FROM JESUS TO THE GOSPELS

More important than the question of authorship in this case would be the question of dating. Were those authors close enough in time to be likely to have their facts straight about Jesus? Here we again find the academic world divided—evangelicals typically, though not unanimously, date Matthew, Mark, and Luke all to the 60s (with Mark sometimes placed as early as in the late 50s), somewhere between twenty-five and forty years after Jesus's death in AD 30 (or possibly 33).[22] The liberal consensus, though not without exception, dates Mark to the late 60s or early 70s and Matthew and Luke to the 80s or 90s.[23]

Obviously the closer in time we can place the composition of a Gospel to the life of Jesus, the stronger the case becomes in principle for historical accuracy. The more conservative dates are partly bound up with external evidence but only partly. We have seen Irenaeus's convictions that Matthew was written while Peter and Paul were still preaching in Rome. This points to the first half of the 60s, since Peter

---

[22] See, e.g., Carson and Moo, *Introduction to the New Testament,* 152–56, 179–82, 207–10; and Köstenberger, Kellum, and Quarles, *Cradle, Cross and Crown,* 185–89, 234–35, 261–64.

[23] See, e.g., Boring, *Introduction to the New Testament,* 518, 536, 587–88; and Delbert Burkett, *An Introduction to the New Testament and the Origins of Christianity* (Cambridge: Cambridge University Press, 2002), 157, 181, 196. Notice how few actual arguments rather than mere affirmations appear for these dates compared to the discussions in the sources noted in note 22.

was most likely martyred in the mid-60s,[24] and Paul did not reach Rome until about 60.[25] If Matthew used Mark, then Mark must be earlier, but by how much we cannot tell. If Luke wrote Acts, then he could not have written before the final events he narrates, which probably occurred in 62 (two years after his arrival in Rome—Acts 28:30). Acts 1:1 refers to Luke's former volume, showing that the Gospel was penned before Acts. And since Luke also used Mark (see below pp. 30–32), the Gospel of Mark must have been written before the Gospel of Luke.

Acts, nevertheless, ends abruptly, with Paul under house arrest in Rome awaiting the outcome of his appeal to the emperor, after being unjustly held in prison by the Roman authorities in Israel. Luke draws out for more than eight chapters the account of Paul's last journey to Jerusalem, his imprisonment there, his various hearings, the threats on his life, his appeal to Caesar, his ill-fated voyage to Rome that left his boat shipwrecked and its passengers wintering on the island of Malta, and then finally his arrival in the capital city of the empire (Acts 20:22–28:31). It is extremely odd that Luke never describes the results of that appeal, especially when early church tradition teaches that Paul was indeed released in about AD 62, only to be reimprisoned and executed a few years later (1 Clem. 5:5–7; Eusebius, *Hist. eccl.* 2.22). But if the reason Luke says nothing is that he was writing in

---

[24] For the various ancient testimonies, see Larry R. Helyer, *The Life and Witness of Peter* (Downers Grove: IVP; Nottingham: Apollos, 2012), 273–80. For another excellent recent defense of Matthean authorship in the 60s, see Donald A. Hagner, "Determining the Date of Matthew," in *Jesus, Matthew's Gospel and Early Christianity: Studies in Memory of Graham N. Stanton*, ed. Daniel M. Gurtner, Joel Willitts, and Richard A. Burridge (New York and London: T & T Clark, 2011), 76–92.

[25] The best study of Pauline chronology is Rainer Riesner, *Paul's Early Period: Chronology, Mission Strategy, Theology* (Grand Rapids: Eerdmans, 1997). For Paul's arrival in Rome, see 224–27.

62 and brought his story up to the present, not knowing what would happen next, then everything falls into place.[26]

This is an argument based on internal evidence. Those scholars who place much more weight on internal than on external evidence often reject the traditional ascriptions of authorship of the Gospels.[27] But, to be consistent, they ought to value this argument concerning dating much more highly than they often do. The problem here is that there is also internal evidence that points to Luke writing after the fall of Jerusalem to Rome in AD 70. Luke's version of Jesus's discourse to his disciples on the Mount of Olives does not speak cryptically about some coming "desolating sacrilege" in the temple like Matthew's and Mark's accounts do (Matt 24:15 NRSV; Mark 13:14 NRSV). Rather Luke reports Jesus as saying, "But when you see Jerusalem surrounded by armies, then know that its desolation has come near" (Luke 21:20 ESV). A common assumption is that Luke has explained what Jesus was prophesying by describing, after the fact, the nature of its fulfillment. This, of course,

---

[26] Cf. Darrell L. Bock, *Luke 1:1–9:50* (Grand Rapids: Zondervan, 1994), 16–18; Evans, *Matthew*, 4–5.

[27] R. T. France (*The Gospel of Mark* [Carlisle: Paternoster; Grand Rapids: Eerdmans, 2002], 38) correctly observes that "modern scholarship has had a remarkable propensity to regard early church traditions of this nature [i.e., about the composition of the Gospels] as automatically suspect. Actual arguments against taking the traditions seriously are not so common." One common claim is that the earliest testimony comes from Papias, whose works are lost and thus he is quoted only secondhand much later by Eusebius, and that all other early church fathers followed him so that we do not have multiple, independent witnesses. To this France (37 n. 72) replies, "This is not at all obvious, since none of the writers before Eusebius mentions Papias as a source of their information," and their wording is never close enough to suggest literary dependence. When scholars are arguing for the independence from the canonical tradition of noncanonical second- and third-century apocryphal and/or Gnostic documents, much closer verbal parallelism with canonical traditions is routinely explained away as still not close enough to support literary dependence!

requires Luke to have been writing after 70.[28] The puzzling ending of Acts can then be explained as Luke's being satisfied with a narrative that got Paul to Rome, the heart of the empire, the springboard from which the gospel could proceed to the uttermost parts of the earth, as Christ commanded in Acts 1:8.[29] Even so, wouldn't Luke have wanted to describe what happened to Paul? Much of Acts presents parallels between the lives of Paul and Jesus;[30] to create a climax with Paul's execution would have drawn those parallels that much more closely.

On closer inspection, moreover, Luke 21:20 actually explains little. Those who were unfamiliar with the details of the destruction of Jerusalem would simply have had their curiosity piqued when they learned that the city was surrounded by armies. What happened next? Were those armies rebuffed, as sometimes in the Old Testament? If not, what did the invaders do that was such a sacrilege when they entered the city? That Luke says nothing about the razing of the temple or the burning of parts of the city leaves his wording almost as cryptic as Matthew's and Mark's, if it is an "after the fact" explanation.[31] A better explanation comes from David Wenham, who has built an impressive case for seeing all three Synoptic accounts excerpting from an original discourse longer than all the existing versions. Matthew 24:15 clarifies that the "desolating sacrilege" (NRSV) or "abomination

---

[28] E.g., John T. Carroll, *Luke: A Commentary* (Louisville: Westminster John Knox, 2012), 4. Again notice how this is just assumed as matter-of-fact with no discussion of any alternatives.

[29] A view that is also perfectly consistent with evangelical convictions. See, e.g., Ben Witherington III, *The Acts of the Apostles: A Socio-Rhetorical Commentary* (Grand Rapids: Eerdmans; Carlisle: Paternoster, 1998), 62.

[30] Especially, via Luke 9:51 and Acts 19:21, with each of them having a prolonged climactic journey to Jerusalem culminating in arrest and imprisonment. See, e.g., Richard I. Pervo, *Acts* (Minneapolis: Fortress, 2009), 482–83.

[31] Cf. Bo Reicke, "Synoptic Prophecies on the Destruction of Jerusalem," in *Studies in the New Testament and Early Christian Literature*, ed. David E. Aune (Leiden: Brill, 1972), 123; Darrell L. Bock, *Luke 9:51–24:53* (Grand Rapids: Baker, 1996), 1675–77.

that causes desolation" (NIV) alludes to the prophet Daniel, which takes us back to Daniel 9:27; 11:31; and 12:11—texts that all use the identical language for a powerful ruler desecrating the temple. Daniel 11:31 proves particularly relevant because the entire verse reads, "His armed forces will rise up to desecrate the temple fortress and will abolish the daily sacrifice. Then they will set up the abomination that causes desolation." Jesus's words in Luke 21:20 conceptually parallel the first half of this text in Daniel, while Matthew 24:15 actually quotes part of the second half. It makes more sense to suggest that Jesus, alluding to the entire verse in Daniel, said both what Luke and what Matthew record, back to back, paraphrasing the entire verse from Daniel, and that each author has excerpted and preserved half of Jesus's teaching as it fit their specific purposes. If this is true, then we may derive nothing about the date of Luke from his wording here. Moreover, the common view that Matthew and Mark must also have been written after 70 because Jesus could not have predicted this event ahead of time, at least not this specifically, must be rejected. None of Jesus's words involve any information he could not have inferred from Daniel, in his own Scriptures.[32]

Once again, though, we should not overestimate the significance of settling the debates between dating the Synoptics in the 60s versus assigning their composition to the 70s and 80s. Whether written thirty, forty, or fifty years after Jesus's death, the Gospels were produced well within the lifetimes of some who were eyewitnesses of Jesus's ministry. By ancient standards this was a short period of time between the life of a famous individual and the appearance of biographies about him.[33]

---

[32] David Wenham, *The Rediscovery of Jesus' Eschatological Discourse* (Sheffield: JSOT, 1984; Eugene, OR: Wipf & Stock, 2003), 185–92.

[33] For a survey of the main existing representatives of Greco-Roman biography from antiquity, see David E. Aune, *The New Testament in Its Literary Environment* (Philadelphia: Westminster, 1987), 29–36. In the fifth-century BC, we find biographers compiling lives of their contemporaries—Isocrates on Evagoras and

Consider, by way of comparison, what we know about the exploits of Alexander the Great, who lived from 356 to 323 BC, dying before his thirty-third birthday after having conquered more of the ancient Middle Eastern world than anyone before him. The oldest existing biographies of Alexander are by Diodorus in the first century BC, Quintus Curtius in the first century AD, and Plutarch and Arrian (the two best works), who wrote in the early second century AD, more than four centuries after Alexander's death. They, in turn, refer to various earlier written sources, sometimes named, on which they relied, but none of these still exists, and we know nothing else about them.[34] Yet, via the standard canons of research, and especially because Arrian regularly names eyewitness sources, historians of ancient Greece can assemble a detailed summary of Alexander's life about which they remain reasonably confident; world civilization textbooks typically rely on these summaries without hesitation.[35] That we have four biographies of Jesus within thirty to sixty years of his death is nothing short of astonishing by ancient standards. No other examples from antiquity have been preserved of this abundance of information from multiple authors in writings so close to the people and events being described. To reject *a priori* the New Testament Gospels as potential sources of excellent historical information about Jesus of Nazareth is to impose a bias on the

---

Xenophon on Ageisalus. But between the fourth century BC and the fourth century AD, an interval of one to four centuries is far more common (Satyrus on Euripides, Cornelius Nepos and Diogenes Laertius on pre-Christian philosophers, Philostratus on Apollonius, and more fragmentary biographies by Lucian, Porphyry, and Iamblichus). Suetonius, *The Lives of the Twelve Caesars*, include some emperors who overlapped with his lifetime, but they begin with Julius, who died about 115 years before Suetonius's birth.

[34] Eugene N. Borza, "The Nature of the Evidence," in *The Impact of Alexander the Great*, ed. Eugene N. Borza (Hinsdale, IL: Dryden, 1974), 21–25.

[35] See, classically, Robin L. Fox, *Alexander the Great*, rev. ed. (London: Penguin, 2004).

study of history, which, if consistently applied elsewhere, would leave us completely agnostic about anything or anyone in the ancient world!

ANCIENT LIFE SPANS

It is, of course, theoretically possible to accept such a depressing result and to add that, because the average life span of a person living in the first-century Mediterranean world who survived to adulthood was somewhere in the forties,[36] it makes a huge difference how long after Jesus's life the Gospel writers wrote. Indeed, even on the earliest reasonable dates for the Gospels, those writers would have been at least thirty years removed from the events they recounted. If they were even as young as in their late teens during Jesus's lifetime, they would already be in their early fifties in the early part of the decade of the 60s and in their seventies by the 80s. Is it credible to imagine people living this long?

The answer is an unequivocal yes! Many babies, children, and young adults in the ancient world died because of rampant disease without modern medicine.[37] An "average" is not a maximum upper limit; it is a figure arrived at by adding a group of numbers together and dividing by the number of elements in the group. Records from all over the ancient world describe a considerable number of people living into their fifties, sixties, seventies, eighties, nineties, and occasionally even beyond 100.[38] The percentage of the population in any given

---

[36] Ian Morris, *Death-Ritual and Social Structure in Classical Antiquity* (Cambridge: Cambridge University Press, 1992), 74.

[37] John Dominic Crossan (*The Birth of Christianity: Discovering What Happened in the Years Immediately After the Execution of Jesus* [San Francisco: HarperSanFrancisco, 1998], 181) cites Morris (see note 36 above) and immediately adds, "a statistic badly skewed by the fact that about one-third of live births were dead by 6 and about two-thirds by 16." Here he is following Thomas F. Karney, *The Shape of the Past: Models of Antiquity* (Lawrence, KS: Coronado, 1975), 88.

[38] See esp. Tim G. Parkin, *Old Age in the Roman World: A Cultural and Social History* (Baltimore: Johns Hopkins, 2003). On pp. 277–98, he gives charts and tables of the number of people likely to have lived into each decade of advancing age, given a certain life span already achieved. A famous rabbinic tradition (*Pirke*

place and time that did so was noticeably smaller than it is in developed countries today, and that percentage shrank even faster from one decade of life to the next than it does today. But nothing precludes Matthew, Mark, and Luke from having lived into their seventies. And because Mark and Luke are never said to have followed Jesus during his earthly life, they may have been younger still. If they were, say, in their early twenties when Paul began his missionary journeys in the late 40s, they would have still been in their mid-forties in 70 and not yet sixty in the early 80s. We must insist that we still have remarkably good reason *a priori* to trust the information presented about Jesus and those around him in the canonical texts.

The Gospel Genre

All the discussion thus far has nevertheless assumed that the correct literary genre for describing the Gospels is that of biography (or historical biography or biographical history). But is that a well-founded assumption? Compared with modern biographies, Matthew, Mark, and Luke appear to be fairly mediocre candidates for that classification at best. Only two of the three tell us anything about Jesus's birth (Matthew 1–2; Luke 1–2). From Matthew we learn about Jesus's parents fleeing with him as a baby from Bethlehem to Egypt and their subsequent return to Nazareth after the death of Herod the Great (Matt 2:13–21). From Luke we read about his experience in the temple at age twelve (Luke 2:41–52). That is the sum total of what we are told in any New Testament document about anything Jesus did until he began his public ministry at about the age of thirty (Luke 3:23). No respectable modern biographer would skip over that much of any famous person's life!

Aboth 5:24) gives stock characteristics of people decade by decade throughout their lives and likewise goes up to age 100.

Even the roughly three years of Jesus's life that the Gospels do cover, they hardly treat uniformly. Large chunks of time pass by with little comment; others are narrated in great detail. Mark reserves almost half of his narrative for Jesus's preparation for and journeying to his crucifixion and its aftermath (Mark 8:31–16:8). Jesus "resolutely set out for Jerusalem" for his last Passover there barely more than a third of the way through Luke's Gospel (Luke 9:51). Sometimes, especially in Matthew, one or more chapters will be wholly devoted to summarizing one of Jesus's great sermons (Matthew 5–7; 18; 24–25; Mark 13). The closer one gets to Jesus's final week in Jerusalem, the more consistently the Gospels narrate material in chronological order, but frequently, especially during the earlier stages of his ministry, episodes are grouped together topically or according to the form of Jesus's deeds or teachings.[39] Explicitly chronological connectives in the Greek text can be few and far between, while a comparison of the Synoptic parallels discloses another Gospel writer placing a certain incident in a different sequence in his Gospel, showing either that he recognized that his predecessor was not writing chronologically or that he knew he was not doing so himself.[40] As one compares parallel texts further, it becomes obvious that one or more of them is abbreviating, expanding, selecting, explaining, or rearranging material, though without necessarily falsifying anything in the process.

Popular Proposals

To further complicate matters, various other suggestions have competed for acceptance among scholarly analysis of the genre of the Gospels. Some have called them "aretalogies"—Greco-Roman

---

[39] For representative outlines of each of the three Synoptics, see Blomberg, *Jesus and the Gospels*, 130, 145–46, 162–63.

[40] A common feature in Greco-Roman biography. See John Fitzgerald, "The Ancient Lives of Aristotle and the Modern Debate About the Genre of the Gospels," *Restoration Quarterly* 36 (1994): 204–21.

accounts of "divine men" that often embellish or exaggerate the famous feats of a warrior or hero of the remote past. Some use the language of the Greek theater and label them "comedies" (focusing on the happy ending of the resurrection) or "tragedies" (highlighting the horrific experience of Jesus in the crucifixion). Perhaps we are to think of a Gospel as an epic narrative, akin to Homer's *Iliad* or *Odyssey*. Because of various quotations of and even more frequent allusions to the Old Testament, still other scholars suggest "midrash" (a kind of Jewish commentary) on the Hebrew Scripture for the genre of one or more of the New Testament Gospels. Focusing on the symbolism of many narratives, especially the miracles and parables of Jesus, still others propose "parable" or "apocalyptic" as the best way to describe these lives of Christ. And still more options are much less influential.[41]

Enough problems surround each of these alternative proposals that none of them has convinced more than a small portion of the academy. Clearly setting stories about Jesus off from all of these suggestions is the fact that the Gospel writers narrate episodes in the life of a genuine, historical human being who lived during their lifetimes. Despite the references to the Old Testament, the Gospels are not primarily interpretations of other ancient documents but depictions of the fulfillment of the hopes enshrined in many of those documents in the life of a recently deceased individual (Matt 5:17; Luke 24:44). They are not glorifying and distorting the exploits of a person

---

[41] On these various options, see further Craig L. Blomberg, *The Historical Reliability of the Gospels* (Nottingham: Apollos; Downers Grove: IVP, rev. 2007), 298–303, and the literature there cited. For a more recent and thorough survey of proposals, see Judith A. Diehl, "What Is a Gospel? Recent Studies in the Gospel Genre," *Currents in Biblical Research* 9 (2011): 171–99. Even more recently, for an example of Luke as a "tragic biography," see DooHee Lee, *Luke-Acts and Tragic History: Communicating Gospel with the World* (Tübingen: Mohr Siebeck, 2013); for an approach akin to midrash, see Mogens Müller, "The New Testament Gospels as Biblical Rewritings: On the Question of Referentiality," *Studia Theologica* 68 (2014): 21–40.

from centuries past, with a narrative no one can falsify. Unbelieving eyewitnesses remained alive, and an increasingly hostile Jewish and Roman leadership had good reasons to squelch this new sect called Christians. Denying or correcting Christian claims about what Jesus did or said would have best achieved this goal, but this is precisely what no ancient document ever discloses.[42]

Those who are insufficiently familiar with Jesus's world often wonder whether the Gospel should be compared to a historical novel or what in the visual media today is called a docudrama.[43] Maybe we should credit the Gospel writers with knowing their culture and customs well and doing enough historical homework to accurately portray life in Israel in the first third of the first century, in order to create an aura of realism surrounding their characters, just as Herman Melville in nineteenth-century America spent four years on a whaling ship to get all the details right when he wrote his most famous novel, *Moby Dick*.[44] On this scenario only the characters in the Gospels and what they specifically did and said would then be either partly or wholly fictitious. As far as we know, however, historical novels as we think of them did not exist in the ancient world. Writers did pen works of fiction that included a handful of realistic details, but usually introduced characters, actions, customs, or locations that were obviously made up in order let their readers know what kind of literary genre they were

---

[42] Cf. Richard A. Burridge, *What Are the Gospels? A Comparison with Graeco-Roman Biography*, 2nd ed. (Grand Rapids: Eerdmans, 2004), 17–24. It is, of course, possible to label the Gospels as unique, fitting into no known genre at all closely, in which case there are no implications for historicity in any direction. See, e.g., Robert A. Guelich, "The Gospel Genre," in *The Gospel and the Gospels*, ed. Peter Stuhlmacher (Grand Rapids: Eerdmans, 1991), 173–208.

[43] E.g., Douglas A. Templeton, *The Gospels as True Fiction: Literature, Literary Criticism, Aesthetics* (Sheffield: Sheffield Academic Press, 1999).

[44] On which, see esp. Wilson Heflin, *Herman Melville's Whaling Years*, ed. Mary K. B. Edwards and Thomas F. Heffernan (Nashville: Vanderbilt University Press, 2004).

employing (see, e.g., the Old Testament Apocryphal works of Judith and Tobit[45]). This is precisely what one *never* finds in the canonical Gospels. These Gospels are vivid but uncluttered, full of incidental detail, ordinary people, and psychological realism, all of which set them off from the fiction of the ancient Mediterranean world.[46]

Still other individuals raise the question of the miracle stories in the Gospels.[47] Our last chapter will address the problem of miracles in some detail. For the debate about genre, suffice it to say that in the ancient Roman world, the presence of miracles in a narrative did not by itself disqualify it from being considered historical or biographical. A striking analogy appears with the four existing accounts of Julius Caesar deciding to cross the Rubicon River between Gaul and Italy, thereby committing himself to the civil war that would lead to the Roman republic becoming an empire and to Julius becoming its emperor. Among many historians Julius's crossing the Rubicon has been used as the classic example of an incontrovertible historical fact from antiquity, better attested than any other.[48] Yet, exactly as with the four Gospels, the four narratives that include this event are not identical, they choose varying items to emphasize, they have small apparent discrepancies among them, and they even include the occasional account of a miracle. Historians who do not believe in miracles or who think *these* miracle stories to be too poorly supported simply discount them and extract reliable history from the rest of the accounts. They

---

[45] Daniel J. Harrington, *Invitation to the Apocrypha* (Grand Rapids: Eerdmans, 1999), 11, 28–29.

[46] Erich Auerbach, *Mimesis: The Representation of Reality in Western Literature*, ed. W. R. Trask (Princeton: Princeton University Press, 2003 [orig. 1953]), 40–49. Cf. also E. M. Blaiklock, *Jesus Christ: Man or Myth?* (Homebush West, New South Wales, Australia: Anzea; Nashville: Nelson, 1984), 38–47, 68–78.

[47] E.g., Robert M. Price, "Jesus at the Vanishing Point," in *The Historical Jesus: Five Views* (Downers Grove: IVP, 2009), 56–62.

[48] Paul Merkley, "The Gospels as Historical Testimony," *Evangelical Quarterly* 58 (1986): 328–36.

do not attach a new generic identification to the works, calling them something other than biography or history.[49]

Greco-Roman Biographies Up Close

By the process of elimination, therefore, we come back to the genre that we suggested at the outset. Can we speak of the Gospels as biographies? If by that we mean modern, Western biographies, then of course not. Jesus lived in the Middle East, not in the West, and he lived long before the modern era. It would be sheer anachronism and a monstrous injustice to evaluate Matthew, Mark, and Luke by twenty-first-century standards of precision, some of which they probably never even could have imagined![50] Theirs was a world without any symbol for a quotation mark or any felt need for one. As long as writers accurately recounted a speaker's intent, they had freedom in how to phrase his or her exact words. Indeed, one of the admirable traits of capable historians or biographers, it was believed, was to so internalize their sources that they could put their own distinctive stamp on their material, writing their works in their own style and with their own language. They did not feel compelled always to quote those sources verbatim, even though they were certainly permitted to do so at particularly crucial junctures.[51]

Historical and biographical writing until just a few centuries ago, moreover, assumed that there was no point in preserving information about the past unless someone could learn valuable lessons from it. All history writing had an ideological spin to it, and not all ideological spins are wrong.[52] A biography of Kareem Abdul-Jabbar would be

---

[49] Craig S. Keener, *Acts: An Exegetical Commentary*, vol. 1 (Grand Rapids: Baker, 2012), 80–81, 346–48, 382.

[50] Cf. Bird, *Gospel of the Lord*, 71.

[51] See esp. Gary Knoppers, "The Synoptic Problem: An Old Testament Perspective," *Bulletin for Biblical Research* 19 (2009): 11–34.

[52] Keener, *Acts*, vol. 1, 148–65; David B. Capes, "*Imitatio Christi* and the Gospel Genre," *Bulletin for Biblical Research* 13 (2003): 1–19.

absolutely justified in highlighting the ways in which he was one of the greatest basketball players in the history of the sport. Someone who would try to make the same claim about me, based on my intramural career in middle school through college, would be extraordinarily misguided! The idea of producing a bare chronicle of all the words spoken in a particular context, such as the *Congressional Record*, may well never have occurred to anyone in antiquity; and, if it did, others would almost certainly have asked, "What could possibly be the point?" So when modern readers raise questions about whether an ancient author erred in some statement they made, the only way to answer those questions is to have a feel for what would have counted as an error in the context in which the statement first appeared. Round numbers, approximations, boiling down a speaker's words to the gist of what they said, omitting less relevant material, paraphrasing their speech, selecting key events out of a much larger pool of possibilities, inserting running commentary on episodes, and the like, were all standard fare. Indeed, they would have been expected of a good writer.[53]

After nearly a century of scholarly debate then, there is fairly widespread agreement today that the Gospels, while certainly containing a few unique features that set them apart from various other works of their genre, are appropriately labeled as Greco-Roman biographies.[54] I often call them, more specifically, theological biographies.[55] If I wanted to create an overly cumbersome label, I could use "theological, literary

---

[53] Darrell L. Bock, "The Words of Jesus in the Gospels: Live, Jive, or Memorex?" in *Jesus Under Fire: Modern Scholarship Reinvents the Historical Jesus*, ed. Michael J. Wilkins and J. P. Moreland (Grand Rapids: Zondervan, 1995), 73–99.

[54] Burridge, *What Are the Gospels?*; Aune, *New Testament in Its Literary Environment*, 17–67. For a recent overview of scholarship which comes to the same conclusion, see Mariusz Rozik, "Klassische griechische Biografie und Evangelium: Die Frage nach der literarischen Gattung," *Studien zum Neuen Testament und seiner Umwelt* 39 (2014): 111–33.

[55] Blomberg, *Jesus and the Gospels*, 122. Cf. I. Howard Marshall, "Luke and His 'Gospel,'" in *The Gospel and the Gospels*, ed. Stuhlmacher, 273–82; Loveday

biographies" because, in addition to consistently promoting various theological perspectives, they are filled with literary artistry. They are not as artistic as classic Greek plays or ancient novels; but, to varying degrees, they disclose the earmarks of well-written prose designed to capture and keep one's attention, with a panoply of narrative techniques that highlight most what the Gospel writers want people to remember and/or implement.[56]

Still, concluding that the Gospels are biographical is not the same as deciding that everything in them actually happened. It makes it unlikely that they are largely fictitious, but some biographies in Jesus's world were poorly researched while others were well researched. How should we rate the Synoptics? Matthew and Mark say nothing about how they came to know what they narrated. Luke's prologue, on the other hand, gives us a wealth of information. It also most closely resembles the prologues of those ancient histories and biographies scholars generally find to be the most trustworthy.[57] Luke declares that he has "carefully investigated everything from the beginning" (1:3), which includes relying on individuals who were the "eyewitnesses and servants of the word" (v. 2).

Alexander, "What Is a Gospel?" in *The Cambridge Companion to the Gospels*, ed. Stephen C. Barton (Cambridge: Cambridge University Press, 2006), 28.

[56] Cf. Jonathan T. Pennington, *Reading the Gospels Wisely* (Grand Rapids: Baker, 2012), 18–35.

[57] Especially Polybius, Herodotus, Thucydides, Ephorus, Lucian, and Josephus. See Witherington, *Acts of the Apostles*, 24–39. Cf. also Loveday C. A. Alexander, *The Preface to Luke's Gospel: Literary Convention and Social Context in Luke 1.1–4 and Acts 1.1* (Cambridge: Cambridge University Press, 1993). Alexander has been misinterpreted by some as denying historical reliability to Luke-Acts because of the parallels to "scientific prose" which she highlights in Luke's prologue. In her *Acts in Its Ancient Literary Context: A Classicist Looks at the Acts of the Apostles* [London and New York: T & T Clark, 2005], 12–19), she clarifies how this generic label does not denigrate historicity any more than a closer link with Greco-Roman historiography would necessarily vindicate it. For a study that argues for a close link between Luke's preface and "decrees" within Greco-Roman history, see John Moles, "Luke's Preface: The Greek Decree, Classical Historiography and Christian Redefinitions," *New Testament Studies* 57 (2011): 461–82.

The use of the single article in the Greek with the two nouns paired in this fashion suggests the eyewitnesses and those who handed down the tradition were at least two closely related groups and most probably one and the same.[58] Luke adds that his purpose is to convince his patron, Theophilus, and the churches who read his writings, of "the certainty of the things you have been taught" (v. 4).[59] Obviously it would be counter-productive if Luke were caught falsifying his account.

At the same time, every ancient noncanonical writer who has written at any length seems to make mistakes in some places. The most reliable writers did their best not to freely invent material they knew bore no resemblance to the people or events they described. They relied on oral and written sources wherever possible. They compared and contrasted multiple sources for the same time period and made judgments as to who seemed more accurate. Lucian's work, *On History Writing*, shows just how sophisticated the ancient Mediterranean author could be and, in educated circles, was expected to be.[60] But many did not live up to the high standards of the profession. Where should we place Matthew, Mark, and Luke on the spectrum of good-to-bad historical and biographical writing?

The most important method to use to try to answer this question, before turning to the specific details of the texts themselves (our task in chapters 2 and 3), is to research how the oral traditions about Jesus functioned and what, if any, previous written sources the Gospel writers used. Then we can also assess to what extent each writer put his own ideological (in this case, theological) stamp on his document

---

[58] Martin M. Culy, Mikeal C. Parsons, and Joshua J. Stigall, *Luke: A Handbook on the Greek Text* (Waco: Baylor University Press, 2010), 3.

[59] Theophilus's name appears where the patron or sponsor of a historical or literary work often appeared. See, e.g., David E. Garland, *Luke* (Grand Rapids: Zondervan, 2011), 56.

[60] For the various kinds of ancient standards for history writing, see Hemer, *Book of Acts in the Setting of Hellenistic History*, 63–100.

and if the theology supported or distorted accurate history. To do this moves us to the disciplines of source, form, and redaction criticism, areas of Gospel scholarship that dominated most of the twentieth century and still produce lively conversations today.

The Composition of the Gospels

Source Criticism

Source criticism is the analysis of the *written* sources Gospel writers employed. Here New Testament scholars regularly speak about "the Synoptic Problem." This expression refers to debates over the nature of the literary interrelationships among Matthew, Mark, and Luke and whatever other documents they may have used. There are enough places where two and even all three Gospels use exactly the same wording in the Greek to make it highly unlikely that they arrived at that wording independently of one another. Of course, God could have chosen to inspire each author to write the identical words at various points, but in light of Luke 1:1, where Luke betrays awareness of "many" who "have undertaken to draw up an account of the things that have been fulfilled among us," it becomes clear that God did not choose this approach.[61] The Gospel writers behaved like normal historians and biographers. Belief in the inspiration of Scripture does not require the conviction that God bypassed the standard processes of research, merely that he superintended those processes and guided the human writers so they wrote exactly what he wanted (cf. 2 Pet 1:21).[62] The term translated "account" (Gk. *diēgēsis*) most commonly refers to

---

[61] Robert H. Stein, *Studying the Synoptic Gospels: Origin and Interpretation*, 2nd ed. (Grand Rapids: Baker, 2001), 44–45.

[62] For a representative articulation of the classic, evangelical doctrine of the inspiration of Scripture, see David S. Dockery and David P. Nelson, "Special Revelation," in *A Theology for the Church*, ed. Daniel L. Akin (Nashville: B&H, 2007), 138–44.

a written narrative, so we should probably envision written sources in view in Luke 1:1, complementing the oral sources cited in verse 2.[63]

Throughout much of the history of the church, as far as we can tell, people paid little attention to the question of the order in which the Gospels were written.[64] Augustine, in the early fifth century, believed the Gospels were written in their canonical order, with each one aware of those that preceded it (*De consens. evang.* 1.2.4, 4.10.11). A substantial majority of modern scholars have come to the conviction, however, that Mark was written first.[65] Overwhelming internal evidence trumps the tiny bit of late external evidence that exists. Mark is by far the shortest of the four Gospels, and more than 90 percent of its information reappears in reasonably similar form in Matthew and/or Luke. At the same time, frequently the episodes common to Mark and at least one of the other Synoptics are narrated with the fullest amount of detail in Mark. If Mark were not written first, we would have to imagine him adding next to nothing to the already existing Gospels of Matthew and/or Luke, abbreviating his overall narrative, leaving out some of the most cherished teachings of Christ from Matthew or Luke (the Sermon on the Mount, the parables of the good Samaritan and prodigal son, etc.), and yet expanding the amount of detail he provided for the passages he did include. And he would have had to do so, often within one and

---

[63] See esp. its use by other historical writers, cited in Joseph A. Fitzmyer, *The Gospel According to Luke I–IX* (Garden City: Doubleday, 1981), 292.

[64] For an intriguing argument, however, that Papias, following the elder John, believed Mark was written first and that Matthew wrote second and in light of Mark, see Robert H. Gundry, "The Apostolically Johannine Pre-Papian Tradition Concerning the Gospels of Mark and Matthew," in *The Old Is Better: New Testament Essays in Support of Traditional Interpretations* (Tübingen: Mohr Siebeck, 2005; Eugene, OR: Wipf & Stock, 2010), 56. There is a Greek *oun* ("therefore") at the beginning of Papias's words in Eusebius. *Hist eccl.* 3.39.16 (on the composition of Matthew), which is often left untranslated in English, that most naturally refers back to Papias's teaching about Mark in 3.39.15.

[65] The classic articulation was B. H. Streeter, *The Four Gospels: A Study of Origins* (London: Macmillan, 1924; Eugene, OR: Wipf & Stock, 2008).

the same passage, by alternating back and forth in terms of when he was following Matthew and when he was following Luke. There *were* epitomizers of lengthy histories in the ancient Greco-Roman world but none that we are aware of who wrote in such an idiosyncratic way.[66]

Further reasons for taking Mark to have written first include details that are the most vivid in his account, suggesting an eyewitness report; a style and syntax that reflects the most rugged Greek of the Gospels, apparently smoothed out by Matthew and Luke; and awkward or embarrassing details the other two synoptists clarify or omit altogether. Mark also contains the highest incidence of Aramaic words preserved in Greek transliteration of any of the Synoptics. Finally, when one applies the kinds of principles regularly used in textual criticism to the relationships among the Synoptics (harder readings tend to be original; later scribes clarified, smoothed out, or expanded their texts; etc.), Mark consistently emerges as the foundational document that Matthew and Luke must have altered in various ways.[67]

What, then, do we do with the early church's conviction that Matthew wrote first? Papias may have already supplied us with the answer. Whatever Matthew's *logia* were may well have preceded Mark, but the final Gospel of Matthew that we know appears to be an expansion of that document, using information from Mark as well. Luke would likewise have used Mark. Perhaps he also used Matthew.[68] But this is a less probable conclusion. When one adopts all the criteria just discussed, and other signs of literal translation from a Hebrew or

[66] See the detailed demonstration throughout R. A. Derrenbacker Jr., *Ancient Compositional Practices and the Synoptic Problem* (Leuven: Leuven University Press and Peeters, 2005).

[67] Matthew C. Williams, *Two Gospels from One: A Comprehensive Text-Critical Analysis of the Synoptic Gospels* (Grand Rapids: Kregel, 2006).

[68] So especially Mark S. Goodacre, *Goulder and the Gospels: An Examination of a New Paradigm* (Sheffield: Sheffield Academic Press, 1996). Cf. also Mark S. Goodacre and Nicholas Perrin, eds., *Questioning Q: A Multidimensional Critique* (Downers Grove: IVP, 2004).

Aramaic original or of an explicitly Jewish background more generally, and analyzes Gospel texts common to Matthew and Luke but not found in Mark, about half of the time it looks like Matthew contains the older tradition, and about half of the time Luke appears to do so.[69]

These observations have led many Bible students, beginning at least with Friedrich Schleiermacher in the early nineteenth century in Germany, to propose that both Matthew and Luke used a common source for what they share that does not appear in Mark. Because the German word for "source" is *Quelle*, this hypothetical source has conventionally been called Q. That no one has found it preserved independently of Matthew and Luke is not surprising because if its contents were largely or wholly reproduced in these two canonical Gospels, early Christians would have felt no need for preserving it separately. When one looks at the roughly 235 verses that make up "Q," the vast majority of them are teachings of Jesus. We know that a popular literary genre in the ancient Mediterranean world was the collection of the most important or influential teachings of famous rabbis or philosophers. In the second century the apocryphal "Christian" document known as the Coptic Gospel of Thomas was precisely such a collection of 114 sayings. A Roman writer named Diogenes Laertius at roughly the same time wrote *The Lives of Eminent Philosophers*, a series of a dozen biographies that often contain a discrete section listing the most famous teachings of the philosopher whose life is being described. From perhaps the end of the second century in Jewish circles comes the work known as *The Sayings of the Fathers*, a compilation of the most famous teachings of the earliest rabbis and post-Christian Jewish sages. So we might expect the first Christians to have composed something similar. For all we know, Papias's testimony about a document with sayings of Jesus might be referring to this very "Q."[70]

---

[69] For examples, see Stein, *Studying the Synoptic Gospels*, 106–11.

[70] So T. W. Manson, *The Sayings of Jesus* (London: SCM, 1949; Grand Rapids: Eerdmans, 1979), 15–20; Matthew Black, "The Use of Rhetorical Terminology in

A lot of theories about Q go far beyond what we can actually demonstrate, which involve a lot of speculation and which compound somewhat improbable hypotheses until they become highly improbable. Some of these dissect Q into multiple layers of editing that reflect discrete theologies, others theorize about the makeup and location of a "Q community" that relied largely or solely on this "Gospel" for their beliefs about Jesus, and still others imagine that the compiler of Q knew nothing about the passion, death, and resurrection of Christ because it does not contain narratives about them.[71] None of these theories seems plausible, but that should not scare us away from the likely existence of a Q document of some kind.[72] On the other hand, nothing requires Q to have been a *single* document; there may have been more than one collection of Jesus's teachings in circulation. Nor need all of the teachings have been written down; what we call Q may in part represent oral sources or tradition.[73]

At any rate a sizable majority of New Testament scholars today accept what they term the "two-document hypothesis," namely, that Matthew and Luke each used Mark and Q.[74] Numerous other models of their interrelationship at times compete,[75] but, to date, none

---

Papias on Mark and Matthew," *Journal for the Study of the New Testament* 37 (1989): 31–41; and Donald A. Hagner, *Matthew 1–13* (Dallas: Word, 1994), xlvi.

[71] For all of these perspectives, see John S. Kloppenborg Verbin, *Excavating Q: The History and Setting of the Sayings Gospel* (Edinburgh: T & T Clark, 2000).

[72] See, e.g., Darrell L. Bock, "Questions About Q," in *Rethinking the Synoptic Problem*, ed. David A. Black and David R. Beck (Grand Rapids: Baker, 2001), 41–64.

[73] See, e.g., throughout Richard A. Horsley with Jonathan A. Draper, *Whoever Hears You Hears Me: Prophets, Performance, and Tradition in Q* (Harrisburg: Trinity Press International, 1999).

[74] For an excellent defense, see Grant R. Osborne and Matthew C. Williams, "The Case for the Markan Priority View of Gospel Origins: The Two-/Four-Source View," in *Three Views on the Origins of the Synoptic Gospels*, ed. Robert L. Thomas (Grand Rapids: Kregel, 2002), 19–96. For a concise summary of the major approaches to Q, see Benedict Viviano, *What Are They Saying About Q?* (New York: Paulist, 2013).

[75] See the survey of options in Craig L. Blomberg, "The Synoptic Problem: Where We Stand at the Start of a New Century," in *Rethinking the Synoptic Problem*,

has even come close to capturing the amount of support the two-document hypothesis has. To be sure, this still leaves almost a third of Matthew and almost half of Luke unaccounted for. Over the years various hypotheses have postulated additional written sources, oral tradition, Matthew's own memory, and Luke's time with Paul in Judea from 57 to 59, during which he could have interviewed eyewitnesses of Jesus's life, to explain the origin of this singly attested material.[76] Many radical scholars have from time to time imagined one or more Gospel writers simply making things up about Jesus or, more often, assuming the oral tradition could not have been counted on to pass everything down without significant distortion.

Form Criticism and Oral Tradition

Addressing this concern shifts our focus from source criticism to form criticism or *Formgeschichte* ("form history"), as the Germans who first popularized it called it.[77] *Formgeschichte* recognizes the diverse literary forms that go into making a Gospel narrative. Jesus's teachings include parables, proverbs, and longer sermons or discourses. Narrative segments of the Synoptics include numerous pronouncement stories (short self-contained episodes of conflict with the Jewish leaders leading to a climactic and controversial pronouncement by Jesus), accounts of miracles, dialogues initiated by Jesus's own questions, and so on. At times there are distinct principles of interpretation for distinct literary forms. But for a study of the historicity of the Gospels, the key question form

---

ed. Black and Beck, 17–40. Of still more recent proposals, the most important is James R. Edwards, *The Hebrew Gospel and the Development of the Synoptic Tradition* (Grand Rapids: Eerdmans, 2009).

[76] See further Craig L. Blomberg, "When Ockham's Razor Shaves Too Closely: A Necessarily Complex Model of the Development of the Jesus Tradition," in the forthcoming *Festschrift*, ed. Todd Still (Waco: Baylor University Press, 2017).

[77] Especially Rudolf Bultmann, *The History of the Synoptic Tradition*, rev. ed. (Oxford: Blackwell; New York: Harper & Row, 1968; Peabody: Hendrickson, 1994 [Germ. orig., 1921]).

critics have scrutinized is how carefully the constituent elements of a Gospel would have been passed on by word of mouth before the first written sources and eventually the complete Gospels were composed.

EARLIER MODELS

In the heyday of Gospel form criticism, throughout the first half of the twentieth century, the assumptions about the nature of the oral tradition did not inspire confidence in the reliability of the canonical texts. It was assumed that each discrete parable, proverb, pronouncement story, and so on, circulated in glorious isolation from the other units of tradition, with few checks and balances to keep it from being altered, intentionally or unintentionally, along the way.[78] Perhaps at times collections of similar traditions might have circulated together but not in large segments.[79] By looking at the most radically different examples of parallel texts, including some that may not have been true parallels at all, "tendencies of the tradition" were postulated.[80] These included the concepts that the tradition regularly changed the audiences of a given teaching or event, added fictitious details ("embellishments") to stories, made up new material inspired by Old Testament passages or popular folklore, and gave stories new introductions and applications.[81] As recently as the 1990s, the Jesus Seminar, who became famous for their voting on and color-coding the passages in the Gospels according

---

[78] See also Martin Dibelius, *From Tradition to Gospel* (New York: Scribner's Sons, 1961 [Germ. orig., 1919]).

[79] E.g., parables or miracle stories. See, respectively, Joachim Jeremias, *The Parables of Jesus*, 3rd ed. (London: SCM; Philadelphia: Westminster, 1972), 90–96; and Paul J. Achtemeier, *Jesus and the Miracle Tradition* (Eugene, OR: Wipf & Stock, 2008), 55–116.

[80] E. P. Sanders, *The Tendencies of the Synoptic Tradition* (Cambridge: Cambridge University Press, 1969; Eugene, OR: Wipf & Stock, 2000).

[81] See my survey and critique of these and other "laws" of transmission of the tradition as applied to parables in Craig L. Blomberg, *Interpreting the Parables*, 2nd ed. (Downers Grove and Nottingham: IVP, 2012), 85–86, 91–108.

to the likelihood that they really happened, relied on such assumptions and added newer ones. A teaching of Jesus that could not be meaningful apart from the narrative context in which it is embedded could not be historical. Jesus only spoke in short, pithy sayings; he never predicted the future; he never spoke about judgment; and he never made claims about himself. All of these are instead the product of the emerging Christian tradition.[82]

At least the original form-critical presuppositions were based on analogies from folk literature in the ancient Greco-Roman world or from the practices of certain traditional societies in the twentieth century that scholars could study. The new assumptions added by the Jesus Seminar made Jesus utterly unlike anyone in his world and like few if any people in the history of the world, but not in any supernatural way. Clearly they were created to ensure the results that Jesus could not have believed himself to be anyone special, could not have prophesied, or taught about heaven or hell, or given any long sermons. Quickly we are left with Jesus the Oriental guru who makes brief, cryptic comments, never more than a parable in length, who promotes love of God and neighbor, and who offends no one. He is politically correct by modern, liberal standards but inconceivable by first-century Jewish ones.[83]

Even the cochairs of the Jesus Seminar, Marcus Borg and Dominic Crossan, in their prolific writings on Jesus and the Gospels[84] are not as skeptical as the combined results of the Jesus Seminar were, masterminded by Robert Funk, whose own book on the historical Jesus was

---

[82] These were their "rules of oral evidence"—Robert W. Funk, Roy W. Hoover, and the Jesus Seminar, *The Five Gospels: The Search for the Authentic Words of Jesus* (New York and Toronto: Macmillan, 1993), 25–34.

[83] See further Craig L. Blomberg, "The Seventy-Four 'Scholars': Who Does the Jesus Seminar Really Speak For?" *Christian Research Journal* 17.2 (1994): 32–38.

[84] See especially Marcus J. Borg, *Meeting Jesus Again for the First Time* (San Francisco: HarperSanFrancisco, 1994); John Dominic Crossan, *The Historical Jesus: The Life of a Mediterranean Jewish Peasant* (San Francisco: HarperSanFrancisco, 1991).

straightforward in its antisupernatural presuppositions and in its admiration of Thomas Jefferson's approach to the Bible, in which he literally cut all the miracles out of it.[85] But the legacy of the most radical and unfounded assumptions of form criticism can clearly be seen when a contemporary scholar like Bart Ehrman continues to liken the oral tradition to the child's game of telephone, in which a fairly detailed, complex message is whispered into one child's ear, who whispers what he thinks he heard to another child, until after even just a dozen or so participants the message becomes hopelessly garbled.[86] April DeConick is only slightly less anachronistic in her otherwise sophisticated studies of what her students in contemporary, undergraduate classes can remember in various exercises designed to test their memory skills.[87]

TRUSTWORTHY TRANSMISSION

Missing in all this scholarship is an adequate answer to the question of how first-century Jewish and later Greek individuals would have handled traditions they deemed sacred. Three important developments beginning around 1960, still being discussed in current scholarship, point the way to more sufficient answers.[88] The first is what has often been called the guarded tradition hypothesis.[89] Jewish schoolboys

---

[85] Robert W. Funk, *Honest to Jesus: Jesus for a New Millennium* (San Francisco: HarperSanFrancisco, 1996).

[86] Bart D. Ehrman, *Jesus: Apocalyptic Prophet of the New Millennium* (Oxford: Oxford University Press, 1999), 51–52.

[87] April D. DeConick, "Human Memory and the Sayings of Jesus: Contemporary Experimental Exercises in the Transmission of Jesus Traditions," in *Jesus, the Voice, and the Text: Beyond the Oral and the Written Gospel,* ed. Tom Thatcher (Waco: Baylor University Press, 2008), 135–79.

[88] For an excellent overview of these and related developments, see Eric Eve, *Behind the Gospels: Understanding the Oral Tradition* (London: SPCK, 2013; Minneapolis: Fortress, 2014).

[89] Classically articulated by Birger Gerhardsson, *Memory and Manuscript: Oral Tradition and Written Transmission in Rabbinic Judaism and Early Christianity* (Lund: C. W. K. Gleerup, 1961; Grand Rapids: Eerdmans, 1998).

regularly attended school in their synagogues, if they were in walking distance of one, receiving an elementary education from the local rabbis that lasted roughly from age five to age twelve or thirteen.[90] They studied one subject, the Hebrew Scriptures, and their rabbis emphasized the memorization of large parts of it. The standard rabbinic practice was to insist that a passage be learned first and then exegeted.[91] Many Jewish men, therefore, had much of the Hebrew Scriptures committed to memory; rabbis often knew all of it.[92] Greek schoolboys studied Homer's *Iliad* and *Odyssey* in similar fashion, and numerous Greek and Roman accounts of prodigious feats of memorization abound in antiquity.[93] Even the shorter of Homer's epics, the Odyssey, contained over 100,000 words, and the Hebrew Scriptures over 600,000! By way of comparison, the longest Gospel, the Gospel of Luke, contains less than 20,000 words in the Greek text. Jews and Christians throughout the ages, and even today, have repeatedly committed works of this length to memory (as have devotees of other religions).[94] This kind of mas-

---

[90] See esp. Rainer Riesner, "Judische Elementarbildung und Evangelienüberlieferung," in *Gospel Perspectives*, vol. 1, ed. R. T. France and David Wenham (Sheffield: JSOT, 1980; Eugene, OR: Wipf & Stock, 2003), 209–23. Cf. Paul Foster, "Educating Jesus: The Search for a Plausible Context," *Journal for the Study of the Historical Jesus* 4 (2006): 7–33.

[91] Samuel Byrskog, *Jesus the Only Teacher: Didactic Authority and Transmission in Ancient Israel, Ancient Judaism and the Matthean Community* (Stockholm: Almqvist & Wiksell, 1994), 223.

[92] Adin Steinsaltz, *The Essential Talmud* (Cambridge, MA: Basic Books, 2006), 23–24. The relevant traditions come from the Talmudic period (ca. fifth century), but there is no reason not to imagine the practices already in use in the first century, given the ubiquity of learning by rote memory in the ancient Mediterranean world. For Jesus's milieu, see esp. Shmuel Safrai and Menachem Stern, eds., *The Jewish People in the First Century*, vol. 2 (Assen, The Netherlands: Van Gorcum, 1978), 946–58.

[93] Whitney Shiner, *Proclaiming the Gospel: First-Century Performance of Mark* (Harrisburg, PA and London: Trinity Press International, 2003), 104–7. Most of her ancient sources are demonstrably pre-Christian in date.

[94] Thomas Meyer, *Oral Transmission in Judaism and Christianity* (Seattle: CreateSpace, 2010).

tery of so much text seldom happens, however, unless one starts at a very young age, uses rhythm and music (or chanting), along with other mnemonic devices, has help from the poetic form of the material itself, and repeats and practices what they have learned extremely regularly throughout their life. But the first-century world was largely an oral culture, with very few of the verbal distractions of today's world, so that such mastery became much more common than it is today.

To memorize the amount of information found in a single Gospel, therefore, was child's play for many first-century Jews and Greeks. As the first generation of Christians, believing Jesus was God's heavenly sent Son, began to treat the accounts of his ministry with the same respect and devotion they did their Scriptures, they would have been careful to pass them on faithfully. The cultures' commitment to rote memorization would have stood them in good stead.

But what about the longer teachings of Jesus not easily memorized by someone after having heard Jesus deliver them just once? First, we have to realize that members of traditional, oral cultures often cultivated the ability to listen and reproduce much longer stretches of speech than we do or can. Kenneth Bailey once tried playing telephone with a class of students in Lebanon from traditional Middle-Eastern village contexts. They were all able to preserve and pass on the message they were given with great accuracy and didn't understand the point of the exercise![95] Second, since even they had their limits, ancient rabbis allowed disciples to take notes on their talks with a kind of shorthand to help preserve the details of longer discourses, even though they then stressed committing them to memory.[96] Third, most of Jesus's teachings would have been repeated dozens of times as the disciples followed

---

[95] Kenneth E. Bailey, "Middle Eastern Oral Tradition and the Synoptic Gospels," *Expository Times* 106 (1995): 563–67.

[96] Alan R. Millard, *Reading and Writing in the Time of Jesus* (Sheffield: Sheffield Academic Press, 2000), 175–76, 202–4, 227–29.

Christ in his itinerant ministry. If Jesus preached in most or all of the more than 200 villages in Galilee (cf. Matt 9:35; Josephus *Life* 45.235), his followers who regularly accompanied him could easily have heard his messages often enough to cement them in their memories.[97] Finally, Jesus sent out the Twelve, even during his lifetime, to replicate his ministry (Matt 10:5–42), so the apostles would have had practice relating many of those identical teachings as they traveled about, announcing the kingdom of God and healing the sick. By going out in pairs, if one person forgot or misrepresented Jesus's message, the other would have been able to help out or correct him.[98]

At the same time, there is no evidence that ancient Jews treated any traditions, however cherished, with the same degree of respect as they did their already written Bible, especially the Torah ("Law") or first five books attributed to Moses. What is more, rabbis and scribes did make occasional mistakes, even in the copying and recitation of the Law. In addition, the fact that parallel accounts of the same events or teaching of Jesus in the Synoptics always vary from one another a little bit demonstrates that the first generation of Christians did not just memorize a narrative about Jesus verbatim and then pass it along unaltered. The culture of memorization inspires a general confidence in the reliability of the Gospel tradition, but it cannot account for the final form of the Gospels themselves.

A second area of study now comes into play. Modern analysts of the most traditional communities of the Middle East, beginning a half century ago, when there were considerably more of them than remain today, speak of three different kinds of oral tradition. One is "formal,

---

[97] Michael F. Bird, *The Gospel of the Lord: How the Early Church Wrote the Story of Jesus* (Grand Rapids: Eerdmans, 2014), 42.

[98] For both of these last two points, see Gerd Theissen, "Jesus as an Itinerant Teacher: Reflections on Social History from Jesus' Roles," in *Jesus Research: An International Perspective,* ed. James H. Charlesworth and Petr Pokorný (Grand Rapids: Eerdmans, 2009), 98–122.

controlled tradition," akin to the guarded-tradition hypothesis just discussed. A second is "informal, uncontrolled tradition," much like "grapevines" or gossip lines worldwide, where numerous distortions and inaccuracies intrude, often unchecked, especially with information not at all deemed sacred or crucially important. In between comes "informal, controlled tradition."[99] Here communities choose official storytellers, who are authorized to recount important, formative traditions to those communities on a regular basis. But, in part because of the amount of material often involved, they have the freedom on any given occasion to leave out or abbreviate less important or less immediately relevant portions, to amplify or explain other more significant sections, and to paraphrase, rearrange, and otherwise modify the tradition to fit their own purposes, so long as numerous fixed points of the story remain intact.[100] Now we are encountering a process that yields something similar to what we find in the Synoptic Gospels.

Inspiring further confidence in such storytelling is the fact that most everyone in a given community already knew the story, especially the fixed points. Variation in its retelling served to highlight certain portions the storyteller believed were particularly important for the audience at a given moment in time. But if any of the unalterable bits were omitted or garbled, the listeners had both the right and the

---

[99] Kenneth E. Bailey, "Informal Controlled Oral Tradition and the Synoptic Gospels," *Asia Journal of Theology* 5 (1991): 34–54; reprinted in *Themelios* 20 (1995): 4–11. Bailey's research was challenged by Theodore J. Weeden, "Kenneth Bailey's Theory of Oral Tradition: A Theory Contested by Its Evidence," *Journal for the Study of the Historical Jesus* 7 (2009): 3–43; but successfully defended by James D. G. Dunn, "Kenneth Bailey's Theory of Oral Tradition: Critiquing Theodore Weeden's Critique," *Journal for the Study of the Historical Jesus* 7 (2009): 44–62.

[100] See esp. A. B. Lord, *The Singer of Tales*, 2nd ed. (Cambridge, MA: Harvard University Press, 2000); and Jan Vansina, *Oral Tradition as History* (Madison: University of Wisconsin Press, 1985).

responsibility to interrupt and correct the speaker.[101] This phenomenon no doubt explains what are often called the "hard sayings of Jesus"— awkward or potentially embarrassing details in the Gospels that could have easily been left out altogether to avoid misunderstanding if the Gospel writers had felt free to do so. One thinks here, for example, of Jesus's teaching that no human being knew the day or hour of the return of the Son of Man (Jesus's favorite self-designation), not even the Son himself (Mark 13:32)! In an environment in which Christians were increasingly emphasizing their conviction that Jesus was divine, highlighting his ignorance as a human being could prove counter-productive.[102] Why not just leave this bit out? Or consider when Luke phrases Jesus's words to the crowds that whoever would be his disciple must "hate" his family members (Luke 14:26). Fortunately, a parallel text in Matthew, probably from a different occasion, explains this pro-nouncement—disciples must love God far more than parents (Matt 10:37). "Hate" in Semitic thought often meant "love less," "not prefer," or "not choose."[103] But the fact that Luke, writing for a Gentile audi-ence, continued to render Jesus's words so starkly and without expla-nation suggests fairly powerful constraints on the oral tradition and Gospel writers alike.

These constraints appear to have also prevented the canoni-cal authors from making up stories out of whole cloth, so to speak.[104]

---

[101] For application to Gospel criticism, see A. B. Lord, "The Gospels as Oral Traditional Literature," in *The Relationships Among the Gospels*, ed. William O. Walker Jr. (San Antonio: Trinity University Press, 1978), 33–91.

[102] Early Christians certainly did not agree on their explanations. See Francis X. Gumerlock, "Mark 13:32 and Christ's Supposed Ignorance: Four Patristic Solutions," *Trinity Journal* 28 (2007): 205–13.

[103] Robert H. Stein, *Luke* (Nashville: Broadman, 1992), 397. Cf. John T. Carroll, *Luke: A Commentary* (Louisville: Westminster John Knox, 2012), 307.

[104] R. T. France, "The Authenticity of the Sayings of Jesus," in *History, Criticism and Faith*, ed. Colin Brown (Downers Grove: IVP, 1976), 130–31. Cf. Alan Kirk, "Orality, Writing, and Phantom Sources; Appeals to Ancient Media in Some

Various topics missing entirely from Jesus's teaching in the New Testament provoked serious, divisive debate in the first generation of church history. If the Gospel writers felt free to include what they believed the risen Lord was teaching them, maybe even through the words of a Christian prophet, but to refer to them as teachings of Jesus, indistinguishable from the teachings of his earthly life, then we should expect to see various topics in the Gospels that we don't.[105]

Where, for example, are Jesus's views about circumcision? More specifically, is circumcision necessary for salvation? Must uncircumcised adult Gentile men in a world without anesthesia subject themselves to this surgery and the prolonged healing process afterwards in order to become Christ-followers? The Apostolic Council in Jerusalem, narrated in Acts 15, like the book of Galatians, shows how divisive this issue proved about twenty years after Jesus's death. Why did the Gospel writers not put an end to the debate once and for all by simply quoting what Jesus taught about the topic? Apparently, they were unaware of any of his teachings that addressed it, and they did not feel free just to invent a story about Jesus teaching on that topic for the sake of settling the argument.[106] Or consider the issue of prophecy and its evaluation, along with speaking in tongues and its interpretation. In the mid-50s, the church at Corinth was almost torn apart by the combative use of these spiritual gifts. First Corinthians cites Jesus's opinion on theological and

---

Recent Challenges to the Two Document Hypothesis," *New Testament Studies* 38 (2012): 21–22.

[105] For this and additional points in response to the view that early Christian prophecy entirely invented some of the sayings of Jesus now found in the Gospels, see Ben Witherington III, *Jesus the Seer: The Progress of Prophecy* (Minneapolis: Fortress, 1994), 293–328.

[106] By contrast, the Coptic Gospel of Thomas does insert an unparalleled logion attributed to Jesus, which reflects its anti-Jewishness: "His disciples said to Him, 'Is circumcision beneficial or not?' He said to them, 'If it were beneficial, their father would beget them already circumcised from their mother. Rather, the true circumcision in spirit has become completely profitable'" (saying 53)!

ethical matters more than any other epistle, but not a word from Jesus appears in chapters 12-14 where these issues are discussed. Paul must not have known anything from the historical Jesus that was relevant. The Synoptic writers, possibly less than ten years later, added nothing either, not knowing of anything Jesus taught on the matter, nor believing that they had the right to invent something that would be relevant.[107]

Conversely, some emphases in the Gospels do not reflect dominant issues or characteristics of Christianity when the Gospels were written. By far the most common title Jesus uses for himself in Matthew, Mark, and Luke is "Son of Man," a title that occurs only once in Acts and once in Revelation in all of the rest of the New Testament. The Synoptic Jesus regularly teaches about the kingdom of God, speaks in parables to illustrate it, and casts out demons to inaugurate it. But in the rest of the New Testament, references to the kingdom are rare, exorcisms sporadic, and parables nonexistent. The Gospel writers, it would seem, are going out of their way *not* to blur the distinctions between what Jesus did on earth before his death and what he, through the Holy Spirit, enabled his church to understand in the generation immediately afterwards.

One common objection to applying these models of careful transmission of tradition to the Gospels involves the claim that a new sect looking for the imminent end of the world would not have been interested in preserving its history for future generations that it believed would never be born. This charge misreads the spirit of the first generation of church history. While numerous texts disclose a lively hope for the *possibility* of Christ's return within the lifetimes of

---

[107] And 1 Corinthians is the letter of Paul in which he most frequently *does* allude to the teachings of Jesus, especially in support of his ethical and theological mandates. See Craig L. Blomberg, "Quotations, Allusions and Echoes of Jesus in Paul," in *Studies in the Pauline Epistles: Essays in Honor of Douglas J. Moo*, ed. Matthew S. Harmon and Jay E. Smith (Grand Rapids: Zondervan, 2014), 136–38.

his followers, none promises it or requires it.[108] The Essene Jews who populated Qumran, a monastic community on the shores of the Dead Sea from about 200 BC to AD 70 likewise frequently thought they could be living in the last days of human history.[109] Yet they protected their library of sacred and community literature, hiding it in pottery at the backs of caves almost impossible to access, most likely at the time of the war with Rome, so that it remained undiscovered for nearly 1,900 years until just after World War II. Within that library are numerous community documents that explicitly or implicitly disclose a wealth of information about Qumran's history and the convictions of its founder, an otherwise anonymous "Teacher of Righteousness." Their beliefs about possibly living in the final generation before God's apocalyptic intervention into human history did not keep them from carefully preserving all this material.[110] Inconsistently, those who dispute the first Christians having enough interest in the historical Jesus to carefully preserve accounts of his words and works usually go on to assume they did have enough interest in him to retroject later fabrications of what he said and did into narratives purportedly about the historical Jesus. But one can't have it both ways.[111]

The third development of the last fifty years of scholarship is in the area of "social memory."[112] Building on the study of the flexibility

---

[108] See esp. A. L. Moore, *The Parousia in the New Testament* (Leiden: Brill, 1966). Cf. Eckhard Schnabel, *40 Questions About the End Times* (Grand Rapids: Kregel, 2011), 257–63.

[109] John J. Collins, "The Expectation of the End in the Dead Sea Scrolls," in *Eschatology, Messianism, and the Dead Sea Scrolls*, ed. Craig A. Evans and Peter W. Flint (Grand Rapids: Eerdmans, 1997), 74–90.

[110] For excellent comparative material, see C. Marvin Pate, *Communities of the Last Days: The Dead Sea Scrolls, the New Testament and the Story of Israel* (Downers Grove: IVP, 2000).

[111] See further Bird, *Gospel of the Lord*, 39.

[112] For an introduction to its application to Gospel studies, see Richard Bauckham, *Jesus and the Eyewitnesses: The Gospels as Eyewitness Testimony* (Grand

of the transmission of oral tradition, studies of social memory focus on what happens to historical or biographical tradition when it is frequently cited in identifiable *groups* of people. Civic or religious organizations even today often have segments of their history that they appeal to repeatedly, especially in the initiation of new members, cementing those details in their memories through their repetition. A church I was once a part of excelled at this process. New attenders within their first months at the church would hear leaders regularly weave a brief account of the church's origins, its vision and mission, and its current strategies for fulfilling that mission into sermons and other messages. A dozen or more key moments in the church's history that shaped it into what it became were quickly cemented into the "social memory." The advantage of such repetition is that there was little danger that anybody would get this part of the story wrong if they retold it to others.[113] The disadvantage was that, by its nature, social memories eliminate many things that could have been highlighted, which then can fade from collective view.

On the other hand, social memory can mask or distort the truth as well.[114] Years ago an administrator at the seminary where I teach frequently felt required to put a positive public spin on what were actually some rather disturbing events that had occurred in our midst. Initially he knew exactly what he was doing; we had conversations in which I at times questioned the wisdom of such lack of candor, and he would acknowledge privately what had really transpired. But he recounted the story so often in so many public contexts in its "revisionist" form

---

Rapids: Eerdmans, 2006), 240–357. Cf. also Robert K. McIver, *Memory, Jesus, and the Synoptic Gospels* (Atlanta: SBL, 2011), 81–182.; and Bird, *Gospel of the Lord*, 95–113.

[113] On this generally conservative strand of social memory, see Samuel Byrskog, "A New Quest for the *Sitz im Leben*: Social Memory, the Jesus Tradition and the Gospel of Matthew," *New Testament Studies* 52 (2006): 319–36.

[114] On which, see esp. Anthony Le Donne, *The Historiographical Jesus: Memory, Typology, and the Son of David* (Waco: Baylor University Press, 2009), 17–64.

that years later, after his retirement, when I again had occasion to talk to him about those events, he could not remember some of them the way they actually happened, only the way he had so often narrated them. He had convinced himself, as it were, that things were not nearly as bad as he had once, off the record, honestly admitted!

Which type of social memory is enshrined in the Gospels? Have early Christian leaders conspired to whitewash Jesus, turning an ordinary Jewish rabbi or prophet into the divine Son of God?[115] Or have they recognized and highlighted the most important facts about his life as they genuinely transpired? Sometimes the claim is made that writers with an inherent bias in favor of the individuals or movements they describe cannot help but skew their stories in unfair ways that are untrue to history. This, however, is demonstrably false. Of course, people can distort history. But those who have a bias against an individual can often do so even more quickly than those who favor a certain person![116] Conversely, supporters of an ideology who have to overcome great odds against them often go out of their way to state things as accurately and fairly as possible so as not to create extra hurdles for themselves.[117] Christianity fell into this second category as it had numerous enemies who would dearly have loved to catch its

---

[115] To borrow some of the language of the title and thesis of Maurice Casey, *From Jewish Prophet to Gentile God: The Origins and Development of New Testament Christology* (Louisville: Westminster John Knox, 1992; Nashville: Ingram, 2001).

[116] For both phenomena, see Alan Kirk and Tom Thatcher, eds., *Memory, Tradition, and Text: Uses of the Past in Early Christianity* (Atlanta: SBL, 2005). For a recent overview of works that span the gamut of perspectives, see Kelly R. Iverson, "Orality and the Gospels: A Survey of Recent Research," *Currents in Biblical Research* 8 (2009): 71–106.

[117] Cf. Doron Mendels, "Societies of Memory in the Graeco-Roman World," in *Memory in the Bible and Antiquity*, ed. Loren T. Stuckenbruck, Stephen C. Barton, and Benjamin G. Wold (Tübingen: Mohr Siebeck, 2007), 151.

first preachers in serious distortion of their accounts of Jesus's life so they could be discredited. But to our knowledge this never occurred.[118]

Conclusion

Scholarship tends to swing the pendulum from one generation to the next in terms of alternately emphasizing written sources and genres and oral/rhetorical processes. The preoccupation with the Synoptic Problem that climaxed with B. H. Streeter in the 1920s was followed by an intense thirty-year fascination with oral tradition and the more radical versions of form criticism. In the 1950s redaction criticism with its preoccupation with the written editorial and compositional work of each Gospel writer came to the fore. This was supplemented in the 1970s by applications of literary criticism more generally. Now, for the last fifteen to twenty years, there has been a return to an interest of the oral stage of the Gospels' formation with the appeal to Greco-Roman oratory, flexible oral tradition, social memory, and what is increasingly called *performance criticism*—focusing on possible indications in the Gospels that significant portions of them were composed for oral recitation.[119]

James Dunn has stressed in a number of recent writings that we need to combine the best insights of these various schools of thought together rather than pitting them against one another.[120] Thus he still strongly defends Markan priority and Matthew's and Luke's use of Mark in its written form. But he also recognizes that Q (or substantial

---

[118] Ibid., 152. Cf. also Markus Bockmuehl, "New Testament *Wirkungsgeschichte* and the Early Christian Appeal to Living Memory," in ibid., 360–61. More generally, see Michael F. Bird, "The Purpose and Preservation of the Jesus Tradition: Moderate Evidence for a Conserving Force in Its Transmission," *Bulletin for Biblical Research* 15 (2005): 161–85.

[119] See esp. David Rhoads, "Performance Criticism: An Emerging Methodology in Second Testament Studies," *Biblical Theology Bulletin* 36 (2006): 118–33, 164–84.

[120] Conveniently collected together in James D. G. Dunn, *The Oral Gospel Tradition* (Grand Rapids: Eerdmans, 2013).

parts of it) may well have been one or more oral collections of Jesus's teachings rather than a formal, written document. Larry Hurtado has even more recently stressed that studies in orality and performance criticism too easily underestimate the amount of literacy that can be shown to have existed in the ancient Mediterranean world, the amount of reading and writing (including silent reading) that occurred and not just among the elites of society, and the different processes involved in the oral recitation (whether memorized or flexible) of written texts on the one hand and in the performance of oratory or rhetoric designed from the outset only to be read aloud on the other hand. Common estimates of rates of literacy at only 5–10 percent of the Roman world are almost certainly too low, especially in Jewish circles and among men.[121]

Our best efforts and reconstructing the processes that went into the formation of the Synoptic Gospels, taking seriously the ancient external evidence as well as the internal evidence for their authorship and dating, give us optimism about the historical reliability of the information the gospels present. The genre of the Gospels does not perfectly match any known literary form but most closely resembles forms of biography and historiography that were generally trustworthy. All this gives us good reason to suspect that we have reliable narratives in hand when we read Matthew, Mark, and Luke. But the only way to move beyond generalizations and probabilities is to examine carefully the actual details the Gospels contain. How exactly do they differ from one another? Are there plausible explanations for those differences?

---

[121] Larry W. Hurtado, "Oral Fixation and New Testament Studies? 'Orality,' 'Performance' and Reading Texts in Early Christianity," *New Testament Studies* 60 (2014): 321–40. Cf. also the data amassed in Craig A. Evans, *Jesus and His World: The Archaeological Evidence* (Louisville: Westminster John Knox, 2012), 63–88. Though he does not challenge the statistic, per se, the data he presents give him every reason to do so, and he does note that 5–10 percent overall would mean 10–20 percent of the men (with women rarely being taught), and he acknowledges a still higher level of literacy among *Jewish* men.

What about the many small *apparent* discrepancies or contradictions one finds when comparing Matthew, Mark, and Luke? What actually *are* the theological biases of each Gospel writer, and how much do they impact their writings? To answer these and related questions lands us in a study of the debates over harmonizing the Gospels and over what is known as redaction (editorial) criticism. Just how much of his own distinctive stamp did each Gospel writer put on his document and in what ways? These are the questions chapter 2 will address.

Chapter 2

Contradictions Among the Synoptics?

H istorians and biographers may at times have a favorable climate
in which to do their work. They may have access to reliable
information, they may be meticulous in preserving it, and they may be
people of outstanding integrity. But the proof is in the pudding. Does
what they write stand up to careful scrutiny by others in the know?
Does it create a coherent narrative internally and correspond exter-
nally to other accurate information? Does the ideological spin that
guides their process of selection and narration overly skew their stories so they cannot be trusted, however well-meaning their intentions
were? Do they just flat out contradict other historical sources? These
are the kinds of questions that must be addressed in order to move us
beyond the general considerations of chapter 1. In this chapter we will
focus specifically on the charge of blatant contradictions.

Issues Arising from Redaction Criticism

One can compile massive lists, of course, of picayune differences among Matthew, Mark, and Luke that would have bothered no one in the ancient world. As we saw in chapter 1, the freedom to rewrite one's sources in one's own words proved pervasive in antiquity and was even expected of an author who was creating a work that was truly his or her own. To speak of apparent contradictions or seeming discrepancies that would have caused even a moment's concern in the ancient Mediterranean world, we have to find two statements that genuinely cannot be simultaneously true. Even then, space prohibits us from examining every candidate for a real error or contradiction that has ever been suggested. We must look at the most commonly suggested ones and those that impinge on historical matters. There are numerous theological distinctives among the Gospel writers that in no way reflect on their skills as historians. Matthew emphasizes Jesus as the Son of David, Mark stresses that he is the Messiah and Son of God, and Luke highlights his true humanity and compassion for outcasts.[1] These are complementary facets of Christ's character, and hardly contradictions. Countless similar examples could be given.[2]

Our interest is in issues that could reflect poorly on the Gospel writers' ability to depict the events they narrate with the levels of accuracy expected in their world. If a pattern of reasonable solutions to the most blatant or striking examples of supposed errors begins to

---

[1] See esp. Richard N. Longenecker, ed., *Contours of Christology in the New Testament* (Grand Rapids: Eerdmans, 2005), 79–147; and Mark A. Powell and David R. Bauer, eds., *Who Do You Say That I Am? Essays on Christology* (Louisville: Westminster John Knox, 1999), 14–65.

[2] See any standard New Testament theology that discusses the distinctive emphases of each author. Cf. especially I. Howard Marshall, *New Testament Theology: Many Witnesses, One Gospel* (Downers Grove and Leicester: IVP, 2004), 57–154; with Frank Thielman, *Theology of the New Testament: A Canonical and Synthetic Approach* (Grand Rapids: Zondervan, 2003), 57–149.

appear, we may decide to give the authors the benefit of the doubt in the remaining instances (an approach sometimes called a "hermeneutic of consent").[3] If, on the other hand, problems repeatedly seem intractable, then it may be appropriate to develop a "hermeneutic of suspicion"[4] and place the burden of proof on the person who would defend the text's reliability at any point.

Alleged contradictions can appear in two forms. There may be places where one Gospel seems impossible to square with another Gospel. Unless we can suggest a plausible solution, we have a genuine problem. Perhaps one Gospel's account can be vindicated but only at the expense of the other, or vice versa. In rare instances tension may be perceived between a Gospel passage and some historical statement elsewhere in the New Testament. Whichever situation obtains, we could then have an error in Scripture. The second kind of contradiction involves dissonance between one of the Gospels and some information from another ancient source outside the Bible. Here we have to assess the likelihood of the other source's being wrong as well as analyzing the biblical account for credibility. Perhaps there *is* a genuine contradiction, while it is not the Bible that has erred but the outside source. All of these possibilities have to be taken into consideration.

We spoke toward the end of chapter 1 about the debates over harmonization and redaction criticism. Many liberal scholars reject the attempt to harmonize two seemingly discrepant accounts as intrinsically inappropriate,[5] even though this is exactly what classical

---

[3] Peter Stuhlmacher, *Historical Criticism and Theological Interpretation of Scripture: Toward a Hermeneutics of Consent* (Philadelphia: Fortress, 1977; Eugene, OR: Wipf & Stock, 2003).

[4] Alison Scott-Baumann, *Ricoeur and the Hermeneutics of Suspicion* (London and New York: Continuum, 2012).

[5] Most recently and passionately, Kenton L. Sparks, *God's Word in Human Words: An Evangelical Appropriation of Critical Biblical Scholarship* (Grand Rapids: Baker, 2008). The label "Evangelical" in the subtitle corresponds to no historic use of the term of which I am aware, given the package of positions Sparks ends up

historians do on a regular basis wherever there are multiple accounts or pieces of data impinging on events from antiquity.[6] Critics may point to extreme examples of harmonizations that most conservatives themselves reject.[7] Others claim not to reject the task intrinsically but seem to assess every attempt by more conservative scholars to do so as "artificial" or "forced," although curiously they rarely give any reasons for those assessments.[8] So the scholar who would defend a certain harmonization is rendered powerless to respond, not knowing the reasons the critic is unconvinced. Some critics resort to this approach so often that it begins to appear like a substitute for actually giving any cogent reasons for their views that could facilitate genuine conversation.[9] In other words, one begins to suspect they have no good reasons

---

supporting. From a more classically liberal perspective, see John Barton, "Biblical Criticism and the Harmonization of Texts," *Princeton Seminary Bulletin* 26 (2005): 144–56.

[6] Craig L. Blomberg, "The Legitimacy and Limits of Harmonization," in *Hermeneutics, Authority, and Canon*, ed. D. A. Carson and John D. Woodbridge (Grand Rapids: Zondervan, 1986; Grand Rapids: Baker, 1994; Eugene, OR: Wipf & Stock, 2005), 135–74.

[7] For a good collection of illustrations of harmonizations he thinks should be rejected, all of them from Saint Augustine, see Dean B. Deppe, "The Use and Abuse of Harmonization in Gospel Studies: A Review Essay," *Calvin Theological Journal* 35 (2000): 316–18. I agree with most but not all of Deppe's examples. I'm not sure one can create formulas for when harmonizations are acceptable or not; one usually has to consider them case by case.

[8] Both of these approaches appear, e.g., in Christian Smith, *The Bible Made Impossible: Why Biblicism Is Not a Truly Evangelical Reading of Scripture* (Grand Rapids: Baker, 2011), 133–34. Smith goes on to present his "Evangelical" alternative, but one wonders how much he believes in it because he has converted to Roman Catholicism.

[9] For an excellent example, see Sparks, *God's Word in Human Words*, 162–64. My harmonizations are called "historically and rationally strained," which "cannot pass as serious scholarly readings," but are "very improbable reconstructions." But Sparks gives not a single reason for his opinions, nor does he interact with the reasons I gave for the positions I took in my previous publications he was citing, nor does he appear to be aware of the other scholars who hold the same positions

for their viewpoint but have discovered they can effectively dismiss others' arguments in this fashion, at least among readers already sympathetic to their perspectives!

On the other hand, many conservatives have been overly suspicious of redaction criticism. Because it was birthed in German, liberal, higher-critical circles and because many of its most well-known uses have considerably impugned the accuracy of Scripture,[10] a handful of evangelicals would throw the baby out with the bathwater.[11] Careful students of the Gospels, however, have recognized differences in theological emphases from one Gospel to the next ever since the second century.[12] If modern redaction critics have often overemphasized the diversity among the Gospels, that does not change the fact that there

---

I do, but with even more detailed defense, whom I would be surprised to find him dismissing so flippantly.

[10] The three pioneering works, one per Gospel, were Günther Bornkamm, Gerhard Barth, and Heinz J. Held, *Tradition and Interpretation in Matthew* (London: SCM; Philadelphia: Westminster, 1963); Willi Marxsen, *Mark the Evangelist* (Nashville: Abingdon, 1969); and Hans Conzelmann, *The Theology of St. Luke* (New York: Harper & Row, 1960; London: Faber & Faber, 1961; Philadelphia: Fortress, 1982), all translated from German originals.

[11] See esp. most of the contributors to *The Jesus Crisis: The Inroads of Historical Criticism into Evangelical Scholarship*, ed. Robert L. Thomas and F. David Farnell (Grand Rapids: Kregel, 1998), especially the chapters by the editors themselves. Cf. also Norman R. Geisler and William C. Roach, *Defending Inerrancy: Affirming the Accuracy of Scripture for a New Generation* (Grand Rapids: Baker, 2011).

[12] See Craig L. Blomberg, "The Gospels for Specific Communities *and* All Christians," in *The Audience of the Gospels: The Origin and Function of the Gospels in Early Christianity*, ed. Edward W. Klink III (London and New York: T & T Clark, 2010), 111–33. Somewhat similar, though weighted somewhat more to favor the Gospels having a general audience, is Justin M. Smith, *Why Bios? On the Relationship Between Gospel Genre and Implied Audience* (London and New York: Bloomsbury T & T Clark, 2015). Michael F. Bird (*The Gospel of the Lord: How the Early Church Wrote the Story of Jesus* [Grand Rapids: Eerdmans, 2014], 278) captures the best balance when he writes, "It might be better to proffer the view that the Gospels were intended for local digestion within a broad network of like-minded churches with a deliberate and conscious intent of disseminating the document further afar."

is diversity, including theological diversity, which must be taken into account.[13] In fact, it is often possible to harmonize two divergent accounts so that there are no necessary contradictions between them but still be puzzled as to why the divergence exists. In many cases, as we will see, redaction criticism provides the answer. The unique way one or both writers narrate their accounts serves to highlight one of their consistent theological distinctives. Contrary to many on both ends of the theological spectrum, redaction criticism and harmonization need not be mutually exclusive methods but can work hand in hand to give the best and fullest explanation of various Gospel parallels, as we will see in several examples below.

Almost thirty years ago, in my first published book, I included a chapter that illustrated what at that time seemed to me to be a representative cross-section of the most famous apparent contradictions among the Synoptic Gospels, which I arranged topically according to the kinds of problems that were raised.[14] Issues involving discrepancies with noncanonical literature were scattered elsewhere in the book. In my revised edition, twenty years later, I thoroughly updated my discussions but did not change my selection of examples.[15] Here I am choosing primarily to proceed chronologically through the life of Christ, according to the main divisions of a standard synopsis of the four Gospels, lumping all the different kinds of problems together. This will avoid needless repetition and also enable us to determine if clusters of problems tend to be concentrated in certain areas of

---

[13] Note how Ben Witherington (*The Indelible Image: The Theological and Ethical Thought World of the New Testament*, 2 vols. [Downers Grove: IVP, 2009–10]) nicely balances diversity and unity by devoting his first volume to "The Individual Witnesses" and his second to "The Collective Witness."

[14] Craig L. Blomberg, *The Historical Reliability of the Gospels* (Leicester and Downers Grove: IVP, 1987), 113–52.

[15] Craig L. Blomberg, *The Historical Reliability of the Gospels*, 2nd ed. (Nottingham and Downers Grove: IVP, 2007), 152–95.

Christ's ministry. Many of the passages treated will be the same as before, but occasionally my preferred solutions have changed, and often the scholarly support for my positions has grown so I cite different and more recent studies. Space prevents us from treating as many problems as in my earlier book, but we will address the hardest ones and allude to several others more briefly. The ones I allude to briefly I will place at the end of the subsection in which I discuss more fully their closest analogues.

The Infancy Narratives

Genealogies

Right at the outset of Matthew's Gospel, we encounter a complicated and puzzling cluster of questions surrounding the genealogies of Jesus. Matthew starts with Abraham and moves forward selectively when compared with the corresponding Old Testament genealogies (Matt 1:2–17). Luke begins with Jesus and goes backward all the way to Adam, who is then called the son of God (Luke 3:23–38). Language of "begetting" (or being the father or son of someone) could often refer to being an ancestor or descendant, so gaps in genealogies prove no problem.[16] Matthew, as the most Jewish of the Synoptics, addressing the most Jewish-Christian audience, understandably stresses Jesus as Son of David (see already Matt 1:1), and arranges his genealogy in three groups of fourteen (sometimes counting inclusively and sometimes exclusively), with David as the fourteenth name, almost certainly because of the numerical value of the consonants in David's name, which added up to fourteen. *Gematria*, a Hebrew practice of totaling the numbers to which the letters of a word corresponded (because Hebrew did not have separate symbols for numerals), was a common device among

---

[16] Michael J. Wilkins, *Matthew* (Grand Rapids: Zondervan, 2004), 58.

the rabbis, used in this case to highlight the role of David in Jesus's genealogy.[17] There are also variant spellings in Greek transliteration of some of the Hebrew names and some puzzling textual variants here and there. But the only really difficult issue is the completely different list of names in the two genealogies in between David and Jesus. Matthew's version, going through Solomon and the kings who succeeded him, would appear to be the legal or royal line of descent,[18] even though from the deportation to Babylon onward, with the exception of Zerubbabel, the relevant men did not actually reign in Israel. But we know absolutely nothing about the people on Luke's list during this time period—Heli, Matthat, Levi, Melchi, Jannai, and so on (Luke 3:23–24).

From the earliest days in church history, two main suggestions have been offered. One is that Mary was also of Davidic descent, given that Jews tended to marry within tribal lineage, so that Heli was Joseph's *father-in-law*.[19] After all, the Greek merely reads, "Joseph, of Heli, of Matthat, of Levi, and so forth. Referring to Joseph, Jesus's adoptive father, would still carry more weight in a patriarchal world, even if the lineage biologically passed through Mary. The second option is that levirate marriages at one or more points in Joseph's biological ancestry accounted for the divergence.[20] This was the practice whereby a man died without children so his widow remarried one of his brothers in hopes of raising up an heir for her first husband (Deut 25:5–6). This could lead the royal line, which would follow other rules for the nearest male kin, to diverge from the biological/inheritance line. In my earlier writings, I leaned in the direction of the latter solution; but the more I

---

[17] W. D. Davies and Dale C. Allison Jr., *A Critical and Exegetical Commentary on the Gospel According to Saint Matthew*, vol. 1 (Edinburgh: T & T Clark, 1988), 163–65.

[18] R. T. France, *The Gospel of Matthew* (Grand Rapids: Eerdmans, 2007), 32–33.

[19] John Nolland, *Luke 1–9:20* (Dallas: Word, 1989), 170.

[20] D. A. Carson, "Matthew," in *The Expositor's Bible Commentary Revised*, ed. Tremper Longman III and David E. Garland, vol. 9 (Grand Rapids: Zondervan, 2010), 88–90.

reflect on the issue, the more I am inclined today to adopt the former. The Palestinian Talmud refers to the father of Mary as Eli (*j. Sanh.* 23c and *j. Hag.* 77d), while apocryphal Christian traditions call him Joachim (*Protev. Jas.*). But Joachim is a Hebrew variation of Eliakim (with *Joa* and *Eli* both coming from names for God), from which Heli could have been derived.[21] At any rate we know that ancient Israelites kept written records and oral traditions about their ancestries in meticulous detail,[22] so it is not difficult to imagine Jesus's genealogies being preserved. It is hard to envision Luke, or the tradition he inherited, just making up names no one had ever heard of, especially when the Old Testament already gave a list of names to adopt (as Matthew did) down through at least the mid-fifth century BC.

For a similar example of how diverse names may have evolved from one original, see Mark 8:10 and Matthew 15:39. Matthew's Magadan may well be a variant form of Magdala, a well-known town on the western shore of the Sea of Galilee. Magdala comes from the Aramaic *migdal nunya*, meaning "fish tower." This could easily have been shortened to *dal nunya* and then Grecized to Dalmanutha.[23] On the other hand, one or both names may just have referred to sites along the shore near one another. Archeologists have recently discovered a biblical-era town right next door to Magdala, which could be an excellent candidate for Dalmanutha.[24]

---

[21] Robert Geis, *Divinity of a Birth* (Lanham, MD: University Press of America, 2011), 109–10, 173–74 n. 20. See also Jacques Masson, *Jésus fils de David: Dans les genealogies de saint matthieu et de saint luc* (Paris: Téqui, 1982), 365–66.

[22] See the survey of scholarly literature on ancient Jewish genealogies in Jason B. Hood, *The Messiah, His Brothers, and the Nations: Matthew 1.1–17* (London and New York: T & T Clark, 2011), 9–62.

[23] A. H. McNeile, *The Gospel According to St. Matthew* (London: Macmillan, 1915; Grand Rapids: Baker, repr. 1980), 234.

[24] Owen Jarus, "Biblical-era Town Discovered Along Sea of Galilee," *Live Science* (September 16, 2013), accessed December 27, 2015, http://www.livescience .com/39661-biblical-era-town-discovered-sea-of-galilee.html.

Quirinius

After the problem of Jesus's two genealogies, nothing else in our entire survey seems nearly as difficult! A well-known issue involves Quirinius, who is described as holding some kind of governing office in Syria (the Greek verb *hēgeomai* was a general term for leading or ruling), apparently at the time of a Roman census (Luke 2:1–2). Quirinius is known from reliable extrabiblical sources to have been governor from AD 6–9 but not at a time early enough to have been in power when Jesus was born (Josephus, *Ant.* 18.1), and there is an uninterrupted record of governors during the relevant time period. For a while it appeared that new archeological evidence would support a joint rule of some kind between Quirinius and another Roman appointee at an earlier date, but this has not materialized.[25] I am now more inclined to suggest a straightforward alternative translation: "This census took place before Quirinius was governing Syria" (NIV mg). Although *prōtos* elsewhere in Luke always means "first," the second most common meaning of the word is "before,"[26] and the entire Greek clause is notoriously ambiguous because Luke did not use any articles to help make his meaning more precise. The most literal translation that is still intelligible in English is, "This census was first/before Quirinius governing Syria" (*hautē apographē prōtē egeneto hēgemoneuontos tēs Surias Kurēniou*). The text certainly can mean, "This census was the first while Quirinius was governing Syria," but one would normally expect an article before *apographē* and again before *prōtē* if that were Luke's intention. But we could translate, "This census was before [one] when Quirinius was governor."[27] The census in

---

[25] For a full discussion of the scholarly options, see Darrell L. Bock, *Luke 1:1–9:50* (Grand Rapids: Baker, 1994), 903–9.

[26] BDAG, 893.

[27] Nigel Turner, *Grammatical Insights into the New Testament* (Edinburgh: T & T Clark, 1965), 23–24.

AD 6 under Quirinius was particularly infamous because it provoked the failed rebellion by Judas the Galilean. So it would be natural for a biographer or historian to refer to an earlier census with reference to the later, much better-remembered one.[28]

Flight to Egypt

Most of Matthew's and Luke's infancy narratives focus on different events surrounding his birth and earliest years, fitting well with their theological purposes. Matthew 1:18–2:23 shows Jesus to be the fulfillment of five key Old Testament prophecies,[29] while Luke 1:5–2:40 compares and contrasts the births of John the Baptist and Jesus. At one point in particular, however, it is often claimed that one Gospel leaves no room for what the other narrates. Specifically, it is alleged that Luke has no space for the flight of Joseph, Mary, and their baby to Egypt, their sojourn there, and their return to Israel possibly up to a couple of years later (Matt 2:13–23).[30] After all, immediately after his description of Jesus's presentation in the temple, which would have occurred between five and six weeks after his birth (see Lev 12:1–5), Luke announces, "When Joseph and Mary had done everything required by the Law of the Lord, they returned to Galilee to their own town of Nazareth" (Luke 2:39).

But how long afterwards did this occur? The next two verses in Luke summarize twelve years, a period of time much longer than we would suspect if it weren't for verse 42 specifying the interval. More dramatically still, 2:52 refers to a period of about eighteen years, as 3:23 discloses, as Luke jumps from the twelve-year-old boy Jesus to his life as a man at about the age of thirty. When we recall, however, that

---

[28] Brook R. W. Pearson, "The Lucan Censuses, Revisited," *Catholic Biblical Quarterly* 61 (1999): 281.

[29] See esp. France, *Matthew*, 40–45.

[30] E.g., C. F. Evans, *Saint Luke* (London: SCM; Philadelphia: Trinity Press International, 1990), 221.

ancient biographers often skipped over large, comparatively unimportant stretches of their subjects' lives, this should not surprise us. Neither should we balk if a source other than Luke tells us more that occurred in between Mary and Joseph's fulfilling their legal requirements in Jerusalem after Jesus's birth and their resettlement in Nazareth. Nor should we assume there is a contradiction between their being guided to Nazareth, which Matthew does not mention until 2:22–23, and Luke's record of their returning to their original home (Luke 2:39).[31] It appears likely that they initially planned to resettle in Bethlehem because the Magi find them living in a home there, possibly up to two years after Jesus's birth (Matt 2:11, 16), no doubt to avoid the stigma and ostracism that would have constantly surrounded them in tiny Nazareth.[32] But, when Herod's orders to kill the babies in and around Jerusalem forced them to flee and when they learned that the worst of his sons, Archelaus, was ruling in Judea after his death, it was clearly better to suffer some social discomfort back in Galilee than to risk the child's life again.

Initial Ministry

The Order and Nature of the Temptations

As Jesus begins the public phase of his life, he is baptized by John and driven by the Spirit into the wilderness to be tempted by the devil. The temptations of Jesus (Matt 4:1–11; Mark 1:12–13; Luke 4:1–13) present an interesting collection of issues that trouble some people. Matthew and Luke each present three distinct temptations the devil

---

[31] John Nolland, *The Gospel of Matthew* (Milton Keynes: Paternoster; Grand Rapids: Eerdmans, 2005), 122.

[32] See esp. Scot McKnight, "Jesus as *Mamzer* ('Illegitimate Son')," in *Who Do My Opponents Say I Am? An Investigation of the Accusations Against the Historical Jesus*, ed. Scot McKnight and Joseph B. Modica (London and New York: T & T Clark, 2008), 133–63.

employed—telling Jesus (1) to satisfy his hunger by turning stones to bread, (2) to throw himself off the temple portico so angels could come and miraculously save his life, and (3) to worship Satan himself in exchange for authority over all the kingdoms of earth. Matthew presents these in the order (1), (2), (3), while Luke has (1), (3), (2). Yet like so many places in the Gospels (which we will not have the space to discuss) where the order of events varies, at least one of the divergent accounts does not make any claims to being in chronological order. Here Luke 4:5 and 9 begin the second and third temptations simply with the Greek conjunctions *kai* and *de* ("and" and "but"), which imply no necessary temporal sequence. Redaction critics have highlighted the importance of the temple for Luke-Acts, so it is not surprising that he would arrange his scenes so that Satan's tempting Jesus on the temple becomes the climactic one.[33] Matthew is more naturally understood as presenting the chronological sequence, as he uses *tote* and *palin* ("then" and "again") to introduce his second and third scenes.[34] Yet even these words in Greek were often used logically rather than chronologically, so even Matthew may not be focusing on the historical order of events.[35]

A different kind of "contradiction" appears with Satan's showing Jesus all the kingdoms of the world from a high mountain. Even the more limited geographical knowledge of people in the first-century Roman Empire included awareness that one couldn't come close to seeing all of the known world from any mountain in Israel—or any other mountain for that matter. This detail is more likely the Gospel writers' way of letting their readers know that Jesus is not literally climbing a tall mountain in his emaciated state after a prolonged fast.

---

[33] Jeffrey B. Gibson, *The Temptations of Jesus in Early Christianity* (Sheffield: Sheffield Academic Press, 1995), 32–37.

[34] Carson, "Matthew," 139.

[35] E.g., Grant R. Osborne, *Matthew* (Grand Rapids: Zondervan, 2010), 129.

That itself would require the kind of miracle Jesus is refusing to perform during his temptations! Rather it suggests a visionary experience—no less real for Jesus but not something any time traveler with a video camera could have recorded.[36]

Sermon in Nazareth

A second example involves the location of an entire passage in the Synoptic narratives. Mark 6:2–6a, followed by Matthew 13:54–58, places Jesus's inaugural sermon in Nazareth well into Jesus's Galilean ministry, while Luke 4:16–30 puts it at the beginning. All three passages begin with *kai* ("and"), so none of them is necessarily implying chronological sequence. But in Matthew and Mark the immediately preceding verses are somewhat closely tied in with the new accounts (Mark 6:1; Matt 13:53), whereas Luke 4:15 ends with a generalizing comment about Jesus's teaching in many Galilean synagogues. So it is most natural to assume Luke has moved this passage nearer to the beginning of his narrative of Jesus's public ministry as a kind of frontispiece or headline over his career more generally—the fulfillment of the Scriptures about his rejection by many in Israel.[37] Redaction criticism highlights both of these as recurring Lukan emphases. Of course, Matthew and Mark have such streamlined accounts compared to Luke's that occasionally it has been suggested that they are narrating a separate event from Luke altogether.[38] But the climactic proverb about no prophet being acceptable in his homeland occurs, in varying

[36] Wilkins, *Matthew*, 160 n. 15; Walter L. Liefeld and David W. Pao, "Luke," in *Expositor's Bible Commentary, Revised*, ed. Tremper Longman III and David E. Garland, vol. 10 (Grand Rapids: Zondervan, 2007), 101; Robert H. Mounce, *Matthew* (Peabody: Hendrickson, 1991; Grand Rapids: Baker, 2011), 31.

[37] I. Howard Marshall, *The Gospel of Luke* (Exeter: Paternoster; Grand Rapids: Eerdmans, 1978), 177–80.

[38] E.g., William L. Lane, *The Gospel of Mark* (Grand Rapids: Eerdmans, 1974; London: Marshall, Morgan & Scott, 1975), 201 n. 2.

forms, in all three Synoptics (Matt 13:57; Mark 6:4; Luke 4:24), so this seems unlikely.

Similar issues surround the differences among Matthew 4:18–22; Mark 1:16–20; and Luke 5:1–11 on the call of the first disciples. Here all three Synoptics agree in putting their accounts early in Jesus's ministry, but Luke again has a much fuller account with enough different, even if not discrepant, details to make one wonder at first if the incidents are even the same. Still they probably are.[39]

Abiathar

Bart Ehrman's theological pilgrimage from a professing evangelical Christian to an avowed agnostic has brought Mark 2:26 into the limelight in recent years. Ehrman tells the story of writing a paper for a doctoral seminar defending one of the classic Christian harmonizations of this verse with its parallels, only to have his Princeton professor ask him why he could not just accept that Mark made a mistake when he referred to Abiathar rather than Ahimelek as the high priest at the time David and his men ate the holy "bread of the Presence" reserved only for priests (see 1 Sam 21:1–6).[40] Because Ehrman had been taught in a conservative branch of evangelicalism that if you acknowledged one error in Scripture, you might as well abandon it all, he fulfilled his teachers' prophecy and slid down the "slippery slope" to unbelief. But no responsible historian would ever treat any other ancient document that way! If it turned out that there were a few minor errors in Scripture, one would have to revise one's understanding of inspiration to one of several Christian alternatives (most notably

---

[39] See further Joseph A. Fitzmyer, *The Gospel According to Luke I–IX* (Garden City: Doubleday, 1981), 560.

[40] Bart D. Ehrman, *Misquoting Jesus: The Story Behind Who Changed the Bible and Why* (San Francisco: HarperSanFrancisco, 2005), 9.

infallibilism, neoorthodoxy, or accommodationism),[41] but there would certainly be no reason to suspect the biblical writers on any widespread basis. That kind of suspicion should follow only after discoveries of considerable amounts of mistaken reporting.

But is there no plausible explanation of Mark's use of Abiathar? Mark here uses none of the standard Greek ways of referring to time. The expression is *epi Abiathar archiereōs*, the most common translation of which would be "upon Abiathar, high priest," an expression that makes no sense at all in this context. Although *epi* is an extremely common preposition in Mark, occurring fifty-one times altogether, only in eighteen cases does it appear with a genitive (rather than dative or accusative) object. Sixteen of those eighteen uses can easily be translated by "on, upon, before or in the presence of," all standard meanings of *epi* when followed by a genitive object.[42] But Mark 2:26 makes no sense with this kind of translation, nor does 12:26, which speaks of reading in the book of Moses *epi tou batou* how God spoke to Moses. God did not speak to Moses upon the bush, before the bush, or in the presence of the bush. The burning bush itself *was* the manifestation of God in this theophany; God spoke from *within* (Heb. *mittōk*) it (Exod 3:4). Thus the major Bible translations use a well-attested subordinate usage of *epi* and translate "in the account/story/passage about the bush."[43]

Why not use that approach, then, in Mark 2:26 as well? Mark would thus be referring to a segment of the Hebrew Scriptures much larger than the six verses in Samuel that talk about David and Ahimelek, just as Jewish readings of the Scriptures in weekly

---

[41] See esp. William P. Brown, ed., *Engaging Biblical Authority: Perspectives on the Bible as Scripture* (Louisville and London: Westminster John Knox Press, 2007).

[42] Mark 2:10; 4:1, 26, 31 (2X); 6:47, 48, 49; 8:6; 9:3, 20; 11:4; 13:9, 15; 14:35, 51.

[43] BDAG, 363.

synagogue worship often recited several chapters at a time.[44] Abiathar is a much more significant character than Ahimelek and is mentioned twenty-eight times in the Old Testament, in the books of Samuel, Kings and Chronicles, as he continues to serve David throughout his reign. Ahimelek, son of Ahitub, on the other hand, appears only thirteen times, three times only because Abiathar was his son, and all the references are clustered in the latter chapters of 1 Samuel. So it should cause no surprise if an ancient Jew referred to a multichapter passage as about Abiathar.[45] A temporal use of *epi*, as is presupposed by most English translations ("in the time of," "in the days of," "when") is much rarer. [46] Had the King James Version not employed it, it is doubtful if so many translators would have followed suit.

Sermon on the Mount/Plain and Other Shifting Sayings[47]

Jesus's Great Sermon (Matthew 5–7; Luke 6:20–49) raises the question of how to deal with teachings of Jesus found in different contexts from one Gospel to the next. On the one hand, both Matthew's and Luke's sermons begin with the Beatitudes, contain teachings on enemy love, proper judgment, and trees and their fruit (in that order), and end with the parable of the two builders. So it is difficult to think the two evangelists are narrating entirely separate messages from two different settings in the life of Christ.[48] On the other hand, much

---

[44] See esp. Michael D. Goulder, *Midrash and Lection in Matthew* (London: SPCK, 1974; Eugene, OR: Wipf & Stock, 2004).

[45] See esp. John W. Wenham, "Mark 2.26," *JTS* 1 (1950): 156. Cf. also Ben Witherington III, *The Gospel of Mark: A Socio-Rhetorical Commentary* (Grand Rapids: Eerdmans, 2001), 130; and James R. Edwards, *The Gospel According to Mark* (Grand Rapids: Eerdmans; Leicester: Apollos, 2002), 95 n. 42.

[46] BDAG, 367, lists it under the eighteenth and last usage of *epi*.

[47] On the "contradiction" between the mount and the plain, it is now widely recognized that Jesus would have had to stand on some level place within the hill country. See, e.g., Carson, "Matthew," 159.

[48] As, e.g., in John F. Walvoord, *Matthew: Thy Kingdom Come* (Chicago: Moody, 1974), 43.

of Jesus's teaching in the far more detailed version of the sermon in Matthew has parallels scattered throughout the Gospel of Luke. There are two common pitfalls to avoid here. The first is to assume collections of teachings of a given person grouped in one place by an ancient writer must refer to teachings the speaker uttered consecutively on one specific occasion. The second is to imagine that Jesus is likely to have spoken any of his proverbs, parables, blessings and woes, or other pronouncements on only one or even just a handful of occasions.[49] No itinerant teacher in the history of the world, to our knowledge, has composed entirely new material for every new educational context in life. The more memorable and widely applicable a given saying is, the more likely a person will reuse it in countless contexts.[50]

Matthew has five major "sermons" of Jesus in his Gospel, which comprise the bulk of chapters 5–7; 10; 13; 18; and (23–) 24–25. Luke 9:51–18:14 is made up almost exclusively of teachings of Jesus, grouped together topically,[51] with almost no indications of time or place among them. In each case there are few textual clues as to the intentions of the Gospel writers. Did Matthew think, and did he expect his

---

[49] For both of these points and a well-balanced intermediate view, see Leon Morris, *The Gospel According to Matthew* (Leicester: Apollos; Grand Rapids: Eerdmans, 1992), 92: "The best solution to a difficult problem seems to be that Matthew has taken a sermon Jesus delivered, and expanded it by including matter given on other occasions." Cf. John Calvin, *Harmony of the Gospels Matthew, Mark and Luke*, vol. 1, ed. D. W. Torrance and T. F. Torrance (Edinburgh: St. Andrew's; Grand Rapids: Eerdmans, 1972 [Lat. Orig. 1555]), 168. Charles Quarles (*Sermon on the Mount: Restoring Christ's Message to the Modern Church* [Nashville: B&H, 2011], 12–14) argues for one sermon also but plausibly sees Matthew and Luke each selecting from a larger whole.

[50] Cf. Carson, "Matthew," 283: "There are few methodologically reliable tools for distinguishing between, say, two forms of one aphoristic saying, two reports of the same saying uttered on two occasions, or one report on one such a saying often repeated in various forms but preserved in the tradition in one form."

[51] Craig L. Blomberg, "Midrash, Chiasmus, and the Outline of Luke's Central Section," in *Gospel Perspectives*, vol. 3, ed. R. T. France and David Wenham (Sheffield: JSOT Press, 1983; Eugene, OR: Wipf & Stock, 2003), 217–61.

readers to think, that each of his five segments of Jesus's teaching was taught by Christ entirely (or only?) on that specific occasion? Other ancient biographers would sometimes use the nucleus of a message as a jumping-off point for adding further teaching by the same person from other settings as a kind of commentary on the message immediately at hand.[52] Did Luke want to be understood as narrating the ministry of Jesus in chronological sequence on the road to the cross, or was he giving samples of Jesus's teaching during this last stage of his itinerant ministry as he traveled *under the shadow of the cross*, knowing that eventually he would have to head more directly for Jerusalem?[53]

Unfortunately, texts like the parable of the lost sheep, which occur in entirely different contexts in Matthew and Luke, with enough difference in detail to make one wonder if Jesus has tailored one basic narrative in two different ways for two different contexts,[54] are often taken as variations of only one original, so that at least one evangelist (in this case, Matthew) is accused of drastically altering the details of Jesus's original instruction.[55] Isn't it historically far more probable that Jesus would have retold this story dozens, if not hundreds of times, because it so wonderfully epitomizes the heart of his ministry—to seek and save the lost (Luke 19:10)?[56] The same is true with

[52] Joachim Wanke, *"Bezugs- und Kommentarworte" in den synoptischen Evangelien* (Leipzig: St. Benno, 1981).

[53] Marshall, *Gospel of Luke*, 9–10.

[54] Craig L. Blomberg, "When Is a Parallel Really a Parallel? A Test Case: The Lucan Parables," *Westminster Theological Journal* 46 (1984): 78–103; Craig L. Blomberg, "Orality and the Parables (with Special Reference to J. D. G. Dunn's *Jesus Remembered*)," in *Memories of Jesus: A Critical Appraisal of James D. G. Dunn's "Jesus Remembered,"* ed. Robert B. Stewart and Gary R. Habermas (Nashville: B&H, 2010), esp. 94–109.

[55] For this and other examples just from the parables, see Craig L. Blomberg, *Interpreting the Parables*, 2nd ed. (Downers Grove: IVP; Nottingham: Apollos, 2012), 100–104.

[56] I. Howard Marshall, *Luke: Historian and Theologian*, 3rd ed. (Downers Grove and Leicester: IVP, 1998), 116.

Matthew's parable of the talents (Matt 25:14–30) and Luke's pounds (Luke 19:11–27 NRSV), and with Matthew's wedding banquet (Matt 22:1–14) and Luke's great supper (Luke 14:16–24).[57]

At the same time, a pair of passages like Matthew's and Luke's parable of the two builders both appear as the climax to Jesus's great sermon (Matt 7:24–27; Luke 6:47–49), so the variations we encounter between those two versions must be attributable either to the early Christian tradition or to the Evangelists themselves.[58] When we recognize, however, that the changes in Luke's account read like a contextualization for a non-Palestinian Gentile audience, it seems most likely that Luke has made them himself—*precisely to keep the point of the passage clear and unchanged for a different audience*.[59] The Palestinian terrain Jesus frequented was filled with wadis or dry gulches that would fill with torrents of water once in a great while after severe storms and cause flash floods endangering anyone or anything in their paths. The rest of the Greek-speaking world Luke inhabited was more familiar with rivers leisurely overflowing their banks after the rainy season, so the imagery of the passage is altered to correspond accordingly.[60]

The Centurion's Servant

The parallel accounts of the healing of the Capernaum centurion's servant in Matthew 8:5–13 and Luke 7:1–10 illustrate the freedom

---

[57] David E. Garland, *Luke* (Grand Rapids: Zondervan, 2011), 754.

[58] Klyne R. Snodgrass, *Stories with Intent: A Comprehensive Guide to the Parables of Jesus* (Grand Rapids: Eerdmans, 2008), 330–31.

[59] Cf. Craig L. Blomberg, "We Contextualize More Than We Realize," in *Local Theology for the Global Church: Principles for an Evangelical Approach to Contextualization*, ed. Matthew Cook, Rob Haskell, Ruth Julian, and Natee Tanchanpongs (Pasadena: William Carey, 2010), esp. 41–43.

[60] Cf. Arland J. Hultgren, *The Parables of Jesus: A Commentary* (Grand Rapids: Eerdmans, 2000), 133, 135. Cf. also Peter R. Jones, "On Rock or Sand? The Two Foundations (Matthew 7:24–27, Luke 6:46–49)," *Review and Expositor* 109 (2012): 236–37.

ancient writers felt in including or omitting material, along with more specific literary conventions like describing one person acting by means of underlings or intermediaries. We have similar conventions today. We may read or hear in a news report that "the president announced today that ..." when in fact his speech writer crafted the document and his press secretary read it out loud to reporters and photographers. Yet we understand the figure of speech and assume (rightly or wrongly!) that the president did peruse the announcement at some point and approve it in the form in which it appeared. Grammarians of Hellenistic Greek regularly speak of the causative use of the active voice.[61] So when Mark 15:15 declares that Pilate flogged Jesus, everyone familiar with Roman customs would have known that no self-respecting Roman prefect would have picked up a whip and struck a prisoner himself. Rather Pilate *caused* Jesus to be flogged by ordering one or more of his soldiers to do it.[62]

No Gospel writer even *appears* to contradict Mark 15:15. But when we apply what we learn there to the earlier account of the Capernaum centurion, we discover the most probable solution to the apparent contradiction between Matthew and Luke. Matthew, of course, has the centurion come and speak with Jesus himself, whereas Luke's much more detailed version has the centurion send two separate embassies to Jesus—the first one made up of Jewish elders and the second comprising personal friends—to plead for him to heal the servant. Luke's is almost certainly the more literal account, whereas Matthew employs a standard literary convention of the day to abbreviate the passage while making the identical point. Once again harmonization averts the need to call this a contradiction, but redaction criticism explains the divergence. Matthew avoids anything that would paint Jewish

---

[61] E.g., Daniel B. Wallace, *Greek Grammar Beyond the Basics* (Grand Rapids: Zondervan, 1996), 411–12.

[62] Ibid., 412, using the parallel passage in John 19:1.

leaders in a positive light and characteristically abbreviates his sources when they contain miracle stories.[63]

Compare this solution with a classic additive harmonization (two seemingly discrepant details viewed as being just part of a larger whole).[64] Jack Shaffer creates one giant account including every detail in both Matthew and Luke. Thus, as in Luke, the two embassies come and dialogue with Jesus, but then as in Matthew the centurion himself finally comes in person. That much alone is not necessarily improbable, but it results in the composite passage quoting both the second embassy and the centurion as repeating the identical speech nearly verbatim when each arrives. If the centurion had the control over his servants that the speech itself claims, he would have assumed they had carried out his orders and would have added something different, probably an even more forceful plea. Additive harmonizations are appropriate in certain contexts (see esp. p. 90) but this one seems too mechanical, improbable, and unnecessary. One begins to understand why many scholars call the entire method into question.

A similar example appears in Matthew 20:20–21 and Mark 10:35–37. Does the mother of James and John (so Matthew) or the sons themselves (so Mark) make the request that they sit on thrones on either side of Jesus when he comes into his kingdom? Both are possible, either could be asking on behalf of the other, and one could imagine both posing the question. But then we would have to make

---

[63] Cf. France, *Gospel of Matthew*, 309–10.

[64] Jack R. Shaffer, "A Harmonization of Matt 8:5–13 and Luke 7:1–10," *Master's Seminary Journal* 17 (2006): 35–50. Shaffer's claim on p. 44 that a solution like ours denies inerrancy and impugns Scripture is simply false. It is based on his application of a modern standard of precision to ancient biographies that was unknown in Jesus's world. Evaluating Scripture by anachronistic criteria is what actually impugns it as God's Word to the people to whom it was first written, however unwitting Shaffer's disrespect may be!

Jesus reply to each with nearly identical words. Better to understand one Gospel reporting the literal request; the other, the most interested source who was really behind it.[65] After all, even in Matthew, when only the mother is mentioned, Jesus replies with the plural "you," saying, "You don't know what you are asking" (Matt 20:22). He clearly has all three individuals in mind.[66]

The Peak of Jesus's Popularity

Jairus's Daughter

As Jesus's public ministry approaches its highest "approval ratings," Matthew employs a similar abbreviation of a narrative in 9:18–26. Whereas Mark 5:21–43 contains both the arrival of Jairus, telling Jesus his daughter is on the verge of death, and the subsequent arrival of someone from Jairus's home announcing her death, Matthew simply has Jairus come and lament that his daughter has just died. What the emissary from Jairus's house spoke later, Jairus is depicted as saying right away so that Matthew can omit much of the detail of the passage. Craig Evans explains, "Matthew, knowing that by the time Jesus and the father arrive they will find the girl dead (as is implied by the public lamentation; cf. Mark 5:38), has the father say, 'My daughter has just died.'"[67] In so doing, nothing about the sequence and timing of the events being narrated is altered in the least.[68]

---

[65] Osborne, *Matthew*, 738–39. Nolland (*Gospel of Matthew*, 819) observes that "one of the main ways a woman in a patriarchal society could exercise power was in terms of her continuing influence over her adult sons" and sees all three individuals involved in the request.

[66] Craig A. Evans, *Matthew* (Cambridge: Cambridge University Press, 2012), 353.

[67] Ibid., 206.

[68] See further Vern S. Poythress, *Inerrancy and the Gospels: A God-Centered Approach to the Challenges of Harmonization* (Wheaton: Crossway, 2012), 203–11.

Compare also Matthew's abbreviation of the withering of the fig tree from Mark 11:12–14, 20–25 in Matthew 21:18–22 [69] and Luke's abbreviation of the two stages of Jesus's trial before the Sanhedrin from Mark 14:53–15:1 in Luke 22:66–71.[70] This latter example introduces the additional problem of whether the Jewish examination of Jesus violated rabbinic laws. This is not the same kind of apparent contradiction as the others discussed in this chapter because it doesn't involve two separate sources reporting things that happened which seem to be at odds with each other, merely things that happened which appear to have been illegal. Still, plenty of political and religious leaders in the history of the world have violated laws for what they deemed to be "higher" purposes. Luke's recasting of the proceedings to the daytime avoids some illegalities, while others may stem from later laws not yet implemented in Jesus's day.[71]

Gadara, Gerasa, and Gergesa

Names of people and places were extremely susceptible to variant spellings and forms in ancient Hebrew and Greek. Did Jesus exorcise the man possessed with a legion of demons in the region of the Gadarenes (Matt 8:28) or of the Gerasenes (Mark 5:1; Luke 8:26)? What looks at first like a straightforward error by one of the Gospel writers turns out to be a much more complicated problem. On the one hand, some manuscripts of Matthew read Gerasenes, and some of Mark and Luke read Gadarenes, but these are almost certainly scribal attempts to solve the problem by simply changing one Gospel's text

---

Cf. also Robert H. Stein, *Difficult Passages in the Gospels* (Grand Rapids: Baker, 1984), 33–34.

[69] Herman N. Ridderbos, *Matthew* (Grand Rapids: Zondervan, 1987), 389–90; Poythress, *Inerrancy and the Gospels*, 144–48.

[70] Marshall, *Gospel of Luke*, 847; Joseph A. Fitzmyer, *The Gospel According to Luke X–XXIV* (Garden City: Doubleday, 1985), 1466.

[71] See further Josef Blinzler, *The Trial of Jesus: The Jewish and Roman Proceedings Against Jesus Christ* (Cork: Mercier; Westminster, MD: Newman, 1959).

to match another rather than what Matthew, Mark, or Luke origi-nally wrote.[72] Intriguingly, some later manuscripts of all three Gospels change the text to Gergesenes.

Where did all these names come from? Gadara was a city south-east of the Sea of Galilee, too far from the lake for pigs to run from the nearby countryside and throw themselves into the sea (Mark 5:13). Gerasa was even farther to the southeast (modern-day Jerash) and not even associated with territory surrounding the sea. The "region" of Gadara, however, could have been viewed as extending northwestward from the town by that name to include some areas just south and east of Galilee. Gergesa, however, was a village close to the Sea of Galilee on its eastern side. Origen (*Comm. Joh.* 5.41) in about AD 200 identi-fied this site with the location the Gospel writers had in mind. Scribes probably also knew this was the correct location and changed their manuscripts accordingly. Why, then, did the synoptists not originally have "the Gergesenes"? The Aramaic name of the town was Khersa (modern-day Qursi, in Arabic). Mark may well have been unaware of the Grecized version of the name and created his own translit-eration, Gerasa (which is actually a bit closer to Khersa than Gergesa is), not knowing that it was a separate location. Luke then followed Mark. Matthew may have recognized the potential confusion Mark had created and so spoke of the region of Gadara that would encom-pass Khersa.[73] There are other possibilities as well, certainly enough to make labeling the various place-names as flat-out contradictions one with the others extremely premature.[74]

---

[72] See further Bruce M. Metzger, *A Textual Commentary on the Greek New Testament*, 2nd ed. (Stuttgart: Deutsche Bibelgesellschaft; New York: United Bible Societies, 1994), 18–19.

[73] Franz Annen, *Heil für die Heiden: Zur Bedeutung und Geschichte der Tradition vom besessenen Gerasener (Mk 5, 1–20)* (Frankfurt-am-Mein: Knecht, 1976), 201–6.

[74] Vassilios Tzaferis, "A Pilgrimage to the Site of the Swine Miracle," *Biblical Archaeology Review* 15.2 (1989): 44–51.

How Many Blind Men?

A synopsis of the Gospels usually prints four columns for the three Synoptics when it comes to Matthew 9:27–31, in which Jesus heals two blind men. In addition to this text, we discover a similar passage in 20:29–34. In the first text the blind men follow Jesus along a road, crying, "Have mercy on us, Son of David," until he enters a house and asks them if they believe he is able to heal them. They reply, "Yes, Lord," receive their sight, are commanded not to spread the news, but go away and tell people everywhere. In the second passage Jesus leaves Jericho, two blind men call to him while sitting by the roadside with the same plea for mercy and using the same title "Son of David." The crowd tells them to be silent, but they cry all the more passionately until Jesus stops and asks them what they want. They want their "eyes to be opened" (NASB), they receive their sight, and they follow him. Whenever two passages are this similar in one Gospel, some scholars will speak of doublets—two variant forms of one original incident.[75] But the question that must always be asked is if it is realistic to imagine something similar happening twice. In Jesus's world there were far more blind people (and people with other disabilities) than today. Some were abandoned to fend for themselves in the world, but people with similar disabilities would naturally have clustered together for support.[76] Jesus probably encountered far more blind people, whether by themselves, in pairs or in small groups, than we are ever told about in Scripture. A plea for mercy is natural, but the recurring use of Son of David probably links with Jewish tradition that David's son, Solomon, was a renowned healer and exorcist.[77] Besides the healing miracles

---

[75] E.g., Ulrich Luz, *Matthew 8–20* (Minneapolis: Fortress, 2001), 46–47.

[76] Carson ("Matthew," 492) notes that there may have been many blind people in and around Jericho because of the balsam produced there, which was believed to be a remedy for eye maladies.

[77] See esp. throughout Ben Witherington III, *Matthew* (Macon: Smyth & Helwys, 2006).

themselves, everything else between the two accounts differs. So there is no good reason not to treat the two accounts as separate incidents in the life of Christ.[78]

But what about Mark's and Luke's parallels to the second healing miracle, which speak only of "a blind man" who was sitting and begging by the roadside (Mark 10:46–52; Luke 18:35–43)? The rest of the details are so closely parallel to Matthew 20:29–34 that there is no question that these three passages describe the same event. If either Mark or Luke had used language to suggest that there was *only* one blind man, we would indeed have a contradiction. But neither does. Why mention only one? Perhaps he was the spokesman for the two throughout. Perhaps he was well known to the later Christian community. Mark, after all, gives his name—Bartimaeus. Perhaps the story was passed along in tradition originating from him.[79] Perhaps he is the only one who persisted in following Jesus for a long time.[80] Any or all of these responses seem plausible. Of course, Matthew must have had access to information that there was indeed more than just the one man Mark mentioned. But the apostles are accompanying Jesus to Jerusalem by this time, so Matthew's source could easily be his memory. And even if one denies that Matthew wrote this Gospel, there are plenty of other possible sources of independent, historically accurate information, as we have seen above.

Matthew also has two demonized men where Mark and Luke have only one (Matt 8:28; cf. Mark 5:2; Luke 8:27); similar exegetical options emerge for this variation. Lest we think that only Matthew has the propensity for "doubling" characters, see Luke 24:4 (vs. both Matt 28:2 and Mark 16:5) with the number of angels at Jesus's empty

---

[78] France, *Gospel of Matthew*, 65.

[79] Richard Bauckham, *Jesus and the Eyewitnesses: The Gospels as Eyewitness Testimony* (Grand Rapids: Eerdmans, 2006), 39–55.

[80] Mark L. Strauss, *Mark* (Grand Rapids: Zondervan, 2014), 468 n. 6.

tomb. Perhaps the most famous "doublet" in the Gospels involves the feedings of the 5,000 and 4,000 (each of which is found in both Matthew and Mark), but different locations and details suggest separate incidents whereby Jesus is showing himself to be the Bread of Life for both Jews and Gentiles, respectively.[81]

Staff or No Staff?

A famous crux involves what Jesus commanded the twelve disciples to take and not take for their travel when he sent them out to replicate his itinerant ministry. In Matthew 10:9–10 and Luke 9:3 they are forbidden from taking a staff, and in Matthew 10:10 sandals, whereas they are allowed these items in Mark 6:8–9. Of a number of proposed solutions,[82] Grant Osborne seems to have articulated the best one. Matthew and Luke are following Q here, with different instructions pertaining to the similar but not identical commissioning of the seventy/seventy-two (see Luke 10:4), which most likely included the Twelve.[83] Even if one takes all the other "sermons" in Matthew as given in exactly their canonical form on the occasion specified, Matthew 11:1 concludes this "message" (Matt 10:5–42) with a vaguer summary statement than is found elsewhere ("after Jesus had finished instructing his twelve disciples" vs., e.g., "when Jesus had finished saying these things" (7:28), allowing for Matthew to have combined material about the mission of the Twelve from more than one context.[84] Matthew 9:35–38, after all, has already presented teaching parallel to that found in Luke 10:1–4, and Matthew elsewhere conflates Q material with

---

[81] See, e.g., R. T. France, *The Gospel of Mark* (Carlisle: Paternoster; Grand Rapids: Eerdmans, 2002), 306–7. For other possible reasons for Matthew's distinctives, see David L. Turner, *Matthew* (Grand Rapids: Baker, 2008), 393.

[82] Bock (*Luke 1:1–9:50*, 815–16) lists seven main options.

[83] Grant R. Osborne, "The Evangelical and Redaction Criticism," *Journal of the Evangelical Theological Society* 22 (1979): 314–15.

[84] Carson, "Matthew," 153.

Markan material in the same passage (see, e.g., Matt 13:31–32, combining details from Mark 4:30–32 and Luke 13:18–19).[85] But what would lead the Gospel writers to include such obviously diverse forms of Jesus's mandates? Many have noted that Matthew 10:9 uses a different verb for "take" than Mark 6:8, which can mean "acquire" (i.e., "take an extra"), but that does not solve the problem of Luke 9:3 where the verb is the same as in Mark. Redaction criticism again provides the most plausible answer. Throughout his Gospel, Mark draws parallels to the Exodus, and the references to staff and sandals recall Exodus 12:11 and the provisions for the original Passover night. Q, on the other hand, may be following a Jewish tradition similar to one found later in the Mishnah, by which "one may not enter the holy mount with his staff or with his shoes or with his money belt" (*Ber.* 9:5), thereby stressing "the holiness of the mission" (see also Exod 3:5). If one assumes the seventy/seventy-two Jesus sent out in Luke included the Twelve, Mark may have conflated Jesus's instructions from the two different sendings and left no material contradiction (much as Matthew did with the two separate parts of the healing of Jairus's daughter).[86]

---

[85] The full evidence for Matthew conflating Mark and Q here is laid out in Robert E. Morosco, "Matthew's Formation of a Commissioning Type-Scene Out of the Story of Jesus' Commissioning of the Twelve," *Journal of Biblical Literature* 103 (1984): 539–56.

[86] Joel B. Marcus, *Mark 1–8* (New York and London: Doubleday, 2000), 389–90. More strained, given the similarities and contexts of the various Synoptic passages, is the attempt to make Mark refer to an altogether different sending of just the Twelve altogether compared to Matthew and Luke, as in Monte A. Shanks, "An Alternate Solution to an Alleged Contradiction in the Gospels," *Bibliotheca Sacra* 169 (2012): 317–27. Shanks interacts with only half of my proposed solution before rejecting it and not at all with either Osborne or Morosco on whom I rely for more detail (324 n. 21), perhaps because he declines to interact with the Q hypothesis altogether (320 n. 12). I would reject my proposal as well if it contained only the part that Shanks acknowledges!

How Many Anointings?

Patrick Mullen has written an entire little book, *Dining with Pharisees*, designed to introduce laypeople and beginning theological students to just how drastically redaction criticism shows the Evangelists could alter accounts of episodes from Jesus's life.[87] Unfortunately, he picks as an example a passage that is almost certainly not a true parallel to those with which he compares it, Luke 7:36–50, thereby calling into question his entire study! In this Lukan episode, Jesus is invited to the home of Simon the Pharisee for dinner, presumably in Galilee. A notoriously sinful woman from that community crashes the party, takes an alabaster flask of ointment she brought with her, and anoints Jesus's feet and wipes them with her hair. Simon concludes that Jesus cannot be a prophet or he would have recognized who this woman was and disallowed her advances. Jesus replies by telling a short parable about how a debtor forgiven a huge debt will show more gratitude than one forgiven a small debt (vv. 41–43). He then berates Simon for his anemic hospitality and praises the woman for offering wholesome love because he has forgiven her sins.[88] In Mark 14:3–9, paralleled in Matthew 26:6–13, an anointing of Jesus takes place during the last week of his life. This occurs in Bethany in Judea at the home of Simon the leper, also over dinner. Simon was the most common Jewish name in the first century,[89] and washing someone with perfume was a common gesture of honor.[90] Doing it at dinnertime when someone was a special guest would ensure that he was publicly honored. So far the similarities should cause no surprise.

---

[87] J. Patrick Mullen, *Dining with Pharisees* (Collegeville, MN: Liturgical, 2004).

[88] For the latest in a series of his articles on this topic, see J. J. Kilgallen, "Faith and Forgiveness: Luke 7, 36–50," *Revue Biblique* 112 (2005): 372–84.

[89] Bauckham, *Jesus and the Eyewitnesses*, 70.

[90] Strauss, *Mark*, 606–7.

Most of the other details differ, often dramatically. In Mark and Matthew, nothing negative is said about the woman at all. She pours her ointment on Jesus's head not his feet. The host does not respond, but Jesus's disciples show indignation, yet not because of who the woman is but because of the financial waste involved. Jesus replies by reminding them they always can and should help the poor but there is a time and place for "one-off" lavish devotion to the Lord. He interprets the anointing as preparation for his burial and promises that wherever the gospel is recounted, this woman's sacrifice will be related as well. If this is the same account we find in Luke, then someone has indeed radically transformed the original story. But why would anyone ever think it was the same story?

The answer lies in the only significant verbal parallelism in the entire passage—the repetition of *alabastron murou* in Mark 14:3 and Luke 7:37. However, this appears to be a stereotyped formula for any fancy long-necked jar of perfume, such as were common in Jesus's context (much like "silverware" is made out of many things besides "silver" today), and an alabaster jar was the container of preference for costly perfume.[91] So it is not surprising, after all, to find these two words reused in two different incidents involving anointing. Someone unfamiliar with papal protocol today might be convinced that two separate accounts of the same pope walking down airplane stairs onto a tarmac, kissing the ground, and being greeted by dignitaries in a formal welcoming line, each of whom kisses his hand, must be doublets of a single original story because those are far too many details to recur repeatedly. In fact, there have been dozens of such papal visits with this exact cluster of details since airplanes were invented! So it is not surprising to find both a Pharisee and a leper with this name.

---

[91] "Unguents Keep Best in Containers of Alabaster" (Pliny, *Hist. nat.* 13.3.19)

Sign or No Sign?

Did Jesus reply to skeptical Jewish leaders asking him to produce a sign from heaven by dismissing their request altogether, promising that no sign would be given (Mark 8:12), or by insisting that no sign would be given except the sign of Jonah (Matt 12:39; 16:4; Luke 11:29)? Probably the latter. Mark presents an abbreviated account because he recognizes that the sign of Jonah is not at all the kind of sign the religious leaders have requested. The death of the Messiah does not fit the Jewish leaders' plans; if Rome is not overthrown, even a resurrection won't convince them! For all realistic intents and purposes the sign of Jonah is no sign at all.[92]

A similar "discrepancy" involves Matthew's exception clause permitting divorce in the case of sexual infidelity (Matt 19:9), when Mark does not portray Jesus offering any permission for divorce (Mark 10:11–12). But permission to divorce and remarry in the case of adultery seems to have been universal in ancient Jewish, Greek, and Roman circles, so Mark may not have felt the need to spell it out. David Instone-Brewer captures the dynamics well: "Matthew's addition ... was a correct reinsertion of well-known details that had been abbreviated out of the account in Mark, because without them the Pharisees' question makes no sense. These additions would have been self-evident to any contemporary Jew, who would have inserted them mentally if they were not present."[93]

Herod and Philip

Another example of apparent tension with noncanonical sources appears with the Synoptic accounts of the death of John the Baptist.

---

[92] Jeffrey B. Gibson, "Jesus' Refusal to Produce a 'Sign' (Mk 8.11–13)," *Journal for the Study of the New Testament* 38 (1990): 37–66.

[93] David Instone-Brewer, *Divorce and Remarriage in the Bible: The Social and Literary Context* (Grand Rapids: Eerdmans, 2002), 187.

Josephus has an account of this event as well, with most of his details fitting in well with the Gospel narratives. The most difficult of the handful of seeming discrepancies is that Mark says Herod (i.e., Herod Antipas, also called Herod the tetrarch [Matt 14:1], son of Herod the Great) married his brother Philip's wife Herodias, who had a daughter named Salome, whereas Josephus calls Herodias's first husband simply Herod, while recounting that Philip's *wife* was Salome. Strauss explains matters well:

> We must first acknowledge that the Herod family tree is enormously complex with a great deal of (sometimes incestuous) intermarriage. This, together with the names we don't know, makes relationships very difficult to untangle. Salome, for example, Herodias's daughter by her first marriage, was at the same time Herod Antipas' niece (the daughter of his half-brother Philip), his grandniece (since Herodias, his wife, was also his half-brother Aristobolus's daughter), and his stepdaughter (his new wife Herodias' daughter). We must add to this the fact that all of the Herods (Antipas, Aristobolus, Philip, Archelaus, etc.) can be referred to simply as "Herod." Finally, there are many people in this tangled genealogy with the same name. The simplest solution is that there were two Herod Philips. Herodias' first husband—referred to simply as "Herod" by Josephus (*Ant.* 18.5.1 §109; 18.5.4 §136)—was actually named Herod Philip, as Mark asserts (6:17). He was a different son of Herod the Great than Philip the Tetrarch (Luke 3:1), who later married Salome, Herodias' daughter (*Ant.* 18.5.4 §137).[94]

"Herod" had become a dynastic name that could apply to any male member of the extended Herodian family. If one finds it too incredible that

---

[94] Mark L. Strauss, *Mark* (Grand Rapids: Zondervan, 2014), 264.

there should have been two men in that family named Philip, consider this: we already know from Josephus that this family contained two different Antipaters, Alexanders, Aristobuluses, Agrippas, Jotapas, Salomes, and Mariamnes.[95] That there could have been two Philips suddenly seems a rather natural possibility. The younger one may even have been named after the older, as happens so often in family trees in all cultures.

Water Walking

A classic example of how harmonization and redaction criticism can work together to make sense of parallel passages comes with the endings of the accounts of Jesus's walking on the Sea of Galilee (Matt 14:22–33; Mark 6:45–52). In Matthew 14:33, we read that the disciples in the boat "worshiped" Jesus, "saying, 'Truly you are the Son of God.'" Dramatically differently, Mark 6:51–52 asserts, "They were completely amazed, for they had not understood about the loaves; their hearts were hardened." Surely two such diametrically opposite reactions couldn't have been simultaneously true! Or could they? A little bit of empathetic imagination suggests that most human beings would have a mixture of the two reactions. How could the miraculous appearance of Jesus on the lake in the middle of the night after the disciples' great toil and peril, leading to the sudden stillness of the surroundings, not have led to awe and adoration? "Son of God" in this context did not mean the second person of the Trinity, coequal with the Father and the Spirit, as in creeds of later centuries. It was a term used in the first-century world for all kinds of apparently personal manifestations of the divine.[96] Whatever the disciples meant, it

---

[95] For helpful visuals of Herod's family tree, see http://www.google.com/search ?q=Herod's+family+tree&sa=X&tbm=isch&tbo=u&source=univ&ei=P5W7Ue7n K4fyqQGRuoC4DQ&ved=0CCwQsAQ&biw=819&bih=521, accessed December 29, 2015.

[96] See especially Adela Yarbro Collins and John J. Collins, *King and Messiah as Son of God: Divine, Human, and Angelic Messianic Figures in Biblical and Related Literature* (Grand Rapids: Eerdmans, 2008).

wasn't as much as Peter did two chapters later when Jesus praises his use of the title as having come from a direct revelation by God (Matt 16:16–17). They still lacked all kinds of understanding; their amazement (and who of us would not have been amazed?) shows that their hearts had only begun to soften at the revelation of Yahweh.[97]

The more interesting question is *why* Matthew and Mark conclude their Gospels so differently, especially since Matthew is most likely aware of Mark's version (recall chap. 1). Here redaction criticism supplies a ready answer. Mark's is the Gospel that regularly portrays the misunderstandings and failures of the disciples in order to encourage a Roman Christian community undergoing hard times that timidity in the face of growing opposition does not prevent God from continuing to work powerfully through a person. Matthew, on the other hand, most highlights acts of reverence and devotion toward Jesus and frequently heightens Mark's already existing "Son of God" Christology, in the context of an apologetic addressed primarily to Jewish individuals, in order to convince them or strengthen their faith about who Jesus truly was. Once we recognize these recurring emphases and distinctives, the variations make perfect sense.

Later Ministry

The Timing of the Transfiguration

As Jesus prepares to journey toward the cross, he reveals himself in another theophany, this time to Peter, James, and John on the Mount of Transfiguration. A fairly minor difference among the parallels

---

[97] Mary Ann Beavis (*Mark* [Grand Rapids: Baker, 2011], 108) adds, "The cowardice of the disciples is underlined by the fact that in ancient Greco-Roman tradition, phantoms (ghosts of the dead) are either stopped short or destroyed by bodies of water; the audience would judge that the disciples are not only fearful but also rather foolish."

nevertheless puzzles the average reader and illustrates again how harmonization and redaction criticism can dovetail. In Mark 9:2 and Matthew 17:1, the transfiguration occurs six days after Christ's prediction of some of his followers seeing the kingdom come with power, probably a reference to this event. Luke, however, says it was "about eight days after Jesus said this" (Luke 9:28). The word "about" obviously leaves room for the number to be an approximation. "After six days" could, of course, mean "seven days later" so the historical reality may have been that exactly one week separated Jesus's prediction from its fulfillment. But *why* did none of the Gospel writers just say "seven days" or "one week" later?

Commentators have frequently suggested that Mark was deliberately making an allusion to the experience of Moses on Mount Sinai who received a divine revelation after six days of God's covering the peak with a cloud of his glory (Exod 24:16).[98] Enough of the other details of the two events are similar enough to make this plausible, especially if one recalls the parallel between Moses's second experience with God on the mountain in Exodus 33:22, in which he reveals himself in "passing by" Moses, and Jesus's walking on the water, in which he passes by the disciples on the lake (a detail found only in Mark 6:48, using the same Greek word as in the LXX of Exodus). Luke, a Gentile writing to the most Gentile Christian audience of the four Gospels, may know that literally the transfiguration took place eight days later but uses "about" so as not to directly contradict Mark. There is also some evidence that the expression was just a Greek idiom for "a week," since ancient cultures often counted inclusively, so that both the first and last days of an interval of time would be enumerated. In this form of reckoning a week would be eight rather than seven days.[99]

---

[98] E.g., Craig A. Evans, *Mark 8:27–16:20* (Nashville: Thomas Nelson, 2001), 35; Strauss, *Mark*, 382.

[99] Colin J. Hemer (*The Book of Acts in the Setting of Hellenistic History*, ed. Conrad H. Gempf [Tübingen: J. C. B. Mohr, 1989; Winona Lake, IN: Eisenbrauns,

The Rich Young Ruler and Jesus

The weaknesses of purely additive harmonization are well illustrated in Jesus's dialogue with the rich young ruler. Mark 10:17 has the man approach Christ, asking, "Good teacher, what must I do to inherit eternal life?" Luke's parallel reads almost identically (Luke 18:18). Matthew 19:16 does not have "good" modifying teacher but does have the man refer to a "good" thing he should do. In Mark and Luke, Jesus replies by asking the man why he calls him good, because "no one is good—except God alone" (Mark 10:18; Luke 18:19). Matthew probably wanted to avoid the misunderstanding that Jesus was denying his own goodness, so he paraphrases Jesus's question as "Why do you ask me about what is good?" (Matt 19:17).[100] Clearly the man *has* asked about one or more good deeds, when he inquired about how to inherit eternal life, even in Mark's and Luke's versions. Matthew 19:16 simply highlights this by making what the man should do explicitly "good" and by not explicitly calling Jesus "good"—because Jesus's reply no longer plays directly off the man's *calling* him good. But Matthew 19:17 ends with, "There is only One who is good," implying the identical conclusion Mark and Luke spell out—only God is ultimately good. Apparently, Matthew didn't understand his rewording to be changing the gist of the conversation since this specific question and answer end at exactly the same place.

Additive harmonization would insist on doubling the length of the exchange so the man would have come to Jesus and asked, "Good teacher, what must I do to inherit eternal life? And, teacher, what good thing must I do to get eternal life?" Or, at the very least, it would

---

1990], 356) labels this the "normal inclusive rendering of a 'week.'" He is followed by Garland, *Luke*, 392.

[100] E.g., France, *The Gospel of Matthew* (Grand Rapids: Eerdmans, 2007), 731; Evans, *Matthew*, 344; Davies and Allison, *A Critical and Exegetical Commentary on the Gospel According to Saint Matthew*, vol. 3 (1997), 555.

require the man to have said, "*Good* teacher, what *good* thing must I do to inherit (or get) eternal life?" Then Jesus would have had to reply, "Why do you call me good? No one is good except God alone. And why do you ask me about the good? There is only One who is good." Or perhaps this kind of harmonizer will acknowledge that "No one is good except God alone" and "There is only One who is good" mean essentially the same thing, but they will still insist on having both "Why do you call me good, and why do you ask me about the good?" included as two separate questions.[101] But this is methodologically akin, even if less dramatic, to the sixteenth-century Reformer, Osiander, harmonizing Matthew's and Mark's accounts of Jesus's encounter with Jairus by insisting that he raised her from the dead on two separate occasions![102]

Matthew and Mark are simply illustrating the freedom that raised no eyebrows in the ancient world to reword one's source material in order to highlight different nuances of the same original statement or question.[103] Whether we can reconstruct that original exactly is less important because the Christian doctrine of Scripture attaches authority to the canonical forms of the text, not any hypothetical reconstruction of what lay beneath them.

The Parable of the Wicked Tenants

Contrast the previous example with the questions raised by the three endings of the parable of the wicked tenants, in which tenant farmers have repeatedly refused to give their absentee landlord his portion of the farm's produce and have beaten his servants and killed his son who have come to try to collect it. Jesus has created a transparent

---

[101] As esp. in Robert L. Thomas, "The Rich Young Man in Matthew," *Grace Theological Journal* 3 (1982): 235–60.

[102] On which, see Stein, *Difficult Passages in the Gospels*, 12.

[103] Carson ("Matthew," 478) suggests the question was, "Why do you ask *me* questions regarding the good?"

allegory for the behavior of the Jewish leaders in Israel of his day, as they have refused to obey God, have persecuted his prophets, and will soon kill his Son.[104] After telling the story, all three Synoptic versions agree that Jesus asked what the vineyard owner would do in response. Matthew then states that the crowd replied, "He will bring those wretches to a wretched end," and "he will rent the vineyard to other tenants, who will give him his share of the crop at harvest time" (Matt 21:41). Mark 12:9 has Jesus answer his own question: "He will come and kill those tenants and give the vineyard to others," while Luke 20:16 mirrors Mark, except that after Jesus's answer, the crowd replies "God forbid!"

One can understand the quick response of some who would assume that if it is not a contradiction for one Gospel to have the crowd support the punishment of the tenants and for another to have them oppose it, then there is no such thing as a contradiction anywhere in the world! Once again, however, one has to try to enter into the scene with some historical empathy. It is not as if the Gospel writers attribute flatly contradictory statements to a single individual. These are the responses of the people milling about in the temple precincts as Jesus teaches there the last week of his life. Apart from prearranged orchestration by a leader, there has probably never been a large group in the history of the world that has responded, in unison, with the identical words to a rhetorical question asked by a public speaker! In part depending on how much of Jesus's allegory someone grasped and in part dependent on their disposition toward the Jewish leaders, different people would have shouted out different things in response to Jesus's question and to one another's comments. If Jesus wanted to let the people know his views, he would have had to answer his own question after receiving different responses from different people in the

---

[104] See esp. Klyne Snodgrass, *The Parable of the Wicked Tenants* (Tübingen: J. C. B. Mohr, 1983; Eugene, OR: Wipf & Stock, 2011).

crowd. Additive harmonization in this instance *is* the most historically responsible way to explain the variant accounts among the Synoptics.[105]

Zechariah, Son of Berekiah

One of the odder anomalies in the Gospels involves Jesus's words at the climax of his woes against certain Pharisees and scribes in Matthew 23:33–36. Here he is predicting God's wrath against the current generation of religious leaders as the culmination of punishment for various Israelite leaders' hostility against God's spokesmen and faithful servants within the nation over the centuries. Specifically, he proclaims, "And so upon you will come all the righteous blood that has been shed on earth, from the blood of righteous Abel to the blood of Zechariah son of Berekiah, whom you murdered between the temple and the altar" (Matt 23:35). Most commentators assume this is a reference to Zechariah son of Jehoiada the priest, who rebuked the disobedient Israelites toward the end of the period of the divided kingdom (2 Chr 24:20).[106] The next verse in this Old Testament account declares that the people plotted against him and stoned him to death in the temple courtyard (v. 21). Jesus, the oral tradition of his words, or perhaps Matthew himself has just accidentally confused this Zechariah with the more famous Zechariah son of Berekiah, who was the prophet whose words appear in the Old Testament book that precedes Malachi.[107] Because 1–2 Chronicles together formed the last

---

[105] Somewhat paradoxically, this traditional harmonization is made more plausible by a postmodern form of interpretation known as reader-response criticism, which stresses the different responses different readers or interpreters will make to narratives, based both on their social locations and the "meaning" they contribute to the story itself from a variety of preunderstandings.

[106] For a recent defense, see Isaac Kalimi, "The Story About the Murder of the Prophet Zechariah in the Gospels and Its Relation to Chronicles," *Revue Biblique* 116 (2009): 246–61.

[107] Or "deliberately conflated" the two, as suggested by Osborne, *Matthew*, 857. But what exactly does this mean in this specific context, and how does it preserve

book in the sequence of the Hebrew canon, the pair of Abel son of Adam, killed by his brother Cain, and Zechariah son of Jehoiada then encapsulates every innocent martyr from the beginning to the end of the Hebrew Scriptures.[108] One could even give the first Christians the benefit of the doubt and presume that Jehoiada's father, who is never mentioned in Scripture or elsewhere in Jewish tradition, was another Berekiah and that "son" is being used to mean "grandson."[109]

But there were plenty of innocent martyrs in Jewish history between the early sixth century BC, during the lifetime of Jehoiada, and Jesus' day.[110] Why would Jesus skip all of them? Why would a first-century generation be punished for their ancestors' sins over a long period of time that did *not* include the six most recent centuries prior to their current rebellion? Maybe only "biblical" history was being traversed, due to the belief in the cessation of prophecy after Malachi,[111] but that still leaves the period of time between the early sixth century and the late fifth century BC. Given that most of the names in the Gospels are not presented along with their patronymics ("son of so-and-so"), why is Zechariah's father's name specified, unless to clarify which Zechariah was being referenced? And if it was

---

Matthew from the charge of error (since Osborne is an inerrantist)? Removing the father's name altogether, as Luke does, would be the obvious way to conflate—i.e., say something that is true about each Zechariah in one place. But "conflation" alone does not make Jesus's statement about Zechariah son of Jehoiada also true of Zechariah son of Berekiah.

[108] Of many possible examples, but with more primary literature cited than most, see Craig S. Keener, *The Gospel of Matthew: A Socio-Rhetorical Commentary*, rev. ed. (Grand Rapids: Eerdmans, 2009), 556.

[109] E.g., Carson, "Matthew," 545.

[110] Consider, classically, the Maccabean martyrs during the persecution by Antiochus Epiphanes and during the Jewish revolt against the Seleucids, which that persecution spawned. Cf. further Étienne Nodet, "Le meurte de Zacharie fils de Barachie (Mt 23,35)," *Revue Biblique* 117 (2010): 430–34.

[111] On which, see especially Benjamin D. Sommer, "Did Prophecy Cease? Evaluating a Reevaluation," *Journal of Biblical Literature* 115 (1996): 31–47.

a conscious decision to specify which Zechariah, is it as likely that the wrong one would be mentioned, especially when we recall the care with which Jews preserved genealogies? By the same logic it seems unlikely that this is some other unknown Zechariah, closer in time to Christ,[112] since adding "son of Berekiah" would naturally make people think of the only Zechariah son of Berekiah known in any ancient writing (Zech 1:1) of whom we are aware.

Intriguingly, two later rabbinic traditions suggest this Zechariah was also martyred in the temple (*Targ. Lam.* 2:20c; late mss. of *Liv. Proph.* 15, 23).[113] Is this just confusion within Jewish tradition, independent from Jesus's teachings? Given the care the later rabbis took to avoid including anything within their literature that would support Christian claims, indeed given their willingness to censor their own literature and take out texts that might abet Christianity,[114] it seems unlikely they would have allowed such confusion to remain. Prophets frequently preached in the temple precincts; it was the only place in Jerusalem with space for a large crowd where people regularly gathered. If action were to be taken against one of God's spokesmen because people disliked his message, this would be the natural place for it to occur. If this is the prophet behind the canonical book of Zechariah, Jesus would be referring to the entire sweep of biblical history, and he would not have made a mistake. This is a good example of a problem that on the one hand, makes little difference to the overall thrust of the passage. Were someone to conclude it were a simple error by the Evangelist, virtually no other passage or topic would be affected. On the other hand, precisely because the issue seems so trivial, many commentators appear just to repeat the "received wisdom" without

---

[112] As in J. M. Ross, "Which Zechariah?" *Irish Biblical Studies* 9 (1987): 70–73.

[113] Charlene McAfee Moss, *The Zechariah Tradition and the Gospel of Matthew* (Berlin and New York: de Gruyter, 2008), 117–20.

[114] On censorship of Jesus traditions themselves, see Peter Schäfer, *Jesus in the Talmud* (Princeton: Princeton University Press, 2007), 133–44.

thinking through if it is actually the most historically probable solution, errancy or inerrancy notwithstanding.

Christ's Return Within One Generation?

Mark 13:30 and parallels no doubt form the most famous text in which Jesus supposedly predicted his return within the lifetime of his disciples. If that is the meaning of the passage, then he was a false prophet. But what is the context for Jesus's solemn asseveration, "Truly I tell you, this generation will certainly not pass away until all these things have happened"? He is speaking to his disciples on the Mount of Olives, having predicted both the destruction of the temple (vv. 2, 14) and the coming of the Son of Man in clouds with great power and glory (v. 26).[115] Verse 30 comes at the end of a short parable or extended metaphor: "Now learn this lesson from the fig tree: As soon as its twigs get tender and its leaves come out, you know that summer is near. Even so, when you see these things happening, you know that it/he is near, right at the door" (vv. 28–29). When Jesus continues to predict that "all these things" will happen in his generation (v. 30), he must be referring back to whatever "these things" referred to in his previous sentence (v. 29). But in verse 29, "these things" cannot include Christ's return because when they occur Christ's return will only be near. If they include his return, then Christ would be *here*, and the signs would be pointless because he would have already come back. So Jesus must be referring to everything he has described earlier in the chapter *prior* to his return, that is, everything leading up to and including the destruction of the temple, which occurred in AD 70,

---

[115] For the overall interpretation of this discourse, see especially George R. Beasley-Murray, *Jesus and the Last Days: The Interpretation of the Olivet Discourse* (Peabody: Hendrickson, 1993; Vancouver: Regent, 2005); and Timothy J. Geddert, *Watchwords: Mark 13 in Markan Eschatology* (Sheffield: JSOT, 1989; London: Bloomsbury, 2015).

exactly forty years after his death—one generation by common biblical definitions.[116]

Mark 9:1 (and parallels) and Matthew 10:23 are the two other main passages that have sometimes been interpreted as failed prophecies of Jesus about his immediate return. But Mark 9:1 is best taken as referring to the transfiguration,[117] while Matthew 10:23 probably alludes to the perennially incomplete Jewish mission.[118] There are other options for each of these three texts, as well, which the standard commentaries survey. But given Jesus's emphasis on ethical living, with provisions for how his followers—and those who came after them—should behave in community after his departure, it is highly likely that he envisioned the movement he founded outlasting him for more than just one generation.[119] On historical grounds alone, then, the interpretation of these passages as Jesus's failed prophecy is about the least likely of all to be the correct one!

Passion, Death, and Resurrection

Most of the biggest problems for harmonization of parallels during the last phase of the Gospel narratives involve one or more of the Synoptics versus John. After all, this is the only place where John runs a reasonably close parallel to Matthew, Mark, and Luke for any prolonged stretch of his text. We will deal with the most important of

---

[116] For similar approaches, see Carson, "Matthew," 569; C. E. B. Cranfield, *The Gospel According to Saint Mark*, rev. ed. (Cambridge: Cambridge University Press, 1977), 408–9.

[117] Cf. Robert H. Stein, *Mark* (Grand Rapids: Baker, 2008), 410–11; Evans, *Mark 8:27–16:20*, 29.

[118] Cf. J. M. McDermott, "Mt. 10.23 in Context," *Biblische Zeitschrift* 28 (1984): 230–40; Keener, *Gospel of Matthew*, 324; Evans, *Matthew*, 224.

[119] See esp. Leonhard Goppelt, *Theology of the New Testament*, vol. 1 (Grand Rapids: Eerdmans, 1981), 77–119.

these issues in our discussion of the Fourth Gospel (see below). But a couple of intra-Synoptic problems merit comment here.

The Sequence of the Last Supper

Additive harmonization works well when one encounters the fact that Mark and Matthew describe Jesus's distributing the bread and the cup, in that order, and investing them with symbolism about his coming death (Mark 14:22–25; Matt 26:26–29), whereas Luke appears to have reversed the order by having Jesus describe the cup first and then the bread (Luke 22:15–19a), with different teaching about the cup. Support for a simple reversal by Luke grows when one observes that some good, ancient manuscripts lack verses 19b–20. But the best textual evidence supports their inclusion, and these verses also refer to the cup as "the new covenant in my blood," much as in Matthew and Mark.[120] In other words, Luke actually has the sequence cup-bread-cup. When one realizes that four cups of wine were drunk during a Passover meal, one before and one after the serving of the main portion of the meal, it seems likely that Luke is simply narrating a fuller account of the meal.[121] Having not mentioned the earlier cup, Mark has the additional teaching about the cup the only place where it can be—when Jesus is drinking one of the prescribed cups of wine immediately after breaking the bread (Mark 14:25; cf. Matt 26:29).

Judas's Suicide

Matthew and Acts create the apparent contradiction in this example. In Matthew 27:3–10, Judas hangs himself, and the chief priests use

---

[120] See esp. Bradly S. Billings, *Do This in Remembrance of Me: The Disputed Words in the Lukan Institution Narrative (Luke 22.19b–20)* (London and New York: T & T Clark, 2006).

[121] Robin Routledge, "Passover and Last Supper," *Tyndale Bulletin* 53 (2002): 203–21. Cf. Graham N. Stanton, *The Gospels and Jesus*, rev. ed. (Oxford: Oxford University Press, 2002), 277.

the money they paid him to betray Jesus, which he had thrown back at them, to buy the "Field of Blood" as a burial ground for foreigners. In Acts 1:16–20, Judas himself buys the field, falls headlong, and his abdomen bursts open, spilling his bowels as he dies. I. Howard Marshall, typically resistant to all but the most convincing of harmonizations, has the best suggestion here:

> (1) Judas hanged himself (Matt.), but the rope broke and his body was ruptured by the fall (possibly after he was already dead and beginning to decompose); (2) What the priests bought with Judas' money (Matt.) could be regarded as his purchase by their agency (Acts); (3) The field bought by the priests (Matt.) was the one where Judas died (Acts).[122]

For a different kind of tension between Matthew and Acts, see the Great Commission on baptizing "in the name of the Father and of the Son and of the Holy Spirit" (Matt 28:19) and the primitive church doing it "in the name of Jesus" (Acts 2:38). The solution here is most likely that neither phrasing is a technical formula that was intended to be the one and only set of words to use for baptism.[123]

Conclusion

As we mentioned at the beginning of the chapter, this is just a selection of the most prominent supposed contradictions either among the Synoptics or between one or more of the Synoptics and some other noncanonical source. We have not considered arguments from silence—why one Gospel omits what another one contains. It is hard enough at times to intuit why certain passages *were* included; it becomes almost hopelessly subjective to speculate as to why some were

---

[122] I. Howard Marshall, *Acts* (Leicester: IVP; Grand Rapids: Eerdmans, 1980), 65.

[123] This also accounts for the appearance of a "Trinitarian" formula this "early"—see further Craig L. Blomberg, *Matthew* (Nashville: Broadman, 1992), 432–33.

not preserved.[124] At any rate, not including a particular episode from the life of Christ or not preserving a particular detail within a given episode does not create a contradiction with a text that does contain that episode or detail; contradictions occur only when information in one Gospel cannot be true if information in another text is also true.

Nor have we dealt with New Testament uses of the Old Testament. This is a study all of its own, and many excellent compilations of research already exist.[125] Suffice it to say that when a passage from the Old Testament is explicitly said to be fulfilled in the New, but when that Old Testament text does not appear to be predicting what the New Testament claims or when that Old Testament text does not even make a future-referring statement, the practice of typology is almost always at work. This was a widely employed hermeneutic in ancient Jewish, Greek, and Roman circles whereby recurring patterns of God (or the gods) acting in history, especially to create and to redeem, were attributed not to coincidence but to divine design. In such instances, the New Testament writer is not claiming to be giving the original meaning of the Old Testament text, merely its contemporary analogue as a divinely intended repetition of God's earlier activity.[126]

For other more minor problems, or for other perspectives on the problems treated here, one should consult the wealth of evangelical commentary literature available these days, especially in the more detailed, recent, and scholarly series or volumes. Not every commentator has the space or desire to deal with every question readers may

---

[124] At times redaction criticism can help, however, when one observes that an omission removes a favorite theme of the earlier source because it is less stressed in the later one. Form-critical studies of the processes of the oral tradition can also lead to informed guesses as to reasons for omission. Recall chap. 1 above for both of these tools.

[125] Most comprehensively, see G. K. Beale and D. A. Carson, eds., *Commentary on the New Testament Use of the Old Testament* (Grand Rapids: Baker, 2007).

[126] Cf. esp. Leonhard Goppelt, *Typos: The Typological Interpretation of the Old Testament in the New* (Grand Rapids: Eerdmans, 1982).

have, but a survey of the half dozen best on any Gospel usually turns up something significant and helpful on just about any worthwhile question.[127] Occasionally, one's research has to range a little bit further.

In a sense this chapter can be thought of as a form of "damage control." How does one approach the various so-called contradictions in the Synoptic Gospels? Our conviction is that there are historically responsible ways to deal with them. Sometimes there is more than one option, and it is not always obvious which is best. Occasionally, none of the options suggested may commend themselves as entirely satisfactory. But we have surveyed enough of them to posit that because plausible solutions have emerged in at least a majority of instances, the texts deserve the benefit of the doubt where we are not as confident in our resolutions of problems. Despite greater scholarly scrutiny of the birth and death of Jesus, due to their theological importance, we have not encountered any greater cluster of problems there than elsewhere, though an examination of the Gospel of John (chaps. 4–5) could change that. All this chapter accomplishes, however, is to bring us back to our starting point, after having had to retreat due to the thrusting and parrying of the critics. We have fended off their biggest attacks, but can we move forward and occupy the high ground by marshaling *positive* evidence for believing in the trustworthiness of the bulk of the Gospel testimony that we have not examined? In particular, are there specific details that can be corroborated by extrabiblical sources? This is the question chapter 3 must tackle.

[127] The Denver Seminary website includes the *Denver Journal*, edited by Richard S. Hess, which is an online journal of book reviews and which also contains Old and New Testament departmental bibliographies that are regularly updated. Among other categories of tools recommended are the departments' choices for the best commentaries for evangelical students, book by book in several classifications. See http://www.denverseminary.edu/resources/denver-journal, accessed December 29, 2015.

Chapter 3

Corroboration of the Synoptics

The archaeological evidence directly or indirectly supporting the details of the Gospels by itself occupies a large volume.[1] When we add other forms of extrabiblical support and the application of the most common criteria of authenticity, still other sizable tomes can be produced.[2] Once again, therefore, our overview will have to be highly

---

[1] See esp. Bargil Pixner, *With Jesus in Galilee According to the Fifth Gospel* (Rosh Pina: Corazin, 1992; Collegeville: Liturgical, 1996); and Bargil Pixner, *With Jesus in Jerusalem According to the Fifth Gospel* (Rosh Pina: Corazin, 1996). Cf. also Jonathan L. Reed, *Archaeology and the Galilean Jesus* (Harrisburg: Trinity Press International, 2000); and James H. Charlesworth, ed., *Jesus and Archaeology* (Grand Rapids: Eerdmans, 2006).

[2] See esp. Craig S. Keener, *The Historical Jesus of the Gospels* (Grand Rapids: Eerdmans, 2009); and Darrell L. Bock and Robert L. Webb., eds., *Key Events in the Life of the Historical Jesus: A Collaborative Exploration of Context and Coherence* (Tübingen: Mohr Siebeck, 2009; Grand Rapids: Eerdmans, 2010). The most commonly employed criteria are multiple attestation, dissimilarity from both previous Judaism and subsequent Christianity, Palestinian environment, coherence, embarrassment, and cutting against the grain of redactional tendencies. For a thorough survey and critique, see Stanley E. Porter, *Criteria for Authenticity in Historical-Jesus Research: Previous Discussion and New Proposals* (Sheffield: Sheffield Academic

selective in dealing with the most important, famous, and/or contested details. We will again proceed roughly in the order of the material as found in a standard Gospel synopsis.

The Birth Narratives

Matthew and Luke both share the belief in Jesus's virginal conception (Matt 1:18–23; Luke 1:26–38). Tellingly, of the otherwise sparse information recorded about Jesus in ancient non-Christian sources, a recurring tradition claims that Jesus was conceived out of wedlock (see especially Origen, quoting Celsus, in *Contra Celsum* 1:32). Here a Roman soldier with a name like Pandera or Panthera is alleged to have been Jesus's father, but these names look suspiciously like corrupt forms of *parthenos*, the Greek word for "virgin." Obviously, non-Christian sources would doubt the biblical account and assume the word for *virgin* meant something else, like a man's name.[3] Among modern skeptics the common charge is that the Gospel writers followed a standard pattern of honoring and deifying great heroes by inventing accounts of their supernatural conception. But on closer inspection no such pattern actually exists.

J. Gresham Machen surveyed the "closest" Greco-Roman and Jewish parallels more than eighty years ago, laying out in detail how little the stories match one another or anything in Matthew or Luke. There are stories of gods appearing in human form to have sex with human women (many of them already married), and there is the legend

---

Press, 2000). For a perspective that finds minimal value in the criteria, see Chris Keith and Anthony Le Donne, eds., *Jesus, Criteria, and the Demise of Authenticity* (London and New York: T & T Clark, 2012). The works of Keener and Bock/Webb, however, show just how much the criteria, appropriately nuanced, can still demonstrate. In German, see esp. Martin Hengel and Anna Maria Schwemer, *Jesus und das Judentum* (Tübingen: Mohr Siebeck, 2007).

[3] See further John P. Meier, *A Marginal Jew: Rethinking the Historical Jesus*, vol. 1 (New York and London: Doubleday, 1991), 96, 106–7 nn. 47–48.

of Alexander's father, Philip of Macedon, being unable to approach his wife on their wedding night due to the sacred python entwined around her. Romulus and Remus, the twins who founded Rome, supposedly were conceived when their mother copulated with a divine phallus emerging from her hearth. Mithraism, a close competitor with Christianity in the second and third centuries for the allegiance of Greeks and Romans, is often cited as containing yet another parallel. The bull-slaying god, Mithras, was believed to have sprung from a rock. Presumably the rock had not had sex, but that is stretching the definition of a virgin considerably! In Jewish circles, the milieu of the Gospel birth narratives, fallen angels could copulate with human women, and in apocryphal Christian documents we read of the actual virgin *birth* of Jesus, not merely his virginal conception (i.e., Mary's hymen remains miraculously unbroken even after Jesus emerges from her body). But nothing remotely approximates the dignity and restraint of the canonical Gospels, in which all we are told is that the Holy Spirit would overshadow Mary and she would become pregnant (Luke 1:35).[4]

---

[4] J. Gresham Machen, *The Virgin Birth of Christ* (New York: Harper & Row, 1930; London: James Clarke, 1987). Cf. W. D. Davies and Dale C. Allison Jr., *A Critical and Exegetical Commentary on the Gospel According to Saint Matthew*, vol. 1 (Edinburgh: T & T Clark, 1988), 214–16. Still other "parallels" are even further removed: The god Adonis is born from a myrrh tree, Dionysus comes from Zeus's sex with his daughter Persephone. Osiris and Horus are born from relations between gods and goddesses. Not a one of these figures was ever even believed to be a human being, and none of the "mothers" are human beings, much less virgins! See Mary Jo Sharp, "Is the Story of Jesus Borrowed from Pagan Myths?" in *In Defense of the Bible: A Comprehensive Apologetic for the Authority of Scripture*, ed. Steven B. Cowan and Terry L. Wilder (Nashville: B&H, 2013), 193–94. Andrew T. Lincoln (*Born of a Virgin? Reconceiving Jesus in the Bible, Tradition, and Theology* [Grand Rapids: Eerdmans, 2013]) appeals to these kinds of "parallels" (and other evidence) to argue that the biblical writers didn't necessarily envisage a literal virginal conception, but his exegesis is not the most straightforward interpretation of the texts; nor, by his own admission, do the "parallels" add up to a pattern of anything other than unusual births.

That Joseph had to be persuaded by an angel in a dream to believe this account (Matt 1:20–21) reminds us that people in the first century knew that it took two human beings to produce a child and that people did not believe that anyone in their day or in recent memory was conceived without normal human parentage, no matter what they might imagine about gods from the distant past! The virginal conception, moreover, is not a doctrine that is stressed in the New Testament. There may be a hint of it in Galatians 4:4 but even that is disputed. John 8:41 suggests that Jesus was slurred because of the claim. As a *mamzer* ("bastard"), Jesus would have been stigmatized in various ways throughout his life,[5] so this is not a story Christians were likely to have invented. And yet consistent post-New-Testament polemic suggests that he continued to be viewed as an illegitimate child.[6] The accounts of Jesus' virginal conception thus appear to be based in historical fact.[7]

People to this day raise their eyebrows the first time they hear that Jesus was almost certainly born before 4 BC (before Christ!). Yet this is not a problem with the Bible but with the calculations of a sixth-century monk, Dionysus Exiguus, who did not have access to

---

[5] Scot McKnight, "Jesus as *Mamzer* ('Illegitimate Son')," in *Who Do My Opponents Say I Am? An Investigation of the Accusations Against the Historical Jesus,* ed. Scot McKnight and Joseph B. Modica (London and New York: T & T Clark, 2008), 133–63.

[6] See esp. James P. Sweeney, "Modern and Ancient Controversies over the Virgin Birth," *Bibliotheca Sacra* 160 (2003): 142–58.

[7] Steve Moyise (*Was the Birth of Jesus According to Scripture?* [Eugene, OR: Cascade, 2013], 101) leaves the door open both for this conclusion and the one that sees Scripture as providing the precedent for the *creation* of the Gospel infancy narratives. He refers to Raymond Brown (*The Birth of the Messiah*, 2nd ed. [New York: Doubleday, 1993], 527) approvingly without quoting his exact words: "The historical evidence for a virginal conception is very thin but none of the alternative theories are especially convincing." On pp. 527–28, Brown states, slightly differently, "I think that it is easier to explain the NT evidence by positing historical basis than by positing pure theological creation."

Josephus when he reconfigured the calendar in the way that would soon become standard throughout the Western world. Josephus, the late first-century Jewish historian, describes the life and exploits of Herod the Great in considerable detail, confirming his ruthlessness and his paranoia that would-be usurpers were trying to take away his throne, along with the names and activities of the three sons who inherited his kingdom, all of whom appear in the Gospels as well— Archelaus (Matt 2:22), Antipas (Mark 6:14–22 pars.; Luke 3:1; 13:31; 23:6–16; Acts 4:27), and Philip (Luke 3:1). Herod even put some of his own sons and wives to death for fear they were plotting against him (*Ant.* 15.222–31).[8]

But if Jesus was born at least by Herod's own death in what we now call 4 BC, how much earlier might it have been? Commentators have always been intrigued by the reference in Matthew 2:16 to Herod's ordering the children two years old and under to be slaughtered. Might this suggest that he realized it had possibly been up to two years since this supposed Messiah had been born? Despite centuries of iconography, paintings, and manger scenes putting the magi with the baby Jesus on the night of his birth, Matthew makes clear that they arrived when the young family was living in a house in Bethlehem (v. 11). That the holy family changes its plans after the flight to and return from Egypt and resettles in Nazareth rather than Bethlehem (vv. 22–23) suggests they had intended to stay in Bethlehem when they initially traveled there from Nazareth.[9] After all, they knew the stigma the child would face in the small, closely knit village in Galilee where few, if any, would believe the story of the virginal conception.

---

[8] For the Josephan passages most relevant to the interpretation of the Gospels, see Cleon L. Rogers Jr., *The Topical Josephus: Historical Accounts That Shed Light on the Bible* (Grand Rapids: Zondervan, 1992). For Herod the Great and his sons, see pp. 17–51.

[9] Cf. Michael J. Wilkins, *Matthew* (Grand Rapids: Zondervan, 2004), 100.

A date of 7–6 BC for Jesus's birth therefore becomes probable.[10] This date also helps us make sense of Luke 2:1–4. We have already discussed the issues surrounding the translation of verse 2 (in chap. 2). But whichever way we take it, we still have to deal with the census that provoked Joseph and Mary to travel to Bethlehem when she was near her due date. It has been objected that we have no evidence of Rome issuing empire-wide censuses. Arguments from silence about fairly ordinary events in the ancient world, however, are precarious because the vast majority of whatever documentation originally did exist has been lost. We do know, though, that Rome periodically issued censuses over various portions of the empire, and *The Deeds of the Divine Augustus* 8.2–4 confirms that Augustus himself ordered a census in 8 BC. With references in this text to 4 million Roman citizens in an empire in which most people were not citizens, and with Rome itself numbering only about a million inhabitants, this census certainly sounds empire-wide in scope. In a world without the ability to travel and communicate nearly as speedily as ours today, it would have been natural for the last stages of such a census still to be unfolding one to two years after the initial decree, especially in "hinterlands" as far from Rome as Israel.[11] All the evidence thus coalesces around a probable birthdate for Jesus in about 7–6 BC. If Matthew and Luke were simply writing fiction at this point, it is highly unlikely that such convergences would appear.

But are we seriously to imagine millions of people around the ancient Roman Empire even over a two-year period traveling from

---

[10] See esp. John M. Lawrence, "Publius Sulpicius Quirinius and the Syrian Census," *Restoration Quarterly* 34 (1992): 193–205. Cf. also D. L. Jones, "Luke's Unique Interest in Historical Chronology," in *SBL Seminar Papers* 28 (1989): 378–89; and T. P. Wiseman, "'There Went Out a Decree from Caesar Augustus . . . ,'" *New Testament Studies* 33 (1987): 479–80.

[11] Cf. further I. Howard Marshall, *The Gospel of Luke* (Exeter: Paternoster; Grand Rapids: Eerdmans, 1978), 97–104; Darrell L. Bock, *Luke 1:1–9:50* (Grand Rapids: Baker, 1994), 903–9.

their current residences to the homelands of their ancestors, and doing so every fourteen years? No, I don't believe we are. Luke 2:3 says that all went to be enrolled, each to his own city. One can understand from verse 4 why readers outside the Roman Empire unfamiliar with its practices could imagine his claiming that every Jew anywhere in the empire who could trace his lineage back to David had to go to Bethlehem, but Luke does not actually say that. "One's own town" is elsewhere language for the city of one's birth or one's present or past residence (Josh 20:6; 1 Sam 8:22; 28:3; 2 Sam 19:37; Ezra 2:1; Neh 7:6; Matt 9:1; 13:57; Mark 6:4). Only a small minority of Jews in the first century lived somewhere other than the city in which they were born, so only they would need to travel for the census. Most tried to return to Israel for at least some of the annual festivals, so that would be a natural time for them to be "enrolled" as well. The reason Luke goes on to give Joseph's ancestry, in addition to showing that Jesus through his adoptive father legally qualified to be the Christ (2:11), is probably because he, like Matthew, knew that Joseph and Mary originally intended to settle in Bethlehem, all the more natural if Joseph had been born there. Perhaps he still had relatives in town (with whom they had hoped to stay, even though the guest room turned out to be full); perhaps he even owned property there.[12] We wish we had more than circumstantial evidence, but again, writers of fiction typically don't even create enough openings for *potential* harmonizations like this to be suggested!

An additional argument from silence questions the likelihood of Herod's massacring the innocent children of Bethlehem because Josephus does not report it. Part of this probably stems from the history of Christian art and storytelling that has imagined hundreds of babies being slaughtered. But Bethlehem probably had only about

---

[12] Marshall, *Gospel of Luke*, 101. Cf. C. F. Evans, *Saint Luke* (London: SCM; Philadelphia: Trinity Press International, 1990), 196.

500–1,000 people in the early first century; the number of boys two and under even in a culture that encouraged large families may well have been no more than twenty or so.[13] When one reads in Josephus of the slaughter of larger numbers of people on multiple occasions under Herod's reign and when one realizes how children were seen much as second-class citizens in the ancient Mediterranean world, one can easily envision Josephus not bothering to mention this event, if he had even heard about it.[14] At the same time there are at least two references in ancient writers that make one wonder if the event *was* known. The Jewish pseudepigraphal *Testament of Moses*, which contains other after-the-fact "prophecies" about Herod the Great, makes an elliptical reference to the fact that "he will kill both old and young, showing mercy to none" (6:4). Since Josephus narrates no murders of children, might the "young" here refer to the incident in Matthew?[15] The Latin writer Macrobius (*Saturnalia* 2.4.11) in the late fourth century states more plainly, "When it was heard that, as part of the slaughter of boys up to two years old, Herod, king of the Jews, had ordered his own son to be killed, [Augustus] remarked 'It is better to be Herod's pig [Gk. *hus*] than his son [Gk. *huios*]'"—a play on words that works only in Greek, not in Latin, so presumably represents older testimony than this Latin account. The pun, of course, does not require the massacre of the children to be valid, but the fact that Macrobius mentions it more tangentially makes it less likely to have been invented. He could, to be sure, know it from the account in Matthew, but he presumably

---

[13] See especially R. T. France, "Herod and the Children of Bethlehem," *Novum Testamentum* 21 (1979): 98–120.

[14] Craig S. Keener, *A Socio-Rhetorical Commentary on the Gospel of Matthew*, rev. ed. (Grand Rapids: Eerdmans, 2009), 110–11; Grant R. Osborne, *Matthew* (Grand Rapids: Zondervan, 2010), 99.

[15] Davies and Allison (*A Critical and Exegetical Commentary on the Gospel According to Saint Matthew*, 264–65) note the reference but recognize it need not refer to this event.

had reason to believe it and not because he was a Christian, since he was not one.[16]

Is the story of the magi credible? We know such people existed, both in Arabia and Persia, and were a combination of what today we would call astronomers and astrologers. If these men were from Persia, traditions of the prophecies of the Hebrew Scriptures could have been passed down over the centuries by the Jews who still lived there. But there was also a pagan hope for a key ruler emerging farther to the West than Persia, part of the reason Augustus was so well received in his imperial role.[17] Given that the appearance of new celestial phenomena was often believed to herald the birth of an important person in the land over which they appeared,[18] it is understandable why these magi could envision the birth of a king. Whether the "star" itself is to be identified with any of a variety of known astronomical anomalies of that day,[19] there seems to be a supernatural dimension at least to the way it led the magi from Jerusalem to Bethlehem. We will have more to say about the explicitly miraculous in chapter 14.

Finally, we may use the reference in Luke 2:36–37 to Anna's age to say a word about ancient life spans. Some skeptics point to an average life span of about forty years for people in the first-century Mediterranean world (lower if you include all those who died in childhood) as a reason for discounting biblical references to the extremely elderly. Apparently they do not understand what an average means.

---

[16] Craig A. Evans (*Matthew* [Cambridge: Cambridge University Press, 2012], 59–60) cites the text as a plausible independent attestation to this event. See now also Barry J. Beitzel, "Herod the Great: Another Snapshot of His Treachery?" *Journal of the Evangelical Theological Society* 57 (2014): 309–22.

[17] N. T. Wright, *Paul and the Faithfulness of God*, vol. 1 (London: SPCK; Minneapolis: Fortress, 2013), 279–347.

[18] Evans, *Matthew*, 52; Keener, *Gospel of Matthew*, 101–2.

[19] For the fullest catalogue of possibilities and a passionate case for identifying the star with a comet seen in 6 BC, see Colin R. Nicholl, *The Great Christ Comet: Revealing the True Star of Bethlehem* (Wheaton, IL: Crossway, 2015).

It does not mean no one lived a lot longer! Especially when so many died at an even younger age in the ancient world,[20] plenty had to live well beyond forty for that to become an average. Roman references cite individuals who lived into their eighties and nineties,[21] while the "Sayings of the Fathers"—some of the oldest Jewish traditions compiled in the Mishnah (ca. AD 200)—envision a few people living even to 100 (*Pirke Aboth* 5.24). Naturally, there would have been far fewer individuals living to these advanced ages than today, but some did. Thus, even if we translate what Luke says about Anna as implying that she lived as a widow for eighty-four years, after seven years of marriage, given that girls could be married as young as twelve or thirteen, she might still have been "only" 103 or 104. More likely, however, the Greek should be translated as saying that she lived as a widow *until* she was eighty-four[22]—much within the bounds of plausibility.

John the Baptist

Josephus clearly knows about John the Baptizer and makes reference both to his ministry and to his death. In *Antiquities* 18.5.2, Josephus writes:

> But to some of the Jews the destruction of Herod's army seemed to be divine vengeance, and certainly a just vengeance, for his treatment of John, surnamed the Baptist. For Herod had put him to death, though he was a good man and had exhorted the Jews to lead righteous lives, to practice justice

---

[20] Craig A. Evans, *Jesus and His World: The Archaeological Evidence* (Louisville: Westminster John Knox, 2012), 110–11.

[21] Robert K. McIver (*Memory, Jesus, and the Synoptic Gospels* [Atlanta: SBL, 2011], 189–209) gives a full demographic of life expectancies for the first century with several subdivisions.

[22] John Nolland, *Luke 1–9:20* (Dallas: Word, 1989), 122; John T. Carroll, *Luke: A Commentary* (Louisville: Westminster John Knox, 2012), 80.

towards their fellows and piety towards God, and so doing to join in baptism. In his view this was a necessary preliminary if baptism was to be acceptable to God. They must not employ it to gain pardon for whatever sins they committed, but as a consecration of the body implying that the soul was already thoroughly cleansed by right behavior.

Not only does Josephus recognize the nature of John's ministry; he even recognizes that it did not automatically accomplish anything without a change in the heart and behavior of those he baptized. This fits well with the Gospels' emphases on John's preaching repentance (Matt 3:2, 8, 11; Mark 1:4 par.; Luke 3:8), on illustrating that repentance behaviorally (Luke 3:10–14), and on rebuking the hypocritical leaders who come to see him as if they think baptism could help them (Matt 3:7–10 par.; cf. Luke 7:30). Although we cannot be sure just exactly when it began, we know Jews at about this time period practiced immersion in water for proselytes to Judaism, that *mikvaoth* (pools for immersion for ritual cleansing) dotted the land of Israel, especially in Jerusalem, and even in the homes of the wealthy there, and that the Essenes at Qumran practiced daily ritual lustrations for the cleansing from sin. We scarcely need to turn outside Judaism for the antecedents to John's and Jesus's practices of baptism, which are completely intelligible in light of all this background.[23]

Luke 3:1 tells us that John's ministry began in the fifteenth year of the reign of Tiberius Caesar, with Pontius Pilate the governor in

---

[23] See esp. Robert L. Webb, "Jesus' Baptism by John: Its Historicity and Significance," in *Key Events in the Life of the Historical Jesus: A Collaborative Exploration of Context and Coherence*, ed. Darrell L. Bock and Robert L. Webb (Tübingen: Mohr Siebeck, 2009; Grand Rapids: Eerdmans, 2010), 95–150. Cf. also Joan E. Taylor, *The Immerser: John the Baptist within Second Temple Judaism* (Grand Rapids: Eerdmans, 1997); Knut Backhaus, "Echoes from the Wilderness: The Historical John the Baptist," in *Handbook for the Study of the Historical Jesus*, vol. 2, ed. Tom Holmén and Stanley E. Porter (Leiden and Boston: Brill, 2011), 1747–85.

Judea, and Herod (Antipas) and Philip the tetrarchs in Galilee and Iturea/Trachonitis, respectively. Tiberius reigned from AD 14 to 37; Pilate from AD 26 to 36; Antipas from 4 BC to AD 39 and Philip from 4 BC to AD 34. Luke also tells us that Jesus was "about" thirty when he began his ministry (3:23). The dating of the beginning and ending of Jesus's public ministry is bound up with the dating of the events in the book of Acts, which will be dealt with later. A minority of scholars prefers AD 29 for the beginning of Jesus's and John's ministries, because fifteen years after 14 clearly brings us to 29. This then leads to a date for the crucifixion of 33, because 30 and 33 were the only two years during Pilate's reign in which the initial day of Passover lasted from Thursday night to Friday night (as we would term them; i.e., the two days just before the Sabbath).[24] But this squeezes the earliest events of Acts and the epistles considerably and would make Jesus about thirty-five at the start of his ministry.

Given the frequency of ancient authors counting inclusively (so that as little as a fourteen-month period, for example, could be called three years if the first month were the last month in one year and the last month the first month in a third year), it seems more likely that John and Jesus began in 28, fifteen years (inclusively) from 14, and that the unnamed feast in John 5:1 is not a Passover.[25] This leaves John narrating events from the time of three Passovers (John 2:13; 6:4; 11:55) spanning a period of two-and-a-fraction years for Jesus's public ministry and leading to his crucifixion in 30.[26] Especially when

---

[24] See esp. Harold W. Hoehner, *Chronological Aspects of the Life of Christ* (Grand Rapids: Zondervan, 1977), 95–114.

[25] Cf. John A. T. Robinson, *The Priority of John*, ed. J. F. Coakley (London: SCM, 1985; Oak Park, IL: Meyer-Stone, 1987), 157; Rainer Riesner, *Paul's Early Period: Chronology, Mission Strategy, Theology* (Grand Rapids: Eerdmans, 1998), 3–10, 57–58.

[26] Cf. also Meier, *A Marginal Jew*, vol. 1, 383–90, 401–6; James D. G. Dunn, *Jesus Remembered* (Grand Rapids: Eerdmans, 2003), 312.

we recognize that one of the ways an ancient writer of fiction tipped his hand to his audience was by using names, dates, and places that were clearly wrong or anachronistic and in no way reconcilable with known historical events, it appears unlikely that the Gospel writers thought they were penning fiction. That everything does not fall into place perfectly neatly, however, suggests that they were not going out of their way to fabricate something with no difficulties whatsoever.

The locations of John's ministry and Jesus's baptism prove similarly plausible. The Jordan River is the only body of living (i.e., fresh, flowing) water in Israel south of the Galilee big enough for the crowds that were coming to John and accessible from the Judean wilderness. It is possible that recent archeology has pinpointed the previously uncertain site of Bethany beyond the Jordan, not far across the river from Jericho.[27] It is unlikely that the first Christians would invent a story of the baptism of their founder for the repentance of sin when he was believed to have been sinless.[28] Jesus could have been repenting on behalf of his nation's people, or he could have simply been putting his stamp of approval on John's ministry as an important example to be imitated,[29] but neither explanation is the first thing readers normally think of. Matthew's distinctive additions to this narrative show that first-century Christians were aware of and wrestled with this issue (Matt 3:14–15).

Josephus at first glance appears to contradict Mark 6:17 and parallel, saying that Herodias had been the wife of a son of Herod the Great also named Herod (when it still functioned as a proper name), rather than Philip the tetrarch (*Ant.* 18.5.4). But Mark and Matthew never

---

[27] Michelle Piccirillo, "The Sanctuaries of the Baptism on the East Bank of the Jordan River," in *Jesus and Archaeology*, ed. James H. Charlesworth (Grand Rapids: Eerdmans, 2006), 437–43.

[28] Meier, *A Marginal Jew*, vol. 2 (1994), 100–105.

[29] John Nolland, *The Gospel of Matthew* (Grand Rapids: Eerdmans; Milton Keynes: Paternoster, 2005), 152.

refer to Philip as the tetrarch, while only Luke mentions a tetrarch by that name but not in this context (Luke 3:1). So it may well be that as the younger of Herod's brothers also began taking the name Herod as a dynastic name, he had to distinguish himself from them by another one of his given names and so used Philip. Nowhere is Philip the tetrarch also called Herod, suggesting that Herod Philip and Philip the tetrarch were two separate individuals. Reusing the same name among children who were given two or three different names was common in the Roman Empire, so this should occasion no surprise.[30]

Jesus's Earliest Ministry

Immediately after Jesus's baptism come his temptations. It has often been observed that there are no mountains in Israel (or anywhere else) from which one can see all the kingdoms of the world (Matt 4:8 par.). Of course the Gospel writers knew this, too; even the known world in the first century extended far beyond any place the devil could have taken Jesus in order for him to see all of it. This fact is probably the tip-off that we are meant to envision some supernatural, visionary experience.[31] After fasting, even just from food, for forty days, Jesus would have been in no condition to climb even a small hill unless he drew on the divine power Satan was asking him to use so as to bypass his suffering. But the temptation to worship Satan was no less real. People can awaken even just from dreams with new ideas that have powerful effects on them as their lives proceed. To the objection that

---

[30] See further Harold W. Hoehner, *Herod Antipas* (Cambridge: Cambridge University Press, 1972; Grand Rapids: Zondervan, 1999), 129–49. Cf. also Paul V. Harrison, "Competing Accounts of the Baptist's Demise," *Faith and Mission* 24 (2007): 26–42.

[31] See esp. David Mathewson, "The Apocalyptic Vision of Jesus According to the Gospel of Matthew: Reading Matthew 3:16–4:11 Intertextually," *Tyndale Bulletin* 62 (2011): especially 99–106.

no one was present to observe or hear Jesus's battle with Satan, we may reply that if it was important enough for Jesus to ask his closest followers to shadow him in Gethsemane so that they heard the gist of his prayers (Mark 14:33–36 pars.), he would surely have communicated the essence of his temptation in the wilderness to them as well.[32]

Once Jesus resists the devil's temptations, he is qualified to begin his public ministry. Calling disciples who had been fishermen from around the Sea of Galilee, including from Capernaum and Bethsaida, fits flawlessly the occupations that many pursued there (Mark 1:16–20 pars.).[33] But no one would have invented a story of a venerable rabbi calling followers from among such ordinary people or being from such an insignificant place as Nazareth.[34] The same is true with calling Levi/Matthew, the toll collector, who would have received customs duties as goods passed in and out of Israel's borders along the Jordan River or across the Sea of Galilee (2:13–17 pars.).[35] Not too many years ago, some scholars were still doubting that synagogue buildings existed already early in the first century; now at least seven have been excavated or identified.[36] The existence of Nazareth in the first century was doubted by some because we had discovered ruins only from a few centuries earlier and a few centuries later than that time. Despite the natural assumption of continuous occupation that would have accompanied the study of almost any nonbiblical site, skeptics reveled in the

---

[32] Marshall, *Gospel of Luke*, 168; Keener, *Gospel of Matthew*, 136.

[33] See esp. Rami Arav and Richard A. Freund, eds., *Bethsaida: A City by the North Shore of the Sea of Galilee*, 3 vols. (Kirksville, MO: Truman State University Press, 1995–2009).

[34] Craig S. Keener, *The Historical Jesus of the Gospels* (Grand Rapids: Eerdmans, 2009), 182–84.

[35] See, classically, John R. Donahue, "Tax Collectors and Sinners: An Attempt at Identification," *Catholic Biblical Quarterly* 33 (1971): 39–61. Cf. also Kathleen E. Corley, "Jesus' Table Practice: Dining with 'Tax Collectors and Sinners' (Including Women)," *SBL Seminar Papers* 32 (1993): 444–59.

[36] Evans, *Jesus and His World*, 44–58.

lack of first-century evidence. Until 2009, that is, when the foundation walls of a first-century home were unearthed,[37] reminding us yet again that the absence of evidence is not the evidence of absence!

Luke 4:44, an apparent parallel to Mark 1:39 and Matthew 4:23, poses a superficial problem with Luke's substitution of Judea for Galilee. But elsewhere Luke uses Judea to refer to the entire land of Israel (Luke 1:5; 6:17; 7:17; Acts 10:37; 26:20), so the problem quickly dissolves.[38] That Jesus called twelve key disciples (Mark 3:13–19 pars.) meshes well with the foundational role of the twelve patriarchs—the sons of Jacob— in the history of Israel. Jesus is claiming, in essence, to be creating a new, true or freed Israel. That he does not "sift among applicants," as it were, to choose the most talented, trained, and gifted students as other rabbis did makes it unlikely the account was made up.[39] That all four Gospels agree in including Judas, the eventual archtraitor, among the Twelve, seems unimaginable if it were not historical. It would have brought such cultural disgrace to any teacher that no one wishing to honor him would have invented the detail.[40] Talmudic tradition also refers to Jesus's having disciples, though the names appear garbled and do not necessarily refer just to members of the Twelve. Specifically, *b. Sanhedrin* 43a contains a statement that "Jesus had five disciples, Mattha, Naqai, Nezer, Buni and Todah." The Hebrew names may correspond to Matthew, Nicodemus, an anonymous Nazarene, John, and Thaddaeus.[41]

---

[37] Henry B. Smith Jr., "First Century House Unearthed in Nazareth," *Associates for Biblical Research* (December 30, 2009), accessed December 29, 2015, http://www.biblearchaeology.org/post/2009/12/30/First-Century-House-Unearthed-in-Nazareth.aspx.

[38] David E. Garland, *Luke* (Grand Rapids: Zondervan, 2011), 218.

[39] See esp. Scot McKnight, "Jesus and the Twelve," in *Key Events in the Life of the Historical Jesus*, ed. Bock and Webb, 181–214; cf. also Ben Witherington III, *The Christology of Jesus* (Minneapolis: Fortress, 1990), 126–31.

[40] See esp. Meier, *A Marginal Jew*, vol. 3 (2001), 208–12.

[41] See further Craig L. Blomberg, *The Historical Reliability of the Gospels*, 2nd ed. (Nottingham: Apollos; Downers Grove: IVP, 2007), 254. Peter Schäfer (*Jesus*

The various conflicts and disputes with groups of Jewish leaders that began early in Jesus's ministry (Mark 2:1–3:6 pars.) all represent exactly the kinds of debates we should expect from an unconventional rabbi in Israel early in the first century. He heals the paralyzed man in Capernaum and pronounces forgiveness of sins apart from the temple hierarchy and the offering of sacrifices there.[42] This was not a debate that would have occurred after the destruction of the temple in AD 70, when there was no further opportunity to offer sacrifices in the one and only place God had prescribed for Israelites to make atonement for their sins. Eating with sinners is a major countercultural theme in Jesus's ministry throughout the Synoptics. Again, no other known Jewish leader or literature went to such extents to embrace the outcast and the wicked of Jewish society, even while calling on them to mend their ways.[43] His teachings on not fasting cut against the tradition of Judaism, especially among the Pharisees, while his behavior on the Sabbath provoked consistent controversy.[44]

All of these were hot-button issues in Palestinian Judaism but less so in the rest of the New Testament that emerged from the Jesus movement. Fasting appears only three times after Pentecost, twice in the context of choosing church leaders for various roles (Acts

---

in the Talmud [Princeton: Princeton University Press, 2007]) finds the Talmudic traditions about Jesus to be deliberate distortions to counter Christian claims.

[42] E.g., Nicholas Perrin, Jesus the Temple (London: SPCK; Grand Rapids: Baker, 2010), 152–54.

[43] See throughout Craig L. Blomberg, Contagious Holiness: Jesus' Meals with Sinners (Leicester and Downers Grove: IVP, 2005). See also Tom Holmén, "Jesus and the Purity Paradigm," in Handbook for the Study of the Historical Jesus, ed. Holmén and Porter, vol. 3, 2709–44. Bruce Chilton, "Jesus and Sinners and Outcasts," in ibid., 2829, speaks of Jesus' approach as reversing "the usual flow of contagion."

[44] See esp. Donald A. Hagner, "Jesus and the Synoptic Sabbath Controversies," in Key Events in the Life of the Historical Jesus, ed. Bock and Webb, 251–92. Cf. also Sven-Olav Back, "Jesus and the Sabbath," in Handbook for the Study of the Historical Jesus, ed. Holmén and Porter, vol. 3, 2597–2633.

13:2–3; 14:23), and once when Saul of Tarsus does not eat while he remains blinded after his vision of the risen Lord (9:9).[45] Three texts also suggest that Sabbath worship was transferred from Saturday to Sunday, the first day of the week (Acts 20:7; 1 Cor 16:2; Rev 1:10). Colossians 2:16–17 makes clear that Saul, now going by Paul, viewed the Sabbath as part of the so-called ritual or ceremonial law that was fulfilled in Christ and no longer needed to be observed literally,[46] a move so shocking for a Pharisaic Jew that it is almost impossible to imagine its occurring without at least implied precedent in the life of Christ.[47] When one sees how many healings Jesus is said to have performed on a Sabbath—not one of which involved an individual whose life was in any imminent danger—one can conclude only that he was deliberately provoking controversy (Mark 3:1–6 pars.; Luke 13:10–17; 14:1–6; cf. John 5:1–15; 9:1–14). Attempts have been made to avoid the sweeping implications of his statements that "the Son of Man is Lord even of the Sabbath" (Mark 2:28 pars.) or that "it is lawful to do good on the Sabbath" (Matt 12:12), but they require reintroducing the kind of casuistry that Christ was portrayed as regularly rejecting.[48]

The sayings that occur in Matthew just before Jesus gives the command for the centurion's servant to be healed (Matt 8:10–12; cf., in a different context, Luke 13:28–29) were likewise scarcely designed to

---

[45] A rare, good book-length overview of the topic is Joseph F. Wimmer, *Fasting in the New Testament: A Study in Biblical Theology* (New York: Paulist, 1982).

[46] See further Craig L. Blomberg, "The Sabbath as Fulfilled in Christ," in *Perspectives on the Sabbath: 4 Views*, ed. Christopher J. Donato (Nashville: B&H, 2011), 305–58.

[47] Colossians 2:16 breathes the same atmosphere as Romans 14:14 (David W. Pao, *Colossians and Philemon* [Grand Rapids: Zondervan, 2012], 185), which in turn is widely viewed as an allusion to Mark 7:18–19 (David Wenham, *Paul: Follower of Jesus or Founder of Christianity?* [Grand Rapids: Eerdmans, 1995], 92–97).

[48] Correctly capturing the implications is R. T. France, *The Gospel of Matthew* (Grand Rapids: Eerdmans, 2007), 465.

win friends and influence people within Judaism. When Jesus praises the faith of the commander of the occupying Roman troops, declaring that he has not found such faith in all of Israel (Matt 8:10), it would be akin to praising a modern-day Taliban chieftain more than all the conservative evangelicals in America and doing so before the man made any formal confession of faith in Jesus, merely faith in Jesus's authority to heal! Who would have dared to invent such a story if it did not have significant roots in historical fact?[49] Even *Gentile* Christians were experiencing Roman persecution by the time most liberal scholars think Matthew and Luke were written, so we can scarcely answer our question just by ascribing the teaching's origin to a Gentile-Christian rather than a Jewish-Christian milieu.

Much the same should be said about Jesus's teaching on true family (Mark 3:31–35 pars.). The ancient Greco-Roman world was not as family friendly as first-century Judaism, but kinship loyalties still remained pervasive. In a culture of honor and shame, children were taught from little up to speak and behave in public in ways that would bring honor rather than shame to their families. Jesus's failure to pay attention to members of his biological family seeking to talk to him and declaring that those who did the will of his Father were his truest family members proved scandalous in a world that mandated intense focus on one's family of origin.[50] Who would have invented such a teaching and attributed it to Jesus had he never taught anything of the kind? The Talmudic traditions about Jesus's teachings are garbled and do not always agree even from one version of the Talmud to another,

---

[49] Nolland, *Luke 1–9:20*, 315; Bock, *Luke 1:1–9:50*, 633.

[50] Stephen C. Barton, *Discipleship and Family Ties in Mark and Matthew* (Cambridge: Cambridge University Press, 1994), 67–96; Cynthia Long Westfall, "Family in the Gospels and Acts," in *Family in the Bible*, ed. Richard S. Hess and M. Daniel Carroll R. (Grand Rapids: Baker, 2003), 125–47.

but they all have the common thread that Jesus challenged traditional Jewish teaching and teachers,[51] just as he does here.

Jesus's Great Sermon

It is humorous to read critics who say Jesus could not have given the Sermon on the Mount (Matt 5:1) "on a level place" (Luke 6:17). Are they imagining him addressing throngs of people who are all trying to balance themselves on a steep slope without falling over and rolling downhill? The traditional site of the Sermon a little northwest of the Sea of Galilee with a Franciscan chapel commemorating Jesus's sermon may or may not be the real location, but it perfectly illustrates how the Galilean hill country is punctuated by level places where large crowds could gather.[52] The Beatitudes with which both Matthew's and Luke's versions of this sermon begin (Matt 5:3–12; Luke 6:20–23), are a thoroughly Jewish rhetorical form (see, e.g., Deut 33:20; Judg 5:24; Ruth 2:19; Pss 1:1; 2:12; 32:1; 33:12; etc.), yet Jesus uses them uniformly to declare blessed all who are not "macho" within his society. Such blessings represented a greater identification with the lowly than had previously emerged in Israel[53] and were not likely invented by someone besides Jesus, especially when his followers must demonstrate these blessings not by monastic withdrawal but right in

---

[51] See Craig A. Evans, "Jesus in Non-Christian Sources," in *Studying the Historical Jesus: Evaluations of the State of Current Research,* ed. Bruce Chilton and Craig A. Evans (Leiden: Brill, 1994), 445.

[52] Cf. D. A. Carson, "Matthew," in *Expositor's Bible Commentary, Revised Edition,* vol. 9, ed. Tremper Longman III and David E. Garland (Grand Rapids: Zondervan, 2010), 159.

[53] Jesus's concern for the poor and outcast is a major theme of his ministry in the Synoptics and widely believed to be authentic. See Heinz Giesen, "Poverty and Wealth in Jesus and the Jesus Tradition," in *Handbook for the Study of the Historical Jesus,* ed. Holmén and Porter, vol. 4, 3269–303; Craig L. Blomberg, *Neither Poverty nor Riches: A Biblical Theology of Material Possessions* (Grand Rapids: Eerdmans; Leicester: IVP, 1999; Downers Grove: IVP, 2001), esp. 111–46.

the midst of the corrupt world (as salt and light—vv. 13–16).[54] That Jesus claimed to "fulfill" the Law—neither abolishing it nor preserving it unchanged—is a delicate balancing act his followers have struggled with ever since (vv. 17–48).[55] Public fasting, praying, and almsgiving (6:1–18) formed three central elements of Second Temple Jewish piety. Again Jesus walks a tightrope, neither condemning them altogether (due to their widespread abuse) nor allowing them in contexts that could promote self-aggrandizement.

One could continue through both versions of the Sermon in similar fashion. Virtually all major topics find at least partial parallels in well-known ancient Jewish literature,[56] but the combinations created by what Matthew and Luke record lead to the crowds' astonishment (Matt 7:28–29). The overall effect of the Sermon sharply distinguishes Jesus from the Jewish leaders who often made similar points piecemeal. This distinction further flowed from the fact that rabbis had to support their pontification by means of Scripture or the authoritative teaching of previous rabbis. Jesus never quotes any merely human authority, and he cites Scripture, in this Sermon at least, only to radically reinterpret it. Who gave him this right and authority?[57]

The main difference between Luke's much shorter account and Matthew's is that most legal material is omitted in Luke. This fits a

---

[54] Craig L. Blomberg, *Matthew* (Nashville: Broadman, 1992), 102.

[55] Donald A. Hagner, *Matthew 1–13* (Dallas: Word, 1993), 106. Cf. further William W. Klein, Craig L. Blomberg, and Robert L. Hubbard Jr., *Introduction to Biblical Interpretation*, rev. ed. (Nashville: Thomas Nelson, 2004), 344–50; Steve Moyise, "Jesus and the Scriptures of Israel," in *Handbook for the Study of the Historical Jesus*, ed. Holmén and Porter, vol. 2, 1137–67.

[56] See esp. Dennis Stoutenburg, *With One Voice/B'Qol Echad: The Sermon on the Mount and Rabbinic Literature* (San Francisco and London: International Scholars Publications, 1996).

[57] Cf. further Sigurd Grindheim, *God's Equal: What Can We Know About Jesus' Self-Understanding in the Synoptic Gospels?* (London and New York: T & T Clark, 2011), 101–23.

Gentile writing to mostly Gentile Christians, far less familiar with the intricacies of Jewish law and its interpretation.[58] Luke's most striking additions emerge in his section on enemy love (Luke 6:27–36), the one topic for which there are few close parallels in either ancient Jewish or Greco-Roman thought.[59] Not surprisingly, that is the dimension of Jesus's ethic that his followers over the centuries have least well followed. Would any of them likely have invented it? Luke also abbreviates the Beatitudes but matches those he preserves with corresponding woes. Deuteronomy 27–28 contains two long lists of curses with an equally long list of blessings in between. Second Enoch 52 alternates blessings and cursings throughout, while 4Q525 from the Dead Sea Scrolls is a substantial, though fragmentary, list of blessings. So it is better to imagine both Evangelists excerpting from a longer original, rather than Luke inventing material on the basis of Matthew (or Q).

Jesus's Great Galilean Ministry

Parables and miracles dominate the Synoptics' presentation of Jesus's ministry in Galilee. We will say more about miracles as supernatural events in chapter 14, but we may look at the settings and imagery for them here, even as also for Jesus's fictitious stories. In each case, as with additional teachings scattered about the Synoptics, the theme of the partial arrival of the kingdom of God (with more to come in the future) dominates Christ's ministry. All but the most skeptical of scholars acknowledge that the kingdom of God was central to the historical Jesus. It builds on the concept of God as King, which permeates the Old Testament even as the actual expression "kingdom of God" never occurs. It does appear occasionally in the intertestamental

---

[58] Bock, *Luke 1:1–9:50*, 554.

[59] For a full catalogue with discussion, see Hans Dieter Betz, *The Sermon on the Mount* (Minneapolis: Fortress, 1995), 301–9.

literature, but Jesus ramps things up a notch by linking King and kingdom, Messiah and messianic age. While God has always reigned over the cosmos whether or not people realize it, he has not yet fulfilled all of his promises in his Word about that reign. In the first century there was a lively expectation of a military, political king/messiah who would liberate Israel from the Romans and inaugurate an era of independence once and for all. Jesus deferred this element largely for his return to earth at the end of the age, focusing on the "mystery" of the kingdom—that it was present in a new and more powerful way but without the irresistible outward force of an empire or army.[60]

The kingdom (*basileia*) appears 107 times in the Synoptics referring to God's reign but only 33 times elsewhere in the entire New Testament with this referent (three times in John, eight times in Acts, fourteen times in Paul, four in the remaining epistles, and four times in Revelation). It is clearly both distinctive and characteristic of the Synoptic Jesus. Although only about half of the parables explicitly mention the kingdom, Jesus is illustrating dimensions of God's unique reign through all of them.[61] Numerous texts point to the central purpose of the miracles as highlighting the inauguration of the kingdom or the arrival of the Messiah (esp. Matt 11:3–6 par.; Mark 2:10–11 pars., 9:1 pars., cf. also Matt 4:23); the clearest of all comes when Jesus declares that if he casts out demons by the power or finger of God, "then the kingdom of God has come upon you" (Matt 12:28 par.).

---

[60] Ben Witherington III, *Imminent Domain: The Story of the Kingdom of God and Its Celebration* (Grand Rapids: Eerdmans, 2009); Mary Ann Beavis, *Jesus and Utopia: Looking for the Kingdom of God in the Roman World* (Minneapolis: Fortress, 2006); Richard A. Horsley, *Jesus and Empire: The Kingdom of God and the New World Disorder* (Minneapolis: Fortress, 2003); Bruce Chilton, *Pure Kingdom: Jesus' Vision of God* (Grand Rapids: Eerdmans, 1996).

[61] See esp. throughout Klyne R. Snodgrass, *Stories with Intent: A Comprehensive Guide to the Parables of Jesus* (Grand Rapids: Eerdmans, 2008). Cf. also Arland J. Hultgren, *The Parables of Jesus: A Commentary* (Grand Rapids: Eerdmans, 2000).

Parables

A parable is a largely realistic, usually fictitious, brief story used to illustrate a key spiritual truth. Rhetorically, it arouses interest, engages people, and makes them think they are outside observers in a narrative about others, only to hook them with the sting in the tale that shows that the story's lessons are intended for them. The parable Nathan used with David to bring about his repentance after his adultery with Bathsheba and his murder of Uriah (2 Sam 12:1–10) forms the classic paradigm for the form of Jesus's parables. Later rabbis used similar stories by the hundreds but almost always to illustrate a specific text of Scripture rather than the nature of the kingdom. They also tend to be a bit more allegorical, whereas Jesus usually intends a second level of meaning only with the main characters of his stories.[62] In the Greco-Roman world of antiquity, they are virtually unknown, and in early Christianity no one we know of even tries to imitate Jesus. The parables are thus therefore usually seen as bedrock, core authentic teachings of the historical Jesus.[63]

The imagery Jesus employs perfectly fits early first-century Israel. Farmers sowed seeds by the "broadcast" method, scattering them over their fields and then plowing them under (Mark 4:3–9 pars.). They did not understand the growing process nearly as well as we do but did their best to prepare the soil and nurture their crops (vv. 26–29). They were familiar with the mustard seed as the smallest of seeds they typically cultivated but which, on rare occasions, could grow as big as a small tree (vv. 30–32 pars.). Bioterrorism was far more primitive than it is today, but there are extrabiblical accounts of people sowing weeds

---

[62] See throughout Harvey K. McArthur and Robert M. Johnston, *They Also Spoke in Parables: Rabbinic Parables from the First Centuries of the Christian Era* (Grand Rapids: Zondervan, 1990; Eugene, OR: Wipf & Stock, 2014).

[63] See throughout Craig L. Blomberg, *Interpreting the Parables*, 2nd ed. (Downers Grove and Nottingham: IVP, 2012).

in an enemy's field to kill his crops (Matt 13:24–30). Leaven makes a whole lump of dough rise, as bakers knew from daily experience (v. 33 par.). Oyster fishermen and treasure hunters dreamed of the one great find that would earn them enough money to live the rest of their lives on "easy street" (vv. 44–46). A dragnet was used to trawl the Sea of Galilee in its shallower regions for fish (vv. 47–50)

Building one's house on sand rather than rock (Matt 7:24–27 par.) is reminiscent of the deep wadis that usually remained dry or with only a small stream of water in them. But they could turn into raging torrents after the occasional heavy rains. Shepherds with small flocks would value every sheep (18:12–14 par.). Everyone would understand that performance counted over promise, as in the parable of the two sons (21:28–32). All of the parables about the Day of the Lord and/or Christ's return similarly use well-known imagery—burglars, masters and servants, wedding customs, bags of gold for investing, and works of mercy for the needy of the world (Matt 24:43–25:46 pars.). The behavior of the friend at midnight (Luke 11:5–8) and the persistent widow (18:1–8) seems unlikely in our culture and probably even in the larger Roman world of the first century but fits the customs of Israel well.

Not everyone had firsthand experience of kings, but the Herodian rulers in Israel were "client kings," while the prefects in Judea were direct appointees from the emperor in Rome. These and other earthly masters could be ruthless in an empire in which up to a third of the people at any given time may have been slaves. That the unforgiving servant should be severely punished after he received pardon of his staggeringly enormous debt (Matt 18:23–35), that tenants hoarding their produce and killing their landlord's servant should be evicted from the vineyard (Mark 12:1–12 pars.), and that the unjust steward should be fired from his job (Luke 16:1–13) would have occasioned no surprise. What shocked people was the graciousness of some of these master figures, including also the father of the two wayward sons (Luke 15:11–32), the banquet giver who welcomes the outcasts

(Luke 14:16–24; Matt 22:1–14), or the employer who pays all the day laborers a full day's wage even though most worked less than a full day (Matt 20:1–14).

Even when Jesus tells a story with a shockingly countercultural character, it is still by means of behavior that is thoroughly rooted in the culture and setting of his world. No one may have actually seen a Samaritan coming to the aid of a dying Jew, because of the frequent enmity between the two people groups. But the Jericho road was notorious for bandits attacking those who traveled alone; with no centers of population between Jericho and Jerusalem, an inn would have been the only recourse for the man offering help, even though they were not normally places "good people" frequented (cf. Luke 10:29–37). The Pharisee's self-centered prayer probably exaggerated tendencies not normally as extreme, just like the tax collector's beating his breast in repentance did (Luke 18:9–14). But if these things ever did happen, the temple would be the place to bring out both extremes. Gross disparities between rich and poor, as in many major world cities today, were often starkly juxtaposed, like the beggar Lazarus right at the gate of the rich man who refused to help him in the least (Luke 16:19–31). Examples could be multiplied, but the point should be clear. A later Christian inventing parables and attributing them to Jesus, especially a Gentile like Luke (whose Gospel contains twice as many parables as anyone else), might well have missed the finer points of the culture here or there in ways we do not see happening in the Synoptics.[64]

---

[64] For the preceding paragraphs, see throughout ibid. and Snodgrass, *Stories with Intent.* Cf. also Kenneth E. Bailey, *Poet and Peasant* and *Through Peasant Eyes,* 2 vols. bd. as 1 (Grand Rapids: Eerdmans, 1983); and Brad H. Young, *The Parables: Jewish Tradition and Christian Interpretation* (Peabody: Hendrickson, 1998; Grand Rapids: Baker, 2008).

Miracles

To this day sudden squalls can come up as tourists cross the Sea of Galilee in motorized vessels and just as quickly dissipate (cf. Mark 4:35–41 pars.). A site known as Qursi on the eastern shore of the lake has a steep cliff and is commemorated by a Byzantine-era church as the probable location of the pigs rushing headlong to their deaths in the Sea of Galilee (Mark 5:1–20 pars.). Because of water usage in modern Israel, the lake is much lower than it once was, but one can easily see how the water used to come up to the cliff's edge. A synagogue ruler typically lived in a large home adjacent to the synagogue, much like twentieth-century pastors often lived in parsonages next door to their churches. The foundations and parts of columns and walls of the fourth-century synagogue in Capernaum are visible and form a popular tourist site today. But separate black basalt foundations are still visible under them, probably from the first century, and portions of walls from a larger than typical adjacent home may well be those of the house Jairus and his family lived in (cf. Mark 5:21–43 pars.).[65] A separate octagonal house was known as Peter's house and was used as a Christian church at least as far back as the fourth century. So the locations of the resurrection of Jairus's daughter and the healing of Peter's mother-in-law may well have been identified (Mark 1:29–31 pars.).[66]

The pejorative comment about the woman with the hemorrhage having spent all she had on doctors (Mark 5:26) rings true to others' experience in the ancient Roman Empire. Her superstitions about

---

[65] Cautiously Bruce F. Harris and Edward M. Blaiklock, "Capernaum," in *New International Dictionary of Biblical Archaeology*, ed. Edward M. Blaiklock and R. K. Harrison (Grand Rapids: Zondervan, 1983), 119; more confidently, H. G. Andersen, "Capernaum," in *The Zondervan Encyclopedia of the Bible*, rev. ed., vol. 1, ed. Merrill C. Tenney and Moisés Silva (Grand Rapids: Zondervan, 2009), 780.

[66] Virgilio C. Corbo, "Capernaum," in *Anchor Bible Dictionary*, ed. David N. Freedman, vol. 1 (New York: Doubleday, 1992), 866–69.

Jesus's garments (vv. 27–28 pars.) do not fit orthodox Judaism but do mesh with folk religion in Israel at that time.[67] A public funeral procession, like the one Jesus encountered for the son of the widow in Nain, was standard (Luke 7:11–17). Luke, the Gentile writer, however, records an authentic Galilean touch that he might not otherwise have known about when he portrays Jesus's speaking to the widow before approaching the bier (vv. 13–14). In Galilee the mourning women walked in front of a casket, whereas the better known Judean custom found them walking behind it.[68] Further, if Luke were making the story up, he would also probably have picked a more significant city than Nain and had the crowds acclaim Jesus as more than just a prophet.

Blind persons had few ways of earning enough money to support themselves, so it is not surprising to find them by the side of busy roads as beggars. The negative account of Jesus's being able to do few miracles in Nazareth due to the people's unbelief would not have been invented by Christians wanting to magnify Jesus's power and honor him. Aramaic words preserved in miracle accounts like *Ephphatha* ("Be opened!"—Mark 7:34) or *Talitha koum* ("Little girl, arise!"—Mark 5:41) suggest memories of ancient Christian tradition rather than later invention.

Withdrawal from Galilee

It is sometimes argued that the historical Jesus never said or did anything to suggest he envisaged a "church" outliving him, much less a

---

[67] Marla J. Selvidge, *Woman, Cult and Miracle Recital: A Redaction-Critical Investigation of Mark 5:24–34* (Lewisburg, PA: Bucknell University Press; London: Associated Presses, 1990), 71–79.

[68] Murray J. Harris, "'The Dead Are Restored to Life': Miracles of Revivification in the Gospels," in *Gospel Perspectives*, vol. 6, ed. David Wenham and Craig Blomberg (Sheffield: JSOT, 1986; Eugene, OR: Wipf & Stock, 2003), 298–99.

ministry to the Gentiles. Only Matthew uses the word *ekklēsia* and then only three times in two passages. But the nature of Jesus's ethical instructions regularly suggests the disciples' continuing to gather together in tightly knit community.[69] The Qumran covenanters thought they were living in the last days and yet had an elaborately organized community that outlived their founding Teacher of Righteousness by more than two centuries. Indeed, it is impossible to have a Jewish Messiah without a Messianic community.[70] That Luke should describe a sending out of seventy/seventy-two followers of Jesus, and not just the initial mission of the Twelve, correlates closely with Genesis 10 and the number of nations into which the rabbis divided the world (Luke 10:1–16). Whether this larger group actually went into Gentile territory is unknown, but they surely prefigure the Gentile mission of the early church.[71] Matthew and Mark do not mention this mission, but they include a significant period of time in which Jesus himself leaves Jewish territory to minister to the north and east of Galilee (Mark 7:1–8:26; Matt 15:1–16:12), which Luke omits.

This section begins with Jesus's strongest challenge to conventional Judaism even while he remains in Galilee—debates with religious leaders over ritual purity involving both hand washing and the dietary laws (Mark 7:1–23 par.). He begins by challenging only the oral law or "tradition of the elders" (v. 5), including their practice of *Corban* (v. 11). This single word, meaning "dedicated to God," has

---

[69] See esp. Gerhard Lohfink, *Jesus and Community: The Social Dimensions of the Christian Faith* (Philadelphia: Fortress, 1984; London: SPCK, 1985). Cf. also Leonhard Goppelt, *Theology of the New Testament*, vol. 1 (Grand Rapids: Eerdmans; London: SPCK, 1981), 207–22.

[70] Keener, *Historical Jesus of the Gospels*, 200.

[71] John L. Nolland, *Luke 9:21–18:34* (Dallas: Word, 1993), 558. Cf. also I. J. du Plessis, "The Church Before the Church—Focussing on Luke 10:1–24," *Neotestamentica* 32 (1998): 343–66.

been found on a Jewish sarcophagus as a guard against grave robbers.[72] Nevertheless, Jesus's sweeping declaration that only what comes out of a person rather than what goes into that person makes them unclean (v. 15) hints at a change in the written law of Moses also. Mark 7:19b is probably Mark's parenthetical comment, possibly learned from Peter, about the significance that Christians came to attach to Jesus's words, though they wouldn't have recognized it at the time. That is why Peter has to have the vision of unclean animals and the heavenly voice commanding him to kill them and eat them before he fully realizes the dietary laws are no longer in force (Acts 10:1–11:18).[73] But as Matthew and Mark composed their Gospels, we can understand why this account formed an appropriate introduction to Jesus's departure from Israel.[74] Theological withdrawal immediately precedes geographical withdrawal. Even today orthodox Jews and Jewish Christians are often scandalized by the thought of Jesus's doing away with the dietary laws and propose less natural ways of interpreting the text to avoid this conclusion,[75] while Gentile Christians typically assume everyone understood the significance of Jesus's teaching on the spot! The mediating position of a sweeping change not clearly understood for another generation seems hardest to imagine and thus would have been hardest to invent.

We learn first of Jesus's ministry in Syrophoenicia, including an encounter with a Gentile woman that reflects an insulting interchange with her (Mark 7:24–30 par.). Early Christians would not have

---

[72] For this and related discoveries and for a full discussion of the term's meaning, see A. I. Baumgarten, "*Korban* and the Pharisaic *Paradosis*," *Journal of Ancient Near Eastern Studies* 16–17 (1984–85): 5–17.

[73] Darrell L. Bock, *Acts* (Grand Rapids: Baker, 2007), 389–90; Robert H. Stein, *Mark* (Grand Rapids: Baker, 2008), 345–46.

[74] Robert A. Guelich, *Mark 1–8:26* (Dallas: Word, 1989), 362; Keener, *Gospel of Matthew*, 414.

[75] See, e.g., Mark S. Kinzer, *Post-Missionary Messianic Judaism: Redefining Christian Engagement with the Jewish People* (Grand Rapids: Brazos, 2005), 54–58.

invented a story about their master calling this woman a dog, even if the Greek word is a diminutive (*kunarion*) and can be translated puppy![76] In context, it certainly sounds as though it demeans her. But Jesus has also shown that he can discern people's faith when others don't, and his repartee provokes the woman's clever retort about dogs eating crumbs from their master's table. Jews for the most part did not use dogs as domestic pets, but Gentiles sometimes did.[77] So it fits that this story takes place outside Jewish territory and that the household setting is envisioned by the woman rather than by Jesus. In the end he both grants her request for her daughter's healing and praises her remarkable faith (Matt 15:28). The whole interchange may have been designed to teach the typically ethnocentric (and chauvinist?) disciples an important lesson.[78]

It is no coincidence that Jesus asked the Twelve about people's opinions of him in the region of Caesarea Philippi (Mark 8:27–30 pars.). That city until recently had been named Paneas (modern-day Banyas), after Pan, the Greek god of the forest. Its new name commemorated the Roman emperor and Philip the tetrarch, son of Herod the Great, who ruled in that region. With a backdrop of pagan mythology, imperial worship and Herodian honor, it was natural for Jesus to raise this topic.[79] Initial answers focused on one of the Jewish prophets, but then he asks the disciples their own opinion. Peter shines for a short moment with his confession of Jesus as Messiah, Son of God. But he turns from "hero" to "goat" in almost no time as he is soon

---

[76] Stressing the pejorative meaning are Glenna S. Jackson, *"Have Mercy on Me": The Story of the Canaanite Woman in Matthew 15,21–28* (London and New York: Sheffield Academic Press, 2002), 54–58; and M. Eugene Boring, *Mark: A Commentary* (Louisville and London: Westminster John Knox, 2006), 210–13.

[77] Keener, *Gospel of Matthew*, 416.

[78] Cf. Robert H. Gundry, *Matthew: A Commentary on His Handbook for a Mixed Church Under Persecution*, 2nd ed. (Grand Rapids: Eerdmans, 1994), 314.

[79] Jerome Murphy-O'Connor, *The Holy Land: An Oxford Archaeological Guide from Earliest Times to 1700*, 5th ed. (Oxford: Oxford University Press, 2008), 203–7.

rebuking his master for talking about suffering and the road to the cross (vv. 32–33 pars.). His understanding of messianic sonship is still limited by conventional expectations of an earthly leader who would rid the land of the Romans. The whole dialogue does not sufficiently acknowledge both Christ's identity and the nature of his mission for it to have been readily invented after Jesus's lifetime.[80]

It is hard to evaluate Jesus's promises to Peter, found only in Matthew, without being inappropriately influenced by centuries of theological interpretation and debate. Roman Catholics have often found support here for their convictions that the pope, in the line of Peter's successors as bishops of Rome, can speak infallibly *ex cathedra*, and that the institutionalized church must follow the principle of apostolic succession, always replacing one pope with another, so that the church always has a worldwide leader, a "vicar of Christ." Yet nothing in Jesus's response to Peter suggests anything beyond the fact that he would be the initial earthly leader of the church as we see in Acts 1–12. On the other hand, Protestants have too often overreacted to Catholic abuse of this text by denying that Peter was the "rock" to which Jesus was referring. Instead they have tended to opt for the belief that it was his confession of Christ, which was the rock on which he would build his church. But this blunts the force of the play on words—*Peter's* name that meant "rock," not Jesus's name. What is more, without Peter as the rock, one altogether loses the contrast between Peter as the solid foundation for the church in this text and his role as a stumbling *stone* in the next.[81]

---

[80] See esp. Michael J. Wilkins, "Peter's Declaration Concerning Jesus' Identity in Caesarea Philippi," in Bock and Webb, *Key Events in the Life of the Historical Jesus*, 293–381.

[81] On the main options for interpretation and the most decisive historical context, see Ulrich Luz, "The Primacy Text (Mt. 16:18)," *Princeton Seminary Bulletin* 12 (1991): 41–55. Cf. also France, *Matthew*, 622–23.

Could Jesus have spoken something in Aramaic corresponding to the words found uniquely in Matthew 16:17–19? Very much so, for they are laden with Semitisms. Behind *ekklēsia* lies *qāhāl*, the Hebrew word for the assembly of the children of Israel. The beatitude form ("Blessed are you"), *bar-Jonah* ("son of Jonah" or possibly a contraction for "son of Johanan"—i.e., John—cf. John 1:42), "flesh and blood" (a stock idiom for mortal humanity), the Aramaic "Cephas" underlying the play on words, the "gates of Hades" as a metaphor for the power of death, and the imagery of the keys of the kingdom along with the language of binding and loosing (see Isaiah 22), all draw on distinctively Hebraic concepts and terminology.[82]

Additional Teachings of Jesus in Matthew or Luke

Almost everything in Mark is repeated in either Matthew or Luke and has been treated above if there is significant corroborative evidence for it and if it comes before Jesus's final Judean ministry. Matthew, however, has two main blocks of teaching that emerge from this period of Christ's life not found in any other Gospel in nearly such detailed form. These two sections comprise Matthew 10:5–42 and 18:1–35. His missionary discourse in chapter 10 contains the restriction that the Twelve go nowhere in Gentile or even Samaritan territory but only to the "lost sheep" of Israel (vv. 5–6). Indirect corroboration for this appears in Romans 1:16 as Paul explains that the gospel was for the Jews first and then also for the Greeks. A postresurrection context for the origin of this teaching makes no sense because by then it was clear the disciples *were* to go into all the world and spread the good news about Jesus.[83]

---

[82] For the various Semitisms, see Ben F. Meyer, *The Aims of Jesus* (London: SCM, 1979; Eugene, OR: Pickwick, 2002), 185–97.

[83] Davies and Allison, *A Critical and Exegetical Commentary on the Gospel According to Saint Matthew*, vol. 2, 167–69.

The restrictions about traveling light, with few provisions, and remaining dependent on the hospitality of those among whom they ministered likewise make sense only within Israel, where there were already sufficient kinship connections and short enough distances between villages to make such restrictions manageable. Matthew 10:17–42 looks beyond anything that happened to the disciples during Jesus's lifetime but accurately reflects conditions they would later experience, as indicated in both Acts and the Epistles.[84] It is no doubt significant that the puzzling verse 23 appears in this context because Jesus's second coming was scarcely mentioned during the initial ministry of the Twelve. The passage is also cryptic enough that it is widely acknowledged as authentic.[85] As we noted above, it may well refer to the perennially incomplete mission of the Jews prior to Christ's return.[86]

Matthew 18 combines a selection of Jesus's teachings on humility and forgiveness, dimensions of his ministry that were reasonably unique. Humility was not considered a virtue in the ancient Greco-Roman world and not always well exemplified in the Jewish world.[87] The language of a millstone being hung around a person who is then drowned in the depths of the sea (v. 6) is particularly fitting for the farmland around the Sea of Galilee. Ancient millstones can still be viewed within the ruins of Capernaum to this day. It is unlikely that any early Christian would have invented the interchange about forgiving seventy times seven (or seventy-seven times, vv. 21–22), when this

---

[84] Wilkins, *Matthew*, 391–92; Evans, *Matthew*, 221–22.

[85] Davies and Allison, *A Critical and Exegetical Commentary on the Gospel According to Saint Matthew*, vol. 2, 187–89.

[86] J. M. McDermott, "Mt. 10:23 in Context," *Biblische Zeitschrift* 28 (1984): 230–40; Evans, *Matthew*, 224; F. F. Bruce, *The Hard Sayings of Jesus* (London: Hodder & Stoughton; Downers Grove: IVP, 1983), 109.

[87] Craig A. Evans, "Jesus' Ethic of Humility," *Trinity Journal* 13 (1992): 127–38.

far exceeded rabbinic limits and the church itself has found it almost impossible to implement![88]

Similarly, countercultural teaching appears in Jesus's rebuke of James and John when they wanted to call down fire from heaven to punish the Samaritan villages that rejected Jesus (Luke 9:52–55). Even more radical were his teachings to let the dead bury the dead and not even to go home to say good-bye to one's family (vv. 59–62 par.).[89] The story of Jesus with Mary and Martha finds him praising the woman who postures herself as equal to the male disciples (Luke 10:38–42), an unlikely action for a first-century Jew in Israel. Again it is harder to conceive of Jesus's followers inventing these teachings than to view Jesus as himself responsible for them. Indeed, while Jesus stopped short of what would today be called a full-fledged egalitarian position with respect to gender roles, his overall affirmation of women was highly countercultural for his world.[90]

No extrabiblical sources corroborate the accounts in Luke 13:1–3 about Pilate's mixing the blood of some Galileans with their sacrifices (a metaphorical way of suggesting that imperial troops slaughtered them in the temple precincts themselves). Nor do they confirm the subsequent reference to a tower in Siloam falling over and killing eighteen people (vv. 4–5). But Pilate's ruthlessness is well attested in Josephus; this murder may have been a minor incident in comparison

---

[88] Cf. Ulrich Luz, *Matthew 8–20* (Minneapolis: Fortress, 2001), 465–67.

[89] On which, see esp. Byron R. McCane, "'Let the Dead Bury Their Own Dead': Secondary Burial and Matt 8:21–22," *Harvard Theological Review* 83 (1990): 31–43. For a summary of his view and three other major options, see Tarsisius Sigho, "Let the Dead Bury Their Own Dead (Matthew 8:22): Four Hypotheses," *East Asian Pastoral Review* 51 (2014): 73–99.

[90] See esp. Kathleen E. Corley, *Women and the Historical Jesus* (Santa Rosa, CA: Polebridge, 2002). Cf. John H. Elliott, "Jesus Was Not an Egalitarian: A Critique of an Anachronistic and Idealist Theory," *Biblical Theology Bulletin* 32 (2002): 75–91.

with the larger-scale murders that made it into his history book.[91] And with buildings much more vulnerable to collapse in antiquity than today, not mentioning that kind of disaster is no more surprising than an American historian not referring to every school shooting in today's America.

Luke 14:26 offers a classic example of the "hard sayings of Jesus," such that almost no one else could be imagined to have concocted it. As we have already seen, the Judaism of Jesus's day was extremely family oriented. How could would-be disciples be expected to respond positively to Jesus's exclamation that "if anyone comes to me and does not hate father and mother, wife and children, brothers and sisters—yes, even their own life—such a person cannot be my disciple"? To be sure, the Greek and Hebrew behind "hate" could mean "love less," or "not prefer,"[92] while Matthew 10:37, in a different context, offers the probable meaning of Jesus's words here: "Anyone who loves their father or mother more than me is not worthy of me; anyone who loves their son or daughter more than me is not worthy of me." But if Luke had the freedom to exclude or even substantially alter Jesus's words in the ways many critics think he did, it is inexplicable why he did not do so here.

The Judean Ministry

Already before formally leaving Galilee for the last time to head toward Jerusalem, Jesus twice predicts his upcoming death and resurrection (Mark 8:31 pars.; 9:31 pars.). En route to Jerusalem he does so a third

---

[91] Similarly, Garland, *Luke*, 537, who also summarizes the atrocities Josephus does record about Pilate.

[92] G. B. Caird, *The Gospel of St. Luke* (Harmondsworth and Baltimore: Penguin, 1963; Philadelphia: Westminster, 1978), 178–79. Cf. Davies and Allison, *A Critical and Exegetical Commentary on the Gospel According to Saint Matthew*, vol. 2, 221; Stein, *Luke*, 397.

time (10:33–34). Critics have often argued that Jesus could not have anticipated his crucifixion, while resurrection lies outside the bounds of historical investigation altogether. We will dispute this latter claim in a later chapter. But even if one does not believe in supernatural prophecy, it is hard to imagine a leading public figure challenging the authorities and crossing a threshold of perceived blasphemy in the numerous ways Jesus did without recognizing that he was in danger of ultimate arrest and execution.[93] Michael Licona goes one step further and uses the standard criteria of authenticity (see above) to argue for the historicity of Jesus's predictions not only of his passion and execution but also of his resurrection.[94]

Jesus's position on divorce and remarriage was stricter than any others we know of in his world, but his affirmation of celibacy as a God-honoring lifestyle was also stronger than most (Matt 19:3–12 pars.).[95] Who else in his milieu would have invented such a combination of positions? He was likewise unusually positive toward little children (19:13–15 pars.) and amazingly harsh to the rich young ruler (vv. 16–30 pars.).

Most of the events toward the end of Jesus's public ministry but before his arrival in the environs of Jerusalem are narrated without reference to specific locations. Once Jesus reaches Jericho, this changes abruptly. As in the earlier portions of his ministry, we can confirm numerous historical and topographical details. Jesus tells the parable of the pounds (Luke 19:11–27 NRSV) when he is in the vicinity of

---

[93] See esp. Hans F. Bayer, *Jesus' Predictions of Vindication and Resurrection* (Tübingen: J. C. B. Mohr, 1986).

[94] Michael R. Licona, "Did Jesus Predict His Death and Vindication/Resurrection?" *Journal for the Study of the Historical Jesus* 8 (2010): 47–66.

[95] Cf. further David Instone-Brewer, *Divorce and Remarriage in the Bible: The Social and Literary Context* (Grand Rapids: Eerdmans, 2002). See also Craig L. Blomberg, "Marriage, Divorce, Remarriage and Celibacy: An Exegesis of Matthew 19:3–12," *Trinity Journal* 11 (1990): 161–96.

Jericho, close to where Herod Archelaus's palace still stood. Not surprisingly, the parable includes imagery reminiscent of the Jewish embassy that went to Rome to get Archelaus removed in AD 6 (though in this fictional parable it does not succeed, and so the nobleman is executed). People would have continued to talk about this event in and around Jericho two decades later, so Jesus could expect them to note the allusion (and the differences).[96]

What we call Palm Sunday today was only one special entry into Jerusalem the week before the Passover when Jesus was executed. Every year the Roman prefect would travel from Caesarea Maritimis, the Roman headquarters in Israel, to Jerusalem in order to be personally present during the holiday. With him would be several hundred armed cavalry and foot soldiers, all of whom would be dressed in full battle regalia. Residing in the barracks at the Antonia Fortress overlooking the temple precincts, the message they sent was unmistakable: Rome is here in force to watch over your proceedings, and if the extra people present to honor your nation's escape from Egypt give anyone the idea to start a revolt against Rome, we will slaughter you all in a heartbeat![97] In (probably) AD 30, however, another procession entered the city from the opposite direction. Coming from the east instead of the west, Jesus and other Galilean pilgrims made their way up the road from Jericho, across the Mount of Olives and down into the holy city. Jesus was not astride the white horse Pilate would ride but a humble beast of burden, a donkey (Mark 11:1–11 par.). Still, he was enacting the role of the royal descendant of David in so doing (Zech 9:9),[98] and

---

[96] Brian Schultz, "Jesus as Archelaus in the Parable of the Pounds (Lk. 19:11–27)," *Novum Testamentum* 49 (2007): 105–27.

[97] Marcus J. Borg and John Dominic Crossan, *The Last Week: A Day-by-Day Account of Jesus's Final Week in Jerusalem* (San Francisco: HarperSanFrancisco, 2006), 2–3.

[98] Brent Kinman, "Jesus' Royal Entry into Jerusalem," in *Key Events in the Life of the Historical Jesus*, ed. Bock and Webb, especially 400–405.

suggesting that the Lord was indeed suddenly coming to his temple (Mal 3:1).[99]

Jesus's "temple tantrum"[100] in at least a corner of the precincts hardly "cleansed" the temple, but it did at least "clear" that one small section. That he was not arrested on the spot is not historically improbable, especially if the "object lesson" was a symbolic prophecy requiring interpretation, as so often in the Old Testament.[101] But it did provide the last impetus needed for the Jewish authorities to seek his arrest (Mark 12:12 pars.). Once again the core events of the narrative are historically credible. So, too, are the controversies that ensued. Only someone familiar with the intricacies of the Jewish leadership groups would recognize how perfectly appropriate each debate was for the people initiating it. The chief priests, scribes and elders comprised the Sanhedrin, the Jewish high court, which therefore oversaw the temple.[102] Naturally they would be the ones to ask where Jesus's authority to create such a mess came from (11:27–33 pars.). The Pharisees and Herodians made strange bedfellows but came together against a common enemy. Realizing that if Jesus supported paying taxes to Rome, the Pharisees would be upset, and if he objected to them, the Herodians would be upset, they forced him into a no-win situation. Still he amazed them with an answer that partly agreed with

---

[99] N. T. Wright, *Paul and the Faithfulness of God* (London: SPCK; Minneapolis: Fortress, 2013), vol. 1, 105–6.

[100] So Witherington, *Christology of Jesus*, 107.

[101] Klyne R. Snodgrass ("The Temple Incident," in *Key Events in the Life of the Historical Jesus*, ed. Bock and Webb, especially 447–54) strikes a judicious balance between terming the episode a merely token protest and envisioning it as occupying the entire Court of the Gentiles. Jostein Ådna ("Jesus and the Temple," in *Handbook for the Study of the Historical Jesus*, ed. Holmén and Porter, vol. 3, 2675) likewise defends its historicity and adds that it remains "crucial to any portrayal of the message of Jesus of Nazareth and his understanding of his own mission."

[102] Craig A. Evans, *Mark 8:27–16:20* (Nashville: Nelson, 2001), 199.

both parties, getting him off the hook (Mark 12:13–17 pars.).[103] The Sadducees did not believe in the resurrection because doctrine for them had to be established from the five books of the Law, and they found nothing about resurrection there. That is why Jesus resorts to what seems like contrived logic, in order to cite a passage from the Torah (Exod 3:6). But it obviously worked and silenced that group of critics (Mark 12:18–27 pars.).[104] A lawyer, finally, would naturally ask about the greatest commandment within the law (vv. 28–34 pars.).

Jesus's Olivet or Eschatological Discourse (Mark 13 pars.) offers a hornet's nest of interpretive cruxes. If Jesus could have predicted his death and resurrection, could he have also prophesied about his second coming? Could he have spoken of final judgment? The Jesus Seminar in the 1990s routinely rejected all the teachings attributed to Jesus on this topic because they found it unworthy of an enlightened teacher like Jesus.[105] But if he never spoke about coming judgment, he would have been the only high profile Jewish teacher in his day who didn't! Everyone would have wanted his opinion on a topic that loomed so large in the Hebrew Scriptures. On the other hand, the division of Old Testament prophecies into certain elements fulfilled in Christ's earthly ministry and others still to come in the future was not adopted by anyone else we know of in antiquity, so it is unlikely that the first Christians would have derived it from anyone other than

---

[103] Stein, *Luke*, 496; Evans, *Mark 8:27–16:20*, 247; Davies and Allison, *A Critical and Exegetical Commentary on the Gospel According to Saint Matthew*, vol. 3 (1997), 216–17.

[104] See further Bradley R. Trick, "Death, Covenants, and the Proof of Resurrection in Mark 12:18–27," *Novum Testamentum* 49 (2007): 232–56. Cf. also Matthew Thiessen, "A Buried Pentateuchal Allusion to the Resurrection in Mark 12:25," *Catholic Biblical Quarterly* 76 (2014): 273–90.

[105] See throughout Robert W. Funk, Roy W. Hoover, and the Jesus Seminar, *The Five Gospels: The Search for the Authentic Words of Jesus* (New York: Macmillan, 1993).

Jesus.[106] A wide swath of New Testament scholarship in fact recognizes an "already but not yet" apocalyptic emphasis as core to the historical Jesus.[107]

Smaller details of Jesus's address likewise stand up to close scrutiny. The Western (or Wailing) Wall in Jerusalem, part of the retaining wall around the temple precincts, was left standing by the Romans when they decimated the city and razed the temple proper in AD 70, as an "in your face" reminder to the Jews of their devastation. But it also confirms Jesus's prophecy that "not one stone here will be left on another; every one will be thrown down" (Mark 13:2) since Jesus was clearly referring to the stones of the temple proper. Verses 5–23 proceed to itemize events that must precede the destruction of the temple, and all of them did indeed occur between AD 30 and 70. Verses 24–33 move beyond the destruction of Jerusalem to some unspecified time in the future when Christ will return; even Jesus in his voluntarily adopted limitations of his earthly life did not know the date of that event (v. 32).[108] In an early Christian context, ever concerned to exalt Jesus, this ignorance would not likely have been invented. Indeed, too

---

[106] See esp. Steven M. Bryan, *Jesus and Israel's Traditions of Judgement and Restoration* (Cambridge: Cambridge University Press, 2002). Cf. also Marius Reiser, *Jesus and Judgment: The Eschatological Proclamation in Its Jewish Context* (Minneapolis: Fortress, 1997).

[107] See esp. Dale C. Allison Jr., *Constructing Jesus: Memory, Imagination, and History* (Grand Rapids: Baker, 2010), 31–220. Cf. also Crispin Fletcher-Louis, "Jesus and Apocalypticism," in *Handbook for the Study of the Historical Jesus*, ed. Holmén and Porter, vol. 4, 2877–909.

[108] For the line of interpretation adopted here, see further George R. Beasley-Murray, *Jesus and the Last Days: The Interpretation of the Olivet Discourse* (Peabody: Hendrickson, 1993; Vancouver: Regent, repr. 2005). Cf. also Keener, *Gospel of Matthew*, 559–93; Witherington, *Matthew*, 444–56; David L. Turner, *Matthew* (Grand Rapids: Baker, 2008), 568–90; C. E. B. Cranfield, *The Gospel According to Saint Mark* (Cambridge: Cambridge University Press, 1977), 387–411; William L. Lane, *The Gospel of Mark* (Grand Rapids: Eerdmans, 1974; London: Marshall, Morgan & Scott, 1975), 444–82.

often in the history of the church, Jesus's followers have pretended to know what he assured them even he did not![109]

The Passion Narrative

A strong case can be made for the authenticity of the Last Supper, especially when shorn of all the later theological overlays that church history bequeathed to it (Mark 14:12–26 pars.).[110] The events of the last night of Jesus's life at table with his disciples dovetail closely with the elements of the Passover *Haggadah* or liturgy.[111] Yet he invests them with shockingly new meaning about his upcoming death on behalf of those who would follow him, which others would not likely have made up. Judas remains present long enough to partake of the parts of the meal Jesus invests with sacrificial significance even though he will reject the offering Christ makes on his behalf by betraying him and hanging himself—a noble suicide if he were Greek or Roman but a shameful death for a Jew—after sounding somewhat sorry for what he did. That Jesus had already given him the bread and wine as if he were a true disciple is unlikely to have been invented. Gethsemane shows Jesus in his full humanity, not wishing to go through with the agony of the crucifixion any more than any other person would have (Mark 14:32–42 pars.). The narrative retains the Aramaic, *Abba*

---

[109] See esp. Francis X. Gumerlock, *The Day and the Hour: A Chronicle of Christianity's Perennial Fascination with Predicting the End of the World* (Atlanta: American Vision, 2000).

[110] I. Howard Marshall, "Jesus' Last Supper with His Disciples," in *Key Events in the Life of the Historical Jesus*, ed. Bock and Webb, 481–588.

[111] Graham N. Stanton, *The Gospels and Jesus*, rev. ed. (Oxford and New York: Oxford University Press, 2002), 277. Cf. the Mishnaic tractate *Pesahim* 10.1–7. Against those who think this *haggadah* originated only after AD 70, see Joel Marcus, "Passover and the Last Supper Revisited," *New Testament Studies* 59 (2013): 303–24.

(v. 36), a distinctively intimate form of address by Jesus to his heavenly "Father," and thus almost universally agreed to be authentic.[112]

The disciples prove to be fickler here than anywhere else. Not only does Judas betray Jesus (vv. 43–46), but the remaining Eleven also all desert him (v. 50 pars.). Unique to Mark is the odd addition, "A young man, wearing nothing but a linen garment, was following Jesus. When they seized him, he fled naked, leaving his garment behind" (vv. 51–52). Commentators throughout church history have wondered if this is Mark's own ignominious signature since we know he came from a family that lived in Jerusalem (Acts 12:12). If it was someone else, we may never know who it was. Perhaps the identity was suppressed to allow him to represent the typical reaction of so many to a suffering Messiah and the fear of suffering with him.[113] But the unflattering portrait of all of Jesus's followers fleeing seems likely to be historical.[114]

Critics have regularly pointed out numerous anomalies in the trial of Jesus by the Sanhedrin according to later rabbinic law. A trial should not have occurred at night, especially not during festival times. Jesus should have had witnesses in his defense. Testimony against him that was internally contradictory should not have been allowed. Can we seriously believe the authorities in Jerusalem, so scrupulous about

---

[112] Though not as entirely unparalleled as once thought. See Scot McKnight, *A New Vision for Israel: The Teachings of Jesus in National Context* (Grand Rapids: Eerdmans, 1999), 49–65.

[113] For the full range of options, see Adela Yarbro Collins, *Mark* (Minneapolis: Fortress, 2007), 688–94. Rupert Allen ("Mark 14.51–52 and Coptic Hagiography," *Biblica* 89 [2008]: 265–68) covers similar ground, noting that the identification of the young man as John Mark goes back at least to sometime before 1208 when it was already reported as an established option in a footnote to a Coptic translation of Mark.

[114] After all, this scene forms the climax of Jesus's followers' shame and failure in the garden. See Howard M. Jackson, "Why the Youth Shed His Cloak and Fled Naked: The Meaning and Purpose of Mark 14:51–52," *Journal of Biblical Literature* 116 (1997): 273–89.

the law, would have allowed these and other illegalities?[115] Two major lines of reply are in order. First, while it is possible that any or all of these laws were in force in Jesus's day, the problem with any rabbinic legislation not explicitly ascribed to a rabbi from the time of Christ (i.e., the vast majority of all the Mishnah and later literature) is that we never know for sure what goes back to the early first century. So many changes in legislation developed after the destruction of Jerusalem in AD 70, and the rabbinic laws involved here refer explicitly to the *beth din* ("house of judgment") that was established in post-70 times, that we just don't know what was in force in Jesus's day.

But second, and perhaps more importantly, desperate times make for desperate people.[116] Various details in the Gospels suggest the Sanhedrin was trying to follow their laws up to a point. They did not initially want to arrest Jesus during the festival, not least because all of his supporters would be present in force and might riot against the action (Mark 14:2 par.). Even after a guilty verdict, they do not stone Jesus themselves according to Mosaic Law (Lev 24:16) but send him to Pilate, who was the local authority in capital cases (John 18:31). Mark 15:1 and parallels may in fact represent a brief early morning reconvening of the Sanhedrin to formalize the charges emerging from the more informal nighttime gathering and to create a greater aura of legality.[117] And we have probable confirmation of Caiaphas as a

---

[115] For a succinct catalogue of the illegalities, see Raymond E. Brown, *The Death of the Messiah*, vol. 1 (New York and London: Doubleday, 1994), 358–59. For full detail of all the problems with Jesus's various hearings before both Jews and Romans, see Laurna L. Berg, "The Illegalities of Jesus' Religious and Civil Trials," *Bibliotheca Sacra* 161 (2004): 330–42.

[116] The fullest defense of the historicity of these anomalous details remains Josef Blinzler, *The Trial of Jesus: The Jewish and Roman Proceedings Against Jesus Christ* (Cork: Mercier; Westminster, MD: Newman, 1959).

[117] R. T. France, *The Gospel of Mark* (Grand Rapids: Eerdmans; Carlisle: Paternoster, 2002), 614, citing *Sanh.* 7:5 in the Mishnah. Cf. also David R. Catchpole, *The Trial of Jesus: A Study in the Gospels and Jewish Historiography*

member of the Jewish elite from the discovery of his ornate ossuary (or bone box) as recently as 1990.[118]

If critics often complain that Herod the Great is more ruthless in the Gospels than in Josephus, because they alone record his massacre of the youngest boys in and around Jerusalem, they often complain that Pilate isn't ruthless enough in the Gospels compared to Josephus. In each instance they regularly fail to give due allowance for the selectivity of both Josephus and the earliest Christian authors to fit their theological and ideological purposes in ways that don't preclude the events narrated from having happened! These critics, moreover, almost never allow for the possibility that Josephus could have been wrong whenever he runs parallel to the New Testament but always assume the Christian authors have erred, even while stressing that Josephus was frequently mistaken elsewhere![119] Clearly this is not evenhanded historical inquiry. In any event the early second-century Roman historian Tacitus confirms that "Christ [was] executed by sentence of the procurator Pontius Pilate in the reign of Tiberius" (*Annals* 15:44). Josephus likewise agrees that Pilate condemned Jesus to be crucified (*Antiquities* 18.64).

We can say more about differing but complementary perspectives. Luke 13:1–3, discussed above, has already demonstrated Pilate's atrocities, even on the pages of the Gospels. Apparently Luke sensed no contradiction between narrating Pilate's instigation of the slaughter of Galileans' offering sacrifices in the temple and his trying unsuccessfully

---

(Leiden: Brill, 1971), 153–203; and A. N. Sherwin-White, "The Trial of Jesus," in *The Historicity and Chronology of the New Testament*, ed. Dennis E. Nineham, et al. (London: SPCK, 1965), 97–116.

[118] William R. Domeris and Simon M. S. Long, "The Recently Excavated Tomb of Joseph Bar Caipha and the Biblical Caiaphas," *Journal of Theology for Southern Africa* 89 (1994): 50–58.

[119] For an assessment of his overall trustworthiness with important exceptions, see Tessa Rajak, *Josephus*, 2nd ed. (London: Duckworth, 2002).

to pawn off responsibility of Jesus's fate on Herod Antipas (Luke 23:5–12). Given the prominence in Greco-Roman religion of the belief that dreams could communicate messages from the gods,[120] it is not difficult to imagine Pilate's wife interpreting a dream as a warning to her husband to have nothing to do with "that innocent man" (Matt 27:19). Given Pilate's delicate situation as an appointee of Rome in the rebellious hinterlands of the empire—no great honor for a would-be prefect—he had to find ways to keep both Rome and the Jewish masses as simultaneously happy as possible. So it is not surprising that he might imagine they would prefer him to release Jesus rather than Barabbas—a notorious terrorist—since the crowds remained generally more favorable to Jesus than the Jerusalem authorities did (Mark 15:9–11 pars.). There is no unambiguous testimony elsewhere to the custom of releasing one prisoner every Passover, but there is so little first-century Jewish history outside the Bible and Josephus that arguments from silence prove nothing here. But there is potentially indirect evidence for this custom in at least three ancient non-Christian sources.[121] *Antiquities* 20.9.3 describes Jewish leaders persuading Albinus, the prefect in 62, to release ten prisoners when he first arrived in Jerusalem at a Passover festival. The Babylonian Talmud, in *Pesahim* 91a, contains legislation for a prisoner's being released at Passover. And the Roman historian, Livy, describes a fourth-century BC event in which Rome released prisoners at a festival in Rome (*History of Rome* 5.13.5–8). So the biblical account actually coheres well with what was historically plausible.[122]

That the Jewish authorities would condemn Jesus of blasphemy (Mark 14:63–64 pars.) flows not from his claim to be Messiah but

---

[120] Derek S. Dodson, *An Audience-Critical Approach to Dreams in the Gospel of Matthew* (London and New York: T & T Clark, 2009).

[121] Keener, *Gospel of Matthew*, 669 n. 181.

[122] Cf. further Blinzler, *The Trial of Jesus*, 218–21; Robert L. Merritt, "Jesus, Barabbas and the Paschal Pardon," *Journal of Biblical Literature* 104 (1985): 57–68.

from his loftier claim to be Daniel's exalted Son of Man coming on the clouds of heaven (vv. 61–62 par.).[123] That they would send him off to the Roman authorities on the charge of claiming to be King fits the fact that they knew the only thing Pilate would care about was if Jesus were a threat to Caesar. Ironically, had he been such a threat in the militaristic sense, all but the Sadducees would have rejoiced, and they might never have sought his arrest.[124] But when it became clear that he was a more direct threat to their own leadership, they had to find a way to make Pilate interested in seeking his crucifixion. Even then Pilate was shrewd enough to recognize Jesus was no political threat, at least not directly, and did not want to create an incendiary situation among the crowds. When he saw that the leaders had whipped up the crowd into an uncharacteristic frenzy, for the same reason—keeping the peace—he decided to release Jesus to them (Mark 15:1–20 pars.).[125]

Compelling a passerby to help carry Jesus's crossbeam when Jesus was unable to continue meshed with the Roman law that a person

---

[123] Darrell L. Bock, *Blasphemy and Exaltation in Judaism: The Charge Against Jesus in Mark 14:53–65* (Tübingen: Mohr Siebeck 1998; Grand Rapids: Baker, 2000). Cf. *idem*, "Blasphemy and the Jewish Examination of Jesus," in *Key Events in the Life of the Historical Jesus*, ed. Bock and Webb, 589–667. Cf. also Joel F. Williams ("Foreshadowing, Echoes, and the Blasphemy at the Cross (Mark 15:29)," *Journal of Biblical Literature* 132 [2013]: 913–33) who shows how the theme of blasphemy ties larger parts of the passion narrative together.

[124] For the diversity and unity of messianic expectation, see Craig A. Evans, "Messianic Hopes and Messianic Figures in Late Antiquity," *Journal of Greco-Roman Christianity and Judaism* 3 (2006): 9–40. For a good, popular-level survey of the militaristic mood of the day, see Reza Aslan, *Zealot: The Life and Times of Jesus of Nazareth* (New York: Random House, 2013), 3–70; his reconstruction of Jesus in the rest of the book, however, is wildly implausible. For the entire history of messianic expectation, see Herbert W. Bateman, Darrell L. Bock, and Gordon H. Johnston, *Jesus the Messiah: Tracing the Promises, Expectations and Coming of Israel's King* (Grand Rapids: Kregel, 2012).

[125] For a full assessment of what we can know most securely about Pilate and his character, see Helen K. Bond, *Pontius Pilate in History and Interpretation* (Cambridge: Cambridge University Press, 2004).

could be commandeered to carry loads for soldiers (the background of Matt 5:41). The crowds' misunderstanding of Jesus's (slurred?) Aramaic as calling for Elijah was likely not invented (Mark 15:35). It is hard to know for sure if the drink offered Jesus on the cross (v. 36) was a mild sedative or a dehydrating liquid that would have increased his agony; both were used at times. In fact, crucifixion was common under Rome, and the descriptions of what happened to Jesus match closely what we know of the gruesome practice from that time period.[126] The only surprising Synoptic detail is how quickly he died—in the course of one afternoon (v. 33). But his preceding flogging would have weakened him considerably (v. 15). Plus, the loud cry with which he died (v. 37) suggests that he could have fought death a little longer but chose voluntarily when to expend all his remaining energy and fulfill his mission. The flogging, along with various aspects of Christ's trials, closely resembles the details of the authorities' treatment of Jesus ben Ananias a generation later (Jos. *War* 6.5.3).[127] The early third-century writer, Julius Africanus, cites an interesting statement from the historian Thallus who wrote a chronicle of world history in Greek in the first century, in which he referred to the darkness that occurred at the time of the crucifixion.[128] The cry of dereliction, finally, in which Jesus shouted, "My God, My God, why have you forsaken me?" (Mark 15:34), is almost certainly authentic because of the embarrassment it caused the first

---

[126] See esp. David W. Chapman, *Ancient Jewish and Christian Perceptions of Crucifixion* (Tübingen: Mohr Siebeck, 2008; Grand Rapids: Baker, 2010). Cf. also Martin Hengel, *The Crucifixion* (Philadelphia: Fortress; London: SCM, 1977).

[127] See further Craig A. Evans, "Jesus and the 'Cave of Robbers': Toward a Jewish Context for the Temple Action," *Bulletin for Biblical Research* 3 (1993): 93–110.

[128] For a full treatment of what we can know of Jesus historically apart from the New Testament, see Robert van Voorst, *Jesus Outside the New Testament: An Introduction to the Ancient Evidence* (Grand Rapids: Eerdmans, 2000).

Christians and because of its preservation in Aramaic as well as in Greek translation.[129]

It is a virtual certainty that Joseph of Arimathea truly did offer an unused tomb for Jesus's burial.[130] Such a detail serves no theological purpose of the Evangelists, is unusual enough that it was not likely made up, and yet it was not implausible. That at least one member of the Sanhedrin should be impressed enough with Jesus to want to give him a proper Jewish burial is completely conceivable. To claim otherwise would be to cast the Council in an extraordinarily anti-Semitic light. That Pilate would be surprised how quickly Jesus died stems from the typical two or three days it might take a crucified victim to die; that he would grant the request reflects his concern to keep the most powerful body of Jewish leaders appeased where possible (Mark 15:42–47 pars.). Josephus likewise attests to a combination of ruthlessness and cowardice before the Jewish authorities on the part of Pontius Pilate (*Ant.* 18.3.1, 18.3.2, 18.4.1–2).

The Church of the Holy Sepulcher in Old Jerusalem has a high chance of being the place Jesus was crucified.[131] Constantine's mother, Helena, traveled there as a pilgrim in the late third century and was shown this site long before an ornate church stood on it. The Romans had already built their own temple there in the second century, and they often erected shrines on top of locations other peoples deemed sacred in order to affirm their sovereignty over those peoples' gods.[132] But the appearance of Golgotha at that time was probably much more

---

[129] James D. G. Dunn, *Jesus Remembered* (Grand Rapids: Eerdmans, 2003), 780–81.

[130] A point stressed repeatedly in the writings of William Lane Craig on the resurrection. See, e.g., his "Opening Address," in *Will the Real Jesus Please Stand Up? A Debate Between William Lane Craig and John Dominic Crossan*, ed. Paul Copan (Grand Rapids: Baker, 1998), 26–27. For full historical background, see J. G. Cook, "Crucifixion and Burial," *New Testament Studies* 57 (2011): 193–213.

[131] Murphy-O'Connor, *The Holy Land*, 49–54.

[132] Keener, *The Historical Jesus of the Gospels*, 327–28.

like Gordon's Calvary—the tourist site today that contains the garden tomb—complete with its skull-shaped rocky crags. The garden tomb and the rolling stone tomb (just south of Jerusalem) are likewise excellent "object lessons" for what ancient tombs looked like, even if neither is in the correct location to have belonged to Joseph and donated for the use of Jesus's corpse. For the historicity of the resurrection narratives, see chapter 14.

Conclusion

The points this chapter has touched on represent only the strongest, most popular, or most influential evidence on behalf of the Synoptic Gospels and the portraits of Jesus they contain. This chapter could be expanded by a considerable length. Whether it is the lay of the land, first-century Jewish customs or beliefs, or actual archaeological or literary confirmation of specific details in these Gospels, a large volume of evidence corroborates the narrative backdrops in the Synoptic Gospels and supports the probability of the teachings and actions of Christ within that context. The criteria of dissimilarity and embarrassment enable us to envision a substantial portion of Jesus's words and deeds being authentic. Few if any others in his world would have dared to invent these details. The Gospel of John will provide similar data for examination. The next two chapters will evaluate the Fourth Gospel in some detail. Sufficient distinctives in its treatment of Jesus's life and ministry make it wise to treat it separately from the Synoptics.

Part Two

The Gospel of John

Chapter 4

The Formation of the Gospel of John

Anyone reading the four Gospels straight through from start to finish in a reasonably short period of time will be struck at how similar Matthew, Mark, and Luke are but how different John is compared with any of the three Synoptic Gospels. Gone are the parables so characteristic of the Jesus of the Synoptics. Absent are all exorcisms. Nothing is said about Jesus's birth or early years. None of Jesus's great sermons like the Mount/Plain (Matthew 5–7 par.) or the Olivet Discourse (Matthew 24–25 pars.) appears anywhere. Jesus undertakes no mission in Gentile territory like his "withdrawal from Galilee" in Mark 7:24–8:26 and parallels. He has no prolonged, final itinerating journey to Jerusalem as in Luke 9:51–18:34. Only three uses of "kingdom" appear amid Jesus's teaching, the topic so central to the Synoptics. Instead, the Fourth Gospel begins with a lofty prologue, explaining Jesus's origins from eternity past (John 1:1–18). John contains Jesus's ministry (John 2–4) before his so-called Great Galilean ministry. It clarifies that Jesus's ministry occupied approximately three years by narrating events that happened when Jesus went up to

151

Jerusalem at festival times (chaps. 5–10). It includes lengthy monologues and dialogues with Jewish leaders and one with a Samaritan woman (4:4–42), and it narrates at length Jesus's teaching in the upper room the night before his death (chaps. 13–17). The most dramatic of all Jesus's miracles, the resurrection of Lazarus, after he had been dead and entombed for four days (11:1–44), appears only in John.

Why is John so different from the Synoptics? Granted their differences, can both be believed, or must we prefer one narrative over the other? Many scholars have argued that the Synoptics stand much closer to the historical Jesus than the Fourth Gospel. John, they believe, has brought out what he believes to be the spiritual significance of Jesus but often at the expense of historical accuracy.[1] A handful of scholars find John theologically offensive as well as historically suspect![2] How should we assess these reactions? This chapter will focus on introductory and background considerations (much like the first of our three chapters on the Synoptic Gospels), which help explain why John is so different. Chapter 5 will then turn to a passage-by-passage exploration of the contents of the Fourth Gospel to see if there are good

---

[1] See esp. J. Louis Martyn, *History and Theology in the Fourth Gospel,* 3rd ed. (Louisville: Westminster John Knox, 2003); less drastic is Raymond E. Brown, *An Introduction to the Gospel of John,* ed. Francis J. Moloney (New York and London: Doubleday, 2003); and Andrew T. Lincoln, *The Gospel According to Saint John* (London and New York: Continuum; Peabody: Hendrickson, 2005). Successfully countering Martyn's two-level reading of John (in which seemingly historical events about Jesus merely represent end-of-first-century issues in the church) is Tobias Hägerland, "John's Gospel: A Two-Level Drama?" *Journal for the Study of the New Testament* 25 (2003): 309–22.

[2] See esp. Maurice Casey, *Is John's Gospel True?* (London and New York: Routledge, 1996). Particularly of concern to Casey is John's supposed anti-Semitism. But John's language reflects an intramural dispute between Christian Jews and Pharisaic-rabbinic Jews and is no stronger than what is regularly found in the Old Testament prophets. See esp. Lers Kierspel, *The Jews and the World in the Fourth Gospel: Parallelism, Function and Context* (Tübingen: Mohr Siebeck, 2006).

reasons for accepting its credibility and if it can be harmonized with the Synoptics.

Authorship

Irenaeus, in the late second century, wrote that after the first three Gospels were written, "John, the disciple of our Lord, who had leaned upon his breast, did publish a Gospel during his residence in Asia" (*Adv. Haer.* 3.1.1). By calling him the Lord's disciple, Irenaeus clarified that he was speaking of the member of the Twelve named John, brother of James and son of Zebedee (cf. Mark 3:17; Matt 10:2). "Leaning upon his breast" is an allusion to John 13:23, where an unnamed disciple Jesus loved was reclining at table at the Last Supper next to him. Five times in this Gospel, the narrator refers to one of the Twelve whom he calls simply "the disciple Jesus loved" (13:23; 19:26; 20:2; 21:7; 21:20). Irenaeus obviously believed this individual was John, the son of Zebedee and the author of this Gospel. Later in his same book, Irenaeus again quoted this document and again attributed the words to "John, the disciple of the Lord" (*Adv. Haer.* 3.11.1). Eusebius also echoed this identical tradition (*Hist. Eccl.* 3.24.5–13).

The issue becomes more complicated, however, when Eusebius cites the testimony of Papias. As we saw with the Synoptics, this is the earliest known information about any of the Gospels so it is particularly important. Papias describes how "if anyone came who had followed the presbyters, I inquired into the words of the presbyters, what Andrew or Peter or Philip or Thomas or James or John or Matthew, or any other of the Lord's disciples had said, and what Aristion and the presbyter John, the Lord's disciples, were saying" (*Hist. Eccl.* 3.39.4). The most straightforward reading of Papias's claim is that he is referring to two groups of individuals, the original Twelve, who have all passed away, so that they must be quoted secondhand, and two additional followers of Jesus who were still alive and could be quoted directly. When one observes that 2 and 3 John are penned by an anonymous individual just called "the elder" (2 John 1; 3 John 1), one can understand why some scholars have speculated that there were two separate individuals named John—the apostle who had known the historical Jesus and an influential church leader in the second generation of Christian history, still alive at the beginning of the second century in Papias's day.[3] Martin Hengel has argued at length that this latter John was the author of the Gospel that bears his name, that he was a follower of the apostle John, and that as a result we still have reliable testimony for the most part in the book that bears his name.[4] But the most common interpretation of Papias's testimony is that John, the only living apostle at that time, is mentioned twice and spoken of in his roles as both a follower of the historical Jesus and a church leader at the end of the first century.[5] What is more, Papias's reference to six of the seven named disciples in John in exactly the distinctive order they are introduced in John, over several discrete passages, strongly suggests he knew the Fourth Gospel.[6] This can only increase the likelihood that he knew accurate information about its composition also.

[3] See esp. Richard Bauckham, *The Testimony of the Beloved Disciple: Narrative, History, and Theology in the Gospel of John* (Grand Rapids: Baker, 2007), 33–72. Bauckham goes on, however, to suggest that the author may have been an anonymous, ideal disciple (pp. 73–91).

[4] Martin Hengel, *The Johannine Question* (London: SCM; Philadelphia: Trinity Press International, 1989).

[5] Charles E. Hill, "What Papias Said About John (and Luke): A 'New' Papian Fragment," *Journal of Theological Studies* 49 (1998): 582–629; Robert H. Gundry, *The Old Is Better: New Testament Essays in Support of Traditional Interpretations* (Tübingen: Mohr Siebeck, 2005; Eugene, OR: Wipf & Stock, 2010), 52–55.

[6] Andrew, Peter, Philip, Thomas, James, and John, in that order. See especially Jake H. O'Connell, "A Note on Papias' Knowledge of the Fourth Gospel," *Journal of Biblical Literature* 129 (2010): 793–94.

When one turns to clues within the Gospel of John itself, one finds oneself in a sleuthing exercise almost worthy of a murder mystery![7] The author is steeped in accurate knowledge of Jewish customs and the geography and topography of Israel.[8] Various touches without any obvious theological motivation strike many readers as details an eyewitness would most likely remember but oral tradition would not necessarily preserve.[9] All of these claims have been disputed but make it natural to think of one of the Twelve as the author. Even more convincing, however, is the context of the five texts about the "beloved disciple." In John 21:24, this disciple is linked directly to the witness of this Gospel, perhaps by his followers who were putting their *imprimatur* or stamp of approval on it. He is obviously one of those present at the Last Supper, though a few more than the Twelve might have been there. But he also joins Mary, the mother of Jesus, at Jesus's crucifixion (19:26–27, 34–35), runs with Peter to see the empty tomb (20:2–5, 8), and is among the seven who return to Galilee and encounter the risen Lord there (21:1–7).

Why would Jesus entrust his aging mother to a disciple and not a family member (19:26–27)? Joseph may well have been dead by this time, and Jesus's half-brothers may not yet have believed in him (cf. 7:5). But it would have had to be someone extremely close to him. Someone outside of the Twelve would appear to be an unlikely

---

[7] The classic discussion, concluding in favor of apostolic authorship, goes back to B. F. Westcott, *The Gospel According to St. John*, rev. ed. (London: J. Murray, 1908), ix–lxvii.

[8] See esp. John A. T. Robinson, *The Priority of John*, ed. J. F. Coakley (London: SCM, 1985; Oak Park, IL: Meyer-Stone, 1987), 123–295. Cf. throughout Bruce E. Schein, *Following the Way: The Study of John's Gospel* (Minneapolis: Augsburg, 1980).

[9] R. L. Sturch ("The Alleged Eyewitness Material in the Fourth Gospel," in *Studia Biblica 1978*, ed. Elizabeth A. Livingstone, vol. 2 [Sheffield: JSOT, 1980], 313–37) notes ways in which this has been exaggerated but still finds a core of details that plausibly reflect eyewitness testimony.

candidate. In the Synoptic Gospels, Peter, James, and John seem to form an inner core of leadership among the Twelve (Luke 8:51; Mark 9:2 par.; 14:33; cf. Gal 2:9), while in Acts John accompanies Peter as his close companion (Acts 1:13; 3:1–11; 4:1–13; 8:14–25). We know the sons of Zebedee are present in John 21 (v. 2), though they are never mentioned by name in this Gospel. The author cannot be Peter since the beloved disciple is distinguished from him. He cannot be James because he was martyred by Herod Agrippa I in AD 44, long before this Gospel was penned. That leaves John as the only plausible person.[10]

One more puzzling feature in the Fourth Gospel falls into place if we equate the beloved disciple with John. Like the Synoptics, the Fourth Gospel refers to a variety of the activities and teachings of John the Baptist. Unlike the Synoptics, it never calls him "the Baptist," merely "John." If anyone other than John the apostle was the author of this Gospel, it would be extremely confusing for him not to have ever specified which John he was speaking of. But if the original addressees knew that John the apostle was the author and that he never referred to himself by name, then they would know that all the references to John would have to refer to the Baptist.[11]

One other prominent individual has to be considered in this sleuthing enterprise. In 11:3, the two sisters, Mary and Martha, send word to Jesus, saying, "Lord, the one you love is sick." This is a strange way of referring to their brother Lazarus unless he was a special friend of Jesus. Ben Witherington has argued forcefully that Lazarus should be viewed as the beloved disciple, since he is the one named individual

---

[10] James H. Charlesworth (*The Beloved Disciple: Whose Witness Validates the Gospel of John?* [Valley Forge: Trinity Press International, 1995]) gives the fullest survey of the history of the discussion of authorship but then implausibly argues for Thomas.

[11] Cf. Leon Morris, *Studies in the Fourth Gospel* (Grand Rapids: Eerdmans, 1969; Eugene, OR: Wipf & Stock, 2006), 277.

in the entire Gospel so identified.[12] On the other hand, two verses later, the narrator explains that Jesus loved all three siblings (v. 5). And it would be even more odd, having identified "the one you love," by name in the rest of John 11, without repeating that epithet for Lazarus anywhere else in the chapter that narrates in detail the events leading up to, including, and following his resurrection, if the narrator would then never again use his name in any of the five later places where he speaks of a beloved disciple.

Finally, we should mention the anonymous disciple who is a companion of Andrew in 1:35 and 40, and an anonymous disciple who is a companion of Peter in 18:15–18. Are these the same individual? Is either or both of them to be linked with the two unnamed disciples in 21:2? Is any or all of them to be understood as the same as the "beloved disciple"? Each narrative would make good sense if these were all elliptical references to John, though they certainly don't have to be. If they are not, it is possible that one of them could be an otherwise unknown author of the Gospel, but he would have been someone in close touch with one or more of the Twelve and thus in at least as good if not better a position to report accurately on Jesus than either Mark or Luke.

When one looks at the arguments used by many scholars to claim a consensus against Johannine authorship, they appear remarkably weak.[13] (1) Wouldn't someone as close to Jesus paint a portrait much more like the synoptists did? Not if he had significantly different purposes, and besides what "lesser light" would dare to be as different? (2) Wouldn't his name appear in the text? Why should it? Neither

---

[12] Ben Witherington III, *What Have They Done with Jesus? Beyond Strange Theories and Bad History* (San Francisco: HarperSanFrancisco, 2006), 141–66; Ben Witherington III, *Invitation to the New Testament: First Things* (Oxford and New York: Oxford University Press, 2013), 124–30.

[13] This paragraph is a summary of Craig L. Blomberg, *The Historical Reliability of John's Gospel* (Leicester and Downers Grove: IVP, 2001), 31–35.

Mark's nor Luke's does. (3) Wouldn't the narrator have the volatile personality of one of the "sons of thunder," as James and John are called in Mark 3:17? Good grief; one's nickname hardly sums up one's entire character or demeanor! (4) Could a Galilean fisherman have written in Greek? Absolutely, especially after up to sixty years after Jesus's death, at least half of which involved living outside Israel. One's occupation and access to early education are unrelated to one's natural intelligence or to the skills one may acquire later in life. (5) Doesn't the author have a better knowledge of Judea and Jerusalem than Galilee? Not really, he just narrates much more of Jesus's time in those locations, so his familiarity with them is more apparent. Anyone accompanying Christ for three years of itinerant ministry would have good knowledge of the entire land. (6) Didn't the Twelve all flee from Jesus in the garden of Gethsemane (Mark 14:50 pars.)? Yes, they did, but all four Gospels agree that Peter came back to the high priest's courtyard (Mark 14:66–72 pars.), so John could have joined him and been present at the crucifixion as well. (7) Isn't there a rivalry between the beloved disciple and Peter in John 20–21 that would be inappropriate for another member of Jesus's inner circle? There are comparisons and contrasts to be sure, whether or not it is a rivalry, but wouldn't it be even less appropriate for someone outside Jesus's closest followers to "compete" with Peter? (8) Could a Galilean fisherman have accessed Caiaphas's courtyard as suggested by 18:15–16? The high priest's family would have required the best fish from Galilee, so at least a few suppliers had to become familiar with the venue. Zebedee's employment of multiple servants or "hired men" (Mark 1:20) suggests he was better off than many, which would fit with one who had opportunity to sell to the Jerusalem elite.[14]

---

[14] The recent, highly touted, liberal textbook by M. Eugene Boring (*An Introduction to the New Testament: History, Literature, Theology* [Louisville: Westminster John Knox, 2012], 630–31] replaces these with six even weaker

None of this is to suggest that John, the apostle, necessarily penned or dictated every last word of the Gospel that now bears his name. As already mentioned, 21:24–25 reads like an epilogue written by those endorsing John's work. Many scholars have observed that 20:30–31, the purpose statement of the Gospel, functions as a fitting ending, so that it is surprising to find chapter 21 following it. Perhaps the entire chapter, therefore, functioned as an epilogue.[15] But it nicely balances the prologue of 1:1–18. In addition, the third-person references to "the beloved disciple" are more natural if penned by someone other than John himself. Might we imagine that John had completed a draft of what he wanted to publish without one or more of these segments and that one of his disciples added them to put it in final form? Might the clarification in 21:23 about what Jesus had promised John stem from the fact that the aged apostle had just died and those who had believed the garbled rumor that he would live until Christ's return were having some kind of crisis in faith?[16] All of this is speculative but

---

arguments: (1) the original text is anonymous; (2) the earliest record of the belief in Johannine authorship is from Gnostics in the mid-second century; (3) early Christian testimony speaks of a community product; (4) the key scenes involving the sons of Zebedee from the Synoptics are missing in John; (5) the distinctive presentation is at odds with eyewitness testimony; (6) the compositional history contradicts apostolic authorship. But (1) is true of all four Gospels so proves nothing; (2) may be an accident of what has and hasn't been preserved but is probably untrue given standard dating of Papias; (3) and (6) are not incompatible with Johannine authorship plus one or more stages of redaction; (4) assumes a main desire of a Gospel writer was to talk about himself rather than about Jesus; and (5) is merely affirmed and nowhere argued.

[15] E.g., C. K. Barrett, *The Gospel According to St. John*, 2nd ed. (London: SPCK; Philadelphia: Westminster, 1978), 576; Ben Witherington III, *John's Wisdom: A Commentary on the Fourth Gospel* (Louisville: Westminster John Knox, 1995), 352.

[16] Stephen S. Smalley, *John: Evangelist and Interpreter* (Exeter: Paternoster, 1978; Eugene, OR: Wipf & Stock, 2012), 120; George R. Beasley-Murray, *John*, 2nd ed. (Nashville: Nelson, 1999), 412; C. H. Talbert, *Reading John* (New York: Crossroad, 1992; Macon: Smyth & Helwys, 2013), 262.

plausible. On the other hand, it is just possible that John penned every word as we now have it.[17]

Reviewers of my earlier work on the Fourth Gospel have sometimes said that a lot of my case for its historical reliability depends on having John as the author.[18] This flies in the face of my explicit comments. Noting that John could have forgotten or skewed a lot over six decades and that other followers of the apostles could have carefully preserved a lot over the same period of time, I concluded, "Thus our consideration of authorship creates some presumption in favour of the historical reliability of John but that presumption might be present even on other theories of authorship."[19] I then moved on, as I do here, to other background considerations.

Date

Although a minority tradition in antiquity affirmed that John was martyred at an early date,[20] most ancient testimony insisted that he lived to a ripe old age and penned the works in the New Testament that now bear his name near the end of the first century. Eusebius cites Clement of Alexandria (ca. 200) to the effect that John remained with the Asian elders at Ephesus until the time of Trajan (AD 98). Irenaeus also presents this identical information (*Adv. Haer.* 2.22.5, 3.3.4). For those who question whether an eyewitness of Jesus's life (AD 27 or 28 through 30)

---

[17] Howard M. Jackson, "Ancient Self-Referential Conventions and Their Implications for the Authorship and Integrity of the Gospel of John," *Journal of Theological Studies* 50 (1999): 1–34.

[18] E.g., Stephen Smalley, in *Theology* 105 (2002): 452–53.

[19] Blomberg, *Historical Reliability of John's Gospel*, 41.

[20] "A seventh-century summary of a fifth-century writer, Philip of Side, reports that Papias said that John and James were killed by the Jews. But Philip was a careless writer and nobody else seems to have found the reference in Papias."—Leon Morris, "John the Apostle," in *International Standard Bible Encyclopedia Revised*, vol. 2, ed. Geoffrey Bromiley (Grand Rapids: Eerdmans, 1982), 1108.

could live so long, recall our discussion about life spans. Intriguingly, a persistent tendency in ancient Christian painting and iconography is to depict John as the one disciple without facial hair.[21] It is impossible to know if this is based on any independent historical information, but if it is, it could mean that John was no more than a young teenager during Jesus's earthly life. Since Jews were considered adults by age twelve or thirteen, a self-styled rabbi like Jesus could have selected anyone younger than him down to the age of fourteen or so to be his disciple. If John were as young as seventeen after Jesus's three years of ministry in AD 30, he would have been only 85 in AD 98, a very conceivable life span.

A handful of conservative scholars have argued for a date for John in the 60s.[22] Clearly this would halve the amount of time that elapsed between Jesus's ministry and the penning of the Gospel. But most of the internal evidence involves arguments from silence. If John were after 70, he would surely have mentioned the destruction of Jerusalem, the defeat of the Zealots at the hands of the Romans, the synagogue's empire-wide condemnation of Jews who decided to follow Jesus, and so on. But this ignores the obvious fact that John is purporting to depict events from Jesus's day, not from later years, even if his selection of episodes to narrate often reflects their relevance to issues from his time. At the same time Andreas Köstenberger has made a plausible case that the reason for John's emphasis on Jesus as the fulfillment of sacred space (John 2:13–22; 4:20–24) and temple festivals (chaps. 5–10) is precisely because the literal temple is no longer standing.[23]

---

[21] "How to Recognize the Holy Apostles in Icons," in *A Reader's Guide to Orthodox Icons* (August 17, 2010), accessed December 29, 2015, http://iconreader .wordpress.com/2010/08/17/how-to-recognize-the-holy-apostles-in-icons.

[22] E.g., John A. T. Robinson, *Redating the New Testament*, rev. ed. (London: SCM; Philadelphia: Westminster, 1976), 257–58, 267–78.

[23] Andreas Köstenberger, "The Destruction of the Second Temple and the Composition of the Fourth Gospel," in *Challenging Perspectives on the Gospel of John*, ed. John Lierman (Tübingen: Mohr Siebeck, 2006), 69–108.

John 5:2 may use a historical present to state that there *is* in Jerusalem a pool by a gate that may have been in ruins by the 90s, but the pool itself was still used as a healing sanctuary for the Roman god Asclepius in later years, so this particular gate may have still been standing or have been rebuilt.[24]

Conservative scholars do no one any favors if they jump on the bandwagon of viewpoints with slender evidence attached to them, like the case for an early date for John. Sixty years by the standards of the ancient Mediterranean world is still a remarkably short span of time between the life of an individual and the appearance of a biography about him. Indeed, the additional length of time between Jesus's ministry and the production of the Fourth Gospel actually helps explain some of its distinctives. John has had plenty of time to reflect on the significance of who Jesus was, so we should not be surprised if his Christology is at times more exalted.[25] He knows what has already been well covered in the first three Gospels and what his audience in and around Ephesus would already have known, both from his own decades of ministry there and from those of other apostolic leaders. In many instances he probably chooses consciously not to repeat what they have well highlighted.[26]

Context and Sources

If John was writing to Christian house churches in and around Ephesus near the end of the first century, this would explain two other dominant

---

[24] Cf., respectively, Westcott, *John*, 181; and J. Ramsey Michaels, *The Gospel of John* (Grand Rapids: Eerdmans, 2010), 288.

[25] See esp. James F. McGrath, *John's Apologetic Christology: Legitimation and Development in Johannine Christology* (Cambridge: Cambridge University Press, 2001).

[26] One does not have to posit direct literary dependence to come to this conclusion. Johannine and Synoptic traditions are more likely "interfluential, augmentive and corrective" (Paul N. Anderson, *The Fourth Gospel and the Quest for Jesus* [London and New York: T & T Clark, 2006], 101–12).

features of the distinctives of his narrative. On the one hand, despite all the lofty Christology, there is also a strong emphasis on Jesus's full humanity. He tires, gets thirsty, becomes angry, weeps, and dies a fully human death. He is the Word become flesh who "tabernacles" among us (1:14).[27] All this naturally counters the growing Gnostic threat that would turn into a full-fledged syncretistic worldview early in the second century that combined elements of Christianity, Judaism, and Greek Neoplatonism. Gnostics had no difficulty believing in Jesus's deity but balked at his complete humanity because they believed that matter was inherently evil![28] At the same time the growing "parting of the ways" between Judaism and Christianity at the end of the first century explains the sustained emphasis on Jesus's interaction with Jewish leaders. John still wants to win over as many Jews who do not yet follow Jesus as Messiah as he can, and he wants to help his Christian audience marshal support for the undertaking.[29]

---

[27] See esp. Marianne Meye Thompson, *The Humanity of Jesus in the Fourth Gospel* (Philadelphia: Fortress, 1988). For a demonstration of both human and divine elements to Jesus's emotions, see Stephen Voorwinde, *Jesus' Emotions in the Fourth Gospel: Human or Divine?* (London and New York: T & T Clark, 2005).

[28] See esp. Udo Schnelle, *Antidocetic Christology in the Gospel of John: An Investigation of the Place of the Fourth Gospel in the Johannine School* (Minneapolis: Fortress, 1992).

[29] Witherington, *John's Wisdom*, 2, 11; Witherington, *Invitation to the New Testament*, 135–36. For a book-length treatment of the originally intended audiences of John as being broad and diverse, see Edward W. Klink III, *The Sheep of the Fold: The Audience and Origin of the Gospel of John* (Cambridge: Cambridge University Press, 2007). The best approach would seem to be a both-and. The Gospels, including John, had specific original audiences in mind but expected their writings to be quickly disseminated to a much broader audience. See Craig L. Blomberg, "The Gospels for Specific Communities *and* All Christians," in *The Audience of the Gospels: The Origin and Function of the Gospels in Early Christianity*, ed. Edward W. Klink III (London and New York: T & T Clark, 2010), 111–33. For the view that the broader audience directly included Christians and non-Christians alike, see Stanley E. Porter, *John, His Gospel, and Jesus: In Pursuit of the Johannine Voice* (Grand Rapids: Eerdmans, 2015).

Much of the last two-thirds of twentieth-century scholarship, however, rejected the traditional view that John was later than, dependent on, and supplementary to the Synoptic Gospels. Careful comparisons of the approximately 20 percent of John that does run parallel to the first three Gospels almost never discloses the extended, verbal parallelism that one often finds when comparing any two (and sometimes all three) of the Synoptic Gospels. At most about five consecutive words in Greek are identical, and two of them are likely to be "the" and "and"![30] But literary independence does not mean John's congregations had never heard one of the earlier Gospels read aloud. Even more to the point, it is virtually certain they were familiar with the major contents of the Synoptics, simply from the common core message that would have frequently been preached and passed along in the fledgling Christian communities.

At the end of the twentieth century, a key work edited by Richard Bauckham, entitled *The Gospels for All Christians*, introduced a paradigm shift for many scholars working in Johannine studies.[31] While possibly exaggerating their case a little, the contributors to this volume more than adequately demonstrated that the Gospel writers would have envisioned the communities to which they first delivered their documents quickly making copies for themselves and then passing the original documents on to neighboring churches, who would then replicate that process. Thirty years would have been more than enough time for Christians in Ephesus to hear about and become familiar with the majority of the contents of the Synoptics. At the same time, by not borrowing directly from the Synoptic outline or core contents, John winds up being noticeably different from them. Another way

---

[30] The pioneering work defending literary independence was P. Gardner-Smith, *Saint John and the Synoptic Gospels* (Cambridge: Cambridge University Press, 1938).

[31] Richard Bauckham, ed., *The Gospels for All Christians: Rethinking the Gospel Audiences* (Grand Rapids: Eerdmans, 1998).

of putting this is that we should not be surprised John is so different from Matthew, Mark, and Luke; we should be surprised that those three texts are so similar. Had they not been interrelated at a literary level, with different writers copying from one another and/or common sources, they might have been as unlike one another as they collectively are unlike John. After all, the core claim underneath the hyperbole of John 21:25 is true of most complex and influential individuals: the whole world would not be able to contain the books that could be written about their exploits.

If John is not literarily dependent on the Synoptics, do any textual data actually support his awareness of their contents and, more importantly, his readers' awareness of them? The answer is yes—in abundance! In numbers of places, John and the Synoptics "interlock" so that either John writes in a way that presupposes knowledge of Matthew, Mark, or Luke or he explains something left cryptic in one of the first three Gospels. We will begin with the first of these phenomena.[32]

John 3:24 functions like a parenthesis in the middle of a narrative about Jesus and John and their ministries of baptism. Tucked into this account is the clarification, "This was before John was put in prison." Anyone familiar with the Synoptic accounts of John the Baptist's imprisonment and execution at the hands of Herod Antipas (Mark 6:14–29 par.) would recognize this passing reference and view it as a helpful chronological clarification. But John's Gospel nowhere says anything else about the Baptist's ultimate demise. John 3:24 would only *raise* questions for a reader or listener unfamiliar with the fuller story of John the Baptist. John was imprisoned? Why? When? By whom? What was the outcome? Only if they already knew what happened to him would this verse form a helpful parenthesis.

---

[32] See esp. Richard Bauckham, "John for Readers of Mark," in ibid., 147–72. Cf. also James D. Dvorak, "The Relationship Between John and the Synoptic Gospels," *Journal of the Evangelical Theological Society* 41 (1998): 201–13.

Or consider John 11:2. At the beginning of the account about Lazarus's death and resurrection, John again adds a parenthesis. Because he has referred to the sisters, Mary and Martha (v. 1), he adds, "This Mary, whose brother Lazarus now lay sick, was the same one who poured perfume on the Lord and wiped his feet with her hair." Mary was by far the most common Jewish woman's name, and several appear in the Gospels alone. So a clarification as to which Mary appears here is natural—but only if this Mary has already been introduced. Nothing in the first ten chapters helps us understand John's supposed clarification. In this example we do read *later* about the episode (12:1–11); perhaps John is simply foreshadowing that event. But he refers to it in the past tense as if his readers would already understand his explanation. Intriguingly, in the Synoptic parallels we are told that the (there unnamed) woman who anointed Jesus would have what she did told wherever the gospel would be preached (Mark 14:9 par.). If Mary's action did become a standard component of early Christian proclamation, then we can understand why John could assume his audience knew about it.

As a final example, take John 18:24 and 28. As in the Synoptics, John knows that Jesus was tried before the high priest Caiaphas (Mark 14:53–65 pars.). Unlike the Synoptics, John says not a word about what happened during that trial. Instead, we read only that Annas sent him bound to Caiaphas and then that the Jewish leaders took him from Caiaphas to Pilate. What happened in between? A narrator can't just raise the matter of Jesus on trial for his life with the highest Jewish court in the land and then say nothing about its proceedings, unless of course he knows his audience already knows that story well.

Interlocking can function in the reverse direction also.[33] Why does the Synoptic Jesus lament *how often* he longed to gather the people of

---

[33] See esp. Morris, *Studies in the Fourth Gospel*, 40–63. Cf. also D. A. Carson, *The Gospel According to John* (Grand Rapids: Eerdmans; Leicester: IVP, 1991), 52–55.

Jerusalem like a mother hen gathers her chicks under her wings? In the Synoptics the only time Jesus is in Jerusalem after age twelve is for the Passover during which he was crucified. But John's roughly three-year chronology for Jesus's ministry narrates his frequent presence in the capital city each year at the time of the major Jewish festivals. In this case John helps explain something puzzling in the Synoptics.

Or think about the charge against Jesus at his trial before the Sanhedrin. The Synoptics claim false witnesses accused him of predicting he would destroy and rebuild the temple during a three-day period of time (Mark 14:58 par.). Nothing in the Synoptics, even in garbled form, corresponds to this prediction. But John 2:19 does. If Jesus declared, "Destroy this temple, and I will raise it again in three days," one could imagine how two or three years later, before anyone understood he was talking about his body (v. 21), his teaching could get distorted in the way the Synoptics report it.[34]

Finally, let us turn to John 18:31. Readers of the Synoptics unfamiliar with the finer points of Jewish law under Rome might wonder why the Sanhedrin involved Pilate and the Roman authorities at all. Blasphemy (Mark 14:64 pars.) in the Torah led to execution by stoning (Lev 24:14). Why didn't the Jewish council simply condemn Jesus to their own executioners according to their own law? Nothing in the Synoptics gives any answer, but John does: Rome had taken away the right of capital punishment in most instances. (The later action taken against Stephen seems to have unfolded more as the result of mob action rather than of any desire to observe the law [Acts 7:57–60].[35])

---

[34] Robinson, *Priority of John*, 127–31.

[35] Or more precisely, with Eckhard J. Schnabel (*Acts* [Grand Rapids: Zondervan, 2012], 391), as an act of institutionally sanctioned violence that nevertheless violated standard procedure of the day. In other words, the Jewish authorities probably allowed and perhaps encouraged matters to escalate, in the absence of immediate Roman presence to stop them and despite the formal illegalities of the action.

In short, John and the Synoptics each help interpret the other and should not be read in isolation from each other.

Can we press behind the Synoptics to any earlier sources on which John may have drawn? If his Gospel is largely the product of eyewitness testimony, there is no need to expect to find any, but he still may have relied on some. Of various theories that have been suggested in modern Johannine source criticism, the most plausible is that there was a "Signs-Source," which accounts for the seven miracles of John 2–11. Robert Fortna spent the better part of his scholarly career defending this hypothesis, based on a meticulous and minute analysis of the distinctive vocabulary and style in these accounts.[36] The otherwise skeptical Jesus Seminar was convinced in the 1990s that such a signs source existed and was written perhaps as early as the 50s.[37] On the other hand, the tendency today is to see a uniformity of style that cuts across all of the Fourth Gospel, making sources too difficult to detect.[38]

To be sure, puzzling literary seams supported the older source criticism. John 6:1 ("Some time after this, Jesus crossed to the far shore of the Sea of Galilee") reads strangely after a chapter in which Jesus has been in Jerusalem (5:1–47). But we should probably just assume John takes for granted that his readers will understand that Galileans celebrating festivals in Jerusalem would return home after the holidays

---

Many countries in the world can point to analogous behavior during particularly volatile times in their history.

[36] See esp. Robert T. Fortna, *The Gospel of Signs* (Cambridge: Cambridge University Press, 1970); Robert T. Fortna, *The Fourth Gospel and Its Predecessor* (Philadelphia: Fortress, 1988).

[37] Robert W. Funk, ed., *The Acts of Jesus: The Search for the Authentic Deeds of Jesus* (San Francisco: HarperSanFrancisco, 1998), 16–18.

[38] Seminal was G. van Belle, *The Signs Source in the Fourth Gospel: Historical Survey and Critical Evaluation of the Semeia Hypothesis* (Leuven: Leuven University Press and Peeters, 1994). A good current anthology is G. van Belle, M. Labahn, and P. Moritz, eds., *Repetitions and Variations in the Fourth Gospel: Style, Text, Interpretation* (Leuven: Peeters, 2009).

concluded.[39] The most famous seam comes in John 14:31, where Jesus addresses his disciples after his Last Supper with them, and after instructing them about his coming departure and the Holy Spirit's role as his replacement, says, "Come now; let us leave." But then he goes on talking for another three chapters! Many scholars have therefore speculated that perhaps two Farewell Discourses have been sutured together at this point.[40]

A study of Greek tragedy, however, calls attention to the dramatic device of a delayed exit. Like some guests who announce it is time for them to leave the home they are visiting but then continue talking at length, an established technique for stressing the importance of upcoming obligations, especially if it included facing opposition, was precisely this kind of narrative where the extended monologue focuses on the significance of the hour.[41] Alternately, perhaps Jesus and his followers did leave for the garden of Gethsemane at this point. After all, the next indication in John of their location comes in 18:1, where they leave and cross the Kidron Valley. It seems a little odd that John says nothing about departing from the city first, though his narrative could just be compressed. The extended metaphor about the vine and its branches in 15:1–8 could have been suggested by the vineyards they would have passed en route. Scott Kellum concludes that 14:31

---

[39] Cf. Colin G. Kruse, *The Gospel According to John* (Leicester: IVP; Grand Rapids: Eerdmans, 2003), 160 and n. 1. The heyday of perceiving dislocations attributed to careless stitching together of divergent sources came in the speculation appearing throughout Rudolf Bultmann, *The Gospel of John* (Oxford: Blackwell; Philadelphia: Westminster, 1971; Eugene, OR: Wipf & Stock, 2014). The rise of literary criticism of the Bible has largely supplanted such theories with approaches to John that see much more unity in composition.

[40] E.g., Fernando Segovia, *Farewell of the Word: The Johannine Call to Abide* (Minneapolis: Fortress, 1991), 320–26.

[41] George L. Parsenios, *Departure and Consolation: The Johannine Farewell Discourses in Light of Greco-Roman Literature* (Leiden: Brill, 2005), 49–76. Somewhat similar is John C. Stube, *A Graeco-Roman Rhetorical Reading of the Farewell Discourse* (London and New York: T & T Clark, 2006), 134–36.

not only signals when the disciples left the upper room but also slows the reader down "immediately before the peak of the discourse."[42] So an awkward stitching together of divergent sources is by no means the only explanation for the odd end to John 14.

Omissions and Outlines

Can we explain John's striking omission of features central to the Synoptics? It seems significant that while there are literally more than a thousand parables scattered throughout the encyclopedic-sized rabbinic literature, not one fictitious narrative at all close in form to Jesus's parables has been discovered in ancient Greco-Roman literature. It appears to have been a uniquely Jewish form of teaching in that day.[43] While John could have chosen to include some of Jesus's parables, he may have felt it was not as appropriate a form for a largely Gentile audience. At the same time, he does include numerous figurative sayings or extended proverbs, which he calls *paroimiai*, so he is certainly aware of Jesus's penchant for this kind of teaching.[44]

Exorcisms in Greco-Roman contexts tended to be more "magical" (see above) than in Jewish contexts. John may have omitted these lest his readership think there were formulae available with which to manipulate God. Still, John knows well that Christ's ministry involved

---

[42] L. Scott Kellum, *The Unity of the Farewell Discourse: The Literary Integrity of John 13.31–16.33* (London and New York: T & T Clark, 2004), 238.

[43] For extensive illustration, see Harvey K. McArthur and Robert M. Johnston, *They Also Spoke in Parables: Rabbinic Parables from the First Centuries of the Christian Era* (Grand Rapids: Zondervan, 1990; Eugene, OR: Wipf & Stock, 2014). Cf. also David Stern, *Parables in Midrash: Narrative and Exegesis in Rabbinic Literature* (Cambridge, MA: Harvard University Press, 1994).

[44] Kim E. Dewey, "*Paroimiai* in the Gospel of John," *Semeia* 17 (1980): 81–99; Ruben Zimmermann, "Are There Parables in John?" *Journal for the Study of the Historical Jesus* 9 (2011): 243–76. For cryptic, metaphorical language in John more broadly, cf. Tom Thatcher, *The Riddles of Jesus in John: A Study in Tradition and Folklore* (Atlanta: SBL, 2000).

the overthrow of Satan (12:31; 14:30; 16:11). In these texts we learn, in turn, that "now is the time for judgment on this world; now the prince of this world will be driven out," that "the prince of this world is coming" but "has no hold over [Jesus]," and that "the prince of this world now stands condemned."[45]

John has nothing about Jesus's birth or early years, but neither does Mark. John does not present the *same* sermons the Synoptics do, but he still has long, extended discourses of Jesus. He does not include Jesus's withdrawal from Galilee, but neither does Luke; and John *does* include Jesus's predicting the Gentile mission in 12:20–36. John 3:3, 5 and 18:36 show that John most certainly knows about the teaching of the kingdom, but again this is a Jewish concept, founded in the Old Testament theocracy and its promises about a descendant of David sitting on his throne in Jerusalem. "Eternal life," on the other hand, occurs nine times in the three Synoptics (including parallels), but twenty-one times in the Fourth Gospel. Matthew 19:16–26 proves particularly instructive here. A rich man asks Jesus what good thing he must do to get "eternal life" (v. 16). The man goes away sorrowful after a brief interchange with Jesus. Jesus replies, "Truly I tell you, it is hard for someone who is rich to enter the kingdom of heaven" (v. 23). He then illustrates his point with his famous metaphor of a camel and a needle's eye but substitutes "kingdom of God" for "kingdom of heaven" (v. 24). Finally, the disciples ask, "Who then can be saved?" (v. 25). At least in this context, gaining eternal life, entering the kingdom of heaven (or kingdom of God), and being saved are synonymous. But eternal life is a concept Greeks regularly discussed so John may have preferred it in composing his Gospel.[46]

---

[45] Eric Plumer, "The Absence of Exorcisms in the Fourth Gospel," *Biblica* 78 (1997): 350–68.

[46] George E. Ladd, *A Theology of the New Testament*, ed. Donald A. Hagner, rev. ed. (Grand Rapids: Eerdmans, 1993), 290–95.

Most of scholars' concerns about omissions in the four Gospels have to do with what *John* leaves out of his narrative, especially since he wrote last. But sometimes the concerns focus on Synoptic omissions. Most strikingly, it is often argued that if Jesus really raised Lazarus from his grave, no Gospel could possibly have avoided including this account. Since it is unique to John, it must be unhistorical. At this point, however, some brief reflections about the outlines of the four Gospels become important. Mark, for whatever reason, decided to narrate only one visit of the adult Jesus to Jerusalem—at the Passover during which he was crucified. Matthew and Luke expanded on Mark's overall outline but left this feature intact. Only John chose to narrate other visits of Jesus to Jerusalem and its vicinity prior to his final, fateful trip there.

This means that any events John chooses to narrate about Jesus's time near Jerusalem that did not coincide with his final trip there, will be omitted no matter how momentous they might have been. The resurrection of Lazarus, in or near Bethany, a "suburb" of Jerusalem, occurs on Jesus's second-to-last visit there. John 11:54 explains that after Lazarus's raising, and because of the death threats on his life, Jesus "no longer moved about publicly among the people of Judea. Instead he withdrew to a region near the wilderness, to a village called Ephraim, where he stayed with his disciples." After an unspecified interval of time, Matthew 12 then proceeds to narrate Jesus's climactic journey to Jerusalem at Passover. The Synoptics thus contain no mention of Lazarus's resurrection because it cannot fit into the self-imposed limitations of their outline.[47] But they do narrate the resurrections of two other individuals, Jairus's daughter (Mark 5:21–24, 35–43 pars.) and the son of the widow at Nain (Luke 7:11–17). The account about Lazarus is quantitatively more spectacular because of

---

[47] Cf. Rudolf Schnackenburg, *The Gospel According to John*, vol. 2 (New York: Seabury, 1980), 345.

the longer time he had been dead, but it is not qualitatively any different. Numerous other "omissions" from either John or the Synoptics can be similarly explained.

Genre and Parallels

A different phenomenon that makes many people skeptical about John's historical reliability involves the way he narrates the events he includes. In the same vein the style of Jesus's speech in the Fourth Gospel seems consistently different from the Synoptics but at times indistinguishable from John's style as narrator. These impressions can be exaggerated; there are, after all, at least 145 words used only by Jesus in John's Gospel that appear nowhere in John's narrative segments.[48] But there is a definite measure of truth in these impressions. Modern English translations of the Bible, for example, regularly note that editors are unsure where Jesus's words leave off and the narrator's begin in John 3 in the dialogue between Jesus and Nicodemus. Many readers have assumed they continue all the way to verse 21. But the last time the first person form ("I" or "we") is used in the passage is in verse 12. Verses 16–21 could easily be the words of John the narrator rather than Jesus's speech. But the style is almost identical so it is hard to be sure.[49]

The same problem recurs later in the chapter between the words of John the Baptist and the narrator of the Fourth Gospel. Some interpreters see the Baptist's words ending at verse 30; others see

---

[48] H. R. Reynolds, *The Gospel of St. John*, vol. 1 (London: Funk & Wagnalls, 1906), cxxiii–cxxv.

[49] Leon Morris (*The Gospel According to John* [Grand Rapids: Eerdmans, 1995], 202 n. 73) notes three Johannine distinctives in vv. 16–21 not found anywhere in the words unambiguously attributed to Jesus in the Fourth Gospel: "one and only" (*monogenēs*), "believing in his name," and "doing the truth." Cf. also E. Earle Ellis, *The Making of the New Testament Documents* (Leiden: Brill, 1999; Atlanta: SBL, 2009), 173–74.

them carrying through to verse 36. A slightly more Johannine style permeates verses 31–36, but the shift is subtle at best.[50] What all this demonstrates is that John the apostle has written up most of his narrative in the same style, whether he is telling the story or someone else is speaking. But in a world without quotation marks or any felt need for them, as we have already seen, no one would have batted an eye at this practice or felt that it impugned John's trustworthiness in the least. The issue was whether he was true to the intent of the characters' speech in the narrative, not how literally he translated their words from Aramaic into Greek.[51]

A distinctive role of the Holy Spirit in John reinforces this point. In John 14:26, we read that Jesus promised his disciples that "the Advocate [Gk. *paraklētos*], the Holy Spirit, whom the Father will send in my name, will teach you all things and will remind you of everything I have said to you." In 15:26, Jesus adds that "when the Advocate comes, whom I will send to you from the Father—the Spirit of truth who goes out from the Father—he will testify about me." Quite likely, the apostle had a strong sense of being guided by the Holy Spirit as he put pen to papyrus (or dictated to a scribe). This sense of inspiration would have given him the confidence to phrase things as he did, even when he knew his wording highlighted the theological significance of speakers' words at times more than a literal translation might have done.[52]

The same is probably true of the literary genre John chose to adopt. While the basic genre is the Greco-Roman biography, just as

---

[50] F. F. Bruce, *The Gospel of John* (Basingstoke: Pickering & Inglis; Grand Rapids: Eerdmans, 1983), 96; Jeffrey Wilson, "The Integrity of John 3:22–36," *Journal for the Study of the New Testament* 10 (1981): 34–41.

[51] Craig S. Keener, *The Gospel of John: A Commentary*, vol. 1 (Peabody: Hendrickson, 2003), 74–76.

[52] Herman N. Ridderbos, *The Gospel According to John: A Theological Commentary* (Grand Rapids: Eerdmans, 1997), 509.

for the Synoptic Gospels, John follows a bit more of a "dramatic" form of that genre, akin to styles sometimes adopted in the Greek theater.[53] This creates a slightly more stylized presentation of the life, death, and resurrection of Jesus, with paradigmatic scenes and episodes conveying the significance of events. It means that phrasing a person's words makes them somewhat more memorable, while still retaining the probability that they are true to the meaning of the speaker's original utterances. In a similar vein the twin themes of truth and witness that permeate the Gospel set clear limits on just how free John, even under the inspiration of the Spirit, would have felt to paraphrase or rephrase the teachings and deeds of his Lord.[54]

A recent dissertation by Philipp Bartholomä demonstrates this last point in meticulous detail for six major discourses of Jesus in the Fourth Gospel. Bartholomä proceeds through each independent clause in John 3:1–21; 4:1–30; 6:22–59; 8:12–59; 14:1–31; and 20:11–29, comparing it with the full range of sayings attributed to Jesus in Matthew, Mark, and Luke. He looks for conceptual and verbal parallels to passages that might appear anywhere in the Synoptics. If neither form of parallel exists, he designates that portion of the text in John as a "[0, 0]." If a moderate conceptual parallel occurs, the first

---

[53] See esp. Jo-Ann Brandt, *Dialogue and Drama: Elements of Greek Tragedy in the Fourth Gospel* (Peabody: Hendrickson, 2004). Particularly important for plotting John on a spectrum about one-fourth of the way from unadorned chronicle to sheer fiction is Derek Tovey, *Narrative Art and Act in the Fourth Gospel* (Sheffield: Sheffield Academic Press, 1997). Cf. also Tom Thatcher, *Why John Wrote a Gospel: Jesus—Memory—History* (Louisville: Westminster John Knox, 2006). At the same time, Bauckham (*Testimony of the Beloved Disciple*, 93–112) points out dimensions in which John is even more like Greco-Roman historiography than the Synoptics.

[54] Gary M. Burge, "Situating John's Gospel in History," in *Jesus in Johannine Tradition*, ed. Robert T. Fortna and Tom Thatcher (Louisville and London: Westminster John Knox, 2001), 35–46. George L. Parsenios (*Rhetoric and Drama in the Johannine Lawsuit Motif* [Tübingen: Mohr Siebeck, 2010]) demonstrates that legal rhetoric and tragic drama are joined together here and elsewhere in Greco-Roman literature, each limiting how much of the other element can be present.

number becomes a 1; if a close conceptual parallel occurs, it becomes a 2. If a moderate verbal parallel occurs, the second number becomes a 1; if a close verbal parallel occurs, it becomes a 2. Despite the fact that most synopses print few parallels from the Synoptics next to any portion of the major discourses of John, Bartholomä demonstrates that only thirty out of the 322 discrete propositions have neither verbal nor conceptual parallels in the Synoptics (only 9.4 percent), while a full 166 (or 51.5 percent) contain not merely conceptual but also verbal parallelism of some significance.[55]

Why then does John at first glance seem so different from the Synoptics? Bartholomä offers three main replies. John's style involves considerably greater repetition of key concepts than is found in the Synoptics. John operates with a noticeably reduced semantic range in his representation of Jesus's words. Finally, his discourses show a greater propensity for abstraction. All of these make sense when we recognize that John is excerpting, abbreviating, and using his own vocabulary and style to summarize much more detailed messages given by Jesus in a different language. After years of preaching to Christian audiences, this material will naturally have taken on his own characteristic style of presentation.[56] Other Christian transmitters will have likewise put their stamp on the tradition.[57] But none of these practices necessarily

---

[55] Philipp Bartholomä, *The Johannine Discourses and the Teaching of Jesus in the Synoptics: A Contribution to the Discussion Concerning the Authenticity of Jesus' Words in the Fourth Gospel* (Tübingen and Basel: Francke, 2012), summarized in chart form on pp. 415–28.

[56] E. Earle Ellis, *The World of St. John: The Gospel and the Epistles* (Grand Rapids: Eerdmans, 1984; Lanham, MD: University Press of America, 1995), 53–54. The same point is stressed by Barnabas Lindars, though with a view of greater freedom on John's part to create than seems warranted, in "Discourse and Tradition: The Use of the Sayings of Jesus in the Discourses of the Fourth Gospel," *Journal for the Study of the New Testament* 13 (1981): 83–101.

[57] See esp. Anthony Le Donne and Tom Thatcher, eds., *The Fourth Gospel in First-Century Media Culture* (London and New York: T & T Clark, 2011).

impugns John's reliability in faithfully communicating the essence of Jesus's teaching en route.[58]

Theological Differences

It is one thing, of course, to dissect a Gospel and show a surprising number of similarities to other documents. It is another to consider it as a whole and the impression it creates by the repetitions, emphases, and diction. Wording may match supposed parallels, while still being used in sufficiently different contexts so as to create substantially different meaning. Does not the distinctive and characteristic theology of the Fourth Gospel vary so consistently and so significantly from that of the Synoptics that we cannot harmonize the differing portraits of Jesus that result? Doesn't the deity of Jesus overshadow his humanity in John far too often to mesh with the Synoptics? Isn't John's eschatology too "realized" or present oriented to fit the futurist emphases of the Synoptics? Isn't his understanding of salvation too centered on personal faith in Jesus to blend with the God-centered understanding of salvation in Matthew, Mark, and Luke? Aren't there frequent dualisms (esp. light vs. darkness, truth vs. falsehood, flesh vs. spirit, and the world above vs. the world below) in John that are absent in the other Gospels? These are perhaps the four most prominent differences that are often highlighted.[59]

---

[58] Bartholomä, *Johannine Discourses and the Teaching of Jesus in the Synoptics*, 344–60. At the same time, 90 percent of Jesus's Johannine vocabulary either also occurs in the Synoptics or is unique to the Gospel of John among the five books traditionally ascribed to him (i.e., including 1–3 John and Revelation). Both observations militate against John having freely invented this vocabulary. See Peter W. Ensor, "Johannine Sayings of Jesus and the Question of Authenticity," in *Challenging Perspectives on the Gospel of John*, ed. Lierman, 20.

[59] Bartholomä, *Johannine Discourses and the Teaching of Jesus in the Synoptics*, 361–81.

Christology

Jesus makes striking claims for himself in the Gospel of John. Only John has the seven "I am" sayings (the bread of life [6:35, 48]; the light of the world [8:12; 9:5]; the gate for the sheep [10:7]; the good shepherd [10:11, 14]; the resurrection and the life [11:25]; the way, the truth, and the life [14:6]; and the true vine [15:1]). Only John has the even more striking association with Exodus 3:14 and/or Isaiah 41:4; 43:10, 13; etc., when Jesus declares, "Before Abraham was born, I am!" (John 8:58).[60] And only John has Jesus declare that the Father and he are one in a way that leads certain Jewish leaders to try to stone him (10:30–31). On the other hand, we have to remember that all of the "I am" statements with predicates employ metaphors susceptible to multiple interpretations. John 8:58 would have proved shocking to some but was still less than fully forthcoming. Because some people heard what they deemed as blasphemous remarks does not mean everyone would have. Strikingly, as late in the Fourth Gospel as 16:30, the disciples exclaim to Jesus, "Now we can see that you know all things and that you do not even need to have anyone ask you questions. This makes us believe that you came from God."[61] Even taking into account their classic hardheadedness, this passage reminds us that Jesus's exalted claims were not nearly as unambiguous before his death and resurrection as they became later (recall texts like 2:22; 8:27; 12:16; and 13:7).[62] The one statement that countless madmen and

---

[60] On which, see Caitrin H. Williams, *I Am He: The Interpretation of "Ani Hu" in Jewish and Christian Literature* (Tübingen: Mohr Siebeck, 1999); David M. Ball, *"I Am" in John's Gospel: Literary Function, Background and Theological Implications* (Sheffield: Sheffield Academic Press, 1996); and Philip B. Harner, *The "I Am" of the Fourth Gospel* (Philadelphia: Fortress, 1970).

[61] Ridderbos (*John*, 542) cites this as the clearest verse in the Gospel to show that John was preserving the distinctions between what people understood during Jesus's lifetime and realizations they came to only after his resurrection.

[62] Cf. esp. D. A. Carson, "Understanding the Misunderstandings in the Fourth Gospel," *Tyndale Bulletin* 33 (1982): 59–91.

dictators have made over the centuries—"I am God"—is the one declaration we have no record of Jesus uttering in such direct or explicit a form.[63]

On the other hand, we dare not underestimate the self-understanding of Jesus in the Synoptics. His favorite form of referring to himself in the third person as the "Son of Man" draws on the background of Daniel 7:13–14, in which one like a "son of man," a true human being, is led into the presence of the Ancient of Days (God) and given authority, power, and everlasting dominion over all the nations of the world, who in turn worship him.[64] This is no mere mortal but an exalted individual. This may explain why in verse 9 Daniel refers to more than one throne set in place in heaven, with the Ancient of Days on one of the (two?) thrones.[65] Various scholars have worked hard to argue for some different background for Jesus's use of "Son of Man" to avoid the implications of Daniel's imagery, but they have consistently disagreed with one another[66] and failed to provide

---

[63] I have occasionally been berated by fellow Christians for not arguing the deity of Christ more forcefully in John's Gospel because some Muslim apologists have misconstrued my words and thought they supported the view that Christ was not divine. But the responsibility of the exegete is to explain what the text does and doesn't say, not to hide or water down certain information because others may misuse it. The Gospel of John still clearly teaches the deity of Jesus, even if not as blatantly and explicitly as some Christians think.

[64] A huge literature has debated the background to Jesus's use of "the Son of Man." Most helpful still are Seyoon Kim, *The "Son of Man" as the Son of God* (Tübingen: J. C. B. Mohr, 1983; Grand Rapids: Eerdmans, 1985; Eugene, OR: Wipf & Stock, 2011); and Chrys C. Caragounis, *The Son of Man: Vision and Interpretation* (Tübingen: J. C. B. Mohr, 1986; Eugene, OR: Wipf & Stock, 2011).

[65] Alan F. Segal, *Two Powers in Heaven: Early Rabbinic Reports About Christianity and Gnosticism*, rev. ed. (Leiden: Brill, 2002; Waco: Baylor University Press, 2012).

[66] For a history of interpretation, see Delbert Burkett, *The Son of Man Debate: A History and Evaluation* (Cambridge: Cambridge University Press, 1999). More recently, for a spirited defense of a nonexalted Son of Man, see Maurice Casey, *The Solution to the "Son of Man" Problem* (London and New York: T & T Clark, 2007).

a more satisfactory explanation of all of Jesus's uses of the title, especially when he is linking himself closely with God (classically in Mark 8:38 pars., where one's response to Jesus on judgment day is counted as one's response to God himself).[67]

A substantial amount of "implicit Christology" appears in the Synoptics as well, as one canvasses the teachings ascribed to Jesus about his self-understanding. Sigurd Grindheim studies nine of these features with chapter-length treatments in his book *God's Equal* (along with treating the titles Son of Man and Son of God in additional chapters).[68] These elements of Jesus's implicit self-understanding include his teaching about the arrival of the kingdom of God (implying that the King has arrived), doing the works of God through Jesus's miracles and his interpretation of their significance (esp. Matt 12:28 par.), Jesus as the eschatological judge (focusing esp. on Matt 25:31–46), speaking with God's authority, articulating the significance of the Law (Matt 5:17–48; 7:28–29), calling the Twelve disciples, metaphorical self-descriptions (esp. bridegroom, mother bird, king, and sower), parallels with other mediatorial figures in Second Temple Judaism (esp. the angel of the Lord, the prince of Light, Melchizedek, and exalted patriarchs and other enthroned figures), and Jesus as the new temple.

Precisely because most of these motifs occur comparatively infrequently, avoid explicit titles, and do not reflect dominant or characteristic language of the early church as represented in the rest of the New Testament, they are likely to derive from authentic tradition. Any given one or two of these might be explained away as something

---

[67] See esp. Larry W. Hurtado and Paul J. Owen, eds., *"Who Is This Son of Man?" The Latest Scholarship on a Puzzling Expression of the Historical Jesus* (London and New York: T & T Clark, 2012).

[68] Sigurd Grindheim, *God's Equal: What Can We Know About Jesus' Self-Understanding in the Synoptic Gospels?* (London and New York: T & T Clark, 2011).

less significant, but the entire package is harder to dismiss.[69] Ben Witherington foreshadowed many of Grindheim's emphases and also included the relationships of Jesus with John the Baptist (esp. Matt 11:11–12 par.), his frequent rebukes to the official leaders of Judaism, especially the Pharisees in their interpretations of the Law, his repeated use of "Amen" ("Truly") at the start of his sovereign pronouncements, and the filial consciousness of his relationship with his heavenly Father implied by *Abba* (Mark 14:36).[70] The specific ways in which the Synoptics illustrate Jesus's exalted self-understanding may often vary from John's approach, but the result seems no less exalted.[71]

One may push matters further. Even in the Synoptics "I am" sayings probably exist, but English translations may mask their presence. When Jesus walks on water, for example, and the disciples catch sight of him, he exclaims, "Take courage! It is I. Don't be afraid" (Mark 6:50 pars.). The Greek for this middle sentence is merely *egō eimi*, which could equally legitimately be rendered "I am." Given that Jesus is behaving in ways only God can (cf. Job 9:8 and Ps 77:19), this "theophany" may well be intending to recall the theophany to Moses in the burning bush and Yahweh's disclosure of his divine name there (Exod 3:14).[72] In the Olivet Discourse, Jesus predicts that many will come in his name, claiming *egō eimi* (Mark 13:6 pars.). This is a

---

[69] Cf. Philip Payne's list of ten expressions used for Yahweh in the Old Testament that Jesus ascribes to himself in the Gospels—sower, director of the harvest, rock, shepherd, bridegroom, father, giver of forgiveness, vineyard owner, Lord, and King—form another excellent example of such a collection, in "Jesus' Implicit Claim to Deity in His Parables," *Trinity Journal* 2 (1981): 3–23.

[70] Ben Witherington III, *The Christology of Jesus* (Minneapolis: Fortress, 1990).

[71] On the complementary rather than contradictory nature of Johannine and Synoptic Christology more generally, see esp. Keener, *John*, vol. 1, 282–320.

[72] Cf. further John P. Heil, *Jesus Walking on the Sea: Meaning and Gospel Functions of Matt. 14:22–33, Mark 6:45–52 and John 6:15b–21* (Rome: Biblical Institute Press, 1981); and Patrick J. Madden, *Jesus' Walking on the Sea: An Investigation of the Origin of the Narrative Account* (Berlin and New York: de Gruyter, 1997).

somewhat more likely candidate for meaning merely, "I am he," but Mark was completely capable of writing *(egō) eimi autos* if he wanted to be perfectly clear that was all he meant. Given the grandiose claims that would-be Messiahs ancient and modern have often made, it would hardly come as a surprise if allegations of deity lay behind this claim as well.[73] Paul Anderson highlights still further "I am" and "I am not" constructions of various kinds in the Synoptics along with all nine predicates used with Johannine "I am" sayings to metaphorically describe Jesus in other contexts. The idiom may be Johannine, but the content is traditional.[74]

Eschatology

Jesus's vision of the future permeates much of the Synoptic accounts of his teaching. Of course the kingdom has arrived in his person and message, but much more remains still to be accomplished. The kingdom is present only in seed form but will grow into something surprisingly large, valuable, and fruitful (Matt 13:1–52 pars.). Jesus will return at some future point to complete what remains as yet undone. Then the kingdom will be present in all its fullness. Then Israel as a whole will declare, "Blessed is he who comes in the name of the Lord" (Matt 23:39). Then judgment day will take place, followed by everlasting life or everlasting punishment (Matt 25:31–46).

The Fourth Gospel, on the other hand, stresses that eternal life and death begin now, in this life. Two verses after the famous summary of the gospel in John 3:16, we read, "Whoever believes in him is not condemned, but whoever does not believe stands condemned

---

[73] Cf. Caitrin H. Williams, "'I Am' or 'I Am He'? Self-Declaratory Pronouncements in the Fourth Gospel and Rabbinic Tradition," in *Jesus in Johannine Tradition*, ed. Fortna and Thatcher, 343–52.

[74] Paul N. Anderson, "The Origin and Development of the Johannine *Egō Eimi* Sayings in Cognitive-Critical Perspective," *Journal for the Study of the Historical Jesus* 9 (2011): 139–206.

already because they have not believed in the name of God's one and only Son" (v. 18). Similarly, John 5:24 depicts Jesus announcing, "Very truly I tell you, whoever hears my word and believes him who sent me has eternal life and will not be judged but has crossed over from death to life." In the Farewell Discourse, it is often hard to know if the Johannine Jesus is looking ahead to the Parousia at all. Statements like, "In a little while you will see me no more, and then after a little while you will see me" (16:16) could refer to Christ's second coming but might merely have his resurrection in view.[75]

There may be a difference of emphasis in John's Gospel, but again it drastically distorts things to speak of contradictions with the Synoptics. After all, immediately after 5:24–27, in which Jesus focuses on the present dimension of eternal life, come verses 28–29 on its future dimension: "Do not be amazed at this, for a time is coming when all who are in their graves will hear his voice and come out— those who have done what is good will rise to live, and those who have done what is evil will rise to be condemned."[76] And the fact that Jesus promises to send the Holy Spirit, the "Paraclete," as his replacement after he has departed from his disciples, shows that he has more than just the period between his death and resurrection in mind. They will need empowerment for a much longer period of time while he goes to prepare a place for them (14:3).[77]

---

[75] The classic statement of realized eschatology in the Gospel of John remains C. H. Dodd, *The Interpretation of the Fourth Gospel* (Cambridge: Cambridge University Press, 1953).

[76] For a more balanced and succinct treatment of Johannine teaching on the topic, see Ladd, *Theology of the New Testament*, ed. Hagner, 334–44; and John T. Carroll, "Present and Future in Fourth Gospel Eschatology," *Biblical Theology Bulletin* 19 (1989): 63–69.

[77] On which, see esp. Steven M. Bryan, "The Eschatological Temple in John 14," *Bulletin of Biblical Research* 15 (2005): 187–98.

Faith

Forms of the main Greek verb for "to believe" in the New Testament (*pisteuō*) occur ten times in Matthew, ten times in Mark, nine times in Luke, but a whopping ninety-eight times in John. Of the twenty-nine Synoptic occurrences, eleven (just over a third) involve belief or trust "in" or "upon" someone or something, usually Jesus. In John that number swells to forty-one (closer to one half). But apart from the sheer frequency of the verbs, are the percentages really so different as to suggest incompatible portraits of Christ's teaching? A little more precision discloses that we are only contrasting 38 percent with 43 percent! The classic language of John 3:16, whether spoken by Jesus or not (recall above) is distinctively and characteristically Johannine to be sure, but only the Synoptics no less than four times depict Jesus's telling someone "Your faith has saved [or "healed"] you" (Mark 5:34 pars.; 10:52 par.; Luke 7:50; 17:19).[78]

The Greek for "faith" is *pistis*, from the same root as *pisteuō*. If English had a verb, "to faith," we would be more familiar with the linkage! As it is, neither "believe" nor "have faith" probably captures as much of the significance of the Greek word group as our English "trust" or "entrust." Neither the Synoptic nor the Johannine Jesus is looking for followers who recite a series of creedal affirmations about him but for those who commit their lives to him in discipleship and trust that his death has atoning significance and that his resurrection guarantees theirs. For whatever reason, John has preferred not to translate Jesus's words with the noun *pistis* at all, or even employ it in other contexts. But it appears twenty-four times in the Synoptics. The ratio between occurrences of the entire *pist-* word group in the

---

[78] On which, see esp. Craig L. Blomberg, "'Your Faith Has Made You Whole': The Evangelical Liberation Theology of Jesus," in *Jesus of Nazareth, Lord and Christ*, ed. Joel B. Green and Max Turner (Grand Rapids: Eerdmans, 1994; Eugene, OR: Wipf & Stock, 1999), 75–93.

Synoptics and in John thus narrows to fifty-four to ninety-eight. If one adds in the adjective *pistos* ("faithful"), the ratio narrows even further to sixty-five to ninety-nine. Of course, we are still comparing three Gospels to one, so the frequencies remain striking, but hardly so much so that we must choose only the Synoptic or the Johannine portrait, if either, as accurate.[79]

One also has to recognize that a mere count of the number of uses of "believe" or "belief" followed by an object or a prepositional phrase does not yield the total number of occurrences of the word group where personal trust is in view. The Synoptic Jesus, for example, tells Jairus when his daughter has just died, "Don't be afraid; just believe" (Mark 5:36 pars.). Even though believing has no explicit direct object here, from the context it is clear Jesus means "believe in me." Similarly, when Jesus proclaims in Mark 9:23 and parallel, "Everything is possible for one who believes," the context makes obvious that the faith in question must be directed toward him. Conversely, even in John, Jesus can use *pisteuō* followed by "me" and not be referring to trust. Thus to the Samaritan woman, he declares, "Believe me, a time is coming when you will worship the Father neither on this mountain nor in Jerusalem" (John 4:21). Here the belief is simply a cognitive acceptance of the truth of Jesus's declaration. Even when believing seems to refer to an initial trust, in John it may not eventuate in abiding faith. Thus, classically, in 8:30, John writes that "even as [Jesus] spoke, many believed in him." But at least some in that same group of individuals are called children of the devil by verse 44, clarifying that it was not full-orbed saving faith John was originally describing.[80] The

---

[79] Cf. Thomas R. Schreiner, *New Testament Theology: Magnifying God in Christ* (Grand Rapids: Baker, 2008), 558–65; Ladd, *Theology of the New Testament*, ed. Hagner, 306–8.

[80] There may be a narrowing of focus, as the passage unfolds, to those with the most artificial faith. See Stephen Motyer, *Your Father the Devil? A New Approach to John and "the Jews"* (Carlisle: Paternoster, 1997), 162–65.

differences between the Synoptics and John are thus those of degrees of emphasis and slight nuances of meaning rather than anything that would force us to have to choose one portrait of Jesus's teaching over the other.

Dualisms

Without a doubt John highlights numerous stark "black-and-white" contrasts, including some attributed to Jesus himself.[81] "Light" is contrasted with darkness nine times in John but only seven times in all the Synoptics, and all of those come in two verses and their parallels. "Truth," with or without an explicit contrast, appears only four times in the Synoptics but twenty-seven times in John. "Flesh" occurs ten times in John but only eight in the three Synoptics. Being "from above" contrasts with "from below" explicitly only once in all four Gospels, in John 8:23.

But these statistics prove little, especially when they are analyzed further. The nine contrasts between light and darkness actually appear in only five discrete passages in John (1:5; 3:19; 8:12; 12:35, and 46). Despite all the references to truth in John, only once in all the documents attributed to him in the New Testament do the words "truth" and "falsehood" actually appear in the same verse—in 1 John (4:6), not the Gospel. "Truth" and "lies" or "liar" are also contrasted in John 8:44–45. There is often an *implicit* contrast in John between what is true and what is false, but that could easily be said of the numerous uses of "truly" in the Synoptics. Seven of the Johannine references to

---

[81] Andreas J. Köstenberger, *A Theology of John's Gospel and Letters* (Grand Rapids: Zondervan, 2009), 282–92. For helpful insights into the relevance of this feature of John to a pluralistic world, see Amos Yong, "'Light Shines in the Darkness': Johannine Dualism and the Challenge for Christian Theology of Religions of Today," *Journal of Religion* 89 (2009): 31–56; "Johannine Dualism and Contemporary Pluralism," in *The Gospel of John and Christian Theology*, ed. Richard Bauckham and Carl Mosser (Grand Rapids: Eerdmans, 2008), 3–18; and Miroslav Volf, "Johannine Dualism and Contemporary Pluralism," in ibid., 19–50.

"flesh" occur in a single passage between 6:51 and 63. Only three times do "flesh" and "spirit" actually appear together in the Gospels, twice in John (3:6; 6:63) and once in the Synoptics (counting Mark 14:38 and Matt 26:41 as one passage because they are parallel). And while John cites Jesus explicitly contrasting the heavenly and the earthly realms more often than the Synoptics do, the Synoptics may actually do so implicitly more often, if Matthew's distinctive use of "kingdom of heaven" (occurring thirty-four times) has in it an implied contrast with earthly kingdoms, as Jonathan Pennington has suggested.[82] Once again nothing of statistical significance allows us to argue that John's and the synoptists' portraits of Jesus are at all incompatible.

Other antinomies appear predominantly within the Fourth Gospel. Among a longer list catalogued by Paul Anderson, particularly striking are the Father-Son relationship (equal and subordinate), the role of the Son in judgment (he both does and doesn't judge), the revelatory and salvific work of Christ (both universal and particular, both freely chosen and divinely predestined), the sacraments (embellished and deconstructed), and the role of the church (both static and dynamic).[83]

Conclusion

John may well have been written by the apostle and son of Zebedee bearing that name. But if not, the author was almost certainly someone no worse off than Mark or Luke in terms of proximity to apostolic tradition. The Gospel was probably written two generations rather than merely one after Jesus's death, but by ancient standards that was

---

[82] Jonathan Pennington, *Heaven and Earth in the Gospel of Matthew* (Leiden: Brill, 2007; Grand Rapids: Baker, 2009), esp. 279–330.

[83] Paul N. Anderson, *The Riddles of the Fourth Gospel: An Introduction to John* (Minneapolis: Fortress, 2011), 25–43. I have rephrased his "either-ors" as "both-ands" since that is his ultimate conclusion and mine.

still a remarkably short period of time. The author's purposes—to promote belief in Jesus by means of a faithful truth-telling witness—support the veracity of his account. The unique style, the degree of how literally the narrator rendered Jesus's words, and the habit of blending the narrator's diction with Jesus's all move the Fourth Gospel into a slightly different category of Greco-Roman biography than the Synoptics. But it is well within the range of what the ancients would have viewed as accurate and trustworthy.

Many of John's choices in what to include or leave out are related to what he believed the Synoptics already covered well. Even if he remains literarily independent of them, he could have assumed that his listeners already knew the common core kerygma—the proclamation of the basic facts about Jesus's life. On closer inspection there are nevertheless many more points of contact between the Jesus of the Synoptics and the Jesus of John than first meet the eye. Differing circumstances in a different community at the end of the first century, in and around Ephesus, further account for a variety of the distinctives of John. Finally, numerous details are present or absent simply because John has chosen to narrate multiple trips of Jesus to Jerusalem at festival times that the Synoptics have omitted.

Theological differences between John and the Synoptics must not be minimized, if for no other reason than they highlight some of the distinctive emphases and concerns John had in the context of late first-century Ephesus. But neither must they be blown out of proportion. Many generalizations about the most well-known of these differences are simply inaccurate, while others are not nearly as meaningful as their proponents suggest. Of course, all of these background and broad-brush considerations could themselves prove little if a more detailed analysis of the Gospel of John, passage by passage, were to turn up repeated examples of incredible details. So it is to that more focused task that we must turn in the next chapter.

Chapter 5

Evidence for the Accuracy of John

C hapter 4 suggested that the frequent global skepticism about the historical trustworthiness of John is misplaced. Indeed, numerous features combine to suggest that one should approach the Fourth Gospel expecting to find reliable history, even if in John's own idiom. This chapter builds on those global impressions by working its way through the material of the book, chapter by chapter and passage by passage, to see if there is more specific corroboration of its contents. Or, if there are apparent contradictions with the Synoptics, can plausible harmonizations be suggested? Because John 1:1–18 forms a prologue that begins at the inception of time with a summary of the mission of Jesus, rather than a historical narrative *per se*, we begin at 1:19.

John the Baptist and Jesus

John 1:19–51 comprises the beginning of the historical narrative of the Fourth Gospel. Here appears significant overlap with the information about John the Baptist and Jesus recorded in one or more of the Synoptics. Characteristic of John's treatment of the Baptist is that he focuses on his role as a witness.[1] The Baptist's identity can be summed up nicely in verses 23 and 26–27 with words closely parallel to those found in the Synoptics (cf. Mark 1:3, 7–8 pars.): he is the voice crying in the wilderness to make straight paths for the Lord. He is also the individual who points to a coming one, the straps of whose sandals he is not even worthy to loosen. The emphasis on his not being Elijah (v. 21) does not contradict Matthew 11:14 and parallel or Luke 1:17, which liken John to Elijah, but it does refute the belief held by some that the literal Elijah carried up to heaven in God's chariot (2 Kgs 2:11) would again return to prepare the way of the Lord (Mal 3:1; 4:5).[2] The location of Bethany beyond the Jordan (John 1:28) has long puzzled commentators, but the site may have been recently discovered near the spring of Wadi Kharrar, to the east of the Jordan River across from Judea, as attested also by ancient writers.[3]

Many readers have balked at the Baptist's claim that he did not previously know Jesus, but all he is claiming in this context is that he did not have full assurance that Jesus would be the Messiah.[4] What John's parents had told him over the years about his celebrated cousin and how often they met each other must remain a mystery; Scripture is entirely silent on these matters. The events surrounding Jesus's and

---

[1] Andrew T. Lincoln, *Truth on Trial: The Lawsuit Motif in the Fourth Gospel* (Peabody: Hendrickson, 2000), 58–65. Cf. Herman N. Ridderbos, *The Gospel of John: A Theological Commentary* (Grand Rapids: Eerdmans, 1997), 62.

[2] Craig S. Keener, *The Gospel of John: A Commentary*, vol. 1 (Peabody: Hendrickson, 2003), 434–36. See further Markus Öhler, "The Expectation of Elijah and the Presence of the Kingdom of God," *Journal of Biblical Literature* 118 (1999): 461–76.

[3] Michele Piccirillo, "The Sanctuaries of the Baptism on the East Bank of the Jordan River," in *Jesus and Archaeology*, ed. James H. Charlesworth (Grand Rapids: Eerdmans, 2006), 433–43.

[4] Cf. Colin G. Kruse, *The Gospel According to John* (Leicester: IVP; Grand Rapids: Eerdmans, 2003), 80. For a variety of other explanations given in the early church, see Joel Elowsky, ed., *John 1–10* (Downers Grove: IVP, 2006), 74–75.

John's birth were no more naturally credible in the first century than in ours. So if John had heard nothing unusual about Jesus in eighteen years or so, it would have been entirely natural to wonder if he truly was God's chosen liberator until the Spirit reaffirmed that fact to him (cf. his doubts after his unexpected imprisonment in Matt 11:2–3 and par.). That the Fourth Gospel narrates the events immediately surrounding Jesus's baptism without ever explicitly narrating the baptism itself remains puzzling. Perhaps the best suggestion is that the Evangelist was trying to quash an exalted view of the Baptist, which we know existed in and around Ephesus in both the mid-first and the mid-second centuries (cf. Acts 19:1–7; Clem. *Recogn.* 1.4, 60; Justin, *Dial.* 80) and therefore may have been present all along throughout that period.[5]

John 1:29–51 stands out because of the amazing cluster of seemingly exalted titles various individuals apply to Jesus even at this earliest date in his public ministry. John calls him the "Lamb of God" (1:29, 36) and "God's Chosen One" (v. 34). Two of John's disciples plus Nathanael refer to him as "Rabbi" (vv. 38, 49), though there is no evidence that he was ever formally trained, much less ordained as an official religious teacher in Israel. Andrew announces that Jesus is the Messiah (v. 41), while Philip declares he is the one that both Moses and the prophets wrote about (v. 45). Nathanael, finally, pronounces him to be the Son of God and "king of Israel" (v. 49). By the time the Fourth Evangelist wrote, of course, all of these terms in their most exalted senses would have been viewed as appropriate for Jesus. But we must not imagine that all these speakers necessarily had such fullness of understanding upon their first encounters with him.

[5] Jey J. Kanagaraj, *John* (Eugene, OR: Cascade, 2013), 4. Cf., more cautiously, Raymond E. Brown, *An Introduction to the Gospel of John*, ed. Francis J. Moloney (New York and London: Doubleday, 2003), 155.

"Rabbi" was an unofficial title for any teacher until after AD 70 when it was reserved for those more formally credentialed.[6] All the other titles in various Jewish contexts at times meant merely Messiah—a longed-for deliverer to be sure but often one envisioned as little more than an earthly ruler and military liberator.[7] That a number of Jesus's first followers had previous exposure to him while John the Baptist was still actively ministering makes it easier to envision them later responding so quickly to Jesus's more formal call along the shores of the Sea of Galilee (Mark 1:16–20).[8] Although Nathanael's name appears nowhere else in the New Testament outside the Gospel of John, he is listed in 21:2 with six other disciples. Here in 1:45, he is associated with Philip, and the Synoptic Gospels consistently pair Philip with Bartholomew, who does not appear by name in John. Bartholomew, moreover, is not a personal name but means "son of Tolmai," making it plausible that Nathanael was his given name.[9] His disparagement of Nazareth, finally, was not likely invented by anyone wanting to honor Jesus but a natural attitude for a small town of perhaps 500 people, never mentioned in the Hebrew Scriptures. As

[6] Andreas J. Köstenberger, "Jesus as Rabbi in the Fourth Gospel," *Bulletin for Biblical Research* 9 (1998): 97–128.

[7] See esp. 4Q 491 and 4Q 246 from the Dead Sea Scrolls. Cf. esp. Richard Bauckham, "Messianism in the Gospel of John," in *Challenging Perspectives on the Gospel of John*, ed. John Lierman (Tübingen: Mohr Siebeck, 2006), 34–68. See also John J. Collins, *The Scepter and the Star: The Messiahs of the Dead Sea Scrolls and Other Literature* (New York and London: Doubleday, 1995; New Haven: Yale University Press, 2007); Andreas J. Köstenberger, *Encountering John: The Gospel in Historical, Literary, and Theological Perspectives* (Grand Rapids: Baker, 1999), 66–69.

[8] Rudolf Schnackenburg, *The Gospel According to John*, vol. 1 (London: Burns & Oates; New York: Herder & Herder, 1968), 306. John A. T. Robinson (*The Priority of John*, ed. J. F. Coakley [London: SCM, 1985; Oak Park, IL: Meyer-Stone, 1987], 168) adds that Acts 1:21–22 shows that Jesus had at least informal followers from the time of John the Baptist onward.

[9] C. Bernard Ruffin, *The Twelve: Lives of the Apostles After Calvary*, rev. ed. (Huntington, IN: Our Sunday Visitor, 1997), 111–19. Cf. Thomas E. Schmidt, *The Apostles After Acts: A Sequel* (Eugene, OR: Cascade, 2013), 143.

we have already seen, skepticism about its existence altogether in the first century has apparently been shown needless by the discovery of the foundations of a small first-century dwelling place there in 2009, though some doubt lingers about its exact date.[10]

From Cana to Cana

John 2–4 begins and ends with the only two episodes ever described in the Bible as occurring at the Galilean city of Cana. Chronologically, the events of these chapters appear to precede Jesus's "Great Galilean Ministry," which occupies so much of the Synoptic accounts (Mark 1:14–6:56 pars.).

Whether one believes Jesus turned water into wine (John 2:1–11) will depend largely on one's view of the supernatural (see chap. 14). For those open to the possibility, a number of factors favor viewing a real event at the core of this narrative. The setting is realistic—a small village wedding. The embarrassment of running out of wine would have brought great shame on the family in a culture of honor and shame. Jesus somewhat distances himself from his mother (v. 4) in a way not likely to have been invented. And the actual miracle is never itself narrated. All we are told is that "the master of the banquet tasted the water that had been turned into wine" (v. 9)! The whole account reminds the reader of Jesus's metaphor in the Synoptics about new wine requiring new wineskins (Mark 2:22 pars.). That John spells out that the water had been in huge jars used for Jewish washing rituals

---

[10] Henry B. Smith Jr., "First-Century House Unearthed in Nazareth," *Associates for Biblical Research* (December 30, 2009), accessed December 29, 2015, http://www.biblearchaeology.org/post/2009/12/30/First-Century-House-Unearthed-in-Nazareth.aspx#Article. Whether or not this particular find proves to be dated correctly, there is more than enough evience to demonstrate that Nazareth existed in the first century. See Bart D. Ehrman, "Did Nazareth Exist?" *The Bart Ehrman Blog: The History and Literature of Early Christianity* (March 1, 2015), accessed April 19, 2016, http://ehrmanblog.org/did-nazareth-exist/.

suggests that he sees a contrast between the old ceremonies of Judaism and the new ways of Jesus. With wine often a symbol or indication of joy (see especially Ps 104:15), it is natural to see in Jesus's miracle an object lesson about the new joy of the kingdom age, a theme consistent with Synoptic emphases.[11]

The account of the temple clearing proves particularly difficult because of its similarities with and differences from the Synoptic incident during the last week of Jesus's life (Mark 11:15–19 par.). All but the most conservative scholars believe Jesus could have done something like this only once, at the end of his life, with it sealing his fate. They therefore take John 2:13–22 to be a topically or thematically relocated version of the incident to function as an ominous kind of headline over Jesus's ministry in John. This is possible, especially when we observe that John's otherwise consistent chronological links in his opening chapters are interrupted at this point. John 1:29, 35 and 43 refer to something happening on "the next day," while 2:1 speaks of "the third day." But 2:13 begins merely with a reference to an upcoming Passover, without any indication of which one. So, too, 3:1 introduces the dialogue between Jesus and Nicodemus without any necessary chronological connection to what precedes it, whereas 3:22 resumes the chronological references with "after this."[12]

On the other hand, the temple leaders reply to Jesus's cryptic prophecy about destroying "this temple" (2:19) by insisting that "it has taken forty-six years to build" it (v. 20). If Josephus's information is accurate (*Ant.* 15.11.1), Herod the Great commissioned the rebuilding of the temple to begin in 20–19 BC. Forty-six years from

---

[11] Cf. Craig L. Blomberg, "The Miracles as Parables," in *Gospel Perspectives*, vol. 6, ed. David Wenham and Craig Blomberg (Sheffield: JSOT, 1986; Eugene, OR: Wipf & Stock, 2003), 333–37. Cf. also Kruse, *Gospel According to John*, 91–96; Ridderbos, *Gospel of John*, 107.

[12] Cf. J. Ramsey Michaels, *John*, rev. ed. (Peabody: Hendrickson, 1989; Carlisle: Paternoster, 1995; Grand Rapids: Baker, 2011), 32–33.

this period of time brings us to no later than AD 27–28, while the earliest possible date for the Passover at which Jesus was crucified is 30. Not surprisingly, the "new look on John" has regularly preferred the Johannine to the Synoptic chronology.[13] But must the accounts be referring to the same event? Randolph Richards has analyzed the events in terms of ancient cultures of honor and shame. It is conceivable that the first incident in John 2 occurred in a comparatively small corner of the temple so that the authorities did not immediately intervene but waited to see if a sign like the one they understood Jesus to have predicted would occur. When it did not, they would assume he was sufficiently shamed, in public, not to be any further danger. But if two or three years later he performed something similar, it showed him to be without shame, unaffected by social constraint, and therefore potentially dangerous.[14] If Jesus spoke something like 2:19 that long before his trial and execution, it is also easier to understand how his words could have been garbled and misconstrued as in Mark 14:58 and parallel.[15] Whether one or two events, however, there are no necessary contradictions between the accounts, and the similarities provide multiple attestation in literarily independent sources to at least one such event.[16]

---

[13] Robinson, *Priority of John*, 130–31; Paul N. Anderson, *The Fourth Gospel and the Quest for Jesus: Modern Foundations Reconsidered*, rev. ed. (London and New York: T & T Clark, 2007), 111–12.

[14] E. Randolph Richards, "An Honor/Shame Argument for Two Temple Clearings," *Trinity Journal* 29 (2008): 19–43.

[15] Gonzalo Rojas-Flores, "From John 2.19 to Mark 15.29: The History of a Misunderstanding," *New Testament Studies* 56 (2009): 22–43. Cf. Robinson, *Priority of John*, 125–31; Andreas Köstenberger, *John* (Grand Rapids: Baker, 2004), 108.

[16] Cf. further Stanley E. Porter, *John, His Gospel, and Jesus: In Pursuit of the Johannine Voice* (Grand Rapids: Eerdmans, 2015), 77. Porter references me in support of the possibility of only one temple cleansing, but he fails to mention that I am equally open to the possibility of two. Other critics have at times noticed only the latter option and assumed, equally erroneously, that I am committed to two temple-clearing incidents.

Jewish literature testifies to two powerful, well-to-do members of the ancient ben-Gurion family named Nicodemus (Jos. *Ant.* 14.37; *b. Gitt.* 56a). It is hard to know if either of these references should be matched with the biblical character by that name, but the verisimilitude of the episode in John 3:1–21 is supported.[17] Here also appear the only two references to the kingdom of God in John (vv. 3, 5; cf. also the use of "kingdom" by itself in 18:36), suggesting that we are in touch with bedrock tradition matching that central Synoptic theme. Being "born again" closely resembles Jesus's Synoptic teaching on entering the kingdom like a little child (Matt 18:3 pars.).[18] Later texts in John and in Christian tradition more generally were more positive in their portrayals of Nicodemus, so it is not likely that anyone would have invented an account here that ends with Nicodemus's last words (John 3:9) showing that as of this moment he just doesn't "get it."[19]

The new look on John regularly acknowledges that a key historical dimension of the Fourth Gospel is the overlap between the Baptist's and Jesus's ministries. When 3:30 declares that Jesus "must become greater" while John "must become less," it may be inferred that Jesus was once not as well known or appreciated as John. John's disciples would not have informed him in an excited fashion about the numbers of people across the Jordan going over to Jesus had John himself not originally been more popular or renowned. But again it is scarcely

---

[17] Richard J. Bauckham, "Nicodemus and the Gurion Family," *Journal of Theological Studies* 47 (1996): 1–37.

[18] See esp. John W. Pryor, "John 3.3, 5: A Study in the Relation of John's Gospel to the Synoptic Tradition," *Journal for the Study of the New Testament* 41 (1991): 71–95. Cf. Barnabas Lindars, *The Gospel of John* (London: Marshall, Morgan & Scott, 1972; Grand Rapids: Eerdmans, 1981), 150.

[19] Craig L. Blomberg, "The Globalization of Biblical Interpretation—a Test Case: John 3–4," *Bulletin for Biblical Research* 5 (1995): 1–15. Cf. Raimo Hakola, "The Burden of Ambiguity: Nicodemus and the Social Identity of the Johannine Christians," *New Testament Studies* 55 (2009): 438–55; Jouette Bassler, "Mixed Signals: Nicodemus in the Fourth Gospel," *Journal of Biblical Literature* 108 (1989): 635–46.

likely that later Christian fabricators would have invented such narratives during the era in which their desires were consistently to exalt
Jesus himself and not to highlight an early period when he was less
acclaimed.[20]

The story of Jesus's dialogue with the Samaritan woman at the
well (4:4–42), while unique to John's Gospel, dovetails nicely with
numerous texts in the Synoptics. Jesus's valuing of a Samaritan, so
despised by orthodox Jewry, recalls his parable in Luke 10:25–37 and
his healing of the ten lepers in Luke 17:11–19. His concern for a morally outcast woman reminds us of Luke 7:36–50 and the woman of
ill repute at the home of Simon the Pharisee. Jacob's well at Sychar
(John 4:5–6), where Jesus and she met, may well be the identical location still commemorated in the basement of the Orthodox church in
modern-day Nablus.[21] The debate over which mountain to worship
on, Mount Gerizim in Samaria or Mount Zion in Jerusalem (v. 20),
remained a live one in Jesus's day and a key point of conflict between
Samaritans and Jews. That Jesus could reveal himself more clearly to
this woman than to any Jewish people this early in his ministry (v. 26)
fits the Samaritan Messianic expectation, which was less distorted
with high hopes for a merely political deliverer.[22] That the woman
becomes an evangelist to her own people dovetails with the role of
Mary Magdalene and the other women at the tomb, who become the

---

[20] And in a culture of honor and shame, John's deference to Jesus who was now
eclipsing him was all the more countercultural. See Jerome H. Neyrey and Richard
L. Rohrbaugh, "He Must Increase, I Must Decrease (John 3:30): A Cultural and
Social Interpretation," *Catholic Biblical Quarterly* 63 (2001): 464–83.

[21] Jerome Murphy-O'Connor, *The Holy Land: An Oxford Archaeological Guide
from Earliest Times to 1700*, 5th ed. (Oxford: Oxford University Press, 2007), 326–37.

[22] Raymond E. Brown (*The Gospel According to John I–XII* [Garden City:
Doubleday, 1966], 172–73) points out that the Samaritans were looking more for a
teacher and lawgiver. Keener (*John*, vol. 1, 619–20) concurs, likening the Samaritan
Taheb to a restorer and prophet like Moses.

first spokespersons for the resurrection, running to tell the male disciples, in the Synoptics (Matt 28:1–10).

The last episode in John 2–4 again poses the problem of whether it is to be equated with a Synoptic passage, in this case the healing of the centurion's servant in Matthew 8:5–13 and parallel, or viewed as a separate but similar incident. The core account of the cure—from a distance—of an official's servant (perhaps loved as a son?) from a serious malady, confirmed later as occurring at precisely the time Jesus spoke the words of healing, is identical in both texts. Nevertheless, most of the remaining details differ. Still they are not contradictory.[23] If, as seems likely, we have two separate events,[24] then the similarities that remain enhance the likelihood of the historicity of the miracle in John.

Fulfilling the Festivals

Only from John do we derive the conviction that Jesus's ministry lasted approximately three years. John 5–11 enables us to construct a partial chronology of events because it makes repeated references to the times of the various annual Jewish festivals, at which times healthy adult males living close enough to Jerusalem to travel were expected to attend, often though not always accompanied by their families. Precisely because the chronology emerges from data not directly designed to depict a chronology but to show Jesus as the fulfillment of the various Jewish holidays,[25] it is probably not tendentiously motivated and therefore is historically probable.

---

[23] For a detailed list of the possible harmonizations of seemingly discrepant data, see E. F. Siegman, "St. John's Use of Synoptic Material," *Catholic Biblical Quarterly* 30 (1968): 182–98.

[24] See, e.g., D. A. Carson, *The Gospel According to John* (Grand Rapids: Eerdmans; Leicester: IVP, 1991), 234; Ridderbos, *Gospel of John*, 174–75.

[25] Francis J. Moloney, *The Gospel of John* (Collegeville, MN: Liturgical, 1998), 164; Brian D. Johnson, "Salvation Is from the Jews," in *New Currents through John: A Global Perspective*, ed. Francisco Lozada Jr. and Tom Thatcher (Atlanta: SBL,

A Sabbath During an Unnamed Feast

John 5:1 refers only to an unnamed Jewish feast day because the main focus of the miracle and teaching of chapter 5 surrounds Jesus's "working" on a Sabbath (vv. 5–18). But it has often been understood to be a Passover,[26] which would potentially yield four distinct Passover festivals mentioned in the Fourth Gospel: the one in which he clears the temple (2:13, 23), this one, the one at the time of the feeding of the 5,000 (6:4) and the one at which he was executed (11:55; 12:1; 13:1; etc.) and hence a ministry of more than three years. If 5:1 does not refer to a Passover, we still have a ministry of somewhere between two and three years. Again it is widely held that some such chronology is historically accurate.[27] While all the events of the Synoptics after Jesus's baptism could have occurred in three to four months, it is unlikely that he would have had the profound impact on his society and his followers that he did over such a short period of time. The Synoptics, moreover, are less inclined than John to give us indicators of when something happened or how much time elapsed between consecutively narrated events, even when they appear in chronological order, which is not always the case.

The healing by the pool of Bethesda (5:1–15) immediately reminds us of the healing in Capernaum of the man lowered through the roof (Mark 2:1–12 pars.). In both cases, the sufferer was paralyzed.

2006), 98. The Passover references may also mark off major sections in John's structure—Gerald L. Borchert, "The Passover and the Narrative Cycles in John," in *Perspectives on John: Method and Interpretation in the Fourth Gospel*, ed. Robert B. Sloan and Mikeal C. Parsons (Lewiston and Lampeter: Edwin Mellen, 1993), 303–16.

[26] Beginning at least as far back as Irenaeus, *Ag. Her.* 2.22.3. Several other Jewish feasts have also been frequently defended.

[27] See especially Robinson, *Priority of John*, 123–57. Cf. Brian D. Johnson, "The Jewish Feasts and Questions of Historicity in John 5–12," in *John, Jesus, and History*, vol. 2, ed. Paul N. Anderson, Felix Just, and Tom Thatcher (Atlanta: SBL, 2009), 117–29; Anderson, *Fourth Gospel and the Quest for Jesus*, 162.

In both accounts Jesus heals him instantaneously. In both instances he has been lying on a mat or pallet, which Jesus then commands him to pick up and carry as he leaves the scene able to walk. In both cases the main point of the passage is not so much about the physical healing but about the spiritual healing to which Jesus points the man. And in both events a controversy ensues over Jesus's perceived disobedience to Jewish law or protocol. The settings are entirely different, and nothing in the Markan passage deals with Sabbath controversy, so few scholars argue that these are the same events. But the similarities make it difficult to argue that John's Jesus is significantly different from the Synoptic Jesus at this juncture.[28] Several other Synoptic texts also disclose Jesus's healing on a Sabbath (Mark 3:1–6 pars.; Luke 13:10–17; 14:1–6).

The description of the pool with five porticoes matches exactly what excavations in the 1890s unearthed—a pair of rectangular pools with four colonnaded walkways around the perimeter and a fifth down the middle, separating the two pools.[29] Today it is increasingly believed that this site would have been a major location just to the north of the temple precincts for ritual immersion, especially by pilgrims to Jerusalem, prior to their entry into the temple precincts.[30] That Jesus has to ask for information from the crippled man and that the man does not express more thanks or a desire for discipleship afterwards suggests the passage was not invented to portray Jesus in the best possible light.[31]

---

[28] Cf. Graham H. Twelftree, *Jesus: The Miracle Worker: A Historical and Theological Study* (Downers Grove: IVP, 1999), 296–98; Rene Latourelle, *The Miracles of Jesus and the Theology of Miracles* (New York: Paulist, 1988), 132–39.

[29] Joachim Jeremias, *The Rediscovery of Bethesda: John 5:2* (Louisville: Southern Baptist Theological Seminary, 1966).

[30] Urban C. von Wahlde, "Archaeology and John's Gospel," in *Jesus and Archaeology*, ed. Charlesworth, esp. 559–66.

[31] Michael H. Burer, *Divine Sabbath Work* (Winona Lake, IN: Eisenbrauns, 2012), 120–24.

The rest of John 5 deals with the accusations against Christ and his defense against them. Verses 19–30 are outlined in a tight chiastic structure (vv. 19–20a and 30, both giving a principle of imitation and its rationale; vv. 20b and 28–29, teaching about marveling; vv. 31–32 and 26–27, supplying illustrations about life and judgment followed by a purpose or reason statement; and vv. 24 and 25, both containing a double amen statement about salvation),[32] not readily created out of disparate materials. Most likely this section formed a rhetorical unity from the beginning. C. H. Dodd made famous the theory that a short parable or metaphor lies at the core of these verses, which he called "the apprentice's father."[33] Just as a son learning a trade or an occupation from his father will imitate him as exactly as possible, so Jesus claims he can do only what he sees his heavenly Father doing, "because whatever the Father does the Son also does" (v. 19). This characteristic parabolic utterance fits the Synoptic Jesus perfectly. But if all of verses 19–30 form a tightly knit unity built up from this initial comparison, then even if John may have abbreviated a much fuller speech and put it in his own words, the entire segment most likely reflects what Jesus actually said.[34] Verses 31–47 flow naturally from the preceding material because they anticipate the charge that Jesus is testifying merely about himself, without any other support. His reply points to four other witnesses—John the Baptist, his works, the Father, and Moses (the latter two as disclosed in the Hebrew Scriptures).[35]

---

[32] Albert Vanhoye, "La composition de Jean 5,19–30," in *Mélanges Bibliques en homage au R. P. Béda Rigaux*, ed. Albert Descamps and André de Halleux (Gembloux: Duculot, 1970), 259–74.

[33] C. H. Dodd, "A Hidden Parable in the Fourth Gospel," in *More New Testament Studies* (Manchester: Manchester University Press, 1968), 30–40.

[34] Craig L. Blomberg, *The Historical Reliability of John's Gospel* (Leicester and Downers Grove: IVP, 2001), 113.

[35] Urban C. von Wahlde, "The Witnesses to Jesus in John 5:31–40 and Belief in the Fourth Gospel," *Catholic Biblical Quarterly* 43 (1981): 385–404. For seeing all of vv. 19–47 as a judicial speech, see A. D. Myers, "'Jesus Said to Them': The

At Passover Time

The feeding of the 5,000 is the one miracle story that appears in all four Gospels and is thus the most multiply attested miracle performed by Jesus prior to his resurrection. The walking on the water follows directly on the heels of the feeding miracle in Matthew, Mark, and John, even though it is absent from Luke. Both episodes in John are extremely similar to their Synoptic parallels, and several scholars have argued for John's being the earliest form.[36] But John alone adds that "the Jewish Passover Festival was near" (6:4). This reference will dovetail with John's extensive addition of Jesus' follow-up sermon in the Capernaum synagogue in which he refers to himself as the Bread of Life (vv. 35, 48). The other key distinctive in John's accounts of the two miracles is the aborted attempt to make Jesus king in verse 15. This detail is widely held to be historical because it reflects the common Jewish expectation of a political and military messiah that Jesus eschewed.[37] Leading up to Jesus's sermon is his interaction with the crowd back on the western shore of the Sea of Galilee, by the synagogue, in which he contrasts working for "food that spoils" with working for "food that endures to eternal life" (v. 27), a characteristic Synoptic-like metaphor.[38]

The homily itself spans verses 32–58 of John 6. In verses 30–31, Jesus has been challenged to produce an ongoing sign like the provision

---

Adaptation of Juridical Rhetoric in John 5:19–47," *Journal of Biblical Literature* 132 (2013): 415–30.

[36] See especially Paul W. Barnett, "The Feeding of the Multitude in Mark 6/John 6," in *Gospel Perspectives*, vol. 6, ed. David Wenham and Craig Blomberg (Sheffield: JSOT, 1986; Eugene, OR: Wipf & Stock, 2003), 273–93.

[37] E.g., John W. Pryor, *John: Evangelist of the Covenant People* (London: Darton, Longman and Todd; Downers Grove: IVP, 1992); C. H. Dodd, *Historical Tradition in the Fourth Gospel* (Cambridge; Cambridge University Press, 1963), 215.

[38] Robinson, *Priority of John*, 205–6; Keener, *John*, vol. 1, 670–71; Pryor, *John*, 31.

of manna in the wilderness,[39] and his questioners have quoted a text that resembles parts of Exodus 16:4; Nehemiah 9:15; and Psalm 78:24–25: "He gave them bread from heaven to eat." Jesus now organizes his comments around this initial "quotation." He then introduces a second text in John 6:45 that cites Isaiah 54:13: "They will all be taught by God." After exposition of this statement, he returns to the initial text in John 6:48–58, unpacking the ways in which he is the Bread of Life. This pattern of first text plus exposition, second text plus exposition, followed by a return to the first text plus exposition closely matches the rabbinic form of homily known as a *proem midrash*.[40] Jesus may well have heard it frequently used in synagogue services he attended over the years so that it would have been one of the most natural forms of address for him to use even without official rabbinic training. Again the passage creates a tightly knit unity, not likely to have been created out of diverse bits of tradition and redaction. The most likely hypothesis is that it goes back to Jesus in precisely this characteristically Jewish form of preaching.[41]

After some in the larger group of Jesus's followers leave him because of his "hard teaching" (John 6:60–66), a discouraging scenario for Jesus so therefore not likely invented, he turns to the Twelve. As often in the Synoptics, Peter proves to be the willing spokesman for the group when Jesus asks if they too wish to stop following him

---

[39] Leon Morris, *The Gospel According to John*, 2nd ed. (Grand Rapids: Eerdmans, 1995), 321; Köstenberger, *John*, 208–9; Kanagaraj, *John*, 68.

[40] See esp. Peder Borgen, *Bread from Heaven* (Leiden: Brill, 1965). Cf. also Paul N. Anderson, *The Christology of the Fourth Gospel: Its Unity and Disunity in the Light of John 6*, rev. ed. (Eugene, OR: Wipf & Stock, 2010).

[41] Carson, *Gospel According to John*, 280. Complicating matters are the parallels between vv. 48–58 and the Last Supper accounts in the Synoptics. But here the language is of flesh and blood, not body and blood, and these are never elsewhere confused. This should be seen as a separate and integral part of John 6, not a transposed and drastically modified segment of Jesus's Eucharistic discourse. See, e.g., Ridderbos, *Gospel of John*, 240–42.

(v. 67). Peter's answer resembles his later, divinely given insight on the road to Caesarea Philippi in the Synoptics (Matt 16:16–19 pars.), as he declares, "Lord, to whom shall we go? You have the words of eternal life. We have come to believe and know that you are the Holy One of God" (vv. 68–69). Peter still has much to learn, especially about the Messiah's need to suffer (see Matt 16:21–23 pars.), but the similarities between the two confessions inspire confidence in their general reliability.[42]

The Feast of Tabernacles

John 7–9 appears to take place at one annual celebration of the Feast (or Festival, in the HCSB) of Tabernacles in Jerusalem, probably in AD 29. The division among Jesus's audiences created by his ministry and highlighted in chapter 7 is entirely what one would expect. An unhistorical, overly exalted portrait of Christ would depict him merely being extolled by the masses. His teachings and miracles could not have gone without creating a large number of "groupies" or superficial adherents, but his conflicts with the Jewish leaders and defiance of traditional interpretations of the law would have also aroused considerable opposition. Particularly striking, however, are the two key metaphors Jesus applies to himself in these three chapters: he is the "living water" (7:38) and the "light of the world" (8:12; 9:5). He immediately illustrates the latter claim by healing a man born blind (9:6–41).

These claims dovetail perfectly with two key rituals performed during the Festival of Tabernacles. One involved a daily libation in the temple, of water drawn from the pool of Siloam that will figure in chapter 9. The Jerusalem Talmud explicitly associates Isaiah 12:3 ("With joy you will draw water from the wells of salvation") with this ritual (j. Sukk. 5.1) But, according to the Mishnah, on the last day

---

[42] Cf. further William J. Domeris, "The Confession of Peter According to John 6:69," *Tyndale Bulletin* 44 (1993): 155–67.

of the festival, this was omitted (*Sukk.* 4.9, 5.1). In this context Jesus offered himself as living water.[43] Second, there were daily services in the temple, during which a giant, brightly lit candelabra was erected, until the final day of the weeklong festivities, in which a service of darkness, remembering God's still unfulfilled promises, took place (*Sukk.* 5.2–4). "On the last and greatest day of the festival" (John 7:37), Jesus claimed to be the light for the whole world (8:12). Just as he believed he fulfilled the Sabbath and Passover, he was alleging that he was the divine fulfillment for Tabernacles as well.[44]

The debate about Jesus's birthplace that punctuates John 7 is no defeater for Jesus's claims. The Fourth Gospel is filled with irony; here appears a classic example. Some reject Jesus as Messiah because the Messiah is not to come from Galilee, but they do not know that he was born in Bethlehem, the proper birthplace for God's anointed deliverer (v. 42). As we saw in the last chapter, John can assume a fair amount of knowledge about the basic contours of Jesus's life among the Ephesian Christians, so they will recognize the irony of Christ's being rejected simply due to some people's ignorance of his proper lineage![45]

We skip over what has come to be labeled 7:53–8:11 because it almost certainly was not in John's original text, though interestingly many fairly skeptical scholars nevertheless believe it preserves a core, historical event from Jesus's life because of its distinctively

[43] Cf. further Bruce Grigsby, "'If Any Man Thirsts . . .': Observations on the Rabbinic Background of John 7.37–39," *Biblica* 67 (1986): 101–8.

[44] Cf. esp. Mary B. Spaulding, *Commemorative Identities: Jewish Social Memory and the Johannine Feast of Booths* (London and New York: T & T Clark, 2009). It is perhaps more likely that John 7:37–38 should be translated as in the NIV footnote rather than as in the NIV. In other words Christ, not the believer, is the source of the living water.

[45] Cf. Warren Carter, *John: Storyteller, Interpreter, Evangelist* (Peabody: Hendrickson, 2006), 119.

and characteristically radical attitude toward forgiveness.[46] The main event of 8:12–59 is the escalating hostility in Jesus's dialogue with some whom John insisted in verse 30 "believed in him."[47] But the careful reader of John will recall that initial "belief" for John is no guarantee of authentic faith. John 2:23 similarly reported that many people "believed in his name" when they saw his miracles, but verse 24 immediately adds that he "would not entrust himself to them, for he knew all people." For John, only those who "abide" or "remain" in Christ demonstrate themselves to be true believers (see esp. 15:1–8; cf. 1 John 2:19).[48]

John 8:44 ("You belong to your father, the devil, and you want to carry out your father's desires") represents what some would consider the most extreme statement of several in the Fourth Gospel that have been labeled anti-Semitic (or more accurately, anti-Jewish).[49] But this requires the author of the Gospel himself to have been Gentile, or he would have been condemning himself! In fact, the text is *more*

---

[46] E.g., Bart D. Ehrman, "Jesus and the Adulteress," *New Testament Studies* 34 (1988): 24–44.

[47] John 8:12–20, like 5:31–40, also takes the legal and oratorical forms of forensic rhetoric, suggesting it was composed as a unity from the outset. See Per Jarle Bekken, *The Lawsuit Motif in John's Gospel from New Perspectives: Jesus Christ, Crucified Criminal and Emperor of the World* (Leiden and Boston: Brill, 2014), 132–47.

[48] Christopher D. Bass, "A Johannine Perspective of the Human Responsibility to Persevere in the Faith Through the Use of MENΩ and Other Related Motifs," *Westminster Theological Journal* 69 (2007): 305–25. For the view that 8:31 introduces a completely different group of people from v. 30, see Terry Griffith, "'The Jews Who Had Believed in Him' (John 8:31) and the Motif of Apostasy in the Gospel of John," in *The Gospel of John and Christian Theology*, ed. Richard Bauckham and Carl Mosser (Grand Rapids: Eerdmans, 2008), 183–92.

[49] For representative polemic, see Maurice Casey, *Is John's Gospel True?* (London and New York: Routledge, 1996), 24–27. For an entire monograph rebutting this identification, see Stephen Motyer, *Your Father the Devil? A New Approach to John and the "Jews"* (Carlisle: Paternoster, 1997).

anti-Jewish if it is *not* historically accurate.[50] If it reflects something the Jewish Jesus actually said, it cannot be anti-Jewish by definition. Moreover, nothing in John, or anywhere else in the New Testament for that matter, condemns every last Jewish person to ever live, nor even every Jew in Jesus's day. The strong language that does appear is precisely the kind of generalized condemnations of the majority of people in a particular context that one often finds in the Old Testament prophets, and they can scarcely be accused of being anti-Jewish when they were canonized in the Jewish Scriptures![51]

The other most problematic passage in John 8 is his striking claim in verse 58 that "before Abraham was born, I am!" Instead of representing bad grammar (i.e., a poorly worded equivalent to "I was"), "I am" most likely alludes to the divine name disclosed to Moses in Exodus 3:14 and/or the unique claims to deity made by Yahweh in texts like Isaiah 43:10, 13; 46:4; and 48:12.[52] Surely, if ever there is a claim on the lips of John's Jesus that makes him too exalted to fit in with the Synoptic portraits, it is this one—or so it is often claimed. Yet Mark 6:50 and parallels (including John 6:20) likewise find Jesus declaring (according to the Evangelists' Greek translation) *egō eimi* ("I am [he]"), often masked in English translation as "It is I." And Mark 13:6 employs the identical language for what false messiahs will come and declare. Christians accustomed to thinking of Jesus in the highest possible terms understandably read the most exalted implications possible into John 8:58, and there is no doubt that Jesus's opponents

---

[50] Motyer, *Your Father the Devil?*, 185–90.

[51] See further throughout Raimo Hakola, *Identity Matters: John, the Jews and Jewishness* (Leiden and Boston: Brill, 2005). Cf. also Thomas D. Lea, "Who Killed the Lord? A Defense Against the Charge of Anti-Semitism in John's Gospel," *Criswell Theological Review* 7 (1994): 103–23; Porter, *John, His Gospel, and Jesus*.

[52] See esp. Catrin H. Williams, *I Am He: The Interpretation of 'Ani Hû" in Jewish and Early Christian Literature* (Tübingen: Mohr Siebeck, 2000); Paul N. Anderson, "The Origin and Development of the Johannine *Egō Eimi* Sayings in Cognitive-Critical Perspective," *Journal for the Study of the Historical Jesus* 9 (2011): 139–206.

heard enough overtones of deity to accuse him of blasphemy (v. 59). But rhetorically, Jesus's wording still remains more muted than the explicit claim that countless madmen have made over the centuries, namely, "I am God."[53] Nor does Jesus ever say in so many words, "I am the Lord," an observation all the more striking because the Roman emperors increasingly demanded that their subjects acknowledge them as "Lord and God."[54]

The Pool of Siloam, which features centrally in John 9, is another location in Jerusalem that escaped correct identification for a long period of time. Even after many identified it with the drainage area at one end of Hezekiah's tunnel, doubt remained. In just the last few years, remnants of a much larger ritual immersion pool slightly farther down the water course have been discovered, leaving little doubt that Bethesda and Siloam formed the two largest such *mikvaoth*, one on the north side and the other on the south side of the temple. Whichever direction pilgrims to the holiest place in Judaism came from, they had ample facilities to be ritually cleansed prior to entering the sacred precincts.[55]

That this is the lone miracle in which Jesus applies mud to a person's body and only one of two in which he uses any additional "helps" (see also Mark 8:22–26) suggests it was not invented as an effort to simulate Jesus's characteristic style of healing miracles. The most problematic verse in the chapter for many scholars is 9:22, which

---

[53] Motyer (*Your Father the Devil?*, 209) argues that Jesus's words would not have been heard as an exact equation of himself with deity so much as "a claim to be a divine agent, anointed with the name and powers of God, and in this case active in the *genesis* of Abraham." But he obviously crossed a threshold within the conventional Judaism of his day that led to the charge of blasphemy (v. 59).

[54] Cf. esp. Warren Carter, *John and Empire: Initial Explorations* (London and New York: T & T Clark, 2008), 195–97.

[55] Urban C. von Wahlde, "The Pool of Siloam: The Importance of the New Discoveries for Our Understanding of Ritual Immersion in Late Second Temple Judaism and the Gospel of John," in *John, Jesus, and History*, vol. 2, 155–73.

reports that these Jewish leaders had already determined "that anyone who acknowledged that Jesus was the Messiah would be put out of the synagogue." Similar claims reappear in 12:42 and 16:2. These critics observe that only toward the end of the first century is there evidence for any organized and sustained measures throughout the empire to excommunicate Jews who followed Jesus from their local synagogues.[56] Yet nothing in any of these three verses in John suggests he is thinking of such widespread efforts. In 9:22 and 12:42 the context refers only to Jerusalem, the most natural location for the earliest forms of this hostility. Chapter 16:2 is phrased prophetically, speaking of what people would do to the disciples after Jesus's death, and even then there is no indication of what scale of persecution Jesus is envisaging. As with 8:44, it is easier to imagine the statements attributed to Jesus as historical when we keep them in the specific contexts they appear rather than trying to make them say something much more than they do and then rejecting them for that reason![57] Recently, Jonathan Bernier has shown that the same motivation that led Caiaphas to sacrifice Jesus to keep the Romans from intervening against Jewish national enthusiasm (11:50) could easily have led some local Jewish leaders in Jerusalem to threaten violence against his followers in expelling them from the synagogues. It would not have been on any widespread scale, but John does not claim that it was.[58]

---

[56] Classically, J. Louis Martyn, *History and Theology in the Fourth Gospel*, 3rd ed. (Louisville: Westminster John Knox, 2003), 46–66.

[57] Edward W. Klink III, "Expulsion from the Synagogue: Rethinking a Johannine Anachronism," *Tyndale Bulletin* 59 (2008): 99–119; Edward W. Klink III "The Overrealized Expulsion in the Gospel of John," in *John, Jesus, and History*, vol. 2, 175–84. Contra Martyn's consistent reading of the Fourth Gospel as referring to later first-century conditions at the time of its compilation, see esp. Tobias Hägerland, "John's Gospel: A Two-Level Drama?" *Journal for the Study of the New Testament* 25 (2003): 309–22.

[58] Jonathan Bernier, Aposynagōgos *and the Historical Jesus in John: Rethinking the Historicity of the Johannine Expulsion Passages* (Leiden: Brill, 2013).

John 10:1–21 appears to continue Jesus's dialogues with certain Pharisees in Jerusalem at Tabernacles, as a result of his curing the man born blind. But the dominant metaphors shift from Christ's being living water and the light of the world to the Good Shepherd (v. 11) and the Gate for the sheep (v. 7). These could be two separate metaphors, with the Good Shepherd referring to the way in which he will lead and nurture his people, in fulfillment of Ezekiel 34, in contrast to the wicked rulers of Ezekiel's and Jesus's day. The sheep gate would then refer to the proper way the flock enters the corral in order to be protected. But it is also possible that Jesus has in mind the custom in which a single shepherd with a small flock in a stone-walled corral would sleep across the threshold of the entrance to the protective area as a guard against predators. He could then be both the Shepherd and the Gate at the same time.[59]

In addition to fitting the culture of rural Israel in the early first century, John 10:1–21 also creates a striking triad. A conspicuous passage from 2 Baruch 77:13–16 contains the identical three elements of flowing water, lamplight, and responsible shepherding:

> For the shepherds of Israel have perished,
> And the lamps which gave light are extinguished,
> And the fountains have withheld their stream whence we used
>   to drink.
> And we are left in the darkness,
> And amid the trees of the forest,
> And the thirst of the wilderness."
> And I answered and said unto them
> "Shepherds and lamps and fountains come from the law:
> And though we depart, yet the law abides.
> If therefore you have respect to the law,

---

[59] Kenneth E. Bailey, "The Shepherd Poems of John 10: Their Culture and Style," *Near East School of Theology Theological Review* 14 (1993): 3–21.

And are intent upon wisdom,
A lamp will not be wanting,
And a shepherd will not fail,
And a fountain will not dry up.[60]

What many Jews ascribed to Torah, therefore, Jesus ascribes to himself. He is the true shepherd, lamp, and fountain. We should not be surprised to see this triad of images all applied at the same Festival of Tabernacles. It is historically credible that Jesus should tailor his claims to his setting, while it is less likely that a later author, writing to a largely Gentile Christian audience, twenty or more years after the fall of Jerusalem and the concomitant abolition of the festivals there, would invent these parallels, expecting everyone to grasp them.

The Feast of Dedication

John 10:22 begins a new scene, a couple of months later, during the Jewish festival better known today as Hanukkah. Not surprisingly, Jesus is again in Jerusalem, again employing the metaphors of sheep and shepherd. The Feast of Dedication, or Hanukkah, commemorated the liberation of Israel from the Syrians by the Maccabees, with the purification and rededication of the temple in 164 BC forming the central event that was memorialized. At first various Jews thought that Judas Maccabeus or one of his brothers might be the messiah. This, of course, did not eventuate, but by the standards of the surrounding centuries, the Maccabees were good shepherds indeed in Israel. But Jesus is the consummate Good Shepherd who guarantees eternal life for his sheep—those who prove to be his true followers (vv. 26–29). Jesus fulfills the festival of Dedication the same way he has fulfilled all of the other Jewish holy days.[61]

---

[60] On which, cf. further Moloney, Gospel of John, 307–8.

[61] "Christ in fact perfectly accomplished what the Maccabees wrought in a figure, and dedicated a new and abiding temple" (B. F. Westcott, The Gospel According

Bridging to the Passion Narrative

John 11–12 is transitional. Most commentators take these two chapters as the conclusion of the "book of signs," prior to the "book of glory"in chapters 13–21. A case can also be made, however, for seeing the end of chapter 11 as the major dividing point in the Gospel. The resurrection of Lazarus, which dominates John 11, is the last miracle John records, and John 12 begins with events less than a week before Jesus's death.[62] But the last account of Jesus's fulfilling a specific festival appears in John 10, so perhaps chapters 11–12 should be viewed simply as a bridge between chapters 5–10 and chapters 13–21.[63]

The Resurrection of Lazarus

We know Mary and Martha already from Luke 10:38–42. While we should be wary of inferring too much about individuals' personalities from single episodes in their lives, it is at least interesting that in John 11, as in Luke 10, Martha seems to be the more active of the two sisters. In John 11:20, she takes the lead to go out to accost Jesus while Mary stays home.[64] On the other hand, both sisters make the same accusation—had Jesus come at once, Lazarus would not have died (vv. 21, 32). They know of Jesus's healing abilities, but they are not expecting a resurrection. Even though Martha's confession in verse 27 employs the identical two titles to Jesus that the Fourth Evangelist wants everyone to acknowledge about him ("Son of God" and "Messiah"—cf. 20:31), when Jesus orders the stone to be rolled away from the entrance to

---

to St John, vol. 1 [London: John Murray, 1908], 187); endorsed by Rodney A. Whitacre, *John* (Downers Grove and Leicester: IVP, 1999), 268.

[62] Cf. Gerald L. Borchert, *John 1–11* (Nashville: B&H, 1996); and Gerald L. Borchert, *John 12–21* (Nashville: B&H, 2002).

[63] Carson, *Gospel According to John*, 403; Köstenberger, *John*, 320, 374.

[64] For the view that Martha is not being as criticized for her "activism" as is often held, see Mary Stromer Hanson, *The New Perspective on Mary and Martha* (Eugene, OR: Wipf & Stock, 2013).

Lazarus's tomb, she protests about the foul odor that will come forth (v. 39). So, too, Mary and her friends' weeping elicits merely Jesus's anger (v. 33), most likely at their unbelief.[65] These are not vignettes invented by later Christians wanting to whitewash the attitudes of Jesus or his first followers!

The resurrection itself outdoes the other biblical revivifications (i.e., where we assume the individuals did die again later on), because Lazarus has been dead for four days. But it is not as if neither the Old Testament nor the Synoptics contain any resurrections—Elijah and Elisha brought people back to life in 1 Kings 17:7–24; and 2 Kings 4:8–37 (cf. also 13:20–21), while Jesus raised both Jairus's daughter (Mark 5:21–43 pars.) and the son of the widow in Nain (Luke 7:11–17). We will say more about the concept of resurrections later (below), and we have already noted reasons the raising of Lazarus is not in the Synoptics (above).[66] The only other issue of a historical nature that is sometimes raised in objection to this narrative is that John takes Lazarus's resurrection, rather than the temple clearing (cf. Mark 11:18 par.), as the catalyst for the plot to execute Jesus (John 11:45–57). But this objection makes the contrast much too stark. All four Gospels include multiple occasions on which various Jewish leaders begin to plot Jesus's demise (see already Mark 3:6 pars.; John 7:1). To argue that the Synoptics give only one cause, and John only a different and contradictory cause, is to oversimplify matters drastically.

---

[65] Moloney, *Gospel of John*, 330; Carson, *Gospel According to John*, 416. Jesus also weeps (v. 35) for Lazarus, but his primary anger at unbelief cannot thereby be dismissed (contra, e.g., Andrew T. Lincoln, *The Gospel According to Saint John* [London: Continuum; Peabody: Hendrickson, 2005], 326–27) because the two verbs in verses 33 (*embrimaomai*) and 35 (*dakruō*) are entirely different and semantically unrelated—see Kanagaraj, *John*, 118.

[66] Cf. also Richard Bauckham, *The Testimony of the Beloved Disciple: Narrative, History, and Theology in the Gospel of John* (Grand Rapids: Baker, 2007), 181.

The Anointing at Bethany

The anointing of Jesus at Bethany should probably be seen as a parallel account to the episodes found in Mark 14:3–9 and Matthew 26:6–13. The divergent details can be readily accounted for. Mark relocates the passage topically because it ties in directly with Jesus's death, and Matthew follows suit. John gives the more precise chronology (John 12:1), specifies who was present in greater detail and both who anointed Jesus (Mary, v. 3) and who objected to it (Judas, v. 4). The core, climactic teaching about Mary's anticipating Jesus's death through her actions and the perennial opportunity to help the poor is identical in all three accounts. Spilling an entire jar of perfume over someone's head (Mark 14:3) would doubtless create runoff on the feet as well (John 12:3), while anointing for burial would require perfume on the entire body (cf. Mark 14:8 par.).[67]

On the other hand, John 12:1–11 should *not* be treated as parallel to Luke 7:36–50. The location, time, characters, dialogue, and point of the two passages are entirely different. The only similarities are that a woman anoints Jesus with the contents of an alabaster jar of perfume. Such behavior was much more common in the first-century Mediterranean world than it is in ours, and alabaster jars were the most recommended kind of container for perfume, as we have seen. So to use the differences in Luke as a paradigm of how drastically one Evangelist might alter his sources is an entirely inappropriate and misleading process.[68]

---

[67] Carson, *Gospel According to John*, 426–27; J. F. Coakley, "The Anointing at Bethany and the Priority of John," *Journal of Biblical Literature* 107 (1988): 246–48.

[68] As, e.g., in J. Patrick Mullen, *Dining with Pharisees* (Collegeville, MN: Liturgical, 2004).

Palm Sunday

Little in John's account of the not-so-triumphal entry is unique to his version of this quadruply attested event. The only striking distinctive is that only from John do we learn about the strewing of *palm* branches. But Jericho, then as now, was the "City of Palms," and Jewish well-wishers had done the same thing to welcome the Maccabean rulers (1 Macc 13:51; 2 Macc 10:7; 14:4; Jos. *Bell.* 7.10–2). So it would be only natural that some of those who hoped Jesus was finally going to disclose his intentions to rid the land of the Romans would be welcomed in similar fashion.[69]

The subsequent dialogue between Jesus and certain disciples about some Greeks to whom Jesus apparently fails to grant an audience (John 12:20–26) is built around a core metaphor closely resembling the seed parables of Mark 4:1–34 and parallels.[70] In John 12:24, Jesus declares that "unless a kernel of wheat falls to the ground and dies, it remains only a single seed. But if it dies, it produces many seeds." Verses 27–28 resemble Jesus's struggle in the garden of Gethsemane in the Synoptics (Mark 14:35–36 pars.),[71] while John's conclusion to this segment of the Gospel views the rejection of Jesus as fulfilling Isaiah 6:10, the passage Jesus cites in Mark 4:11–12 and parallels for

---

[69] Cf. further J. F. Coakley, "Jesus' Messianic Entry into Jerusalem (John 12:12–19 par.)," *Journal of Theological Studies* 46 (1995): 470–71.

[70] Just as Jesus must die so others can live, so his followers must imitate his servant leadership. Cf. Lindars, *John*, 430; J. Ramsey Michaels, *The Gospel of John* (Grand Rapids: Eerdmans, 2010), 689, 692.

[71] Brown, *John I–XII*, 471. In both settings, "Jesus, in turmoil of spirit, shrinks from the fearful experience before him, and in his address to God, seeks avoidance of it; yet he acknowledges that to endure it is the reason for his mission from God; in an act therefore of total obedience to the Father's will his spirit rises in unreserved affirmation."—George R. Beasley-Murray, *John*, 2nd ed. (Nashville: Thomas Nelson, 1999), 212.

why many don't grasp the significance of his teaching in parables.[72] All of these parallels inspire confidence that the Fourth Evangelist is not making things up.

Death and Resurrection

The Upper Room and the Last Supper

John 13 moves us to the last night of Jesus's earthly life. Just as chapter 1 contained considerable information about the ministry of John the Baptist without ever formally narrating John's baptizing Jesus, so too chapters 13–17 give greatly more detail about Jesus's last words with his followers on "Maundy Thursday" evening but without ever mentioning his words over the bread and the cup. If John the Evangelist were concerned to play down a growing sacramentalism accompanying a growing institutionalization of the church at the end of the first century, we can understand these omissions.[73] The foot-washing of 13:1–17 fits perfectly, however, with Jesus's teaching about servant leadership in Mark 10:42–45 and parallels.[74] Interestingly, Luke's parallel likewise inserts this into Jesus's upper room conversation with the Twelve on Thursday night (Luke 22:24–27). We do not know of such a ritual in Judaism or the Greco-Roman world, and it proved extremely countercultural. So by the criteria of both multiple attestation and dissimilarity, it is likely to be historical.[75] The rest of John 13 closely parallels the Synoptics with Jesus's predicting Judas's betrayal

---

[72] On which, see Craig L. Blomberg, *Interpreting the Parables*, 2nd ed. (Downers Grove and Nottingham: IVP, 2012), 44–46.

[73] See throughout Gary M. Burge, *The Anointed Community: The Holy Spirit in the Johannine Tradition* (Grand Rapids: Eerdmans, 1987).

[74] Jey J. Kanagaraj, "Johannine Jesus, the Supreme Example of Leadership: An Inquiry into John 13:1–20," *Themelios* 29 (2004): 15–26; Keener, *John*, vol. 2 (2003), 901.

[75] Bauckham, *The Testimony of the Beloved Disciple*, 191–206.

and Peter's denial. All of this suggests that the meal occurring in this chapter (see v. 2) is the Passover meal, rather than a separate meal a day earlier as many critics have alleged.[76] Verse 1 does indeed state that "it was just before the Passover Festival." But verse 1 forms a short paragraph all its own, suggesting that what took place *before* the festival was Jesus's knowledge that his time had come and his commitment to carry things through to the end (the rest of the contents of v. 1). When verse 2 proceeds to announce that "the evening meal was in progress," we should then understand the meal to be the Passover meal that occurred the first evening of the weeklong festival, which has just been mentioned.[77] When we read in verse 29a that some of the disciples thought Judas exited the dinner to buy "what was needed for the festival," this must then refer either to further provisions for that evening or to supplies for the rest of the week. After all, shops stayed open on the night of the first day of Passover for precisely these purposes. When others thought he might be going "to give something to the poor" (v. 29), this reinforces this conclusion. Part of the Passover evening ritual in Jerusalem involved giving alms to beggars who gathered near the gates to the temple.[78]

---

[76] Rightly Cullen I. K. Story, "The Bearing of Old Testament Terminology on the Johannine Chronology of the Final Passover of Jesus," *Novum Testamentum* 31 (1989): 317.

[77] Gary M. Burge, *John* (Grand Rapids: Zondervan, 2000), 365–67; Ridderbos, *Gospel of John*, 455; Köstenberger, *John*, 400; Carson, *Gospel According to John*, 455–58; Kruse, *Gospel According to John*, 279. If this view is rejected, the next most probable is that either Jesus celebrated the meal as a Passover meal (as in the Synoptics) one day early, knowing he would not be alive twenty-four hours later or that he was following a different Passover calendar, perhaps with the Essenes and/or other sectarian Jews. For the most persuasive version of the latter option, see Stéphane Saulnier, *Calendrical Variations in Second Temple Judaism: New Perspectives on the "Date of the Last Supper" Debate* (Leiden and Boston: Brill, 2012).

[78] For documentation and elaboration, see Joachim Jeremias, *The Eucharistic Words of Jesus* (London: SCM; New York: Scribner's, 1966), 54 and 82. Cf. Carson, *Gospel According to John*, 471; Kruse, *Gospel According to John*, 290.

Chapters 14–16 are often referred to as Christ's Farewell Discourse. Here Bartholomäi's work proves particularly instructive. While a typical synopsis might print only a couple Synoptic parallels to individual verses in all three chapters in John, Bartholomäi lists thirty-six verbal echoes of Synoptic material in the thirty-one verses of chapter 14 alone.[79] The idiom overall may be John's, but the concepts are clearly Christ's, along with numerous individual words or turns of phrase. Conceptually, the main theme of sending the Holy Spirit to empower the disciples for bold testimony, especially in contexts of persecution in the interim between his resurrection and his second coming, matches exactly topics we find repeatedly addressed in the Synoptics (especially in Mark 13 pars.).

Specific subordinate points line up even more closely. Jesus as the true and living way (John 14:6; taking the trio of nouns as a hendiadys), just as when he called himself the Gate for the sheep in 10:7, reminds us of Jesus's call in the Sermon on the Mount to enter by the narrow way and gate (Matt 7:13–14). Receiving whatever the disciples ask in Jesus's name (John 14:13–14; 15:7; 16:24) recalls Jesus's promises moments earlier in the Sermon (Matt 7:7–11) and elsewhere (esp. Luke 11:9–13). The metaphors of the vine and the branches (John 15:1–8) resemble Jesus's teaching about fruit bearing just a few verses earlier still in his great Sermon (Matt 7:1–21).[80] Remaining in God's love (John 15:10) and loving one another sacrificially (v. 13) match the double love commandment from Deuteronomy 6:5 and Leviticus 19:18, cited clearly in Matthew 22:34–40 and parallels. The proverb that "a servant is not greater than his master" (John 15:20) parallels

---

[79] Philipp Bartholomä, *The Johannine Discourses and the Teaching of Jesus in the Synoptics: A Contribution to the Discussion Concerning the Authenticity of Jesus' Words in the Fourth Gospel* (Tübingen and Basel: Francke, 2012), 251–306.

[80] And the form approximates the Synoptic parable/simile form as closely as anywhere in John and is therefore likely authentic. See further E. Earle Ellis, *The Making of the New Testament* (Leiden: Brill, 1999), 177–79.

Matthew 10:24. The image of labor pains for the agony just before Christ returns carries over from Mark 13:8 to John 16:21. The prediction of all the disciples scattering to their homes and abandoning Jesus (John 16:32) is fulfilled in the Synoptic account of everyone except the arresting authorities fleeing from him in the garden (Mark 14:50).

Is the language of 16:2 too strong to be credible in an early first-century Jewish context? This goes beyond the simple excommunication from the synagogue mentioned in 9:22. Here a time is predicted "when anyone who kills you will think they are offering a service to God." But that is precisely what Saul of Tarsus thought he was doing as he tried to round up believers to imprison and perhaps murder them. In Galatians 1:11–14 he even describes this zeal as advancing beyond his other countrymen of that day. We must not envisage Saul as a troubled soul, like the medieval Luther, more and more aware of his inability to live up to the law, but as an ancient terrorist, motivated by religious zeal, convinced he was helping purify his people by ridding apostates from the earth![81]

The entire Farewell Discourse has often been viewed as composite, particularly because of the seemingly awkward literary seam in 14:31. Here Jesus exhorts the Twelve, "Come now; let us leave." But he continues talking for another three chapters! It is possible that they did leave the upper room at this point and that the vineyards they would have passed by en route to the garden of Gethsemane inspired Jesus's teachings about the vine and the branches. After all, the next geographical reference comes in 18:1 when the little troupe is set to cross the Kidron ravine, outside the city and down a steep slope to the base of the Mount of Olives.[82] It is also possible that 14:31 is a rhetorical

---

[81] Cf. Ben Witherington III, *John's Wisdom: A Commentary on the Fourth Gospel* (Louisville: Westminster John Knox, 1995), 262.

[82] D. A. Carson, "Historical Tradition in the Fourth Gospel: After Dodd, What?" in *Gospel Perspectives*, vol. 2, ed. R. T. France and David Wenham (Sheffield:

device to highlight the significance of the two remaining chapters[83] or a dramatic action to delay departure in the tradition of Greco-Roman tragedy when protagonists know they must go to meet their opponents but try to delay the inevitable as long as they can.[84] The probable chiastic structure of John 14–16 further supports its unity.[85]

Jesus's so-called high priestly prayer, comprising John 17, again reflects uniquely Johannine idiom and an unparalleled circumstance— Jesus's petition to the Father, especially for the disciples, just before the arresting party arrives. What is intriguing, however, are the close conceptual parallels within this prayer to all but one of the petitions of what is traditionally called the Lord's Prayer in Matthew 6:9–13. The following chart discloses the parallels:

Matthew 6	John 17
Our Father in heaven	Looking to heaven … "Father"
Hallowed be your name	Son glorifies Father
Your kingdom come	The time [hour] has come …
Your will be done on earth as in heaven	Completing heavenly work on earth
Give us this day our daily bread	Giving them everything from God
Forgive our debts as we forgive our debtors	Make them holy
Lead us not into temptation	Not taken out of world,
Deliver us from evil	but protected from evil one[86]

JSOT, 1981; Eugene, OR: Wipf & Stock, 2003), 123. Cf. Ernst Haenchen, *John 2* (Philadelphia: Fortress, 1984), 128; Westcott, *Gospel According to St John*, vol. 1, 187.

[83] L. Scott Kellum, *The Unity of the Farewell Discourse: The Literary Integrity of John 13.31–16.33* (London and New York: T & T Clark, 2004), 238.

[84] George L. Parsenios, *Departure and Consolation: The Johannine Farewell Discourses in Light of Greco-Roman Literature* (Leiden: Brill, 2005), 49–76.

[85] Of various proposals, the most persuasive is Wayne Brouwer, *The Literary Development of John 13–17: A Chiastic Reading* (Atlanta: SBL, 2000).

[86] William O. Walker Jr., "The Lord's Prayer in Matthew and John," *New Testament Studies* 28 (1982): 237–56.

Most of these parallels are not blatant or explicit, as one might expect from an imitator. They are subtle, yet still present, more consistent with the hypothesis of the same speaker behind each prayer.

The Passion of the Christ

A consistent distinctive of John's portrait of Jesus's passion (chaps. 18–19) is that he shows Jesus still in charge.[87] Thus he voluntarily lays down his life; he is not outwitted by the Jewish authorities. But here we find the closest and greatest number of parallels to the Synoptics of any two chapters in the Gospel. Both the Synoptics and John agree that Jesus and his disciples went to the garden and that Jesus was betrayed by Judas, who came guiding a detachment of soldiers from the Jewish and/or Roman authorities. Both agree that the disciples left without being arrested. Both know of Simon Peter's aborted efforts to begin the revolution, involving his use of a sword to cut off an ear of a servant of the high priest. Both agree Jesus was taken to Caiaphas, the current high priest, and then to Pontius Pilate, the Roman governor of Judea. Both recount Peter's three denials before a rooster crows. Both agree that Pilate could find no reason for executing Jesus and tried to release him in favor of Barabbas but failed.

Examples of Jesus's being in control, especially in chapter 18, abound. Soldiers fall down backwards when he says, "I am [he]" (vv. 5–6), another possible allusion to the divine name? Although the Synoptics portray the disciples as running away, John depicts Jesus's requesting that the soldiers leave them alone (v. 8). Obviously he realized they all could be rounded up if the authorities wanted to do so. After rebuking Peter for using his sword, John's Jesus adds, "Shall I not drink the cup the Father has given me?" (18:11). John alone adds the accounts of Jesus's hearing before Annas, Caiaphas's father-in-law and former high priest (vv. 13, 19–24). Despite Rome's

---

[87] See esp. Donald P. Senior, *The Passion of Jesus in the Gospel of John* (Collegeville, MN: Liturgical, 1991).

frequent depositions of high priests, in Jewish law the office was to be held for life (Num 35:25), so the courtesy of bringing a celebrated captive to Annas is historically plausible (see also Josephus, *Bell.* 4.151, 160).[88] Here again Jesus holds his own in dialogue, even to the point of being slapped by a nearby official for his directness (v. 22). An anonymous disciple, perhaps the "beloved disciple" himself, enables Peter to join him in the high priest's courtyard (vv. 15–16; recall above) but he plays no further role in the story of Peter's denials, which could explain his absence from the Synoptic accounts.

Chapter 18:28 is the next text that has led many to imagine John's contradicting the Synoptics with respect to the Passover chronology. A cursory reading of this sentence would indeed make it sound like the festival had not yet begun at all: "By now it was early morning, and to avoid ceremonial uncleanness [the Jewish leaders] did not enter the palace, because they wanted to be able to eat the Passover." But Jewish days began at sundown. If the uncleanness they feared incurring was the kind that would last only until the end of the day, then they *would* have been able to eat the inaugural Passover meal that evening, if the festival had yet to start. On the other hand, the noontime meal at the end of the morning *after* the initial evening Passover feast was a second important meal of the weeklong festival. It was known as a *Hagigah*, and an entire Mishnaic tractate is devoted the laws surrounding its celebration.[89] It is more likely, then, that John has this midday meal in mind.

---

[88] C. K. Barrett, *The Gospel According to St. John*, 2nd ed. (London: SPCK; Philadelphia: Westminster, 1978), 524; Keener, *John*, vol. 2, 1089–90.

[89] See esp. Barry D. Smith, "The Chronology of the Last Supper," *Westminster Theological Journal* 53 (1991): 29–45. Another entire tractate is devoted to "mid-festival days" (*Moed Katan*) more generally. Cf. also Köstenberger, *John*, 524; Carson, *Gospel According to John*, 589–90.

The next particularly striking Johannine distinctive in his passion narrative appears in verse 31. Only in the Fourth Gospel does a group of Jews acknowledge the reason that explained what the Synoptics took for granted as common knowledge—under most circumstances the people Rome had conquered were not permitted to implement the death penalty for those they found guilty of capital offenses (*j. Sanh.* 1.1, 7.2). The rest of chapter 18 and part of 19 describe the dialogue between Jesus and Pilate. In the Synoptics, Christ simply remains silent, a scenario with which John is also familiar (19:10). But he has expanded his account of Jesus's "examination"[90] before Pilate with additional detail that seems more realistic than Jesus's just remaining mute the entire time. If one asks how the disciples could have found out what Jesus said here or in other private conversations when no one else was present, the most obvious answer would be that he told them. If one protests that, at least in this instance, there is no occasion before his death for him to have disclosed such details, we must remember that Luke depicts Jesus's appearing to the apostles over a period of forty days (Acts 1:3) and teaching them how everything in the Scriptures that pointed to him had to be fulfilled (Luke 24:44–48). This would have afforded him ample time to include a handful of key details surrounding his passion that the disciples themselves had not previously known. Or, less supernaturally, Pilate or one of his guards could easily have confided in Caiaphas about the unusual hearing, who could have reported it to the Sanhedrin. With at least Joseph of Arimathea and Nicodemus secretly friendly to Jesus and his followers, they in turn could have passed the word on to one or more of the disciples.[91]

---

[90] The term preferred by Darrell L. Bock, *Blasphemy and Exaltation in Judaism and the Final Examination of Jesus* (Tübingen: Mohr Siebeck; Grand Rapids: Baker, 2000).

[91] Cf. further Carson, *Gospel According to John*, 587.

Chapter 19:12 brings us to the next key Johannine distinctive also regularly deemed historical. Why would Pilate allow himself to be pressured by Jewish authorities to have Jesus crucified if he found in him nothing worthy of death according to Roman law? The answer is that appointment to a post in Judea and Samaria was not entirely an honor. This was near the eastern end of the empire in a province filled with residents with a reputation for rebellion. Pilate was caught between a rock and a hard place. He had to keep the Roman emperor, Tiberius, convinced that he had everything under control and that the Israelites were loyal to Rome. But he could not rule so oppressively that the Jewish leaders would start a revolt or send an embassy to Rome requesting Pilate's replacement as they had successfully done in the days of Archelaus. So the sacrifice of a would-be king, however misguided, was a small price to pay for peace in Judea.

Trying the patient outdoors at *Gabbatha* ("the Stone Pavement," v. 13) conforms to what we have thus far unearthed in archaeological digs at the Praetorium.[92] Second-century paving stones can be viewed to this day with etchings in them, representing games Roman soldiers played, not unlike the gambling for Jesus's clothes in 19:23–24.[93] That 19:14 calls this "the day of Preparation of the Passover" again fuels the fires of those who would insist that Johannine and Synoptic chronology contradict each other. But the Greek expression can also be translated as "the day of Preparation in Passover week." The "day of Preparation" (*Paraskeuē*) was an expression that meant Friday, the day of Preparation for the Sabbath (cf. *Did.* 8.1, *Mart. Polyc.* 7.1). Verse 31 confirms that the next day was indeed the Sabbath, and a special one because it was the Sabbath during Passover week. Verse 42 reiterates that it was "the day of

---

[92] Paul N. Anderson, "Aspects of Historicity in the Gospel of John: Implications for Investigations of Jesus and Archaeology," in *Jesus and Archaeology*, ed. Charlesworth, 603–4.

[93] Peter L. Walker (*In the Steps of Jesus* [Grand Rapids: Zondervan, 2006], 173) notes the possibility of a recently discovered site being the actual location of *Gabbatha*.

Preparation" with no reference to the Passover at all. So we should understand "the day of Preparation" throughout John 19 as meaning *Friday* in all three contexts, not the day before the Passover Festival began.[94]

Chapter 19:13–14 contains another passing reference, the significance of which has been blown out of proportion to its brevity. John adds that "it was about noon" (v. 14)—literally, the sixth hour, the time when the lambs would begin to be slaughtered on the day leading to the inaugural evening Passover meal. Surely now we can say that the Passover has not yet begun and that John is deliberately recasting events so that Jesus is crucified as the Lamb of God, a uniquely Johannine concept.[95] But several fallacies here are rarely discussed. (1) John's largely Gentile audience in Ephesus would not likely have known about the precise timing of Jewish Passover ritual. (2) Even if they had, John does not say Jesus died at the sixth hour; rather, this is the time Pilate delivers Jesus over to the Jewish authorities. (3) There is no mention of the slaughter of the lambs in the passage, nor any mention of Jesus as Lamb of God here. (4) Indeed, in John's Gospel, "Lamb of God" is a term used only in John 1:29 and 36, on the lips of John the Baptist. It has been a long time since John has employed this title in his narrative, and it can scarcely be called a dominant one. (5) While "lamb" *will* characterize John's Christology in the book of Revelation, that book was most likely not yet written when the Gospel of John was, and the word for "lamb" is consistently a different one (*arnion* rather than *amnos*).[96]

---

[94] Cf. Story, "The Bearing of Old Testament Terminology on the Johannine Chronology of the Final Passover of Jesus," 318; Ridderbos, *Gospel of John*, 806; Burge, *John*, 108; Kruse, *Gospel According to John*, 364.

[95] So most commentators. Perhaps none is more exaggerated in his enthusiasm for this view than Kenton L. Sparks, *God's Word in Human Words: An Evangelical Appropriation of Critical Biblical Scholarship* (Grand Rapids: Baker, 2008), 162–64.

[96] For what can fairly be said about John's "Lamb of God" theology in the Gospel, see Andreas J. Köstenberger, *A Theology of John's Gospel and Letters* (Grand Rapids: Zondervan, 2009), 414–15.

But what of a different kind of supposed contradiction? Mark 15:25 says it was nine o'clock in the morning (literally, the third hour) when they crucified him, referring to the beginning of a six-hour ordeal (cf. vv. 33–34). So was it 9:00 a.m. or noon when the process began? Here one must recognize that John wrote merely "about [Gk. *hōs*] noon." In the first-century Mediterranean world, the most precise instrument for measuring time was the sundial, and its use was scarcely widespread. Most people estimated time by where the sun was in the sky and often were no more precise in reporting than according to the quarters of the day or night—the third, sixth, ninth, and twelfth hours. An event happening midway between two of these markers could easily be "rounded off" to one or the other.[97] It is only when we demand modern standards of precision of ancient documents that such discrepancies become labeled full-fledged errors or mistakes!

Did Christ carry his own cross(bar) (John 19:17) or was Simon of Cyrene commandeered to do it for him (Mark 15:21)? A long history of Christian art and pageantry has resolved that issue by plausibly assuming that Jesus would have been ordered to carry his own crossbeam as was the common procedure. But so weakened by his preceding flogging, it is not realistic to imagine him making it all the way to Golgotha (or even very far along the way) without collapsing and requiring help.[98]

---

[97] Johnny V. Miller, "The Time of the Crucifixion," *Journal of the Evangelical Theological Society* 26 (1983): 157–66; Borchert, *John 12–21*, 28; Carson, *Gospel According to John*, 604–5; Morris, *John*, 708; Robert H. Stein, *Mark* (Grand Rapids: Baker, 2008), 713; Darrell L. Bock, *Jesus According to Scripture* (Grand Rapids: Baker; Leicester: Apollos, 2002), 504.

[98] On the details of crucifixion and the preceding torture that often accompanied it, see especially Martin Hengel, *Crucifixion* (London: SCM; Philadelphia: Fortress, 1977); and for the way such execution was viewed, see especially David W. Chapman, *Ancient Jewish and Christian Perceptions of Crucifixion* (Tübingen: Mohr Siebeck, 2008). For this harmonization, see, e.g., Raymond E. Brown, *John XIII–XXI* (Garden City: Doubleday, 1970), 899; Robinson, *Priority of John*, 276.

That Jesus was concerned for his mother and the beloved disciple in the midst of his agony (John 19:26–27) occasions little surprise after we read in Luke that he could pronounce forgiveness on his executioners even as they were tormenting him (Luke 23:34).

That he would be thirsty is the most natural element in the entire scene (John 19:28), and "It is finished" (v. 30) is almost as natural a way to declare the end of one's life at hand. John would have rightly understood both statements as far more profound at a spiritual level, as he does his various typological fulfillments of Scripture in the Passion Narrative and elsewhere.[99] But these additional elements in no way detract from the probable historicity of Jesus's words. Indeed, as in the Synoptics, the more the Old Testament text seems *not* to have been originally about an event in the life of the Messiah, the less likely it is that John made it up. Rather, the events of Jesus's life were the constraints with which he had to work, as he mined the Scriptures to find precedent for them.[100] Giving up his spirit in death (v. 30b) corresponds closely to the committing of his spirit to God in Luke 23:46. That the soldiers did not break Jesus's bones to speed his death because a spear thrust confirmed that he was already dead (John 19:33–34) likewise typologically fulfilled prophecies of David and Zechariah (vv. 36–37; cf. Ps 34:20 and Zech 12:10) but were also the expected consequences of Jesus's dying unusually rapidly on a cross, again doubtless due to his greatly weakened state.[101] The outflow of water and blood points to a true, human death—blood from the heart

---

[99] On which, see esp. Andreas J. Köstenberger, "John," in *Commentary on the New Testament Use of the Old Testament*, ed. G. K. Beale and D. A. Carson (Grand Rapids: Baker; Nottingham: Apollos, 2007), 415–512. For the quotations in John 19, see David E. Garland, "The Fulfillment Quotations in John's Account of the Crucifixion," in *Perspectives on John*, 229–50.

[100] Douglas J. Moo, *The Old Testament in the Gospel Passion Narratives* (Sheffield: Almond, 1983; Eugene, OR: Wipf & Stock, 2008), 278.

[101] At the same time, in keeping with John's theme of Jesus's remaining in control of events during his passion, the rapid death described as his bowing his

and water from the pericardial sac, precisely what emerges immediately after expiry before fluids begin to coagulate and the corpse begins to harden.[102]

The Synoptics (Mark 1:43–45 pars.) agree with John 19:38–42 on the role of Joseph of Arimathea in Christ's burial. The strong Jewish concern not to desecrate the Sabbath with an unburied corpse makes Joseph's actions highly probable (cf. Deut 21:23; Josephus, *Bell.* 4.317), notwithstanding what some authorities might have done or not done to a convicted criminal's body at another time during the week.[103] John adds that Nicodemus accompanied him, bringing enough aromatic spices for the corpse of a king.[104] If he had been growing in his appreciation for Jesus since his nighttime interview in chapter 3, which his defense of Jesus's right to a fair hearing in 7:50–51 suggests, then this lavish honor proves less surprising.

As in our survey of the Synoptics, we will save questions about the resurrection narratives until our treatment of miracles and resurrections together (chap. 14). We could have gone into more detail even without a discussion of the final two chapters of John's Gospel. But for now it is enough to bring this chapter to a conclusion and to prepare the way for a study of the Acts of the Apostles.

---

head and giving up his spirit may well imply that he voluntarily chose when to stop struggling against death. See especially Michaels, *Gospel of John*, 965.

[102] John Wilkinson, "The Incident of the Blood and Water in John 19.34," *Scottish Journal of Theology* 28 (1975): 149–72.

[103] A point repeatedly stressed by William L. Craig. See, e.g., his "Opening Address," in *Will the Real Jesus Please Stand Up? A Debate Between William Lane Craig and John Dominic Crossan*, ed. Paul Copan (Grand Rapids: Baker, 1998), 26–27. Cf. Beasley-Murray, *John*, 38. Philo (*Flacc.* 83) knows of others taken down from crosses when a holiday was at hand, and the Mishnah makes provision for the court to provide tombs for those they execute (*Sanh.* 6.5).

[104] Ben Witherington III, *John's Wisdom: A Commentary on the Fourth Gospel* (Louisville: Westminster John Knox, 1995), 312.

Conclusion

Not every detail in the Gospel of John can be corroborated. Many details in most ancient histories cannot be corroborated because most ancient evidence is forever lost. But key details in virtually every passage in the Gospel fit in well with some elements in the Synoptics, cut against the grain of John's overall theological emphases, or have been supported by archaeology, topography, or other ancient literature. Several authors are today calling for a fourth quest of the historical Jesus.[105] The first, nineteenth-century quest largely re-created Jesus in the philosophical or religious image of the questers. The second, mid-twentieth century quest rehabilitated a key core of the Synoptic sayings and deeds of Jesus. The third, late twentieth and early twenty-first century quest has finally placed Jesus squarely within his early first-century Jewish context and suggested that a substantial majority of the multiply attested features of the Synoptic tradition appear to be historical.[106] A fourth quest would take John's Gospel as seriously as the Synoptics as a source for discovering historical information about Jesus. It is time for such a quest to begin.[107]

---

[105] See esp. Anderson, *The Fourth Gospel and the Quest for Jesus*, 192.

[106] See esp. Ben Witherington III, *The Jesus Quest: The Third Search for the Jew of Nazareth*, rev. ed. (Downers Grove: IVP, 1997); Craig A. Evans, "Assessing Progress in the Third Quest of the Historical Jesus," *Journal for the Study of the Historical Jesus* 4 (2006): 35–54.

[107] See further Craig L. Blomberg, "The Historical Jesus from the Synoptics and the Fourth Gospel? Jesus the Purifier," in *The Message of Jesus: John Dominic Crossan and Ben Witherington III in Dialogue*, ed. Robert B. Stewart (Minneapolis: Fortress, 2013), 163–79.

Part Three

Acts and Paul

Chapter 6

The Credibility of Acts

W hen we turn from the Gospels to the Acts of the Apostles, our task becomes both easier and harder. It is easier because we have only one document covering the first generation of church history, so we don't have to deal with apparent discrepancies between parallel accounts. It is harder because we have no other accounts of this same period with which to compare Acts for any purposes, including corroborating material attested independently. There is a "Synoptic problem" on a small scale as one compares information in Acts, mostly about Paul's life and ministry, with what Paul discloses firsthand in his letters, and we will reserve chapter 7 for this topic. Here we want to assess, to the extent we are able, the historical credibility of Acts on its own, apart from the epistles of Paul.

Background Considerations

Setting

Traditionally the church has ascribed Acts to Luke, the author of the Third Gospel. Acts 1:1–2 clearly intends to tie this narrative together with the Gospel of Luke, as the author begins, "In my former book, Theophilus, I wrote about all that Jesus began to do and to teach until the day he was taken up to heaven, after giving instructions through the Holy Spirit to the apostles he had chosen." Given that Jesus is no longer physically present with his followers throughout most of this latter book, it is striking that the author refers to his Gospel as containing what Jesus *began* to do and teach. Presumably he understands the Acts as what Jesus *continues* to do and teach, through his Spirit, in the lives of his closest followers. [1]

Virtually all modern scholars agree that Luke and Acts were written by the same person.[2] The style of writing remains similar throughout both volumes, and many of the same themes are emphasized as well. We have already discussed reasons for accepting the tradition

---

[1] I. Howard Marshall, *The Acts of the Apostles* (Leicester: IVP; Grand Rapids: Eerdmans, 1980), 56; John B. Polhill, *Acts* (Nashville: Broadman, 1992), 79–80.

[2] But see Patricia Walters, *The Assumed Authorial Unity of Luke-Acts: A Reassessment of the Evidence* (Cambridge: Cambridge University Press, 2009). Even the dominant view of authorial unity does not necessarily require the two volumes to have been written back-to-back in a short period of time or with the identical themes, style, or literary genre throughout. For the most dramatic emphasis on the differences between the two volumes, see Mikeal C. Parsons and Richard I. Pervo, *Rethinking the Unity of Luke-Acts* (Minneapolis: Fortress, 1993). Cf. also several of the essays in Andrew F. Gregory and C. Kavin Rowe, eds., *Rethinking the Unity and Reception of Luke and Acts* (Columbia: University of South Carolina Press, 2010). For a full exploration of the topic from diverse perspectives, see Giuseppe Alberigo, ed., *The Unity of Luke-Acts* (Leuven: Peeters, 2009). For a persuasive defense of the unity, see Joel B. Green, "Luke-Acts, or Luke and Acts? A Reaffirmation of Narrative Unity," in *Reading Acts Today*, ed. Steve Walton, Thomas E. Phillips, Lloyd Keith Pietersen, and F. Scott Spencer (London and New York: T & T Clark, 2011), 101–19.

that the medical doctor Luke, a part-time traveling companion of the apostle Paul, is the author in each case, while acknowledging that many today doubt this attribution (see above). A key phenomenon in Acts, not found in the Gospel of Luke, is the sudden shift in several places from third-person narration to first-person plural form (16:10–17; 20:5–21:18; 27:1–28:16). Without preparation the author begins to refer to what "we" did and then just as suddenly returns to speaking exclusively about what others did. In each case these shifts occur in places where Paul is present, supporting the idea that the author is at times his companion and at times absent.[3]

Two other theories have competed with this one, especially in modern scholarship. Might the author have been copying the travel diaries of one who had been a companion of Paul and eyewitness of the events narrated in the first person?[4] It is not entirely obvious why such an author would not modify his wording, either to indicate that this was what he was doing or to make the narrative in the third person throughout. For purposes of assessing historicity, however, the written record of an eyewitness copied verbatim is as valuable as the remembered record of an eyewitness turned into writing later. For all we know, Luke might have been quoting his *own* diaries, thus creating

---

[3] See William S. Campbell, *The "We" Passages in the Acts of the Apostles: The Narrator as Narrative Character* (Atlanta: SBL, 2007), for a literary study that demonstrates the narrative role of such passages in Acts and other Greco-Roman histories as defending and projecting "the narrator's personal knowledge as eyewitness or researcher, and, therefore, his credentials for telling the story accurately" (p. 90) without weighing in on the accuracy of that projection for Acts itself.

[4] See esp. Stanley E. Porter, "The 'We-Passages,'" in *The Book of Acts in Its Greco-Roman Setting*, ed. David W. J. Gill and Conrad H. Gempf (Carlisle: Paternoster; Grand Rapids: Eerdmans, 1994), 545–74; Stanley E. Porter, *The Paul of Acts* (Tübingen: J. C. B. Mohr, 1999 [= *Paul in Acts* (Peabody: Hendrickson, 2001)]), 10–46. More cautiously, cf. A. J. M. Wedderburn, "The 'We-' Passages in Acts: On the Horns of a Dilemma," *Zeitschrift für die neutestamentliche Wissenschaft* 93 (2002): 78–98.

the doubly helpful written record of an eyewitness later copied into a larger account written by that same individual.

The other theory is that the first-person plural is a fictional device used especially in narratives of sea voyages.[5] Each of Acts' "we-passages" is closely related to a part of Paul's journeying that includes boat trips, but first-person-plural narration is found in other ancient genres as well, both fictional and factual, and it is not always present in fiction, not even in fictional voyages, so this solution seems improbable.[6] Besides, a writer of fiction would have most likely integrated his material better, creating smoother seams between the first- and third-person sections. Historical constraints of some kind must have prevented him from doing so.

We suggested in our discussion of the Gospel of Luke that a good case could be made for dating Luke and Acts to AD 62 because nothing at the end of Acts that has happened took place any later than that date and because Acts ends surprisingly abruptly. Luke has been following the journeys of Paul and, from the end of chapter 21 onwards, his arrest, trials, and imprisonments. Now he is awaiting the outcome of his appeal to the emperor in Rome, but the narrative simply breaks off. We also noted that Luke may have wanted to tell the story just as far as Paul's making it to Rome, the capital of the empire, and that he would have thought it a perfectly proper ending to conclude with the kingdom of God being proclaimed boldly even while Paul was under house arrest. The paradox of Paul's teaching "without hindrance" (Acts 28:31), when he was personally hindered by being loosely chained to a rotation of soldiers day and night, creates a sufficiently striking and

---

[5] See esp. Vernon K. Robbins, "By Land and by Sea: The We-Passages and Ancient Sea-Voyages," in *Perspectives on Luke Acts*, ed. C. H. Talbert (Danville, VA: NABPR, 1978), 215–42.

[6] See esp. Colin J. Hemer, "First Person Narrative in Acts 27–28," *Tyndale Bulletin* 36 (1985): 79–109. Cf. also Susan M. Praeder, "The Problem of First Person Narration in Acts," *Novum Testamentum* 29 (1987): 193–218.

dramatic ending. The open-ended nature of Acts could link the narrative "to an expansive story that stretches to the end of the age," as suggested by 1:1, 8, and 11.[7]

All this is true. Yet none of it explains why Luke has spent a disproportionate time highlighting each of Paul's hearings. Nor does it clarify why Luke repeats Paul's testimony at each of them, creating a fair amount of redundancy on a scroll that could not have been much bigger than what the twenty-eight chapters of Acts would have occupied. Luke certainly knows how to streamline accounts elsewhere. Andrew Clark has highlighted in considerable detail all the parallels Luke deliberately indicates between the ministries of Peter and Paul on the one hand and Jesus on the other.[8] All three heal chronically crippled individuals (Luke 13:10–13; Acts 3:1–10; 14:8–10), all three cure those bedridden with illness (Luke 4:38–39; Acts 9:32–35; 28:7–10), and all three bring people back to life (Luke 7:11–17; Acts 9:36–42; 20:9–12). Jesus, Peter, and Paul perform miracles of destruction or punishment (Luke 8:32–33; Acts 5:1–11; 13:6–11), all testify boldly before their Jewish interrogators (Luke 22:67–71; Acts 4:18–20; 23:1–6), and all have enemies who intend to put them to death (Luke 23:16–24; Acts 12:1–4; 23:12–22). With Jesus, it is God's plan that he indeed be executed, but it is not his will for Peter to die, at least not at the time in which he is imprisoned within the narrative of Acts (12:5–11). Surely if Luke knew whether Paul was executed after his house arrest in Rome, he would have wanted to recount that information.

Some scholars have drawn the connections even more tightly. It is widely agreed that Luke 9:51, without any parallel in other Gospels,

---

[7] Troy M. Troftgruben, *A Conclusion Unhindered: A Study of the Ending of Acts Within Its Literary Environment* (Tübingen: Mohr Siebeck, 2010), 188. This work also thoroughly surveys all the main proposals for the reason for Acts' ending as we find it.

[8] Andrew Clark, *Parallel Lives: The Relation of Paul to the Apostles in the Lucan Perspective* (Carlisle: Paternoster, 2000), 150–260.

marks the beginning of Luke's unique central travel narrative and indicates an emphasis in his Gospel on Jesus's journeying to the cross. Acts 19:21 can then be seen as Luke's equivalent passage in his second volume: "After all this had happened, Paul decided to go to Jerusalem, passing through Macedonia and Achaia. 'After I have been there,' he said, 'I must visit Rome also.'"[9] This explains why Luke can view his narrative as complete after Paul reaches Rome but not why he refuses to tell us the outcome of Paul's appeal, if he knows it. If Paul were executed (as he was at least by AD 68), the parallels with his Lord would be so striking that Luke could scarcely have omitted them.

But what if Paul were initially acquitted and released, freed for further ministry, only to be rearrested and condemned several years later, as two key early Christian sources allege (1 Clem. 5:5–7; Eusebius, *Hist. eccl.* 2.22)? What if Luke were writing between Paul's release and his second arrest? One could argue that Luke didn't want to portray Paul's escaping a fate that Jesus himself couldn't avoid. But then it would be hard to understand why Luke includes Acts 20:25 within his narrative. Here Paul declares confidently to the Ephesian elders, "Now I know that none of you among whom I have gone about preaching the kingdom will ever see me again." No doubt that was Paul's genuine conviction based both on his own travel plans and whatever premonitions of the future the Lord had given him. But if he were a free man again when Luke was writing, Luke could easily have envisioned his returning to Ephesus, especially because Paul speaks in Philippians about returning eastward from Rome at least as far as Philippi when he is released from prison, as he believes he will be (Phil 2:24). On this scenario it would have made more sense for Luke to omit such a potentially falsifiable prediction by the apostle.

---

[9] C. H. Talbert, *Reading Acts* (New York: Crossroad, 1997; Macon: Smyth & Helwys, 2005), 12.

Not only does Acts end abruptly with the events of AD 62, with no mention of what happened to Paul subsequently, but it also contains no reference to the persecution of Christians by Nero (64–68), the martyrdom of Peter during that persecution, the Jewish rebellion against Rome beginning in 66, or the fall of Jerusalem in 70. Of course these are all arguments from silence, but the accumulation of the silences can be deafening. Acts *does* contain frequent references to persecution of Christians prior to 62, the earlier martyrdom of Stephen, the tensions between Jews and Romans elsewhere, and Roman authorities squelching Jewish protests. One would normally have expected that if Acts were written after 70, the culmination of these various trends, then some hint of these events would appear somewhere in Luke's second volume.[10]

As we saw earlier, most of the arguments for a late date for Luke-Acts surround the assumption that the Gospel knows that the destruction of Jerusalem has occurred (recall above). Take away this plank from their platform, and proponents have little reason to support a post-70 date. Indeed, one wonders if Luke at a later time would have taken such a consistently pro-Roman approach in Acts as he does. In every instance local Jews (and occasionally a few local pagans) are the ones who persecute Paul and his companions, whereas the Roman government consistently winds up rescuing him or declaring his innocence (Acts 16:35–40; 18:12–17; 23:23–35; 26:31–32). Only prior to the beginning of Nero's persecution in AD 64 would this pattern reflect what the regular experience of believers was. None of this proves the reliability of Acts, of course, but it does place the author within one generation in a time and place to be able to gather large amounts of

---

[10] See further Eckhard J. Schnabel, *Acts* (Grand Rapids: Zondervan, 2012), 27–28.

accurate information about the fledgling church.[11] Conversely, if Acts turns out to have been written in the 80s, with a majority of more liberal scholars, the nature of the oral tradition along with the presence of living eyewitnesses from the years canvassed would still have placed the author in an excellent position to report reliable history by ancient standards. And this would remain true even if the writer turned out to be some anonymous Christian other than Luke.[12]

A tiny group of contemporary scholars date Acts as late as about 110, on the assumption that its anonymous author knew and drew on the collected letters of Paul, partook of a theological and ecclesiastical atmosphere that did not exist until the early second century, and did not have access to reliable, independent sources of information besides Paul's epistles.[13] A number of these scholars participated in the Acts Seminar in the 2000s that dissected Acts the way the Jesus Seminar dismembered the Gospels in the 1990s. But they assert their position as a presupposition of their work far more than genuinely arguing for it. And the few arguments they do put forward include the improbable positions that Luke knew and used Josephus and the letters of Paul, that the Pastoral Epistles should be dated to the second century, and that a linear, evolutionary trajectory can be traced between first- and second-century Christianity, so that when Acts resembles

---

[11] See esp. Colin J. Hemer, *The Book of Acts in the Setting in Hellenistic History*, ed. Conrad H. Gempf (Tübingen: J. C. B. Mohr, 1989; Winona Lake, IN: Eisenbrauns, 1990), 365–410.

[12] Conservatives supporting a date in the 70s or 80s include David J. Williams, *Acts*, rev. ed. (Peabody: Hendrickson, 1990; Grand Rapids: Baker, 2011), 11–13; Ben Witherington, *The Acts of the Apostles: A Socio-Rhetorical Commentary* (Grand Rapids: Eerdmans; Carlisle: Paternoster, 1998), 62; and Craig S. Keener, *Acts: An Exegetical Commentary*, vol. 1 (Grand Rapids: Baker, 2012), 383–401.

[13] See esp. Richard I. Pervo, *Dating Acts: Between the Evangelists and the Apologists* (Santa Rosa: Polebridge, 2006).

the Pastorals, it too should be dated almost a century after the beginning of the church.[14]

When it comes to source criticism, we actually know how the author of the Gospel of Luke treated his sources—quite conservatively by ancient standards. He consistently abbreviated Mark's Gospel rather than embellishing it. And he is regularly viewed as preserving a form of Q closer to the original than Matthew does.[15] But the only reason we know this is because we have all three Synoptic Gospels. We have no reason to assume he operated any differently for the Acts; we just have little ability to determine any written sources he may have used. But it is most natural to envision his treating them with the same care and relative conservatism we can observe him employing in his Gospel.[16] We do know that Greek and Roman orators often wrote speeches down and then memorized them to deliver them orally, so it is even possible that Luke had access to such documents when he was summarizing the various main characters' speeches in Acts.[17]

Genre

After a variety of proposals competed for acceptance, the Gospels today have been widely acknowledged to be a form of ancient Greco-Roman biography, as we have seen. Unfortunately, a consensus on Acts

---

[14] See throughout Dennis E. Smith and Joseph B. Tyson, eds., *Acts and Christian Beginnings: The Acts Seminar Report* (Salem, OR: Polebridge, 2013). For a response, see Keener, *Acts*, vol. 1, 395–400.

[15] See throughout James M. Robinson, Paul Hoffmann, and John S. Kloppenborg, *The Critical Edition of Q* (Minneapolis: Fortress, 2000).

[16] Sean A. Adams, "On Sources and Speeches: Methodological Discussions in Ancient Prose Works and Luke-Acts," in *Christian Origins and Classical Culture: Literary and Social Contexts for the New Testament*, ed. Stanley E. Porter and Andrew W. Pitts, vol. 1 (Leiden: Brill, 2012), 389–411. For a valiant effort at reconstructing these sources, see Joseph A. Fitzmyer, *The Acts of the Apostles* (New York and London: Doubleday, 1998), 80–88.

[17] Schnabel, *Acts*, 127–28.

has been harder to achieve.[18] On the one hand, we might imagine that if Luke and Acts are taken as two halves of a combined work they should each share the same literary genre. But the Gospels are clearly about one main character—Jesus—while no one individual dominates all parts of Acts. Peter takes center stage in the opening chapters after Jesus ascends to heaven as the first leader of the Twelve. Stephen is the main character in 6:8–8:3. Philip unites the rest of chapter 8. Chapter 9:1–31 describes Saul's conversion, who will become better known by his Latin name Paul. Chapter 9:32 through 12:24 can be seen as unified around Peter's activities again, though a few of the subsections of this segment of Acts do not contain any reference to Peter (11:19–30 and 12:19b–24). Finally, from 12:25 to the end of the book Saul/Paul becomes the clear protagonist.

One attractive option is to label Acts what Sean Adams calls "collected biography."[19] Hellenized writers like Cornelius Nepos, Philo, Plutarch, Diogenes Laertius, and many others wrote and compiled multiple biographies in single volumes, often highlighting the parallels among them. Clark's work demonstrates that the parallels between Peter and Paul at times extend to other early Christians in Luke's narrative, like Stephen and Philip.[20] Yet it does not appear that Luke set out to create a complete biography of any of his Christian protagonists, even by the selective standards of the ancient world. What unifies Acts, despite its traditional title as the Acts of the Apostles, is that it is the equally selective account of the progress of the gospel as itemized in Acts 1:8 under the power and guidance of the Holy Spirit.

---

[18] Thomas E. Phillips ("The Genre of Acts: Moving Toward a Consensus?" *Currents in Biblical Research* 4 [2006]: 365–96) offers a good survey of recent proposals, but his claim of an emerging consensus applies only to the milieu of the Acts Seminar and a handful of other scholars!

[19] Sean A. Adams, *The Genre of Acts and Collected Biography* (Cambridge: Cambridge University Press, 2013).

[20] Clark, *Parallel Lives*, 261–93.

A handful of recent scholars have argued strongly for viewing Acts as much more fictional in nature than Greco-Roman biography typically was. Leading this movement is Richard Pervo, who highlights the numerous signs of literary artistry, adventure, and entertainment throughout Luke's second volume. He believes Acts should be characterized as an "ancient novel," which he defines as "a relatively lengthy work of prose fiction depicting or deriving certain ideals through an entertaining presentation of the lives and experiences of a person or persons whose activity transcends the limits of ordinary living as known to its implied readers."[21] Scholars like Dennis MacDonald and Marianne Palmer Bonz have gone one step farther and likened Acts to classic Greco-Roman epics like Homer's *Iliad* and *Odyssey* or Virgil's *Aeneid*, respectively.[22]

The problem with the latter proposal is that epics in the ancient world were consistently composed as poetry. Their scale and scope were much vaster and their focus on heroic values much more central.[23] The thematic parallels offered between Homer or Virgil on the one hand and Luke's narrative on the other are often either the kinds of stereotypical scenes found in historical and fictional works alike, or they are vague enough as to prove fairly little. Pervo rightly notes that ancient novels could at times involve some genuine historical characters, but no known parallels from antiquity have such an intense concentration of known individuals, exact locations, accurate customs, and which dovetail with the autobiographical and factual writings of

---

[21] Richard I. Pervo, *Profit with Delight: The Literary Genre of the Acts of the Apostles* (Philadelphia: Fortress, 1987), 105.

[22] Dennis R. MacDonald, *Does the New Testament Imitate Homer? Four Cases from the Acts of the Apostles* (New Haven and London: Yale University Press, 2003); Marianne Palmer Bonz, *The Past as Legacy: Luke-Acts and Ancient Epic* (Minneapolis: Fortress, 2000).

[23] Loveday C. A. Alexander, *Acts in Its Ancient Literary Context: A Classicist Looks at the Acts of the Apostles* (London and New York: T & T Clark, 2005), 181.

one of the main characters in the novel as Acts does. In fact, historical novels as we think of them today, with fictional activities and at least partly fictional characters set in a carefully researched and historically plausible setting, barely existed at all in antiquity and are largely the creation of the last several centuries of world history.[24] Of course, one could choose to highlight simply how no genre fits Acts exactly, leaving one free to posit whatever combination of history and fiction one perceives based on parallels to small, constituent literary forms within the book.[25] But such a combination actually leaves Acts overall less like *any* work from antiquity than the various specific proposals for an identifiable genre do.

In the ancient Mediterranean world, far more common were novels with deliberate, obvious historical "errors" to tip the author's hand to his intent to write fiction. For example, early on the Jewish intertestamental novel Judith, canonized in the Catholic Apocrypha, is riddled with inaccuracies and improbabilities that most ancient readers would have immediately recognized. Bruce Metzger sums up matters forcefully:

> The consensus, at least among Protestant and Jewish scholars, is that the story is sheer fiction. Apart from exaggerations in numbers (1:4, 16; 2:5, 15; 7:2, 17), such as are found even in acknowledged historical works of the time, the book teems with chronological, historical, and geographical improbabilities and downright errors. For example, Holofernes moves an immense army about three hundred miles in three days (2:21). The opening words of the book, when taken with 2:1ff. and 4:2f., involve the most astonishing historical nonsense, for the author places Nebuchadnezzar's reign over the Assyrians (in

---

[24] The classic work here is Erich Auerbach, *Mimesis: The Representation of Reality in Western Literature* (Princeton: Princeton University Press, 1953).

[25] As, e.g., with Alan J. Bale, *Genre and Narrative Coherence in the Acts of the Apostles* (London and New York: Bloomsbury T & T Clark, 2015).

reality he was king of Babylon) at Nineveh (which fell seven years before his accession!) at a time when the Jews had only recently returned from the captivity (actually at this time they were suffering further deportations)! Nebuchadnezzar did not make war on Media (1:7), nor capture Ecbatana (1:14). It is passing strange that Bethulia, a city of such strategic importance, is otherwise unknown. The rebuilding of the Temple (4:13) is dated, by a glaring anachronism, about a century too early. Moreover, the Jewish state is represented as being under the government of a high priest and a kind of Sanhedrin (6:6–14; 15:8), which is compatible only with a post-exilic date several hundred years after the book's presumed historical setting.[26]

The same is true of Tobit, another popular novel from the Old Testament Apocrypha, though not to the same extent. In 1:4, Tobit claims to have lived through events spanning the years 928–722 BC, even though later he is said to have lived only 112 years (14:2). In 1:15, Shalmaneser is said to be the father of Sennacherib, rather than Sargon II, his true father. Tobit 5:6 claims that the journey from Ecbatana to Rages takes two days and that Ecbatana "is in the middle of the plain." But the two locations were 185 miles apart and Ecbatana was located in the mountains.[27] Daniel Harrington, a Roman Catholic commentator, notes that "the sequence of Assyrian kings is incomplete and inaccurate (no mentions of Tiglath-pileser III and Sargon II), and the geographical information is sometimes confused. The book is best

---

[26] Bruce M. Metzger, *An Introduction to the Apocrypha*, rev. ed. (New York: Oxford University Press, 1977), 50–51. Cf. Carey A. Moore, *Judith* (Garden City: Doubleday, 1985), 46–49.

[27] Amy Jill-Levine, "Tobit," in *The New Oxford Annotated Apocrypha*, 4th ed. (Oxford: Oxford University Press, 2010), 11, 13, 18.

understood not as a memoir but rather as a historical novel set in the distant past."[28]

Even when an ancient novel did not tip its hand as obviously as this, numerous additional features set them off as a distinct genre. Witherington lists several key features absent from the Acts of the Apostles: romance, the reuniting of two parties long separated, a happy ending or closure at the conclusion, "encounters with colorful pirates or bandits," and a consistent focus on one or two main characters. The interest is in developing biographical detail of these individuals to a much greater extent than what we find in Acts.[29] And unlike the occasional novel that is littered with geographical information to generate delight in holy places or demonstrate authorial expertise, "Luke usually uses exact geographical information only when it is there in the tradition and is significant for the narrative or for his theology."[30] Loveday Alexander concludes that

> we may note it as significant in this regard that Luke's presentation of the travel element in detail is closer to the factual, pragmatic *periplous* [a "sailing around" of a body of water to report in detail on geography and topography] tradition than to the novels, at least to Chariton and Xenophon. Paul's adventures, unlike those of Callirhoe or Anthia [protagonists in mid-first-century romantic novels], happen in a realistic, contemporary landscape, a world of trading ships not of triremes.[31]

---

[28] Daniel J. Harrington, *Invitation to the Apocrypha* (Grand Rapids: Eerdmans, 1999), 11. Carey A. Moore (*Tobit* [Garden City: Doubleday, 1996], 17–21) discusses the book's fictional genre, and unpacks it as ironic comedy (24–26).

[29] Witherington, *Acts of the Apostles*, 376–81, esp. 377–78.

[30] Martin Hengel, "The Geography of Palestine in Acts," in *The Book of Acts in Its Palestinian Setting*, ed. Richard Bauckham (Grand Rapids: Eerdmans, Carlisle: Paternoster, 1995), 67.

[31] Alexander, *Acts in Its Ancient Literary Context*, 119.

Pervo peppers his commentary on Acts with references to alleged parallels from ancient myths and legends, but if one looks up a representative sampling of them and reads them in context, precious few prove at all close.[32]

The most likely genre for Acts is therefore some form of ancient history writing. The term *praxeis* ("acts") was not widely used with Jewish or Greco-Roman book titles, but when it was, it was typically attached to accounts of "the deeds of a single great individual, such as Alexander the Great (Diodorus Siculus, *Library of History* 17.15; 18.1.6) or Augustus," with the Latin equivalent, *Res gestae divi Augusti*. At times, however, it referred to a group as with the "Acts of the Early Kings" (Diodorus Siculus, *Library of History*, 3.1.1.).[33] That numerous, largely fictional acts of various apostles (e.g., Acts of Andrew, Acts of John, Acts of Peter, Acts of Thomas, Acts of Paul and Thecla) were produced in the second and third centuries does not suggest that the original Acts of the Apostles was fictional any more than apocryphal epistles demonstrated anything about the authenticity of the New Testament letters. They were later, sometimes fanciful attempts to fill in the perceived gaps in Luke's account. It is historically backwards or anachronistic to use later documents to interpret earlier ones.[34]

The two most common and helpful suggestions for a more precise delineation of the kind of history Luke intended to write are

---

[32] Thanks to my research assistant, Clint Wilson, who did precisely this for a large number of the most accessible sources Pervo cites. When one reads these sources by themselves without having just read a specific passage from Acts, one is often hard-pressed to guess even what passage in Luke's second volume Pervo has linked them with because the parallels are so vague or else so commonplace.

[33] Darrell L. Bock, *Acts* (Grand Rapids: Baker, 2007), 1–2.

[34] On these later writings, see especially Hans-Josef Klauck, *The Apocryphal Acts of the Apostles: An Introduction* (Waco: Baylor University Press, 2008). On the greater parallels between the apocryphal acts and fictitious biographies than with the canonical Acts, see François Bovon, "Canonical and Apocryphal Acts of the Apostles," *Journal of Early Christian Studies* 11 (2003): 165–94.

the "historical monograph" and "apologetic history."[35] The former would account for the comparatively short length of Acts; the latter, for Luke's repeated defense of the legality and legitimacy of the early Christian movement, especially in the eyes of Rome.[36] But, as with the Gospels when compared with ancient biography, Acts does not perfectly match any one subgenre of ancient history, so it is best to recognize it as a mixture of forms.[37] Given its clear theological emphases, it may be best simply to refer to it as theological historiography, just as the Gospels can be considered theological biography.[38]

While it was universally assumed that history was recounted for ideological reasons, that is, to inculcate lessons from the past to guide one's living in the present and future, the people of the ancient Mediterranean world nevertheless clearly distinguished between well-written, reasonably reliable history and sensationalizing, skewed history.[39] Which kind did Luke author? His prefaces resemble the opening sections of "scientific" prose.[40] His careful attention to detail that can be corroborated resembles the work of the best of ancient Greco-Roman historians, including Polybius, Herodotus, Thucydides, and Ephorus. His structure and contents suggest that he is drafting

---

[35] For these, along with less likely proposals, and their advocates, see the survey in Todd Penner, "Madness in the Method? The Acts of the Apostles in Current Study," *Currents in Biblical Research* 4 (2002): 233–41.

[36] See esp. Paul W. Walaskay, *"And So We Came to Rome": The Political Perspective of St. Luke* (Cambridge: Cambridge University Press, 1983).

[37] This is the conclusion throughout Claire K. Rothschild, *Luke-Acts and the Rhetoric of History: An Investigation of Early Christian Historiography* (Tübingen: Mohr Siebeck, 2004).

[38] Daniel Marguerat, *The First Christian Historian: Writing the "Acts of the Apostles"* (Cambridge: Cambridge University Press, 2002), 21.

[39] A. W. Mosley, "Historical Reporting and the Ancient World," *New Testament Studies* (1965): 10–26. The classic ancient Greco-Roman source was Lucian's *On Writing History*.

[40] Loveday Alexander, *The Preface to Luke's Gospel: Literary Convention and Social Context* (Cambridge: Cambridge University Press, 2005).

an institutional history, in this case of the fledgling church, a form of history-writing for which greater objectivity was important than with the military histories that proliferated.[41] His use of numbers (of people, of length of time elapsed, of chronology and dates—areas that were difficult for many to get right in Luke's world) are realistic, coherent, and at times can even be corroborated.[42] The way he integrates his source material, only rarely citing it directly, resembles the work of the better historians of his day.[43] His speeches are short, comparatively unadorned, but memorable, all of which support a fair degree of reliability in their transmission. Despite some claims to the contrary, they have enough details not characteristic of Luke's style to suggest they were really spoken by the people to whom they were attributed.[44]

All of these background considerations create a favorable impression of Luke as one whose writing is likely to have a high degree of historical accuracy by the standards of his day. None of them, however, proves the trustworthiness of any specific feature of the book of Acts.

---

[41] Hubert Cancik, "The History of Culture, Religion and Institutions in Ancient Historiography: Philological Observations Concerning Luke's History," *Journal of Biblical Literature* 116 (1997): 673–95.

[42] Cf. Paul L. Maier, "Luke as a Hellenistic Historian," in *Christian Origins and Classical Culture: Literary and Social Contexts for the New Testament*, ed. Stanley E. Porter and Andrew W. Pitts, vol. 2 (Leiden: Brill, 2013), vol. 1, esp. 426–30.

[43] Andrew W. Pitts, "Source Citation in Greek Historiography and in Luke (-Acts)," in *Christian Origins and Classical Culture*, ed. Porter and Pitts, 349–88.

[44] Colin J. Hemer, "The Speeches in Acts," *Tyndale Bulletin* 40 (1989): 77–85, 239–60; G. H. R. Horsley, "Speeches and Dialogue in Acts," *New Testament Studies* 32 (1986): 609–14; Conrad Gempf, "Public Speaking and Published Accounts," in *The Book of Acts in Its Ancient Literary Setting*, ed. Bruce W. Winter and Andrew D. Clarke (Grand Rapids: Eerdmans; Carlisle: Paternoster, 1993), 259–303. For categorization of the speeches under Hellenistic historiography, including Hellenistic Jewish forms, cf. also Marion L. Soards, *The Speeches in Acts: Their Content, Context, and Concerns* (Louisville: Westminster John Knox, 2004), 134–61. For a wide-ranging study, containing many of these summary conclusions about the book as a whole, see Martin Hengel, *Acts and the History of Earliest Christianity* (London: SCM; Philadelphia: Fortress, 1979; Eugene, OR: Wipf & Stock, 2003).

For an impression of Luke's reliability as a historian, we must survey the most significant details in Acts that can either be corroborated or reasonably be called into question. As mentioned at the beginning of this chapter, we will reserve treatment for comparisons with the letters of Paul for our next chapter but deal with a broad cross-section of the remaining kinds of issues here. As with the Gospels, we will reserve treatment of the miraculous for chapter 14.

Specific Details in Acts

The Church in Jerusalem (Acts 1:1–6:7)

Despite its dominance in the Synoptics, "the kingdom of God" is comparatively rare in the rest of the New Testament. It appears only eight times in Acts but always at strategic junctures.[45] Jesus continues to teach about it in his resurrection appearances to his disciples (Acts 1:3; cf. v. 6). Philip proclaims the good news of the kingdom in 8:12, as the gospel moves from Judea to Samaria. Paul on his first missionary journey teaches that "we must go through many hardships to enter the kingdom of God" (14:22) and summarizes his ministry when he addresses the Ephesian elders just before his final trip to Jerusalem as "preaching the kingdom" (20:25; cf. 19:8). Acts 28:23 and 31 round out the book with Paul's explaining about the kingdom in Rome also, forming an inclusio with 1:3. This is a reminder that Luke has not strayed far from bedrock Synoptic tradition even as he describes the gospel moving out, but neither does he have his characters employ a largely Jewish expression very often in non-Jewish contexts, which would be more historically implausible anyway.

Jesus's command not to start the world mission effort immediately (1:4) seems counterintuitive and would not likely have been invented.

---

[45] David G. Peterson, *The Acts of the Apostles* (Nottingham: Apollos; Grand Rapids: Eerdmans, 2009), 105.

The reference back to the nature of John's and Jesus's ministries (v. 5) corresponds closely to what all four Gospels agree on (Matt 3:11; Mark 1:8; Luke 3:16; John 1:33). Not knowing the times or seasons of Jesus's return (Acts 1:7) fits his own ignorance of the day and hour in his Olivet Discourse (Mark 13:32 pars.). Verse 8 might be viewed as Luke's invention because it matches closely the structure of his narrative, except for the fact that the "ends of the earth" for someone in the first-century Roman Empire, moving westward, would have more naturally been the west coast of the Iberian Peninsula, not Rome, where Luke ends.[46]

"A Sabbath day's walk" (1:12) was about a kilometer or five-eighths of a mile, an accurate figure for the distance from the Mount of Olives to Jerusalem.[47] The differences between Acts' account of Judas's death (Acts 1:18–19) and the one Gospel account of the same event (Matt 27:3–10) are well known. As we saw previously, I. H. Marshall, typically resistant to straightforward harmonizations if they are in the slightest implausible, nevertheless acknowledges the plausibility of one here. The consistent rockiness of the terrain around Jerusalem makes point 1 (p. 96) all the more likely. But why would the two accounts differ the way they do? Here redaction and literary criticism help answer the question as Matthew stresses the fulfillment of Scripture (though certainly not in any straightforward fashion that would suggest the narrative was created on the basis of the Scripture), while Acts highlights Judas's ignoble nature, programmatic for the persecution believers will receive throughout the volume.[48]

---

[46] E. Earle Ellis, "'The End of the Earth' (Acts 1:8)," *Bulletin for Biblical Research* 1 (1991): 123–32. Eckhard J. Schnabel (*Early Christian Mission*, vol. 1 [Downers Grove: IVP; Nottingham: Apollos, 2004], 372) believes no one fixed location is meant but "literally to the farther reaches of the inhabited world (known at the time)."

[47] For various options for even more exact distances, see Bock, *Acts*, 75–76.

[48] See esp. Jesse E. Robertson, *The Death of Judas: The Characterization of Judas Iscariot in Three Early Christian Accounts of his Death* (Sheffield: Sheffield Phoenix, 2012).

Peter's decision to replace Judas and preserve twelve persons as the disciples' "leadership team" would not likely have been invented on the basis of Psalms 69:25 and 109:8 (Acts 1:20) because the passages represent David's prayers against his enemies. But once Peter had decided that at the outset of this new movement there should still be twelve apostles, probably to match the twelve tribes of Israel,[49] one can see how he could have combed the Scriptures, and especially the psalms of David, looking for support, typologically, from what David wanted God to do to his archenemies.[50] That the candidates for replacing Judas had to have been with the larger group of disciples "beginning from John's baptism" and had to be able to testify to the resurrection (1:21–22) demonstrates Peter's (and Luke's) desire for credibility as the story about Jesus is transmitted. Casting lots to determine God's will (v. 26) was an accepted Jewish procedure (e.g., Lev 16:8; Josh 18:6, 8, 10; Jud 20:9; 1 Chron 24:5, 31; etc.); what is striking is that it never occurs again as the New Testament unfolds. Apparently guidance by the Holy Spirit, who permanently indwells believers from Pentecost onwards, is a more than sufficient substitute.[51] It is most unlikely, therefore, that a Christian author would have fictitiously ascribed this particular decision-making process to Jesus's followers at the beginning of the Christian movement.

Pentecost was one of the annual festivals when Jewish and God-fearing pilgrims from throughout the ancient world would converge

---

[49] James D. G. Dunn, *Beginning from Jerusalem* (Grand Rapids: Eerdmans, 2009), 152.

[50] Tzvi Novick ("Succeeding Judas: Exegesis in Acts 1:15–26," *Journal of Biblical Literature* 129 [2010]: 795–99) suggests that Peter saw the tension between leaving an enemy's place deserted and having another take his place of leadership and solved it by having Judas's replacement be someone who had been with the disciples all along so that he was really not new to the group, replacing Judas, just moving to a different role or office.

[51] Williams, *Acts*, 35. Cf. Polhill, *Acts*, 95; J. Bradley Chance, *Acts* (Macon: Smyth & Helwys, 2007), 41.

on Jerusalem. So Luke's depiction of individuals from all major parts of the Roman Empire (Acts 2:5–12) fits exactly what was expected. The subsequent Christian celebration of Pentecost makes sense only if ecstatic phenomena were experienced by the disciples on that date.[52] Peter's explanation of the phenomena of speaking in tongues draws on Old Testament passages quite differently than in chapter 2. Although plenty of scholars demur, a good case can actually be made for each of the three main prophecies he quotes being intended as Messianic predictions from the outset. Joel 2:28–32 (cited in Acts 2:17–21) appears in the context of restoration of God's people to an age of eschatological abundance after he has judged them for their sins in the present or near future.[53] Psalm 16:8–11 (quoted in Acts 2:25–28) cannot have been exhaustively fulfilled in the life of David for the reason Peter highlights: his body did decay in the grave (Acts 2:29).[54] Finally, while Jesus did silence his critics and amaze the crowds by using Psalm 110:1 in a Messianic fashion (Mark 12:36 pars.), there is evidence that at least some Jews had already recognized that this text must refer to a Messiah, as Peter insists here (Acts 2:34–35).[55]

The response to Peter's Pentecostal preaching leads to the baptism of 3,000 new adherents to the Jesus movement (2:41). Those who have scoffed at the credibility of the logistics required are apparently unfamiliar with the topography of ancient Jerusalem. A crowd of even larger size pressing in to hear Peter would have been easily contained in just a portion of the giant temple precincts. Approximately 150

---

[52] For the logic and rationale, see Dunn, *Beginning from Jerusalem*, 164–71.

[53] Cf. Duane A. Garrett, *Hosea, Joel* (Nashville: B&H, 1997), 367–69; Leslie C. Allen, *The Books of Joel, Obadiah, Jonah and Micah* (Grand Rapids: Eerdmans; London: Hodder & Stoughton, 1976), 98.

[54] Geoffrey W. Grogan, *Psalms* (Grand Rapids: Eerdmans, 2008); 63; Derek Kidner, *Psalms 1–72* (Leicester: Tyndale; Downers Grove: IVP, 1973), 86.

[55] For texts and discussion, see Craig L. Blomberg, "Matthew," in *Commentary on the New Testament Use of the Old Testament*, ed. G. K. Beale and D. A. Carson (Grand Rapids: Baker; Nottingham: Apollos, 2007), 83–84.

mikvaot or ritual immersion pools dotted the Jerusalem landscape, including the sizable pools of Bethesda and Siloam.[56] With at least 120 followers of Jesus already gathered together (cf. 2:1 with 1:15), they could have each taken on average twenty-five people to one of the pools, which was in regular use for ritually cleansing those offering sacrifices at the temple, and had them immersed to indicate the forgiveness of their sins. Or a smaller group of the 120 could have spent the next couple of hours with a larger number of new believers in one of the large pools, just as John had overseen the crowds at the Jordan River.[57]

Subsequent gatherings could have occurred only in the temple precincts if the entire group of believers had wanted to be together somewhere in Jerusalem. But while the apostles' instruction and prayers could readily occur in such a crowd, breaking bread and intimate fellowship would have required small groups in countless private homes. And these are precisely the activities and the locations that 2:42–47 depict the young church undertaking. The communal sharing of verses 44–45 must be interpreted in light of Luke's further unpacking of the procedures involved in 4:32–37. The NIV nicely brings out the iterative imperfects in verses 34–35: "For *from time to time* those who owned land or houses sold them, brought the money from the sales and put it at the apostles' feet." There was no once-for-all divestiture of possessions as an entrance requirement into the primitive church, as there was for full membership in the Essene community at Qumran.[58] But even if there had been, the Qumran model shows that communal sharing as an exemplary religious ideal was certainly known in the

[56] Keener, *Acts*, vol. 1, 995.

[57] On numerous related details, cf. further idem, "The Plausibility of Luke's Growth Figures in Acts 2:41; 4:4; 21:20," *Journal of Greco-Roman Christianity and Judaism* 7 (2010): 140–63.

[58] Rightly Schnabel, *Early Christian Mission*, vol. 1, 413; Witherington, *Acts of the Apostles*, 162; Marshall, *Acts*, 84.

world into which the first Christians came.[59] The common notion that Luke follows a Greek ideal of a utopian community to fictionally portray early Christian commensality founders on the fact that proponents of such an ideal could not have imagined it crossing socioeconomic boundaries. They envisioned only peers who were intimate friends as participants. In the words of Reta Halteman Finger, "The idea of redistributing possessions with the goal of eliminating poverty would have been unthinkable in Greco-Roman society."[60] Rather, the background is Levitical and thus the historicity probable.

In Acts 3:1, Luke correctly identifies the afternoon time of Jewish prayer as 3:00 p.m. (lit., the ninth hour—counting from 6:00 a.m.). Beggars frequented the areas outside the temple precincts because of the throngs that passed by (v. 2). The gate called Beautiful (vv. 2, 10) may well have been the lavishly adorned Nicanor Gate, with "Beautiful" as a nickname, though we are not sure.[61] Solomon's colonnade was a well-known location on the east side of the temple precincts, mentioned also in 5:12 and independently in John 10:23. The early speeches in Acts contain several titles for Jesus that are not often used in the rest of early Christianity, nor elsewhere in Acts, so that they appear to be early and accurately reported Christological depictions.[62] In 3:13, Peter calls him "servant," in verse 14, "the Holy and Righteous One," and in verse 15, "the author of life." The latter two

[59] On which, see esp. Brian Capper, "The Palestinian Cultural Context of Earliest Christian Community of Goods," in *Book of Acts in Its Palestinian Setting*, ed. Bauckham, 323–56.

[60] Reta Halteman Finger, *Of Widows and Meals: Communal Meals in the Book of Acts* (Grand Rapids: Eerdmans, 2007), 53.

[61] For a brief discussion, see Keener, *Acts*, vol. 2, 2013, 1048–49. Schnabel (*Acts*, 194) identifies the Nicanor gate and the gate by Robinson's Arch as the two main possibilities. Cf. further Justin Taylor, "The Gate of the Temple Called 'The Beautiful' (Acts 3:2, 10)," *Revue Biblique* 106 (1999): 549–62.

[62] See esp. Richard N. Longenecker, *The Christology of Early Jewish Christianity* (London: SCM; Naperville, IL: Allenson, 1970; Vancouver: Regent, 1994).

represent an exalted view of Jesus, suggesting that this understanding emerged with revolutionary speed rather than slowly evolving over decades.[63] Peter's quotation of parts of Deuteronomy 18:15, 18, and 19 in Acts 3:22 adds to this mix the portrait of Jesus as the eschatological prophet like Moses. Stephen will make a similar reference in Acts 7:37, but again we do not see later New Testament uses of the title.

It is historically accurate that the Sadducees, the one leadership sect in Judaism that did not believe in bodily resurrection, would be the most incensed at the disciples' teaching about Jesus's resurrection (4:1–2). They would also have formed the majority on the Sanhedrin that voted to hand Jesus over to Pilate. Legal proceedings typically did not occur in the evening, so Peter and John, when arrested, are jailed overnight (v. 3).[64] The continued growth of the Jesus movement in Jerusalem (v. 4), based on another miracle done with large crowds witnessing it (3:1–10) and Peter's subsequent explanation (vv. 11–26) is exactly what we should expect. We have seen Annas (v. 6) attested independently in both John 18:13 and 24 and Josephus (*Ant.* 20.9.1), with Luke mentioning him previously in Luke 3:2. Caiaphas, his son-in-law, is mentioned in all four Gospels. John could be Annas's son, Jonathan, who was high priest after Caiaphas (AD 36–37). Alexander we don't know about otherwise, but the name was common enough an among Hellenized Jews, which many of the Sadducees were.

There is at least some non-Christian Jewish use of Psalm 118:22 as a messianic prophecy (Acts 4:11). *Agrammatos* and *idiōtēs* in verse 13 have been widely mistranslated and misinterpreted to suggest that the disciples were illiterate. But Louw and Nida correct this misunderstanding. Under their lexicon entry for *agrammatos* they write:

---

[63] Cf. throughout Larry W. Hurtado, *Lord Jesus Christ: Devotion to Jesus in Earliest Christianity* (Grand Rapids: Eerdmans, 2003).

[64] Keener, *Acts*, vol. 2, 1133; Schnabel, *Acts*, 234.

Pertaining to one who has not acquired a formal education (referring primarily to formal training)—"uneducated, unlearned." . . . Some persons have assumed that ἀγράμματος in Ac 4.13 means "illiterate" in the sense of not being able to read or write, but this is highly unlikely in view of the almost universal literacy [of Jewish men] in NT times, and especially as the result of extensive synagogue schools. Evidently, ἀγράμματος in Ac 4.13 refers to a lack of formal rabbinic training.[65]

Idiōtēs, as in 1 Corinthians 14:16, then refers to someone "who has not acquired systemic information or expertise in some field of knowledge or activity," that is, a layperson or amateur.[66] The Jewish authorities marveled at the disciples' understanding, given that they had no advanced schooling beyond the elementary education for boys from roughly ages five to twelve. Without detailed knowledge of Israelite practices, the Gentile Luke could easily have misrepresented the disciples as less literate, like many in the Greco-Roman world, but he has done his homework well.

The Sanhedrin's response is similarly realistic. We must not foist anti-Semitic caricatures onto our perceptions of these men. They were charged with doing what they believed was consistent with their Scriptures and in the best interests of their people (recall John 11:50).

---

[65] Johannes P. Louw and Eugene A. Nida, *Greek-English Lexicon of the New Testament Based on Semantic Domains,* vol. 2 (New York: United Bible Societies, 1988), 329. Cf. also Thomas J. Kraus, "'Uneducated,' 'Ignorant,' or Even 'Illiterate'? Aspects and Background for an Understanding of ἀγράμματοι (and ἰδιῶται) in Acts 4.13," *New Testament Studies* 45 (1999): 434; Rainer Riesner, *Jesus als Lehrer: Eine Untersuchung zum Ursprung der Evangelien-Überlieferung* (Tübingen: Mohr Siebeck, 1981), 413.

[66] Louw and Nida, *Greek-English Lexicon of the New Testament,* vol. 2, 329; Kraus, "'Uneducated,' 'Ignorant,' or Even 'Illiterate'?" 441–42; Mikeal C. Parsons and Martin M. Culy, *Acts: A Handbook on the Greek Text* (Waco: Baylor University Press, 2003), 70; Schnabel, *Acts,* 243.

It was one thing to execute Jesus at the low point of his popularity in Jerusalem; it would be quite another to put to death the leaders of his followers, with more than 5,000 men, plus no doubt many in their families, now in their number (Acts 4:4). Besides, some in their midst were more positive toward Jesus and the story of his resurrection than others (esp. Joseph of Arimathea). Severe threats at the moment (4:18–21) and serious flogging shortly thereafter (5:40) are probably the most they could have gotten away with if they didn't want to cause massive city riots![67]

Chapter 5 brings us to the first internal threat to the fledgling church, with the sins of deception and lying by Ananias and Sapphira. Completely apart from questions related to the apparently miraculous side of God's response is the question of its severity. It is closely reminiscent of the sin of Achan and God's response in Joshua 7, even down to the use of the rare verb *nosphizō* ("to swindle") in verse 1 (cf. Acts 5:2). Theologically, in both Testaments, God's behavior may be explained as an unusually harsh punishment needed at the beginning of the new life of his covenant communities to prevent total fragmentation at the outset.[68] But historically, Luke, who is by all accounts eager to play down conflict within the church throughout the book of Acts, would hardly have invented something that cuts this much against the grain of his redactional emphases.

The other major historical question in Acts 5 surrounds Gamaliel's reference to Theudas in verse 36. We know from later Jewish literature that Gamaliel was a highly esteemed rabbi. The Mishnah, for example,

---

[67] On the historical realism of the persecution of the first Jesus followers by Sadducees in Jerusalem out of zeal for the purity of God's temple, see Eyal Regev, "Temple Concerns and High-Priestly Prosecutors from Peter to James: Between Narrative and History," *New Testament Studies* 56 (2010): 64–89.

[68] Richard N. Longenecker, "Acts," in *The Expositor's Bible Commentary*, rev. ed., eds. Tremper Longman III and David E. Garland, vol. 10 (Grand Rapids: Zondervan, 2007), 786. Cf. Polhill, *Acts*, 160–62.

declares that "when Rabban Gamaliel the elder died, the glory of the law ceased and purity and abstinence died (*m. Sotah* 9:15)."[69] Josephus gives fuller accounts of the uprisings led by men named Judas the Galilean in AD 6 and Theudas in AD 44 (cf. Jos. *Ant*. 20.97, 102, 171; *War* 2.259–64). But Theudas's insurrection had not yet occurred when Gamaliel was addressing the Sanhedrin in the early to mid 30s. Most scholarship routinely accuses Luke of being mistaken, therefore, even though Josephus demonstrably errs more often than Luke![70] Another possibility, given the number of uprisings Josephus depicts from Judas's day until the destruction of Jerusalem by Rome in AD 70, is that this is another, perhaps smaller, insurrection led by a different Theudas. When we realize that Theudas was also an abbreviation for names such as Theodotus or Theodosius, themselves the Greek equivalents (meaning "given by God") to the Hebrew names Jonathan, Nathanael, and Matthias, the probability of this option increases.[71] Interestingly, Calvin argued that "after this" in verse 37 means merely "moreover" or "besides."[72] This would account for the order of the two incidents in Luke but not for how Gamaliel could have referred to Theudas's uprising before it happened! With Joseph of Arimathea presumably present, the problem of how the disciples could have learned of Gamaliel's words is also easily resolved. At any rate, a confident proclamation that Luke has erred here is certainly premature![73]

---

[69] Schnabel, *Acts*, 314.

[70] Keener, *Acts*, vol. 2, 1231–32. Witherington (*Acts of the Apostles*, 238) notes specifically how Josephus often rearranges the order of events.

[71] Polhill, *Acts*, 173 n. 132. Cf. Witherington, *Acts of the Apostles*, 239; Marshall, *Acts*, 122–23.

[72] John Calvin, *Commentary upon the Acts of the Apostles* (Grand Rapids: Baker, 1979 [orig. 1585]), 224.

[73] Pervo (*Acts*, 149 n. 86) insists that "those who believe that Acts 5:35–39 includes a historical report of Gamaliel's words and beliefs must explain why he did not raise the same objection some months earlier at the trial of Jesus." The simplest answer is that he did not yet have the positive appreciation of Jesus and his

The second internal church conflict leads to the selection of seven Hellenistic Jewish Christians to oversee the distribution of either food or money (or both) to needy widows within their ranks (6:1–7).[74] With both Greek- and Aramaic-speaking Jews living in Jerusalem, and with all of the apostles presumably being Aramaic speaking, the oversight is completely understandable and another reminder that Luke is not trying to portray an unrealistic utopian community, even if he could say that for a short period of time "there were no needy persons among them" (4:34). The criteria for the selection of these additional leaders (6:3) show that they had to be just as "spiritual" as the apostles, so we should not be surprised that Luke focuses on that dimension of their ministry—at least with respect to Stephen and Philip—in the next two chapters.

The Church in Judea, Samaria, and Environs (6:8–9:31)

Jerusalem would have contained numerous synagogues in Jesus's day; inscriptional evidence of one has even been found.[75] Divisions along class and ethnic lines ran deep in the ancient Mediterranean world, and Judaism was scarcely immune to them. A Synagogue of Freedmen (6:9a) would scarcely have been surprising. That Stephen, a Hellenistic Jewish Christian, preached among Hellenistic Jews (v. 9b) is likewise

---

followers before the resurrection and the first miracles and ministry of the church as he did after them.

[74] See further Craig L. Blomberg, *Neither Poverty nor Riches: A Biblical Theology of Possessions* (Grand Rapids: Eerdmans; Leicester: IVP, 1999; Downers Grove: IVP, 2001), 167–69. Pervo (*Acts*, 152) complains that appointing seven from one party doesn't explain how both parties' widows would be served, but Luke says specifically that it was only the one party that was being excluded. Pervo does at least acknowledge that "Luke's repeated stress on unity and harmony makes it unlikely that he invented a disagreement where none existed" (p. 156).

[75] Craig A. Evans, *Jesus and His World: The Archaeological Evidence* (Louisville: Westminster John Knox; London: SPCK, 2012), 41–44. More broadly, cf. Rainer Riesner, "Synagogues in Jerusalem," in *Book of Acts in Its Palestinian Setting*, ed. Bauckham, 179–211.

THE CREDIBILITY OF ACTS | 261

just what we would expect. The false charges against Stephen (vv. 11–14) remind us of those trumped up against Jesus (Mark 14:56–59 par.). Luke did not include that information in his Gospel, so it is unlikely he would invent it or move it here simply to make Stephen look more like Jesus.[76]

Stephen's lengthy "defense speech" before the Sanhedrin (7:2–53) seems more rambling and disjointed than any other in Acts and therefore not merely characteristic of Lukan style. On close inspection, Stephen is highlighting how God blessed the Israelites and their ancestors even when they weren't living in the land or worshipping in the temple, while Stephen appeals to Moses the Lawgiver to show how he pointed to the Messiah.[77] In other words, the charges of speaking against "this holy place" (6:13; the temple but probably also the land) and Moses (vv. 11 and 14; especially the law) were not entirely false, merely misconstrued. Stephen's martyrdom can be attributed to his having gone further than anyone before him in dissociating the Jesus movement from Judaism in these respects. But his direct "disrespect" for and charges against the authorities at the end of his speech (vv. 51–53) may well have turned legal proceedings into a lynch mob—whether or not the Jewish authorities had the right to do so under Rome![78] The reference to Saul's presence and participation (7:58, 8:1a) literarily foreshadows the large role he will play in Acts later on, but it also shows that Luke was not trying to whitewash Saul's anti-Christian past.

Several discrepancies appear between details in Stephen's summary of Old Testament events and information in the Hebrew Bible itself.

---

[76] As alleged, e.g., by Antonio Piñero and Jesús Peláez, *The Study of the New Testament: A Comprehensive Introduction* (Leiden: Deo, 2003), 405.

[77] See further Craig L. Blomberg, *From Pentecost to Patmos: Acts to Revelation, An Introduction and Survey* (Leicester: Apollos; Nashville: B&H, 2006), 36–37.

[78] Keener, *Acts*, vol. 2, 1453–55. Cf. Torrey Seland, *Establishment Violence in Philo and Luke: A Study of Non-Conformity to the Torah and Jewish Vigilante Reactions* (Leiden: Brill, 1995), 241–42.

These involve when Abram left Haran (7:4; cf. Gen 11:26, 32; and 12:4), how many people went to Egypt (7:14; cf. Gen 46:27), and where Jacob was buried (7:16; cf. Gen 49:29–32). Other information Stephen includes is simply not found in the Masoretic Text of the Hebrew Scriptures (e.g., Moses's education in the wisdom of Egypt—7:22; visiting his people specifically at age forty—7:23; and angels mediating the revelation of the law (7:53). Most of three details, however, appear in Jewish tradition, sometimes even in the Septuagint, so Stephen is unlikely to have invented them.[79] More importantly, *Luke's* accuracy does not depend on the inerrancy of Stephen's speech; it means merely that he has accurately reported what Stephen declared.[80] That he allows these seeming discrepancies to stand shows his care as a historian.

The most puzzling piece historically about the subsequent persecution unleashed on the disciples (8:1b–3) is why everyone *except* the apostles scattered. It has often been suggested that they represent, by synecdoche, the Hebraic Jewish Christian wing of the church, which was not as theologically radical as Stephen and the Hellenistic Jewish Christian wing.[81] That view has fallen out of favor in recent times, though not based on any new evidence.[82] But it is also possible that Luke does not intend to suggest that anyone was immune from persecution, so that the Twelve had to go "underground," as it were, in order to stay in Jerusalem, but were committed to doing so in order to preserve a witnessing presence there whenever they felt it safe to come out of hiding.[83] On either interpretation, "all" has to be hyper-

---

[79] See the charts in Chance, *Acts*, 110; and Keener, *Acts*, vol. 2, 1336.

[80] Rex A. Koivisto, "Stephen's Speech: A Theology of Errors?" *Grace Theological Journal* 8 (1987): 101–14.

[81] E.g., Martin Hengel and Anna Maria Schwemer, *Paul Between Damascus and Antioch: The Unknown Years* (London: SCM; Louisville: Westminster John Knox, 1997), 137.

[82] E.g., Richard Bauckham, "James and the Jerusalem Church," in *Book of Acts in Its Palestinian Setting*, ed. Bauckham, 429.

[83] Keener, *Acts*, vol. 2, 1469. Cf. Schnabel, *Acts*, 394.

bolic in light of texts that show other believers still in Jerusalem (9:26; 11:22; 15:4).[84]

The rest of Acts 8 presents two vignettes from the ministry of the Philip who was chosen to help minister to the needy widows in 6:5 (not Philip the apostle). Simon, the Samaritan magician, became the object of considerable subsequent Christian speculation. Whether any of these later traditions was based on genuine historical information is harder to determine, but they mostly insist that he became an opponent of the church, not a true believer, in sync with where Luke ends the account about his spiritual condition (vv. 18–23; v. 24 falls noticeably short of a personal repentance speech!).[85] Given the number of ambiguous characters in the New Testament that apocryphal traditions turned into full-fledged Christians (including both Nicodemus and Pilate), it would appear that people recognized that Simon's initial profession of faith was a sham. This leaves the door wide open for the explanation that the other Samaritans' belief and baptism was premature, too (vv. 12–13). The otherwise consistent pattern in Luke of the Spirit's coming when and only when someone truly began to follow Jesus (cf. vv. 14–17) was not broken here.[86] But the diverse narratives show that Luke wasn't running roughshod over the "messiness" of the actual events, just in order to portray a uniform theological position.

Philip's ministry to the Ethiopian eunuch (vv. 26–40) demonstrates numerous features of historical verisimilitude. God-fearing Gentiles regularly came to worship in Jerusalem, especially at festival times. *Kandakē* was the title used for a succession of queens in ancient

---

[84] Parsons and Culy, *Acts*, 148.

[85] See esp. Iren. *Adv. Haer.* 1:23, and Just. *Apol.* 1.26. For a full reception history, see Alberto Ferreiro, *Simon Magus in Patristic, Medieval, and Early Modern Traditions* (Leiden: Brill, 2005).

[86] James D. G. Dunn, *Baptism in the Holy Spirit* (London: SCM; Philadelphia: Westminster, 1980), 64–65.

Ethiopia during this period.[87] Eunuchs were regularly employed in the harems of the king, though it is possible here that the term refers simply to a wealthy official in the court, which would also explain this man's access to chariot travel, an Isaiah scroll, and the education he would have needed to have had to read it (vv. 27–28). The interpretation of Isaiah 52:13–53:12 to refer to the Messiah (Acts 8:32–35) fits other early Christian understanding (Matt 8:17; Luke 22:37; John 12:38; Rom 10:16; 1 Pet 2:22) and at least one minority strand of interpretation in Judaism prior to the time of Jesus.[88] The older view that stock, liturgical language has intruded into Luke's narrative when the eunuch asks, "What can stand in the way of my being baptized?" (8:36; cf. Mark 10:14 pars.) has largely been abandoned. More likely the eunuch phrased his question as he did because he knew well that either his castration or his occupation made him ritually unclean and unfit for circumcision as a full-fledged proselyte to Judaism, but he was unaware of similar hurdles in Christian theology.[89]

Most of Acts' information about Saul of Tarsus can be tested only by comparing it with his letters, so we will save this task for the next chapter. Other important matters will be mentioned here. The most significant for the conversion narrative is the fact that Luke three times includes versions of Saul-Paul's testimony (twice later in his own words; 22:3–21 and 26:2–23). The minor variations among the accounts form a classic illustration of the freedom ancient speakers and writers felt in retelling the same story. The only detail that even

---

[87] Keener, *Acts—3.1–14.28*, 1573–75.

[88] Martin Hengel with Daniel P. Bailey, "The Effective History of Isaiah 53 in the Pre-Christian Period," in *The Suffering Servant: Isaiah 53 in Jewish and Christian Sources*, ed. Bernd Janowski and Peter Stuhlmacher (Grand Rapids: Eerdmans, 2004), 75–146.

[89] Keener, *Acts*, vol. 2, 1590. C. K. Barrett (*A Critical and Exegetical Commentary on the Acts of the Apostles*, vol. 1 [Edinburgh: T & T Clark, 1994], 432–33) believes the idiom "what can hinder me?" was common and meant little more than "why not?"

borders on an actual contradiction involves what Paul's traveling companions heard. In 9:7, we read that "they heard the sound [of Jesus's voice] but did not see anyone." In 22:9, Paul states that his companions "saw the light, but they did not understand the voice of him who was speaking to me." In 26:14, he does not mention at all what his companions did or did not hear or understand. The NIV masks the fact that in both 9:7 and 22:9 Luke uses the verb *akouō*—"to hear" or "to listen." But the case of the noun for voice (*phonē*) is genitive in the first passage and accusative in the second. In classical Greek the former meant to hear without understanding; the latter, to hear with understanding. The NIV, like the ESV, GWN, NASB, NET and NLT, translates Luke's words in these two passages according to this distinction. Luke does not uniformly preserve this difference in his writing elsewhere, but he may have chosen to do so here.[90] After all, this is not a "contradiction" between Luke and some other source of information. Luke presumably did not think he was contradicting himself and that his audience would understand.

Further Geographical Advances of the Gospel (9:32–12:24)

Acts 9:32–43 presents Peter taking the gospel further afield, from Jerusalem to towns in the coastal plains of Judea. Not only is the gospel continuing to move out from Israel's capital, but Peter even stays with a Jewish tanner (Simon) in Joppa (v. 43), a man who almost certainly would have been unclean by his trade, working with the skins of dead animals. This experience prepares him for the astonishing vision he has at Simon's home, with God three times declaring unclean foods clean (10:1–11:18). We have mentioned this already in conjunction with Mark 7:19 above. Here we need add only that

---

[90] Polhill (*Acts*, 235 n. 15) notes that the generalization does not hold up for Luke but adds, "The distinction is perhaps to be seen in the qualifying participial phrase of 22:9, hearing a 'voice' (φωνή) *which was speaking*, whereas 9:7 need mean no more than hearing a 'sound.'"

further verisimilitude appears in the reference to the Italian Regiment (Acts 10:1),[91] a God-fearing centurion (v. 2), his sending of servants and a soldier (v. 7), the way they couch their message to be as attractive as possible to a Jewish person (v. 22), and Peter's report of objections to association (perhaps referring to table fellowship) and visiting (probably in their homes) with Gentiles, at least in the strictest of the Pharisaic laws (v. 28).[92] Peter's deduction that God's declaring all foods clean[93] meant he was declaring all peoples clean (vv. 34–35) follows naturally because Gentile meals with unclean food was one of the biggest hindrances to intimate fellowship with them.

A superficial reading of 10:44–46 could suggest another exception to the Pentecostal package of belief, water baptism, and the reception of the Spirit all as a closely unified cluster of events (2:38). Here it appears that the Spirit interrupts Peter's preaching and comes on Cornelius and company before anyone ever makes a profession of faith! But the fact that Peter has just spoken about believing in Jesus and receiving forgiveness of sins through his name (v. 43) means that almost certainly they were starting to believe in their hearts at exactly that moment.[94] Luke does not skirt around the actual events in order to produce a tidy, cut-and-dried pattern of conversion for everyone, as a writer of fiction might have done. Yet neither does Luke ignore the fact that some of the more Torah-obedient Jewish Christians in

---

[91] For the main details, see Barrett, *A Critical and Exegetical Commentary on the Acts of the Apostles*, vol. 1, 499. For a thorough study, cf. Craig S. Keener, "Acts 10: Were Troops Stationed in Caesarea During Agrippa's Rule," *Journal of Greco-Roman Christianity and Judaism* 7 (2010): 164–96.

[92] For the evidence and the debate that still remains, see Bock, *Acts*, 394.

[93] Against those who would deny this straightforward understanding of Peter's vision and God's commands to him, Schnabel (*Acts*, 492) observes that "the interpretation of the vision in 10:28 makes sense only if it is related to food that Gentiles ate but was prohibited for Jews and that made intimate encounters between Jews and Gentiles difficult."

[94] Dunn, *Baptism in the Holy Spirit*, 80.

Jerusalem criticized Peter for his ministry (11:2–3). Nor does he delete the demeaning "even" from their otherwise eventual acceptance of matters: "When they heard [Peter's story], they had no further objections and praised God, saying, 'So then, even [Gk. postpositive *kai*] to Gentiles God has granted repentance that leads to life'" (v. 18). James Dunn observes that "something like this [event with Peter and Cornelius] must have happened if the presuppositions and traditions of centuries were to be so quickly overturned in the initial expansion of the new messianic sect."[95]

It is equally plausible that most of the Jewish Christians who left Jerusalem at the time of the persecution of 8:1 would testify to fellow Jews (11:19). But it would be almost inevitable that someone somewhere, so elated at their own experiences, would share with Gentile friends or acquaintances. Those from Cyprus and Cyrene (modern Libya) were used to being minorities in Gentile communities, so it should occasion no surprise that they would pioneer outreach to full-fledged Greeks, who had no background in Judaism (v. 20). Given the irregular experiences surrounding the gospel going to Samaria, it would be only natural for the Jerusalem church to send someone to check things out, and a fellow Cypriot (Barnabas; v. 22; cf. 4:36) was a natural choice. Barnabas will soon play second fiddle to Saul of Tarsus, so, like John the Baptist originally being more significant than Jesus, it is doubtful if Luke would have gratuitously portrayed Barnabas as the more prominent person in verses 22–26 (cf. v. 30; 12:25; 13:2). *Christianoi* was probably a title given Jesus's followers by outsiders akin to the Grecized Latin labels *Hērōdianoi, Kaisarianoi, Nerōnianoi,* and so on.[96] That this development should occur in the place where those followers first preached to full-fledged Gentiles is only fitting. Josephus (*Ant.* 20.51; cf. also Suet., *Claud.*18.2) confirms the famine

---

[95] Dunn, *Beginning from Jerusalem*, 400.
[96] Fitzmyer, *Acts of the Apostles*, 478.

that afflicted most of the Roman Empire to one degree or another in the late 40s but was most severe in Judea.[97]

Acts 12 relates two episodes involving "King Herod." This is Herod Agrippa I, grandson of Herod the Great. From Roman histories we learn that he grew up with Caligula, in Rome, so we should not be surprised when Caligula became emperor that he appointed Agrippa to rule in Israel.[98] To keep Rome happy, client kings had to keep the peace locally while remaining loyal to the emperor. Persecuting the believers, whom Jews and Romans increasingly disliked, would fit the bill admirably (12:1–5). The martyrdom of one of the three members of Christ's inner circle, James the brother of John, is mentioned in a single verse (v. 2), yet "Luke did not feel free to choose to elaborate a far too skimpy death notice."[99] Peter is hardly praised too much in the story of his miraculous release; at first he can't believe it is really happening (cf. vv. 9 and 11). The local believers are laudably praying for him but initially unwilling to believe their prayers have actually been answered (v. 15). Rhoda's role reads like the touch of an eyewitness; it scarcely supports any particular theology (vv. 13–14).[100] Recognizing the danger he was still in, Peter leaves Jerusalem "for another place" (v. 17). If Luke were the early catholic theologian so many have claimed he was, falsifying history in support of ideology,[101] he would have told us that Peter went to Rome, as later tradition claimed (beginning

---

[97] See further Bruce W. Winter, "Acts and Food Shortages," in *The Book of Acts in Its Graeco-Roman Setting*, ed. David W. J. Gill and Conrad Gempf (Grand Rapids: Eerdmans; Carlisle: Paternoster, 1994), 59–78.

[98] For references and additional background information, see Keener, *Acts*, vol. 2, 1867–68.

[99] Dunn, *Beginning from Jerusalem*, 406.

[100] Bock (*Acts*, 428) adds, "The fact that a slave girl would answer the door is one of those little details that point to authenticity."

[101] Classically, Hans Conzelmann, *The Theology of St. Luke* (New York: Harper & Row, 1960; London: Faber & Faber, 1961; Philadelphia: Fortress, 1982).

already with the most likely interpretation of 1 Pet 5:13). Instead, he leaves us in the dark about Peter's travels.

Josephus confirms the second episode about Agrippa (Acts 12:19b–23) in considerable detail. The accounts are phrased sufficiently differently to preclude direct dependence of either author on the other, but the basic events are clearly corroborated:

> Here he celebrated spectacles in honor of Caesar, knowing that these had been instituted as a kind of festival on behalf of Caesar's wellbeing. For this occasion, there were gathered a large number of men who held office or had advanced to some rank in the kingdom. On the second day of the spectacles, clad in a garment woven completely of silver so that its texture was indeed wondrous, he entered the theater at daybreak. There the silver, illumined by the touch of the first rays of the sun, was wondrously radiant and by its glitter inspired fear and awe in those who gazed intensely upon it. Straightway his flatterers raised their voices from various directions—though hardly for his good—addressing him as a god. "May you be propitious to us," they added, "and if we have hitherto feared you as a man, yet henceforth we agree that you are more than mortal in your being." The king did not rebuke them nor did he reject their flattery as impious. But shortly thereafter he looked up and saw an owl perched on a rope over his head. At once, recognizing this as a harbinger of woe just as it had once been of good tidings, he felt a stab of pain in his heart. He was also gripped in his stomach by an ache that he felt everywhere at once and that was intense from the start. Leaping up he said to his friends: "I, a god in your eyes, am now bidden to lay down my life, for fate brings immediate refutation of the lying words lately addressed to me. I, who was called immortal by you, am now under sentence of death. But I must accept my lot

as God wills it. In fact, I have lived in no ordinary fashion but in the grand style that is hailed as true bliss." Even as he was speaking these words, he was overcome by more intense pain. They hastened, therefore, to convey him to the palace; and the word flashed about to everyone that he was on the very verge of death. Straightway the populace, including the women and children, sat in sackcloth in accordance with their ancestral custom and made entreaty to God on behalf of the king. The sound of the wailing and lamentations prevailed everywhere. The king, as he lay in his lofty bedchamber and looked down on the people as they fell prostrate, was not dry-eyed himself. Exhausted after five straight days by the pain in his abdomen, he departed this life in the fifty-fourth year of his life and the seventh of his reign. (*Ant.* 19.343–50)

Both accounts confirm that the Phoenicians acclaimed Herod as a god and not merely a mortal, that Herod did not resist the acclaim, and that supernatural powers struck him down by means of a gastrointestinal disorder.

Paul's First Missionary Travels and the Apostolic Council (12:25–16:5)

The names of the prophets and teachers in the church at Antioch, besides Barnabas and Saul (13:1), fit the multiethnic nature of the congregation (recall 11:19–21). *Niger* means "black man"; Simeon may well have been from Africa. Cyrene was part of modern-day Libya, so Lucius was clearly a foreigner. If Manaen grew up with Agrippa, he would have come from Rome. Barnabas and Saul set off for Cyprus (13:4), Barnabas's homeland (4:36). Traveling from east coast to west coast, as they would have to do after coming from Seleucia on the east coast of the Mediterranean Sea, they make significant stops at Salamis and Paphos, the two biggest cities of the island, on each of those two coasts (13:5–6). That a sorcerer in Paphos who opposes them has a Jewish name (bar-Jesus), as well as a Greek one (Elymas), makes his syncretism particularly heinous. Here is the one (more temporary) miracle of judgment performed by Saul, now called Paul as he consistently ministers in almost exclusively Gentile settings (vv. 6–12). The existence of the family of the proconsul in Paphos who becomes a believer, Sergius Paulus, is confirmed by two gravestones and one inscription.[102] Roman sources, moreover, "tell us of more than one high-born Roman who was attracted by the 'superstitions' stemming from the East. And several Roman rulers had magicians and soothsayers among their personal staff."[103] John Mark's heading for home in verse 13 would have been a major embarrassment and not likely to have been invented.

From Cyprus Paul and company head to the south-central coast of what we would call Turkey. All the places can be identified, and all of Luke's geography proves accurate. Even Pisidian Antioch, so-called by Luke to distinguish it from Paul's home base for his travels in Syrian Antioch, is correctly labeled (Acts 13:14). Technically it was across the border from Pisidia into Phrygia, but another Antioch was more squarely located in Phrygia, so it became known as Pisidian Antioch to distinguish those two cities. All in all, sixteen cities in Paul's day were called Antioch because of the historic influence of the four Seleucid rulers during the Hellenistic period by the name of Antiochus.[104]

They begin by ministering in the local synagogue, the foundations of which have been excavated. A "word of exhortation" (13:15) was a homily or sermon; Paul may well have been viewed as a rabbi

---

[102] Keener, *Acts*, vol. 2, 2037–38. Cf. Douglas A. Campbell, "Possible Inscriptional Attestation to Sergius Paul[l]us (Acts 13:6–12) and the Implications for Pauline Chronology," *Journal of Theological Studies* 56 (2005): 1–29.

[103] Dunn, *Beginning from Jerusalem*, 421.

[104] Longenecker, "Acts," 918.

who was qualified to address the congregation.[105] Luke accurately represents Paul as addressing both Jews and God-fearers (vv. 16, 26).[106] Paul's words center on the Hebrew Scriptures (vv. 16–41) as the congregation would have expected. Paul shows how Israelite history unfolded, culminating in the arrival of Jesus the Messiah. Some of his logic and the texts he cites match those Peter expounded in Jerusalem, not surprisingly, since by now Paul has met and spent time with the apostles (9:27; 11:29–30). The polarized response matches the reception Jesus and the other apostles consistently received, exactly as we would expect. Paul's story is compelling, so some Jews will accept it. But it so threatens their conventional interpretations of many Scriptures and challenges the adequacy of life without following Jesus that many nevertheless reject it and want to do away with those who promote it (13:42–45). The pattern of Jewish persecution and Gentile acceptance (vv. 46–52) will recur throughout Paul's ministry.

But why did Paul and his companions make their way to begin with from the large coastal cities to the smaller communities in the high-plateau country, over daunting and arduous roads and terrain? Inscriptional evidence has shown that members of the extended family of Sergius Paulus were among the leaders in Pisidian Antioch.[107] Might he have requested that the emissaries whose message transformed his life go to his relatives in hopes of having a similar effect among them? Luke, of course, says nothing about this, as he might

---

[105] Barrett (*Acts*, vol. 1, 629), also citing Philo, *de Spec. Leg.* 2.62: "The scholars sit . . . while one of special experience rises and sets forth."

[106] For the definitive study squelching the claim that God fearers did not exist, see Irina Levinskaya, *The Book of Acts in Its Diaspora Setting* (Grand Rapids: Eerdmans; Carlisle: Paternoster, 1996), 51–126.

[107] See Barrett, *A Critical and Exegetical Commentary on the Acts of the Apostles*, 195; Schnabel, *Early Christian Mission*, vol. 2, 1088.

have if he were fictitiously inventing a connection. Such undersigned coincidences, however, rarely appear behind works of fiction![108]

For the longest time scholars did not know where ancient Lystra and Derbe, the cities Paul visits in 14:1–23, were located. Some even questioned whether they ever existed. Then inscriptions for each were discovered in archeological explorations, in 1885 and 1956, respectively.[109] Now they can both be viewed on display at a small museum in modern-day Konya, not far from the ancient site of Iconium in central Turkey. Luke not only uses real locations in his account; he also correctly identifies Lystra and Derbe as part of the ancient territory of Lycaonia (v. 6). He knows there is a separate indigenous Lycaonian language spoken there (v. 11), although, as throughout the empire, many people would have been able to speak at least some Greek. Luke does not just arbitrarily choose Lystra as the place where some townspeople wanted to sacrifice to Barnabas and Paul as if they were Zeus and Hermes, the head of the Greek pantheon of gods and the messenger god, respectively. Apparently, Barnabas was the larger, stronger-looking man while Paul was the talkative one, proclaiming a particularly urgent message from God after working a miracle of healing (vv. 8–13)! An altar and an inscription to Zeus and Hermes dating to about AD 250 were found just outside the ancient city.[110] And precisely in this region, according to Ovid in his *Metamorphoses*, the legend was passed on that centuries earlier the gods had appeared in human form but were rejected by the local people leading to the entire area being judged in some devastating fashion (8:626–724). Clearly some of the more credulous townspeople were eager that this not

---

[108] Cf. the lists of "specialized knowledge," "latent internal correlations within Acts," "unstudied allusions," and "peculiar selection of detail," in Hemer, *Book of Acts in the Setting of Hellenistic History*, 108, 190–93, 201–2, and 206–9, respectively.

[109] Clyde E. Fant and Mitchell G. Reddish, *A Guide to Biblical Sites in Greece and Turkey* (Oxford: Oxford University Press, 2003), 174–75, 240–41.

[110] Marshall, *Acts*, 232–33.

happen again. When Paul and Barnabas convinced them they were not gods, and when some Jews from Pisidian Antioch and Iconium came to continue to persecute them, that same superstitious tendency drove the people to the opposite extreme, so that they began to stone Paul (vv. 19–20). It is difficult to imagine either of these extremes occurring in a major, urban location, but a smaller more out-of-the way site was precisely where the old myths died hard.[111]

Luke presents the barest skeleton of Paul's address to the Lystrans (vv. 14–18). But he gives just enough for us to see that Paul contextualized his message in a way that stood the best chance of gaining a positive hearing among these superstitious Gentiles, apparently uninfluenced by any significant knowledge of Judaism. Instead of appealing to the fulfillment of the Jewish Scriptures, Paul speaks about the revelation of God in nature. But he still includes the core of the gospel message—repentance and turning from idolatry to the living God (v. 15). Looking on a map, one could easily imagine Paul and Barnabas continuing east overland to Tarsus and then back to Syrian Antioch. But although this was the closest route mileage-wise, it required traversing the rugged Taurus Mountains. Plus, they wanted to follow up with their new converts in the cities they had evangelized and where they had received the greatest opposition (vv. 21–23).

Retracing their steps to the Mediterranean Sea, Paul and Barnabas preach in Perga, a major port city in Pamphylia, on the south-central coast of modern-day Turkey (v. 24–25). Extensive ruins of Perga are today open to the public. Nearby Antalya has grown out of the smaller site of ancient Attalia, where they head next, and Roman ruins can still be seen near the harbor there (v. 25). Landing at Perga when coming from Cyprus, but sailing for Attalia when heading to Syria

---

[111] See, e.g., Dean Béchard, "Paul Among the Rustics: The Lystran Episode (Acts 14:18–20) and Lucan Apologetic," *Catholic Biblical Quarterly* 63 (2001): 84–101.

corresponds to the most common routes of the day.[112] Even just by the end of Paul's first missionary journey, we begin to recognize a feature that sets Acts off from ancient epic narratives and other legends: one can trace in detail his travels, identify every location, and understand something from the local culture or Paul's past experience that explains his movements, behavior, and forms of public address. And the historical existence of even minor characters and details can often be confirmed from extrabiblical sources.[113]

Several of the components of the Apostolic Council in Jerusalem (15:1–35) will be discussed in chapter 7 in conjunction with Paul's autobiographical information in his letter to the Galatians. Here we may observe that again Luke's geography is perfectly accurate. From Syrian Antioch, Phoenicia is farther south and Samaria farther still, en route to Jerusalem in Judea (v. 3). James, the half brother of Jesus, the chief elder and leader of the church in Jerusalem since Peter's previous departure, is known from numerous ancient sources to have been a pious conservative Hebraic Jewish believer.[114] We are not surprised, then, when Luke uses the name Simeon, a variant of Simon, Peter's Hebrew name, for how James referred to him, rather than his Greek nickname, Peter (for "rock").

It is often pointed out that James appears to quote from the Septuagint of Amos 9:11–12 in Acts 15:16–18, which would be unlikely for so conservative a Jewish Christian. Two replies prove relevant. First, with attendees to the Council potentially coming not

[112] Douglas A. Campbell, "Paul in Pamphylia (Acts 12.13–14a; 14.24b–26): A Critical Note," *New Testament Studies* 46 (2000): 595–602.

[113] For a lengthy list of these and related phenomena, see Hemer, *Book of Acts in the Setting of Hellenistic History*, 108–58.

[114] Bruce Chilton and Craig A. Evans, eds., *James the Just and Christian Origins* (Leiden: Brill, 1999); Patrick J. Hartin, *James of Jerusalem: Heir to Jesus of Nazareth* (Collegeville: Liturgical, 2004); Matti Myllykoski, "James the Just in History and Tradition: Perspectives of Past and Present Scholarship," *Currents in Biblical Research* 5 (2006): 73–122; 6 (2007): 11–98.

just from Israel but also from the diaspora, they would naturally have chosen Greek in which to speak and the Greek translation of the Scriptures to cite.[115] Second, while it is true that James's point about treating Gentiles and Jews the same way can be derived more clearly from the Septuagint, it is implicit in the Hebrew as well. To be sure, one can interpret the Hebrew of Amos 9:12 ("so that [Israel] may possess the remnant of Edom and all the nations that bear my name") as referring to some domineering role for Jews. Nevertheless, given the emphasis on the equality of Israel with the nations in verse 7 ("'Are not you Israelites the same to me as the Cushites?' declares the LORD. 'Did I not bring Israel up from Egypt, the Philistines from Caphtor and the Aramaeans from Kir?'"), an overly ethnocentric interpretation seems inappropriate. Thus even if all Luke knew was that James cited Amos 9:11–12, so that Luke merely copied the Greek translation with which he was familiar, he would not have been unfaithful to James's point.[116]

Why did the Council decide on the four restrictions for Gentiles that they did—abstaining from food sacrificed to idols, sexual immorality, the meat of strangled animals, and [eating] blood (Acts 15:20)? The two most likely answers are that either (1) these exemplified the Noahic laws that Jewish tradition believed were incumbent on Gentiles, or (2) they represented common pagan worship practices, associated with local temples, which were particularly offensive to Jews.[117] Either way, the Gentile author of Acts must have had fairly

---

[115] Cf. also Keener, *Acts*, vol. 3, 2247–48.

[116] J. Paul Tanner, "James' Quotation of Amos 9 to Settle the Jerusalem Council Debate in Acts 15," *Journal of the Evangelical Theological Society* 55 (2012): 65–85. It is actually possible, however, that the LXX is a translation of an older Hebrew form of the text, in light of two texts discovered among the Dead Sea Scrolls. See Jan de Waard, *A Comparative Study of the Old Testament Texts in the Dead Sea Scrolls and in the New Testament* (Leiden: Brill, 1965), 24–26.

[117] See further Craig L. Blomberg, "The Christian and the Law of Moses," in *Witness to the Gospel: The Theology of Acts* (Grand Rapids: Eerdmans, 1998), esp. 408–10.

detailed knowledge of Jewish tradition and scruples if he were just making up these restrictions to create historical realism. More likely the restrictions reflect the actual decision of a real council. Even more significantly we can scarcely underestimate how shocking the decision was not to require circumcision, God's ordained rite of initiation for his people from the days of Abraham (Gen 17:10–14) onward, long before the giving of the Law. It would scarcely have been invented had it not actually occurred. What is more, Paul's temporary compromise with select parts of the Christian world via the "apostolic decree" is even less likely to have been created, because it provides no ultimate or final solution to the debate about circumcision.[118]

As Paul prepares to embark on his second missionary journey, a serious rupture with Barnabas occurs (the Greek is *paroxusmos*— a "paroxysm"—Acts 15:39).[119] Once again Luke cannot rightfully be accused of whitewashing a major internal Christian division. Circumcising Timothy in Lystra (16:3) at first glance flies entirely in the face of the decision just made in Jerusalem. A writer of fiction would scarcely allow such an apparent contradiction to stand. But the debate over circumcision that triggered the council was whether it was necessary for salvation (15:1). That is not the issue here, but facilitating Jewish evangelism is. Even one who was half Jewish should have been circumcised, according to Jewish tradition, and Paul does not want to place unnecessary stumbling blocks in the paths of those he hopes will come to Christ.[120]

---

[118] Keener, *Acts*, vol. 3, 2269, 2277–79.

[119] Louw and Nida, *Greek-English Lexicon of the New Testament*, vol. 1, 440: "a severe argument based on an intense difference of opinion."

[120] William O. Walker Jr., "The Timothy-Titus Problem Reconsidered," *Expository Times* 92 (1981): 231–35.

New Missionary Fields Farther West (16:6–19:20)

Right at the outset of this fifth section of Acts comes a clue that Luke has extraordinarily accurate and detailed knowledge of Roman provincial organization. Granville Sharp's rule indirectly suggests that Luke's wording implies that there was one single region jointly encompassing both Phrygia and Galatia (16:6; cf. 18:23).[121] This is exactly the arrangement Rome created in 25 BC as it reorganized its empire into ten provinces, often blurring historic territorial divisions along ethnic lines.[122] The territories of Asia (minor), Mysia, Bithynia and Macedonia, and the city of Troas, are all real places, listed in a way that makes sense of Paul's attempted and actual travels. The same is true of his itinerary in Greece—from the island of Samothrace to the cities of Neapolis (16:11), Philippi (16:12), Amphipolis, Apollonia, Thessalonica (17:1), Berea (17:10), Athens (17:16), and Corinth (18:1). Paul is visiting the major towns on the eastern side of the peninsula in sequence as he progresses from north to south.

The description of Philippi in 16:12 has proved puzzling, both in terms of the original text and with respect to its meaning. A woodenly literal translation of the poorly attested text favored by the UBS would state that Philippi "is of the first part of Macedonia, a city, a colony." But the best and majority of the manuscripts have that it "is the first of the part of Macedonia, a city, a colony." If we translate with the RSV, "which is the leading city of the district of Macedonia, and a Roman colony," the descriptor seems patently false; Thessalonica

---

[121] Technically, the rule that equates two substantives does not apply with the 100 percent level of reliability it does for a pair of singular, personal, and nonproper nouns, because *Phrugian* and *Galatikēn* are singular, impersonal, and proper *adjectives*. But there is consistently a conceptual unity between the two. See Daniel B. Wallace, *Granville Sharp's Canon and Its Kin: Semantics and Significance* (New York: Peter Lang, 2009), 87–177.

[122] Colin J. Hemer, "The Adjective Phrygia," *Journal of Theological Studies* 27 (1976): 122–26.

deserved that label. The NRSV therefore reads, "a leading city," which would be true but seems a less natural translation of the Greek. The NIV solves this second problem with "the leading city of that district of Macedonia," which would be true, and the article before "part" or "district" could easily have the sense of a demonstrative pronoun. But if Paul wanted to be clear, we would have expected the actual demonstrative pronoun to be present. Most other translations adopt equivalents to one of these three options, although the recent CEB has "a city of Macedonia's first district." The 2011 NIV's footnote is honest: "The text and meaning of the Greek for *the leading city of that district* are uncertain"—uncertain enough that it would be premature to accuse Luke of an error.[123]

Lydia, a dealer in purple cloth, comes from Thyatira (16:14), a region well known for that particular business.[124] "A Latin inscription from Philippi refers to dealers in purple, an inscription from Thessalonica documents a guild of purple dyers, and an inscription from Philippi mentions purple dyers from Thyatira."[125] The use and abuse of fortune-tellers in the ancient Greco-Roman world (vv. 16–18) is equally well attested.[126] A small jail cell has been excavated at Philippi and is regularly shown to tourists, though we have no way of knowing if this is where Paul and Silas were held. The description of being stripped, beaten severely with rods, and put in foot stocks also rings true to documented experiences of the day (vv. 22–24).[127] Guards could be executed for allowing prisoners to escape, and suicide was

---

[123] See further Witherington, *Acts of the Apostles*, 489–90; Peterson, *Acts of the Apostles*, 459–60; Keener, *Acts*, vol. 3, 2382–83.

[124] Fitzmyer, *Acts of the Apostles*, 585. Even Pervo (*Acts*, 403 n. 26) has to acknowledge this.

[125] Schnabel, *Acts*, 680.

[126] Witherington, *Acts of the Apostles*, 494; Bock, *Acts*, 535–36.

[127] Brian Rapske, *The Book of Acts and Paul in Roman Custody* (Grand Rapids: Eerdmans; Carlisle: Paternoster, 2004), 123–27.

considered a noble form of death after dereliction of duty in various Greco-Roman circles, so the jailer's behavior in verse 27 is normal enough. What was unprecedented was all the prisoners remaining present, so the jailer's question about how to be saved in verse 30 is completely understandable. With his home probably being right next door, he may well have heard some of the words of the hymns Paul and Silas sang before he went to sleep, and thus had a religious meaning with his question.[128] Providing a midnight meal to make up for their mistreatment (v. 34) is also easily believable in a culture that valued hospitality and table fellowship immensely.

We can plausibly fill in the gaps in Luke's story by envisioning the jailer's sending word the next morning to the town magistrates about what had happened. The simplest way for them to save face would be for Paul and Silas to leave town quietly. But Paul plays his trump card by appealing to his Roman citizenship in order to secure the public recognition of the legality of the young church in Philippi and of the behavior of everyone associated with it (vv. 35–40).[129] Would a writer of fiction be this subtle, or would he have had Paul reveal his hand the previous night to avoid the hours of suffering that he and Silas already endured?

But is Paul's Roman citizenship credible? Not many Jews received citizenship but a few did. Paul will later explain that he was born a citizen (22:28), suggesting that his father may have distinguished

---

[128] Even without this specific knowledge, the jailer would have known why Paul and Silas were there and have heard the gist of the message they had been preaching around town (Bock, *Acts*, 541; Marshall, *Acts*, 272). Keener (*Acts*, vol. 3, 2510) adds, "Urban prisons normally kept logs of prisoners and their alleged offenses, and so the jailor would understand Paul and Silas in religious terms; before he understood them as charlatans, but now as divine messengers."

[129] Justo L. González, *Acts: The Gospel of the Spirit* (Maryknoll, NY: Orbis, 2001), 196.

himself in military service or some other activity for the government.[130] Given the hints scattered about Acts and Paul's own letters that he may have come from a family of some wealth,[131] such service, accompanied by citizenship as a reward, becomes sufficiently plausible. But could Paul then still have credibly maintained that he was a Pharisee? Wouldn't citizenship and its concomitant demand of loyalty to Rome have placed insuperable burdens on the orthodoxy of Saul of Tarsus? It might have. We have no claims recorded of how Saul might or might not have regarded or tried to use his citizenship as an orthodox Jew. We know only that he appealed to it on a few key occasions as a follower of Jesus, by which time he had already rejected sizable portions of his previous identity (Phil 3:7–9). John Lentz characterizes Luke's portrait as one of Paul taking pride in his citizenship, and thus rejects the likelihood of this portion of Acts being accurate.[132] But it is hard to see how Acts shows Paul taking any pride in this status. The only times he ever refers to it are in tactical situations where he employs it to avoid punishment that would harm the church more generally. And if he inherited it from his father, then he would never have aspired to attain this status that could put him at odds with his Judaism; he simply used it on rare occasions for the sake of the gospel after he had become a Christ follower.[133]

About the only new feature not already seen in Luke's account of Paul's ministry in Thessalonica and Berea (17:1–15) is the twofold

---

[130] For these and other options, see Rapske, *Book of Acts and Paul in Roman Custody*, 86.

[131] Gillian Clark, "The Social Status of Paul," *Expository Times* 96 (1985): 110–11.

[132] John C. Lentz, *Luke's Portrait of Paul* (Cambridge: Cambridge University Press, 1993), 43.

[133] It is also likely that Paul's citizenship did not bring him into as much tension with Judaism as Lentz alleges, given other examples from the first century of individuals in similar circumstances. See Rapske, *Book of Acts and Paul in Roman Custody*, 72–112, esp. 87–90.

reference to a number of "prominent Greek women" being among the new believers (vv. 4, 12). Luke has been highlighting the participation of women in the Jesus movement throughout the Acts (1:14; 2:18; 5:14; 8:3, 12; 9:2; 13:50; 16:13; cf. also 22:4), so this could just reflect a redactional emphasis.[134] On the other hand, calling attention to women at the center of a new religious movement wouldn't necessarily have commended the gospel in Luke's world, so one suspects the information is also historically accurate. The city officials in Thessalonica are literally "politarchs" (Acts 17:8), a term unattested elsewhere in antiquity until an inscription on the Vardar Gate in town was discovered.[135] One of the striking signs of Luke's historical accuracy is the plethora of different terms used for local rulers in the numerous town his narrative spans, all of them precisely accurate![136] Finally, inscriptional evidence for a synagogue in Thessalonica came to light for the first time in 1965.[137]

Paul's preaching in Athens stands out as noticeably different from everywhere else (vv. 22–31). For this reason, many scholars have found it historically suspect. But once we observe that Paul's preaching, when it is depicted in any detail, is noticeably different *each* time Luke records it, we suspect Luke is accurately portraying Paul's skill at contextualizing his message. Ancient Greek and Roman authors attest to altars to unknown gods in Athens, as does various inscriptional evidence,[138] so the picture of an altar to a single unknown god (v. 23) fits Athens' milieu nicely. Ruins of temples in honor of various gods

---

[134] See, e.g., Ivoni Richter Reimer, *Women in the Acts of the Apostles: A Feminist Liberation Perspective* (Minneapolis: Fortress, 1995).

[135] Today more than thirty inscriptions from the second century BC to the third century AD have been recovered, most of them in Macedonian cities. See F. F. Bruce, *The Book of the Acts*, rev. ed. (Grand Rapids: Eerdmans, 1988), 324 n. 8.

[136] For a long list of "local names and titles illustrative of the text" of Acts, see Hemer, *Book of Acts in the Setting of Hellenistic History*, 221–39.

[137] Schnabel, *Early Christian Mission*, vol. 2, 1163.

[138] Bock, *Acts*, 564; Schnabel, *Early Christian Mission*, vol. 2, 1176–77.

and goddesses, along with their appropriate altars and statues, still can be viewed in and around the Acropolis, just as Paul saw them in much better condition centuries ago. Epicureans and Stoics (v. 18) likewise proved plentiful in Athens;[139] Paul's sermon is a masterpiece of playing the views of each group against each other in service of Christian truth. The Cretan Epimenides and the Cilician Stoic Aratus are quoted in verses 27–28 to support God's immanence, but only after his transcendence, in agreement with the Epicureans, was well established (vv. 24–26). That his message in the agora had already focused on Jesus and the resurrection (vv. 18–19) meant he didn't have to say anything specifically about them at this juncture. Or perhaps Luke, in his abbreviation of Paul's address, recognized that *he* didn't have to traverse that terrain again.[140]

That Paul would be queried by the city council, the Areopagus (vv. 19, 22, 34), is natural enough because one of their functions was to serve as custodian of the accepted gods and goddesses who could be legally worshipped in town.[141] Whether the council still met atop the hill named after them is hard to determine, but the original "Mars Hill"—the meaning of the term Areopagus, from Ares (Gk.) or Mars (Lat.), the god of war—can still be viewed and climbed by tourists. The seemingly more modest positive response to Paul's preaching (vv. 32–34) is just what we should expect in this university town and center of all manner of philosophy. But neither do we hear of the extreme

---

[139] Hans-Josef Klauck, *The Religious Context of Early Christianity: A Guide to Graeco-Roman Religions* (Minneapolis: Fortress, 2003), 335–400.

[140] Schnabel (*Early Christian Mission*, vol. 2, 1177–78), who notes that Paul's address may be a summary of a written source that circulated as part of the process for determining if Paul's "new religion" could occupy a valid place within Athens' pantheon.

[141] Ibid. Cf. also Bruce W. Winter, "On Introducing Gods to Athens: An Alternative Reading of Acts 17:18–20," *Tyndale Bulletin* 47 (1996): 71–90.

reactions of those who persecuted Paul elsewhere, also in keeping with the Athenian reputation for tolerance.[142]

As Paul begins his ministry in Corinth, he meets Aquila and Priscilla who have come from Rome after the expulsion of the Jews from that city (18:1–2). Suetonius (*Claud.* 25.4) declares that this happened due to a riot at the instigation of *Chrestus*. This name is either an alternate or a garbled form of *Christus*, Latin for "Christ." Probably Jewish persecution of Jewish Christians led to Claudius ordering them all to leave. The event can be most likely dated to AD 49; Cassius Dio also speaks of a prohibition of Jews to gather in 41, which some have equated with this expulsion, but which should probably be viewed as a separate event.[143] An inscription has been found to a synagogue in Corinth, which *could* be from the building in which Paul preached (vv. 4, 7).[144] The reference to Gallio in verse 12 forms a major synchronism with extrabiblical history. Thanks to an inscription discovered at Delphi, we can date Gallio's proconsulship in Corinth to a single year's period of time, most likely AD 51–52, though just possibly 50–51.[145] His behavior in Acts comports closely with what we know of him from other sources.[146] Tourists can view a plausible site for Gallio's seat of judgment to this day. "A novelist would not dare fabricate a precedent about the ruling of a recent, historical, named figure, nor would an ancient novelist have cared to research the details Luke has accurately provided."[147] The pagan crowd's turning on the

---

[142] That Luke offers neither of these extremes supports authenticity. Cf. Keener, *Acts*, vol. 3, 2567–69.

[143] C. K. Barrett, *A Critical and Exegetical Commentary on the Acts of the Apostles*, vol. 2 (Edinburgh: T & T Clark, 1998), 861–62.

[144] Levinskaya, *Book of Acts in Its Diaspora Setting*, 162–66.

[145] Rainer Riesner, *Paul's Early Period: Chronology, Mission Strategy, Theology* (Grand Rapids: Eerdmans, 1997), 208–10.

[146] Bruce W. Winter, "Rehabilitating Gallio and His Judgement in Acts 18:14–15," *Tyndale Bulletin* 57 (2006): 291–308.

[147] Keener, *Acts*, vol. 3, 2760.

synagogue ruler for being a leader among those inciting procedures against Paul in the city courts (v. 17) reflects the latent anti-Semitism that took little provocation to become apparent in the first-century Mediterranean world.[148]

Luke moves rapidly through Paul's voyage to Israel and return to Syrian Antioch. But he knows it was natural to sail directly across the Aegean Sea and dock at Ephesus (v. 19) before making the much longer journey to the eastern Mediterranean (v. 18). He knows Caesarea was a major port city on the coast of Israel (v. 22a) and that one goes "up" to Jerusalem because of its elevation and "down" to Antioch in Syria (v. 22b) at a lower altitude, even though it was north of Jerusalem.

On his third missionary journey, Paul retraces many of the steps he took on his second trip. A major stopping place for him is Ephesus. It might seem far-fetched to find a group of followers of John the Baptist such a long way from Judea (19:1–7), but this is what often happened with new religious movements in the Roman world. Far from where John originally ministered, however, information could easily become garbled or truncated.[149] That these "disciples" didn't even know there was a Holy Spirit shows they couldn't have been Jews. It also means they couldn't have had much accurate detail even about John's teaching since he regularly contrasted his baptism with Jesus's coming baptism "with the Holy Spirit" (Mark 1:8 pars.). There is second-century evidence of a sect in and around Ephesus that worshipped the Baptist as the Messiah;[150] did it evolve from a group similar to this band of twelve men?

Mention of a Jewish *archiereus* (lit., "high priest") in Ephesus (Acts 19:14) at first glance appears like a blatant error; only one high

---

[148] See also Moyer V. Hubbard, "Urban Uprisings in the Roman World: The Social Setting of the Mobbing of Sosthenes," *New Testament Studies* 51 (2005): 416–28.

[149] Dunn, *Baptism in the Holy Spirit*, 83–89; Marshall, *Acts*, 306.

[150] Pseudo-Clementine, *Recognitions* 1.54, 60; cf. Justin Martyr, *Dialogue* 80.

priest held power at any time, and he lived in Jerusalem. But the term could also refer to leading priests, including retired ones, who might have migrated to any major imperial city.[151] Ephesus was known as a center for ancient magic, similar to what we would call the occult today. Hundreds of magical papyri from a slightly later date have been preserved or recovered, presenting spells and incantations invoking countless deities with all kinds of nonsense words (as far as we know).[152] Little wonder this was the site for the first Christian book- (or scroll-) burning ceremony (v. 19), a practice known from rulers who "ordered books to be burned in order to repudiate their content regarded as offensive, seditious, or dangerous."[153]

Final Travels (19:21–28:31)

Even more prevalent in Ephesus was the worship of the local goddess of the hunt, who also became a fertility goddess, Artemis. Not much of her once grand temple has been preserved in the otherwise spectacular ruins of Ephesus, but some foundation stones and small parts of pillars do remain. The many-breasted statue that once occupied a central place in the temple can now be viewed in the Ephesus Archeological Museum. Various idols or shrines have been dug up that could correspond to the products of the local artisans, including a marble replica of her temple (though no silver ones have been found yet—as in Acts 19:24).[154] Ephesus was also the leading city of the

---

[151] Sceva may also have been a nickname meaning "left-handed" because we know of no Jewish high priest by that name. While many think he may have been a renegade Jew serving as a high priest in a *Roman* cult, Howard C. Kee (*To Every Nation Under Heaven: The Acts of the Apostles* [Harrisburg: Trinity, 1997], 231) thinks he may have simply made a false claim to being a high priest. But Luke reports it as if he believes it is accurate.

[152] See esp. Clinton E. Arnold, *Ephesians: Power and Magic* (Cambridge: Cambridge University Press, 1989; Grand Rapids: Baker, 1992).

[153] Schnabel, *Acts*, 799.

[154] Ibid., 802.

province of Asia Minor (19:27).[155] Shouting the praises of Artemis for two hours (vv. 28–34) seems excessive until one observes some of the modern protests and shouting in the Middle East that have lasted at least as long. The 24,000-seat theater in which the Ephesian chanting took place (v. 31) is still in excellent condition, as ruins go. Like many ancient Greek and Roman semicircular theaters, it had excellent acoustics, where a solitary voice onstage with the ability to project well could (and still can) be heard without amplification by thousands of people sitting on the steeply banked tiers of seats. The speech by the city clerk that finally quiets and ultimately disperses the crowd accurately recounts the legal procedures that should have been followed instead of rioting (vv. 35–41).[156]

Much of Paul's subsequent journeying is narrated almost like a travel itinerary, with only sporadic additional information about what happened at the various locations. All of the sites were real places—Troas (20:5), Assos (v. 13), Mitylene (v. 14), Chios, Samos, and Miletos (v. 15). Troas, Assos, and Miletos still have easy-to-reach Roman-period ruins for tourists to view. Acts 20:18–35 contains the one address of Paul in Acts that has often been said to closely resemble the style and contents of Paul's writing in the epistles,[157] not surprisingly, because like the letters it is the one message in Acts addressed to Christians rather than as part of evangelistic efforts with outsiders. The travel itinerary continues in chapter 21, with every city in the right order forming a logical sequence—Kos, Rhodes, and Patara (v. 1), passing by Cyprus en route to Tyre in Syrophoenicia (vv. 2–3). Then would come Ptolemais (v. 7) and Caesarea (v. 16), prior to Jerusalem (v. 17). Incidental details like Philip's unmarried daughters

---

[155] See throughout Paul Trebilco, *The Early Christians in Ephesus from Paul to Ignatius* (Tübingen: Mohr Siebeck, 2004).

[156] Hemer, *Book of Acts in the Setting of Hellenistic History*, 121–24.

[157] Steve Walton, *Leadership and Lifestyle: The Portrait of Paul in the Miletus Speech and 1 Thessalonians* (Cambridge: Cambridge University Press, 2000), 140–85.

prophesying bespeak authenticity, because nothing is made of the fact and in a patriarchal world Luke would not likely have made up a story about women giving authoritative teaching.[158]

The more theologically conservative Jewish Christians alert Paul to exaggerated and false rumors circulating about the degree to which he has broken from Judaism (21:21). In a world without modern mechanisms for reporting and checking information, this is exactly what we might have expected to happen. When a crowd starts to attack Paul, the Roman guards intervene and have to arrest him to rescue him from violent attack (vv. 27–36). Paul now relies on his multicultural and multilinguistic background to his greatest advantage. The soldiers probably assumed he was just some local upstart who spoke only Aramaic. When Paul speaks to them in Greek, they wonder if he is a famous Egyptian terrorist, possibly the same as the individual Josephus describes in *Ant.* 20.168–72; *Bell.* 2.261–63 (vv. 37–39). When he gains permission to address the crowd from the safety of the Roman barracks,[159] he surprises *them* by speaking in Aramaic. Perhaps he hasn't wandered so far from his Judaism after all, they may have surmised, so they quiet down (21:40–22:2).

Intriguingly, he is able to tell much of his life story while the Jerusalemites continue to listen (22:3–20). Only when he mentions his commission to go to the Gentiles do they start to shout him down, the key sticking point about this Jesus movement for many of the most conservative Jews of the day (vv. 21–22). The Roman soldiers take him inside the barracks and begin to flog him, a privilege they could exercise without a trial, unless the victim was a citizen. Paul announces that he does hold this status and perhaps shows his captors the small,

---

[158] Bock, *Acts*, 637.

[159] To the claim that it is inconceivable that a Roman tribune would give Paul this permission, Bock (*Acts*, 658) replies, "Given that Paul is a Jew, perhaps the tribune thinks that the crowd can be quelled by noting a crucial misidentification like the one the tribune has made."

wooden diptych with a waxed surface that included his *testation* as a citizen, much like we show our passports, which he may have carried with him as he traveled (vv. 23–29).[160] This begins the succession of events that allows Luke to narrate Paul's defense speeches before the Jewish Sanhedrin, the Judean governor Felix, his successor Festus, and the Galilean ruler Herod Agrippa II (22:30–26:32). This happened when Ananias was high priest (23:2); he served in this capacity from about AD 47 to 58. The combination of Roman justice, the best the ancient Mediterranean world had ever known, which saves Paul's life more than once with a system that still often depended on bribes (24:26) to enable a prisoner to go free, is exactly what other ancient sources depict.[161]

That Paul divides the Sanhedrin along party lines, pitting Pharisees against Sadducees with respect to the resurrection (23:6–10), corresponds to what we know about the two groups from Josephus and the rabbinic sources.[162] That Paul had relatives in town (v. 16) could explain how he had the opportunity to come to study with Gamaliel in the first place (22:3). The one piece of correspondence we would not have expected any Christian to know about is Claudius Lysias's private letter to Felix (23:26–30). But in verse 25, Luke introduces it as a letter, literally, "having this type" (*echousan ton tupon touton*—my translation). The HCSB translates "of this kind"; the ESV, "to this effect"; and the NASB, "having this form." Here is where Thucydides's famous statement about including speeches in his histories may prove relevant (*History* 1.21.1). While trying to adhere to the actual words of a speaker or writer as often as possible, he acknowledged that

---

[160] Rapske, *Book of Acts and Paul in Roman Custody*, 131.

[161] Ibid., 166–67. On the nature of Roman rule under Felix and other procurators more generally, see David W. J. Gill, "Acts and Roman Policy in Judaea," in *The Book of Acts in Its Palestinian Setting*, ed. Bauckham, 15–25.

[162] See esp. Steve Mason, "Chief Priests, Sadducees, Pharisees and Sanhedrin in Acts," in *The Book of Acts in Its Palestinian Setting*, ed. Bauckham, 115–77.

sometimes it was not possible, and then he had them say what he assumed they must have said.[163] Is Luke tipping his hand that he is following this convention here? If so, then he has deceived no one and told the truth by saying that a letter was written of this type.[164]

The high priest Ananias (23:3; 24:1) corresponds to the individual Josephus describes in *Antiquities* 20.5–10. Tertullus is a Hellenistic name, probably the best prosecutor the Jewish leadership could hire, irrespective of his ethnic background. The portion of his address that Luke records begins with a classic *captatio benevolentiae*, a sycophantic introduction to curry the greatest possible favor with the governor (vv. 2–4).[165] People were held in custody under Rome while they were awaiting the outcome of their court cases, but the state did not normally provide food or other necessities for them. That would depend on friends or acquaintances from outside who were allowed to visit and bring provisions for the prisoners (thus 24:23).[166] Paul's appeal to the emperor meant that his case would go to the highest judge in the land (25:11–12). "Historical evidence indicates that the right of Roman citizens to appeal to the Emperor was absolute."[167] Festus had no choice but to grant Paul's request.

Agrippa II often went about in public with his sister, Bernice (25:13), but rumors suggested the relationship was more than platonic

---

[163] On which, see esp. Stanley E. Porter, "Thucydides 1.22.1 and Speeches in Acts: Is There a Thucydidean View?" *Novum Testamentum* 32 (1990): 121–42.

[164] Marshall, *Acts*, 370. On the other hand, Witherington (*Acts of the Apostles*, 701) thinks Felix would have read the letter out loud in Paul's presence as a prelude to his hearing. Keener (*Acts*, vol. 3, 3196–97) attributes the extra detail to this and the other defense speeches of Paul to Luke's presence (as indicated by the "we" passages) and his ability to interview people about the proceedings even of what he wasn't directly present for.

[165] Bruce W. Winter, "The Importance of the *Captatio Benevolentiae* in the Speeches of Tertullus and Paul in Acts 24:1–21," *Journal of Theological Studies* 42 (1991): 505–31.

[166] Rapske, *Book of Acts and Paul in Roman Custody*, 171.

[167] Chance, *Acts*, 466.

(Jos. *Ant.*20.145–47; *Bell.* 2.217). The pomp and circumstance fits the context very naturally.[168] The conversations between Agrippa and Festus (25:14–22; 26:31–32) would have occurred in private, one would assume, so how would Luke come to know about their contents? Witherington observes that the information is largely "a rehearsal of material that, for the most part, we have already heard about earlier in the chapter," and wonders if this is another case of Luke presenting what he assumes must have been said. Witherington adds, however, that he would not rule out the possibility of an attendant being present who could have informed others later.[169] Winter goes even further and argues that all of the speeches in Acts 24–26 would have been recorded in public documents.[170]

The ill-fated trip from Caesarea to Rome occupies Acts 27:1–28:16. There is not an unrealistic detail in this entire account. The mid-nineteenth-century commentator, James Smith, wrote a classic work on *The Voyage and Shipwreck of St. Paul.*[171] In meticulous detail he examined every aspect of ancient seafaring relevant to Paul's experiences in these chapters, concluding that the author of Acts must have either accompanied Paul, as is implied by the "we"-narrative, or was relying on another person's eyewitness account of the events. Every element of the route, the danger yet desire to travel late in the fall while still before winter, the outfitting of the vessel, the measures taken to survive during the storm, the hurricane-force wind blowing from the northeast, soundings as land became closer, and the danger of running aground at too great a speed all correspond perfectly to

---

[168] Bock, *Acts*, 705, citing a variety of primary references.

[169] Witherington, *Acts of the Apostles*, 728 and n. 397.

[170] Bruce W. Winter, "Official Proceedings and the Forensic Speeches in Acts 24–26," in *Book of Acts in Its Ancient Literary Setting*, ed. Winter and Clarke, 305–36, noting that more than 250 documents of official proceedings have been discovered.

[171] (Minneapolis: James Family, 1856; Eugene, OR: Wipf & Stock, 2001).

what we know of the practices and technology of the day.[172] The more superstitious yet hospitable nature of the Maltese (28:1–10) likewise discloses historical verisimilitude.[173] There are no vipers on Malta as we think of them, but the Greek *echidna* was used for a variety of snakes and small reptiles, including some that were present.[174] Those who question whether the crew would have listened to Paul underestimate the power of a charismatic personality believed by some to be in touch with the divine in the midst of desperate circumstances.[175]

The completion of the trip to Rome on a new boat after winter had ended likewise fits what we know of Paul's era. Castor and Pollux were the twin gods of seafaring, so they formed a natural figurehead for a ship (28:11). Syracuse, Rhegium Puteoli, and Three Taverns were towns on the Appian Way as travelers made their way northward on the Italian Peninsula toward Rome (vv. 12–15). House arrest, with a prisoner lightly chained to a series of rotating guards (v. 16) was a common practice with individuals not considered to be dangerous. They could receive visitors and supplies; they simply could not leave the property. To add insult to injury, they had to pay their own rent for their accommodation (v. 30).[176] That the local Jews had heard about Paul and yet had received no official orders from the Jerusalem authorities likewise proves realistic. The Sanhedrin did not exercise empire-wide control over Jewish people; most synagogues were

---

[172] For briefer updates of the work of Smith, see Brian M. Rapske, "Acts, Travel, and Shipwreck," in *The Book of Acts in Its Graeco-Roman Setting*, 1–47; J. M. Gilchrist, "The Historicity of Paul's Shipwreck," *Journal for the Study of the New Testament* 61 (1996): 29–51.

[173] See the lengthy list of details evaluated in Hemer, *Book of Acts in the Setting of Hellenistic History*, 132–52.

[174] Kee, *To Every Nation under Heaven*, 337, n. 62.

[175] Bock, *Acts*, 727–28. Besides, Paul had extensive experience with traveling by ship and with at least two other shipwrecks (2 Cor 11:25).

[176] Rapske, *Book of Acts and Paul in Roman Custody*, 236–39.

independent.[177] Still, reports and rumors about false teaching and practice could spread widely (vv. 21–22).[178] Appeals to the emperor were supposed to be heard within eighteen months (Philo, *Contra. Flacc.* 16.128). Does Luke's reference to Paul's remaining in his rented house for "two whole years" (v. 30) imply that Luke knew Paul had been freed but didn't want to say so explicitly? That hypothesis seems to make little sense; what reason would he have for withholding the information after building the suspense for so many chapters as to the outcome of Paul's case? An early date for Acts, before Luke knew what happened, still makes the best sense of the data.

Conclusion

Even with all these illustrations, we have highlighted only the most important or striking examples of information in Acts that can be corroborated by other sources or that display all the earmarks of authenticity. Colin Hemer's magisterial work, *The Book of Acts in the Setting of Hellenistic History*, cited throughout this chapter already, highlights numerous other instances of such phenomena. The five-volume series edited by Bruce Winter, *The Book of Acts in Its First-Century Setting*, adds considerably more background information.[179] The extraordinarily thorough four-volume commentary on Acts by Craig Keener, which we have also used extensively, includes virtually every conceivable reference to relevant ancient primary literature to verify in passage after passage how consistent Luke's writing was with first-century *history*.

---

[177] Levinskaya, *Book of Acts in Its Diaspora Setting*, 186.

[178] Chance (*Acts*, 524) complains that only the credulous would believe the Roman Jews who visited Paul had heard nothing bad about him, but Luke goes on to note that they say they have heard plenty of bad things about Christianity. Presumably, it is not Paul's person or character that has been attacked but his message.

[179] Bruce W. Winter, ed., *The Book of Acts in Its First-Century Setting*, 5 vols. (Grand Rapids: Eerdmans; Carlisle: Paternoster, 1993–96).

If Luke composed fiction within this elaborate a historical framework, he was a millennium and a half ahead of his time, so that no one in his world would have recognized what he was doing. In comparison, the claims of the Acts Seminar, who voted on the probability of large portions of Acts the way their larger and more influential predecessor, the Jesus Seminar, did with the Gospels, consistently presents sheer affirmation unsupported by actual argument or documentation.[180] And the rationales to which the Seminar does sporadically appeal are methodological presuppositions that are questionable in the extreme. Once it is assumed that Luke is a *second*-century document, then the likelihood of it using sources or recovering history is diminished. Almost anything that fits Luke's theological emphases is dismissed as unhistorical, as is much that is aesthetically pleasing, as if genuine history must be free of ideology and artistry. If a narrative is unified, then it cannot have used source material or be historical; apparently no editors were smart enough to smooth out composite documents. If a story, especially a miracle, shows even superficial similarities to other ancient legendary accounts, it is dismissed as a comparable myth. Hardly anything of Acts is left at the end of the day. But by the same principles, hardly anything of ancient history at all would be left if the Seminar were to apply its approach to other ancient texts. But this, of course, would be a self-defeating exercise for the Seminar, because it is "contradiction" with other "historical" sources that often functions as their reason for rejecting the historicity of Acts.

The truth is that the members of the Acts Seminar, like those of the Jesus Seminar before it, have so stacked the deck from the outset that they couldn't discover a significant amount of history in Acts if they were hit over the head with it. And they talk only among themselves. The bibliography in their book-length report contains nothing of significantly dissenting points of view. There are no rebuttals to

---

[180] Smith and Tyson, ed., *Acts and Christian Beginnings*.

the arguments of Hemer, Winter and cohorts, Keener, Dunn, Bock, Marshall, Schnabel, Witherington, or numerous other like-minded scholars.[181] There is not even a hint of awareness of their views, though a handful of the most prominent members of the Acts Seminar, like Richard Pervo, do interact with them in their other works, so such awareness could have been passed on. Yet in the Acts Seminar's report there is almost no interaction even with more standard liberal perspectives. It is one thing to note that works of fiction did at times in the ancient world include a smattering of references to real people and places, particularly well-known ones. It is something else altogether to read the lists of literally hundreds of synchronisms of data that Hemer, Keener, and even Barrett enumerate with the book of Acts, including fairly trivial and incidental corroborations and verisimilitude, and then find any parallel literature from the ancient Mediterranean world not solidly in the camps of generally trustworthy historical literature. The truth of the matter is far more likely to be that Luke wrote in the *first* century, based on good sources and oral tradition, including eyewitness sources and tradition, about real people and what they did in real places to show how the real church grew from its inception onwards.

---

[181] Including two slightly older, shorter works not otherwise cited in this chapter that still contain a wealth of helpful information supporting the historicity of Acts: Martin Hengel, *Acts and the History of Earliest Christianity* (London: SCM; Philadelphia: Fortress, 1979; Eugene, OR: Wipf & Stock, 2003); and A. N. Sherwin-White, *Roman Society and Roman Law in the New Testament* (Oxford: Clarendon, 1963; Eugene, OR: Wipf & Stock, 2004).

Chapter 7

Paul in Acts and in the Epistles

D espite all the details surveyed in the last chapter, there is still much more that supports the trustworthiness of Acts when we compare what it discloses about the apostle Paul with the details Paul himself reveals in his letters. To begin with, the fact that countless scholars throughout the ages have been able to put the information found in Acts together with what Paul himself reports in his epistles and create a harmonious outline of his life and ministry goes a long way toward disproving the notion that Acts is primarily fiction. Nor is it merely the case that broad contours fit together. A work like F. F. Bruce's classic textbook, *Paul: Apostle of the Heart Set Free*, shows how a plausible biography of Paul prior to his major missionary journeys and a detailed itinerary of those missionary journeys emerge from a comparison of Acts and the letters.[1]

---

[1] (Grand Rapids: Eerdmans, 1977) = F. F. Bruce, *Paul: Apostle of the Free Spirit* (Exeter: Paternoster, 1977).

In a few places more complicated and controversial questions emerge, but the vast majority of the data fit together neatly so there is an astonishing amount of agreement on what happened, where, and when, among scholars who take all of the relevant data as accurate.[2] Luke would have had to have been an extraordinarily sophisticated writer, centuries ahead of his time, to have created a largely fictitious narrative that dovetails so remarkably with the information from the seven undisputed epistles of Paul, which are almost universally accepted as authentic. Little wonder, then, that the handful of recent revisionists who want to argue that Acts is primarily fictitious have had to invent a late date for his authorship, after those letters were well known *as a corpus,* and have had to claim that Luke knew and used the letters of Paul for much of his information (see chap. 6). But then they are left with no good explanation of Luke's absolute silence about Paul's letter-writing activity. And, of course, they must discount or ignore the numerous arguments for an early date for Luke-Acts.[3]

On the other hand, precisely because Paul's letters for the most part date to as early as the 50s, we cannot envision a scenario in which Paul could have made false claims about his life based on information he found in Acts. Firsthand testimony is almost always preferred over secondhand narrative anyway. But once we realize that Acts cannot be dated any earlier than 62 (due to the events with which it ends), then all of Paul's letters (except for 1–2 Timothy and Titus), if they

---

[2] Cf. Richard N. Longenecker, *The Ministry and Message of Paul* (Grand Rapids: Zondervan, 1971); John B. Polhill, *Paul and His Letters* (Nashville: B&H, 1999); John McRay, *Paul: His Life and Teaching* (Grand Rapids: Baker, 2003); David B. Capes, Rodney Reeves and E. Randolph Richards, *Rediscovering Paul: An Introduction to His World, Letters and Theology* (Downers Grove and Nottingham: IVP, 2007); and Anthony C. Thiselton, *The Living Paul: An Introduction to His Life and Thought* (Nottingham and Downers Grove: IVP, 2010).

[3] E.g., Richard Pervo, *Dating Acts: Between the Evangelists and the Apologists* (Santa Rosa: Polebridge, 2006).

are authentic, must have been written before Acts was penned. In other words, we need to treat Acts and Paul's letters as literarily independent sources of information.

This chapter will therefore again proceed through the narrative of Acts, this time limiting ourselves to the texts in which Saul of Tarsus, later better known by his Roman name Paul, appears. We will identify the major places where Acts and material from one or more of Paul's letters overlap, noticing how regularly they reinforce each other. In the handful of places where there are apparent contradictions, we will explore the solutions that have been suggested to resolve the problems, and we will assess their plausibility. We include information from the disputed letters of Paul because as a subsequent chapter will show, there are no compelling reasons for designating any of the thirteen letters attributed explicitly to Paul to a later, pseudonymous author. But it will also become clear that a substantial majority of the parallels to Acts come from the undisputed letters anyway, so someone unpersuaded by our later discussion of pseudonymity need not discount this chapter's findings for that reason.

Saul of Tarsus as a Zealous Pharisaic Jew

The first time the book of Acts introduces us to Saul is in 8:1. As if we already knew who Saul was, Luke tells us simply that he approved of the stoning of Stephen. Of course, even on the earliest date for Acts, the readers (or listeners) *did* know about this extraordinary individual, so no introduction was necessary. In 8:3, Luke expands on this one clause by adding that "Saul began [or "tried"][4] to destroy the church. Going from house to house, he dragged off both men and women and

---

[4] The imperfect tense of *elumaineto* could be inceptive ("began to destroy") or, perhaps more likely, conative ("tried to destroy"), since there is no evidence that whatever successful persecution Saul may have at first instigated had any effect on destroying the church. As people fled hostility, they took their message elsewhere,

put them in prison." These brief references to Saul classically illustrate the literary device of foreshadowing. Even if some did not know who Saul was, they would remember his cameo appearance when he comes to center stage in chapter 9.

Paul has much more to say about his pre-Christian life in his letters.[5] He clearly affirms his Jewish identity in Romans 9:3 and laments his countrymen's misguided zeal in 10:2–3. In 11:1, he announces that he is "an Israelite" himself, "a descendant of Abraham, from the tribe of Benjamin." In 2 Corinthians 11:22, he reiterates that he is a Hebrew, an Israelite and a descendant of Abraham. Galatians 1:13 dovetails particularly closely with Acts 8:3, when Paul admits that he intensely "persecuted the church of God and tried ["began"][6] to destroy it." Verse 14 adds that he "was advancing in Judaism beyond many of my own age among my people and was extremely zealous for the traditions of my fathers."[7] This raises the question of whether Saul's pres-

---

and numbers in the young movement actually grew. Cf. Mikeal C. Parsons and Martin M. Culy, *Acts* (Waco: Baylor University Press, 2003), 149.

[5] On which, see especially Martin Hengel, *The Pre-Christian Paul* (London: SCM; Philadelphia: Trinity Press International, 1991). Cf. also N. T. Wright, *What Saint Paul Really Said: Was Paul of Tarsus the Real Founder of Christianity?* (Oxford: Lion; Grand Rapids: Eerdmans, 1997), 25–35. For the possibility that Paul had been a Zealot more formally, see Mark R. Fairchild, "Paul's Pre-Christian Zealot Associations: A Re-examination of Gal 1.14 and Acts 22.3," *New Testament Studies* 45 (1999): 514–32.

[6] This time the verb is *eporthoun*, but again it is in the conative imperfect— Douglas J. Moo, *Galatians* (Grand Rapids: Baker, 2013), 100. This time the NIV appropriately translates it "tried to destroy," which is probably how it should have rendered Acts 8:3 as well.

[7] Giving the lie to the popular view that he was psychologically ripe for conversion. See esp. the classic study of Krister Stendahl, "The Apostle Paul and the Introspective Conscience of the West," *Harvard Theological Review* 56 (1963): 199–215. More recently, cf. Terence L. Donaldson, "Zealot and Convert: The Origin of Paul's Christ-Torah Antithesis," *Catholic Biblical Quarterly* 51 (1989): 655–82. For an overview of approaches, see Larry W. Hurtado, "Convert, Apostate, or Apostle to the Nations: The 'Conversion' of Paul in Recent Scholarship," *Studies in Religion* 22 (1993): 273–84.

ence at Stephen's stoning implies that he had already been appointed to the Sanhedrin. Because members of that court lay their garments at Saul's feet (to free themselves from all but an inner garment and make stone throwing easier and more accurate), some have envisioned Saul's playing an official role in the proceedings.[8] Later in Acts, Paul will himself refer to casting his vote against the Christians he was persecuting (26:10). But while this language could support Saul's being a part of the court, it can also simply be metaphorical terminology for agreeing with or approving of the court's action.[9]

Tied in with this discussion is Paul's reference to having studied with Gamaliel (Acts 22:3). This would have been his educational preparation for becoming a rabbi. Did he complete his study? If so, was he ordained? Did ordination even exist this early, or did it come into play only after AD 70? If he had become a rabbi, he could have been on the Sanhedrin. If so, he almost certainly would have been married.[10] But 1 Corinthians 7:8 reveals that he is single, at least in the mid-50s. But he divulges this information in the context of talking about widows and (probably) widowers.[11] So perhaps Paul had

---

[8] A balanced conclusion appears in David G. Peterson, *The Acts of the Apostles* (Grand Rapids: Eerdmans; Nottingham: Apollos, 2009), 268: "The fact that the witnesses laid their clothes at Saul's feet suggests that he was already the acknowledged leader in the opposition to the early church (cf. 8:1, 3)." In n. 89, Peterson observes that in 4:35, 37; and 5:2, "Laying something at someone's feet implies a recognition of that person's authority." Cf. also Brice C. Jones, "The Meaning of the Phrase 'And the Witnesses Laid Down Their Cloaks' in Acts 7:58," *Expository Times* 123 (2011): 113–18.

[9] Peterson, *The Acts of the Apostles*, 663. Cf. Darrell L. Bock, *Acts* (Grand Rapids: Baker, 2007), 715; Ben Witherington III, *The Acts of the Apostles: A Socio-Rhetorical Commentary* (Grand Rapids: Eerdmans; Carlisle: Paternoster, 1998), 741–42.

[10] E.g., Polhill (*Paul and His Letters*, 42), who nevertheless notes that these are later rabbinic traditions. Cf. Gillian Beattie, *Women and Marriage in Paul and His Early Interpreters* (London and New York: T & T Clark, 2005), 26.

[11] The Greek *agamos*, often translated just as "unmarried," is the form used for "widowers" before the masculine of *chēra* ("widow") began to be used, well after the first century. Given that the two words are paired here, one masculine and one

become a widower. All these questions leave enough uncertainty that we have to remain somewhat agnostic about them.

Philippians 3:4–6 contains the fullest catalog of the credentials Saul of Tarsus once placed great confidence in: "circumcised on the eighth day" (after his birth, according to Torah), "of the people of Israel, of the tribe of Benjamin, a Hebrew of Hebrews; in regard to the law, a Pharisee; as for zeal, persecuting the church; as for righteousness based on the law, faultless." He was not an individual who could have been easily persuaded by other human beings to turn from his spiritual commitments.[12] Yet in 1 Thessalonians 2:14–16, he distances himself so much from that lifestyle that he can speak about other Jewish individuals who "killed the Lord Jesus and the prophets and also drove us out." Thus he concludes, "In this way they always heap up their sins to the limit. The wrath of God has come upon them at last."[13] The Pastoral Epistles (1–2 Timothy and Titus) are often considered deutero-Pauline. Yet whatever differences they may exhibit from the undisputed Paulines on other topics, they disclose no difference on this one. "Paul" declares that he "was once a blasphemer and a persecutor and a violent man" (1 Tim 1:13). There is not the slightest tension between Acts and the epistles on this front and much that reinforces the brief glimpses Luke gives us into Saul's pre-Christian life.[14]

---

feminine, it is likely that Paul is referring to "widowers and widows." Cf. Gordon D. Fee, *The First Epistle to the Corinthians*, rev. ed. (Grand Rapids: Eerdmans, 2014), 318–20; and J. Dorcas Gordon, *Sister or Wife? 1 Corinthians 7 and Cultural Anthropology* (Sheffield: Sheffield Academic Press, 1997), 120 and n. 78.

[12] Cf. further Peter T. O'Brien, *The Epistle to the Philippians* (Grand Rapids: Eerdmans; Exeter: Paternoster, 1991), 366–81; John Reumann, *Philippians* (New Haven and London: Yale University Press, 2008), 511–16.

[13] This is not to be taken as anti-Jewish, however; Paul is vilifying only a certain group of leaders. See esp. Michael A. Rydelnik, "Was Paul Anti-Semitic? Revisiting 1 Thessalonians 2:14–16," *Bibliotheca Sacra* 165 (2008): 58–67.

[14] Michael Wolter ("Paulus, der bekehrte Gottesfeind: Zum Verständnis von 1. Tim 1:13," *Novum Testamentum* 31 [1989]: 48–66) finds the writer of the Pastorals

Saul's Conversion

Acts 9 picks up the narrative of Saul exactly where Luke left off a chapter earlier. He is "still breathing out murderous threats against the Lord's disciples" (v. 1). He has asked the high priest for letters, presumably commissioning him to (or at least endorsing him for) the task,[15] so that he can go to another large Jewish community, Damascus in Syria, where a fair number of Jews had apparently come to believe that Jesus was the Messiah. There he would continue his persecuting activity and try to bring prisoners back to Jerusalem for trial (vv. 1–2). Close to the city a heavenly light flashed around him, he fell to the ground, and he heard the risen Lord Jesus speak to him. Temporarily blinded, he had to be led into the city to the home of a man named Judas on Straight Street. There he would meet a believer named Ananias who would teach him the truth about Jesus and baptize him (vv. 3–18).

Saul does so, spends several days with the believers in Damascus and begins to tell his story in the synagogues, now convinced that Jesus is both Messiah and Son of God (vv. 19–22).[16] Not surprisingly his personal testimony proves irrefutable, so the same mind-set that led Saul to try to quash this new Messianic sect through violence leads the unconvinced Jewish authorities in Damascus to try to do the same—by killing Saul. The close watch set by various guards at each of the city gates left Saul's newfound friends no recourse but to lower him in a basket to the ground after spiriting him off through a hole in the city wall somewhere (vv. 23–25). A cloudy night, a place in the

---

(whom he believes to be pseudonymous) closer to Acts than to the undisputed Paulines on this point!

[15] For details, see Craig S. Keener, *Acts*, vol. 2, 1619–21.

[16] See esp. N. T. Wright, *Paul and the Faithfulness of God*, vol. 2 (London: SPCK; Minneapolis: Fortress, 2013), 690–701.

wall with no torch or candlelight nearby, and unsuspecting guards all doubtless contributed to the success of the subterfuge.[17]

For this episode Acts teaches us more than Paul's letters do. But they are not entirely devoid of reference to these events. Galatians 1 refers to Saul's conversion as the occasion "when God . . . was pleased to reveal his Son in me" (vv. 15–16). Is it coincidence that God's Son is also the title that first characterizes Saul's preaching in Damascus according to Acts 9:20? In Galatians, Paul does not immediately say that this happened near Damascus, but at the end of verse 17, after some time in Arabia, he speaks of returning to Damascus, suggesting that he had been there previously. Second Corinthians 11:32–33 presents a much more striking correspondence. There Paul notes that in Damascus in the days of King Aretas, the governor of the city kept a guard in order to arrest Paul. In order to escape, he had to be lowered in a basket from "a window in the wall." Given that most ancient "windows" were simply holes in walls, without glass or any other covering material, there is no contradiction here with Acts. In fact, the specific features of Paul's description mesh in detail with Acts' depiction.

Philippians 3 reinforces the clean and quick break he made from his previous beliefs about Jesus, as Luke describes it, when Paul writes in verses 7–9 that

> whatever were gains to me I now consider loss for the sake of Christ. What is more, I consider everything a loss because of the surpassing worth of knowing Christ Jesus my Lord, for whose sake I have lost all things. I consider them garbage, that I may gain Christ and be found in him, not having a righteousness of my own that comes from the law, but that which is through faith in Christ—the righteousness that comes from God on the basis of faith.

---

[17] Cf. Keener, *Acts*, vol. 2, 1674–75.

Even before the instruction from Ananias, the moment Saul realized Jesus was speaking to him from heaven on the Damascus road, he would have recognized that it was his message, not traditional Jewish attitudes to the law, to which he should adhere. No doubt the contrast between Jesus and the Jewish leaders on this topic was one of the most well-known elements of Jesus's theology as those leaders explained to one another, and to anyone else who was interested, why they viewed Jesus as so apostate and dangerous. He was, in their eyes, an antinomian—a lawbreaker who would bring down God's wrath on the Jewish people unless the virus of his teaching was eradicated from their midst.[18]

The other key detail from Saul's conversion in Acts that his letters frequently confirm is his calling or commissioning to proclaim the message of Jesus, not merely to Israelites but throughout the Gentile world and to their authorities (Acts 9:15). The passages in the epistles are too numerous to list them all. But we may observe, in Romans alone, how Paul includes in his introductory greeting that through Christ he "received grace and apostleship to call all the Gentiles to the obedience that comes from faith for his name's sake" (Rom 1:5). In what is widely regarded as part of the two-verse thesis of the letter (vv. 16–17),[19] Paul adds that the gospel "is the power of God that brings salvation to everyone who believes: first to the Jew, then to the Gentile" (v. 16), while Acts regularly confirms that sequence once Paul begins his missionary journeys. Whenever he can find a Jewish

---

[18] See Michael F. Bird, "Jesus as Law-Breaker," in *Who Do My Opponents Say That I Am? An Investigation of the Accusations Against the Historical Jesus*, ed. Scot McKnight and Joseph B. Modica (New York and London: T & T Clark, 2008), 3–26. Cf. Alan F. Segal, *Paul the Convert: The Apostolate and Apostasy of Saul the Pharisee* (New Haven: Yale University Press, 1990).

[19] E.g., Ben Witherington III with Darlene Hyatt, *Paul's Letter to the Romans: A Socio-Rhetorical Commentary* (Grand Rapids: Eerdmans, 2004), 47–48; Colin G. Kruse, *Paul's Letter to the Romans* (Grand Rapids: Eerdmans; Nottingham, Apollos, 2012), 66.

presence in a community, he begins proclaiming Jesus there (Acts 13:5, 14; 14:1; 16:13; 17:1, 10, 17; etc.). But consistently a measure of hostility leads him at some point to turn from the local Jews to the larger, Gentile population in which they are embedded (Acts 13:46; 14:1, 6–7; 17:4, 12, 17; 18:6, etc.).[20] As he winds up his letter, Paul emphasizes his calling or commissioning again. In Romans 15:15–16, he reminds his audience that God's grace enabled him "to be a minister of Christ Jesus to the Gentiles," and that in preaching he strove "that the Gentiles might become an offering acceptable to God, sanctified by the Holy Spirit."[21]

Indeed, two passages in his letters in particular stress how passionate Paul remained about obeying this call. Four verses later in Romans, he explains that "it has always been my ambition to preach the gospel where Christ was not known, so that I would not be building on someone else's foundation" (Rom 15:20). In 2 Corinthians 10:16, Paul stresses his goal to preach the gospel in "regions beyond" the Corinthians, an expression that has lent itself to the name of more than one missionary organization.[22] While Paul would have encountered Jewish individuals at numerous points of the Roman Empire, the further afield he went from Israel and from the major cities in other parts of his world, the more he would be speaking predominantly with Gentiles, thus fulfilling his Christ-ordained mission revealed to him on the Damascus Road as highlighted in Acts 9.

---

[20] See further Eckhard J. Schnabel, *Early Christian Mission* (Downers Grove and Leicester: IVP, 2004), vol. 2, 1300–1301, 1385–92.

[21] Most translations take "of the Gentiles" as an objective genitive—i.e., offering the Gentiles to God as a sacrifice. It is possible, however, to take it as subjective, referring to the collection for Jerusalem—i.e., the offering the Gentiles gave. See David J. Downs, "'The Offering of the Gentiles' in Romans 15.16," *Journal for the Study of the New Testament* 29 (2006): 173–86.

[22] Note especially Regions Beyond Missionary Union, Regions Beyond International, and Regions Beyond Ministry.

Saul's First Visit to Jerusalem

Frequently in the Gospels and Acts, events that are separated by a significant period of time are narrated one right after the other in a fashion that could make the unsuspecting reader imagine that no time elapsed at all. Acts 9:26 contains one of these literary seams. Luke continues, after Saul's escape from Damascus, by narrating that "when he came to Jerusalem, he tried to join the disciples." But when exactly was that? Verse 23 has already referred to a long period of time after Saul's conversion that he remained in Damascus. The expression "many days" in Greek was an indefinite expression that at times encompassed years.[23] And Luke gives no hint how long it was between Saul's departure from Syria and his visit to Jerusalem. Galatians 1 answers our questions in part: three years after his conversion on the Damascus Road, he traveled to Jerusalem for the first time as a Messianic believer (v. 18). Commentators who glibly speak of a contradiction between Acts and Galatians here simply have not read carefully enough.[24]

---

[23] C. K. Barrett (*A Critical and Exegetical Commentary on the Acts of the Apostles*, vol. 1 [Edinburgh: T & T Clark, 1994], 463) refers to the Greek here and in v. 19b as each representing "a vague expression of time," with "no precise length" in mind, but with this expression a longer period is suggested than in the earlier verse.

[24] Mark Harding ("On the Historicity of Acts: Comparing Acts 9:23–5 with 2 Corinthians 11.32–3," *New Testament Studies* 39 [1993]: 518–38) argues that Luke's emphasis on Jewish opposition is irreconcilable with Paul's reference to tensions with the local Roman government and that we should see Luke's perspective as invented because of his redactional emphasis on Jewish opposition. This founders on two grounds: (1) Luke is the most nuanced of the Gospel writers in his presentation of the Jewish leadership; i.e., he has more positive references (along with other negative ones) than any other Evangelist; and (2) Jews working through the Roman government to oppose Jesus and early Christians is exactly the consistent approach we see throughout all four Gospels and Acts and the only historically realistic option they had under imperial domination. Richard I. Pervo (*Acts* [Minneapolis: Fortress, 2009]), 247, n. 10) cites Harding approvingly; and against those who would see Jews and Romans working together, he states merely that this is "a methodologically dubious ploy" without any explanation as to what makes it dubious. These kinds of

Acts 9 continues by noting that the Jerusalem Christians were at first afraid of Saul, not surprisingly, because of his previous persecuting activity (v. 26). So Barnabas, introduced as an encouraging and generous member of the fledgling Christian community already in 4:36–37, brings Saul to the apostles, corroborating his story about his experience in and around Damascus (9:27). Luke concludes this episode by explaining that Saul spoke boldly in Jesus's name in Jerusalem and debated especially with other Hellenistic Jews (those most like him). Eventually some became upset enough that they wanted to murder him, so he was again spirited out of the city and returned to his hometown of Tarsus (vv. 28–30).

Commentators often claim that Galatians 1:17–24 flatly contradicts Acts 9. Such individuals appear to have too little historical imagination or appreciation of how different authors can describe the identical events from different angles.[25] In Galatians 1:17, Paul insists he did not go immediately to Jerusalem to consult with the apostles there after his conversion. Instead he spent up to three years in "Arabia," a territorial designation that in the first century included parts of the Nabatean kingdom that Aretas oversaw just a little to the southeast of Damascus.[26] Although there is a long-standing tradition in some Christian circles that Saul went away for some kind of spiritual retreat, nothing in any Scripture positively supports this notion. It

---

footnotes prove pervasive throughout Pervo's commentary; he thinks he can refute views simply by sheer affirmation that they involve faulty method. Presumably he is arguing against every form of harmonizing two differing documents by combining information from both of them together, in which case he is flying in the face of the actual practices of almost all responsible historians of all eras!

[25] Contrast Martin Hengel and Anna Maria Schwemer, *Paul Between Damascus and Antioch: The Unknown Years* (London: SCM; Louisville: Westminster John Knox, 1997), 33–50.

[26] See esp. Schnabel, *Early Christian Mission*, vol. 2, 1035–42.

is more likely that he simply continued the ministry of preaching he had begun already in Damascus.[27]

Either way, however, Paul does go to Jerusalem three years later, which, as we have already seen, in no way contradicts anything Acts actually states. Acts never states which apostles Saul saw (Acts 9:27), so when he specifies that it was only Cephas (i.e., Peter) and James, the Lord's brother (Gal 1:19–20), there is again no contradiction.[28] At this early stage of things, it is unlikely that "apostle" had yet become a technical term for "the Twelve," especially since this James was not one of them. Acts 9 likewise is consonant with Galatians 1:22, which declares that Saul was personally unknown to the churches in Judea, which would have included the various house congregations in Jerusalem. The Greek employs the metaphor that Saul was not known "by face," but this cannot be taken literally because some of them would have recognized Saul from his years there before his conversion. Rather "to know by face" was a Semitic idiom for having a close acquaintance with someone, which the Jerusalem Christians would not have had, especially not with Saul now as one of their number.[29] Most of them may not have even seen him during this visit since he was spending time not with fellow Jewish Christians but with non-Christian Jews (Acts 9:28–29).[30] That a few believers (but only a few)

---

[27] Hengel and Schwemer, *Paul Between Damascus and Antioch*, 80–90; Schnabel, *Early Christian Mission*, vol. 2, 1031–32.

[28] F. F. Bruce (*The Book of the Acts*, rev. ed. [Grand Rapids: Eerdmans, 1988], 193–94) speaks appropriately of a "generalizing plural" and a "generalizing report" in Acts 9:27. Eckhard J. Schnabel (*Acts* [Grand Rapids: Zondervan, 2012], 456) observes that the article "should not be pressed to mean that all twelve apostles are present in Jerusalem at this time and meet Saul in a meeting arranged by Barnabas."

[29] Martinus C. de Boer, *Galatians: A Commentary* (Louisville: Westminster John Knox, 2011), 100–102; Ben Witherington III, *Grace in Galatia: A Commentary on Paul's Letter to the Galatians* (Grand Rapids: Eerdmans, 1998), 124.

[30] I. Howard Marshall (*Acts* [Leicester: IVP; Grand Rapids: Eerdmans, 1980], 176) perceptively remarks, "It seems likely, however, that in Galatians Paul is dealing with some kind of accusation that he had been involved in a mission in

accompanied him at his departure (v. 30) scarcely contradicts this, and we could not imagine the majority of the already thousands of Judean Christians throwing a massive farewell party for one they were trying to secret out of town and away from death threats! The majority had not seen him; they merely heard that their former archenemy was now passionately on their side (Gal 1:23).

Saul's Second Visit to Jerusalem

Acts does not say anything more about Saul until chapter 11. Then, in verses 27–30, Luke tells us that a Christian prophet named Agabus came to Syrian Antioch and foretold a famine that would spread throughout the whole Roman world (Gk. *oikoumenē*). This food shortage turned out to afflict the Judeans particularly severely,[31] so that the disciples sent material aid to Jerusalem delivered by Barnabas and Saul.

It is unclear whether Luke intends to narrate the sending of a gift that arrived before the famine ensued or to recount a lengthy, multiyear collection with the barest of details. The initial number of believers who swelled the ranks of the church in and around Jerusalem undoubtedly created material strains on the community, especially since many

---

Judea during which he had been happy to insist on circumcision (Gal. 5:11). J. B. Lightfoot claims: 'To a majority therefore of the Christians at Jerusalem he *might*, and to the churches of Judea at large he *must* have been personally unknown. But though the two accounts are not contradictory, the impression left by St Luke's narrative needs correcting by the more precise and authentic statement of St Paul.' Since, according to Acts, Paul's activity was among the Hellenists, *i.e.* Jews from the Diaspora resident in Jerusalem, it is clear that he did not do missionary work in the country areas of Judea."

[31] The word often refers to representative parts of the Roman world (cf. Luke 2:1; Acts 17:6; 19:27; 24:5; Rom 10:18). For primary sources attesting to the number of parts of the empire plagued by famine, with the worst being Judea in 46–48, see Joseph A. Fitzmyer, *The Acts of the Apostles* (New York and London: Doubleday, 1998), 481–82. Cf. Schnabel, *Acts*, 525–26.

were from out of town, originally intending to celebrate Pentecost and then return home (Acts 2:8–11). By Agabus's time many would have made arrangements to settle permanently in or near the Holy City. Liquidating assets for even a partially common treasury (2:43–47; 4:32–37) would not have been a long-term solution.[32] So perhaps the drought began to be most severe first in Judea, even as Agabus predicts it will spread considerably. In either event Paul's own letters describe him to still be collecting funds for these poor people almost a decade later (1 Cor 16:1–4; 2 Cor 8–9; Rom 15:25–27), so it is clear there were long-term, adverse effects of the famine that still had to be addressed.[33]

The second trip to Jerusalem for the converted Saul of Tarsus, according to Galatians, involves a different set of circumstances, at least at first glance. Barnabas goes with him, exactly as in Acts 11:30. But Titus comes along as well (Gal 2:1). It is a private meeting with the leaders (v. 2), just as Acts 11:30 speaks of the emissaries meeting with the elders in Jerusalem. But from that point on, it seems that the main topic of discussion was whether Saul's "law-free" gospel was on target. Specifically, circumcision becomes a central issue. Does a Gentile follower of Jesus have to be circumcised as if he were Jewish and Torah obedient? Fortunately for men like Titus, in a world without anesthesia, the conclusion was no (Gal 2:2–3).[34] Some Jewish Christians had been arguing the opposite (v. 4), but their opinions

---

[32] This is not to return to the older, discredited view that Luke viewed communal sharing as a mistake. For a balanced perspective, see esp. Steve Walton, "Primitive Communism in Acts? Does Acts Present the Community of Goods (2:44–45; 4:32–35) as Mistaken?" *Evangelical Quarterly* 80 (2008): 99–111.

[33] On the collection, see esp. David J. Downs, *The Offering of the Gentiles: Paul's Collection for Jerusalem in Its Chronological, Cultural, and Cultic Contexts* (Tübingen: Mohr Siebeck, 2008). Cf. also Dieter Georgi, *Remembering the Poor: The History of Paul's Collection for Jerusalem* (Nashville: Abingdon, 1992).

[34] The view that while Titus was not *compelled* to be circumcised, he voluntarily underwent the process is appropriately labeled an "artificial construction" by Hans Dieter Betz (*Galatians* [Philadelphia: Fortress, 1979], 80 n. 298).

did not carry the day (vv. 5–6). This discussion then broadened in order to deal with the general spheres of ministry in which Peter and Saul would function: Peter to the Jews and Saul to the Gentiles (vv. 7–9). Completely apart from Acts, it becomes obvious that these are extremely generalized "marching orders." As we saw above, even the Paul of the letters continues to preach to Jews, but a substantial majority of his ministry does focus on the Gentile world. And 1 Corinthians knows that Peter has been in Corinth (1:12; 3:22; 9:5), where it would have been hard for him to avoid Gentile ministry, even if he concentrated largely on the small Jewish population there. If the first letter of Peter has any authentic parts to it at all, then it too, addressed as an encyclical to Christians in five provinces in what we would call Turkey today, had to have included plenty of Gentiles as well as Jews in the congregations Peter had visited and/or established.[35]

Could Galatians 2:1–10 possibly refer to the same visit to Jerusalem as Acts 11:27–30? Two small items suggest we should envision the discussion about law-keeping as occurring at the same time as the delivery of monies for the famine-stricken believers. First, Galatians 2:2 explicitly states that Paul went in response to a revelation. While this could have taken many forms, the prophecy by Agabus fits hand in glove. Second, the final and probably climactic point of the gathering in Galatians 2:10 states that the Jerusalem leaders were concerned that Paul continued to remember the poor, and he declares that he was eager to do this. This detail likewise fits perfectly a delivery of support for the impoverished and a recognition that this was going to be a long-term problem. In fact, it is hard to imagine Barnabas and Saul,

---

[35] James D. G. Dunn (*The Epistle to the Galatians* [London: A & C Black; Peabody: Hendrickson, 1993], 111–12) notes the problems of pressing any division of labor too much and suggests the translation in v. 9, "that we should be for the Gentiles, and they for the circumcision," i.e., that Paul and Barnabas "should represent, or act for, or be responsible for the Gentile converts, while the pillars [Peter, John, and James] should represent, or act for, or be responsible for the Jewish disciples."

with the time and rigors of travel in the ancient world, making a trip of this nature, dropping the gift off in a "mailbox" and leaving again! Simple hospitality, not to mention theological questions that would have emerged at the beginning of any religious movement growing out of Judaism, would no doubt have led to a stay of a few days. Can we seriously imagine them not having some vigorous theological conversation about the most pressing issues of the young church?[36]

Why then does Luke say nothing about all this? The simplest answer is that he knows he will be narrating a more formal, prolonged council in Acts 15 that returned to this topic and hashed out a more official agreement. He knows these were more preliminary conversations that did not prevent further controversy from arising.[37] Besides at this juncture, from 8:1 onwards, he is primarily describing the growth of the Christian movement outside Jerusalem.[38] The reason Acts 11:27–30 appears at all is because it reflects an important incident in *Antioch* of Syria, in a segment of three vignettes involving this city (11:19–21, 22–26, and 27–30).[39] It would disrupt his narrative flow for Luke to say any more at this point.

But does not Acts 15:5–29 closely resemble Galatians 2:1–10? In certain ways, yes, of course it does. Paul, Barnabas, Peter, and James appear in both accounts. There is a debate over circumcision, with the conclusion

---

[36] Especially if James D. G. Dunn (*Jesus, Paul and the Law: Studies in Mark and Galatians* [London: SPCK; Louisville: Westminster John Knox, 1990; Grand Rapids: Baker, 2011], 108–28) is correct that *historēsai* in Gal 1:18 means "to interview or acquire information from someone, not merely to get to know someone in a casual way."

[37] Cf. Witherington, *Acts of the Apostles*, 444–46. See also L. Ann Jervis, *Galatians* (Peabody: Hendrickson, 1999), 7–15; and Colin J. Hemer, "Acts and Galatians Reconsidered," *Themelios* 2 (1977): 81–88.

[38] For a representative outline of Acts reflecting this progression in detail, see Richard N. Longenecker, "Acts," in *The Expositor's Bible Commentary*, rev. ed., ed. Tremper Longman III and David E. Garland, vol. 10 (Grand Rapids: Zondervan, 2007), 108–12.

[39] Ibid., 709; Peterson, *The Acts of the Apostles*, ix; Pervo, *Acts*, viii.

that Gentile believers need not be circumcised. And in both instances none of the named individuals are arguing otherwise but other unnamed Jewish Christians whom Paul sees as highly misguided. But beyond this, nothing in Acts 15 says anything about anyone coming to the gathering in response to a revelation, nor is there anything about remembering the poor. Nor does Galatians 2 include any mention of Pharisaic Jewish Christians, the specific testimony and viewpoints of Peter, Paul, and James, any appeal to Scripture at all, any reference to the presence of the apostle John, Judas Barsabbas, or Silas, any formal conclusion regarding highly offensive practices Gentiles should abstain from for the sake of Jewish evangelism,[40] or any letter sent off to various churches itemizing these practices and explaining the council and its results.

Precisely because the vast majority of the details in Acts 15 are not found in Galatians 2 but in no way contradict them, it is certainly possible to argue that the two gatherings depicted in these two chapters *do* refer to the same event. No insuperable contradictions emerge between the two if one comes to this conclusion.[41] But is it the most probable relationship between Acts and Galatians? To answer this query, we must examine the sequel to Galatians 2:1–10 in verses 11–14.

At some unspecified time after Paul and Peter appeared to be on the same page in Jerusalem, Peter came to Syrian Antioch while Paul was still there. Peter stayed long enough to establish the practice of enjoying table fellowship with Gentile believers (v. 12b). This meshes with the lesson he learned in Acts 10:1–11:18. God had declared all food clean, which meant there were no longer any inherently impure people because of their regular contact with impure

---

[40] See further Craig L. Blomberg, "The Christian and the Law of Moses," in *Witness to the Gospel: The Theology of Acts*, ed. I. Howard Marshall and David G. Peterson (Grand Rapids: Eerdmans, 1998), 407–10. Cf. Bruce, *Paul*, 187.

[41] See esp. Craig S. Keener, *Acts*, vol. 3, 2195–2202.

food.[42] Then "certain men came from James," presumably meaning from the Jerusalem church (Gal 2:12). It is impossible to know from this expression whether James agreed with their views or not. He could have sent them for some other reason, but when they saw the Christian practices in Antioch, their objections ensued. For all we know, they could have come without any formal endorsement by James at all, but appealed to their membership in the Jerusalem church by referring to its chief elder to try to gain support for their viewpoints.[43] In any event the Jewish Christians in Antioch, led by Peter and even Barnabas, withdrew from the table fellowship they had been enjoying with their Gentile brothers and sisters (v. 12c), which led Paul to charge Peter with standing condemned as a hypocrite (vv. 11, 13–14).

If Galatians 2:1–10 describes the so-called apostolic or Jerusalem Council of Acts 15:5–29, then we have to imagine virtually every Jewish Christian present except for Paul consciously reneging on a formal dictum from James himself, the man these "Judaizers" newly arrived in Antioch claim to represent. It is not just that Peter, who denied Jesus three times, would have capitulated; we could probably envisage that! But every other Jewish Christian would have done so likewise, in opposition to the chief elder of the Jewish wing of the mother church in Jerusalem, even after a formal council had decided to the contrary, which also took place in the presence of those who were challenging its views from a more traditional, law-abiding approach. Stranger things have happened in the history of the world, but it is

---

[42] See esp. van Thanh Nguyen, *Peter and Cornelius: A Story of Conversion and Mission* (Eugene, OR: Pickwick, 2012). Cf. Schnabel, *Acts*, 492.

[43] More likely, they were sent by James to find out what was going on and express some concern over issues that hadn't been settled in Galatians 2:1–10 (assuming that these verses do not correspond to Acts 15). How accurately or hyperbolically they expressed those concerns is impossible to know. See Thomas R. Schreiner, *Galatians* (Grand Rapids: Zondervan, 2010), 140.

far easier to imagine this duplicity occurring merely after the more informal caucus of Galatians 2:1–10, with the events of Acts 15:5–29 having not even happened yet when Paul penned Galatians.[44]

Acts 15:1 appears to offer confirmation of this hypothesis. What originally precipitated the apostolic council was that "certain people came down from Judea to Antioch and were teaching the believers: 'Unless you are circumcised, according to the custom taught by Moses, you cannot be saved.'" This sounds all too suspiciously like the same people Galatians 2:12 calls "certain men . . . from James."[45] After all, even though what Paul is most exercised about in Galatians is the withdrawal of Peter and Barnabas from table fellowship, he does refer to this group of visitors as "the circumcision group" (v. 12). Circumcision was even more foundational to Judaism than the dietary laws, so it is not surprising that a (probably pejorative) nickname for these visitors who insisted on keeping kosher would involve their similarly law-based insistence that circumcision was a requirement for salvation. Both Luke and Paul, as consistently elsewhere, are disclosing selectively just the historical details that most fit the issues at hand in the contexts of each of their documents. But a careful reading discloses how much more complex each was as well.

It is far easier to imagine all the Jewish Christians in Antioch capitulating under pressure of some they believed represented James if only informal conversations and "gentlemen's agreements" had been previously reached. *Who knew?*, they might have thought, *Maybe James*

---

[44] Richard N. Longenecker, *Galatians* (Dallas: Word, 1990), lxxx; Witherington, *Grace in Galatia*, 17; Schreiner, *Galatians*, 139. On the greater likelihood of the possibly strained relationship between James and Paul occurring earlier rather than later, see also Jim Reiher, "Paul's Strained Relationship with the Apostle James at the Time of Writing Galatians (and How It Contributes to the Debate on the Destination of the Letter)," *Evangelical Quarterly* 87 (2015): 18–35.

[45] Peterson, *The Acts of the Apostles*, 420–21; Longenecker, "Acts," 939–42; Bruce, *Book of Acts*, 286.

had changed his mind as well? This scenario would also explain why Paul in Galatians does not mention any previous agreement, to say nothing of a letter that could easily have still been in the Antiochene Christians' possession. He had no conciliar decision to remind them of because none had yet been reached. Almost certainly Peter did not repent on the spot, or Paul would surely have told us, bolstering his point that much more.[46] But that does not mean Peter could not have realized his duplicity in the days and weeks ahead so that at the subsequent apostolic council of Acts 15 he could confidently side with Paul again (vv. 7–11).[47] Finally, Paul's whole point in Galatians 1:12–2:14 is to demonstrate his independence from the Jerusalem apostles and his authority equal to theirs. To have omitted any trip he made to Jerusalem in which he had opportunity to converse with the apostles would have jeopardized his case considerably. Anyone who was at all suspicious of him who discovered that he had been there on an additional occasion would doubtless have alleged that he kept silent about such a trip because that is when the apostles did not support him or agree with his theology.[48]

We are suggesting, therefore, with many evangelical commentators (and the occasional other), that Paul's first postconversion trip to Jerusalem is narrated in Acts 9:26–31 (= Galatians 1:18–24), that his second such trip appears in Acts 11:30 (= Galatians 2:1–10), that Acts 15:1 corresponds to the time of Galatians 2:11–14, and that Acts 15:5–29 takes place after the letter to the Galatians has been written

---

[46] Longenecker, *Galatians*, 79; Dunn, *Epistle to the Galatians*, 130; David A. deSilva, *Global Readings: A Sri Lankan Commentary on Paul's Letter to the Galatians* (Eugene, OR: Cascade, 2011), 111.

[47] John Nolland, "A Fresh Look at Acts 15.10," *New Testament Studies* 27 (1980): 105–15; Schnabel, *Acts*, 636.

[48] Robert K. Rapa, *The Meaning of "Works of the Law" in Galatians and Romans* (New York; Peter Lang, 2001), 79–80; Scot McKnight, *Galatians* (Grand Rapids: Zondervan, 1995), 89.

and sent.[49] To see if these equations can be sustained, it is time to discuss matters of dates and chronology.

The earliest fixed date of any event in Paul's career is his ministry in Corinth under Gallio. We know this because an inscription at Delphi enables us to date Gallio's rule in Corinth for a single year from AD 51–52. If we limit ourselves to Acts for the moment, that means we can work backwards from 18:1–17 where Paul is in Corinth. It is usually estimated that the events described in Acts 15:30–17:34, with the travels involved, would have taken about two years. So the Apostolic Council of the immediately preceding verses in Acts 15 is commonly dated to AD 49.[50] There is almost nothing in Acts to indicate when Saul's conversion in Acts 9 should be dated, otherwise than sometime after Stephen's stoning and after Philip's ministry in Samaria and Gaza (chap. 8). Nor do we have any way of dating Acts 11:27–30 other than sometime in conjunction with or slightly before the famine, which seems to have been at its height in the mid-to-late 40s. We do know from a study of the Gospels' chronology that Jesus must have been executed in either AD 30 or 33, based on when the Passover would have fallen on a Thursday evening through Friday afternoon.[51]

Now we may factor in Galatians. If our reconstruction of events above is correct, Saul's conversion occurred either fourteen or seventeen

---

[49] F. F. Bruce, *The Epistle to the Galatians* (Exeter: Paternoster; Grand Rapids: Eerdmans, 1982), 3–32; Moo, *Galatians*, 2–18; deSilva, *Paul's Letter to the Galatians*, 28–39; Longenecker, *Galatians*, lxxii–lxxxiii; Witherington, *Grace in Galatia*, 13–20; Timothy George, *Galatians* (Nashville: Broadman & Holman, 1994), 46–50.

[50] Raymond E. Brown, *An Introduction to the New Testament* (New York and London: Doubleday, 1997), 287; Delbert Burkett, *An Introduction to the New Testament and the Origins of Christianity* (Cambridge: Cambridge University Press, 2002), 292; Donald A. Hagner, *The New Testament: A Historical and Theological Introduction* (Grand Rapids: Baker, 2012), 335.

[51] Either 14 or 15 Nisan. If the Passover began on 14 Nisan, as seems most likely, then only AD 30 is a possible date. See Herman H. Goldstine, *New and Full Moons, 1001 BC to AD 1651* (Philadelphia: American Philosophical Society, 1975), 86.

years before his second postconversion trip to Jerusalem, after which comes his first missionary journey followed by the apostolic council. We need to leave at least a year or a little more for that missionary journey, taking us back to about 48. Subtracting either fourteen or seventeen years yields a date for Paul's conversion in either 31 or 34. The uncertainty has to do with whether "then after fourteen years" (Gal 2:1) is to be added to the "after three years" of Galatians 1:18. Adding the numbers together is the most natural way to take the Greek,[52] in which case there would be seventeen years between Saul's conversion and his second trip to Jerusalem. If it is determined that Jesus died in 33, then we almost certainly have to assume a fourteen-year interval. Moreover, because people in the ancient Mediterranean world often dated events by inclusive as well as exclusive reckoning, the seventeen years could actually be a figure that would round off to sixteen years. So with a date of 30 for the crucifixion, Saul could have been converted as late as early 32 with the famine visit to Jerusalem as early as late 47. Further precision is impossible. If we combine an early crucifixion with an inclusive reckoning of a fourteen-year period between events, the dates of Paul's early ministry can vary yet again.[53] Nevertheless, it seems unlikely that all these synchronisms would be permitted by a writer who was penning Acts as sheer fiction, unconcerned with accurate chronology.

There is still a tension between the fact that the most likely date for Jesus's death is 30, whereas the earliest possible date for the beginning of Aretas's reign over Damascus (recall 2 Cor 11:32), on the assumption that Caligula's policy of reinstituting client kings gave

---

[52] Betz, *Galatians*, 83; Dunn, *Epistle to the Galatians*, 87; Witherington, *Grace in Galatia*, 127. Many commentators do not prefer one solution over the other and allow different factors to determine their chronology of events at this juncture.

[53] Schnabel (*Acts*, 43–44; cf. 455), opting for an early crucifixion of Jesus and conversion of Saul and the fourteen years before the famine visit beginning with his conversion and reckoned inclusively, is able to date the famine visit to as early as 44.

this Nabatean ruler power over that city, is 37.[54] Of course, nothing precludes the events of Acts 1–8 being spread out over a seven-year period. Saul could have come to faith in Jesus in 37, left Damascus in that same year, early during Aretas's tenure, and then we would have to assume that the fourteen years of Galatians 2:1 was calculated inclusively and referred to the whole time from Saul's transformation to the apostolic council, and we arrive at 50, which can still (just) allow for brief stops at the places Acts designates for Paul's second missionary journey before he arrives in Corinth in 51. On the other hand, the Greek term Luke uses for Aretas's emissary is *ethnarchēs* (ethnarch). Both Josephus and Strabo use this term to refer to the head of an ethnic quarter or trade colony within a major city who represented the interests of a province and acted as a kind of consul to the governor of that region.[55] Aretas had ruled Nabatea since 9 BC so he could have had an ethnarch in this sense in Damascus well before 37. If that is the correct scenario, a date of 32 for Saul's conversion would work absolutely fine.[56]

Paul's First Missionary Journey

Thus far we have been referring to Saul (his Jewish name) when we have been following the book of Acts and Paul (his Roman name) when referring to something he says in his letters because that is how he has been identified in those two sources. It is often erroneously

---

[54] Victor P. Furnish, *II Corinthians* (Garden City: Doubleday, 1984), 522.

[55] Rainer Riesner, *Paul's Early Period: Chronology, Mission Strategy, Theology* (Grand Rapids: Eerdmans, 1998), 85.

[56] Douglas A. Campbell ("An Anchor for Pauline Chronology: Paul's Flight from 'The Ethnarch of King Aretas' [2 Corinthians 11:32–33]," *Journal of Biblical Literature* 121 [2002]: 299–302), using inclusive dating, is only one year different, placing Saul's conversion in 33 and his first Jerusalem visit in 36. In fact, he finds the synchronism between Acts 9 and 2 Cor 11 one of the most helpful data to construct a Pauline chronology.

thought that he began to take the name of Paul immediately following his conversion. Acts, however, does not begin to use "Paul" until 13:9, when he has set off on what is regularly referred to as his first missionary journey. It would appear that only when he began to minister regularly and for a prolonged period of time among Gentiles did he stop using his Jewish name.[57] After that, the only remaining occurrences of this name in Acts are in Paul's later speeches when he refers back to how the Lord addressed him on the Damascus Road (22:7; 26:14) and to what Ananias the Jewish high priest called him later (22:13). He is still called Saul in 13:1, 2, and 7, but we will use the name Paul exclusively from here on out.

Paul and Barnabas are chosen and commissioned by the church in Syrian Antioch to engage in missionary work further afield, as directed by the Holy Spirit (13:1–4). As we have seen, Galatians 2:11 confirms that this Antioch was a key location for Paul's activity. Second Timothy 3:11 also indicates that Paul had ministered and suffered there, presumably at the hands of outsiders to the faith. None of the ministry of Paul and Barnabas on the island of Cyprus is mentioned in the epistles, but none of the epistles is addressed to any community or collection of communities on that island, so this should cause no surprise.

Our intrepid pair's time in Pisidian Antioch, Iconium, Lystra, and Derbe (13:13–14:24) may well form the backdrop for the entire letter to the Galatians. A huge debate has raged in scholarship as to whether this epistle addressed believers in "North" or "South" Galatia.[58] Ethnic Galatians, individuals who would use that name naturally to identify themselves, lived farther north in central "Turkey" from these four cities. But under Roman provincial reorganization in 25 BC, the territory that included these cities was joined with what had historically

---

[57] Cf. Keener, *Acts*, vol. 2, 2019–22; Schnabel, *Acts*, 559.
[58] See the thorough survey of the debate in Donald G. Guthrie, *New Testament Introduction*, 4th ed. (Leicester and Downers Grove: IVP, 1990), 465–83.

been called Galatia to form a larger province by the same name. If, as seems probable, Galatians was written to the inhabitants of Antioch, Iconium, Lystra, and Derbe,[59] then we may hear echoes of events in Acts 13–14 in Paul's letter. Galatians 3:1 uses the comparatively rare word "bewitched" (*ebaskanen*)[60] for the way in which the Judaizers have tricked the local Christians into believing their warped theology. But it seems appropriate for locations like Lystra where locals were quick to believe that ancient legends might have repeated themselves with the gods becoming men (Acts 14:11). Galatians 4:13 declares that "it was because of an illness" that Paul came first to the Galatians. Some have speculated that malaria, commonly contracted in the marshlands along the coast of south-central "Turkey" would explain Paul's departure for the high, inland plateau country, where those afflicted frequently went to try to be cured in a higher, dryer locale. This could also have been Paul's thorn in the flesh (2 Cor 12:7), which would explain how he was healthy enough for long, arduous travel yet from time to time had to stay in one location much longer than normal, if recurring bouts of the disease afflicted him after months or years of comparative health.[61] But all this is entirely speculative; little weight should be placed on these particular correlations.

Other synchronisms between Acts and Paul's letters with respect to his first missionary journey prove even more limited. Paul's

---

[59] See especially Colin J. Hemer, *The Book of Acts in the Setting of Hellenistic History*, ed. Conrad H. Gempf (Tübingen: J. C. B. Mohr, 1989; Winona Lake: Eisenbrauns, 1990), 277–307. Cf. Frank J. Matera, *Galatians* (Collegeville, MN: Liturgical, 1992), 19–24.

[60] The verb may refer to the ancient practice of casting an evil eye on a person in an attempt to curse them. On this practice, see Jerome H. Neyrey, "Bewitched in Galatia: Paul and Cultural Anthropology," *Catholic Biblical Quarterly* 50 (1988): 72–100.

[61] See esp. William M. Ramsay, *St. Paul the Traveller and Roman Citizen*, ed. Mark Wilson (London: Angus Hudson; Grand Rapids: Kregel, 2001 [based on 15th ed. of 1925]), 90–92.

preaching in Pisidia (Acts 13:16–41) has reminded many readers more of Stephen's speech, with its long survey of key Old Testament events, than of Paul's preaching elsewhere, even in Acts. But this is precisely how to establish common ground with a Jewish audience. There are also parallels in the uses of one of the texts of the Hebrew Scriptures that Peter cited at Pentecost (cf. Acts 13:35–37 with 2:25–32, both citing Ps 16:10), but it should hardly be surprising that early Christians would repeatedly cite key texts they believed confirmed the truth of their message.[62] Paul's focus on the crucifixion and resurrection (Acts 13:27–31) matches his emphases in 1 Corinthians 1:18–2:5 and 15:1–58, respectively. Acts 13:39 provides a particularly suggestive parallel to the recurring theme in the epistles of justification by faith rather than by works of the law: "Through [Jesus] everyone who believes is set free from every sin, a justification you were not able to obtain under the law of Moses."[63]

Galatians is filled with some of the harshest language anywhere in Scripture as Paul combats the Judaizers. If he recalls the repeated persecution and even physical violence he experienced in Galatia, beginning in Acts 13:50 at the hands of non-Christian Jews, one can understand the emotion and passion behind his warnings all the more. Second Timothy 3:11 refers more explicitly to the persecutions and sufferings Paul endured "in Antioch, Iconium and Lystra."[64] But

---

[62] Leading to the influential hypothesis of collections of *testimonia*—OT passages that witnessed to the truth of the Gospel—which may have regularly been used by numerous early Christian preachers. On the variety of uses of the Old Testament in Acts more generally, see esp. Loveday Alexander, "'This Is That': The Authority of Scripture in the Acts of the Apostles," *Princeton Seminary Bulletin* 25 (2004): 189–204.

[63] Many translations make it seem as if Paul's point is that the law can forgive people of some but not all sins and the gospel covers the rest. The 2011 NIV rectifies this point, as the quotation here demonstrates. Cf. Peterson, *The Acts of the Apostles*, 394; Bock, *Acts*, 458–59; Marshall, *Acts*, 228; Schnabel, *Acts*, 584.

[64] "The point of this return to the past is not to introduce new information, for Timothy probably joined Paul not too many months after these episodes (Acts

otherwise we find no further unambiguous trace in his letters of this first major stop among the cities of Southern Galatia.

In Iconium, Paul's second stop, he is enabled by the Lord to work a variety of signs and wonders (14:3). In Lystra, stop number three, Luke narrates one of these—the healing of a lame man (vv. 8–10). This may be why Paul in Galatians 3:5 writes about how God has worked miracles among his congregations.[65] The summary of Paul's message in Lystra, according to Luke, is different from the account of his synagogue sermon in Antioch. But this is a non-Jewish audience with no appreciation of the Hebrew Scriptures, so Paul has to begin with what theologians today would call general revelation, the witness of God in nature (Acts 14:17). The eventual reaction of the crowd, after the Jews who came from Antioch and Iconium turned it against Paul, is confirmed in 2 Corinthians 11:25: "Once I was pelted with stones" (cf. Acts 14:19).[66] Little wonder, as he continues to minister in the cities of southern Galatia, he teaches that "we must go through many hardships to enter the kingdom of God" (v. 22). This passage calls to mind his similar generalization in 2 Timothy 3:12: "Everyone who wants to live a godly life in Christ Jesus will be persecuted." Acts 14:23 reminds us that the early Christians had elders from their earliest days. They would have taken over the concept from the synagogue; it was not an office that was established only at a late date in the

---

16:1), and he would have known well the experiences of Paul in Lystra and Iconium (16:2). What Paul does is to remind him of the pattern that is still in effect; therefore, in a sense, Paul's Roman imprisonment is simply a matter of consistency."— Philip H. Towner, *The Letters to Timothy and Titus* (Grand Rapids: Eerdmans, 2006), 574.

[65] Cf. Graham H. Twelftree, *Paul and the Miraculous: A Historical Reconstruction* (Grand Rapids: Baker, 2013), 190.

[66] Murray J. Harris, *The Second Epistle to the Corinthians* (Milton Keynes: Paternoster; Grand Rapids: Eerdmans, 2005), 804.

evolution of New Testament ecclesiology.[67] So when we see it recurring throughout 1 Timothy and Titus, we should not use it as a reason for assigning a late, post-Pauline date to those epistles.

The Apostolic Council

Most of what needs to be said about Acts 15:1–35 has already been covered in our comparisons between this text and Galatians 2 above. If, however, we conclude that the apostolic council took place just after Galatians was written, we may at least ask if parallels to it appear in any of Paul's later letters. One of the most cited topics is the Council's conclusion that Gentiles should abstain from food sacrificed to idols (Acts 15:20, 29). How does this square with Paul's teaching in 1 Corinthians 8 and 10 that eating such food is a morally neutral issue? Shouldn't believers expect to agree to disagree in love (cf. also Rom 14:1–15:13) rather than just refraining altogether?

The answer would seem to be that the Council is not introducing a new law. Sometimes commentators have argued that the four restrictions of abstaining from food polluted by idols, blood, the meat of strangled animals, and sexual immorality represent Gentile obligations according to Jewish tradition under the category Jews developed known as the Noahic laws incumbent even on the Gentiles.[68] Others try to find parallels to all of these prohibitions in Leviticus 17–18,

---

[67] See esp. R. Alastair Campbell, *The Elders: Seniority Within Earliest Christianity* (Edinburgh: T & T Clark, 1994), although Campbell plays down the sense of "office" of elders in both Judaism and Christianity a little too much. Cf. also Arthur G. Patzia, *The Emergence of the Church: Context, Growth, Leadership and Worship* (Downers Grove: IVP, 2001), 171–74.

[68] E.g., Markus Bockmuehl, "The Noachide Commandments and New Testament Ethics, with Special Reference to Acts 15 and Pauline Halakhah," *Revue Biblique* 102 (1995): 93–95.

arguing that for Paul the Torah is still in force.[69] The language of Acts 15:19, 21, 28–29 seems too mild for this conclusion. James states that these prohibitions reflect merely his "judgment," that Moses is read regularly in local synagogues (so these are particularly sensitive matters of Jewish scruples that should not be threatened when evangelizing the Jewish community in a given location[70]), that "it seemed good to the Holy Spirit and to us," and that "you will do well to avoid these things." This language appears far too casual or informal for the four restrictions to represent some timeless, new law.[71] That they are written only to the churches in Antioch, Syria, and Cilicia, and then only to the Gentile believers in those churches, rather than to all Christians everywhere, reinforces this conclusion. First Corinthians 9:6 also confirms the ongoing role of Barnabas as one of Paul's ministry helpers. Not only do Galatians 2:1, 9–10, and 13 also mention Barnabas as a key traveling companion of Paul, but so does Colossians 4:10.

Philemon, an undisputed epistle, features Mark as one of the key persons present with Paul (cf. Acts 15:36–41), who is sending greetings to Philemon (v. 24). Timothy, who is introduced in Acts 16:1–4, appears eighteen times in Paul's letters, and two entire letters are addressed to him. Acts 16:6 proceeds to mention "Galatia" as a territory, and this name recurs not merely in the epistle to the Galatians (1:2; 3:1) but also in 2 Timothy 4:10 when Paul writes that "Crescens has gone to Galatia." Acts 16:9–10 forms Paul's Macedonian call, as

---

[69] E.g., Terrance Callan, "The Background of the Apostolic Decree (Acts 15:20, 29, 21:25)," *Catholic Biblical Quarterly* 55 (1993): 284–97.

[70] E.g., Bruce, *Paul*, 187. On this passage, see further Blomberg, "The Christian and the Law of Moses," 407–10. Charles H. Savelle ("A Reexamination of the Prohibitions in Acts 15," *Bibliotheca Sacra* 161 [2004]: 449–68) notes that this would have also promoted unity among Jewish and Gentile believers.

[71] Witherington (*The Acts of the Apostles*, 469) notes, however, that "it seemed good to us" *is* the language of a formal decree not just a mere opinion, while Marshall (*Acts*, 255) suspects that "you will do well" means "you will prosper," as part of "a courteous request to accept the proposal."

he accepts the appeal to come and minister on the European continent. Macedonia appears thirteen times by name in the epistles, twelve of which occur in his undisputed letters. But otherwise there is little more to add to our earlier discussion of the council in Jerusalem and its immediate aftermath.

Paul's Second Missionary Journey

Second Corinthians 2:12 confirms that Paul traveled through Troas en route to Macedonia, just as we read in Acts 16:11 that "from Troas [they] put out to sea and sailed straight for Samothrace" (a Greek island in the Aegean Sea) and then on to Neapolis (a port city on the Macedonian coast). Second Timothy 4:13 likewise refers back to a period when Paul had been in Troas, though probably more recently. That Paul spent time in Philippi (Acts 16:12–40) is confirmed by the entire little epistle to the Philippians. The specific mistreatment and persecution he experienced, leading to a half a night in prison (vv. 19–24), dovetails with the serious mistreatment and suffering in Philippi to which Paul alludes in 1 Thessalonians 2:2.

Paul's time in Thessalonica (Acts 17:1) leads to two follow-up epistles: 1 and 2 Thessalonians. Luke's one verse summary of Paul's preaching there meshes well with the Christology of the epistles overall: he used Scripture to explain and prove "that the Messiah had to suffer and rise from the dead" and that the Messiah was Jesus (Acts 17:2–3). Messiah (or Christ, from the Gk. *christos*) is a central Christological category in Paul's letters likewise, even as the crucifixion and resurrection are the central focus of Jesus's work or accomplishments for humanity throughout Paul's thought.[72] Paul vividly harks back to the

---

[72] In brief, see Craig L. Blomberg, "Messiah in the New Testament," in *Israel's Messiah in the Bible and the Dead Sea Scrolls*, ed. Richard S. Hess and M. Daniel Carroll R. (Grand Rapids: Baker, 2003), esp. 125–32. For a suggestive unpacking, see Matthew V. Novenson, *Christ Among the Messiahs: Christ Language in Paul*

persecution of verses 5–9 when he writes in 1 Thessalonians 2:14–16 about the Thessalonians the same kind of hostility and persecution in their area as that which led to Jesus's demise in Judea.[73] The misleading charges in Acts 17:7—that Paul is defying Caesar's decrees and teaching that there is another king—are true up to a point if Paul is refusing to offer the sacrifice to the emperor as a god. They also fit the royal imagery used throughout 1 Thessalonians, likening the ministry and return of Christ to a *parousia* or coming of an emperor or one of his key ambassadors.[74] The Jason who appears as a supporter of Paul in Acts 17:6–9 could be the same person who greets the Romans in Romans 16:21, but since Paul writes that letter from Corinth, we really have no way of knowing.

Paul has left no letters behind to the churches in Berea and Athens, the next stops on his journey, so we should expect little or nothing in his other epistles to correlate with the rest of Acts 17. In fact, he does allude to his time in Athens in 1 Thessalonians, which creates some complexities for the reader who wants to chart the travels of his coworkers. The two named individuals who have been

---

and Messiah Language in Ancient Judaism (Oxford: Oxford University Press, 2012). For a forceful defense of the titular sense of *Christos* even throughout Paul, see N. T. Wright, *The Climax of the Covenant: Christ and the Law in Pauline Theology* (Edinburgh: T & T Clark, 1991), 41–55.

[73] For this and numerous other correlations between Acts and 1 Thessalonians, see Riesner, *Paul's Early Period*, 366–67. Even more recent persecution of Jesus's followers in Jerusalem had occurred under the emperor Claudius in 48–49, on which see Markus Bockmuehl, "1 Thessalonians 2:14–16 and the Church in Jerusalem," *Tyndale Bulletin* 52 (2001): 1–31.

[74] See esp. throughout Ben Witherington III, *1 and 2 Thessalonians: A Socio-Rhetorical Commentary* (Grand Rapids: Eerdmans, 2006). On Christ's *parousia* itself, see Robert H. Gundry, "The Hellenization of Dominical Tradition and Christianization of Jewish Tradition in the Eschatology of 1–2 Thessalonians," *New Testament Studies* 33 (1987): 161–69; and Robert H. Gundry, "A Brief Note on 'Hellenistic Formal Receptions and Paul's Use of ΑΠΑΝΤΗΣΙΣ in 1 Thessalonians 4:17,'" *Bulletin for Biblical Research* 6 (1996): 39–41.

accompanying Paul on his second missionary journey are Silas and Timothy. Luke mentions Paul and Silas specifically, in Acts 17:10, as those whom the Thessalonian believers sent off to Berea. Timothy is obviously in their company as well, because in verse 14, when Paul leaves Berea for Athens, Luke explicitly states that Silas and Timothy remained behind. The next time in Acts we hear of these two men is in 18:5, when we read that Silas and Timothy came from Macedonia, the northern half of the Greek peninsula that included Philippi, Thessalonica, and Berea, and rejoined Paul in Corinth (which, along with Athens, was in Achaia, the southern half of the peninsula).

In 1 Thessalonians 3:1–2, however, it appears that at least Timothy had already left Berea and met up with Paul in Athens because Paul is willing to be left alone so that Timothy could return to encourage and strengthen the Thessalonians. Then in verse 6 Paul notes that he has returned to where Paul is now—presumably Corinth—with good news of the Thessalonians' spiritual condition. It is possible, though not necessary, that Silas likewise accompanied Timothy south to Athens and then back north to Thessalonica. If he didn't do so, staying in Berea the whole time, then most likely Timothy met up with him in Macedonia, and the two returned to Corinth together.[75] Nothing in 1 Thessalonians contradicts anything Luke says in Acts, these verses just remind us of what we already knew: Luke writes selectively, noting only what is necessary for his purposes. History is always more complex than what historians have time to cover.

What scholars have spilled enormous amounts of ink discussing, however, is if Paul's Mars Hill address in Athens differs too much from his preaching in the epistles to be authentic. Four theological topics appear to distinguish the theology of this speech (and of Paul

---

[75] Cf. further Gene L. Green, *The Letters to the Thessalonians* (Grand Rapids: Eerdmans; Leicester: Apollos, 2002), 157–58; D. Michael Martin, *1, 2 Thessalonians* (Nashville: B&H, 1995), 25.

in Acts in various other places as well) from the Paul of the letters: a positive view of natural theology, the resurrection rather than the crucifixion as central, an absence of justification by faith, and the delay of Christ's return.[76] On the other hand, these are scarcely the only emphases in Acts; more "Pauline" strands on all of these topics can be found.[77] More importantly, the Paul of the letters likewise believes the existence of God should be plain from the created order (Rom 1:19–20); 1 Corinthians 15 on the resurrection more than balances out 1:18–2:5 on the crucifixion; the entire word group of "justification, justify, etc." when used to mean "declared righteous" is absent from one of Paul's undisputed letters altogether (1 Thessalonians); and 2 Corinthians 5 and Philippians 1 both disclose Paul's realizing the end might be well beyond his lifetime. Luke can better be seen as portraying Paul as the master contextualizer—tailoring each message to its audience in order to maximize their chances of responding positively to Jesus.[78] Stanley Porter aptly concludes that while Paul's missionary speeches have elements in common with the other public addresses in Acts, they have enough distinctives to suggest they present accurate historical information, especially in light of the parallels with Romans 1:18–32.[79]

---

[76] The classic study was Philipp Vielhauer, "On the 'Paulinism' of Acts," in *Studies in Luke-Acts*, ed. Leander E. Keck and J. Louis Martyn (Nashville: Abingdon, 1966; London: SPCK, 1978; Philadelphia: Fortress, 1980 [Germ. orig. 1950]), 33–50.

[77] See especially David Wenham, "Acts and the Pauline Corpus II: The Evidence of Parallels," in *The Book of Acts in Its Ancient Literary Setting*, ed. Bruce W. Winter and Andrew D. Clarke (Grand Rapids: Eerdmans, 1993), 215–58.

[78] Dean Flemming, *Contextualization in the New Testament: Patterns for Theology and Mission* (Downers Grove: IVP, 2005), 56–88. For analogous situations among other Greco-Roman historians of antiquity, see especially T. Hillard, A. Nobbs, and B. Winter, "Acts and the Pauline Corpus I: Ancient Literary Parallels," in *The Book of Acts in its Ancient Literary Setting*, ed. Winter and Clarke, 183–213.

[79] Stanley E. Porter, *The Paul of Acts* (Tübingen: J. C. B. Mohr, 1999) [= *Paul in Acts* (Peabody: Hendrickson, 2001)], 150.

Paul's time in Corinth spans Acts 18:1–18a. With two later letters addressing the Corinthian Christians, we could expect numerous points of contact between Luke's and Paul's writings, and we are not disappointed. In Corinth, Paul met Aquila and Priscilla, fellow tent makers (vv. 2–3), who would both become disciples and valued coworkers. Romans 16:3; 1 Corinthians 16:19; and 2 Timothy 4:19 refer to them as well. First Corinthians 9:1–18 likewise confirms that Paul did not rely on the Corinthian church for any support while he ministered to them, but was engaged in manual labor to meet his material needs.[80] In 1:14, Paul mentions that Crispus was one of the few Corinthians he personally baptized. While we cannot be sure this is the same Crispus who was the leader of the synagogue in Corinth who becomes a believer (Acts 18:8), the conversion of such a prominent individual could easily explain why Paul singled him out for special mention.[81] Crispus's replacement is Sosthenes, whom a group of Gentiles in town beat up after his unsuccessful attempt to have Paul convicted of a crime for preaching the gospel (Acts 18:17). The opening verse of 1 Corinthians announces that this letter comes from Paul *and Sosthenes*. Did the combination of Gallio's dismissal of the case against Paul, followed by the abuse Sosthenes received, contribute to his also becoming a believer?[82]

Before setting sail for the eastern end of the Mediterranean, Paul makes a brief stop in Cenchreae (18:18), a coastal town just a few

---

[80] Ronald F. Hock (*The Social Context of Paul's Ministry: Tentmaking and Apostleship* [Philadelphia: Fortress, 1980], 59–62) notes the strings that were often attached to financial support of clients by their patrons, constraints by which Paul refused to be encumbered.

[81] On the probable correlation of the two references to a Crispus, see Anthony C. Thiselton, *The First Epistle to the Corinthians* (Grand Rapids: Eerdmans, 2000), 140–41.

[82] For the probable equation of the two references to a man named Sosthenes, see, e.g., Raymond F. Collins (Collegeville, MN: Liturgical, 1999), 51. Cf. Schnabel, *Acts*, 765.

miles from Corinth. Romans 16:1 tells us that Phoebe, the letter carrier for the epistle to the Romans, was a deacon and patron from the church in Cenchreae.[83] Paul probably evangelized this town during his year-and-a-half stay in the area of Corinth (Acts 18:11) and got to know Phoebe on that occasion. Apollos, to whom we are introduced in verses 24–28, also reappears in 1 Corinthians in six different places, five of them in chapters 1–4, which lament the way the Corinthians have divided themselves into factions (perhaps based on the early Christian leaders under which they came to faith).[84] These divisions may explain the final reference in 16:12 where Paul admits that Apollos is no longer eager to visit the church in Corinth.[85] Paul also asks Titus to send Apollos on his journey, after providing for his needs, in Titus 3:13.

In addition to all of the synchronisms just noted, we are able to date the letters to the Thessalonians to around 51, give or take a year, because they were written from Corinth on Paul's second missionary journey. At least that is the only time we know of when Paul, Silas,[86] and Timothy were all together in that city, and their names

---

[83] On both terms, see R. A. Kearsley, "Women in Public Life in the Roman East: Iunia Theodora, Claudia Metrodora and Phoebe, Benefactress of Paul," *Tyndale Bulletin* 50 (1999): 189–211. Cf. also Caroline F. Whelan, "Amica Pauli: The Role of Phoebe in the Early Church," *Journal for the Study of the New Testament* 49 (1993): 67–85.

[84] Fee, *The First Epistle to the Corinthians*, 66; Lyle D. Vander Broek, *Breaking Barriers: The Possibilities of Christian Community in a Lonely World* (Grand Rapids: Brazos, 2002), 40.

[85] Fee, *The First Epistle to the Corinthians*, 910–11; Ben Witherington III, *Conflict and Community in Corinth: A Socio-Rhetorical Commentary on 1 and 2 Corinthians* (Grand Rapids: Eerdmans; Carlisle: Paternoster, 1995), 317.

[86] Known as Silvanus (Gk. *Silouanos*), the full form of the name, in the epistles (2 Cor 1:19; 1 Thess 1:1; 2 Thess 1:1; 1 Pet 5:12), but always abbreviated to Silas (Gk. *Silas*) in the book of Acts. The distinction is preserved in most formally and optimally equivalent translations, though not in the NIV (or in the dynamically equivalent NLT).

appear as the writers in the opening verses of both letters. Of course, if 2 Thessalonians is pseudonymous, then it only *appears* to fit this chronology, but 1 Thessalonians is almost universally viewed as authentic and datable to this time period. Because Paul's stay in Corinth comes just before his return to Jerusalem and to Syrian Antioch, we may estimate that this second missionary journey came to an end in about 51 or 52.

Paul's Third Missionary Journey

Most of this "journey" actually involved a three-year residence in Ephesus (Acts 20:31), probably from 52 to 55.[87] Daily lecturing for about two years in Tyrannus's hall led a huge number of people from the province of Asia Minor to come to hear Paul, and through them most of the rest of the province came to learn about the gospel as well (19:9–10). As an illustration the church in Colossae a little to the east was planted by Epaphras (Col 1:7), a Colossian himself (4:12). There is no indication that Paul was ever in Colossae, so Epaphras may well have become a believer by coming to Ephesus and encountering Paul there.[88] If Acts 19:10 is accurate, even granted a little hyperbole, in its claim that "all the Jews and Greeks who lived in the province of Asia heard the word of the Lord," this could support the theory that Ephesians is an encyclical letter, addressed to a number of churches throughout Asia Minor (see chap. 8). Verse 26 makes a similar grandiose claim for Paul's influence in Asia. The central theme of spiritual

---

[87] Riesner, *Paul's Early Period,* 296–99; Schnabel, *Acts,* 45.

[88] James D. G. Dunn, *The Epistles to the Colossians and to Philemon* (Carlisle: Paternoster, 1996; Grand Rapids: Eerdmans, 63; Douglas J. Moo, *The Letters to the Colossians and to Philemon* (Grand Rapids: Eerdmans, 1996; Nottingham, Apollos, 2008), 90. For more plausible speculation about this little known individual, see Michael Trainor, *Epaphras: Paul's Educator at Colossae* (Collegeville: Liturgical, 2008).

warfare that permeates Ephesians does in any case mesh nicely with Luke's narratives of magic-like miracles (vv. 11–12), backfiring exorcisms (vv. 13–16), and scroll burnings of magical spells and incantations (vv. 17–20).[89]

There is no straightforward, mechanical borrowing of names from Paul's letters to create the characters in Acts. People who have already appeared in Acts in narratives about Paul but who are never mentioned in the epistles include Ananias, Agabus, Lydia, Dionysus, and Damaris. Conversely, key companions of Paul who appear in his letters, including Titus and Epaphroditus, never show up in Acts. So Luke is not slavishly inventing accounts for all Paul's coworkers just to create the strongest historical verisimilitude possible. It is intriguing, nevertheless, how many people overlap between the two bodies of literature. Even as isolated a reference as Acts 19:22, which mentions that Paul sent Timothy and Erastus ahead of him into Macedonia, employs a name that appears only here in Acts and twice in Paul's letters—Erastus. In Romans 16:23, he is described as the director of public works and is among those who send greetings from Corinth to the Roman church.[90] In 2 Timothy 4:20, Paul notes merely that he left Erastus in Corinth. To this day one can see a portion of paving stone in the outdoor part of the archaeological museum of the Corinthian ruins that has inscribed on it in Latin the name of Erastus as the "aedile" (a municipal director of public projects) who financed the laying of this street at his own expense. All these undesigned coincidences inspire all the more confidence in Acts' historical accuracy.

---

[89] See esp. throughout Clinton E. Arnold, *Ephesians* (Grand Rapids: Zondervan, 2010); and Clinton E. Arnold, *Power and Magic: The Concept of Power in Ephesians* (Cambridge: Cambridge University Press, 1992; Eugene, OR: Wipf & Stock, 2001).

[90] Cautiously, David W. J. Gill, "Erastus the Aedile," *Tyndale Bulletin* 40 (1989): 293–301. Confidently, Schnabel, *Acts*, 801.

Acts 19:29 introduces Gaius and Aristarchus, traveling companions of Paul from Macedonia. Gaius was an extremely common Roman name, so we should not be surprised to hear of a Gaius from Derbe in 20:4 and another one in Corinth in Romans 16:23 and 1 Corinthians 1:14. If Luke were simply trying to use as many names as he could from Paul's letters to make his fiction appear historical, he would have made at least one of these men named Gaius be from Achaia, the province which contained Corinth.[91] Similarly, Alexander was a common Greek name, so we should not try to create any links between the Jew with that name in Acts 19:33 and the later Christian whom Paul disciplined in 1 Timothy 1:20. It is possible that the man in Acts is the Alexander, the metalworker of 2 Timothy 4:14, who did Paul great harm because he appears in Acts in the context of the riot provoked by the guild of silversmiths. If he were staunchly opposed to Christianity, given the length of time Paul spent in Ephesus, he could have been a consistent opponent of Paul's ministry. The term used in 2 Timothy is usually translated "coppersmith," though, whereas the issue in Acts 19 was stirred up by the craftsmen who worked with silver. On the other hand, the two groups of metalworkers would have naturally sympathized with each other, and Luke does speak of those working in related trades being present (v. 25). But the man in 2 Timothy would be more likely to be the same person with that name in 1 Timothy, making the link with Acts altogether unlikely.[92]

The problem of matching names continues with Luke's list of Paul's travel companions as his third journey begins to wind down (Acts 20:4). Sopater of Berea could be the same individual as Sosipater in Romans 16:21, but we have no way of knowing. Aristarchus from

---

[91] On this second Gaius, see esp. L. L. Welborn, *An End to Enmity: Paul and the "Wrongdoer" of Second Corinthians* (Berlin: de Gruyter, 2011), 241–50.

[92] For all five Alexanders in the New Testament and which ones *might* be equated with one another, see George W. Knight III, *The Pastoral Epistles* (Carlisle: Paternoster; Grand Rapids: Eerdmans, 1992), 110–11.

Thessalonica is presumably the same person by that name mentioned in Acts 19:29 because there he is said to be from Macedonia, and Thessalonica was a city in the province of Macedonia. But should he be identified with Paul's fellow prisoner in Colossians 4:10, who also sends greetings in Philemon 24? It is hard to know. Secundus appears nowhere else in the New Testament. We have already mentioned Gaius from Derbe, and we know Timothy much better. Tychicus is presumably the letter carrier for Ephesians and Colossians (Eph 6:21; Col 4:7), who is also mentioned in Titus 3:12 and 2 Timothy 4:12. He is never associated with his hometown, as if to distinguish himself from another Tychicus from elsewhere, and the name is less common than many of the others we have debated, so it appears that he was well enough known to be identified simply by a single name. Trophimus from Asia is probably Trophimus the Ephesian later in Acts' narrative (21:29) and could well be the Trophimus Paul left ill in Miletus (a community close to Ephesus) in 2 Timothy 4:20.[93] In spite of the various uncertainties, even the handful of correlations that do occur would almost certainly not have appeared if Luke were ranging through the full thesaurus of names open to him simply to give fictitious characters plausible identities.

Paul's farewell address to the Ephesian elders at Miletus (20:18–35) has been viewed as the one speech in Acts most consistent with the Paul of the epistles.[94] This should occasion no surprise; it is the one speech in Acts addressed to a Christian audience just as the letters are. The others are sermons or messages to Jews, defense speeches before hostile authorities, or evangelistic addresses to Gentiles. Perhaps most significant in the context of Paul's farewell address is the equation of elders, overseers, and shepherds (vv. 17, 28). We have seen *elders* earlier

---

[93] For each of these judgments, see also Schnabel, *Acts*, 833.

[94] Colin J. Hemer, "The Speeches of Acts: I. The Ephesian Elders at Miletus," *Tyndale Bulletin* 40 (1989): 77–85.

(above); *overseers* is what Paul calls these leaders in Philippians 1:1. The term *shepherd* (or "pastor") in Paul's epistles appears only in the context of spiritual gifts (Eph 4:11). The institutionalization of the church that would differentiate these and additional leadership titles according to clear divisions of office has not yet occurred. Luke knows only one office, borrowed from Judaism and fluid in labels (and the precedent for the second office in the Pauline epistles—that of deacon—in Acts 6:1–7).[95]

Acts 20:28 contains an additional expression that narrows the gap between the Paul of the letters and the Paul of Acts. Some argue that Acts knows nothing of Christ's sacrificial atonement, but this verse ends by referring to the church as having been "bought" by God's (or maybe Christ's) own blood.[96] Paul's emphasis on putting others' financial needs above his own in verses 33–35 matches his recurrent attitude throughout his epistles. His goal of counting his life as nothing but wanting to finish the race and complete the task the Lord had given him (v. 24a) calls to mind Philippians 3:7–14. And his emphasis on the gospel of God's grace (v. 24b) reflects a central theme throughout almost all of his letters.

How far have we progressed in time since the end of Paul's second missionary journey about 52? Brief stops overland in Galatia plus three years in Ephesus, a return trip to Macedonia and Achaia, followed by a retracing of his steps in Greece, a stop in Miletus, and the trip to Jerusalem would add up to about five years altogether. We are most likely in the year 57.[97] We can also correlate still more of Acts with the

---

[95] Cf. further Joseph A. Fitzmyer, *The Gospel According to Luke I–IX* (Garden City: Doubleday, 1981), 251–57.

[96] Most translations have "his own blood," but the Greek (*dia tou haimatos tou idiou*) could also be rendered "the blood of his Own One" (i.e., Jesus). Hence, NET, NJB, and NRSV have "the blood of his own Son." For further discussion of the options for interpretation, see Keener, *Acts*, vol. 3, 3038–40.

[97] Riesner, *Paul's Early Period*, 218–19; Witherington, *The Acts of the Apostles*, 85.

various letters of Paul. First Corinthians 16:5–9 shows that Paul wrote this letter from Ephesus, not long before he set out for his return trip to Greece, most likely in 55.[98] Second Corinthians was written from Macedonia after Paul left Ephesus and before he arrived in Corinth (2 Cor 2:12–13; 7:5–7), so probably in 56.[99] Romans was penned in Corinth (or maybe nearby Cenchreae) as Paul gets set to return to Judea (Rom 15:23–29), hence in the winter of 57–58.[100] Once again, for all these details in both Acts and the epistles to fit together in just the right periods of time to create a coherent chronology makes it highly unlikely that Luke was composing fiction.

Paul's Arrest and Imprisonments

When Paul returns to Judaism's Holy City, he is informed about a large number of Jewish believers who remain zealous for the law. They have heard garbled rumors about Paul that he is even more averse to the law than he actually is. So the leaders of the Jerusalem church devise a plan to convince the locals that their view of Paul is misguided. He will purify himself, go to the temple with some men who have completed a vow, and pay for their sacrificial offerings (Acts 21:20–25). Can we seriously imagine Paul going to such lengths to placate his opponents when he has already clearly articulated Jesus as the sole and final means of redemption and atonement (Rom 3:21–26)? It is possible. First Corinthians 9:19–23 discloses his strategy of becoming all things to all people so as by all means to save some. This includes

---

[98] Craig L. Blomberg, *1 Corinthians* (Grand Rapids: Zondervan, 1994), 21. Cf. Pheme Perkins, *First Corinthians* (Grand Rapids: Baker, 2012), 18.

[99] Linda L. Belleville, *2 Corinthians* (Downers Grove and Leicester: IVP, 1996), 20; Margaret E. Thrall, *A Critical and Exegetical Commentary on the Second Epistle to the Corinthians*, vol. 1 (Edinburgh: T & T Clark, 1994), 76–77.

[100] Richard N. Longenecker, *Introducing Romans: Critical Issues in Paul's Most Famous Letter* (Grand Rapids: Eerdmans, 2011), 46–50.

becoming as one under the law to win those under the law (v. 20).[101] On the other hand, perhaps Paul went one step too far. The ploy failed miserably, Paul was falsely accused of bringing a Gentile into that part of the temple reserved for Jews, crowds rioted, and the Romans had to arrest Paul to save his life (Acts 21:26–36). Perhaps this is Luke's narrative technique for suggesting that the scheme cooked up by the Jerusalem leadership was unwise and not to be imitated.[102] Whether or not this is the case, it is interesting to reflect back on all the examples of Paul's Torah obedience in Acts, especially with respect to the ritual Law. None is presented as prescriptive, merely descriptive; all are natural as part of the Jesus movement's Jewish origins and the non-linear, gradual movement away from those origins. What *does* stand out in Acts are the zealous Saul's major steps toward Gentiles as equal partners with Jews in a church free from the *requirement* to follow Jewish ritual, exactly as in his letters.[103]

When Paul tells his story in 22:2–21, there are numerous points of contact with Luke's original account of his conversion in chapter 9. But there are also distinctive details, some of which mesh with the epistles in ways not already surveyed. Only Acts ever tells us that Saul came from Tarsus (9:11; 21:39; 22:3). In both of Paul's autobiographical

---

[101] E.g., Keener, *Acts*, vol. 3, 3141–43; Fitzmyer, *Acts*, 692. Schnabel (*Acts*, 878–80) appears to opt for this view but stresses it is not mere missionary tactics but the expression of a consistent theological position.

[102] E.g., Barrett, *A Critical and Exegetical Commentary on the Acts of the Apostles*, vol. 2 (1998), 328. Porter (*Paul of Acts*, 172–86) appears to opt for this view among the options he presents, though not unambiguously.

[103] For all the details, see Craig L. Blomberg, "The Law in Luke-Acts," *Journal for the Study of the New Testament* 22 (1984): 53–80. Daniel Marguerat (*Paul in Acts and Paul in His Letters* [Tübingen: Mohr Siebeck, 2013], 64–65) also highlights the value for Luke in portraying Christianity as still deeply rooted in Judaism, in a Roman world that conferred the most legitimacy on its *oldest* religious movements. A similar ambiguity can be seen in Luke's portrayal of the historical significance of the temple, even as Jesus's followers, especially under Paul, increasingly substitute the home as the location of worship (106–29).

accounts he calls it Tarsus in/of Cilicia (21:39; 22:3). Cilicia does appear in the epistles, in Galatians 1:21, when Paul describes where he went in between his first two trips to Jerusalem after his conversion. With Tarsus as a major university town, he would have surely included it in his itinerary, all the more naturally if that is where he spent most of his childhood years.[104] The epistles have no natural place where we would have expected Paul to describe his upbringing in any detail, including his study under Gamaliel for the rabbinate (Acts 22:3). But in Philippians 3:5 he identifies himself as a "Hebrew of Hebrews; in regard to the Law, a Pharisee." While Jews in the diaspora could be extremely nationalistic, these labels make best sense if Paul had actually lived in Israel for a while, and as far as we can tell the center of Pharisaism was Jerusalem.[105] So his advanced study with Gamaliel fits this scenario perfectly.

Paul's subsequent imprisonment in Jerusalem and Caesarea and his various hearings before Felix, Festus, and Herod Agrippa II do not feature in the epistles. Acts 24:17, however, merits attention. While it has been disputed, it seems likely that Paul's reference to bringing gifts to the poor among his people refers to the collection for the Judean poor that occupied his attention off and on for several years, according to 1 Corinthians 16:1–4; 2 Corinthians 8–9; and Romans 15:25–27.[106] Indeed, the diversity of people from different parts of the empire who accompanied Paul back to Jerusalem (Acts 20:4) may include the unnamed individuals chosen to keep the transportation and distribution of the monies "squeaky clean" (2 Cor 8:16–24).[107]

---

[104] See further Hengel, *Pre-Christian Paul*, 18–39.

[105] Oskar Skarsaune, *In the Shadow of the Temple: Jewish Influences on Early Christianity* (Downers Grove: IVP, 2002), 121.

[106] Schnabel, *Acts*, 960–61. Cf. Barrett, *A Critical and Exegetical Commentary on the Acts of the Apostles*, vol. 2, 1108.

[107] Agreed on by commentators as otherwise far apart as Bock, *Acts*, 618–19; and Pervo, *Acts*, 508–9. The link was vigorously disputed throughout Downs,

Acts 24:27 notes that two years passed while Paul languished in prison, bringing us to the year 59. As we noted in the last chapter that is exactly the date when Festus succeeded Felix, according to extra-biblical evidence. The chronology continues to fall into place flaw-lessly. The Prison Epistles—Ephesians, Colossians, Philemon, and Philippians—have traditionally been believed to have been written from Rome. But from time to time scholars have argued for Caesarea as the provenance for one or more of these letters, in which case the period of time for their writing would be 57–59. An Ephesian impris-onment has also been suggested. Second Corinthians 1:8–9 reveals that Paul despaired of surviving some ordeal in Asia Minor, which could mean Ephesus, and it felt like a death sentence. First Corinthians 15:32 speaks of Paul's fighting wild beasts at Ephesus, but no Roman citizen was ever forced to face literal animals so he is probably refer-ring metaphorically to opposition. One early church tradition refers to an Ephesian imprisonment, but only one (the anti-Marcionite pro-logue to Colossians). If any of the Prison Epistles come from such an imprisonment, they would date to 52–55 (recall above).[108]

Most likely we should follow the dominant church tradition and view them as coming from Rome (see especially Jerome, John Chrysostom, and Theodoret). That will mean sometime between 60 and 62.[109] Little in Colossians, Philemon, or Ephesians helps decide the issue, although Luke's presence with Paul (Col 4:14; Phlm 24) fits both Caesarea and Rome, because the "we passages" of Luke include Paul's detention in both of those communities. But in Philippians, Paul speaks of how his imprisonment has actually served to advance

---

Offering for the Gentiles, but see the response by Verlyn D. Verbrugge and Keith R. Krell, *Paul and Money: A Biblical and Theological Analysis of the Apostle's Teachings and Practices* (Grand Rapids: Zondervan, 2015), 197–99.

[108] For these various options, see further Guthrie, *New Testament Introduction*, 489–95, 545–55, 577–80. More succinctly, cf. Hagner, *New Testament*, 554–57.

[109] Riesner, *Paul's Early Period*, 318–19; Witherington, *The Acts of the Apostles*, 85.

the gospel (Phil 1:12). Those who have guarded him have heard his message and spread it throughout the whole Praetorian Guard (v. 13). Caesarea had a Praetorium but was a long way from Philippi. Ephesus was close by but had no imperial guard. Rome again emerges as the best option, especially since the Praetorium can also be translated as the "palace guard"—soldiers in the emperor's palace.[110]

The surprising success of the gospel, despite Paul's imprisonment, dovetails precisely with the end of Acts. Paul's dramatic statement about turning to the Gentiles in Acts 28:25–28 does not imply a final rejection of the Jews, contradicting Romans 11:25–26. Rather it is simply the climactic example in Luke's narrative of a pattern we have seen recur almost everywhere Paul has preached: at some point enough local Jews reject Paul's message that he turns to the Gentiles where he finds greater success.[111] Despite his house arrest, Paul's ministry in Acts concludes with how he "proclaimed the kingdom of God and taught about the Lord Jesus Christ—with all boldness and without hindrance" (Acts 28:31). Despite always being loosely chained to a soldier, Paul preached the Word to any who would come to hear him. No doubt some of the soldiers wondered who exactly the captive audience was! At any rate, with imprisonment in Philippi, Jerusalem, Caesarea, and Rome all explicitly mentioned in Acts, we can understand Paul's claim in 2 Corinthians 11:23 that he had been in prison more frequently than the false teachers in Corinth.

Indeed, Paul's catalog of sufferings in 2 Corinthians 11:23–28 goes well beyond anything we would know from Acts alone. But we

---

[110] See NIV, NKJV, and NLT. HCSB, ESV, NET, and NRSV have "imperial guard." For the possibility that Philippians should be dated to the same second Roman imprisonment often postulated for the setting of 2 Timothy (below), see Jim Reiher, "Could Philippians Have Been Written from the Second Roman Imprisonment?" *Evangelical Quarterly* 84 (2012): 213–33.

[111] James D. G. Dunn, *Beginning from Jerusalem* (Grand Rapids: Eerdmans, 2009), 1006; Bock, *Acts*, 755.

do know of a later shipwreck in Acts 27:39–28:6 ending on the island of Malta, so the reference to three earlier, similar (but probably less dramatic) experiences in verse 25 rings true. All of the travels in Acts certainly mesh with his affirmation that "I have been constantly on the move" (2 Cor 11:26). His travels would have included numerous river crossings and the common dangers of bandits in remote, unguarded rural areas (v. 26b). "Danger from my fellow Jews" and "danger from Gentiles" (v. 26) corresponds to the frequent persecution that Acts has narrated. The combination of persecution and the normal dangers of life and travel in the Roman Empire accounted for "danger in the city," "danger in the country," and "danger at sea" (v. 26) "Danger from false believers" (v. 26) corresponds to the warnings of Acts 20:29–30.[112]

Conclusion

It matters little whether one turns to the pre-Christian life of Saul of Tarsus, his conversion and call (or commissioning), his early years as a believer, his specific missionary journeys, or the years he was detained in one prison after another. In every instance there are close correlations between the narrative of Acts and the autobiographical information his letters disclose.[113] It is only to be expected that some details are found only in one corpus or the other. But only rarely does even an *apparent* conflict occur in the portions of Paul's life that both touch on. In those few instances resolutions are readily available. Nothing is even as complicated as the most famous supposed contradictions among Gospel parallels, with the possible exception of the comparisons between Acts and Galatians on Paul's postconversion trips to Jerusalem. Many of the details that are corroborated are incidental

---

[112] Cf. David E. Garland, *2 Corinthians* (Nashville: B&H, 1999), 495–502.
[113] Cf. also Michael B. Thompson, "Paul in the Book of Acts: Differences and Distance," *Expository Times* 122 (2011): 425–36.

ones for which a writer of fiction would make no effort to create historical verisimilitude. Enough of the details between Acts and the letters are different enough, without being contradictory, to suggest that Luke was not composing any of his narrative simply on the basis of information he learned about in Paul's epistles.

Most of the corroboration of Acts from Paul's letters comes from his seven undisputed epistles: Romans, 1–2 Corinthians, Galatians, Philippians, 1 Thessalonians, and Philemon. So even if one takes the other six letters attributed to him in the New Testament as pseudonymous and, thus, as off-limits for assessing Acts' historicity, plenty of evidence remains in the undisputed letters that dovetails with details in Acts. Porter concludes that "there are legitimate grounds for seeing the Paul of Acts as sharing a similar voice to that of the Paul of the letters," and that "there must have been some close lines of connection between the authors of the book of Acts and of the Pauline letters."[114] If the book of Acts were second century and the connections were only that its author knew the finished form of the entire collection of Paul's epistles, then we would not expect even the apparent contradictions we have surveyed. A writer of fiction would have had the freedom to create a less dissonant narrative. But neither are the distinctives in Acts so great that one cannot imagine Paul and Luke having been travel companions. If, on the other hand, the author of Acts breathed the second-century air of a church that valued the deutero-Pauline letters highly, then the majority of parallels would not have come from Paul's undisputed letters. There is enough evidence, to be sure, to demonstrate that *Paul* did not write Acts(!) but much too little to suggest that a close associate of his could not have penned this book.[115]

Thomas Phillips meticulously catalogs the portraits that emerge from the Paul of Acts and the Paul of the letters, concluding that the

---

[114] Porter, *Paul of Acts*, 170, 199.
[115] Ibid., 187–206.

issue of coordinating the journeys of Paul to Jerusalem in Acts and the Galatians is the linchpin to determining if the two portraits of Paul are more dissimilar or more similar to each other. He opts for matching Galatians 2:1–10 with Acts 15 so that the dissimilarities wind up being stressed, but he acknowledges that harmonization with Acts 11 is possible, just awkward.[116] But it is even more awkward to postulate a major, persistent tension between Paul and the Jerusalem apostles, which requires Acts and the deutero-Paulines to be written to rehabilitate Paul in a semifictitious fashion to try to smooth over ongoing differences in the church for which there is otherwise no independent evidence![117] The vast majority of second-century Christianity has to then also be viewed as part of the conspiracy to pretend that unity existed where there was only diversity. Soon a tiny minority of the total evidence—the undisputed letters of Paul, and really only a minority of them (primarily Romans and Galatians, though also to a certain degree 1–2 Corinthians)—become the tail that wags the dog. Everything else must be the corruption of the true Paul who was lost by almost all other early Christians.

It is not surprising that such theories originally began largely within German Lutheranism, whose origins lay in making similar sweeping claims against Roman Catholicism and whose legacy was perpetuated by sharply separating itself from all other branches of emerging Protestantism. It is not surprising that Lutheran scholars would privilege Romans and Galatians, but today we must recall that even the entire undoubted Pauline corpus was not designed to supply Paul's full-orbed theology, occasional as each letter was. Even if one rejects Acts as reliable, one has to assume that there is much more that we do not

---

[116] Thomas E. Phillips, *Paul, His Letters, and Acts* (Peabody: Hendrickson, 2009).

[117] For a classic example of this approach, which has to rely almost entirely on "mirror reading" the internal evidence of the epistles, see Michael D. Goulder, *Paul and the Competing Mission in Corinth* (Peabody: Hendrickson, 2001).

know about Paul's thought than what can be gleaned from his epistles. Jacob Jervell called this "the unknown Paul" but stressed that a fair amount of this additional thought could well be that which is gleaned from Acts, especially where it reflects Paul's undeniably Jewish roots.[118]

But has it not been demonstrated on other grounds? Were not other New Testament documents frequently ascribed to an author who did not actually write them? Does this not make a substantial portion of the New Testament and Christian origins based on what we would today call forgeries? The mantras have been frequently repeated, but what is the actual evidence for believing that various New Testament documents were not written by those whom Christian history has largely believed penned them? How much is at stake in our decision concerning the presence and/or legitimacy of pseudonymity? Chapter 8 must turn to these questions.

---

[118] Jacob Jervell, *The Unknown Paul: Essays on Luke–Acts and Early Christian History* (Minneapolis: Augsburg, 1984). See also a number of the essays in Daniel Marguerat, *Paul in Acts and Paul in His Letters* (Tübingen: Mohr Siebeck, 2013).

Chapter 8

Forgeries Among the
Epistles of Paul?

One of the byproducts of remaining in the guild of New Testament scholarship for a generation or longer is getting to watch interpretive fashions change without any fresh discoveries. Of course, genuine progress and new finds do occur, but that is not what I am thinking about here. Rather, perhaps in large part due to the nature of what often qualifies as a PhD dissertation (i.e., some challenge to the status quo of the past), diametrically opposite viewpoints can be derived from identical data. When these take turns defining a generation of scholarship, it is appropriate to talk about fashions.

Forty years ago source criticism still dominated both Old and New Testament studies, so that it was standard fare to parcel up the five books of Moses and the Synoptic Gospels into numerous separate sections, confidently assigning them to specific sources, and then reconstructing those sources, complete with author profiles and distinctive theologies. Certain epistles were equally confidently declared to be composite, with the conviction that ancient editors stitched together two or more pieces of correspondence to a particular Christian community into an artificial whole.[1] Then came literary and canonical criticisms, which read the identical documents in ways that found far more unity than the previous generation had discerned. Sometimes they presupposed the findings of the older source criticism; sometimes they simply ignored them altogether. But it was not as if new data had actually been discovered about the origins of these documents. It was simply a methodological choice to privilege plausible readings that perceived literary unity rather than those that labeled as literary seams every slightly awkwardly juxtaposed set of sentences or paragraphs.[2]

A similar phenomenon has occurred with the theories of pseudonymity. First, we will consider briefly the odyssey of scholarship on this topic over the last generation. Then we will look in some detail at the arguments for and against Pauline authorship of the books that are often doubted.

The Changing Winds of Scholarly Fashion

Throughout my undergraduate and graduate studies, countless scholars identified biblical documents they believed were not written by the people to whom the Bible appears to attribute them. When students asked questions about the apparent moral duplicity of this behavior, with rare exceptions they were reassured that this was a standard feature of ancient writing. It was understood as an accepted literary device, and was no more morally objectionable than modern celebrities using a ghostwriter who has actual literary skills to help them pen

---

[1] Esp. 2 Corinthians and Philippians. Today one rarely encounters supporters of a composite origin for Philippians, and even 2 Corinthians is increasingly viewed as a unity, though by no means universally so.

[2] See esp. the major, pioneering works of Brevard Childs: *An Introduction to the Old Testament as Scripture* (Philadelphia: Fortress, 1979); and *An Introduction to the New Testament as Canon* (Philadelphia: Fortress, 1985).

their autobiographies. Indeed, in a world without footnotes, bibliographies, or other more recent forms of documentation, pseudonymity was actually a way of crediting one's teacher with thoughts that were not primarily one's own. If a disciple of Paul, for example, chose to write a letter to a Christian congregation in the generation after Paul died, trying to imagine what Paul would say to that community were he still alive, then it would have been laudable for him to put Paul's and not his own name on the document.[3]

Today all this has changed in many scholarly circles. Careful studies have stressed what was already known and articulated a generation ago, but they have received much more press: there are no actual examples in early Christian history of a document known to have been written by someone other than the person to whom it was attributed, which were deemed acceptable by any sizable segment of the Church. Certainly there are no known examples of books being accepted into the New Testament which were believed to have been written by someone other than the person to whom they were ascribed, with the possible, partial exception of 2 Peter (on which, see below).[4] As a

---

[3] See esp. Kurt Aland, "The Problem of Anonymity and Pseudonymity in Christian Literature of the First Two Centuries," in *The Authorship and Integrity of the New Testament*, ed. Kurt Aland (London: SPCK, 1965), 1–13; James D. G. Dunn, *Unity and Diversity in the New Testament Theology* (London: SCM, 1977), 344–59; and David G. Meade, *Pseudonymity and Canon: An Investigation into the Relationship of Authorship and Authority in Jewish and Earliest Christian Tradition* (Tübingen: J. C. B. Mohr, 1986; Grand Rapids: Eerdmans, 1987).

[4] See esp. Terry L. Wilder, *Pseudonymity, the New Testament, and Deception: An Inquiry into Intention and Deception* (Lanham, MD: University Press of America, 2004); and Jeremy Duff, "A Reconsideration of Pseudepigraphy in Early Christianity" (DPhil Thesis: University of Oxford, 1998). Cf. also Eckhard J. Schnabel, "Paul, Timothy, and Titus: The Assumption of a Pseudonymous Author and of Pseudonymous Recipients in the Light of Literary, Theological, and Historical Evidence," in *Do Historical Matters Matter to Faith? A Critical Appraisal of Modern and Postmodern Approaches to Scripture*, ed. James K. Hoffmeier and Dennis R. Magary (Wheaton: Crossway, 2012), 383–403.

result, Bart Ehrman has made the view popular that we should speak of New Testament books widely held to be pseudonymous today as forgeries—works meant to deceive their readers into thinking they had apostolic origin in order to gain credence for their views. Had the works been published under the names of the real authors, so the theory goes, their views would have gained too little currency.[5]

The remarkable feature about this academic odyssey is that it has occurred *without any new discoveries from antiquity.*[6] The handful of Qumran fragments or gnostic texts not already translated by 1982 when I completed my doctorate have disclosed nothing new to change the course of studies of pseudonymity. It is almost as if what has transpired is that more liberal scholars finally decided to stop contesting the conservative claim that there was no benign pseudonymity in the early church and say, "Fine. But we're still convinced certain documents were pseudonymous. So if you can't see any positive way of couching this, we'll just have to call them forgeries. There—is that what you wanted?"

Compounding the problem are certain conservative scholars closing the door on pseudonymity *a priori*. Because they personally cannot envision a scenario in which the practice could be morally acceptable, they do not even investigate the data. They simply announce that the theory is unacceptable, and they build into their doctrinal statements affirmations (or interpretations of affirmations) that anyone believing

---

[5] Bart D. Ehrman, *Forged: Writing in the Name of God—Why the Bible's Authors Are Not Who We Think They Are* (New York: HarperOne, 2011); and Bart D. Ehrman, *Forgery and Counterforgery: The Use of Literary Deceit in Early Christian Polemics* (Oxford and New York: Oxford University Press, 2012).

[6] This is not to say that there was not a lot of additional research and examination of already known sources; there was. For both the most relevant sources and the latest research summarized, see Armin D. Baum, "Authorship and Pseudepigraphy in Early Christian Literature: A Translation of the Most Important Source Texts and an Annotated Bibliography," in *Paul and Pseudepigraphy*, ed. Stanley E. Porter and Gregory P. Fewster (Leiden and Boston: Brill, 2013), 11–63.

or teaching that Paul did not write all thirteen books attributed to him in the New Testament cannot be a part of their institution or organization.[7] Yet they seem oblivious to the fact that it is such *a priori* dismissal that often pushes people into positions like Ehrman's! If there is no middle ground for acceptable pseudonymity and certain people are not convinced by arguments for traditional claims of authorship, they are left with nowhere to turn except to charge the New Testament writers with duplicity.[8] The fallacy of the false dilemma stands out glaringly. There are numerous legitimate intermediate options.

Missing in most of these conversations are a number of crucial topics. We do not have evidence that early Christianity accepted pseudonymity as a legitimate device in the testimony that exists. Unfortunately, we have no evidence at all for Christian perspectives on the topic earlier than the late second century. In the middle of the second century, however, the Jewish wing of the Christian movement was becoming small compared to the Gentile wing. Allegorical interpretations of scriptural narratives that had never previously been accepted

---

[7] Certain views of apostolic authorship may also be assumed rather than demonstrated.

[8] The most egregious recent example of this from a mainstream evangelical publisher appears throughout Norman L. Geisler and William C. Roach, *Defending Inerrancy: Affirming the Accuracy of Scripture for a New Generation* (Grand Rapids: Baker, 2011), with their interpretation of the International Council on Biblical Inerrancy's Chicago Statement. Article 18 includes the following: "We deny the legitimacy of any treatment of the text or quest for sources lying behind it that leads to relativizing, dehistoricizing, or discounting its teaching, or rejecting its claims to authorship." But does the appearance of an individual's name in the opening verse of a letter automatically make a "claim to authorship" and, if so, what kind of authorship? Ironically, in Norman L. Geisler and William Nix, *A General Introduction to the Bible*, 2nd ed. (Chicago: Moody, 1986), 225, we read, "It should be noted that a book might use the literary device of impersonation with no intent to deceive, by which the author assumes the role of another for effect. Such a view is not incompatible with the principle herein presented, provided it can be shown to be a literary device and not a moral deception." Apparently, for Geisler, now it not only *is* incompatible; it is also worthy of anathematizing any who articulate it!

were becoming standard. The seeds of a distinctively *Roman* Catholic movement were affecting doctrine and church hierarchy. Gnosticism was a significant threat to orthodoxy here and there. Persecution by Roman emperors, while not consistent, at times reached a peak beyond what it had ever been before. These and other factors led the church to tighten the reins on a variety of practices that had once been considered acceptable and to introduce new ones that had not previously existed.[9] To assume without further evidence that any attitude or practice from this era onward *must* have been agreed upon already by the mid-first century at the heart of the writing of the books that would eventually form the New Testament is a risky venture.

Conversely, it is beyond any reasonable doubt that pseudonymity existed in Second Temple Judaism. Large numbers of the Old Testament Apocrypha and Pseudepigrapha are ascribed to the Patriarchs (Enoch, Abraham, Isaac, Jacob and his sons, Moses, Job), later prominent figures in Israelite history (Ezra, Solomon, Jeremiah, Manasseh), or to characters otherwise unknown from Jewish history (Tobit, Judith, ben Sira), and the like. Most of these can be dated to the first or second centuries BC. Some of them exist with enough copies to suggest they were somewhat widely known. It is difficult to imagine the majority of Israelite readers who read one or more of these documents believing that someone had just unearthed ancient treasure troves of writings that had been written centuries or even millennia earlier but then lost. Nothing in the documents even presents them in such a light. It is much more likely that the fiction was transparent, while the preservation and use of the documents suggests that at least for a significant number of readers the practice was not

---

[9] For an excellent study of the formative role of Jewish Christianity and its gradual diminution of influence on the Jesus movement with the changes attending to that diminution, see Oskar Skarsaune and Reidar Hvalvik, eds., *Jewish Believers in Jesus: The Early Centuries* (Peabody: Hendrickson, 2007).

duplicitous.[10] The least amount of evidence exists for pseudepigraphal *epistles*, but we can point to the Letter of Jeremiah and the Letter of Aristeas. On the other hand, these are not the same subgenre of letters we find in the New Testament.[11] In the Greco-Roman world, however, the practice appears much more commonly.[12]

More controversial is whether any of the documents in the Hebrew Scriptures themselves were pseudonymous. Such an investigation would take us well beyond the purview of a book on the reliability of the *New* Testament. There is precious little external evidence to help us anyway; the vast majority of the discussion proceeds on the grounds of internal evidence—whether there is reason to date a given document early enough for it to have been written by the named individual or it shows signs of having come from a later era. What we *do* know is that the early rabbinic debates about certain Old Testament books and their inclusion in the canon did not involve questions about authorship but about contents. The Song of Songs proved questionable because of its glorification of sexual love, Ecclesiastes because of its almost unrelentingly pessimistic outlook on life, and Esther because God never appears explicitly in the text.[13]

Meanwhile, a recent international symposium on pseudepigraphy in early Christian literature found reasonably centrist biblical scholars

---

[10] Vicente Dobroruka, *Second Temple Pseudepigraphy: A Cross-Cultural Comparison of Apocalyptic Texts and Related Jewish Literature* (Berlin and New York: de Gruyter, 2013), has made the most detailed case for this to date. But he limited himself to apocalyptic literature, so there is no guarantee that his results apply to epistolary literature as well.

[11] On the possibility of nondeceptive Christian pseudepigraphal epistles outside the New Testament, see esp. Richard Bauckham, "Pseudo-Apostolic Literature," *Journal of Biblical Literature* 107 (1988): 469–94.

[12] See esp. Charles D. N. Costa, *Greek Fictional Letters* (Oxford: Oxford University Press, 2001).

[13] For full details, see Roger Beckwith, *The Old Testament Canon of the New Testament Church and Its Background in Early Judaism* (Grand Rapids: Eerdmans, 1985; Eugene, OR: Wipf & Stock, 2008), 274–337.

suggesting that the consensus of a generation ago is more likely to be accurate.[14] But these scholars are more nuanced in identifying a variety of reasons for this literary device. In some cases, *mimēsis* or imitation (the sincerest form of flattery, as it would later be called) formed the motive.[15] Certain literary genres like apocalyptic literature seemed to be dominated by pseudepigraphy. Various possible psychological or sociological correspondences between the real author and his purposes and the ancient individual in whose name he wrote (or to whom others may have credited an originally *anonymous* text) may have provoked the particular ascription of authorship.[16] In fact, David Aune itemizes at least six different kinds of pseudepigraphy among the ancients: (1) works that are partly authentic but have been supplemented by later authors, (2) works written largely by later authors but relying on some material from the named authors, (3) works that are generally influenced by the earlier authors who are named, (4) works from a "school" of writers ideologically descended from the named authors, (5) originally anonymous works later made pseudonymous for one of these previous reasons, and (6) genuine forgeries intended to deceive.[17] With only one of these six categories involving any intent to deceive, scholars on both far left and the far right would appear to be simply wrong when they claim some inherently immoral quality to the practice of pseudepigraphy or pseudonymity. Here, finally, we do

---

[14] Jörg Frey, Jens Herzer, Martina Janssen, and Clare K. Rothschild with Michaela Engelmann, eds., *Pseudepigraphie und Verfasserfiktion in frühchristlichen Briefen/Pseudepigraphy and Author Fiction in Early Christian Literature* (Tübingen: Mohr Siebeck, 2009).

[15] Leo G. Perdue, "Pseudonymity and Graeco-Roman Rhetoric: *Mimesis* and the Wisdom of Solomon," in ibid., 59.

[16] Eigbert Tigchellar, "Forms of Pseudepigraphy in the Dead Sea Scrolls," in ibid., 85–101.

[17] David E. Aune, "Reconceptualizing the Phenomenon of Pseudepigraphy: An Epilogue," in ibid., 794.

have some significant advances in the state of scholarly knowledge and understanding.

Even looking more narrowly into the concept of *authorship* in the ancient Mediterranean world, we find a broad spectrum of options. (1) To say that someone authored a document could mean they wrote the words on the papyrus or parchment. (2) It could mean they dictated word for word to a scribe (technically known as an amanuensis). (3) It could be they had collaborated with one or more other individuals to agree on wording to be written or dictated. (4) They could have authorized another individual to write a selection of their thoughts. (5) Finally, they could have written as best as they could envision how a teacher of theirs would have written had he been alive or present.[18] All five of these options appear in Cicero's *Letters to Atticus*. An excellent example of (5) appears in Iamblichus's late third century *Life of Pythagoras* 31.198:

> But the men shut out all lamentation and tears and the like, letting neither gain nor desire nor anger nor love of honor nor any other such thing become a cause of difference. Rather, all the Pythagoreans have the same attitude toward each other as a diligent father would have toward his children. And they consider it a noble thing to attribute and allot all of their investigations to Pythagoras, claiming none of the honor for themselves—unless perhaps rarely, for there are very few whose writings are known to be their own.

Frank Thielman cites the ten *Epistles of Anacharsis* and the *Epistles of Socrates and the Socratics* as additional good examples.[19] More famously, the Jewish Mishnah at the end of the second century declared that "a

---

[18] Jerome Murphy-O'Connor, *Paul the Letter Writer: His World, His Options, His Skills* (Collegeville, MN: Liturgical, 1995), 6–36; C. H. Talbert, *Ephesians and Colossians* (Grand Rapids: Baker, 2007), 7–9.

[19] Frank Thielman, *Ephesians* (Grand Rapids: Baker, 2010), 1.

man's representative is like himself" (*Berak.* 5.5). In Christian circles the closest we come to these sentiments is Tertullian's late second-century insistence "that which Mark published may be affirmed to be Peter's, whose interpreter Mark was. For even Luke's form of the Gospel, men usually ascribe to Paul" (*Contra Marc.* 4.5). Thielman also thinks the fictional exchanges between Paul and Seneca and between Christ and Abgar were "honest fictions" and that "their form as an exchange of correspondence may have been intended to signal that they were not authentic documents but edifying fabrications."[20] At the same time, there is plenty of evidence for false attribution of works to authors that was not viewed as acceptable, though practiced. Achtemeier, Green, and Thompson, therefore, substantially outrun the evidence when they allege that "according to Greco-Roman practice, if one got one's ideas from another, custom demanded that the writing identify the source of those thoughts as the document's author," and that "it was dishonest to do otherwise."[21]

In the sixth century AD, a Neoplatonic philosopher, Olympiodorus, writing about pseudepigraphical commentaries on Aristotle and Pythagoras, observes that there was "a time when the books were falsely ascribed because of the gratitude of the pupil over against their teachers" (*Introduction to Aristotle's Logic* 14). Salvian, a fifth-century AD elder in the church of Marseille, wrote about a book falsely attributed to Timothy that its author "thought that what he had done for the honor of his Lord should be known only to God himself, and that the work might please God the more as it ignored public recognition." Salvian continues to explain that this writer chose Timothy for what he believed was the same self-effacing, humble demeanor that he wanted to reflect. He also berates those in his day who overemphasize

---

[20] Ibid., 2.

[21] Paul J. Achtemeier, Joel B. Green, and Marianne Meye Thompson, *Introducing the New Testament: Its Literature and Theology* (Grand Rapids: Eerdmans, 2001), 380.

authorship instead of content. What should count is the merits of what is written in a book rather than whether the author used his own name or a pen name.[22]

The question that unfortunately cannot be answered unless new evidence is discovered is how *first-century Christians* would have envisaged these practices. Did many of them, given their Jewish roots, see it as at least sometimes acceptable and involving no intention to deceive, only to have their Gentile counterparts 150 years later proffer a different opinion? Or was the reason later Christians unanimously rejected the practice because of some development at the outset of the Christian movement that led believers to differentiate themselves from previous Jewish convictions on the topic? Both hypotheses are realistic enough, but neither can be demonstrated given the current limitations in what we know about the ancient Mediterranean world.

It is tragic, therefore, when pseudepigraphy becomes a "hill," on which some scholars have to "die." It is heartbreaking when an excellent professor is fired from an institution or a good pastor ousted from a church merely for defending pseudonymity somewhere in the canon. It is appalling that some in the church or academy feel they have to draw their confessional lines so tightly that such a practice is categorically excluded. Whether a certain New Testament book was written by the person whose name appears in what we now consider to be the first verse of its first chapter is a matter ultimately for students of historical and literary criticism to determine.[23] On the other hand, just as far too many individuals have simply *assumed* that pseudepigraphy

---

[22] Both authors are quoted in Baum, "Authorship and Pseudepigraphy in Early Christian Literature," 45 and 49.

[23] A chapter on pseudonymity is thus rightly included in David A. Black and David S. Dockery, eds., *Interpreting the New Testament: Essays on Methods and Issues* (Nashville: B&H, 2001). Cf. Andreas J. Köstenberger and Richard D. Patterson, *Invitation to Biblical Interpretation: Exploring the Hermeneutical Triad of History, Literature, and Theology* (Grand Rapids: Kregel, 2011), 461–63.

could not have been an acceptable phenomenon, so also have way too many assumed that all the arguments marshaled *against* traditional ascriptions of authorship for certain biblical books have proved conclusive.

With respect to the letters, seven are almost universally accepted as authentic today. Few serious scholars of any ideological stripe deny that Paul wrote Galatians, 1 Thessalonians, 1 and 2 Corinthians, Romans, Philemon, and Philippians. On the other hand, a fair number deny 2 Thessalonians, slightly more reject Colossians, even more find Ephesians pseudonymous, and outside of evangelical circles almost all New Testament scholars—that is, nearly half of the guild (since evangelicals number approximately half as well)—deny that Paul wrote the Pastoral Letters—1 and 2 Timothy and Titus. What are the specific arguments used in each instance, and how strong are they?

Are Any of Paul's Letters Pseudonymous?

2 Thessalonians

The most common reasons for concluding that 2 Thessalonians was not written by Paul are as follows:

1. Second Thessalonians includes non-Pauline vocabulary. Expressions like "we ought always to thank God for you" (1:3; 2:13), the use of the verb *saleuō* ("unsettled"—2:2), and the use of *trechō* to mean "spread rapidly" rather than literally "run" (3:1) occur in no other letters attributed to Paul. But every one of Paul's epistles has at least a similar amount of distinctive vocabulary and usage, so this argument proves little.[24] In addition, the two short letters have 146 words in

---

[24] So also Delbert Burkett, *An Introduction to the New Testament and the Origins of Christianity* (Cambridge: Cambridge University Press, 2002), 348, who notes that both letters to the Thessalonians have "about the same percentage of" distinctive vocabulary.

common, all but four of which appear in any or all of Galatians, 1–2 Corinthians, and Romans.[25] A forger would have needed not only to imitate 1 Thessalonians carefully throughout while still choosing to diverge noticeably in word choice at other points, but he would have had to know and use words common to all of Paul's major epistles to fit into a context not determined by the content of those epistles. No examples exist in the ancient world of forgeries nearly this subtle!

2. Second Thessalonians has a more advanced Christology than the first epistle. Instead of addressing the audience as brothers and sisters "loved by God" (1 Thess 1:4), this letter calls them "loved by the Lord," that is, "Jesus" (2 Thess 2:13). But 1 Thessalonians is filled with references to the Lord Jesus, so this claim collapses almost immediately. Attempts to draw significance from even more trivial observations like the order of references to God and Jesus barely merit mention.[26]

3. Second Thessalonians relies more on tradition and Old Testament allusions, less relevant to a primarily Gentile church, than does 1 Thessalonians.[27] For example, the UBS Greek New Testament lists fourteen allusions to passages in the Hebrew or Greek Old Testaments in a book of forty-seven verses (2 Thess) but only thirteen such allusions in a book of eighty-nine verses (1 Thess). But this is hardly a statistically significant variation. Much of 2 Thessalonians involves coming events related to God's judgment, which are described in Jewish apocalyptic language, so such allusions are only natural. Given Paul's short period of time in town before he was run

---

[25] Andreas J. Köstenberger, L. Scott Kellum, and Charles L. Quarles, *The Cradle, the Cross, and the Crown: An Introduction to the New Testament* (Nashville: B&H, 2009), 434.

[26] Again presented and rebutted in Burkett, *Introduction to the New Testament and Origins of Christianity*, 349.

[27] Supported by M. Eugene Boring, *An Introduction to the New Testament: History, Literature, Theology* (Louisville: Westminster John Knox, 2012). Rejected by D. A. Carson and Douglas J. Moo, *An Introduction to the New Testament*, 2nd ed. (Grand Rapids: Zondervan, 2005), 537.

out and given that his initial converts came from the synagogue before he turned to the Gentiles, there could easily have been enough of a Jewish element in the congregation to make such allusions meaningful. Those believers would have then readily explained anything missed by Gentile converts.

4. More significant is the noticeably harsher tone of 2 Thessalonians, especially as the author calls for God to avenge their enemies.[28] The first three chapters of 1 Thessalonians constitute the longest uninterrupted segment of praise for the Christians addressed in any of the letters attributed to Paul. By the beginning of 2 Thessalonians 2, however, the author is sternly warning his audience against being duped by false reports of his teaching, whether orally or in writing (2:1–2; cf. v. 15). He urges them not to be deceived by those who argue for too imminent a return of Christ (2:3–4). What was just a passing warning against the idle Christians in town in 1 Thessalonians 5:14 (who were possibly in view in 4:11–12 as well), becomes a full-on mandate to disassociate with anyone who refuses to work in 2 Thessalonians 3:6–15.

The author of this second letter also contains several harsh announcements about the judgment of those who are oppressing and persecuting the Thessalonian Christians. They will ultimately go to hell (1:6–10), as will a mysterious figure called "the man of lawlessness" (2:3) whom Jesus himself will destroy upon his return (2:8–10). All of his followers have refused to love the truth and be saved; as a result, God sends them a powerful delusion so that they are confirmed in their disobedience and unbelief (vv. 11–12).

On the other hand, all it would have taken was for the problems with the idle and the persecutors to have gotten worse after 1 Thessalonians for Paul to have had to write the way he does in

---

[28] See esp. Carl R. Holladay, *A Critical Introduction to the New Testament: Interpreting the Message and Meaning of Jesus Christ* (Nashville; Abingdon, 2005), 294–96, though he does not find this decisive.

the second letter. And neither of these problems requires a period of decades, much less years, to increase. A few weeks or months could have easily exacerbated such problems, especially if the Thessalonian church was growing rapidly, as both letters suggest it was (1 Thess 1:3–10; 2 Thess 1:3–4).[29] While it is sometimes argued that no one would have forged a letter in Paul's name until his authority and reputation were more widespread, nothing suggests that such a forgery was known by anyone outside Thessalonica. Given the widespread use of forgeries in the Greco-Roman world, a point Bart Ehrman *has* successfully demonstrated,[30] nothing more than the presence of a new, annoying, monotheistic sect in Thessalonica would have been needed before one person, aware of the contents of 1 Thessalonians, might have tried to undermine Paul's work in this fashion. It could have even come from some disaffected person in-house.

This would be plenty to create a more official, aloof tone to Paul's instructions in 2 Thessalonians. And it is not as if 1 Thessalonians has nothing harsh in it about outsiders. Chapter 2:14–16 has long been noted as reminiscent of Jesus's invective against select Pharisees in Matthew 23.[31] When the restrictive clause in verse 15 is not punctuated properly, it can sound as if Paul is accusing all Jews of killing Christ rather than referring specifically to the ones who did.[32] Of course, for this reason some have argued that these verses must be a post-Pauline interpretation,[33] but this borders closely on arguing in a

---

[29] See, e.g., Gordon D. Fee, *The First and Second Letters to the Thessalonians* (Grand Rapids: Eerdmans, 2009), 237–42.

[30] See the works cited in n. 5 above.

[31] David Wenham, *Paul: Follower of Jesus or Founder of Christianity?* (Grand Rapids: Eerdmans, 1995), 319–26.

[32] Frank D. Gilliard, "The Problem of the Antisemitic Comma Between 1 Thessalonians 2.14 and 15," in *New Testament Studies* 35 (1989): 481–502.

[33] This view has been increasingly abandoned, not least because of studies like Jon A. Weatherly, "The Authenticity of 1 Thessalonians 2.13–16: Additional Evidence," *Journal for the Study of the New Testament* 42 (1991): 79–98.

circle: Why can't 2 Thessalonians be Pauline?—because it's harsher than 1 Thessalonians, which *is* Pauline. What about 1 Thessalonians 2:14–16, which *is* as harsh as anything in 2 Thessalonians? Oh, it must not be Pauline!

Turning to 2 Thessalonians 2:2 more specifically, its language in no way requires that the threat about which the author is concerned was a forged letter. If the author knew for sure that a *document* written falsely in his name were the source of the believers' confusion, there is no reason for him to have been so vague—"whether by a prophecy or by word of mouth or by letter" (2 Thess 2:2). And given this vagueness, I. Howard Marshall's suggestion that it could have been 1 Thessalonians itself that had been misinterpreted by some proves persuasive.[34] In Greek the phrase *hōs di' hēmōn* (lit., "as through us") appears after the triad of options and most likely modifies all three.[35] Whether it was a misunderstanding of Paul's oral teaching when he was in town, someone's subsequent claim in the name of the Lord about what that teaching meant, or his letter that had been misinterpreted, Paul offers the necessary theological corrective in 2 Thessalonians. This suggestion is made even more likely by 2:15, which does not refer to anything that merely appeared to be Pauline but instead commands: "Stand firm and hold fast to the teachings we passed on to you, whether by word of mouth or by letter." In other words, follow the plain meaning of Paul's preaching and writing, not some creative distortion of it.[36]

---

[34] I. Howard Marshall, *1 and 2 Thessalonians* (London: Marshall, Morgan & Scott; Grand Rapids: Eerdmans, 1983), 28–45. Similarly, Abraham J. Malherbe, *The Letters to the Thessalonians* (New York and London: Doubleday, 2000), 351.

[35] Marshall, *1 and 2 Thessalonians*, 187.

[36] Ben Witherington III, *1 and 2 Thessalonians: A Socio-Rhetorical Commentary* (Grand Rapids: Eerdmans, 2006), 234. Witherington thinks that only here and not also in 2:2 is the misrepresentation of Paul's own writing in view because of the difference in language. But except for the omission of "prophecy," the wording is actually strikingly similar.

If there is any merit to this line of argumentation, then 2 Thessalonians does not indicate that a forged letter had been produced at all. The problem in town was not with a new letter claimed to be by Paul but with a misinterpretation of the real Paul. Marshall goes on to suggest a plausible line of developments that could easily have occurred within a period of months: Paul established the fledgling Thessalonian congregation, inculcated in them the basics of the faith, but then was persecuted to such an extent that he had to leave the area. Questions about nonessentials of the faith would naturally have lingered. Maybe a new believer died and the church was unsure of all of the details of what he or she would experience in the life to come. Maybe there were doubts about whether Jesus could fairly be described as still coming back soon, now that twenty years had elapsed since his death and resurrection. So Paul pens 1 Thessalonians, among other reasons, to stress that he did still have a lively hope of the second coming of Christ and that no believer who died before Jesus's return would miss out on any of the blessings of the coming age.

As with any corrective, however, some can swing the pendulum too far in the opposite direction. The problem with the idle may or may not have been connected to the notion that Christ would return so soon that people didn't need to continue working. Some were apparently interpreting 1 Thessalonians as claiming that the Day of the Lord had already come. It was not merely in later full-blown Gnosticism but also in Greek philosophy more generally, which for the most part did not believe in the resurrection of bodies but only in the immortality of souls, that the idea flourished of a new form of existence intruding into this life in entirely invisible, spiritual fashion. Could that be what Paul had been teaching, some might well have wondered—or confidently claimed. In response Paul pens 2 Thessalonians to describe visible signs that must yet occur (2:3–7). If anything along the lines of this scenario did in fact unfold, it would have not required years to elapse, unknown theological positions to develop, or Paul's teaching to spread around the empire. Within months of writing 1 Thessalonians, the word that was brought to Paul in Corinth, where he ministered for at least a year, could naturally have necessitated his second epistle to that community.[37]

5. Perhaps the two most common charges against the authenticity of 2 Thessalonians are the fifth and sixth issues to be considered. One is that the two letters are too similar to each other to have come from the same author.[38] Both begin with similarly worded greetings (1 Thess 1:1; 2 Thess 2:1–2). Both continue with prayers of thanksgiving for the Thessalonians' growth, including as reported by outsiders, in the midst of suffering and persecution (1 Thess 1:2–10; 2 Thess 1:3–12). Both at some point turn to eschatological concerns about the timing of the end and preceding and accompanying events (1 Thess 4:13–5:11; 2 Thess 2:1–17). Both refer to the idle in briefer exhortational material (1 Thess 5:14; 2 Thess 3:10–15). And both end with almost the identical closing verses (1 Thess 5:28; 2 Thess 3:18).

It is true that the wording and contents of much of these two epistles are more alike than for any other two of the undisputed epistles. Of course, two other pairs of letters demonstrate the same phenomena—Colossians and Ephesians, and 1 Timothy and Titus—but that is also one of the reason one or both of the members of each of those pairs of epistles are often doubted (see pp. 378–411). Yet if six of the thirteen letters ascribed to Paul exhibit close parallels to one other letter, there is hardly a large enough majority of letters that do not exhibit such parallelism (seven others) to use that as a reason for rejecting the

---

[37] Cf. esp. Marshall, *1 and 2 Thessalonians*, 23–25. See also Gary S. Shogren, *1 and 2 Thessalonians* (Grand Rapids: Zondervan, 2012), 34–36.

[38] Boring, *Introduction to the New Testament*, 362–63; Udo Schnelle, *The History and Theology of the New Testament Writings* (Minneapolis: Fortress, 1998), 320–22; Christina M. Kreinecker, "The Imitation Hypothesis: Pseudepigraphic Remarks on 2 Thessalonians with Help from Documentary Papyri," in *Paul and Pseudepigraphy*, ed. Porter and Fewster, 197–219.

authenticity of any of them! If Paul wrote both letters to Thessalonica in close proximity to each other, the similarities are understandable. If Paul wrote the second letter to correct misunderstandings of the first letter, he could have felt it necessary to repeat many of the same details of the first letter, but in a context of clarification. If both letters were written in a short period of time, from the same location, with the same coauthors, to the same audience, to a similar but deteriorating situation, it would be natural for the same exhortational (or advice-giving) letter genre,[39] a similar outline, and similar rhetorical structures and devices to be used. The similarities argue more for common authorship than for different sources of composition. The two letters are certainly not so slavishly similar as to require the theory of a forger meticulously imitating an original in an effort to fool an audience that he was really Paul.[40] In light of 2 Thessalonians 3:17 ("I, Paul, write this greeting in my own hand, which is the distinguishing mark in all my letters. This is how I write"), a supporter of pseudonymity would appear to have to admit that the real author of 2 Thessalonians was trying to be highly deceptive.

6. That the final main argument against the authenticity of 2 Thessalonians points to the differences between the two letters reinforces this conclusion. The last argument commonly put forward is that, theologically, the eschatology in 2 Thessalonians is diametrically opposite that of 1 Thessalonians and that, ethically, the issues have narrowed to the single matter of the idle.[41] But if Marshall's

---

[39] Beverly R. Gaventa, *First and Second Thessalonians* (Louisville: Westminster John Knox, 1998), 5. Charles A. Wanamaker, *The Epistles to the Thessalonians* (Grand Rapids: Eerdmans; Carlisle: Paternoster, 1990), 46–48, sees a slight difference between the two categories.

[40] Malherbe, *Letters to the Thessalonians*, 356–61.

[41] Cf. Schnelle, *History and Theology of the New Testament Writings*, 316–17; Mark A. Powell, *Introducing the New Testament: A Historical, Literary, and Theological Survey* (Grand Rapids: Baker, 2009), 391–93, although Powell does not choose sides in the debate.

scenario (even apart from his specific conclusions about the source of the Thessalonians' misunderstanding) is even close to being correct, then Paul must have stressed the flip side of his overall eschatological teaching. Nothing in 1 Thessalonians excludes the possibility that there were still certain signs that had to take place before Christ returned. When a group of people have overreacted in a certain direction, a corrective influence may have to overreact in the opposite direction. This does not create contradiction; it creates balance.

If the Thessalonians were already doing as well as Paul said they were when he wrote 1 Thessalonians, we should not be surprised that they heeded his advice on most of the ethical issues he addressed in his first letter. This would mean that all he had left to address was the problem with the idle. So again, pitting one letter against the other on these grounds drives a false wedge between the two.[42] Donald Hagner sums up the situation well: "The single most important fact that must be taken into consideration when examining 2 Thessalonians is its special character as a brief, appendix-like response written for the main purpose of correcting an erroneous understanding of a particular point." As a result, the two letters must always be studied together. "The shortness of time between the letters, on the traditional view, can account reasonably well for both the similarities and the differences between them." In other words, "similarities in structure and language appear because of the proximity in time in which they were written, while differences appear because the very purpose of the second letter is to clarify a misunderstanding possibly caused by the first."[43]

It is almost humorous that the two most commonly advanced arguments against the authenticity of 2 Thessalonians pretty much cancel

---

[42] See esp. Paul Foster, "Who Wrote 2 Thessalonians? A Fresh Look at an Old Problem," *Journal for the Study of the New Testament* 35 (2012): 150–75.

[43] Donald A. Hagner, *The New Testament: A Historical and Theological Introduction* (Grand Rapids: Baker, 2012), 465.

out each other.[44] Is the letter pseudonymous because it is too similar to its predecessor or because it is too different? At some point it appears that critics are simply looking for reasons to reject a particular document because they do not like its contents. Final judgment of God's enemies is not a fashionable topic in the Western world today, though people in many other parts of the world understand it well. When we recognize that the topic was brought up in the New Testament largely to encourage beleaguered and persecuted Christians, things take shape somewhat differently (cf. 1 Thess 4:18; 5:11; 2 Thess 1:6).[45] Many liberal biblical critics still rightly stress the need for social justice. But justice often cannot occur without punishment for the oppressors. We understand the dynamics with injustice in this life, and yet some then protest that God has to be completely different when it comes to eternal life. The inconsistency proves telling. The biggest problem with 2 Thessalonians is that it is not politically correct enough for many modern critics.[46] Yet all that proves is that modern political correctness is at times based on values not derivable from the Christian Scriptures, a point almost all of us already knew. It proves nothing about whether Paul wrote 2 Thessalonians!

Eugene Boring provides an excellent catalog of the wide array of scholarly proposals that have tried to account for the diversity of

---

[44] Carson and Moo, *Introduction to the New Testament*, 537.

[45] "The emphasis on the vengeance of God is calculated to encourage the brothers and sisters in the face of great adversity, supplying them with an eschatological perspective that will enable them to evaluate their present situation rightly."—Gene L. Green, *The Letters to the Thessalonians* (Grand Rapids: Eerdmans; Leicester: Apollos, 2002), 287.

[46] At the same time, 2 Thess 1:9 is a crucial text on hell—"shut out from the presence of the Lord and from the glory of his might." Fire and darkness, the most common ways of referring to eternal punishment elsewhere in the New Testament, cancel each other out if either is absolutized, suggesting that they are metaphors. Here in 2 Thessalonians is a text that can be taken literally. Those who want nothing to do with God ultimately get what they want—forever!

phenomena within 1 and 2 Thessalonians.[47] These include theories that see one letter addressed to the entire church but the other one to a minority of people within it; that find one addressed to a different church besides Thessalonica and errantly ascribed to that city; or that envision Timothy or Silas, listed with Paul in the first verse of each letter, writing one of them with Paul's approval. The last of these is completely possible, but stylistic differences are so minor as to scarcely require it. The first two hypotheses have no hint of support from the actual text of the two letters. Still others have dated 2 Thessalonians prior to 1 Thessalonians, which is possible, since nothing within the text of either letter requires a particular chronology of composition. But the perceived tensions between the two letters still remain. Theories of pseudonymity subdivide into those who see it written by one of Paul's close followers after his death to correct false understandings of Paul's eschatology in a way that would have deceived no one, and those who see it as an "orthodox" forgery to counter heterodoxy. As we have noted, in view of the contents of 2 Thessalonians 3:17, which strongly stress Pauline authorship, this last option would appear particularly duplicitous. The first option could be attractive if the arguments against authenticity were stronger. As it stands, there is no compelling reason to reject the unanimous verdict of the first 1,800 years of church history that Paul wrote the letter, from Corinth, shortly after his first letter to Thessalonica.[48]

Colossians and Ephesians

Colossians and Ephesians form the next pair of letters that in many ways appear remarkably similar to each other. In this instance both

---

[47] Boring, *Introduction to the New Testament*, 360–62.

[48] Likewise Holladay, *Critical Introduction to the New Testament*, 290; Luke T. Johnson, *The Writings of the New Testament*, 3rd ed. (Minneapolis: Fortress, 2010), 255–58; Achtemeier, Green, and Thompson, *Introducing the New Testament*, 445 (cautiously).

letters have often been doubted, though some who reject Ephesians accept Colossians and argue that the pseudonymous author of Ephesians relied on the genuinely Pauline Colossians the way the supposedly pseudonymous author of 2 Thessalonians relied on the genuinely Pauline 1 Thessalonians. As a result, we need to look at Colossians and Ephesians separately.

Colossians

As with 2 Thessalonians, we may dispense with a few arguments of little merit before moving on to the major reasons many scholars challenge the Pauline authorship of Colossians.

1. A few people have argued that the Colossian heresy opposed explicitly starting in Colossians 2:8 is too akin to second-century or late first-century philosophies, especially Gnosticism, to have been a danger in Colossae during Paul's lifetime.[49] This can be immediately set to one side by the observation that there are more competing yet plausible theories for the Colossian heresy than for any other false teaching mentioned anywhere in the New Testament, and not the slightest hint of any consensus as to its makeup.[50] That is because we are simply not given enough details in the letter to affirm with any degree of confidence that we have identified the precise philosophy that was competing with Christianity. A generation or more ago there might have been a plurality, though certainly not a majority, of scholars who found it gnostic; today that view is only infrequently held.[51]

---

[49] A view surveyed in detail but rejected by R. McL. Wilson, *A Critical and Exegetical Commentary on Colossians and Philemon* (London and New York: T & T Clark, 2005), 35–51.

[50] Among evangelicals, however, a plurality of support may be discernible for the mixture of Jewish and local, pagan folk beliefs and practices outlined in Clinton E. Arnold, *The Colossian Syncretism: The Interface Between Christianity and Folk Belief at Colossae* (Tübingen: J. C. B. Mohr, 1995; Grand Rapids: Baker, 1996).

[51] Important alternatives today include mainstream Judaism (Allan R. Bevere, *Sharing in the Inheritance: Identity and the Moral Life in Colossians* [London and

2. The household code in 3:18–4:1 resembles second-century household codes too much to come from the mid-first century.[52] The problem here is that the only first-century literature we have with household codes is in New Testament books. These appear particularly clearly in Ephesians (5:22–6:9) and 1 Peter (2:13–3:7; 5:1–5), which are also often viewed as pseudonymous and therefore late. But if the only known relevant first-century literature is excluded from consideration, then the argument is decided in advance. It is not as if we do not have pre-Christian *Jewish* household codes that bear some similarities to the ones in the New Testament. But we should *expect* first-century Christian codes to look more like slightly later Christian codes than like earlier non-Christian ones!

3. An earthquake destroyed much of Colossae in about AD 61, and we have no evidence that the city was ever rebuilt. So Paul could not have written to a Christian community in a city that no longer existed.[53] But the chronology for Paul's arrival in Rome, the traditional location for the writing of Colossians from his house arrest, places Paul in the imperial capital by the spring of 60 (recall above), giving

---

New York: Sheffield Academic Press, 2003]); ascetic and apocalyptic Jewish mysticism (Thomas J. Sappington, *Revelation and Redemption at Colossae* [Sheffield: JSOT, 1991]); Jewish and Greek Middle Platonic views of wisdom (Richard E. DeMaris, *The Colossian Controversy: Wisdom in Dispute at Colossae* [Sheffield: JSOT, 1994]); and cynicism (Troy W. Martin [*By Philosophy and Empty Deceit: Colossians as Response to a Cynic Critique* (Sheffield: Sheffield Academic Press, 1996]).

[52] Burkett, *An Introduction to the New Testament and the Origins of Christianity*, 365–66; Jerry L. Sumney, *Colossians: A Commentary* (Louisville and London: Westminster John Knox, 2008), 2.

[53] Boring (*Introduction to the New Testament*, 336–37) thinks "a teacher in the Pauline school in Ephesus composed a letter in the 70s or 80s CE, ostensibly directed to 'Colossae,' which all the readers knew no longer existed." This way they could apply it more indirectly to themselves. Holladay (*Critical Introduction to the New Testament*, 396) proves more persuasive when he declares how difficult it is "to imagine that someone writing years later would compose a Pauline letter addressed to Colossae unless there had been an actual connection between Paul and Colossae and some correspondence between them."

him perhaps up to a year or a little more to have written the letter. If the letter is to be dated to an Ephesian or Caesarean imprisonment, as a minority of scholars has proposed, then it was written even earlier (52–55 or 57–59, respectively). If indeed, the city was largely abandoned after the earthquake, why would any later pseudonymous writer address it at all? And if it was at least partially repopulated, then Paul could have written it sometime after the earthquake but before his death in the mid- to late-sixties.[54]

4. A few theological issues are sometimes said to distinguish Colossians from the undisputed Pauline letters, but the alleged distinctions cannot stand up to careful scrutiny. (1) Did the author of the letter have a stronger (later) view of apostolic succession, with Paul as an undisputed final authority and Epaphras as the successor to Paul (Col 1:7)?[55] All this verse does is remind the readers that Epaphras was the founding pastor of the church in Colossae, since Paul had never visited there personally. (2) Does the author have a much higher view of the importance of traditions and creedal formulations for Christian thought than the real Paul?[56] The letter contains plenty of potentially pre-Pauline, with the clearest and most well-known being 1:15–20.[57] But the most similar passage in form to this Christological confession elsewhere in the letters comes in Philippians 2:6–11, in an undisputed epistle. (3) Is it significant that there is no unambiguous reference

---

[54] On the other hand, Carson and Moo (*Introduction to the New Testament*, 522) may not exaggerate much when they declare "that it is inconceivable that the destruction would not have been mentioned by any informed and compassionate writer."

[55] Willi Marxsen, *Introduction to the New Testament*, rev. ed. (Philadelphia: Fortress, 1968), 177–79. Cf. Schnelle, *New Testament Writings*, 286.

[56] Boring, *Introduction to the New Testament*, 334–35. Schnelle (*History and Theology of the New Testament Writings*, 286) thinks this manifests itself with the author's defining faith as "holding fast to tradition."

[57] See esp. George E. Cannon, *The Use of Traditional Materials in Colossians* (Macon: Mercer University Press, 1983).

to the Holy Spirit in Colossians?[58] The Greek *pneuma* ("S/spirit") occurs only in 1:8 and 2:5, which could refer to the human spirit, though probably references the Holy Spirit. But even if not, it would be more surprising for a later second- or third-generation Christian letter not to mention all three persons of the Trinity, as that doctrine was becoming more and more fleshed out, than in the first generation.

This leaves three main reasons for us to consider.

5. The language and style are noticeably different from the rest of the Pauline corpus, save for Ephesians.[59] Some might wish to dispute this, but repeated study of the Greek, not merely in terms of distinctive vocabulary (much of which could have been borrowed from the heresy) but also in terms of sentence length and structure (for which there would be little reason for the same author to change), confirms this distinctive.[60] Yet Timothy is listed as a cosender in the opening verse of the letter, and he could well be a coauthor also.[61] In fact, Paul could have given Timothy his thoughts and outline and asked him, as his scribe or amanuensis, to write it up in his own words. This also fits Colossians 4:18, where Paul then would have taken pen in hand

---

[58] Sumney, *Colossians*, 3; Schnelle, *History and Theology of the New Testament Writings*, 287.

[59] See esp. Mark C. Kiley, *Colossians as Pseudepigraphy* (Sheffield: Sheffield Academic Press, 1987).

[60] See esp. Eduard Lohse, *Colossians and Philemon* (Philadelphia: Fortress, 1972), especially 85–87. Ben Witherington III (*The Letters to Philemon, the Colossians, and the Ephesians: A Socio-Rhetorical Commentary on the Captivity Epistles* [Grand Rapids: Eerdmans, 2007], 102–3), nevertheless thinks that once traditional materials, especially the Colossian hymn, and the natural amount of variation from one Pauline epistle to another are taken into account, the only other piece necessary to affirm complete Pauline authorship is "Asiatic rhetoric and its characteristic features of style."

[61] Cf. James D. G. Dunn, *The Epistles to the Colossians* (Grand Rapids: Eerdmans; Carlisle: Paternoster, 1996), 35–39; Michael F. Bird, *Colossians, Philemon* (Eugene, OR: Cascade, 2009), 9; Robert W. Wall, *Colossians and Philemon* (Downers Grove and Leicester: IVP, 1993), 15; and Hagner, *New Testament*, 566 (tentatively).

to write the last verse (recall 2 Thess 3:17). Even nonevangelicals have proposed this scenario on more than one occasion.[62] The difference in style can also be used as an argument against pseudepigraphy. Wouldn't a forger follow Paul's style even *more* closely? The close similarity in style between 1 and 2 Thessalonians, we recall, was put forward as a reason for seeing 2 Thessalonians as pseudepigraphal. Now it is the differences between Colossians and the rest of Paul's letters that are being cited for the same reason. But these comparatively small differences "speak louder [*sic*] in favor of Colossians as a product of the creative mind of Paul than do the obvious harmonies."[63]

6. The Christology and eschatology seem to differ substantially from the emphases in those areas of the undisputed Paulines.[64] Jesus is the cosmic Christ, the Creator of the universe, the Head of the body which is his church (Colossians 1:15–20), having rescued us from the kingdom of darkness and brought us into the kingdom of light (1:12–13). The author fills up what is lacking in the afflictions of Christ (1:24), who represents the fullness of deity in bodily form (2:9). Instead of a largely future hope for Christ's return, we are already sharing in our inheritance (1:12), in which we have redemption and forgiveness of sins (v. 14). We have been reconciled to God (v. 22), and God's mysterious plan of salvation has already been revealed to us (vv. 26–27). Believers have already been raised with Christ (2:12). Christ himself has already disarmed the spiritual powers arrayed against us and him (2:13–15, 20). In 3:1–2, it would appear we have a kind of Christ mysticism, in which believers are to set their hearts on things

---

[62] E.g., Eduard Schweizer, *The Letter to the Colossians* (London: SPCK; Minneapolis: Augsburg, 1982), 23–24; David M. Hay, *Colossians* (Nashville: Abingdon, 2000), 24 (tentatively).

[63] Markus Barth and Helmut Blanke, *Colossians* (New York and London: Doubleday, 1994), 121.

[64] Raymond E. Brown, *An Introduction to the New Testament* (New York and London: Doubleday, 1997), 611–13.

above, in the heavenly realm, where Christ is seated at the right hand of God.

Still, all these are contrasts in degree not of kind, all of which were most likely necessitated by the false teaching Paul has to oppose and the preformed traditions he has chosen to use to counter the heresy. After all, we have died to sin in Romans 6:2, are buried and raised with Christ in baptism in verses 3–4, with no power able to separate us from the love of God in 8:39. First Corinthians 8:6 affirms the creation of all things through Christ who likewise holds them all together. Second Corinthians 4:8–12 shows that Paul believed his physical sufferings manifested the presence of Christ in his body, while Philippians 2:6 declares that Christ was in the form or nature of God.[65]

Plenty of thoroughly Pauline concepts, moreover, are present in Colossians. We read Paul's thanksgiving for the Colossians' growth (1:3, 6; cf. most of the thanksgivings in the undisputed Paulines), his prayer for their faith, hope, and love (vv. 4–5, 8; cf. 1 Thess 1:3; 1 Cor 13:13), his proclamation of the gospel throughout creation (1:23; cf. Rom 10:18), his distinctive commission to the Gentiles (v. 27; Rom 1:16), and his emphasis on spiritual unity (2:1–3; cf. 1 Cor 1:10), on "present ... in the spirit" despite being "absent ... in body" (v. 5; cf. 1 Cor 5:3–4). Furthermore, Paul combats Judaizing, especially with respect to circumcision (vv. 11–13; cf. Gal 2:1–10; Phil 3:3–6), highlights the centrality of Christ's cross-work (v. 14; cf. 1 Cor 1:18–2:5) and counters legalistic attitudes toward food and drink (vv. 16–17, 20–22; cf. Rom 14:1–4; 1 Corinthians 8). What appears at first to be mysticism turns out to be defined, fairly mundanely, as holy living in interpersonal relationships in the affairs of this world (Colossians 3:5–17). And a clearly future-oriented eschatology appears immediately after the statement that believers died so that their lives are "now

---

[65] Cf. the helpful chart in Powell, *Introducing the New Testament*, 363. See also Johnson, *Writings of the New Testament*, 347–49.

hidden with Christ in God" (3:3): "When Christ, who is your life, appears, then you also will appear with him in glory" (v. 4), an event which has clearly not yet happened.[66] With respect to arguments (5) and (6) overall, F. F. Bruce adds the important reminder that the apostle "whose settled policy was to be 'all things to all men' for the gospel's sake" (1 Cor 9:19–23) could surely have varied his style and contents to some degree to counter specific false teaching in language borrowed from the heresy, which would nevertheless present the truth as he understood it.[67]

7. The similarities and differences between the greetings in Philemon and Colossians suggest that Colossians was both imitating and modifying key details from Philemon.[68] This little undisputed prison epistle mentions Paul and Timothy also as cosenders or coauthors (v. 1), Epaphras is described as Paul's fellow prisoner (v. 23), while Mark, Aristarchus, Demas, and Luke (his fellow workers) also offer greetings (v. 24). In verse 12, Paul clarifies that he is sending Onesimus back to his master Philemon, and in verse 2 he mentions Archippus as one of the people to whom the letter is addressed. In Colossians, however, Epaphras is simply called "one of you and a servant of Christ Jesus" (Col 4:12) who is working hard for the believers in Colossae and neighboring cities (v. 13). Mark, Luke, Demas, and Aristarchus are again greeted, though in a different order and with

---

[66] See further esp. the detailed analysis of Paul's identity as it emerges from Colossians in Gregory S. MaGee, *Portrait of an Apostle: A Case for Paul's Authorship of Colossians and Ephesians* (Eugene, OR: Pickwick, 2013), 80–127. More briefly, cf. Douglas J. Moo (*The Letter to the Colossians and to Philemon* [Grand Rapids: Eerdmans; Nottingham: Apollos, 2008], 32–37), who also compares Colossians' ecclesiology and apparent "early Catholicism" with the undisputed letters. For a more balanced assessment of Colossians' eschatology, see Todd D. Still, "Eschatology in Colossians: How Realized Is It?" *New Testament Studies* 50 (2004): 125–38.

[67] F. F. Bruce, *The Epistles to the Colossians, to Philemon, and to the Ephesians* (Grand Rapids: Eerdmans, 1984), 29.

[68] Boring, *Introduction to the New Testament*, 331–32.

varying details. Aristarchus is now called a fellow prisoner (v. 10) and Luke a doctor (v. 14). Archippus is given the specific command to complete some ministry (v. 17), and other names appear not found in Philemon (vv. 7, 11, 15), while Philemon's and Apphia's names (Phlm 1, 2) are absent.

This cluster of similarities and differences actually makes it much more likely that the letters to Philemon and to the Colossians were sent out about the same time.[69] Not giving the identical information about each person in two different letters creates a problem only if contradictory information is actually present, which it is not. Unless Paul were copying slavishly from a previous letter of his, there is no reason for the wording to have been any closer. Philemon was an individual believer and host of a house church in Colossae, and every detail in Paul's letter to him fits that occasion.[70] Additional information involving the entire Christian church in that community can appear in a letter addressed to the whole collection of congregations, but it is irrelevant for the personal remarks and requests that characterize Philemon. That in both letters Onesimus is on his way home to Philemon (see Col 4:9; Phlm 10–12) is almost inexplicable if one is authentic and the other a pseudonymous composition of a later era, especially since that detail makes no difference for the theology and exhortation of Colossians.

Boring again nicely catalogs the major options for explaining all of these data: Paul could have written to the Colossians; Timothy, with Paul's approval, could have written to the Colossians; a member of the "Paulinist school" of Paul's disciples could have written to

---

[69] David W. Pao, *Colossians and Philemon* (Grand Rapids: Zondervan, 2012), 22–23; Dunn, *Epistles to the Colossians and to Philemon*, 37–38; Donald G. Guthrie, *New Testament Introduction*, 4th ed. (Leicester and Downers Grove: IVP, 1990), 576–77.

[70] See esp. Markus Barth and Helmut Blanke, *The Letter to Philemon* (Grand Rapids: Eerdmans, 2000), 121–28 and throughout.

the Colossians; such a Paulinist could have written to the church as a whole; or a Paulinist could have written to the Pauline churches of Asia Minor, especially Colossae, Hierapolis, and Laodicea.[71] These are the two larger cities nearest Colossae; both are mentioned in Colossians 4:13, and a letter to the Laodiceans is mentioned in verse 16 along with Paul's desire to have Colossians read in Laodicea. This last option is Boring's preference, but it suggests a sixth possibility: Paul, with Timothy's help, wrote with at least the two churches of Colossae and Laodicea in mind and perhaps others in the same region. Carl Holladay modifies this theory to suggest that a pseudonymous writer edited and supplemented authentic Pauline memoirs,[72] but it is not obvious that this complication is at all needed.

In short, it seems unnecessary to postulate a date beyond Paul's lifetime for the writing of Colossians. The only significant barrier to straightforward Pauline authorship is the grammatical style of the letter, though even this is ameliorated when probable pre-Pauline material is bracketed. Andrew Pitts argues that we should examine an author's register much more than his or her style. Pitts defines *register* broadly "as contexts for language varieties ranging from literary genres to social situations." "Audience design" would be another dimension.[73] The amount of variation in style and vocabulary among the letters attributed to Paul is consistent with the amount of variation of register. Of the six disputed Pauline epistles, Colossians demonstrates the least variation of register from the seven undisputed letters.[74] That the opening verse explicitly links Paul with Timothy, moreover, makes it reasonable to suggest that Timothy may have had a role in the composition of the letter that accounts for whatever differences remain.

---

[71] Boring, *Introduction to the New Testament*, 329–31.

[72] Holladay, *Critical Introduction to the New Testament*, 394–96.

[73] Andrew W. Pitts, "Style and Pseudonymity in Pauline Scholarship," in *Paul and Pseudepigraphy*, ed. Porter and Fewster, 117.

[74] See the chart in ibid., 146.

The close but not slavish resemblances with Philemon strongly argue for the two letters' being written and sent out about the same time to the same community. If Philemon is authentic, as is almost universally acknowledged, then Colossians should be accepted as coming from Paul as well.[75]

EPHESIANS

Some of the same issues just discussed with Colossians recur in analyzing the letter to the Ephesians, but new ones appear also. The most significant involves a textual variant in 1:1. The original copies of Sinaiticus and Vaticanus, the two oldest, most complete copies of the New Testament, from the fourth century, along with one of the Chester Beatty papyri (p[46]), dated to the end of the second century and the oldest known copy of this part of Ephesians, all lack the words "in Ephesus" at the beginning of the letter. So, too, do a handful of later documents, even though the vast majority of all ancient copies contain them. This leads critical reconstructions of the Greek New Testament to express considerable doubt as to whether these words were original.[76] The text reads awkwardly without them, though:

---

[75] Similarly, Peter T. O'Brien, *Colossians, Philemon* (Waco: Word, 1982), xli–xlix; Lee M. McDonald and Stanley E. Porter, *Early Christianity and Its Sacred Literature* (Peabody: Hendrickson, 2000), 473–76; N. T. Wright, *Colossians and Philemon* (Leicester: IVP; Grand Rapids: Eerdmans, 1986), 31–34; David A. deSilva, *An Introduction to the New Testament: Contexts, Methods and Ministry Formation* (Downers Grove: IVP; Leicester, Apollos, 2004), 696–701; Bonnie Thurston, *Reading Colossians, Ephesians, and 2 Thessalonians*, 2nd ed. (Macon: Smyth & Helwys, 2007), 10–12; Marianne Meye Thompson, *Colossians and Philemon* (Downers Grove and Leicester: IVP, 2005), 2–5; David E. Garland, *Colossians/Philemon* (Grand Rapids: Zondervan, 1998), 17–22.

[76] Rudolf Schnackenburg, *The Epistle to the Ephesians: A Commentary* (Edinburgh: T & T Clark, 1991), 39–42; Schnelle, *History and Theology of the New Testament Writings*, 304–5; Holladay, *Critical Introduction to the New Testament*, 412. The UBS Greek New Testament includes them, but in brackets and with only a {C} level of confidence. The Nestle-Aland text likewise brackets the words.

"Paul, an apostle of Christ Jesus by the will of God, to *the holy ones who are* (*tois hagiois tois ousin*), and to the faithful in Christ Jesus." It is possible to translate the italicized words more smoothly as "to those who are holy ones," but if that is what Paul meant, why did he not simply do as he did frequently elsewhere and write merely, "to (all) God's/his holy people" (cf. 1 Cor 1:2, 2 Cor 1:1, Phil 1:1)?

On the other hand, it has frequently been suggested that Ephesians was an encyclical letter, intended for more than one congregation.[77] The original copy could have had a space after *tois ousin* large enough for a local church to add the name of the addressees. Ephesus was by far the largest and most significant city in Asia Minor. Once Christians started copying the version of the letter that would have begun with "to the holy ones who are in Ephesus" and disseminated those copies, there would have been little need to save those with a different address. Further reason to suspect Ephesians of being an encyclical is the less personal nature of the letter when compared with the undisputed Paulines.[78] Next only to Romans, Ephesians is Paul's most orderly, systematic presentation of the truths of the gospel, splitting the letter almost exactly in half between theology and ethics (3:21/4:1). Statements like "Surely you have heard about the administration of God's grace that was given to me for you" (3:2) and "surely you have heard about him [Christ] and were taught in him" (4:21a NRSV) seem odd if Paul is writing simply to Ephesus where he spent a three-year period of time (recall above). But if he were also including communities he had not evangelized, they would make perfectly good

---

[77] Burkett (*Introduction to the New Testament and the Origins of Christianity*, 373) claims scholarly agreement on this point, though this is probably an overstatement. Cf. Clinton E. Arnold, *Ephesians* (Grand Rapids: Zondervan, 2010), 28–29.

[78] Boring, *Introduction to the New Testament*, 345; Arthur G. Patzia, *Ephesians, Colossians, Philemon*, rev. ed. (Peabody: Hendrickson, 1990; Carlisle: Paternoster, 1995; Grand Rapids; Baker, 2012), 125.

sense. He then could not take for granted that everyone reading his letter knew the true gospel or Paul's distinctive commission.

Maybe the strangest part of Ephesians, on the assumption it was written solely to Ephesus, is its ending.[79] Paul consistently sends greetings from a handful of those fellow believers he is with at the time he writes and gives greetings to specific people he knows in the churches he is addressing. Yet Ephesians ends with reference to only one person, Tychicus, who is the letter carrier and can give the Ephesians more information as they desire it (Eph 6:21–22). Contrast the opposite extreme in the last chapter of the letter to the Romans, which contains approximately thirty names of people sending greetings or being greeted (Rom 16:1–23).

A generation ago it was standard among nonevangelical scholars to argue that Romans 16 actually contained the misplaced ending to Ephesians.[80] After all, why would the most number of personal links between Paul and a given church appear precisely in a letter written to a community he had never yet visited? The doxology in what we call Romans 16:25–27, moreover, is found in a variety of places in the ancient manuscripts. It appears as early as after 14:23 in some ancient texts, as if the copyists knew that some manuscripts contained nothing else beyond this juncture. Origen himself claimed that Marcion had copies that altogether lacked anything after Romans 14. Some manuscripts contain the doxology here *and* at the end of chapter 16. Some place it at the end of Romans 15; others have it at the end of

---

[79] Cf. Schnelle, *History and Theology of the New Testament Writings*, 302: "The whole document makes a very impersonal impression, so that e.g., there is not a single greeting to members of the church in Ephesians."

[80] Robert Jewett (*Romans* [Minneapolis: Fortress, 2007], 8–9) itemizes a key list of scholars who reflected this consensus, notes that he once believed it, details the key studies that turned the tide in the academy, esp. Karl P. Donfried, ed., *The Romans Debate*, 2nd ed. (Minneapolis: Augsburg, 1991; Grand Rapids: Baker, 2011), and observes that today it has been widely abandoned.

both chapters 14 and 15 but not at the end of 16. One minuscule (1506) lacks Romans 16 altogether, except for the doxology, but it is late, dating to AD 1320.[81]

Of course, Marcion was highly anti-Jewish and condemned as a heretic who had excised passages from various New Testament documents. The theory that Romans once lacked both chapters 15 and 16 seems highly unlikely. It may have lacked chapter 16 in more than one manuscript, perhaps at much earlier times, explaining the varying positions of the doxology, but this could be precisely because the scribes also were surprised to find Paul having so many personal connections with a church he had never visited. But that does not mean it originally lacked this chapter. Even if it did, that would scarcely suggest it once belonged with Ephesians. Today it is far more common for scholars of numerous theological stripes to assert that Paul was mentioning everyone he had ever met or heard about during his mission work who was currently in the Roman church in order to build bridges with a church he hadn't previously visited.[82] We know that to be the case with Prisc(ill)a and Aquila (Rom 16:3; cf. Acts 18:1–4), so it is plausible to assume it to be the case with the rest of the people, most of whom appear nowhere else in Scripture. "All roads lead to Rome" was not merely a geographical proverb from antiquity; in the first century large numbers of people migrated from other parts of the empire to settle in the capital.

We still have to account for the lack of greetings, however, in the letter to the Ephesians. A circular letter would not try to list names from every city to which it was addressed, even if the author knew people at every location, precisely because a majority of those names would not be meaningful to the majority of the addressees. We have

---

[81] UBS *Greek New Testament*, 4th rev. ed., 18*.

[82] See esp. Harry Gamble Jr., *The Textual History of the Letter to the Romans: A Study in Textual and Literary Criticism* (Grand Rapids: Eerdmans, 1977).

already seen that Colossians refers to an otherwise unknown letter to the Laodiceans (Col 4:16). What if that were the letter we know as Ephesians but in the version addressed to Laodicea?[83] We know of one New Testament document that was addressed to seven churches in Asia Minor—the book of Revelation (see Revelation 2–3)—and two of those churches were Ephesus and Laodicea, so this hypothesis gains further plausibility. Marcion even claimed to have a document identical to our Ephesians that was addressed to the Laodiceans. But the state of the evidence does not allow us to move from plausibility to probability. The theory that Ephesians was an encyclical, however, does not *require* it to have been the missing letter to the Laodiceans.

The general nature of Ephesians has also proved an impediment to the acceptance of Pauline authorship.[84] After a highly theological blessing (rather than the customary thanksgiving) and prayer for God's rich provision for believers, divided according to the three persons of the Trinity (1:3–14), then a proper thanksgiving prayer ensues with gratitude for all of the spiritual privileges we have in Christ (1:15–23). The prayer seamlessly transitions into theological declarations of how we have been made alive with Christ, raised with him and seated with him in the heavenly realms (2:1–10). The author uses or creates compound verbs with prepositional prefixes to express

---

[83] E.g., Andrew T. Lincoln, *Ephesians* (Dallas: Word, 1990), 5–7. Michael D. Goulder ("The Visionaries of Laodicea," *Journal for the Study of the New Testament* 43 [1991]: 15–39) thinks Paul wrote what we call Ephesians but that it was originally intended *primarily* for Laodicea. Ernest Best (*A Critical and Exegetical Commentary on Ephesians* [Edinburgh: T & T Clark, 1998], 20–21) discounts this view because he thinks it requires what we call Ephesians to have predated Colossians, but in fact it simply requires that Paul know when he wrote Colossians that he was also sending out what we call Ephesians.

[84] See esp. Lincoln, *Ephesians*, xxvi–xliv. Johnson (*Writings of the New Testament*, 359) counters that "if written pseudonymously, the author in this case failed to create a plausible impression of intimacy between Paul and a church he apparently knew so well."

these actions (*suzōopoieō*—v. 5; *sunegeirō* and *sunkathizō*—v. 6) and five times in the letter refers to something "in the heavenlies" (i.e., places or realms) with an expression found nowhere else in the Bible (*en tois epouraniois*—1:3, 20; 2:6; 3:10; 6:12).[85] Then he turns to the reconciliation between Jew and Gentile in Christ that this unity should produce (2:11–22). Chapter 3 contains the author's description of the administration of this mystery of reaching the Gentiles followed by yet another prayer. Chapters 4–6 then present, in equally orderly fashion, the concomitant ethics that flow from the gospel's theology.

Is this what a church with which Paul had recently spent three years most needed to hear? Repetition may be the secret to learning, but given the time and expense related to letter writing in antiquity, would this have been the best use of Paul's resources? On the other hand, if Ephesus was just one of several churches, one could appreciate the contents much more. At the same time, as Clinton Arnold has repeatedly stressed, a clear thread runs throughout the entire epistle corresponding to the dangers of the demonic realm but Christ's triumph over it that makes good sense if addressed to Ephesus, a key center for the ancient practice of magic (akin to our occult). This triumph over the demonic world led to the first known Christian scroll-burning ceremony (of "magical papyri," still preserved in abundance from later times and other locations) in Acts 19:11–20 (see esp. v. 19).[86]

The motif of spiritual warfare is, in fact, woven throughout Ephesians. It begins with the blessings we have received in the

---

[85] On which, see esp. M. Jeff Brannon, *The Heavenlies in the Ephesians: A Lexical, Exegetical, and Conceptual Analysis* (London and New York: T & T Clark, 2011).

[86] See esp. Clinton E. Arnold, *Ephesians: Power and Magic* (Cambridge: Cambridge University Press, 1989 [= *Power and Magic: The Concept of Power in Ephesians* (Eugene, OR: Wipf & Stock, 2001)]); Clinton E. Arnold, "Ephesians, Letter to the," in *Dictionary of Paul and His Letters*, ed. Gerald F. Hawthorne, Ralph P. Martin, and Daniel G. Reid (Downers Grove and Leicester: IVP, 1993), 238–49.

heavenly realms in 1:3 (viewed probably as the place where angels and demons battle; cf. 2:2 where Satan is called "the ruler of the kingdom of the *air*"). It may account for the emphasis on predestination, to encourage the tiny handful of Christians with the promise that God has safely secured their preservation for eternity despite the hostile forces all around them (1:4–12), along with the promise that the Spirit has sealed us and given us himself as a deposit guaranteeing the full array of blessings to come (vv. 13–14). The incomparably great power Paul wants his readers to fathom (v. 19) would fit a context of spiritual warfare nicely, as would his reminders that Christ has already placed all things under his feet in exercising his authority as head of his body, the church (vv. 20–23).

The thread continues with the triumphs we have experienced in both real and future time in 2:1–7. The gospel creates peace to counter the hostility of evil powers (2:14–18). Unity across ethnic lines demonstrates the effective outworking of God's previously secret plan of salvation even as the unseen world of "rulers and authorities in the heavenly realms" look on (3:10). Understanding the power believers have recurs again in the doxology in 3:20. Spiritual gifts come as a result of Christ's taking many captives (4:7, 11). We are no longer "darkened in [our] understanding" (v. 18); we "do not give the devil a foothold" (v. 27); indeed, we are no longer "darkness" itself (5:8) because we should "have nothing to do with the fruitless deeds of darkness, but rather expose them" (v. 11). Commands not to be drunk with wine but to be filled with the Spirit (v. 18) take on extra poignancy at the center of the cult of Bacchus/Dionysus, the god of wine. Submitting to one's husband and loving one's wife as sacrificially as Christ loved the church (vv. 22–27) contrast radically with the heavy-handed patriarchy of ancient paganism, punctuated periodically by grandiose claims of female superiority in Artemis/Diana worship, also centered in Ephesus. With all these foreshadowings, the expansive metaphor of the armor of God, with its detailed call to engage in spiritual warfare against "the world powers of this darkness" in 6:10–20, does not hit us like a bolt out of the blue but forms the climax of a motif that has been weaving its way throughout the letter and is particularly appropriate for the church in Ephesus.[87]

Questions of vocabulary, structure, and style again come to the fore as well. As already noted, Ephesians and Colossians are similar though not identical in style. But they are more like each other than either is like the undisputed letters of Paul.[88] Traditional reconstructions of the setting of these prison epistles date them to a time during Paul's house arrest in Rome in 60–62. If Philemon is undisputed, and Colossians is closely linked with Philemon by the names of Paul's friends and companions they share, then Ephesians and Colossians are noteworthy because Tychicus is mentioned as the letter carrier in both letters (and nowhere else). Indeed, the place where the two letters are most verbally parallel is precisely at this point, with Ephesians 6:21–22 and Colossians 4:7–8 containing thirty-two consecutive words that are identical in the standard Greek New Testaments. So it would seem at least as likely that Colossians and Ephesians were both sent out at the same time with the same traveling party as it is that Colossians and Philemon were.[89] If all three letters left Paul's hands in Rome via Tychicus at the same time, Ephesus would have been in a direct line for the travelers to stop en route to Colossae, and all the necessary deliveries could have been made. As with Colossians, it is arguable that the use of traditional materials accounts for a fair amount of the distinctive vocabulary. Plus, the use of three separate prayer sections in

---

[87] A somewhat analogous thread can be identified on the assumption that the imperial cult forms the key background for Ephesian Christian perception of powerlessness and oppression from powers and principalities. See Thielman, *Ephesians*, 20–23.

[88] For details, see C. Leslie Mitton, *Ephesians* (London: Marshall, Morgan & Scott, 1976; Grand Rapids: Eerdmans, 1981), 11; Lincoln, *Ephesians*, xlix.

[89] See esp. Johnson, *Writings of the New Testament*, 360–64.

the letter (1:3–14; 1:15–23; and 3:1, 14–21) also dictates some differences in style and wording.[90]

Why then is there no reference to Timothy in the opening lines of Ephesians as there is in Colossians? Several options appear plausible; none can be proven. Perhaps Timothy contributed to the style and/or contents of Colossians in a way he did not with Ephesians. Perhaps Timothy was present when Paul penned the one letter but not when he drafted the other, and he did not materially contribute to the style or contents of either letter. Differences could then be ascribed to other unmentioned scribes or amanuenses, given a certain amount of freedom to put Paul's thoughts in their own words and style.[91] Paul may not have relied on as many preformed traditions for Ephesians as he did for Colossians, even while still relying on some. Paul may have deliberately chosen a different style for a different genre of letter—an encyclical. Even despite the similarities between Ephesians and Colossians, the former can plausibly be identified as an encomium in epistolary form, praising God as patron or benefactor, in a way that doesn't work as readily with Colossians, which could also explain the distinctive diction.[92]

The similarities between Ephesians and Colossians, however, extend considerably further. A whole array of similar topics and forms, often in the same order, appears in both letters. A partial list of these includes redemption and forgiveness (Eph 1:7; Col 1:14), prayer for wisdom (Eph 1:17; Col 1:9), riches of a glorious inheritance (Eph 1:18; Col 1:12, 27), being made alive in Christ (Eph 2:5; Col 2:13), foreigners reconciled through Christ's death (Eph 2:11–22;

---

[90] Markus Barth, *Ephesians 1–3* (Garden City: Doubleday, 1974), 6–10.

[91] E.g., E. Randolph Richards, *The Secretary in the Letters of Paul* (Tübingen: J. C. B. Mohr, 1991), 190–92, 201, while admitting the hypothesis is only "probable."

[92] See esp. Holland Hendrix, "On the Form and Ethos of Ephesians," *Union Seminary Quarterly Review* 42 (1988): 3–15. Thurston (*Reading Colossians, Ephesians, and 2 Thessalonians*, 90) prefers the term "panegyric," i.e., a "festal address praising someone, in this case, God."

Col 1:20–22; 2:14–15), Paul's suffering for the addressees (Eph 3:1, 13; Col 1:24), his divine commission (Eph 3:2–9; Col 1:25), God's mystery made known to him (Eph 3:3–6; Col 1:26–27), the need for a worthy life of humility, patience, and forbearance (Eph 4:1–2; Col 1:10–11; 3:12–13), Christ as head of the body (Eph 4:15; 5:23; Col 1:18; 2:19), re-creation in God's moral image (Eph 4:24; Col 3:10), putting off the old nature and putting on the new defined in terms of immoral and moral living (Eph 4:25–5:2; Col 3:5–14), walking wisely (Eph 5:15; Col 4:5a), making the most of the time (Eph 5:16; Col 4:5b), giving thanks to God (Eph 5:20; Col 1:3, 12; 3:15–17; 4:2), a household code addressing the same six categories of the extended Greco-Roman family (Eph 5:22–6:9; Col 3:18–4:1), Paul as prisoner asking for prayers (Eph 6:19–20; Col 4:3–4, 10, 18), and the role of Tychicus (Eph 6:21–22; Col 4:7–9).[93]

Do these parallels really suggest two separate pseudonymous works by two different authors (with one possibly using the other) or at least one pseudonymous work imitating Colossians? Wouldn't it be more natural for the same writer, composing two letters at the same time under the same circumstances, to want to include a few similar topics when addressing two congregations in the same general geographical region? Wouldn't the differences that remain more likely reflect the different needs that would inevitably be attached to separate congregations, even despite their proximity? If the other features about Ephesians discussed here can be accounted for, the combination of similarities and differences between Colossians and Ephesians should actually support common, Pauline authorship rather than calling it into question.[94] Luke Johnson perceptively remarks, "It

---

[93] Cf. the charts in Powell, *Introducing the New Testament*, 330; and Brown, *Introduction to the New Testament*, 628.

[94] See esp. Barth, *Ephesians 1–3*, 41–43. Cf. also Harold W. Hoehner, *Ephesians: An Exegetical Commentary* (Grand Rapids: Baker, 2002), 32–35; and Guthrie, *New Testament Introduction*, 511–13.

is difficult to believe that a later writer who followed Colossians so assiduously would use the shared vocabulary in such different ways. The whole idea behind pseudepigraphy is to replicate the thought and style of the exemplar as closely as possible."[95] If one envisions the parallels in language being so close that the author of Ephesians had to have had Colossians in his possession and copied it in places, Paul could have copied his own work. After all, scribes regularly retained at least one copy of a letter that was sent to someone else in case it got lost and its contents needed to be reproduced.[96]

The same is true when one looks at the distinctive concepts found in Ephesians, coupled with the numerous parallels to the undisputed Paulines.[97] On the one hand, there seems to be much more realized eschatology with the blessings of salvation already available now in this present age (Eph 2:1–10), a focus on Jews and Gentiles molded into one new human person (2:11–22), the supersession of the law (2:14–15), a positive view of marriage (5:22–33). Yet these may actually be Paul's more timeless emphases, with the apparent contrasting themes in his other letters representing more occasional remarks. He has to stress future eschatology, for example, in 2 Thessalonians 2, because of that church's imbalanced views (v. 2). First Corinthians 7 seems negative toward marriage because Paul is trying to agree with a pro-celibacy faction in Corinth as much as he can (v. 1) while still

---

[95] Johnson, *Writings of the New Testament*, 361. More than fifty years ago, H. J. Cadbury ("The Dilemma of Ephesians," *New Testament Studies* 5 [1958–59]: 101) phrased it this way: "Which is more likely—that an imitator of Paul in the first century composed a writing ninety or ninety-five percent in accordance with Paul's style or that Paul himself wrote a letter diverging five or ten percent from his usual style?"

[96] Lynn H. Cohick, *Ephesians* (Eugene, OR: Cascade, 2010), 14–15.

[97] Best (*A Critical and Exegetical Commentary on Ephesians*, 20–25) acknowledges this much, even though he ultimately opts for pseudonymity. Cf. also Hoehner, *Ephesians*, 37.

having to disagree with them in key places.[98] Unity in a new humanity actually appears centrally in Galatians 3:28 but is not as emphasized because of the major threat of the Judaizers in Galatia. And "setting aside . . . the law with its commandments and regulations" (Eph 2:15) focuses on the deleterious emphasis on externals, without in any way contradicting Paul's emphasis that the law is fulfilled in Christ and in the love commandment (Gal 5:14; 6:2; Rom 13:9–10).[99]

Other minor differences have been noted but seem less significant.[100] Maybe the only other one meriting brief mention is Andrew Lincoln's claim that Ephesians' view of the Old Testament lacks the true Pauline letters' promise-fulfillment scheme.[101] But that conviction relies largely on the conclusion that the contrast of 3:5 is to be understood as absolute rather than relative, speaking of the mystery of Christ "which was not made known to people in other generations as it has now been revealed by the Spirit to God's holy apostles and prophets." But the "as" (Gk. *hōs*) more likely means "to the degree that" or "in the same way that" rather than implying that no one had God's plans revealed to them at all in Old Testament times.[102]

---

[98] See esp. Gordon D. Fee, *The First Epistle to the Corinthians*, rev. ed. (Grand Rapids: Eerdmans, 2014), 302–93.

[99] William W. Klein ("Ephesians," in *Expositor's Bible Commentary*, rev. ed., ed. Tremper Longman III and David E. Garland, vol. 12 [Grand Rapids: Zondervan, 2006], 83), cites Klyne R. Snodgrass (*Ephesians* [Grand Rapids: Zondervan, 1987], 133) approvingly: "What is abolished is the law as *a set of regulations that excludes Gentiles*" (emphasis his) and adds, "This is helpful; clearly, Paul did not mean that Christ abolished the law completely (cf. Ro 3:31) but only some of its implications, functions, and effects." If one allows Romans to help in interpreting Ephesians, this is a logical conclusion. If one is already committed to Ephesians' being at odds with Romans, then this recourse will be rejected.

[100] See further Barth, *Ephesians 1–3*, 31–36.

[101] Lincoln, *Ephesians*, xciii.

[102] Chrys C. Caragounis, *The Ephesian Mysterion* (Lund: Gleerup, 1977), 102–3 (*contra* many). Cf. Stephen E. Fowl, *Ephesians: A Commentary* (Louisville: Westminster John Knox, 2012), 26–27. As for the claim that Ephesians uses the OT differently and less than Colossians does, see the contrary perspective defended

Donald Hagner, arguing for pseudonymity, makes the intriguing observation that "all the designations of the great church of later centuries are here." He explains:

> The church is *one*: "There is one body . . . one faith, one baptism" (4:4–5); *holy*: "that he might present the church to himself in splendor, without spot or wrinkle or any such thing, that she might be holy and without blemish" (5:27); *catholic*: "the church, which is his body, the fullness of him who fills all in all" (1:22–23); and *apostolic:* "the household of God, built upon the foundation of the apostles and prophets, Christ Jesus himself being the cornerstone" (2:19–20 . . .).[103]

On the other hand, one could just as easily argue that "one, holy, catholic and apostolic church" was a *legitimate* later Christian formula based on authentic Pauline teaching.

Perhaps the upshot of such a survey is the reminder that we dare not just focus on Galatians and Romans to capture the heart of Paul's theology. A certain question-begging nature to the argument is never spelled out as follows but often amounts to the same thing: the heart of Paul's thought appears when he is countering an improper dependence by people on works of the Law. This appears particularly in Romans and Galatians. There are enough commonalities with this central thrust in five other epistles to ascribe them to Paul as well. Other letters deviate sufficiently from this center and therefore cannot be accepted. But what if one constructed the argument differently? One could reason in this way: thirteen letters were unanimously ascribed to Paul in the ancient church. Given that doubts about the authorship of Hebrews, 2 Peter, John, and Revelation *were* raised, we

---

in Thorsten Moritz, *A Profound Mystery: The Use of the Old Testament in Ephesians* (Leiden: Brill, 1997).

[103] Hagner, *New Testament*, 592.

know Christians didn't just blindly ascribe all of their favorite books to a single undisputed apostolic authority. If we derive the synthesis of Pauline theology from all of these thirteen letters, justification by faith rather than works of Torah will emerge as an important topic but not necessarily become *the* central, unifying theme of all Paul's epistles. Perhaps the reconciliation of Jew and Gentile as one new humanity, and as the true Israel, may emerge as even more central.[104] Or maybe a promise-fulfillment scheme is more all-encompassing.[105] None of the letters so far discussed deviates from either of these possible centers to such an extent that it must be rejected as inauthentic.

But what of the domestic codes that enjoin submission of wives to husbands and slaves to masters (Eph 5:22–33, 6:5–9)? Aren't these the sign of the repatriarchalization of the church that began in the late first or early second century?[106] If so, it disproves the authenticity of Colossians as well (see the parallel commands in 3:18–19 and 3:22–4:1). Of course, some scholars are prepared to grant that, even though more accept the authenticity of Colossians than accept Ephesians. But the author of Colossians has just also penned 3:11—"Here there is no Gentile or Jew, circumcised or uncircumcised, barbarian, Scythian, slave or free, but Christ is all, and is in all."[107] And this text, in turn, strikingly resembles one in the undisputed letter of Galatians, central

---

[104] This is in essence the most important consideration that leads Barth (*Ephesians 1–3*, 44–48) to accept the authenticity of Ephesians. This is also close to the heart of the center of Pauline thought articulated throughout N. T. Wright, *Paul and the Faithfulness of God*, 2 vols. (London: SPCK; Minneapolis: Fortress, 2013).

[105] Craig L. Blomberg, *The Fulfillment of God's Promises: A New Testament Theology* (Waco: Baylor University Press, forthcoming).

[106] See, classically, Elisabeth Schüssler Fiorenza, *In Memory of Her: A Feminist Theological Reconstruction of Christian Origins* (New York: Crossroad, 1983), 251–59, 266–70.

[107] Cf. Bruce, *Epistles to the Colossians, to Philemon and to the Ephesians*, 148–51; Moo, *Letter to the Colossians and to Philemon*, 271–72.

to that "charter" of Christian liberty: "There is neither Jew nor Gentile, neither slave nor free, nor is there male and female, for you are all one in Christ Jesus" (Gal 3:28). If Galatians 3:28 is the classic proof of Paul's egalitarianism, by those who argue for it, then Colossians 3:11 must be a close second. If one argues that Colossians has deliberately omitted "male and female" because its author didn't believe in gender egalitarianism, then that same logic would require Paul in Galatians not to have believed barbarian and Scythian were equal since he does not use that pair there. But if the author of Colossians 3:11 could also write 3:22–4:1 (the Colossian household code), then either he did not understand claims like Galatians 3:28 as so sweeping as we moderns often have, or his instructions to wives and slaves were situation specific in some respect.[108] Either way, it follows that the Paul of Galatians could have written the household code of Colossians and therefore the parallel code of Ephesians also.

Less significant issues surrounding the authorship of Ephesians include slight differences in phraseology with either Colossians or the undisputed Paulines. It is hard to place much weight on the difference between a mystery revealed by God to be Christ himself (Col 1:27) or to be the unity of Jew and Gentile in Christ (Eph 3:4–6); the one flows naturally from the other. In a context that viewed Jesus as divine, the difference between Christ as the agent of reconciliation (Eph 2:16) and God playing that role (Col 1:20) seems even more insignificant. Is the foundation of the church Jesus (1 Cor 3:10) or the apostles and prophets (Eph 2:20)? It depends on whether one is using the metaphor in an absolute sense or just comparing human roles. After all, this verse in Ephesians also calls Christ the cornerstone! Is Ephesians even

---

[108] The so-called complementarian and egalitarian perspectives, respectively. With respect to Gal 3:28, for the former, see especially Richard W. Hove, *Equality in Christ? Galatians 3:28 and the Gender Dispute* (Wheaton: Crossway, 1999); for the latter, cf. Pauline N. Hogan, *"No Longer Male and Female": Interpreting Galatians 3.28 in Early Christianity* (London and New York: T & T Clark, 2008).

more "flowery" than Colossians? The long, convoluted sentences, pil-
ing up of adjectives, and chains of nouns in the genitive actually make
the two letters more like each other than unlike each other.

More so than with 2 Thessalonians or Colossians, scholars have at
times proposed that Ephesians could contain an authentically Pauline
core, thoroughly edited and supplemented by a later redactor.[109] So
many parallels to the undisputed Paulines appear in individual verses
or clauses in Ephesians,[110] even as they are at times combined together
in much longer and more cumbersome sentences. Ephesians 1:9
recalls Romans 16:25 on God's mystery, 1:10 matches Galatians 4:4
on the fullness of time, 1:11 parallels Romans 8:28–29 on predestination for those called according to God's purpose, and 1:14 resembles
2 Corinthians 1:22 on our inheritance. Ephesians 2:5 echoes Romans
6:13 on being dead to sin, verse 8 fits Galatians 2:16 on being saved
through faith and Romans 3:28 on the contrast with works of the
Law, not boasting ties verse 9 together with 1 Corinthians 1:29, and
the covenants of promise in verse 12 remind us of Romans 9:4. One
could proceed through the book of Ephesians finding close conceptual
parallels and verbal echoes of other passages in the undisputed Pauline
epistles with at least the same frequency.

Ephesians 3:1–13, moreover, contains so many personal disclo-
sures by the author that if it were not Paul it would be harder than
elsewhere to exonerate the author from the charge of trying to deceive
his readers concerning his identity. Here he speaks of himself as a
prisoner of Jesus for the sake of the Gentiles (v. 1), of the administration of God's grace that had been given to him (v. 2), of the mystery
made known to him by revelation (v. 3), of his role as a servant of

---

[109] See esp. John Muddiman, *The Epistle to the Ephesians* (London and New
York: Continuum, 2001; Peabody: Hendrickson, 2004).

[110] Bruce, *Epistles to the Colossians, to Philemon, and to the Ephesians*, 29–40 and
throughout.

God's grace by his power (v. 7), of how he is less than the least of God's people (v. 8), and of his suffering for the Ephesians' sake (v. 13). The best solution, therefore, may be to combine the encyclical hypothesis with the theory of a distinctive amanuensis given the freedom, possibly in imitation of Colossians, to put in his own words Paul's desired contents.[111]

The Pastoral Epistles

Discussions of pseudonymity become even more complex when one turns to 1 and 2 Timothy and Titus. Now we have three letters to look at both together and individually. On the one hand, one discovers yet a third noticeably distinct style of writing. Of 848 words in these letters that are not names, 306 occur in none of the other letters attributed to Paul; 175 do not otherwise occur in the New Testament. Of the 542 words found elsewhere in Paul, only 50 are distinctive (i.e., not found elsewhere in the New Testament). Of the 175 words unique to the Pastorals within the New Testament, 131 appear in the earliest known second-century Christian writings. Similar comments could be made about grammatical features.[112] If the undisputed Paulines

---

[111] See esp. A. van Roon, *The Authenticity of Ephesians* (Leiden and New York: Brill, 1974); Peter T. O'Brien, *The Letter to the Ephesians* (Leicester: Apollos; Grand Rapids: Eerdmans, 1999), 4–47.

[112] The classic study was P. N. Harrison, *The Problem of the Pastoral Epistles* (Oxford: Oxford University Press, 1921). For these numbers, see pp. 20, 24, and 70. Numerous statistical analyses have attempted to support or disprove Harrison's claims, but none has commanded widespread approval. Perhaps the most extensive, conclusive, and little known is James A. Libby's unpublished Denver Seminary master's thesis, "A Proposed Methodology and Preliminary Data on Statistically Elucidating the Authorship of the Pastoral Epistles," 2 vols. (1987). Cf. also Armin D. Baum, "Semantic Variation Within the Corpus Paulinum: Linguistic Considerations Concerning the Richer Vocabulary of the Pastoral Epistles," *Tyndale Bulletin* 59 (2008): 271–92. These are the most statistically sophisticated refutations of the validity of Harrison's argument, but, of course, they only refute a thesis. They do not prove Pauline authorship. For a detailed list of all 306 distinctive words in the Pastorals categorized as to possible reasons they occur on

and 2 Thessalonians thus offer us one style, Ephesians and Colossians provide a second, and now the Pastoral Epistles present the third. First Timothy and Titus also closely resemble each other in content at several points (especially with criteria for church leaders and instruction for different ages and genders of people in the church), while 1 and 2 Timothy are unified by both claiming to be addressed to Paul's younger adult companion and spiritual son.

In terms of the Pastorals' theology, it is also frequently suggested that they represent a developed form of ecclesiology not otherwise known until the late first or early second century.[113] First Timothy 3:1–7 and Titus 1:6–9 both give us detailed commands for choosing elders or overseers, while 1 Timothy 3:8–13 adds information on a second leadership office—that of deacon. First Timothy 5:3–10 assumes an order of elderly widows who are to be supported by the church and prescribes criteria for being enrolled in the list of these specific widows. Christianity has become a deposit of doctrine, regularly referred to as "the faith" (1 Tim 1:2; 3:9; 5:8; 6:12; Titus 1:13; 3:15; etc.), and five times these letters contain specific sayings that apparently stem from older Christian tradition the author labels as faithful or trustworthy (1 Tim 1:15; 3:1; 4:9; 2 Tim 2:11; Titus 3:8).[114] Culturally

---

the assumption of Pauline authorship, see William D. Mounce, *Pastoral Epistles* (Nashville: Nelson, 2000), civ–cxiii. His categories include those dictated by the historical situation, those generated by the beliefs or behaviors of the opponents, positive antidotes to the same, words about church leadership, words in vice lists, words from traditional material, Latinisms, words topically grouped with Pauline words, and words cognate to Pauline words. Suddenly the list has shrunk to only 74 distinctive, noncategorized words.

[113] A. T. Hanson, *The Pastoral Epistles* (London: Marshall, Morgan & Scott; Grand Rapids: Eerdmans, 1982), 31–38.

[114] On which, see esp. George W. Knight, *The Faithful Sayings in the Pastoral Letters* (Grand Rapids: Baker, 1979). Knight, however, does not find them as signs of lateness or pseudonymity. Cf. also R. Alastair Campbell, "Identifying the Faithful Sayings in the Pastoral Epistles," *Journal for the Study of the New Testament* 54 (1994): 73–86.

these three epistles are supposed to represent a bourgeois Christianity, little different from the cultivated virtues of the noble Greco-Roman man or woman.[115] Second Timothy 2:2, lastly, has been seen as teaching the doctrine of apostolic succession, otherwise not found until the end of the first century.[116]

A final topic for consideration involves chronology. Unlike the previous epistles we have considered, there is no natural place during Paul's missionary journeys, as described in Acts, in which to place the Pastorals. They must have been written after Paul had spent his three-year time in Ephesus (Acts 20:31), so that he could assign Timothy the responsibility to be his apostolic delegate in and around that community (1 Tim 1:3). Paul is not in prison when he purportedly writes 1 Timothy (3:14–15; 4:13). But after his extended time in Ephesus, Paul travels through Macedonia, Achaia, and then back to Israel. There he is arrested, and the book of Acts ends with him not yet released from his series of imprisonments. Titus has to have been written after a church has been planted on Crete (Titus 1:5), and there is no indication in Acts of a church being planted there. In fact when the ship bound for Rome makes a stop there (Acts 27:8), not a word is said about Paul's greeting local Christians, as he does so consistently elsewhere during his travels, including later in this journey (28:13–14) whenever his ship makes port and there is a believing community nearby. Titus also discloses Paul's writing as a free man. In 2 Timothy, however, Paul is again in prison, presumably some time later than when he wrote the first letter to Timothy. Now, however, things sound much bleaker than they did during his four earlier epistles from prison, as he senses the end is near. Gone is the hope found even in Philippians for eventual

[115] See, e.g., Hanson, *Pastoral Epistles*, 3–5, 13, 31–42.

[116] Burkett, *Introduction to the New Testament and the Origins of Christianity*, 439. Robert W. Wall with Richard B. Steele (*1 & 2 Timothy and Titus* [Grand Rapids: Eerdmans, 2012], 9–11) prefers to see all three letters as succession letters.

release (Phil 1:25–26), and he urges Timothy to come soon to him, because he may not have much longer to live (2 Tim 4:9, 21). He has fought the good fight and finished the race and is ready to move on to his heavenly reward (4:7–8).

Traditionally, then, Christians who accept Paul as the author of these three letters assign them to a time after the events covered in Acts, that is, after AD 62.[117] On the assumption that Paul was released from house arrest because he was acquitted by Nero, he could have traveled on to Spain and/or returned to the eastern part of the empire and penned 1 Timothy and Titus. He would then have been rearrested later, after the start of Nero's official pogrom against believers in 64, and executed perhaps shortly after writing 2 Timothy. Nero took his own life in AD 68, putting an end to the persecution, but we have no way of determining how long before this date Paul was executed. So there are at least five, maybe six years potentially unaccounted for in Paul's life, after what is narrated in Acts—more than enough time for all these extra events to have unfolded.[118] DeSilva further observes that even though they don't fit into the time frame of Acts, each of the Pastorals "does presuppose a strikingly detailed historical framework," uncharacteristic of most pseudonymous works.[119] J. N. D. Kelly asks why a later Christian wanting to gain authority and credibility for his writings would not select more readily recognizable settings in Paul's life to make his pseudepigraphy more plausible.[120]

---

[117] For a plausible, twelve-step chronology of events, see Aida Besançon Spencer, *1 Timothy* (Eugene, OR: Cascade, 2013), 11–12.

[118] Boring (*Introduction to the New Testament*, 373) notes this solution but, because of other factors he believes promote pseudonymity, does not even give any arguments against it.

[119] DeSilva, *Introduction to the New Testament*, 739.

[120] J. N. D. Kelly, *A Commentary on the Pastoral Epistles: I Timothy, II Timothy, Titus* (New York: Harper & Row, 1960; London: A & C Black; 1963; Peabody: Hendrickson, 1993), 9.

A minority of scholars opting for Pauline authorship have suggested an alternate scenario, by which these letters *can* fit into the period depicted in Acts.[121] A period of several months could easily have intervened between Acts 19:20 and 21, between the end of Paul's time in Ephesus (foreshadowed here, since he is still in that city during the riot of vv. 23–41). Either before or after that incident, Paul could have traveled back westward, leaving Timothy in charge in Ephesus. After all, if Paul did actually evangelize representative portions of the territory all the way around from Jerusalem to Illyricum (Rom 15:19), this would be the most natural time for him to have gone to the territory of Illyricum, just north of ancient Macedonia along the Adriatic Sea. And the argument from the silence of Acts 27 with respect to Crete is precisely that— an argument from silence. It is unlikely that Acts would not mention a church there if *Paul* had founded it, but if it had been planted by Titus, Paul might have known no one there to go visit. Furthermore, Crete is a large island, not a single town, so the location of the Christian community or communities there need not have been anywhere close to Fair Havens, where Paul's ship docked (27:8). If 1 Timothy and Titus can be dated to a period of time *within* the framework of Acts, 2 Timothy could then have been written as early as the time of the house arrest with which the book ends.[122] Of course, it could still come from a later, second imprisonment, but those who deemed the evidence inadequate to postulate Paul's release after his Acts 28 imprisonment, could still place 2 Timothy as Paul's last letter, written from that same imprisonment after things took a turn for the worse.[123]

---

[121] See esp. Peter Walker, "Revisiting the Pastoral Epistles," *European Journal of Theology* 21 (2012): 4–16. Cf. also Towner, *Letters to Timothy and Titus*, 12–15; John A. T. Robinson, *Redating the New Testament* (Philadelphia: Westminster, 1976; Eugene, OR: Wipf & Stock, 2000; London: SCM, 2012), 81–84.

[122] See esp. Walker, "Revisiting the Pastoral Epistles," 4–16, 120–32.

[123] But this would probably have required transfer to a much more brutal Roman prison, with all the pain and shame attached to it, for which there is no

The linguistic issues become even more interesting when one makes a close comparison between the style and vocabulary of the Pastorals and their counterparts in Luke-Acts. Stephen Wilson a generation ago and Ben Witherington more recently have both defended in detail the Lukan authorship of the Pastorals.[124] Given that Acts discloses Luke's accompanying Paul more consistently toward the end of the missionary journeys Luke narrates, it is natural to envision him still with Paul during any years he may have lived after his Acts 28 imprisonment. On either of the above scenarios for dating the Pastorals, then, Paul could easily have delegated Luke to write Paul's instructions to Timothy and Titus in his own style, checking them afterward to ensure they corresponded to his intentions. When one reads in 2 Timothy 4:11 that only Luke is with Paul, this hypothesis becomes even more attractive.

A second, possibly complementary approach to the question of style in the Pastorals, as in Colossians, has to do with preformed traditions. Mark Yarbrough has used a sophisticated and detailed set of criteria for identifying these, at least in 1 Timothy, concluding that the clearest examples appear in 1:8–10, 15a–b, 17; 2:5–6a; 3:1, 16; 4:8, 9–10; 5:24–25; 6:7, 10a, and 11–16. A disproportionate percentage of the distinctive vocabulary of this letter occurs in these poetic, tightly packed, creedal statements of key teachings of

---

actual evidence. See Gregory S. MaGee, "Paul's Response to the Shame and Pain of Imprisonment in 2 Timothy," *Bibliotheca Sacra* 165 (2008): 338–53.

[124] Stephen G. Wilson, *Luke and the Pastoral Epistles* (London: SPCK, 1979)— after Paul's death; Ben Witherington III, *Letters and Homilies for Hellenized Christians, vol. 1: A Socio-Rhetorical Commentary on Titus, 1–2 Timothy, and 1–3 John* (Downers Grove: IVP, 2006), 57–62 *et passim*—during Paul's life with his endorsement. Jerome D. Quinn and William C. Wacker (*The First and Second Letters to Timothy* [Grand Rapids: Eerdmans, 2000], 19–20) allow for both options but prefer the later date; while Jerome D. Quinn (*The Letter to Titus* [New York and London: Doubleday, 1990], 18–19) opts more unambiguously for the later date. Apparently Wacker was the voice of caution in the coauthored volume.

orthodoxy or orthopraxy, which could easily have led to the author's repeated use of the same terminology elsewhere.[125] For example, the word "godliness" (*eusebeia*) is frequently cited as a classic example of the unique style and theology of the Pastorals. The word appears ten times in the Pastorals, eight of them in 1 Timothy, nowhere else in Paul, and elsewhere in the New Testament only in Acts (once) and 2 Peter (four times). But three of the eight uses in 1 Timothy are in preformed tradition (3:16; 4:8; 6:11), and the other five in closely adjacent verses to these traditions (2:2; 4:7; 6:3, 5, 6). So it could well have been the case that this term's presence in preexisting creedal material influenced Paul's use of it in the context surrounding those creeds.

Luke Johnson, followed by Philip Towner, has suggested another key reason the style and vocabulary in the Pastoral Epistles may have varied from the rest of the Pauline corpus. The epistolary subgenre of 1 Timothy and Titus appears to be that of a mandate letter, a series of instructions from a superior to a subordinate, about the way he should exercise his public responsibilities. Typically, these were sent by provincial governors to local city leaders or by other political officials to those under them.[126] Johnson and Towner think it is better to understand Timothy and Titus not merely as Paul's sometime traveling companions, coworkers, and now local pastors. Rather they refer to them as "apostolic delegates," those commissioned by the apostle Paul to oversee the churches in more than one single location (in and around Ephesus, or throughout Crete), who in turn would have

---

[125] Mark M. Yarbrough, *Paul's Utilization of Preformed Traditions in 1 Timothy: An Evaluation of the Apostle's Literary, Rhetorical, and Theological Tactics* (London and New York: T & T Clark, 2009).

[126] Luke T. Johnson, *The First and Second Letters to Timothy* (New York and London: Doubleday, 2001), 46–47; Towner, *Letters to Timothy and Titus*, 33–36 (cautiously).

supervised the work of the pastors or elders of individual house churches.[127] Combine this difference of genre with the fact that we don't know if these letters were meant to be read aloud to the local congregations exactly as Paul had written them or they were just for Timothy and Titus, who would then implement the instructions and communicate the relevant parts of the letters to their congregation. At least some of the differences in form may well be accounted for by this distinct subgenre of epistle.

Second Timothy then becomes what Johnson and Towner call a personal parenetic letter, a letter of more intimate instruction, exhortation, and encouragement to Timothy.[128] It need not have been read out, at least at first, to any congregation, even though it informed Timothy's ongoing ministry in Ephesus. (Eventually, of course it would have been read aloud to instruct entire congregations.) There are so many personal details in 2 Timothy that even some scholars who find 1 Timothy and Titus pseudonymous are willing to countenance the possibility that 2 Timothy is authentic.[129] A few have tried to explain all three Pastoral Epistles that way, as well, although this hypothesis is probably the least commonly held of the various approaches to these letters.[130] Arguments about internal contradic-

---

[127] Luke T. Johnson, *Letters to Paul's Delegates: 1 Timothy, 2 Timothy, Titus* (Valley Forge: Trinity Press International, 1996), 29–31; Towner, *Letters to Timothy and Titus*, 10, 107–8 n. 19, 271.

[128] Johnson, *Letters to Paul's Delegates*, 39–41. Features of the testamentary genre also account for some of 2 Timothy's distinctives. See, e.g., Schnelle, *New Testament Writings*, 339. But these do not require the work to be pseudonymous unless all other biblical testaments are similarly labeled (*contra* Raymond F. Collins, *I & II Timothy and Titus: A Commentary* [Louisville and London: Westminster John Knox, 2002], 7), a patently circular argument.

[129] See esp. Michael Prior, *Paul the Letter Writer and the Second Letter to Timothy* (Sheffield: Sheffield Academic Press, 1989).

[130] See esp. James D. Miller, *The Pastoral Letters as Composite Documents* (Cambridge: Cambridge University Press, 1997).

tions within the Pastorals seem to be grasping at straws to come up with reasons for rejecting them.[131]

All this leaves only one really significant impediment to the Pauline origin of the Pastorals—the apparently later theology.[132] Do these three little documents reflect the growing institutionalization of Christianity, which we know took the form of a "monarchical episcopacy" at least by the early second century? In other words, were the overseers or bishops over larger groups of Christians or churches than just one local congregation? No, not from anything they explicitly disclose. The instructions for overseers and deacons do not in any way suggest that they have oversight over more than one fellowship. Does the lack of any reference to spiritual gifts and the active participation of all members in worship or the public life of the congregation as found in 1 Corinthians 12–14 and Romans 12:3–8 mean that we are into second- or third-generation Christianity when the charismata had allegedly ceased? No, not unless the lack of reference to these gifts in Galatians, 2 Corinthians, 1 Thessalonians, Philippians, and Philemon also places *them* decades later than the dates to which the

---

[131] E.g., Boring (*Introduction to the New Testament*, 373–74) pits 2 Tim 1:15; 4:10–11; and 4:16 against 4:21 (in which Paul sends greetings from various fellow Christians after stressing how he was abandoned by believers from Asia, has only Luke with him, and no one came to his first defense). But we have no idea when and where the Christians in v. 21 were when they asked Paul to communicate greetings; 1:15 and 4:16 have explicit limitations on whom Paul is referencing; and Luke is probably the only person among Paul's *closest* companions left near him. Boring cannot reconcile Paul's sense of impending death with his call to Timothy to come soon, before winter. But in the ancient world a couple of months would be soon; these statements reinforce rather than contradict one another. Finally, Boring thinks Titus 3:12 and 1:5 contradict each other. But he inserts words not in Titus when he says that the former verse asks Titus to come "as quickly as possible."

[132] After presenting arguments and counterarguments on all of the other points, Holladay (*Critical Introduction to the New Testament*, 424) concludes, "More than anything else, what pulls the Pastorals toward the end of the first century are the similarities and outlook with texts such as the *Didache*, *1 Clement*, and even Ignatius and Polycarp."

same critics typically assign them. Philippians 1:1, moreover, as an undisputed letter, still refers explicitly to both overseers and deacons, just as 1 Timothy 3 does. Does the presence of an order of widows in 1 Timothy 5 mean the Ephesian church more resembles emerging Catholic monastic orders of later eras than the vibrant, fluid, and formless church of the first generation of the Jesus movement? No—we have no evidence of such an order outside of this one local congregation, and as early as Acts 6:1–7 in the first year or two of the church's history, believers are portrayed as showing deep concern for needy widows.

Why would one assume in the first place that the original congregations were without form and void? The model of 1 Corinthians 14:26–33 of everyone's using their gifts on one occasion appears only in that single epistle—why not label *it* pseudonymous? Elders existed already in pre-Christian Judaism and in Greco-Roman civic organizations. Synagogues had structure, offices, an order of service, and various fixed policies and procedures, all of which directly influenced Christianity from the beginning. First Thessalonians 5:12–13, one of Paul's earliest letters, presupposes some kind of leadership structure. The reconstruction of early Christianity as comparatively formless stems from German Lutheran scholars in the nineteenth and twentieth centuries still fighting the medieval battles with Catholicism's elaborate hierarchy, but the extremes of both fully innovative and fully institutionalized churches are anachronistic when imposed on the first century. There is evidence of both structure and spontaneity in various combinations throughout all segments of the New Testament church.[133] The charismata did not cease at the end of the first century; one can

---

[133] On just the thirteen letters ascribed to Paul, see esp. the outstanding quartet of articles by Ronald Y. K. Fung, "Charismatic Versus Organized Ministry? An Examination of an Alleged Antithesis," *Evangelical Quarterly* 52 (1980): 195–214; Ronald Y. K. Fung, "Some Pauline Pictures of the Church," *Evangelical Quarterly* 53 (1981): 89–107; Ronald Y. K. Fung, "The Nature of the Ministry According to

find testimony in abundance to prophecy and miracles well into the third century before they begin to diminish noticeably.[134] Second Timothy 2:2, finally, scarcely teaches apostolic succession, merely the need for local churches to keep teaching the great truths of the faith to new generations of faithful teachers who can in turn keep "passing it on."[135]

What about bourgeois Christianity? Must the Pastorals be read as promoting the settled, humdrum life of ordinary Christian living, little different from virtuous Greek and Roman lifestyles, in the second or third generation of the church's history? Nothing of a more developed ecclesiology is in the Pastorals than can be discerned in 1 Corinthians. Contextualizing Christian thought in Hellenistic language where overlaps exist appears already in Acts 17:22–31, at least as depicted by Luke.[136] The letter to Titus in particular can be seen as the creative and effective contextualization of Paul's message in light of numerous specific and distinctive facets of Cretan culture.[137] But the basis for the Pastorals' ethics is thoroughly Christian.[138] In light of 1 Timothy 4:1; 6:13–14; Titus 2:13; 2 Timothy 3:1; and 4:1, it is hardly accurate to say that the hope for a near return of Christ has receded into the

---

Paul," *Evangelical Quarterly* 54 (1982): 129–46; and Ronald Y. K. Fung, "Ministry, Community, and Spiritual Gifts," *Evangelical Quarterly* 55 (1983): 3–20.

[134] Cecil M. Robeck Jr., *Prophecy in Carthage: Perpetua, Tertullian, and Cyprian* (Cleveland: Pilgrim, 1992).

[135] To borrow the label from a tiny but excellent commentary by Robert H. Mounce, *Pass It On: 1 and 2 Timothy* (Ventura, CA: Regal, 1979; Eugene, OR: Wipf & Stock, 2005).

[136] See further John J. Wainwright, "*Eusebeia*: Syncretism or Conservative Contextualization," *Evangelical Quarterly* 65 (1993): 211–24.

[137] George M. Wieland, "Roman Crete and the Letter to Titus," *New Testament Studies* 55 (2009): 338–54.

[138] See esp. Philip H. Towner, *The Goal of Our Instruction: The Structure of Theology and Ethics in the Pastoral Epistles* (Sheffield: JSOT, 1989). Cf. Philip H. Towner, "Pauline Theology or Pauline Tradition in the Pastoral Epistles: The Question of Method," *Tyndale Bulletin* 46 (1995): 287–314.

background in these epistles.[139] "Bourgeois Christianity" appears to be a label invented by people who wanted Paul to be as hard-hitting as he was in Galatians or as majestic and definitive as in Romans in all his letters, possibly also due to their latent anti-Semitism. They have also wanted to blunt the authority of the Pastorals, especially in its teaching on submission, and so have looked for every way possible to declare it not Pauline and thereby diminish its authority.[140]

Why are so many basic themes of the undisputed Paulines absent in the Pastorals? Why are there no expositions of the great truths of sin and justification, sanctification and glorification like in Romans? Why is there no focus on wisdom as so centrally in 1 Corinthians? Other omissions could be added. Gordon Fee answers these questions cogently, stunned how rarely the point is made in scholarly circles. These three letters were first of all written to advise Timothy and Titus how to deal with real, pastoral problems in the church. They were not written to a church Paul had not visited, which he wanted to hear the gospel in all its fullness to make sure they got it right, like Romans. They were not written to be read or heard directly by those caught up in heterodoxy or heteropraxy, as at Corinth. They were Paul's guidance to his delegates as to how to deal with unique, specific problems in their churches.[141]

As in Ephesians and Colossians, one can find high Christology in passages like Titus 2:13 and 1 Timothy 2:5 and 3:16. But Romans 9:5 equates Christ with God, and 1 Corinthians 8:6 ascribes to Jesus the same activities as it does to God, without any sense of tension of speaking of one divine being. As we have already seen, the Philippian hymn (Phil 2:6–11) contains as high and elaborate Christology as any

---

[139] See esp. Philip H. Towner, "The Present Age in the Eschatology of the Pastoral Epistles," *New Testament Studies* 32 (1986): 427–48.

[140] Cf. Johnson, *First and Second Letters to Timothy*, 42–48.

[141] Gordon D. Fee, *1 and 2 Timothy, Titus*, 2nd ed. (Peabody: Hendrickson, 1988; Carlisle: Paternoster, 1995; Grand Rapids: Baker, 2011), 16.

passage in the New Testament.[142] So one has to be selective about which passages one cites if one tries to defend a trajectory that moves from a simpler primitive Christology in the undisputed Paulines to a more developed and exalted Christology in the deutero-Paulines. As Larry Hurtado has demonstrated, the development of New Testament Christology was revolutionary rather than evolutionary, with exalted titles and ascriptions of worth given to Jesus from the earliest days onward.[143]

If there is a benign form of pseudonymity behind the Pastorals, Johnson, who rejects the hypothesis, nevertheless sketches out the most probable scenario. A follower of Paul adapts Paul's message for a new generation to stress structure and order in the church, without supporting either asceticism or egalitarianism, but recognizing the delay of the Parousia and the need to determine how best to live in the world as the church awaits the day of the Lord.[144] In only partial agreement with this scenario, I. Howard Marshall coins the terms *allonymity* and *allepigraphy* to refer to authorship by an author similar in nature to Paul, not in keeping with the later deceptive practices of "Christian" pseudonymity.[145] He recognizes that nothing in the ecclesiastical situation behind these letters cannot plausibly be dated to the years immediately after Paul's death.[146] He envisages one or

---

[142] On which, see esp. Ralph P. Martin and Brian J. Dodd, *Where Christology Began: Essays on Philippians 2* (Louisville: Westminster John Knox, 1998).

[143] Even just in Paul, a trajectory of linear growth in ever more exalted Christology cannot do justice to the data. See esp. Chris Tilling, *Paul's Divine Christology* (Tübingen: Mohr Siebeck, 2012; Grand Rapids: Eerdmans, 2015); Gordon D. Fee, *Pauline Christology: An Exegetical-Theological Study* (Peabody: Hendrickson, 2007; Grand Rapids: Baker, 2013).

[144] Johnson, *Writings of the New Testament*, 381.

[145] I. Howard Marshall with Philip H. Towner, *A Critical and Exegetical Commentary on the Pastoral Epistles* (Edinburgh: T & T Clark, 1999), 84.

[146] Ibid., 52–57. Cf. I. Howard Marshall with Philip H. Towner, "The Christology of the Pastoral Epistles," *Studien zum Neuen Testament und seiner Umwelt* 13 (1988): 157–77; I. Howard Marshall with Philip H. Towner, "'Sometimes

more people within the Pauline circle of disciples using authentic, unfinished memoirs to create 2 Timothy as we now know it. Then, on the basis of that letter, and perhaps also using authentic Pauline fragments, probably on a smaller scale and no longer extractable from the larger texts, 1 Timothy and Titus were composed. The stylistic differences, combined with a gradual but discernible development of Paul's thought, tip the scales for Marshall in this direction.[147] It is not clear why a theory like that of Luke's being given enough freedom to write up Paul's thoughts in his own words, at the end of Paul's life, would not also account for these phenomena, but it should be clear that Marshall's hypothesis scarcely warrants being grouped together in the same category as Ehrman's confident pronouncements about early Christian forgeries! Myriam Klinker-De Klerck has independently covered much the same ground, for and against the authenticity of the Pastorals, and finds no conclusive reason for rejecting their authenticity.[148] And if works like hers fail to convince, James Aageson's book-length treatment of *Paul, the Pastoral Epistles, and the Early Church* demonstrates the possibility of the thoughts being understood as "what would Paul say?" from a disciple of Paul in the generation after his death.[149]

Conclusion

Gentile Christian attitudes to pseudepigraphy by the mid- to late-second century increasingly crystallized around the end of the spectrum

---

Only Orthodox'—Is There More to the Pastoral Epistles?" *Epworth Review* 20.3 (1993): 12–24.

[147] Marshall with Towner, *A Critical and Exegetical Commentary on the Pastoral Epistles*, 59–63.

[148] Myriam Klinker-de Klerck, "The Pastoral Epistles: Authentic Pauline Writings," *European Journal of Theology* 17 (2008): 101–8.

[149] James W. Aageson, *Paul, the Pastoral Epistles, and the Early Church* (Peabody: Hendrickson, 2008).

of opinion that treated them as deceptive. Pre-Christian Judaism apparently accepted a broad cross-section of pseudepigraphal genres as a legitimate literary device, although we do not know if they believed any of the Hebrew canon of Scripture was pseudepigraphal. When did these attitudes change? What were Jewish and Gentile Christian reactions to pseudonymity in the mid-first century? The only honest answer is that we simply don't know.

Are there ways, therefore, to envisage pseudonymity as an acceptable practice for the early Christian community? Marshall has surely demonstrated that the answer to that question is yes, even if one chooses to use a different term for the practice. Is this then the best way to account for any or all of the disputed Pauline letters? Not necessarily. We have surveyed the arguments most commonly brought against straightforward Pauline authorship of 2 Thessalonians, Colossians, Ephesians, and the Pastoral Epistles. In the case of 2 Thessalonians, they seem exceedingly weak. The stylistic, and to some degree the theological, issues in Colossians could point to a significant role for Timothy in helping Paul, exactly as the opening verse of the letter could readily be interpreted. Preformed traditions and the needs of addressing the Colossian heresy most likely account for many of the remaining distinctives of this epistle. But the connections with the undisputed letter to Philemon make it difficult to distance Colossians from Paul himself. Ephesians is similar enough to Colossians to suggest that they were written at the same time in the same setting and sent out together by Tychicus. Since Timothy is not mentioned as a cosender with Paul in Ephesians, we may envisage Paul partly following their joint efforts, combined with the exigencies of composing an encyclical. Plus, the sustained motif of Christ's and the believers' conquest of the demonic realm fits what we know of circumstances in Ephesus hand to glove.

In writing the Pastoral Epistles, Paul may well have used Luke as his amanuensis with the freedom for his beloved physician to write

Paul's thoughts in his own style. The formalities and style of mandate letters explain several of the distinctive features of 1 Timothy and Titus, while 2 Timothy as a personal parenetic letter may be the one truly nonpublic epistle in the Pauline canon. The number of personal details in 2 Timothy make it the hardest to view as the composition of somebody a generation later to a broader audience. But the similarities among the three letters mean that if a case can be mounted for the authenticity of 2 Timothy, then perhaps we should not be so quick to dismiss a Pauline origin for 1 Timothy or Titus either.

In every instance we must recall what register analysis has demonstrated on a sophisticated level but which previous statistical studies of distinctive vocabulary and style also often stressed. The more similar the topic, audience, setting, and literary genre, the more likely the same author will reuse key elements of his or her distinctive linguistic range and style. The greater similarities between 1 and 2 Thessalonians than between either letter and other Pauline epistles is exactly what should be expected of two letters on the same topic to the same community within a short period of time. Similar settings, audiences, and genres make it natural for Colossians and Ephesians to contain key similarities with each other, but the differences in the communities and their challenges mean those similarities will not be as great as between 1 and 2 Thessalonians. The differences in audiences will account for a significant portion of the changes in topics. Colossians is a church Paul has not founded, and Ephesians is most likely written to several other churches as well that Paul has not founded. Not surprisingly, these two letters are closest to Romans in the sense of giving a carefully structured presentation of the gospel as Paul understands it, with a clear division into theological and exhortational sections. Pitts's register analysis shows the two letters closest to Ephesians and Colossians when all the variables he examined are taken into account, including style and vocabulary, are Philemon and Philippians, precisely what we should expect given that they all were most likely written from Paul's same imprisonment closely in time to each other.[150]

The Pastorals also cohere as a cluster of three similar epistles on register analysis and are by far and away the most divergent from the ten remaining letters of Paul. But again this makes sense because only here is Paul writing to two individuals functioning as pastors or apostolic delegates in local churches and/or regions, with no indication whether these letters would have been read aloud. Paul may have been able to use language and refer to topics he knew Timothy and Titus understood without having to be concerned to explain them to anyone else. Paul is also apparently near the end of his ministry and, eventually, his life. Churches have grown and become more organized, he is more concerned to train others to carry on without him, and the amount of time Paul has spent in Rome by now explains the increase in imperial imagery and Latinisms in his style that advocates of pseudonymity often point to.[151]

Harold Hoehner notes that Galatians is approximately the same size as Ephesians and each has approximately the same number of unique words not found elsewhere in the New Testament (35 vs. 41, respectively) and about the same number of words unique within Paul but found elsewhere in the New Testament (90 vs. 84, respectively). Yet virtually no one today argues for Galatians' pseudonymity.[152] Indeed, 1 and 2 Corinthians are different from each other in topics and style, but these differences are not considered grounds for labeling one or both as pseudonymous. One suspects that the specter of Luther and the key epistles that inspired his theology the most loom larger than is acknowledged in this debate. If scholars can relegate other letters to a second tier, then they can focus on those whose teaching they

---

[150] Pitts, "Style and Pseudonymity in Pauline Scholarship," 139.

[151] Ibid., 142–46.

[152] Hoehner, *Ephesians* 24.

appreciate the most. One sees this dramatically on an issue like gender roles, where if Ephesians, Colossians, 1 Timothy, and Titus can be discounted, the way to full-fledged egalitarianism becomes far easier.

At the same time, many scholars have highlighted how a deutero-Pauline epistle like Ephesians reads as if it were "the quintessence of Paulinism"—what one might imagine a writer penning if he were to create a mosaic of the best in Paul.[153] But then why could Paul himself not have created such a letter? Good authors, moreover, are typically versatile in what they write. Maybe the most important lesson in all of these comparisons of style, vocabulary, and themes is the small "sample space" of data we have when examining the writings even of someone who has contributed as much to the New Testament as Paul. Pitts insists, "In the cases where an author's sample includes writings on varying topics, the only way of increasing accuracy for authorship discrimination is by substantial increases in corpus sizes for a given author, far beyond what we have available for any of the authors of the New Testament."[154]

Suppose, then, that one accepts all thirteen epistles attributed to Paul as authentic. That still leaves some dramatic differences between his letters and the Gospels' account of the life of Jesus to explain. More than one scholar has argued that Paul was the true founder of Christianity as we think of it. Did he transform the message of the simple Galilean rabbi Jesus into something extremely different from what the teacher from Nazareth could have ever imagined or endorsed? Or do the letters of Paul actually disclose considerable continuity with the Jesus of the Gospels? If Paul were conscious of continuing the Jesus tradition in his ministry, why does he quote the teaching of Jesus so rarely? Or are there actually an abundance of allusions, if not exact quotations, that support Paul's indebtedness to tradition? To these and related questions we must turn in our next chapter.

---

[153] Famously, Bruce, *Paul*, 424.

[154] Pitts, "Style and Pseudonymity in Pauline Scholarship," 118.

Chapter 9

Is Paul the True Founder of Christianity?

In chapter 8, we saw how some can read the epistles of Paul and pit them against the picture of Paul that emerges in Acts. Not surprisingly, then, even more readers try to make Paul contradict *Jesus*. Reading any one of the Gospels followed by the major letters of Paul makes it apparent that they do not always emphasize the same themes. For someone raised in a Christian context that gave disproportionate attention to Paul's letters compared to the rest of the canon, it is understandable when they go back to Jesus and wonder if they are in the same religious environment.[1] Of course, to some degree they

---

[1] Notice, e.g., the wording of the title of the widely acclaimed talk by John Piper, "Did Jesus Preach Paul's Gospel?" delivered at the Together for the Gospel 2010 conference (Louisville, April 27, 2010). While doubtless chosen for effect, historically this is exactly backwards from the way the question should be asked, namely, did Paul preach Jesus' Gospel? Jesus came first, not Paul; and Jesus, according to Piper's own convictions, was God incarnate, while Paul was not! Jesus should never be measured by Paul as a standard, only Paul by Jesus.

are not, since Jesus ministered almost exclusively in a Jewish context within the land of Israel, while Paul increasingly had to contextualize his message so Gentiles outside of Israel would understand it.

The charges, however, go well beyond this observation.[2] The famous English playwright of a century ago wrote about Paul's letters as "the monstrous imposition on Jesus," while the late nineteenth-century nihilistic philosopher, Friedrich Nietzsche, called Paul "the first Christian" and "the Jewish dysangelist" (i.e., a bearer of bad rather than good news)![3] Much more recently, atheist historian Gerd Lüdemann has dubbed Paul the true founder of Christianity,[4] and Michael Goulder has resurrected F. C. Baur's mid-nineteenth-century hypothesis that pits Paul against Peter as the two main streams of early Christian thought, with Peter preserving much more of the true nature of the historical Jesus.[5] Maurice Casey, finally, sums up the difference between Jesus's and Paul's teaching with his book title, *From Jewish Prophet to Gentile God*.[6] If any of these claims is at all on target,

---

[2] A large portion of this chapter from here on covers the same territory or is unpacked in fuller detail in Craig L. Blomberg, *Making Sense of the New Testament: Three Crucial Questions* (Grand Rapids: Baker; Leicester: IVP, 2004), 71–106.

[3] For these quotations and excerpts of both men's writings on Paul, see *The Writings of St. Paul: A Norton Critical Edition*, ed. Wayne A. Meeks (New York: Norton, 1972), 288–302.

[4] Gerd Lüdemann, *Paul: The Founder of Christianity* (Amherst, NY: Prometheus, 2002). Only slightly less sweeping in his similar claims is James D. Tabor, *Paul and Jesus: How the Apostle Transformed Christianity* (New York: Simon and Schuster, 2013).

[5] Michael D. Goulder, *Paul and the Competing Mission in Corinth* (Peabody: Hendrickson, 2001).

[6] Maurice Casey, *The Origins and Development of New Testament Christology* (Louisville: Westminster John Knox, 2001). See also Bart D. Ehrman's broader thesis, scarcely new, epitomized in his title, *How Jesus Became God: The Exaltation of a Jewish Preacher from Galilee* (New York: HarperOne, 2014) and well refuted in Michael F. Bird, Craig A. Evans, Simon J. Gathercole, Charles E. Hill, and Chris Tilling, *How God Became Jesus: The Real Origins of Belief in Jesus' Divine Nature* (Grand Rapids: Zondervan, 2014).

then we had better pay little attention to Paul's letters and expend all our energies in understanding the historical Jesus if we don't want to be led astray in investigating Christianity's origins. But are these charges well founded? Numerous surveys of the evidence suggest they are not.[7]

Paul's Use of the Jesus Tradition

Many readers of his letters have wondered why Paul did not quote Jesus more often. If Paul believed him to be the risen Lord and divine Messiah, then surely his words would have provided the most authoritative support for Paul's perspectives imaginable. Assuming the two agreed with each other, one might have expected Paul to be referring to what Jesus said on a given topic at almost every turn. After all, he regularly quotes the Hebrew Scriptures, what we call the Old Testament, to support his views. That he doesn't cite Jesus nearly as often or as clearly could thus call into question his knowledge of the oral tradition of Jesus's teachings and therefore of that tradition itself. Maybe not much of any substance about Jesus was accurately preserved after all.

A Direct Quotation of Jesus's Teaching: Remembering His Atoning Death

The first response to these charges is to highlight a number of passages that clearly *do* disclose Paul's citing Jesus's teachings on a given

---

[7] In addition to the literature cited elsewhere in this chapter, see especially Herman N. Ridderbos, *Paul and Jesus: Origin and General Character of Paul's Preaching of Christ* (Phillipsburg, NJ: Presbyterian & Reformed, 1957; Grand Rapids: Baker, 1958); J. W. Fraser, *Jesus and Paul: Paul as Interpreter of Jesus from Harnack to Kümmel* (Appleford, England: Marcham Manor Press, 1974); A. J. M. Wedderburn, "Paul and Jesus: Similarity and Continuity," *New Testament Studies* 34 (1988): 161–82; and Michael F. Bird and Joel Willits, eds., *Paul and the Gospels: Christologies, Conflicts and Convergences* (London and New York: T & T Clark, 2011).

topic.[8] The most extensive appears in 1 Corinthians 11:23–25, Paul's so-called words of institution of the Lord's Supper. Here we read:

> For I received from the Lord what I also passed on to you: The Lord Jesus, on the night he was betrayed, took bread, and when he had given thanks, he broke it and said, "This is my body, which is for you; do this in remembrance of me." In the same way, after supper he took the cup, saying, "This cup is the new covenant in my blood; do this, whenever you drink it, in remembrance of me."

All three Synoptic Gospels contain similar words attributed to Jesus on the last night of his earthly life (Mark 14:22–24; Matt 26:26–28; Luke 22:19–20). What is particularly interesting is that at several points Paul's wording is extremely close to Luke's even though Luke varies a little from Mark and Matthew. Thus both Luke and Paul include after "the body," the words, "which is [given] for you." Both add the command, "Do this in remembrance of me." Both add in the narrative material, "in the same way," and "after supper." And both explicitly label the covenant a "new" one.

We have seen earlier that Luke almost certainly wrote after Mark, using and editing him, and that a date in the early 60s is the earliest realistic date for the composition of the Gospel of Luke. That means

---

[8] In addition to the literature cited below in this section, see especially Dale C. Allison Jr., "The Pauline Epistles and the Synoptic Gospels: The Pattern of the Parallels," *New Testament Studies* 28 (1982): 1–32; Stephen G. Wilson, "From Jesus to Paul: The Contours and Consequences of a Debate," in *From Jesus to Paul: Studies in Honour of Francis Wright Beare,* ed. Peter Richardson and John C. Hurd (Waterloo, ON: Wilfrid Laurier University Press, 1984), 1–21; Eric K. C. Wong, "The De-Radicalization of Jesus' Ethical Sayings in Romans," *Novum Testamentum* 43 (2001): 245–63; Eric K. C. Wong, "The De-Radicalization of Jesus' Ethical Sayings in 1 Corinthians," *New Testament Studies* 48 (2002): 181–94; and David A. Fiensy, "The Synoptic Logia of Jesus in the Ethical Teachings of Paul," *Stone-Campbell Journal* 13 (2010): 81–98.

that when Paul was writing 1 Corinthians, dated by virtually all scholars of any theological persuasion to the mid-50s, he could not have been copying Luke's Gospel. It had to have been the oral tradition that was circulating on which he relied. So even the distinctive redactional form of a later Gospel, at least at this point, was relying on pre-Pauline tradition and was not rewording tradition for the sake of later, theological emphases.[9] Some have argued that these verses were preserved so carefully because they had already come to be used liturgically, in the church's Eucharistic services.[10] But this hypothesis doesn't explain the minor variations that do remain among the four accounts nor the supposed liturgy's appeal to the latest rather than the earliest form of the tradition. What is more, Paul does not appeal to human tradition here as he does sometimes elsewhere (e.g., 1 Cor 15:3). This information has come specifically "from the Lord" (11:23). This need not mean some direct revelation from God or Christ, but it does suggest a level of reliability or confidence in the tradition that goes beyond what mere human transmission can provide.[11] Both Jesus and Paul, therefore, believed that Christ's death provided a substitutionary atonement for the sins of humanity (his death is *huper humōn*—"on your behalf" or "for your sake"—1 Cor 11:24; Luke 22:29; cf. Rom 3:25; Mark 10:45), a central tenet of Christianity throughout its history.[12]

---

[9] See esp. I. Howard Marshall, *Last Supper and Lord's Supper* (Exeter: Paternoster; Grand Rapids: Eerdmans, 1980; Vancouver: Regent, 2006), 30–56, for this conclusion as well as a thorough comparison of all the parallels.

[10] E.g., Victor P. Furnish, *Jesus According to Paul* (Cambridge: Cambridge University Press, 1993), 31–32.

[11] Cf. David E. Garland, *1 Corinthians* (Grand Rapids: Baker, 2003), 545; Gordon D. Fee, *The First Epistle to the Corinthians*, rev. ed. (Grand Rapids: Eerdmans, 2014), 607–8.

[12] Cf. Roy E. Ciampa and Brian S. Rosner, *The First Letter to the Corinthians* (Grand Rapids: Eerdmans; Nottingham: Apollos, 2010), 551. Raymond F. Collins (*First Corinthians* [Collegeville: Liturgical, 1999], 432) adds, "In cultic language *hyper* ("for [your] sake") specifies the beneficiaries of the sacrifice or dedication. More than thirty NT texts use the preposition in reference to Jesus' death. This

Allusions to Jesus's Ethical Instruction

We should not be surprised that a consistent purpose for Paul's appeal to the Jesus tradition would have been to back up his ethical injunctions, especially when they proved countercultural. Paying one's religious teachers was not a Jewish practice, so the disciples no doubt raised their eyebrows when Jesus told them, in the context of their ministry, that "the worker deserves his wages" (Luke 10:7; cf. Matt 10:10b). First Corinthians 9:14 likewise maintains that that "the Lord has commanded that those who preach the gospel should receive their living from the gospel." Were it not for the introductory words, "the Lord has commanded," we might be uncertain as to whether Paul was alluding to anyone else's claims. In light of that introduction, it is hard to avoid the conclusion that he is referring to teaching like that given in the context of Jesus's missionary discourses.[13] When we realize that Jews almost always forbade rabbis from receiving money for ministry, lest it compromise their motives, Paul's countercultural teaching almost certainly requires an authority like Jesus behind it. First Timothy 5:18 reuses Jesus's command again in what is almost a direct quotation.[14]

---

does not preclude other interpretations of Jesus' death as well." Beverly Gaventa ("Interpreting the Death of Jesus Apocalyptically: Reconsidering Romans 8:32," in *Jesus and Paul Reconnected: Fresh Pathways into an Old Debate*, ed. Todd D. Still [Grand Rapids: Eerdmans, 2007], 125–45) finds important congruence between Jesus and Paul on the so-called classic view of the atonement also.

[13] See further Anthony C. Thiselton, *The First Epistle to the Corinthians* (Carlisle: Paternoster; Grand Rapids: Eerdmans, 2000), 692–98. Cf. Richard B. Hays, *First Corinthians* (Louisville: Westminster John Knox, 1997), 152.

[14] If Paul intends *graphē* ("writing" or "scripture") in this verse to cover both quotations, then he must be quoting Luke's Gospel, and the passage is irrelevant for a discussion of Paul's dependence on oral tradition (e.g., I. Howard Marshall with Philip H. Towner, *A Critical and Exegetical Commentary on the Pastoral Epistles* [Edinburgh: T & T Clark, 1999], 616). If *graphē* refers only to the quotation from Deut 25:4 preceding it, then his source for the saying could be oral tradition (e.g., William D. Mounce, *Pastoral Epistles* [Nashville: Nelson, 2000], 311).

First Corinthians 7:10 and 12 contain an intriguing pair of somewhat different commands from different sources. In verse 10, Paul stresses that those who are already married must not leave their spouses, but if they do divorce, then they must remain single. Paul ascribes this conviction not merely to himself but to "the Lord." Two verses later, however, he commands a wife not to leave her husband (and vice versa) and does so by his own authority rather than Christ's ("I, not the Lord"). This cannot mean, as some have alleged, that Paul did not think he was inspired when he wrote verse 12 but he did when he wrote verse 10.[15] After all, in verse 25 he repeats the statement about having no command from the Lord but giving a judgment "as one who by the Lord's mercy is trustworthy." At the end of the chapter in a seemingly ironic aside, countering those in Corinth who were promoting celibacy as the Christian ideal, Paul declares: "And I think that I too have the Spirit of God" (v. 40). We must not use Paul's language, therefore, to argue that verse 10 came from the risen Lord, while verse 12 expresses Paul's merely human opinion.[16] Both are equally inspired and authoritative; one just comes from the oral tradition about the teaching of the historical Jesus whereas the other does not. Jesus had taught that the intention of marriage was for spouses to stay together (Mark 10:7 par.). He had not addressed the situation, now common a quarter century later in the Gentile world, of the non-Christian

---

[15] As, e.g., in Joseph A. Fitzmyer, *First Corinthians* (New Haven and London: Yale University Press, 2008), 292. Peter Richardson ("'I Say, Not the Lord': Personal Opinion, Apostolic Authority, and the Development of Early Christian Halakah," *Tyndale Bulletin* 31 [1980]: 65–86) thinks the difference is between oral tradition and quasi-legal decisions akin to Jewish halakah required by new circumstances.

[16] As noted earlier, for outstanding commentary on all of 1 Corinthians 7, including these perspectives on these verses, see Fee, *First Epistle to the Corinthians*, 301–93.

partner in a mixed marriage of believer and unbeliever sometimes wanting to initiate divorce.[17]

A cluster of allusions to Jesus's ethical instructions appears in Romans 12–15. Romans 12:14 may be even more countercultural than 1 Corinthians 9:14 was. If Jesus had not taught, in opposition to dominant interpretation of the Old Testament, that his followers should bless those who persecute them rather than cursing their persecutors (Luke 6:28), it is doubtful if Paul would have dared to command the same radical response in his letters.[18] Romans 12:17 may likewise allude to Jesus's great sermon but this time to a portion found only in Matthew (5:38–40) on not resisting an evil person (i.e., not repaying evil for evil). Romans 12:18–19 and 21 then repeat the identical concepts if not the exact wording of Jesus's call to love one's enemies, especially as found in Luke 6:27 and 36 in that same sermon.[19] That Paul can in the same context selectively cite disparate portions of Jesus's teachings scattered about a lengthy discourse suggests he may have been familiar with at least one version of the entire discourse or sermon. With the *occasional* nature of Paul's letters (i.e., addressing specific occasions and concerns), only a minority of all the tradition about Jesus that Paul knew would have been relevant to the issue at hand. That he can cite multiple parts of a greater whole under these conditions makes it likely that he knew much more of that entire message.[20]

---

[17] Cf. further Craig L. Blomberg, "Marriage, Divorce, Remarriage and Celibacy: An Exegesis of Matthew 19:3–12," *Trinity Journal* 11 (1990): 161–96.

[18] The saying thus passes the standard criteria of authenticity with flying colors. See esp. William Klassen, "The Authenticity of the Command: 'Love Your Enemies,'" in *Authenticating the Words of Jesus,* ed. Bruce Chilton and Craig A. Evans (Leiden and Boston: Brill, 2002), 385–407.

[19] On all of the allusions to Jesus's teaching in Romans 12–15, see esp. Michael B. Thompson, *Clothed with Christ: The Example and Teaching of Jesus in Romans 12.1–15.13* (Sheffield: JSOT Press, 1991; Eugene, OR: Wipf & Stock, 2011).

[20] See esp. Christopher L. Carter, *The Great Sermon Tradition as a Fiscal Framework in 1 Corinthians: Toward a Pauline Theology of Material Possessions*

The next chapter of Romans discloses Paul's familiarity with Jesus's teaching in the temple the last week of his life. Trapped by the Pharisees and Herodians, who had diametrically opposite views of whether or not Jews should pay taxes to Rome, Jesus evaded the trap by making concessions to both parties: "Give back to Caesar what is Caesar's and to God what is God's" (Mark 12:17 pars.). In Romans 13:7, Paul insists, contrary to most Jews except those same Herodians, that Christians must give to everyone what is owed them, whether taxes, revenue, respect, or honor. That he uses the rarer, compounded form *apodote* ("give back"), rather than just *dote* ("give"), just as the Gospel accounts do also, makes it likely that he is indeed alluding to what Jesus said not quite thirty years earlier.[21]

Paul's chapter-and-a-half discussion of dietary laws and related matters in Romans 14:1–15:13 is likewise radical enough that his reference to being "persuaded in the Lord Jesus" (14:14) most likely harks back to the tradition of Jesus's teachings.[22] Paul's conviction in this verse that "nothing is unclean in itself" fits nicely with Mark 7:18–19, which culminates with Mark's parenthetical observation in verse 19b that Jesus thus declared all foods clean. No one seems to have recognized just how sweeping the significance of Jesus's claims was when he declared that only what came out of a person rather than what went into a person made them unclean (7:15; cf. 20–23). Only after Peter's thrice-repeated vision of unclean animals accompanied by God's command to him to kill and eat them (probably in the late 30s or early

---

(London and New York: T & T Clark, 2010). Cf. also F. F. Bruce, *Paul and Jesus* (Grand Rapids: Baker, 1974), 71–72. For further possible allusions to the missionary discourses of Matthew 10 and Luke 10, see David Wenham, *Paul: Follower of Jesus or Founder of Christianity* (Grand Rapids: Eerdmans, 1995), 190–99.

[21] C. E. B. Cranfield, *A Critical and Exegetical Commentary on the Epistle to the Romans*, vol. 2 (Edinburgh: T & T Clark, 1979), 669–70; Thomas R. Schreiner, *Romans* (Grand Rapids: Baker, 1998), 686.

[22] Thompson, *Clothed with Christ*, 185–89; Robert Jewett, *Romans* (Minneapolis: Fortress, 2007), 858.

40s) did the disciples fully understand that the new covenant did not preserve the dietary restrictions of the Mosaic law (Acts 10:1–11:18).[23] But Paul wrote Romans in about 57, so he would have learned about the full significance of Jesus's words by then.

The verse immediately preceding Romans 14:14 may well allude to Jesus's teaching also. "Let us stop passing judgment on one another" (v. 13) reminds the reader of Matthew 7:1 and Jesus's command not to judge—in the sense of not *condemning* others. That Jesus warned about God's treating us the way we treat others could explain why Paul has also just reiterated in verse 12 that "each of us will give an account of ourselves to God." Paul's treatment of similar dietary questions in 1 Corinthians 8:1–11:1 may also rely on the Jesus tradition. The concluding summary, to "eat whatever is put before you without raising questions of conscience" (10:27) could likewise be based on Mark 7:18–19 and its larger context. But it could equally well recall Jesus's commands to the seventy(-two) disciples for their short-term itinerating mission: "Stay there, eating and drinking whatever they give you" (Luke 10:7). Given that we have already seen Paul allude to the second half of this verse ("the worker deserves his wages"), this conclusion becomes all the more probable. Finally, Romans 15:1–3 refers to the model of Christ's not pleasing himself, using language that probably alludes to his own teachings about his role as a servant in Mark 10:45 and parallel.

Allusions to Jesus's Theological Instruction: Eschatology

The major *theological* topic that recurs in Paul's allusions to the teachings of Jesus is eschatology. First Thessalonians 2:15–16 likens the

---

[23] Joel Marcus (*Mark 1–8* [New York and London: Doubleday, 2000], 455) uses appropriate caution in concluding that at the very least Mark and Paul "moved in the same sort of circles." Cf. pp. 73–75, where a wide swath of parallels between the two authors is noted. On the clear break implied between the two ages here, see Eckhard J. Schnabel, *Acts* (Grand Rapids: Zondervan, 2012), 491–92.

persecution the Thessalonians have been enduring to similar hostility unleashed by non-Christian Jews against their Christian brothers and sisters in and around Jerusalem. We should not be surprised, then, if Paul were to allude to the teaching of Jesus himself, and it appears he does just that when he concludes that these Jewish leaders "in this way ... always heap up their sins to the limit. The wrath of God has come upon them at last [or "fully"]" (v. 16). Numerous portions of Jesus's invective against a select group of scribes and Pharisees in Matthew 23 resemble Paul's outburst in 1 Thessalonians. The closest parallel comes in verse 32: "Go ahead, then, and complete what your ancestors started!" The words translated "heap up" and "complete" both come from the same *pleroō* word group and can also mean "fulfill." The imagery is so striking with the ironic command to continue defying God's will that one suspects Paul did not invent it but adopted it from the Jesus tradition.[24] The parallels do not stop here, however. The Jews "who killed the Lord Jesus and the prophets and also drove us out" (1 Thess 2:15) resemble those "who murdered the prophets" in Matthew 23:31 and who will still "kill and crucify" other "prophets and ... teachers" in verse 34.

In addition to knowing at least parts of Matthew 23, Paul seems to be familiar with the eschatological discourse that spans all of chapters 24 and 25 (and in shorter form in Mark 13 and Luke 21:5–36). In 1 Thessalonians 4:15 Paul proclaims that "according to the Lord's word," those who are still alive when Christ returns will have no advantage over those believers who have already died. In verses 16–17 he proceeds to describe this future occasion. Christ will return from heaven with a loud shout, the voice of an archangel, and a trumpet call of God. The previously deceased believers will rise to life and join the living Christians as they are caught up in the air to meet the Lord. Is

---

[24] See further David Wenham, *Paul*, 320–21; Gary S. Shogren, *1 and 2 Thessalonians* (Grand Rapids: Zondervan, 2012), 112.

all this "the Lord's word" signaled in verse 15? It is at least intriguing that partial parallels to most of these concepts appear in Christ's eschatological discourse. Mark 13:26 portrays the Parousia—the second coming—as Jesus sends out his angels from heaven. The parallel passage in Matthew (24:31) adds a reference to a loud trumpet. Both Mark and Matthew, then, go on to recount the gathering together of all God's people.[25]

Still other parts of Jesus's eschatological discourse emerge even more clearly as we continue into 1 Thessalonians 5. The comparison in verse 2 to the coming of "a thief in the night" is so striking and potentially misleading and unflattering that no early Christian is likely ever to have created it. But once Jesus himself used it to explain the unexpected nature of his return (and in no other way is he likening himself to a burglar!), then other believers would have felt free to reuse it (see Matt 24:43–44; Luke 12:39–40).[26] The sudden arrival of the end of history as we know it (1 Thess 5:3), with its striking metaphor of a woman in labor pains, matches Matthew 24:37–42 and Mark 13:8. Being sober and alert, as children of the daytime rather than of darkness (1 Thess 5:4–6), meshes with the call to watchfulness (with the same verb *grēgoreō*) in Mark 13:33 and the entire parable of the ten bridesmaids (Matt 25:1–13).[27] Second Thessalonians 2:3–6,

---

[25] See further David Wenham, "Paul and the Synoptic Apocalypse," in *Gospel Perspectives*, vol. 2, ed. R. T. France and David Wenham (Sheffield: JSOT, 1981), especially 347–52; and P. H. R. van Houwelingen, "The Great Reunion: The Meaning and Significance of the 'Word of the Lord' in 1 Thessalonians 4:13–18," *Calvin Theological Journal* 42 (2007): 308–24. For the view that 4:15 is a prophetic utterance, not a teaching of the historical Jesus, cf. Michael W. Pahl, *Discerning the "Word of the Lord": The Word of the Lord in 1 Thessalonians 4:15* (London and New York: T & T Clark, 2009).

[26] Wenham, "Paul and the Synoptic Apocalypse," 347. Cf. also Gordon D. Fee, *The First and Second Letters to the Thessalonians* (Grand Rapids: Eerdmans, 2009), 187–88.

[27] David Wenham, *The Rediscovery of Jesus' Eschatological Discourse* (Sheffield: JSOT Press, 1984; Eugene, OR: Wipf & Stock, 2003), 63.

finally, describes the same anti-Christian figure that Jesus referred to as "the abomination that causes desolation" (Mark 13:14 par.). All in all, there is a good chance he knew the entire discourse. That he drew on sections unique to Matthew as well as parts common to Mark and Matthew again suggests that Jesus did originally speak something at least as long as the later, fuller Matthean version.[28]

One can move beyond both individual sayings and entire discourses of Jesus and suggest that Paul's "new creation eschatology" shares the identical "already but not yet framework" as that which so consistently characterizes Jesus. Unlike the standard Jewish expectation of the old age giving way to the new Messianic age of Jeremiah's new covenant (Jer 31:31–34), both Jesus and Paul see the new age as having broken into the old era of humanity without entirely obliterating it (Matt 13:1–52 pars.; 12:28 pars.; 27:51–53). Thus believers still retain their fallen human natures with their propensity to sin (Rom 6:11–14; 7:14–25), even as their new status as forgiven beings begins the process of transforming them increasingly into God's likeness (Col 3:10; Eph 4:24). Jesus's resurrection shows that the end has begun, but believers still wait for their resurrection bodies even as Jesus provides the "firstfruit" of that promise, thereby guaranteeing it will happen for everyone else (1 Cor 15:20–28).[29]

Other Possible Allusions to Jesus's Teachings

A handful of scholars have gotten carried away with the idea of an epistle writer's using the Jesus tradition and postulate allusions or echoes to words of Christ every time a key word or striking image

---

[28] See esp. ibid., throughout. So also Grant R. Osborne, *Matthew* (Grand Rapids: Zondervan, 2010), 864.

[29] See esp. Gerry Schoberg, *Perspectives of Jesus in the Writings of Paul: A Historical Examination of Shared Core Commitments with a View to Determining the Extent of Paul's Dependence on Jesus* (Eugene, OR: Pickwick, 2013), 242–331.

proves parallel.[30] Given the frequency of much of this language in other ancient Jewish, Greek, or Roman sources, this approach remains unhelpful. On the other hand, it seems likely that the allusions to Jesus's teaching in the Pauline epistles are more frequent than merely these reasonably clear references just surveyed.[31] Richard Hays has suggested seven major criteria for determining when similarities between Paul and an Old Testament text are sufficiently significant to suggest he is consciously alluding to Scripture. These seem helpful in determining his uses of the Jesus tradition as well. The names Hays gives for the criteria are "availability," "volume," "recurrence," "thematic coherence," "historical plausibility," "history of interpretation," and "satisfaction."[32]

"Availability" for Hays means acquaintance with the text allegedly referenced and the probability that Paul's audience would likewise be familiar with the text. "Volume" refers primarily to "the degree of explicit repetition of words or syntactical patterns" but also to how prominent the proposed background text is both in its original context and in Paul's. "Recurrence" asks how often Paul elsewhere refers to the same text. "Thematic coherence" has to do with how well the older text fits into Paul's context if we presuppose its use. "Historical plausibility" asks if Paul and his readership could have understood the alleged "meaning effect" if such a reference were consciously intended.

---

[30] Among recent scholars the clearest example is Dean B. Deppe, *The Sayings of Jesus in the Epistle of James* (Chelsea, MI: Bookcrafters, 1989). For Paul, Seyoon Kim ("Jesus, Sayings of," in *Dictionary of Paul and His Letters*, ed. Gerald F. Hawthorne, Ralph P. Martin, and Daniel G. Reid [Downers Grove and Leicester: IVP, 1993], 481) seems a bit overconfident with his chart of thirty-one items.

[31] See esp. throughout David Wenham, *Paul: Follower of Jesus or Founder of Christianity* (Grand Rapids: Eerdmans, 1995). Cf. also David Wenham, *Paul and Jesus: The True Story* (London: SPCK; Grand Rapids: Eerdmans, 2002); and David Wenham, *Did St. Paul Get Jesus Right?* (Oxford: Lion Hudson, 2011).

[32] Richard B. Hays, *Echoes of Scripture in the Letters of Paul* (New Haven and London: Yale University Press, 1989), 29–32.

"History of interpretation" inquires as to how often other scholars as well as ordinary people have heard the same echoes. "Satisfaction," finally, asks how much sense the proposed reading makes. Not all of these criteria apply to the Jesus tradition in exactly the same way as they do to the Hebrew Scriptures, but their application is sufficiently similar to make it worthwhile to use them.[33]

All of the passages so far itemized pass with flying colors. Another cohort that seems likely to comprise conscious allusions includes Romans 12:18—Paul's call to live at peace with all people, to the extent that our actions make that possible. Given the other allusions already noted in this context to the Sermon on the Mount/Plain, we may envision Paul's having the beatitude now found in Matthew 5:9 in mind about the blessedness of peacemakers. First Corinthians 4:12, with its claims about blessing when cursed and enduring persecution, probably alludes to the same parts of Jesus's Sermon as Romans 12:14 did, even if it is a little less exact in its verbal parallelism.[34] Romans 13:8–10, in this context of so many parallels to the Jesus tradition, may then offer one more—Jesus's teaching on fulfilling the law and the double-love command (Matt 5:17; Mark 12:31 pars.). Galatians 5:14 has a similar allusion; interestingly, Jesus's words on loving one's neighbor appear in the same context as his teaching on paying one's taxes, already identified as a passage Paul uses.[35]

In 1 Corinthians 6:2, Paul reminds his readers that they already know that believers will judge the rest of the world. This is not

---

[33] This is the thrust of Craig L. Blomberg, "Quotations, Allusions, and Echoes of Jesus in Paul," *Studies in the Pauline Epistles: Festschrift for Douglas J. Moo*, ed. Matt Harmon and Jay Smith (Grand Rapids: Zondervan, 2014), 129–43.

[34] Cf. Harm W. Hollander, "The Words of Jesus: From Oral Traditions to Written Records in Paul and Q," *Novum Testamentum* 42 (2000): 345.

[35] Thompson, *Clothed with Christ*, 121–40. Douglas J. Moo (*Galatians* [Grand Rapids: Baker, 2013], 346) plausibly believes Paul also knows the parable of the good Samaritan in its historical context, with its expansion of the definition of "neighbor" (Luke 10:25–37).

standard Jewish eschatology, so where did Paul get the concept? In a partial parallel in Matthew 19:28, Jesus speaks of the Twelve sitting on thrones and judging the twelve tribes of Israel, which could have led him to conclude that the rest of the church would be involved in judging the rest of the world. First Corinthians 8:13 resembles Mark 9:42 and parallel, even though the only verbal parallelism involves the verb *skandalizō* (to cause to stumble or sin). Both passages use drastic hyperbole to warn against the danger of causing a fellow believer to be led into sin. *Skandalizō* occurs 26 times in the Gospels (20 of those times in speech attributed to Jesus), while elsewhere in the New Testament it is found only in this Pauline text and in 2 Corinthians 11:29. It appears nowhere in the Greek Old Testament and only four times in the Apocrypha. These statistics increase the likelihood of Paul's picking up the concept from the Jesus tradition.[36]

Rabbis did occasionally speak metaphorically of faith moving mountains (e.g., *b. Bat.* 3b, *b. Sanh.* 241, *Lev. Rab.* 8:8), so 1 Corinthians 13:2 need not have come from Jesus. Mark 11:22–23 and parallel, nevertheless, use the same imagery in the context of either the Mount of Olives or Mount Zion, making a promise so striking that it is likely to have been well embedded in the oral tradition of Jesus's sayings. So again Paul may well have thought of this metaphor's use because of his familiarity with the words of Christ.[37]

All of these possible allusions are, of course, in Greek. Particularly striking is Galatians 4:6, with its use of the Aramaic *Abba* for God's role as believers' Father. While a few uses of this noticeably intimate word—somewhere between "Daddy" and "Dad" perhaps—have been

[36] Cf. Michael F. Bird, "Mark: Interpreter of Peter and Disciple of Paul," in *Paul and the Gospels*, ed. Bird and Willits, 51; Seyoon Kim, *Paul and the New Perspective: Second Thoughts on the Origin of Paul's Gospel* (Grand Rapids: Eerdmans, 2001), 325.

[37] Maureen W. Yeung, *Faith in Jesus and Paul: A Comparison with Special Reference to "Faith That Can Remove Mountains" and "Your Faith Has Healed/Saved You"* (Tübingen: Mohr Siebeck, 2002), 39–50.

discovered in other ancient Jewish sources, it still remains comparatively rare.[38] For the New Testament reader, Jesus's use of *Abba* in his prayer in the garden of Gethsemane (Mark 14:36) comes immediately to mind. Of course, that same term may lie behind any or all of the other, common uses of the Greek *patēr* in the Gospels, but at least this one passage was so noteworthy that the Aramaic was preserved in the Jesus tradition that Mark eventually used. Paul would almost certainly have known about it, and he apparently assumes his readers in Galatia, already influenced strongly by other Jewish Christians, would recognize it and understand it, too.

Less distinctive but still important is Philippians 4:6 ("Do not be anxious about anything"), especially in light of the frequency of Paul's allusions to the Sermon on the Mount/Plain. One thinks immediately of Matthew 6:25/Luke 12:22 and their larger contexts on not being anxious about what we will eat or drink or wear. The same Greek verb *merimnaō* appears in both passages even though many English versions use "worry" instead of "be anxious" to translate it. No form of *merimnaō* occurs in the New Testament in the imperative mood except in these three texts, and all forms of the verb are rare outside of the Synoptics and the words of Jesus.[39] First Thessalonians 5:13b, finally, with its teaching about being at peace with yourselves calls to mind Mark 9:50.[40]

Echoes of the Jesus Tradition

Many possible echoes of the Jesus tradition, not even large or clear enough to be called allusions, could be added to our list. A scan of the instances the UBS Greek New Testament cross-references a passage

---

[38] Cf. esp. Scot McKnight, *A New Vision for Israel: The Teachings of Jesus in National Context* (Grand Rapids: Eerdmans, 1999), 49–65.

[39] Cf. Gordon D. Fee, *Paul's Letter to the Philippians* (Grand Rapids: Eerdmans, 1995), 408.

[40] Cf. Shogren, *1 and 2 Thessalonians*, 220.

from the Gospels in its footnotes to the epistles of Paul will high-light the most likely echoes. One thinks especially of the numerous similarities between Paul's discussion of the wisdom in 1 Corinthians 1–2 that hides itself from the world's powerful and noble but reveals itself to the weak and disadvantaged, and Jesus's teaching to the same end in Matthew 11:25–27/Luke 10:21–22.[41] We could explore 1 Thessalonians 4:8 and Luke 10:16 with their parallel structures on rejecting Paul's or Jesus' teaching as rejecting God's teaching. We could compare what was not revealed by "flesh and blood" in Galatians 1:15–16[42] and Matthew 16:17, or the commands for disfellowship-ping in 1 Corinthians 5:1–5 and Matthew 18:15–17.[43]

The metaphors of the gospel's "bearing fruit and growing" in Colossians 1:5–6 might rely on Jesus's seed parables, especially the parable of the sower (Mark 4:3–9 pars.). Some have even speculated that the strange reference to Paul as a *spermologos* (etymologically, someone who makes words with seeds), could have been referring to his use of Jesus's seed parables, distinctive in a Greco-Roman con-text.[44] The frequent contrast in Paul between flesh and S/spirit (see,

---

[41] See the chart in Peter Richardson, "The Thunderbolt in Q and the Wise Man in Corinth," in *From Jesus to Paul*, ed. Peter Richardson and John C. Hurd (Waterloo, ON: Wilfrid Laurier Press, 1984), 96. For a longer but more specula-tive treatment of possible allusions to Jesus's teachings in 1 Corinthians 1–4 (and also in chap. 9), see Biorn Fjärstadt, *Synoptic Tradition in 1 Corinthians* (Uppsala: Teologiska Institutionen, 1974).

[42] Although Matt 16:16–19 is not found in Mark, numerous Semitisms in Matthew's additions make it likely Jesus did say these things. See especially Ben F. Meyer, *The Aims of Jesus* (London: SCM, 1979; Eugene, OR: Wipf & Stock, 2002), 185–97.

[43] Paul Foster ("Paul and Matthew: Two Strands of the Early Jesus Movement with Little Sign of Connection," in *Paul and the Gospels*, ed. Bird and Willits, 111–12) acknowledges the connection but is uncertain of the relationship between the two texts.

[44] So Maurice A. Robinson, "Σπερμολόγος: Did Paul Preach from Jesus' Parables?" *Biblica* 56 (1975): 231–40.

e.g., Gal 5:16–17; Rom 8:12–13; 1 Cor 13:1–3) resembles Jesus's words in the garden (Mark 14:38 par.) that "the spirit is willing but the flesh is weak." A number of Pauline passages refer to serving one another and often use Christ as the model of how to do it (e.g., Rom 15:1–4; 1 Cor 10:33–11:1; Phil 2:5–11), suggesting knowledge of his own self-identification as a servant (esp. Mark 10:45 par.).[45] Second Corinthians 1:17, finally, presents Paul as changing his travel plans not due to duplicity or fickleness but to a changed situation at Corinth. Paul's question, "Or do I make my plans in a worldly manner so that in the same breath I say both 'Yes, yes' and 'No, no'?" closely resembles Matthew 5:37: "All you need to say is simply 'Yes,' or 'No'; anything beyond this comes from the evil one."

Additional examples start to become more speculative. But we have canvassed enough text to make the point sufficiently obvious. Paul did know the tradition of Jesus's teachings, and he appears to have preserved it reasonably carefully. That he did not use direct quotations more often is in keeping both with the fact that there was no single, fixed, canonical form of Jesus's teaching at this early date and with the practice in antiquity of authors deliberately varying the wording of their sources a little so as to show they owned it for themselves (recall chap. 1).

Jesus's Actions

When one comes to Jesus's actions, Paul's biggest focus is on Christ's death and resurrection. This should occasion no surprise because without an atoning crucifixion or a bodily resurrection, Jesus becomes just one more tragic religious martyr in world history. Paul does not have a huge number of references to Jesus's earthly life, but there are some. Stanley Porter has assembled and summarized these as follows:

---

[45] See esp. Larry W. Hurtado, "Jesus as Lordly Example in Philippians 2:5–11," in *From Jesus to Paul*, ed. Hurd and Richardson, 113–26.

He was born as a human (Rom. 9.5) to a woman and under the law, that is, as a Jew (Gal. 4.4), that he was descended from David's line (Rom. 1.3; 15.12); though he was not like Adam (Rom. 5.15), that he had brothers, including one named James (1 Cor. 9.15; Gal. 1.19), that he had a meal on the night he was betrayed (1 Cor. 11.23–25), that he was crucified and died on a cross (Phil. 2.8; 1 Cor. 1.23; 8.11; 15.3; Rom. 4.25; 5.6, 8; 1 Thess. 2.15; 4.14, etc.), was buried (1 Cor. 15.40, and was raised three days later (1 Cor. 15.4; Rom. 4.25; 8.34; 1 Thess. 4.14, etc.), and that afterwards he was seen by Peter, the disciples and others (1 Cor. 15.5–7).[46]

We should probably extend this list. "Born of a woman" in Galatians 4:4 is just odd enough, if all Paul wants to say is that Jesus was truly human, that perhaps he is alluding to his virginal conception—that humanly he was related *only* to a mother.[47] Paul's language about Jesus's rescuing us from God's coming wrath (1 Thess 1:10) echoes John the Baptist's command to flee the coming wrath (Matt

---

[46] Stanley E. Porter, "Images of Christ in Paul's Letters," in *Images of Christ: Ancient and Modern*, ed. Stanley E. Porter, Michael A. Hayes, and David Tombs (Sheffield: Sheffield Academic Press, 1997), 98–99. See also J. P. Arnold, "The Relationship of Paul to Jesus," in *Hillel and Jesus: Comparative Studies of Two Major Religious Leaders*, ed. James H. Charlesworth and Loren L. Johns (Minneapolis: Fortress, 1997), 256–88.

[47] Most commentators correctly argue that all that can be demonstrated with certainty from this reference is Paul's belief in Jesus's full humanity. But Timothy George (*Galatians* [Nashville: B&H, 1994], 302–3), whose commentary deals more with broader systematic and historical-theological concerns than most, rightly observes that "it is inconceivable that Paul, the travel companion of Luke, would not have known about the virginal conception of Jesus. The fact that he nowhere mentions the virgin birth in his letters could only mean that it was so universally accepted among the Christian churches to which he wrote that he deemed no elaboration or defense of it necessary. As J. G. Machen noted, 'The virgin birth does seem to be implied in the profoundest way in the entire view which Paul holds of the Lord Jesus Christ.'"

3:7 par.). Second Corinthians 5:21, with its affirmation of Christ's sin-lessness, shows Paul knew numerous dimensions of Jesus's life, most likely including his resistance to the temptations by the devil (Matt 4:1–11; Luke 4:1–13). In 1 Corinthians 1:22, Paul talks about Jews' demanding signs, even though they do so nowhere else in information included in his letters. But Mark 8:11–13; Matthew 12:38–39; Luke 23:8–9; and John 4:48 show them doing so during Jesus's ministry and thus Paul may well have had one or more of those occasions in mind. The language of 2 Corinthians 3:18 is reminiscent of the transfigura-tion (Mark 9:2 pars.)—"being transformed into his image with ever-increasing glory."[48]

Though more speculative, we may add still more detail, following Stephen Stout's recent comprehensive catalog of elements of the life of the historical Jesus that Paul may have known. In addition to all the items so far listed, it may be that Romans 6:3 and Colossians 2:12 assume knowledge of Jesus's own baptism by John as a prototype for subsequent Christian baptism. The "preaching of Jesus Christ" (KJV, RSV, NASB, ESV) in Romans 16:25 is usually taken as containing an objective genitive—the preaching *about* Jesus—but it could be subjec-tive and refer to the preaching ministry Jesus had. A decision on this will likely be influenced by the famous debate over the many references in Paul to "the faith of Jesus," with more and more scholars opting for the subjective genitive there, too, referring to Jesus's faithfulness to his mission and calling.[49] Ephesians 2:17 seems more secure as this kind

---

[48] See esp. A. D. A. Moses, *Matthew's Transfiguration Story and Jewish-Christian Controversy* (Sheffield: Sheffield Academic Press, 1996), 226–38, who argues not only that Paul knew the account but that he phrased his treatment of it in 2 Corinthians 3 so as to refute an abuse of it among the Corinthians. The latter conclusion, of course, does not necessarily follow from the former.

[49] For the debate, see esp. Michael F. Bird and Preston M. Sprinkle, eds., *The Faith of Jesus Christ: Exegetical, Biblical, and Theological Studies* (Milton Keynes: Paternoster; Peabody: Hendrickson, 2010).

of allusion with its reference to Jesus's coming to preach peace to those both far and near—Gentile and Jew respectively. In Romans 9:30–32 Paul references the "cornerstone" and "stumbling stone" imagery of Isaiah 28:16 and 8:14, that Jesus does by means of Psalm 118:22 and Isaiah 8:14 in the parable of the wicked tenants (Matt 21:42 pars.). Might the clause about Jesus's being seen by angels in 1 Timothy 3:16 refer to one or more of the incidents recorded in the Gospels in which angels appeared, especially at the beginning and end of his life? After all, 1 Timothy 1:15 already appeals to the same central mission of Jesus as Luke does in Luke 19:10: Christ came into the world to save sinners/he came to seek and to save the lost. "Christ's perseverance" (2 Thess 3:5), finally, recalls Luke 9:51 with Jesus's resoluteness to go to Jerusalem.[50]

To conclude this section, we may note the numerous passages in Paul that commend the imitation of Christ.[51] Sometimes the command is explicit (1 Cor 11:1; 1 Thess 1:6); often it is more implicit (Phil 1:21; 2 Cor 3:18; Rom 6:17; 8:15–16; 13:14; 15:1–6). But how can Paul tell people in the churches he founded to imitate Jesus across the board in every walk of life unless they had fairly thorough knowledge of how Jesus lived? And how could they have learned this information unless Paul communicated it to them because he had detailed access to information about Christ's lifestyle? Whatever else this included, it certainly would have highlighted his servanthood, obedience, and willingness to suffer, as in the Philippian hymn's first half (Phil 2:6–8). Indeed, in 1 Corinthians 11:1, Paul explicitly declares, "Follow my example, as I follow the example of Christ." So he acknowledges that

---

[50] Stephen O. Stout, The "Man Christ Jesus": The Humanity of Jesus in the Teaching of the Apostle Paul (Eugene, OR: Wipf & Stock, 2011), 64–142.

[51] See esp. David Stanley, "Imitation in Paul's Letters: Its Significance for His Relationship to Jesus and to His Own Christian Foundations," in From Jesus to Paul, ed. Hurd and Richardson, 127–41. Cf. also John B. Webster, "The Imitation of Christ," Tyndale Bulletin 37 (1986): 95–120.

he knows enough about the historical Jesus to emulate him on a day-to-day basis and to teach others how to do so, not least by telling them to watch him![52]

Paul's Nonuse of the Jesus Tradition

Paul was well aware of many details about the life of Christ. Some of what we have labeled allusions and echoes can be explained in some alternate way, but enough parallels between Jesus and Paul are secure enough to refute those who would say Paul knows little or nothing about the historical Jesus. Yet the question remains, why didn't Paul cite Jesus *much more* often and plainly? Six factors go a long way toward answering this question.[53]

First, we must remember that none of Paul's letters represents first-time evangelism of unsaved people or even the beginning of the discipleship process for brand-new Christians. These had already taken place before Paul ever penned a single one of his epistles. Rather, Paul is addressing specific problems in the churches to which he writes. Sometimes false teachers from outside have intruded, sometimes there is internal dissension or questioning, and often there is some of each. Occasionally Paul is preparing the way for a hoped-for visit, including to churches like Rome and Colossae to which he hadn't

---

[52] Cf. Kathy Ehrensperger, *Paul and the Dynamics of Power: Communication and Interaction in the Early Christ-Movement* (London and New York: T & T Clark, 2007), 144–54. Cf. Kathy Ehrensperger, "At the Table: Common Ground Between Paul and the Historical Jesus," in *Jesus Research: New Methodologies and Perspectives*, ed. James H. Charlesworth with Brian Rhea and Petr Pokorný (Grand Rapids: Eerdmans, 2014), 531–50, in which she applies Romans 15:7 to the whole area of table fellowship, suggesting that Paul was familiar with the whole tradition of Jesus's fellowship meals, not just with the Last Supper.

[53] Cf. esp. Rainer Riesner, "Paulus und die Jesus-Überlieferung," in *Evangelium, Schriftauslegung, Kirche*, ed. Jostein Ødna, Scott J. Hafemann, and Otfried Hofius (Göttingen: Vandenhoeck und Ruprecht, 1997), 356–65.

previously been able to travel. If one wants to envision what first-time gospel instruction looked like, the speeches in Acts are a better model. Peter's words in Acts 10:36–38 prove particularly instructive, as Peter includes reference to Jesus's life beginning with his baptism all the way through to his crucifixion. These verses almost certainly summarize what Peter took a good chunk of time to say and flesh out with all the necessary supporting detail.[54]

Second, none of the rest of the New Testament epistles has any greater frequency in using the Gospel tradition of Jesus's words and deeds. James and 1 Peter, we will see in the next chapter, allude to Jesus's teaching a fair number of times, but the same difficulties reappear in deciding just when a conscious reference to a saying of the Lord was in the original epistle-writer's mind. And the one set of letters written by the same person who actually wrote a Gospel actually has *no* unambiguous reference to any of the teachings or deeds of Jesus mentioned in that Gospel! I speak, of course, of John. The oldness and newness of the love command in 1 John 2:7–11 *might* allude to John 13:34,[55] but it is hard to be sure. The language could easily have entered common Christian, or at least Johannine, parlance. After that, there is nothing. Even if a certain scholar views the Fourth Gospel and the Epistles traditionally ascribed to the apostle John as produced by different writers, neither of whom was the apostle and son of Zebedee, he or she is likely at least to see a Johannine school of editors, composers, or adherents to the Johannine trajectory within the early church as responsible for both the Gospel and the Epistles. On either scenario, if ever one would have expected letters to refer to the Gospel tradition, it is here. We may not yet have explained why the

[54] See esp. C. H. Dodd, *The Apostolic Preaching and Its Developments* (London: Hodder & Stoughton, 1936; Grand Rapids: Baker, 1982), 54–56.

[55] Stephen S. Smalley, *1, 2, 3 John* (Waco: Word, 1984), 54; Raymond E. Brown, *The Epistles of John* (Garden City: Doubleday, 1982), 286.

Jesus tradition is so muted in the Epistles, but the regular recurrence of the phenomenon shows that Paul's practices were not anomalous. And if John could write letters without alluding to details of the life or teaching of the one he wrote an entire Gospel about, then Paul can have comparatively few allusions in his letters and still may have known at least enough to have written an entire Gospel about Jesus had he chosen to do so!

Third, following from these first two points, early Christian epistles were apparently not the preferred genre or context for catechetical instruction about the life and teaching of Jesus. This occurred by word of mouth, as preachers and teachers orally passed on what they believed people needed to know. This would change after the middle of the second century, when Jesus's teachings *were* regularly used to buttress ethical and theological instruction in the letters of the later apostolic and other ante-Nicene Church Fathers. No doubt this change coincided with the emerging canon consciousness of Christianity—that the first-century Christian documents carried an authority on a par with the Hebrew Scriptures, which were so abundantly cited in the New Testament and earlier second-century Epistles. But until that point arrived, the Old Testament remained the norm to cite if one needed to buttress one's arguments.[56]

Fourth, as briefly noted above, Jesus's followers quickly recognized that the most important features of his life were his death and resurrection. It would be absurd, for example, to say that the framers of the Apostles' Creed in the third century knew nothing of the wealth of material in the Gospels about Jesus's life. The Gospels had long been in existence, and the early Christians were steeped in them. But this creed's concise summary of essential Christian

---

[56] See further Donald A. Hagner, "The Sayings of Jesus in the Apostolic Fathers and Justin Martyr," in *Gospel Perspectives*, vol. 5, ed. David Wenham (Sheffield: JSOT, 1985; Eugene, OR: Wipf & Stock, 2004), 233–68.

belief proceeds from saying that Jesus was "born of the virgin Mary" immediately to "suffered under Pontius Pilate, was crucified, dead and buried."[57] What made Jesus not just another wise, religious teacher was that he was of divine descent and supernaturally born, and atoned for our sins through his death, vindicated by the resurrection. Little wonder, then, that his death and resurrection would be what Paul would most refer to, especially before there were any written Gospels (especially Gal 3:10–14; 1 Cor 2:1–4; 15:1–59; 2 Cor 5:11–21; Rom 3:21–31).

Fifth, the sense of divine inspiration or guidance that Paul experienced would have freed him up to write in the words he sensed he was supposed to use.[58] Even when he was citing a passage out of the Old Testament, he felt free not to use a word-for-word translation from the Hebrew into Greek, or even always to quote the Septuagint verbatim.[59] If Paul handled these sacred documents with this kind of freedom, how much more should we not expect him to treat an oral tradition, not yet written down much less canonized, with whatever flexibility fit his needs yet without altering the gist of what he was repeating? It is even possible that there were two forms of tradition to which Paul had access: one with fairly fixed wording, perhaps especially for liturgical use in the church, and one for which there was

---

[57] Philip Schaff, ed., *The Creeds of Christendom*, vol. 1, rev. David S. Schaff (New York: Harper & Row, 1931; Grand Rapids: Baker, 1998), 21.

[58] James D. G. Dunn, "Paul's Knowledge of the Jesus Tradition," in *Christus Bezeugen*, ed. Karl Kertelge, Traugott Holtz, and Claus-Peter März (Leipzig: St. Benno, 1989), 206–7.

[59] Out of the wealth of literature on Paul and the Old Testament, see esp. Christopher D. Stanley, *Paul and the Language of Scripture: Citation Technique in the Pauline Epistles and Contemporary Literature* (Cambridge: Cambridge University Press, 1992). Cf. also James W. Aageson, *Written Also for Our Sake: Paul and the Art of Biblical Interpretation* (Louisville: Westminster John Knox, 1993); and Steve Moyise, *Paul and Scripture: Studying the New Testament Use of the Old Testament* (Grand Rapids: Baker, 2010).

greater flexibility to reword from one retelling to the next. This would concord closely with the roles of the written and oral laws in Judaism as well.[60]

Sixth, on more than one occasion Paul has to stress that he has as much authority as the apostles in Jerusalem do, against those who doubt or oppose him (esp. Galatians 1–2; cf. Acts 15). On the one hand he takes pains to stress that what he teaches does not differ in any material way from the instructions of those who were among Jesus's closest followers. On the other hand, he emphasizes his independence from them by highlighting the Lord's direct revelation to him. In such contexts it could prove counterproductive to rely very much on the traditions of Jesus's earthly teachings that he could have learned only from other human believers, including the Twelve.[61]

Broader Theological Agreement

The most telling kinds of comparisons between Paul and Jesus are not, however, the frequency of Pauline quotations, allusions, or echoes of Jesus's teachings or deeds. What really matters is if the two men substantially agreed or considerably differed with each other with respect to the major topics they expounded. A cursory reading of the Gospels (even just the Synoptics) and the letters of Paul could make it appear as though they had little in common. A closer look leads to a different assessment.

---

[60] Traugott Holtz, "Paul and the Oral Gospel Tradition," in *Jesus and the Oral Gospel Tradition*, ed. Henry Wansbrough (Sheffield: JSOT, 1991), 380–93.

[61] More pointedly, Paul's emphasis in Galatia on "a circumcision-free and law-free gospel for the Gentiles is *not* based on common apostolic tradition, going back to the beginning," because that was precisely what was still being debated, unlike, e.g., the agreed-upon significance of the resurrection and list of eyewitnesses in 1 Cor 15:1–11. So Martinus C. de Boer, *Galatians: A Commentary* (Louisville: Westminster John Knox, 2011), 84.

Justification by Faith and the Kingdom of God

Little doubt surrounds the claim that the kingdom of God was central to the message of the historical Jesus.[62] The expression and its equivalents ("kingdom," "kingdom of heaven") occur more than 100 times in the Synoptics alone. The present and future arrival of God's reign in a new, more powerful way on earth through the mission and ministry of Jesus encapsulates a large amount of what the Gospels remember Jesus as being about. In all of Paul's letters, however, the term appears only 14 times.

If we examine the Pauline epistles further, we discover that "justification by faith" is often viewed as their central theme, especially in 2 Corinthians, Romans, and Galatians.[63] Throughout Paul's writings, the noun *dikaiosunē* ("justification") appears 58 times; the verb *dikaioō* ("to justify"), 27 times. Compare these figures with 2 and 7 uses in the Synoptic Gospels, respectively, with none of either form in the Gospel of Mark. How do we account for this shift in emphasis? To begin with, the Greco-Roman world would have not been nearly as familiar with the Hebrew concept and background of "the kingdom of God," so its infrequency in Paul's letters to diaspora churches should cause no surprise. Second, the Greek term *dikaiosunē* ("justification") also means "righteousness" or "justice." It is the same noun appearing in the translation of Jesus's Sermon on the Mount in Matthew 6:33: "But seek first his kingdom and his righteousness, and all these things

---

[62] In addition to the works cited above, see N. T. Wright, *How God Became King: The Forgotten Story of the Gospels* (New York: HarperOne, 2012); and Christopher W. Morgan and Robert A. Peterson, *The Kingdom of God* (Wheaton: Crossway, 2012).

[63] E.g., Mark Seifrid, *Christ, Our Righteousness: Paul's Theology of Justification* (Downers Grove and Leicester: IVP, 2000); D. A. Carson, Peter T. O'Brien, and Mark A. Seifrid, *Justification and Variegated Nomism*, 2 vols. (Tübingen: Mohr Siebeck; Grand Rapids: Baker, 2001–4); John Piper, *The Future of Justification: A Response to N. T. Wright* (Wheaton: Crossway, 2007).

shall be given to you as well. "Righteousness" or "justification" therefore defines what God's kingdom comprises; the two concepts mesh rather than compete with each other.[64]

Moreover, frequency of usage does not always equate to importance. Many of the Gospel references to "kingdom" come in parallel texts, making the number of occurrences artificially high. The fourteen appearances in Paul are scarcely negligible. In Romans 14:17, the kingdom of God is defined, in part, as righteousness (*dikaiosunē* again). In 1 Corinthians 4:20, the kingdom is about power, reminiscent of the linkage of those two concepts in Mark 9:1.[65] Four times Paul speaks of someone's inheriting or not inheriting the kingdom (1 Cor 6:9, 10; 15:50; Gal 5:21), while five times someone in the Gospels talked about inheriting something synonymous with the kingdom— the earth in the age to come (Matt 5:5) or eternal life (Matt 19:29; Mark 10:17; Luke 10:25; 18:18). The list could go on. Conversely, righteousness even in the "Pauline" sense of a legal declaration of right standing is scarcely absent from the Gospels. Jesus's statement at the end of his parable of the Pharisee and tax collector carries the exact sense of many of Paul's uses: "I tell you that this man, rather than the other, went home justified before God" (Luke 18:14).[66] Matthew 12:37, referring to justification or acquittal by one's words, in the context of Judgment Day, affords another close parallel.

---

[64] See further James D. G. Dunn and Alan M. Suggate, *The Justice of God* (Carlisle: Paternoster, 1993; Grand Rapids: Eerdmans, 1994); and Elsa Tamez, *The Amnesty of Grace: Justification by Faith from a Latin American Perspective* (Nashville: Abingdon, 1993; Eugene, OR: Wipf & Stock, 2002).

[65] For additional possible allusions in Gal 2:9 to Mark 9:1 and the transfiguration narrative, see David Wenham and A. D. A. Moses, "'There Are Some Standing Here...': Did They Become the Reputed Pillars of the Jerusalem Church? Some Reflections on Mark 9:1, Galatians 2:7, and the Transfiguration," *Novum Testamentum* 36 (1994): 146–63.

[66] See esp. F. F. Bruce, "Justification by Faith in the Non-Pauline Writings of the New Testament," *Evangelical Quarterly* 24 (1952): 66–69.

But what about justification *by faith*? Four times Jesus uses the expression, "Your faith has saved [or, healed] you" (Mark 5:34 par.; Mark 10:52 par.; Luke 7:50; 17:19). In three cases an individual was physically healed but then also spiritually redeemed. Maybe a better translation would be, "Your faith has made you whole."[67] Jesus teaches a lot about judgment according to works but very much in the same way we will see James doing so—as a demonstration of the genuineness of one's faith, not as a substitute for faith itself.[68]

A final comparison draws Jesus and Paul even more closely together. Ephesians 2:8–9 reminds us that "justification by grace through faith" is the fuller and more accurate summary of Paul's key concept. And grace is extremely important to Jesus, even if the word itself appears infrequently in the Gospels. The parable of the prodigal son (Luke 15:11–32) forms the classic illustration, but the much less well-known parable of the unworthy servant teaches the flip side equally powerfully—our inability to merit anything from God (Luke 17:7–10). Not only are both Jesus and Paul sharply criticized by the religious "right wing" of their day for their views and behavior in this respect; they reply in kind. Jesus and Paul both reserve their sharpest rebukes for the religious insiders who knew better but nevertheless drew the boundaries of their faith too narrowly.[69] John Barclay compares Jesus's table fellowship with sinners and Paul's mission to the Gentiles and is struck by their congruity: "Both enact and express a paradigm of God's grace that is simultaneously welcoming to the

---

[67] Craig L. Blomberg, "'Your Faith Has Made You Whole': The Evangelical Liberation Theology of Jesus," in *Jesus of Nazareth, Lord and Christ*, ed. Joel B. Green and Max Turner (Grand Rapids: Eerdmans, 1994), 75–93.

[68] See further Yeung, *Faith in Jesus and Paul*; Alan P. Stanley, *Did Jesus Teach Salvation by Works? The Role of Works in Salvation in the Synoptic Gospels* (Eugene, OR: Pickwick, 2006).

[69] See further Craig L. Blomberg, "The New Testament Definition of Heresy (or When Do Jesus and the Apostles Get Really Mad?)," *Journal of the Evangelical Theological Society* 45 (2002): 59–72.

lost outsider and deeply challenging to the insider—challenging to the point of scorching away the secure marks of a bounded system."[70]

The Role of the Law

Few topics, if any, have commanded as much interest in the last generation of scholarship about Jesus and Paul than the relationship of the teaching of each to the Jewish law. It has been increasingly recognized that first-century Judaism was more diverse than some past eras of scholarship have acknowledged. By no means primarily pure legalists (belief that obedience to God's law makes a person right with God), they had large components of covenantal nomism (living *out* one's covenant relationship with God by means of the law) and ethnocentrism (the famous "badges of national righteousness," such as circumcision, the dietary laws, offering animal sacrifices in only one place [the temple in Jerusalem], Sabbath keeping, and belief that God had given them a uniquely holy land with the territory they occupied in Israel).[71] As a result Jesus's and Paul's emphasis on justification by faith must be addressed as not opposing a predominantly legalistic first-century Judaism but one that operated out of covenantal nomism or ethnocentrism.

But what of Jesus's and Paul's teaching vis-à-vis the written laws of Moses and the Hebrew Scriptures? Neither figure argued for the overthrow or abolition of the law. Jesus, in the paragraph-long thesis to his Sermon on the Mount in Matthew 5:17–20, explains that he

---

[70] John M. Barclay, "'Offensive' and 'Uncanny': Jesus and Paul," in *Jesus and Paul Reconnected*, ed. Still, 17.

[71] See the helpful survey of research in James D. G. Dunn, *The New Perspective on Paul*, rev. ed. (Tübingen: Mohr Siebeck, 2005; Grand Rapids: Eerdmans, 2008), 1–97. For perhaps the best balance between the major Reformation and so-called "new" perspectives on Paul, recognizing the strengths and avoiding the pitfalls of each, see Michael F. Bird, *The Saving Righteousness of God: Studies on Paul, Justification and the New Perspective* (Milton Keynes and Colorado Springs: Paternoster; Eugene, OR: Wipf & Stock, 2007).

did not come to abolish the Law or the Prophets. Yet neither does Jesus proceed with the expected antinomy that he continues to preserve them unchanged. Instead he uses the concept of fulfillment. Paul, likewise, in Galatians 5:14 sums up the entire ethical responsibility placed on the Christian as the fulfillment of the central Levitical command to love your neighbor as yourself.[72]

Unpacking this concept, both Jesus and Paul recognize that the moral principles enshrined in the Mosaic commandments remain an abiding authority for the people of God. Many of these are encompassed by the Ten Commandments, but there are plenty of moral principles elsewhere in the Mosaic legislation, and at least one of the Ten (Sabbath keeping) is defined as being part of the so-called ceremonial or ritual law in Colossians 2:17–18.[73] Jesus, likewise, so redefined Sabbath keeping that literal rest from work one day in seven would no longer necessarily be required (see esp. Mark 2:27 pars., 3:4 pars.).[74] Paul recognizes the same trap that beset those who often tried to catch Jesus out in his words—guarding against defining godly living as rule keeping or legal obedience to the "dos and don'ts" of the Christian faith (see esp. Gal 2:15–21; cf. Matt 19:3). Yet at the same time neither man promotes antinomian or lawless living. Paul twice mysteriously refers to the "law of Christ" as what binds him, without defining its

---

[72] Indeed, on the consistency of this theme throughout the New Testament, see esp. Thomas R. Schreiner, *New Testament Theology: Magnifying God in Christ* (Grand Rapids: Baker, 2008), 617–72. On Jesus and Paul, cf. also Stephen Westerholm, "Law and Gospel in Jesus and Paul," in *Jesus and Paul Reconnected*, ed. Still, 19–36.

[73] Douglas J. Moo, *The Letters to the Colossians and to Philemon* (Grand Rapids: Eerdmans; Nottingham: Apollos, 2008), 218–24; Michael F. Bird, *Colossians and Philemon* (Eugene, OR: Cascade, 2009), 83–86.

[74] See further Craig L. Blomberg, "The Sabbath as Fulfilled in Christ," in *Perspectives on the Sabbath: 4 Views*, ed. Christopher J. Donato (Nashville: B&H, 2011), 305–58. See also the entire collection of essays in D. A. Carson, ed., *From Sabbath to Lord's Day: A Biblical, Historical, and Theological Investigation* (Grand Rapids: Zondervan, 1982; Eugene, OR: Wipf & Stock, 2000).

contents (Gal 6:2; 1 Cor 9:21), but it appears akin to Jeremiah's new covenant, written and thus internalized in believers' hearts.[75]

Whatever else had or hadn't changed, animal sacrifices were clearly no longer to be a part of regular temple or synagogue worship. The Jesus of the Synoptics predicts the destruction of the current temple (Mark 13:2 pars.), the Johannine Jesus sees his resurrected body as the new temple (John 2:21), and Paul views Jesus's death as a propitiation, the sacrifice offered in the temple to appease God's wrath (Rom 3:25; recall Mark 14:22–25 pars.). Paul, like Jesus, recognizes the change in the dietary laws; now all foods are clean (cf. Mark 7:19). This means all people, even Gentiles, are clean and can be associated with on equal terms as fellow Jews (cf. Gal 2:14). Philippians 3:18–19 may also refer to those Judaizers who still insist on maintaining the kosher laws: "Their god is their stomach"![76]

A final example of the continuity and discontinuity between the law and kingdom ages can be seen in both Jesus's and Paul's attitude toward parents. Both recognize the abiding validity of the command to honor one's parents (Mark 7:9–13 par.; Eph 6:2–3) but place honor of God so far above family as to make statements that would have shocked standard Jewish sensibilities (esp. Luke 14:26 par.). In Mark 3:31–35 and parallels, Jesus redefines true family not as biological but

---

[75] Femi Adeyemi, "The New Covenant Law and the Law of Christ," *Bibliotheca Sacra* 163 (2006): 438–52. John Ziesler (*The Epistle to the Galatians* [London: Epworth, 1992], 95) surveys the main options and helpfully but more generally concludes, "The law of Christ is the law as brought to fulfilment in love, and as exemplified and taught by Christ."

[76] Confidently, John Reumann, *Philippians* (New Haven and London: Yale University Press, 2008), 519–20. More cautiously, Demetrius Williams (*Enemies of the Cross of Christ: The Terminology of the Cross and Conflict in Philippians* [London and New York: T & T Clark, 2002], 221–22) notes that 3:18–19 most naturally refers back to the various descriptions of the Judaizers earlier in the chapter, while leaving the door open for seeing these opponents as libertines, as many commentators do.

as spiritual kin.[77] He acknowledges those who are called to remain celibate for the kingdom of heaven (Matt 19:12) or who must respond to the call to discipleship so immediately and completely that they cannot return home to say good-bye to their family or wait to bury their parents (Luke 9:57–62).[78] Paul similarly recognizes that God calls some not to marry and thinks they will actually be happier and able to devote more time to Christ's service than if they had been weighed down with a family (1 Cor 7:8, 26–27, 32–35, 38, 40).[79]

The Gentile Mission and the Church

At times various scholars have tried to defend the claims that Jesus never envisioned going outside of the Jewish world of his day, that he preached the restoration of the kingdom to his people, and that he would have been surprised to discover that what emerged instead was the multiethnic church![80] Paul, of course, seems to be teaching about the church in most chapters in most of his letters. Can these varying emphases be plausibly harmonized? Yes, most definitely.[81]

While Jesus undertakes only one discrete segment of his ministry outside of Jewish territory—his so-called withdrawal from Galilee

---

[77] Cf. esp. David M. May, "Mark 3:20–35 from the Perspective of Shame/Honor," *Biblical Theology Bulletin* 17 (1987): 83–87. For just what an upheaval this was in its context, from a literary rather than a sociological perspective, see George Aichele, "Jesus' Uncanny 'Family Scene,'" *Journal for the Study of the New Testament* 74 (1999): 29–49.

[78] For a reasonably balanced view of Jesus's "asceticism," see Dale C. Allison Jr., *Jesus of Nazareth: Millenarian Prophet* (Minneapolis: Fortress, 1998), 172–216.

[79] Cf. Vincent L. Wimbush, *Paul, the Worldly Ascetic: Response to the World and Self-Understanding in 1 Corinthians 7* (Macon: Mercer University Press, 1987; Eugene, OR: Wipf & Stock, 2012).

[80] So classically Alfred Loisy, *The Gospel and the Church* (London: Isaac Pitman & Sons, 1908), 166.

[81] See further George E. Ladd, *A Theology of the New Testament*, ed. Donald A. Hagner (Grand Rapids: Eerdmans, 1993), 103–17. Cf. also Richard Bauckham, "Kingdom and Church According to Jesus and Paul," *Horizons in Biblical Theology* 18 (1996): 1–26.

(Mark 7:24–8:30), he certainly drops plenty of hints that his is not to be a mission exclusively for Jews, nor should the ministries of his followers focus on them alone.[82] In Luke 4:16–27, what irritated the Nazareth synagogue attenders the most was Jesus's pointing out God's preference for the needy outside of Israel in the days of Elijah and Elisha (vv. 25–27). In Matthew 8:10–12, Jesus declares the faith of the Gentile centurion to be greater than that of any of his fellow Israelites. He goes on to predict that many of them will take their places at the heavenly banquet while various Jews, who are trusting in their ethnicity as their saving virtue, will find themselves excluded from it. If the sending out of the Twelve (Matt 10:5–42) reflected ministry to fellow Israelites (see esp. vv. 5–6; cf. Matt 15:24), the sending out of the 70/72 (Luke 10:1–24) suggests a ministry to the entire world.[83] Of course, after his resurrection, Jesus is *clearly* commissioning his followers to go to the whole world (see especially Matt 28:18–20; Acts 1:8; but cf. also John 20:21 and Mark 16:15[84]).

Jesus's countercultural concern for Gentiles, moreover, is just a part of his larger care for and ministry to those who would have typically been deemed outcast by orthodox Jewish leaders. Other people in this category would have included the lepers and others with particularly contagious illnesses or those which made them ritually unclean, tax collectors and others deemed particularly notorious sinners, the poorest of the poor, women (to varying degrees), and Samaritans.

---

[82] See esp. Michael F. Bird, *Jesus and the Origins of the Gentile Mission* (London and New York: T & T Clark, 2007). Cf. also Eckhard J. Schnabel, *Early Christian Mission*, vol. 1 (Downers Grove: IVP; Leicester: Apollos, 2004), 327–48.

[83] The number 70/72 comes from the table of nations in Genesis 10; even the textual variants are based on the varying numbers of nations in the MT vs. the LXX. Cf. Schnabel, *Early Christian Mission*, vol. 1, 316–26; David E. Garland, *Luke* (Grand Rapids: Zondervan, 2011), 425.

[84] Though Mark 16:9–20 is almost certainly a scribal addition, the inclusion of a statement like that found in v. 15 still testifies to the centrality of the Great Commission in the early church.

Even scholars who find only a small portion of the Synoptic Gospels historical typically include a fair number of events and teachings that focus on this dimension of Jesus's ministry.[85] Paul, too, quickly imbibes a passion for the Gentiles and begins to teach that they should be accepted on equal terms as the Jews into the community of Jesus's followers. Galatians 1–4 combats the Judaizers who would reject this idea, Philippians 3 opposes similar intruders into the Christian community in Philippi, while Romans and Ephesians both stress the unity of Jew and Gentile in Christ throughout their letters.[86] As for the poor Paul's multiyear passion for his collection for the impoverished saints in Jerusalem (1 Cor 16:1–4; 2 Corinthians 8–9; Rom 15:25–28), not to mention programmatic remarks like Galatians 2:10 on remembering the poor, shows just how central this element is in his letters.[87]

But did Jesus envision the church—a community of his followers—carrying out his commands? Only Matthew uses the term "church" (*ekklēsia*) and then only three times in two verses (16:18; 18:17), but the concept of his followers acting in community pervades the Gospels. *Ekklēsia* regularly translates *qāhāl* (assembly, congregation—usually of the Israelites) in the Septuagint, while the sociology of the ancient Mediterranean world was much more corporate than individualistic, so it is not inappropriate to envision Jesus approving what Paul would unpack in detail in his ecclesiology. Jesus, after all, called his followers a "little flock" (Luke 12:32) of previously "lost sheep" (Luke 15:3–7 par.) and a new family (Mark 3:31–35 par.).

---

[85] E.g., Luise Schottroff and Wolfgang Stegemann, *Jesus and the Hope of the Poor* (Maryknoll: Orbis, 1986; Eugene, OR: Wipf & Stock, 2009); Greg Carey, *Sinners: Jesus and His Earliest Followers* (Waco: Baylor University Press, 2009). From a more optimistic view of what can be recovered about Jesus, see Craig L. Blomberg, *Contagious Holiness: Jesus' Meals with Sinners* (Downers Grove: IVP; Nottingham: Apollos, 2005).

[86] See esp. Schoberg, *Perspectives of Jesus in the Writings of Paul*, 64–136.

[87] Bruce W. Longenecker, "Good News to the Poor: Jesus, Paul, and Jerusalem, in *Jesus and Paul Reconnected*, ed. Still, 37–65.

These metaphors may be part of what lay behind Paul's use of the "body" imagery in 1 Corinthians 12.[88] As David Wenham sums up, "Jesus may not have seen himself as founding the church as we think of it today but he did see himself as gathering together the saved people of God."[89]

Women's Roles

Neither Jesus nor Paul would probably have thought of gender roles as a major topic in their ministries. Because it has become so in our modern world, it is interesting to compare them here. Careless over-generalizations have sometimes spoken of Jesus as the friend of women and Paul as the misogynist who stifled them.[90] But, in fact, their positions seem extremely comparable.

Jesus did indeed encourage women in numerous countercultural roles. He praised Mary for wanting to learn from him like a male disciple rather than following Martha's domestic preoccupations (Luke 10:38–42). He affirmed the woman at the well to such a degree that she became an evangelist to her own people (John 4:4–42). His relationship with Mary Magdalene is tantalizingly unspecified, other than that he cast seven demons out of her, and she became one of a small group of women who at times traveled with the disciples in their

---

[88] Although Greco-Roman philosophical and civil imagery may have also contributed. See Michelle V. Lee, *Paul, the Stoics, and the Body of Christ* (Cambridge: Cambridge University Press, 2006). For the view that, regardless of the background, the function of the metaphor in 1 Corinthians 12 is to create a countercultural community of reconciliation, see Yung Suk Kim, *Christ's Body in Corinth: The Politics of a Metaphor* (Minneapolis: Fortress, 2008).

[89] Wenham, *Paul*, 190.

[90] For a balanced response to this caricature, see J. Daniel Kirk, *Jesus Have I Loved, but Paul? A Narrative Approach to the Problem of Pauline Christianity* (Grand Rapids: Baker, 2011), 117–39. For an entire book just on women in Paul, see Craig S. Keener, *Paul, Women, and Wives: Marriage and Women's Ministry in the Letters of Paul* (Peabody: Hendrickson, 1992).

itinerant ministry (Luke 8:1–3).[91] She became close enough to Jesus to be with another small group of women who stood by him at the cross, saw where he was buried, went to the tomb early that first "Easter" morning, and reported what they saw to the male disciples. Jesus also forgave an unnamed woman of a notoriously sinful past and accepted her potentially scandalous overtures of lavish love (Luke 7:36–50).[92] But for whatever reason he never invited a woman to be a part of his innermost circle of twelve leaders in training—the apostles.[93]

Paul likewise had a remarkable number of female coworkers about which we wish we knew more. Phoebe was most likely a deacon in the church in Cenchrea and a patron of Paul's ministry (Rom 16:1–2). Priscilla and Aquila (vv. 3–4), a wife and husband team, are mentioned seven times in the New Testament, with Priscilla mentioned first in five of the references, an uncommon order in Paul's world unless she were a leader of some kind in their joint ministry, which at least on one occasion involved correcting Apollos in what appears to be doctrinal matters (Acts 18:26). Andronicus and Junia (Rom 16:7) are male and female names, respectively, who are jointly called apostles (NIV). Obviously they are not part of the Twelve, but Paul regularly uses the term in a broader sense, including as a spiritual gift (Eph 4:11). Given the root meaning of *apostolos* as someone sent on a mission of some kind, this couple was probably akin to what we would call church planters or missionaries.[94]

---

[91] See further Ben Witherington III, *Women in the Ministry of Jesus* (Cambridge: Cambridge University Press, 1984), 116–18; David C. Sim, "The Women Followers of Jesus: The Implications of Luke 8:1–3," *Heythrop Journal* 30 (1989): 51–62.

[92] See further Blomberg, *Contagious Holiness*, 132–34.

[93] Agreeing, from a liberal and a conservative perspective, respectively, that Jesus stopped just short of being a full-fledged egalitarian are Kathleen Corley, *Women and the Historical Jesus: Feminist Myths of Christian Origins* (Santa Rosa, CA: Polebridge, 2002); and Grant R. Osborne, "Women in Jesus' Ministry," *Westminster Theological Journal* 51 (1989): 259–91.

[94] On both of these passages, as well as those discussed in the next paragraph, see further Craig L. Blomberg, "Neither Hierarchicalist nor Egalitarian: Gender

All this must be kept in mind when we come to the so-called problem passages in Paul. Whatever Paul means by a husband's being "head" of his wife (1 Cor 11:3; Eph 5:23), it cannot preclude her from all leadership or teaching roles in Christian ministry, unless we assume Paul flatly contradicted himself. Because he allows women to pray and prophesy publicly (1 Cor 11:5), the silence commanded in 1 Corinthians 14:34 must also be contextually restricted in some way. The combination of verbs meaning "to teach" and "to assume authority"[95] in 1 Timothy 2:12 suggests the sole position Paul has in mind is the office of elder or overseer, which in 3:1–13 seems also, unlike the office of deacon, to be reserved for men. I have written about all of this at much greater length elsewhere;[96] my point here is a fairly modest one. On several different nuancings of these texts, the overall result is the same. Paul counterculturally affirms women's participation in the congregation to an unprecedented degree, given his Jewish background, but stops just short of endorsing a fully egalitarian approach. It is hard, therefore, to see how one can fairly drive a wedge between Jesus and Paul on this topic.

Roles in Paul," in *Paul and His Theology*, ed. Stanley E. Porter (Leiden and Boston: Brill, 2006), 283–326.

[95] The 2011 NIV adopted this translation because (a) it seemed to reflect what the rare *authentein* meant in this context; (b) it had been proposed by various complementarians and egalitarians alike (including at least as far back as Calvin) for either or both of the meanings "to exercise appropriate authority" or "to negatively usurp authority" (cf. KJV); and therefore (c) it did not foreclose being naturally interpreted in either of these lights, both of which have had strong scholarly cases made for them. All statements or resolutions to the contrary claiming an egalitarian rationale, motive, or meaning in this decision, are in error. No such statements have been authored by anyone present for the NIV Committee on Bible Translation's discussion of the matter, whereas I was personally present for the conversation.

[96] See also Craig L. Blomberg, "Women in Ministry: A Complementarian Perspective," in *Two Views of Women in Ministry*, rev. ed., ed. James R. Beck (Grand Rapids: Zondervan, rev. 2005), especially 147–75.

Christology and Discipleship

Maybe the most serious charge made against Paul by those who envision him as the true founder of Christianity is the one that insists he was the first to turn the Galilean rabbi, Jesus, into a divine figure. That Paul believed in Jesus's deity is beyond question. He regularly refers to him as "Lord," "Messiah" (in the most exalted sense), and "Son of God," as well as probably directly calling him God in Romans 9:5 and Titus 2:13.[97] The Philippian (Phil 2:6–11) and Colossian (Col 1:15–20) hymns clearly associate Jesus with the loftiest heavenly positions both before and after his incarnation.[98] But what did Jesus himself think?

Here if ever analysis is complicated by the views that the highest, titular Christology of the Gospels represents the later creation of the early church.[99] One risks arguing in circles at this point: Why do we know Paul contradicts Jesus? We know because Paul's Christology is so much loftier. But how do we explain the high Christology of the Gospels? It is a redactional addition. How do we know this? Because we know the historical Jesus did not hold such a high view of himself. How do we know that? Because Paul exalted and deified him later![100]

---

[97] Murray J. Harris, *Jesus as God: The New Testament Use of* Theos *in Reference to Jesus* (Grand Rapids: Baker, 1992; Eugene, OR: Wipf & Stock, 2008), 143–85. On Pauline Christology more generally, see especially Gordon D. Fee, *Pauline Christology: An Exegetical-Theological Study* (Peabody: Hendrickson, 2007).

[98] See, respectively, Ralph P. Martin and Brian J. Todd, *Where Christology Began: Essays on Philippians 2* (Louisville: Westminster John Knox, 1998); and Vincent A. Pizzuto, *A Cosmic Leap of Faith: An Authorial, Structural, and Theological Investigation of the Cosmic Christology in Col. 1:15–20* (Leuven: Peeters, 2006).

[99] Classically articulated in Ferdinand Hahn, *The Titles of Jesus in Christology: Their History in Early Christianity* (London: Lutterworth, 1969; London: James Clarke, 2002); and Reginald H. Fuller, *The Foundations of New Testament Christology* (London: Lutterworth, 1965; London: James Clarke, 2002).

[100] For rebuttals to the classic paradigm, see esp. C. F. D. Moule, *The Origin of Christology* (Cambridge: Cambridge University Press, 1977); I. Howard Marshall, *The Origins of New Testament Christology*, rev. ed. (Downers Grove and Leicester:

Of course, the circularity is seldom expressed so unguardedly, so it can easily be missed.

There are several ways to respond. One is to apply the standard criteria of authenticity in a painstaking way to the Synoptic sayings of Jesus and see what the Christological results are for those that have the strongest case for authenticity.[101] A second is to point out possible development within Paul's theology, so that not all of his uses of all the Christological titles equally reflect an unambiguous declaration of deity.[102] A third is to grant the premise, at least for the sake of argument, that the more explicit the Christology in the Gospels, the more suspect it is. But plenty of "implicit Christology" still remains in the Synoptics alone, which would not likely have been left as implicit as it is if the Evangelists felt free to "doctor" *all* their material. Precisely because it has not been highlighted any more than it has, it is all the more likely to be authentic even if other parts of the Gospels turned out to have been "tampered with."[103] We discussed this concept ever so briefly above. Here we may enumerate thirteen examples of this implicit Synoptic Christology in just a bit more detail.

1. The Gospel writers would not have invented Jesus's baptism by John because it creates the problem of his apparently having to repent of sin. Yet all the Synoptics agree that the baptism was the occasion of

IVP, 1990); and Martin Hengel, *Studies in Early Christology* (Edinburgh: T & T Clark, 1995).

[101] See esp. Darrell L. Bock and Robert L. Webb, eds., *Key Events in the Life of the Historical Jesus: A Collaborative Exploration of Context and Coherence* (Tübingen: Mohr Siebeck, 2009; Grand Rapids: Eerdmans, 2010); or, in popularized form, Darrell L. Bock, *Who Is Jesus? Linking the Historical Jesus with the Christ of Faith* (New York: Howard Books, 2012).

[102] See several of the essays in *Paul and the Gospels*, ed. Bird and Willits.

[103] See esp. Ben Witherington III, *The Christology of Jesus* (Minneapolis: Fortress, 1990), 33–118; and N. T. Wright, *Jesus and the Victory of God* (London: SPCK; Minneapolis: Fortress, 1996), 477–539.

identifying Jesus as both the Messiah and the Suffering Servant by the heavenly voice's allusions to Psalm 2:7 and Isaiah 42:1, respectively.[104]

2. Even fairly liberal scholars agree Jesus worked something perceived to be miraculous, especially in healing and exorcising people. They also agree that a bedrock, authentic saying links Jesus's understanding of his miracle-working ministry with the arrival of the kingdom (Matt 12:28 par.). But if the kingdom had come, then its King must be present—a Messiah with supernatural, miracle-working power.[105]

3. The poorly named "triumphal entry" (Mark 11:1–11 pars.) was embarrassing enough not to have been invented, since it led to no triumph for Jesus. But it clearly fulfilled Zechariah 9:9, a messianic prophecy about God's anointed coming in peace, not in warfare.[106]

4. The subsequent temple clearing (Mark 11:15–19 par.) would also not have been invented because it shows Jesus's rebelling against his own people's leadership rather than the Romans and creating a scandalous mess in the process. But the event makes sense only as a foreshadowing of the temple's destruction, which in turn necessitated another way to achieve forgiveness of sins, apart from the temple sacrifices. Jesus must have envisaged a replacement arrangement, which only God could authorize.[107]

---

[104] See esp. John P. Meier, *A Marginal Jew: Rethinking the Historical Jesus*, vol. 2 (New York and London: Doubleday, 1994), 100–116.

[105] For extensive detail, see ibid., 509–1038.

[106] Brent Kinman, "Jesus' Royal Entry into Jerusalem," in *Key Events in the Life of the Historical Jesus*, ed. Bock and Webb, 383–427.

[107] See, e.g., E. P. Sanders, *Jesus and Judaism* (London: SCM; Philadelphia: Fortress, 1985), 61–76 (without endorsing his belief in a literal rebuilt temple). For similarities with Paul, see esp. James Sweeney, "Jesus, Paul and the Temple: An Exploration of Some Patterns of Continuity," *Journal of the Evangelical Theological Society* 46 (2003): 605–31. Both envisaged Jesus and his followers as creating a spiritual temple even while the literal one was still standing.

5. Jesus's Last Supper draws on Passover imagery to explain his coming death. Particularly important is Mark 14:24 and parallels: "This is my blood of the covenant, which is poured out for many." Here are the more muted, symbolic actions to justify the later epistle to the Hebrews' more explicit Christology of Jesus as the once-for-all sacrifice for humanity's sin.[108]

6. Jesus declares that John the Baptist was the greatest person of the old age of humanity (Matt 11:11a par.). But who has the right to make such a sovereign declaration? Moreover, he speaks of himself as someone greater than both Jonah and Solomon (Matt 12:41–42 par.) and announces that the least in the new age of the kingdom will be greater than John (Matt 11:11b par.).

7. Jesus's relationships with the Jewish leaders disclose a stunning audacity. He claims to proclaim in God's name how to interpret the law they are trained and credentialed to explain while he is not.[109] Conventional understandings of the badges of Jewish national righteousness are in various ways challenged—especially the dietary laws, the role of the temple, the nature of the Sabbath, and the significance of the land.

8. Jesus must have had twelve central disciples. Given Judas's treachery, had he not been one of the Twelve and had Jesus not been known to have had twelve, he would never have been included.[110] But that number consciously associates the core disciples with the twelve tribes of Israel, as does Matthew 19:28 more explicitly. Jesus believes he is constituting a new, true, and freed Israel in the community of his followers.

---

[108] I. Howard Marshall, "The Last Supper," in *Key Events in the Life of the Historical Jesus*, ed. Bock and Webb, 481–588.

[109] See esp. Chris Keith, *Jesus Against the Scribal Elite: The Origins of the Conflict* (Grand Rapids: Baker, 2014).

[110] James H. Charlesworth, "Should Specialists in Jesus Research Include Psychobiography?" in *Jesus Research*, ed. Charlesworth and Pokorný, 440–41.

9. More than once Jesus declares that someone's response to him on Judgment Day will determine how God will respond to that person (Mark 8:38 pars.; Matt 10:32–33; Luke 12:8–9). But what mere mortal can play such a role as the sieve or filter determining who truly are God's people and who are not?

10. So, too, the manner in which Jesus claims to forgive sins goes beyond what a mere human being is authorized to claim. He bypasses the entire system of temple rituals prescribed by God himself and simply pronounces someone forgiven who has had faith in him (see esp. Mark 2:1–12 pars.).[111]

11. On numerous occasions Jesus applies metaphors to himself that in the Old Testament normally or exclusively are reserved for Yahweh himself. These include bridegroom, rock, director of the harvest, shepherd, sower, vineyard owner, dispenser of forgiveness, father, king, and one who receives children's praise (Matt 21:16).[112]

12. Jesus's use of the Aramaic *Abba* as a title of endearment for one's dad is, as we have seen, *comparatively* unprecedented (Mark 14:32). Who would so consistently speak of God as Jesus does, so casually and intimately (recall above)?

13. Even the little transliterated Greek introductory word *Amēn* for "Truly," so punctuates the Gospel narratives at the beginning of Jesus's sayings that he must have regularly used it. It gives an "up close and personal" take on how he viewed the authority of his teachings and deeds.[113]

There are still more examples of the implicit Christology of the Synoptics, but these should make our point clear. One does not even need to defend the use of Messiah or Son of God or Lord on Jesus's

[111] Cf. further Tobias Hägerland, *Jesus and the Forgiveness of Sins: An Aspect of His Prophetic Mission* (Cambridge: Cambridge University Press, 2012).

[112] Philip B. Payne, "Jesus' Implicit Claim to Deity in His Parables," *Trinity Journal* 2 (1981): 3–23.

[113] Daniel Doriani, "Jesus' Use of *Amen*," *Presbyterion* 17 (1991): 125–27.

lips for the Synoptics to disclose a rich amount of detail that can point readers in the direction of concluding that the historical Jesus even of just the Synoptics can be trusted to paint a credible portrait of Jesus of Nazareth. And that portrait complements Paul's nicely.

But what about Jesus's repeated insistence that disciples must be prepared to follow him on his way to the cross, to suffer with him and even die with him if necessary? They are to be slaves to all rather than lords, and the Eucharist not only memorializes Christ's death but shows the disciples' participation in it (see especially Mark 8:34–38 pars.; cf. also Mark 10:42–45; 14:22–24 pars.). They must die to this life in order to find true life (Matt 10:39; Luke 17:33) and be baptized with the metaphorical baptism of suffering that Christ will experience (Mark 10:38–40 par.). Paul's central motif of dying with Christ, as symbolized in baptism and the Lord's Supper (Rom 6:3–6; 1 Cor 10:16–21) follows entirely naturally from this emphasis, as does his participationist Christology of believers being united with Jesus in many dimensions of their lives (see especially Ephesians 1–2).[114]

The Role of Paul's Conversion

If Paul learned so much from historically reliable tradition of the kind preserved in the Synoptics, then how do we explain his emphatic insistence that he did not receive his gospel from any human source but only from divine revelation (Gal 1:11–12)? Obviously, elsewhere he does acknowledge following tradition (see esp. 1 Cor 15:3), so he must be referring to the main points of his understanding of Jesus. Clearly much would have become plain to Paul on the Damascus Road when the risen Lord appeared to him in the heavens. His Christology would have been transformed as he recognized that Jesus was the Messiah

---

[114] See esp. Schoberg, *Perspectives of Jesus in the Writings of Paul*, 128–41.

after all and not an arch-apostate. His soteriology would have changed from one based on Torah obedience, however its fine points were understood, to one relying on faith in Jesus apart from works of the law. Paul's ecclesiology would have been upended, as he recognized God's people now to be those who were followers of Jesus of any ethnicity rather than those who were born into the Mosaic covenant community or became proselytes to Judaism to attach themselves to that community. Finally, his eschatology would have changed from looking forward to a coming Messianic age to the conviction that the era of the Messiah had been inaugurated even without being fully consummated.[115]

Those four points alone would have created such a seismic upheaval in Paul's thinking that one can see why he penned Galatians 1:11–12. But beyond this, no revelations enabled him to learn the list of the eyewitnesses of Jesus's resurrection; the names of Jesus's disciples; Jesus's views on marriage and divorce, wealth and poverty, or any other of the wide array of details found in the Gospels. Paul did spend two weeks, though, with Peter and James only three years after his conversion (Gal 1:18–24); it is impossible to imagine their not filling him in on countless details about Jesus's life at that point.[116] Indeed, he would almost certainly have learned a fair amount of information even while staying in Damascus with various believers at the time of his baptism (Acts 9:19).[117]

---

[115] See esp. Seyoon Kim, *The Origin of Paul's Gospel* (Grand Rapids: Eerdmans, 1981; Tübingen: J. C. B. Mohr, 1984; Eugene, OR: Wipf & Stock, 2007). Cf. also Richard N. Longenecker, "A Realized Hope, a New Commitment, and a Developed Proclamation: Paul and Jesus," in *The Road from Damascus: The Impact of Paul's Conversion on His Life, Thought, and Ministry*, ed. Richard N. Longenecker (Grand Rapids: Eerdmans, 1997; Eugene, OR: Wipf & Stock, 2002), 18–42.

[116] Richard N. Longenecker, *Galatians* (Dallas: Word, 1990), 37–38.

[117] John B. Polhill, *Acts* (Nashville: Broadman, 1992), 238.

Conclusion

Paul had a profound influence on the history of early Christianity, to be sure. He systematized its theology to a considerable extent. He contextualized it for numerous Greco-Roman as well as diaspora Jewish contexts. He mediated debates, opposed false teaching, bent over backwards to bring people to Christ, and traveled thousands of miles, many of them by foot. For these efforts he often received little but hardship or persecution. Only the conversions he saw occur compensated for his suffering. But to call Paul Christianity's true founder misses the mark badly. Paul learned a large amount of information about the historical Jesus from early on after his own conversion and commissioning. He cited or alluded to a fair amount of that information in his writings, but one has to be familiar with Jesus's teaching to recognize all of the allusions, and some suggestions are more secure than others. The purpose and genre of letter writing was not the primary way, however, in which people learned about the details of Jesus's life, so we should not expect to find more of them in the epistles than we do. The Hebrew Scriptures were still the canonical authority, even if Paul increasingly interpreted them Christologically. His own sense of inspiration or guidance by the Spirit, like his awareness of his apostolic authority, similarly reduced any felt need he might have otherwise had to quote Jesus more frequently to back up his instruction.

A careful scrutiny of both Paul's ethical teachings and his eschatology discloses the most frequent clusters of references back to the sayings of Jesus. But a sampling of the two men's views on as diverse topics as the role of the law in the age of the new covenant, the mission to the Gentiles, the nature of the church, and the role of women in the young movement all show profound overlap as well. And where Jesus and Paul diverge, they complement rather than contradict each other. The same holds true for what many have seen as the central teachings of each, at first seemingly unrelated to each other—the kingdom of God and justification by faith. On closer inspection we discover that both Paul and Jesus promoted both concepts, even if to varying degrees, and that they are in fact intimately interrelated once properly understood. When it comes to Christology, the same major titles for Jesus appear in both corpora, while the implicit Christology of the Synoptics, even if every other strand of Gospel Christology be bracketed, by itself presents a sufficiently high messianic self-understanding by Jesus so that Paul's Christology can only be said to have built directly on it. Paul did have good reasons for distinguishing himself from the Jerusalem apostles on various occasions, but these did not mean the content of his message contradicted theirs. Paul may have been the "second founder" of Christianity but only by building on and in submission to the true founder—Jesus of Nazareth.

Part Four

The Rest of the New Testament

Chapter 10

The Non-Pauline Epistles—
New Testament Anomalies?

T he Gospels and the letters of Paul are by far the two best-known parts of the New Testament. Next probably comes the Acts of the Apostles. The letters not attributed to Paul in the back of the New Testament are the ugly stepchildren for many Christians, receiving not nearly as much attention. But a complete survey of issues surrounding the reliability of the New Testament requires at least one chapter of treatment for these documents as well. As we have seen in several places already, issues of authorship and setting beguile these letters also. But, as we saw in our last chapter with Paul's letters, allusions to the Jesus tradition also suggest important lines of continuity with the Gospels. As we saw in chapter 9 with Paul as well, although each writer of the non-Pauline epistles has his own distinctive and dominant themes, they are not at odds with the rest of the New Testament. They supplement and complement its better known parts, rather than contradicting them.

Authorship and Setting

We will proceed through the letters in one possible chronological order, recognizing that dating these documents, even following traditional ascriptions of authorship, is often more difficult than with the letters of Paul.

James

Early church tradition is nearly unanimous that the author of this letter is James, the half brother of Jesus.[1] Josephus (*Ant.* 20.9.1—after the governor, Festus, had died and Ananus became high priest) tells us that this James was martyred in AD 62, so obviously if the tradition is accurate, it must have been written by that date. Hypotheses about the setting of the letter, on the assumption of authenticity, tend to cluster around what may be called an earlier date and a later date. The earlier date typically places the letter between AD 44 and 49, making it probably the earliest of all the New Testament documents.[2] That later date places it in the early 60s just before James's death.[3]

The main reason for the debate is James's classic apparent contradiction with Paul on the role of faith and works. Where Paul stresses justification by faith apart from works of the law, even appealing to Abraham as his model (Rom 4:3, 9, 22; Gal 3:6), James is adamant that faith alone cannot save. It must demonstrate itself through good deeds, and James cites the identical text in Genesis concerning Abraham for

---

[1] Jerome and Eusebius, however, each know of a belief by some that the letter was published under James's name by someone else. See Dale C. Allison Jr., *A Critical and Exegetical Commentary on the Epistle of James*, vol. 1 (London and New York: Bloomsbury T & T Clark, 2013), 18–19.

[2] So, e.g., Douglas J. Moo, *The Letter of James* (Grand Rapids: Eerdmans; Leicester: Apollos, 2000), 25–27; Donald G. Guthrie, *New Testament Introduction*, 4th ed. (Leicester and Downers Grove: IVP, 1990), 753.

[3] So esp. Ralph P. Martin, *James* (Waco: Word, 1988), lxviii–lxxvii. Martin also postulates a later redactor putting the letter in its final form as we know it.

support (Jas 2:21–24)! Of course, many scholars, scarcely limited to evangelical ones, recognize that this contradiction is only apparent. Paul has trust in Jesus in mind when he uses the word "faith," and he knows that faith must work itself out through love (Gal 5:6). So, too, immediately after one of his classic statements on being saved by grace through faith (Eph 2:8–9), he adds that we are Christ's workmanship created for good works (v. 10). James, conversely, has Jewish monotheism in mind when he declares that belief in God is not enough, while the works he requires are those of Christian mercy. Once one understands the two writers' different lexicons, the supposed contradiction evaporates.[4]

But why would the two authors have made even such apparently divergent affirmations? One option is that one was correcting the other, but that assumes that one thought the other wrong,[5] which is unlikely if the two perspectives are harmonizable. A second option is that one of the writers was correcting a misinterpretation, probably a one-sided appropriation, of the other author.[6] If this is the situation, it is far more likely that James was reacting to a distortion of Paul than vice versa because almost all of the existing evidence suggests Paul was much better known and used earlier than James. This situation also pretty much requires the later date, just before 62, by which time Paul's major letters, especially Galatians and Romans, would have become

---

[4] See, already and succinctly, Joachim Jeremias, "Paul and James," *Expository Times* 66 (1955): 568–71. Cf. also Frances Gench, *Hebrews and James* (Louisville: Westminster John Knox, 1996), 106; and C. Ryan Jenkins, "Faith and Works in Paul and James," *Bibliotheca Sacra* 159 (2002): 62–78.

[5] So esp. Martin Hengel, "Der Jakobusbrief als antipaulinische Polemik," in *Tradition and Interpretation in the New Testament*, ed. Gerald F. Hawthorne and Otto Betz (Tübingen: J. C. B. Mohr, 1987), 248–78.

[6] So esp. Margaret M. Mitchell, "The Letter of James as a Document of Paulinism?" in *Reading James with New Eyes: Methodological Reassessments of the Letter of James*, ed. Robert L. Webb and John S. Kloppenborg (London and New York: T & T Clark, 2007), 75–98.

known well enough to be potentially misconstrued. If, on the other hand, James wrote in the 40s, then he could easily have written before any of Paul's letters were even composed, without any knowledge of the exact ways Paul would choose to phrase things. So he can scarcely be blamed for not phrasing things more closely in agreement with wording that didn't yet exist! This date would also account for the lack of any reference to the issues debated at the apostolic council in 49.[7]

But did James, the chief elder of the church in Jerusalem, especially after Peter left there for his own missionary activity, actually pen this letter? The earliest traditions about this James that are most likely to be reliable view him as representing a fairly conservative Jewish form of Christianity, of being widely respected and influential even outside explicitly Christian circles, a pious, law-abiding man, and a great prayer warrior.[8] All of these characteristics match features of the letter of James that have widely been observed. The letter is addressed to the twelve tribes in the dispersion (1:1)—Jewish Christians outside Israel. It continues to hold Torah in high regard (2:8–10; 4:11–12), while recognizing that it must be filtered through the grid of fulfillment in Jesus (1:25; 2:11–12). The importance of prayer recurs in 1:5; 4:2–3, 15 and throughout 5:13–18. It may be pure coincidence, but it is intriguing that, given how rarely James appears in the rest of the New Testament, the one significant address we have from him elsewhere (in Acts 15:13–21, 23–29) contains the expression, "If you [do such-and-such], you do well" (v. 29), exactly as in James 2:8 and (minus the

---

[7] Other data in the letter, however, may also point to an early date, so a conclusion is by no means dependent on the resolution of this one debate alone. See, e.g., Jim Reiher, "Violent Language—a Clue to the Historical Occasion of James," *Evangelical Quarterly* 85 (2013): 228–45.

[8] For a full survey, see John Painter, *Just James: The Brother of Jesus in History and Tradition*, rev. ed. (Columbia: University of South Carolina Press, 2004). Cf. also Hershel Shanks and Ben Witherington III, *The Brother of Jesus: The Dramatic Story and Meaning of the First Archaeological Link to Jesus and His Family* (San Francisco: HarperSanFrancisco, 2003), 91–223.

explicit condition) in 2:19. The Greek varies in Acts, but then Luke is probably translating James's Aramaic words there anyway. [9]

Why then do some scholars find James pseudonymous and written later than the lifetime of James the elder?[10] Four main reasons recur in the scholarly literature. First, it is argued, the style of the epistle represents a more elegant form of Greek, drawing on more sophisticated forms of Hellenistic culture than could be expected of a Galilean fisherman.[11] But this view represents about as blatant a classist and ethnic prejudice imaginable. Simply because a person does not have the opportunity for formal educational training in a particular language or culture demonstrates nothing about his or her inherent aptitude for language learning. Assuming James used an amanuensis, as almost all letter writers did, all that is necessary is that in the multi-ethnic context of Jerusalem where he traveled and/or lived almost twenty years before writing his letter, he heard the public rhetoric of enough Greek-speaking people that he picked up the language well enough to dictate it to someone else. Cultural idioms and references he used were never so technical that they were not "in the air," as it were, easily imbibable by someone accustomed to conversing with others even if only for the purposes of evangelism. And the early church had plenty of Pentecostal pilgrims who spoke Greek as their first language who remained in Jerusalem after AD 30 with whom James would

---

[9] For additional expressions found in both James and the speech attributed to him in Acts 15, see Karen H. Jobes, *Letters to the Church: A Survey of Hebrews and the General Epistles* (Grand Rapids: Zondervan, 2011), 153.

[10] For a thorough discussion of the issues, see Luke T. Johnson, *The Letter of James* (New York and London: Doubleday, 1995), 89–123, who concludes that James could well have written the letter.

[11] E.g., M. Eugene Boring, *An Introduction to the New Testament: History, Literature, Theology* (Louisville: Westminster John Knox, 2012), 439. But even Udo Schnelle, who favors pseudonymity on other grounds, recognizes that this argument no longer carries any weight (*The History and Theology of the New Testament Writings* [Minneapolis: Fortress, 1998], 385).

have mingled. Finally, it is possible that a later redactor accounted for a little of the literary polish.[12]

Second, some argue that the contents of the letter are not sufficiently Christian. Christ appears only twice, in 1:1 and 2:1.[13] The Spirit appears at most once, in 4:5, but *pneuma* there may well refer to the human spirit indwelling people and not the Holy Spirit at all.[14] Almost all of the ethical maxims that form the book's backbone can find fairly close parallels in pre-Christian Jewish and/or Greco-Roman literature.[15] On the other hand, nowhere does James mandate obedience to anything that formed part of the uniquely ritual or civil law of Israel, and his qualifiers for *nomos* ("law") suggest he is not just endorsing the 613 commandments of Moses (as the rabbis thought of them) unchanged. The law his community must follow is the "royal law" (2:8, perhaps meaning "law of the kingdom"—Gk. *nomos basilikos*)—of neighbor love.[16] This was first articulated in Leviticus 19:18 but also endorsed and elaborated by Jesus in Mark 12:31, 33, and parallels. This law is likewise "the perfect law of liberty" (James 1:25 KJV), a strange expression to use if Torah pure and simple is

[12] For most of these points, see esp. Scot McKnight, *The Letter of James* (Grand Rapids: Eerdmans, 2011), 31–34.

[13] Allison (*A Critical and Exegetical Commentary on the Epistle of James*, 382–84) reduces the list of references to one (1:1) by conjectural emendation, arguing that the words "Jesus Christ" were not in the original form of 2:1!

[14] For a wide array of options for interpreting the verse, see Richard Bauckham, "The Spirit of God in Us Loathes Envy: James 4:5," in *The Holy Spirit and Christian Origins*, ed. Graham N. Stanton, Bruce W. Longenecker, and Stephen C. Barton (Grand Rapids: Eerdmans, 2004), 270–81. For an attractive possible solution, see Craig B. Carpenter, "James 4.5 Reconsidered," *New Testament Studies* 47 (2001): 189–205.

[15] For a thorough presentation, see James R. Strange, *The Moral World of James: Setting the Epistle in Its Greco-Roman and Judaic Environments* (New York: Peter Lang, 2010).

[16] Cf. J. Alec Motyer, *The Message of James: The Tests of Faith* (Leicester and Downers Grove: IVP, 1985), 97.

still meant, since it has just been cited in James 2:10–11 without such qualifiers. The reference in 1:21 to "the implanted word" (ESV), combined with the continuities and discontinuities between James's teaching and Old Testament law, suggest he understood the new covenant to have been inaugurated with Torah written now on human hearts.[17] Schnelle finds it inconceivable that James would not refer to Jesus as an example of suffering (rather than Job) in 5:11 if he were the Lord's brother,[18] but the point of the illustration is perseverance over years not severity over a matter of hours.

Furthermore, several references to "the Lord" in this letter probably refer to Jesus.[19] "The Lord's coming" in James 5:7–8 must denote Christ's Parousia. The uses of "the Lord" in James 5:14–15 may well refer specifically to Jesus also, since early Christians consistently prayed for healing in his name. This, in turn, suggests that praying, "If the Lord wills" in 4:15 may also refer to Christ. More significant, however, are the numerous allusions to Jesus's teaching scattered throughout all portions of James's letter. The clearest comes in 5:12 ("Do not swear—not by heaven or by earth or by anything else. All you need to say is a simple 'Yes' or 'No.'"), which reads like an epitome of Matthew 5:34–37. But there are another 35 texts where an allusion could well be present, many times to Jesus's Great Sermon as found in

---

[17] Mariam J. Kamell, "Incarnating Jeremiah's Promised New Covenant in the 'Law' of James," *Evangelical Quarterly* 83 (2011): 19–28. Paul J. Achtemeier, Joel B. Green, and Marianne Meye Thompson (*Introducing the New Testament: Its Literature and Theology* [Grand Rapids: Eerdmans, 2001], 498) observe that "the 'Jewishness' of James turns out on closer inspection not to distinguish the document from that which is distinctly Christian, but to align it with the prophets of the OT and the teaching of Jesus."

[18] Schnelle, *History and Theology of New Testament Writings*, 386.

[19] See esp. William R. Baker, "Christology in the Epistle of James," *Evangelical Quarterly* 74 (2002): 47–57. Cf. also Carl R. Holladay, *A Critical Introduction to the New Testament: Interpreting the Message and Meaning of Jesus Christ* (Nashville; Abingdon, 2005), 473.

either Matthew 5–7 or Luke 6:20–49.[20] For example, blessing in trials appears in James 1:2 and Matthew 5:11–12, asking and receiving from God in James 1:5 and Matthew 7:7, God giving only good gifts in James 1:17 and Matthew 7:11, being doers of the Word and not hearers only in James 1:22 and Luke 6:46–47, God choosing the poor in James 2:5 and Luke 6:20, and so on. The claim that there is little that marks James out as clearly Christian, therefore, can be decisively set to one side.[21]

Third, it has been argued that this letter is not sufficiently *Jewish* Christian to have come from James. This argument sits uneasily next to the previous one that found James thoroughly Jewish but not sufficiently Christian. Usually what is meant is that there is little sign of the late first- and early second-century Jewish Christian sect known as Ebionism, the Christology of which was less than fully orthodox with Jesus as less than fully divine. It was also a form of Messianic Judaism that *required* Torah observance for everyone, for which there is little or no trace in James.[22] All this objection proves, in fact, is that James is orthodox, fitting squarely within the mainstream of the early Christian movement. And if it is *not* pseudepigraphical, then there

---

[20] Peter H. Davids, *The Epistle of James* (Exeter: Paternoster; Grand Rapids: Eerdmans, 47–48). This, in turn, raises the question of James's possible knowledge of Q, which is explored in detail in Patrick J. Hartin, *James and the Q Sayings of Jesus* (Sheffield: JSOT, 1991; London: Bloomsbury, 2015).

[21] See esp. Jobes, *Letters to the Church*, 183–99. Cf. also throughout Christopher W. Morgan, *A Theology of James: Wisdom for God's People* (Phillipsburg, NJ: P & R, 2010).

[22] But see Matt A. Jackson-McCabe, *Logos and Law in the Letter of James* (Leiden: Brill, 2001), who argues as strenuously as anyone for precisely such a Torah-obedient perspective and finds *that* a key reason for pseudonymity. Just about any Jewish or Christian distinctive is taken by some scholars as a demonstration of pseudonymity if they are committed to finding it. This tendency probably goes back to the hegemony of Paul in New Testament theology since the Reformation. If even Jesus can't escape being evaluated in light of Paul (as with Piper), we should hardly expect James to be exempt!

is no reason to look in it for theological developments from beyond the lifetime of James. Later Christian hagiography did occasionally portray James as fully keeping even the ritual law of Torah, but this is more likely an exaggeration and a legendary embellishment of his true character than sober historical fact. Scot McKnight's and Dale Allison's recent commentaries have nevertheless demonstrated how permeated in Jewish and Jewish-Christian thought James is, with both envisioning Messianic Jewish communities as the addressees, in which boundaries between Judaism and Christianity were still fluid.[23]

Finally, the comparatively slow acceptance into the emerging canon in the second through fourth centuries has been cited as a reason for James's pseudepigraphy.[24] But there are a few allusions to James in 1 Clement and the Shepherd of Hermas from the first half of the second century, showing awareness of and respect for the letter already.[25] Indeed, it is likely that 1 Peter and 1 John allude to and expand on James in the first century.[26] The supposed tension with Paul on faith versus works adequately accounts for the controversy surrounding its canonical acceptance; we hardly need to postulate pseudonymous authorship to explain that debate or vice versa.[27] The limited audience of largely poor Jewish believers experiencing economic

---

[23] McKnight, *Letter of James*; Allison, *A Critical and Exegetical Commentary on the Epistle of James*.

[24] Boring, *Introduction to the New Testament*, 439; Schnelle, *History and Theology of New Testament Writings*, 387.

[25] For charts of the most noteworthy parallels, see Dan G. McCartney, *James* (Grand Rapids: Baker, 2009), 21–22.

[26] For possible parallels in the full range of New Testament documents, see James B. Mayor, *The Epistle of St. James*, 3rd ed. (London and New York: Macmillan, 1910; Grand Rapids: Kregel, 1990), lxxxv–cix.

[27] But in ways not true for the Protestant Reformers, the early church's support for James was ultimately linked to its emphasis on faith plus works. Both Origen and Augustine "celebrated the letter for its ability to bridge the ethical injunctions of the Gospels with Pauline teaching on justification by faith."—David R. Nienhuis and Robert W. Wall, *Reading the Epistles of James, Peter, John and Jude as Scripture:*

persecution in their roles as agricultural day laborers at the eastern end of the Mediterranean[28] also means it would have taken a while for the letter to circulate and be valued more widely.

David Nienhuis stands on its head the traditional understanding of the relationship between James and second-century authors, thinking James was *very late*—around 150—composed to complete the emerging collection of "Catholic Epistles" (the non-Pauline epistles minus Hebrews). This collection was then canonized to balance out a one-sided appropriation of the Pauline letter collection. Nienhuis also observes how different the James of the epistle is from his portrayal in later Christian tradition as following the ritual law. So he assumes the letter must have been written well after even the memory of the historical James was largely lost.[29] Yet one would have expected a pseudepigrapher to make this letter conform more closely to the James of history, if he truly were a pious, fully Torah-observant Jew. More likely, again, it is the tradition that is exaggerated. As for the argument that those later legends say nothing about James writing this letter, most later traditions about *any* of the apostles and their associates say nothing about their letter-writing activity. It appears that travels, evangelism, and miraculous exploits were the order of the day for the genre of apocryphal Acts and related literature.

Dan McCartney highlights five features typically present in known pseudepigraphy that are not normally even alleged to be present in James. There is no elaboration of the author's identity or authority;

The Shaping and Shape of a Canonical Collection (Grand Rapids: Eerdmans, 2013), 78–79.

[28] A perspective best highlighted in Elsa Tamez, *The Scandalous Message of James: Faith Without Works Is Dead,* rev. ed. (New York: Crossroad, 2002); and Pedrito U. Maynard-Reid, *Poverty and Wealth in James* (Maryknoll: Orbis, 1987; Eugene, OR: Wipf & Stock, 2004).

[29] David R. Nienhuis, *Not by Paul Alone: The Formation of the Catholic Epistle Collection and the Christian Canon* (Waco: Baylor University Press, 2007).

this James is just a servant/slave of Jesus (1:1)! There are no warnings against heresies or false teachings afoot. There is no emphasis on or appeal to tradition. There is no demand for submission to proper authorities, and there is no apparent delay of Christ's return.[30]

The letter of James should be accepted as authentic and probably as the oldest existing work of distinctively Christian literature. It preserves the wisdom tradition of Old Testament poetry, the radical edge of Old Testament prophecy, and a voice that is faithful to the ethics of Jesus. If Martin Luther vacillated over its value when he was combatting an overemphasis on works-righteousness within medieval Catholicism,[31] we should welcome it today in an age of easy believism, at least in the Western world. For those questioning whether the teachings of Jesus in the Gospels rely on early, accurate tradition, the numerous allusions in existence already in the mid-to-late forties, perhaps a scant fifteen years after Jesus's life and death, should inspire considerable confidence.[32]

Hebrews

Here we may proceed much more rapidly. The ancient Greek manuscripts of Hebrews make no claim for the authorship of this letter. The title in the King James Version, "The Epistle of Paul the Apostle" prior to the words "to the Hebrews" is not a translation from any Greek manuscript but an editorial guess based on one common

---

[30] McCartney, *James*, 30.

[31] Many summaries of Luther's perspectives do not do justice to the complexity of his opinion. Luther's real complaint was that there was not enough of the "gospel" in James. See Donald A. Hagner, *The New Testament: A Historical and Theological Introduction* (Grand Rapids: Baker, 2012), 683–84; David B. Gowler, *James through the Centuries* (Oxford and Malden, MA: Wiley Blackwell, 2014), 177–78.

[32] Cf. esp. Peter H. Davids, "James and Jesus," in *Gospel Perspectives*, vol. 5, ed. David Wenham (Sheffield: JSOT, 1985; Eugene, OR: Wipf & Stock, 2004), 63–84.

ancient Christian tradition.[33] The KJV also contains in a subscript at the end of the letter, "written to the Hebrews from Italy by Timothy," presumably imagining him to be the amanuensis and letter carrier on the basis of 13:23b, but these words correspond to nothing in any Greek manuscripts either. To be accurate, therefore, one should refer to this document as anonymous, like the four Gospels and Acts. Issues of pseudonymity do not come into play.[34]

Is there any reason to treat Hebrews at all, then, in a book on the historical reliability of the New Testament? To the extent that a later chapter will discuss the formation of the Christian canon, yes. If we do not know who wrote the letter, how could it pass the test of apostolicity (authored by an apostle or a close associate of an apostle) for inclusion in the New Testament? The answer is relatively straight-forward. The ancient church likewise debated the issue of author-ship. Many did hold to Pauline authorship,[35] though that is almost universally dismissed today on grounds that need not detain us here.[36] Those who supported someone else suggested Clement, Barnabas, Silas, or Luke. For the most part these claims came *not* in debates explicitly about canonization but in broader discussions of the

---

[33] Mark A. Powell, *Introducing the New Testament: A Historical, Literary, and Theological Survey* (Grand Rapids: Baker, 2009), 431.

[34] Unless one argues that 13:20–25 was written to make the work look Pauline from the outset, in which case it could be treated as a pseudepigraphon. So Clare K. Rothschild, *Hebrews as Pseudepigraphon: The History and Significance of the Pauline Attribution of Hebrews* (Tübingen: Mohr Siebeck, 2009).

[35] Beginning at least as early as p^{46} at the end of the second century, which places Hebrews between Romans and 1 Corinthians (according to the principle of decreasing length).

[36] An important exception is David A. Black, "On the Pauline Authorship of Hebrews (Part 1): Overlooked Affinities Between Hebrews and Paul," *Faith and Mission* 16.2 (1999): 32–51; and David A. Black, "Who Wrote Hebrews? The Internal and External Evidence Reexamined," *Faith and Mission* 18.2 (2001): 3–26.

composition of the earliest Christian writings.[37] So when one looks at the list of names and recognizes that every person put forward as a possible author was a close associate of Paul, we see that the criterion of apostolicity was fulfilled.[38]

What about historical information contained within Hebrews? There is not a lot, but what appears is accurate enough. References to the roles of angels (1:5–14), the creation of humanity to exercise godly stewardship over the earth (2:5–13), Jesus's temptations both in the wilderness and the garden of Gethsemane (2:14–18), the roles of Moses and Joshua respectively in leading the children of Israel out of Egypt and into the Promised Land (3:1–11; 4:8–11), the rebellion and punishment of many in the wilderness (3:12–4:7), the role of the Levitical and Aaronic priesthoods (5:1–4; 7:11–13, 20–28; 8:3–5), the appearance of the enigmatic Melchizedek (7:1–10), worship in the tabernacle (9:1–10; 10:1–20), and the roll call of Old Testament heroes of the faith (chap. 11) all correspond to what Jewish people in the first century knew from their Scriptures, with a small amount of supplementary information from Second Temple Jewish tradition.[39]

---

[37] For a full discussion of the various proposals, ancient and modern, see Paul Ellingworth, *The Epistle to the Hebrews* (Carlisle: Paternoster; Grand Rapids: Eerdmans, 1993), 3–21. Ellingworth's conclusion would be echoed by many: Luther's suggestion at the time of the Reformation of Apollos "is perhaps the least unlikely of the conjectures which have been put forward" (21), but that is hardly a ringing endorsement! Cf. Luke T. Johnson, *Hebrews: A Commentary* (Louisville and London: Westminster John Knox, 2006), 44: "with just enough support to make it plausible."

[38] Modern scholarly suggestions have ranged more widely, but none has garnered much support: Jude, Stephen, Philip the deacon, Aristion, Priscilla, Mary (the mother of Jesus), and Epaphras (Ellingworth, *Epistle to the Hebrews*, 17–20).

[39] But filtered through a distinctively Christian grid of interpretation. See Elke Tönges, "The Epistle to the Hebrews as a 'Jesus-Midrash,'" in *Hebrews: Contemporary Methods—New Insights*, ed. Gabrielle Gelardini (Leiden and Boston: Brill, 2005), 89–105.

A few anomalies have generated a flurry of research. That angels helped Moses in mediating the law between heaven and earth (Heb 2:2) was a staple of Jewish tradition (cf. also Acts 7:53 and Gal 3:19), even though it is not mentioned in the Hebrew Scriptures.[40] Hebrews 5:7 could be taken to mean God heard Christ's prayers and saved him from the crucifixion but, given this letter's frequent references to his atoning death elsewhere (2:9, 14–15; 7:27; 9:14, 28; 10:10, 12–14; 12:2), that hardly seems possible. Much more likely, our author means that God saved him from remaining dead by raising him again to life.[41] The puzzling descriptors of Melchizedek in 7:3 as "without father or mother, without genealogy, without beginning of days or end of life" should probably be taken to mean without *record* of any of these, so that his priesthood is not based on his ancestral lineage nor passed along to his biological progeny.[42] It is hard to imagine any author as steeped in the Old Testament as the author of Hebrews not knowing that the altar of incense was in the court immediately outside the holy of holies rather than inside of it, as 9:4a seems to suggest. The verb usually translated "had" here may therefore mean "belonged" in this context, just as 1 Kings 6:22 describes this altar as belonging to the inner sanctuary even while not actually positioned in it.[43] Finally, although not all of the sufferings of the heroes of the faith in Hebrews 11 appear in the Old Testament, the other ones are mentioned somewhere in Jewish tradition.[44] By citing them, our author is not claiming

---

[40] For the text, especially in Jubilees, see Harold W. Attridge, *The Epistle to the Hebrews* (Philadelphia: Fortress, 1989), 65 n. 28.

[41] Ellingworth, *Epistle to the Hebrews*, 286–91.

[42] So NLT, GNB, and God's Word to the Nations. Cf. M. J. Paul, "The Order of Melchizedek (Ps 110:4 and Heb 7:3)," *Westminster Theological Journal* 49 (1987): 207.

[43] Donald Guthrie, *The Letter to the Hebrews*, rev. ed. (Leicester: IVP; Grand Rapids: Eerdmans, 1983), 180.

[44] For fullest detail, see Pamela M. Eisenbaum, *The Jewish Heroes of Christian History: Hebrews 11 in Literary Context* (Atlanta: Scholars, 1997).

that the apocryphal or pseudepigraphal works in which they are found are inspired or even entirely accurate, merely that he believed in the truth of these particular details of the suffering of Old Testament saints.

The only other question for a survey of historical reliability worth mentioning is the setting envisioned for the audience of the epistle. Is it one that ever actually existed? Chapter 12:4 contains the enigmatic reminder to the addressees that "in your struggle against sin, you have not yet resisted to the point of shedding your blood." If the author is speaking about resisting the temptation to sin, it is hard to imagine what he could have in mind by "to the point of shedding your blood." If the sin is that which those persecuting these Christians are committing by their oppressive activity, then the statement makes perfect sense as a declaration that no one has yet been martyred for their faith.[45] In 13:24, "Those from Italy send you their greetings," could mean people with the author in Italy greeting churches somewhere else in the empire. But the preposition *apo* (which can also mean "away from") a little more naturally suggests that the author and his Christian companions are writing to Italy from some other location.[46]

With Italy as the province dominated by Rome, and the first government-sponsored persecution against Christians, beginning under Nero in 64, affecting believers in Rome and scattered other parts of the Italian peninsula, it seems best to view the letter as written to Jewish Christians in Rome prior to the outbreak of the persecution in 64 that produced numerous Christian martyrs. Chapter 10:34 then falls into place as an allusion to the time when Jews, including Jewish believers, were expelled from Rome due to the edict of Claudius in 49. That is the only obvious time when they would have had property

---

[45] Jobes, *Letters to the Church*, 34; Hagner, *New Testament*, 651–52.

[46] Cf. R. McL. Wilson, *Hebrews* (London: Marshall, Morgan & Scott; Grand Rapids: Eerdmans, 1987), 9–12.

confiscated because the government took over their abandoned homes. All this adds up to a probable date just before 64 as circumstances are becoming bleaker for believers in Rome. Jewish believers would have been particularly tempted to revert to identifying themselves merely as Jews, thereby gaining freedom from having to worship the emperor because they were considered a *religio licita* by Rome. To the extent that far more Gentiles than Jews were becoming Christians by this time, those who maintained their explicit allegiance to Jesus were no longer being viewed as just another Jewish sect and thus no longer exempt from persecution. So the author stresses that there is no source of salvation apart from Jesus and repeatedly warns his house churches not to shrink back from full-fledged faith in Christ.[47] He stresses that what he has written is a "word of exhortation" (13:22), a term found elsewhere in the New Testament only in Acts 13:15 where it refers to a sermon. Hebrews can easily be viewed as a sermon in written form, accounting for its lack of epistolary opening.[48] But its epistolary closing shows that it does have specific congregations in view. Because the letter makes so few explicit claims about its circumstances, it is hard to find much that would call into question its authenticity. For the same reason, neither does it contribute as much to the main topic of our book.

1 Peter

With 1 Peter we discover a clearer contribution. The early church unanimously agreed that Peter, the disciple of Jesus and leader of the early church, penned this epistle. The addressees at first glance sound as Jewish as the audience of James ("God's elect, exiles scattered"—1:1),

---

[47] For this reconstruction, see esp. William L. Lane, *Hebrews 1–8* (Dallas: Word, 1991), li–lxvi; Peter T. O'Brien, *The Letter to the Hebrews* (Grand Rapids: Eerdmans; Nottingham: Apollos, 2010), 9–20.

[48] William L. Lane, "Hebrews: A Sermon in Search of a Setting," *Southwestern Journal of Theology* 28 (1985): 13–18.

but they are much more likely to be of mixed Jewish and Gentile origin. Not only their location—five provinces in what we today would call Turkey—but also their background tips us off. Peter declares that they have spent enough time in debauched, orgiastic living (4:3–4). This is not a generalization likely to have fit many people of Jewish background, but the activities mentioned would have occurred frequently among Gentiles. Once again it appears that suffering is becoming more common for these believers, though suffering for doing good is still comparatively rare (3:13–14). Peter sends greetings from the church in "Babylon"—a code word for Rome (5:13)[49]—so the context may be almost exactly that of Hebrews (the early 60s), just with the location of sender (Rome) and recipients (outside Rome) reversed.[50]

Nevertheless, a fair number of scholars prefer to support pseudonymity, roughly comparable to the percentage who classify James or Colossians that way. Key arguments include (1) the excellent Greek in which the letter is written, (2) the primary use of the Septuagint for Old Testament quotations, (3) the absence of any of the theological tension that pitted Paul against Peter in Galatians 2:11–14 and the close similarities to Pauline thought found throughout (including the deutero-Pauline Epistles), (4) the lack of references to the historical Jesus, and (5) the impression from 1 Peter 5:9 that persecution

---

[49] Occasionally it is argued that this is a sign the letter could not have been written until the end of the first century because nowhere else before Revelation is Babylon used this way. But if 1 Peter should be dated to the 60s on other grounds, then *this* letter is the first example of this use. Someone had to be first; to reject a document for this reason would lead to a *reductio ad absurdum* such that no document employing the code could ever be authentic!

[50] Similarly, Thomas R. Schreiner, *1, 2 Peter, Jude* (Nashville: B&H, 2003), 36–41; Wayne Grudem, *The First Epistle of Peter* (Leicester: IVP; Grand Rapids: Eerdmans, 1988), 33–38. Ben Witherington III, however, bucks the trend and mounts a credible case for a primarily *Jewish-Christian* audience, in *Letters and Homilies for Hellenized Christians*, vol. 2 (Downers Grove: IVP; and Nottingham: Apollos, 2007), 22–39.

is occurring on an empire-wide basis, which would never have been true during Peter's lifetime, since he was martyred under Nero in the mid-60s,[51] and no "fiery trial" (4:12 ESV) had occurred prior to Nero's lighting Christians ablaze as human torches. In addition, some would argue for (6) a more developed ecclesiology behind the letter than existed by the mid-60s, (7) the unlikelihood of Christianity having permeated these five provinces by this early a date, (8) the lack of numerous substantive allusions to events from Peter's life, and/or (9) the contradiction between Peter's ministering to Gentiles in 1 Peter and having been assigned Jews as his mission field in Galatians 2:7–8.[52]

On the other hand, as we have already seen, it is impossible to determine how fluent Peter might have become, especially orally, in the dominant language of the regions in which he may have ministered for twenty years already (if he left Israel ca. 42–44 and wrote from Rome ca. 62–64). We have seen that Acts 4:13 does not mean Peter was unschooled, much less illiterate, but rather not formally trained as a rabbi. Thomas Schreiner rightly warns that "we must beware of an educational snobbery that refuses to recognize the intellectual and literary gifts of those in business."[53] Karen Jobes, moreover, has argued that the Greek of 1 Peter shows signs of "bilingual interference that is consistent with a Semitic author for whom Greek is a second language." When this affects syntax—in this instance, the use of prepositions, the genitive personal pronoun, the position of attributive adjectives and the use of the dative case—we appear to be

---

[51] See esp. Markus Bockmuehl, "Peter's Death in Rome: Back to Front and Upside Down," *Scottish Journal of Theology* 60 (2007): 1–23. J. Ramsey Michaels (*1 Peter* [Waco: Word, 1988], lvii–lxvii) is a rare scholar who finds the evidence insufficient to support this early a date for Peter's death and therefore holds the door open both to Petrine authorship and a post-70 date.

[52] For details, see esp. John H. Elliott, *1 Peter* (New York and London: Doubleday, 2000), 120–23.

[53] Schreiner, *1, 2 Peter, Jude*, 34.

on particularly secure ground. These features emerge almost subconsciously for a writer and are difficult to imitate.[54] Use of the Greek translation of the Hebrew Scriptures would have been only natural in the diaspora, where even the majority of Jews no longer used Hebrew or Aramaic. Peter wrote to be understood by his audiences.

As for (3), nothing in Galatians or anywhere else in the New Testament suggests the conflict between Peter and Paul was anything other than short-lived, despite the scholarly tradition that has tried to pit them against each other for life, with schools of followers perpetuating that division even after their deaths![55] There is some definite irony when one observes the same critics objecting to the authenticity of a letter attributed to Paul because of its differences from other letters of Paul now objecting to the authenticity of a letter attributed to Peter because of its similarities to Paul. Apparently one author is never allowed to express himself differently in different contexts, and two authors are never allowed to agree with each other very much! With respect to (4), we have already spent the better part of the last chapter showing both (a) why Christian epistles weren't the place to expect numerous citations of the teachings of Jesus, and (b) that a good smattering of allusions does in fact dot the letters of Paul. Both principles apply likewise to 1 Peter. The genre and purpose of the letter do not lend themselves to numerous quotations from the Jesus tradition, but a fair number of possible allusions do emerge.

Examples begin as early as 1 Peter 1:4 (cf. Luke 12:33); 1:8 (cf. John 20:29); 1:13 (cf. Luke 12:35); 1:17 (cf. Matt 6:9); and 1:23 (cf. John 3:3, 7). Sometimes larger chunks of Jesus's teaching appear to be alluded to. Peter's teaching on taxes and the government in 1 Peter 2:13–17 recalls Matthew 17:24–27. His appeal to Jesus's example of nonretaliation in 1

---

[54] Karen H. Jobes, *1 Peter* (Grand Rapids: Baker, 2005), 7; cf. 325–38.

[55] Beginning with F. C. Baur and the famous Tübingen School of the mid-nineteenth century.

Peter 2:18–23 closely parallels Jesus's teaching in Luke 6:27–36. Being blessed when persecuted for being a Christian (1 Pet 4:13–14) reminds us of the climax of the Matthean beatitudes (Matt 5:10–11). The lists continue.[56] Altogether Gerhard Maier finds 18 pairs of parallels "probable" evidence of awareness of an accurate Jesus tradition and another eight pairs of parallels "possible."[57] To the extent that some of these come from John as well as the Synoptics, we may speak of a reliable Proto-Johannine tradition circulating already too.

Concerning (5), Peter refers to believers throughout the world undergoing similar sufferings. This would not at all have depicted the pogrom by Nero, which was limited largely to the Italian peninsula. But then neither the persecution unleashed by Domitian in the 90s nor that initiated by Trajan in the 110s were so widespread as to span the known world or even the empire. It is much more likely that Peter has in mind the more informal, homegrown hostilities that did seem to plague the preaching of the gospel just about anywhere it made effective inroads. In this case it could refer to the situation throughout the empire already before the Neronic persecution began. "Fiery" in 4:12 is probably a metaphor for "painful" (so NIV). Achtemeier nicely summarizes the conclusions of many even outside of evangelical circles:

> The persecutions faced by the readers of 1 Peter were in the nature of the case due more to unofficial harassment than to official policy, more local than regional, and more at the imitation of the general populace as the result of a reaction against the lifestyle of the Christians than at the initiation of Roman

---

[56] Hagner, *New Testament*, 693–94.

[57] Gerhard Maier, "Jesustradition im 1. Petrusbrief?" in *Gospel Perspectives*, vol. 5, ed. Wenham, 85–128.

officials because of some general policy of seeking out and punishing Christians.[58]

Questions about the authorship of 1 Peter are complicated further by the reference in 5:12 to Peter's having written "with the help of Silas [lit., Silvanus]." Many have wondered if that phrase meant Silas was not merely an amanuensis but someone given the freedom to write Peter's thoughts in his own words. And since Silas was a companion of Paul, parallels to Pauline language could emerge all the more naturally. On the other hand, outside the New Testament, writing "through" a person (*dia* + the genitive of the person) normally means using someone not as a secretary but as a letter carrier and interpreter. Of course, that doesn't mean Silas (or someone else) could not have functioned as an amanuensis with a certain measure of literary freedom, just that 5:12 is not making that specific claim.[59]

The question of a developed ecclesiology ties in closely with the presence of domestic codes, extended now to include government and citizens (1 Pet 2:13–17), and elders and their congregations (5:1–6). But if these literary forms do not require a late date (recall above), neither does anything else point in that direction.[60] Only the office of elder is mentioned, a carryover from Judaism as we have seen, while there is still a focus on the charisms or gifts of the Spirit (1 Pet 4:10–11)

---

[58] Paul J. Achtemeier, *1 Peter* (Minneapolis: Fortress, 1996), 35–36. For a good overview of the ways Christians were perceived and treated and for the underlying rationales, see Reinhard Feldmeier, *The First Letter of Peter* (Waco: Baylor University Press, 2008), 2–13. Travis B. Williams (*Persecution in 1 Peter: Differentiating and Contextualizing Early Christian Suffering* [Leiden and Boston: Brill, 2012]) argues that this more informal harassment did in various instances turn into local, legal accusations against Christians.

[59] See further E. Randolph Richards, "Silvanus Was Not Peter's Secretary: Theological Bias in Interpreting διὰ Σιλουάνου ἔγραψα in 1 Peter 5:12," *Journal of the Evangelical Theological Society* 43 (2000): 417–32.

[60] Cf. J. N. D. Kelly, *A Commentary on the Epistles of Peter and of Jude* (London: A & C Black; New York: Harper, 1969), 11–15.

as in Romans and 1 Corinthians. If James is criticized because its author does *not* call himself an apostle, 1 Peter cannot escape criticism when its author *does* do so (1 Pet 1:1)! If Peter spent much of the decades of the 40s and 50s evangelizing territories in between Israel and Rome, there would have been plenty of time for the gospel to permeate Pontus, Galatia, Cappadocia, Asia, and Bithynia, without necessarily overlapping with places Paul had visited. As far as links with the earlier periods of Peter's life go, this argument can be stood on its head. Wouldn't a pseudepigrapher be even more inclined to make direct tie-ins to try to convince others Peter was the true author? The brief reference to Mark in 5:13 fits the early church tradition that Mark wrote his Gospel based particularly on information from Peter while the two of them were in Rome (recall chap. 1). It could be argued that we have just the right balance of fit with what we know about Peter from elsewhere without its becoming heavy-handed and seemingly contrived.

Not much else from 1 Peter itself discloses details about the background of its author. In 1:1, he is an apostle. In 5:1, he calls himself a "fellow elder." For those who can envision Peter making only lofty claims for himself as the first bishop of Rome, this modest role could suggest pseudonymity. But a pseudepigrapher trying to pass himself off as Peter would probably be the one more likely to make only lofty claims.[61] If these are still the early 60s, and Peter is coming under increased pressure in Rome just as his charges are in Pontus, Galatia, Cappadocia, Asia, and Bithynia (1:1), "fellow elder" would be a natural way for him to describe himself. That he is also a "witness of Christ's sufferings" (5:1) does not necessarily mean "eyewitness." *Martus* means

---

[61] Even Achtemeier (*1 Peter*, 43), who opts for pseudonymity, acknowledges that "the very absence of identifiably Petrine elements in the letter argues strongly for some internal association with the apostle Peter; otherwise, it is difficult to imagine why the letter would have been ascribed to him," and therefore assumes the unknown author "drew on traditions historically associated with Simon Peter."

one who testifies. It would become the word for "martyr" after enough of the Christians who testified to their faith were executed for it. In 1 Peter it still means "one who bears testimony to the truth of the gospel."

The context of the entire letter is missional, a further indication that we are most likely in the first rather than the second or third generation of Christianity.[62] Peter's ministering to a mixed congregation of Jews and Gentiles counts against his authorship no more than Paul's doing the same counts against his. The division of labor in Galatians 2:7–8 was informal, possibly limited in time, and who is to say Peter did not begin with Jews he discovered in the diaspora communities he evangelized, only to discover as Paul did a greater door open among the Gentiles? In fact, nothing actually says he founded these communities at all, though obviously he has some important links with them.[63] There are additional phrases scattered around the letter that some have thought counted for or against Petrine authorship,[64] but no arguments appear as frequently as these we have just mentioned. One may decide that someone like Silvanus or some other member of a Petrine "school" played a significant role in the production of the letter, but there is nothing to prevent ascription of the epistle in its heart and soul to Peter.

Jude and 2 Peter

We treat these letters together because of the literary relationship between Jude and 2 Peter 2. A sizable majority of scholars believes 2 Peter to have depended on Jude, not vice versa, which makes the

---

[62] See esp. Christoph Stenschke, "Reading First Peter in the Context of Early Christian Mission," *Tyndale Bulletin* 60 (2009): 107–26.

[63] Luke T. Johnson, *The Writings of the New Testament*, 3rd ed. (Minneapolis: Fortress, 2010), 426.

[64] Ernest Best, *1 Peter* (London: Marshall, Morgan & Scott, 1971; Grand Rapids: Eerdmans, 1982), 51–54.

earliest date for Jude difficult to determine. Its midrashic form suggests Jewish roots, and suggestions of dates in the 40s and 50s are scarcely implausible.[65] But if the literary relationship between the two letters suggests any proximity in date of composition, and if 2 Peter has anything to do with the historical Peter, then we are looking at a date for each in the 60s. Plus, various scholars have seen the false teachers in Jude as antinomians who have distorted Paul's teaching on grace,[66] which would also require Jude to be at least as late as the 60s. We place the two letters here in our historical survey, however, because 2 Peter must come after 1 Peter, and the discussions of Jude and 2 Peter belong together.

Jude

Perhaps less is known about the origin and composition of Jude than any other New Testament document. An older generation often speculated about Gnostic backgrounds; today apocalyptic Judaism is often favored.[67] That these two movements had significantly different perspectives on numerous major issues shows how little we should actually claim we know with any confidence. We learn more about the teachers' licentious behavior and the Jewish characters and analogies to which they are likened than about the ideologies they promoted. The letter is written in reasonably good Greek, but we have already seen how few issues of historical background that settles (above).

One might imagine that with so little to go on, and so obscure an author as Jude in the opening verses, there would be few charges of pseudonymity. This Jude (Gk. *Ioudas* or Judas) is a "servant of Jesus"

---

[65] Richard Bauckham, *Jude, 2 Peter* (Waco: Word, 1983), 10–14.

[66] Boring (*Introduction to the New Testament*, 450–51) itemizes ten main places he takes to be Jude's deliberate echoing of Pauline language as well.

[67] Cf. Rudolf Bultmann, *Theology of the New Testament*, vol. 1 (London: SCM; New York: Charles Scribner's Sons, 1951; Waco: Baylor University Press, 2007), 170; and Jobes, *Letters to the Church*, 239–40, respectively.

(just like James) and "a brother of James" (so presumably another half brother of Jesus—see Mark 6:3). But why ascribe an early Christian letter to him unless he were actually behind it?[68] Eusebius quotes a tradition from Hegesippus that the emperor Domitian in the 90s summoned Jude's grandsons, thinking they were a political threat to him (*Church History* 3.19.1–3.20.7), which suggests they may have been part of a prominent family whose Davidic lineage was well known. They replied that they were mere workmen, tilling the earth and awaiting a spiritual kingdom. Nothing suggests even this much prominence for their grandfather thirty to fifty years earlier that would lead someone to write a letter in his name.[69]

A lot of attention paid to Jude has involved the claim that his letter epitomizes what German scholarship dubbed *Frühkatholisizmus* ("early Catholicism"), typically defined as that stage of emerging Christianity beginning at the end of the first century that was characterized by a dwindling hope for Christ's quick return, an increasing institutionalization of the organized church, and the transformation of "the faith" into a fixed body of doctrine. Thus verse 3 urges Jude's audience to "contend for the faith that was once for all entrusted to

---

[68] "Jude was too obscure a person for someone to use his name to add authority to a document, and if the point was to add authority to the document surely Jude's being Jesus' brother would have been mentioned."—Ben Witherington III (*Letters and Homilies for Jewish Christians: A Socio-Rhetorical Commentary on Hebrews, James and Jude* (Downers Grove: IVP; Nottingham: Apollos, 2007), 571. Cf. also Peter H. Davids, *II Peter and Jude: A Handbook on the Greek Text* (Waco: Baylor University Press, 2011), xviii–xix.

[69] For a full treatment of *Jude and the Relatives of Jesus in the Early Church*, see the book so entitled by Richard Bauckham (Edinburgh: T & T Clark, 1990), who also defends this letter's authenticity on these and other grounds. Earl J. Richard (*Reading 1 Peter, Jude, and 2 Peter: A Literary and Theological Commentary* [Macon: Smyth & Helwys, 2000], 237) argues that identifying Jude as the brother of James links the pseudonymous author of this letter with the successful pseudepigraphy of the earlier letter ascribed to James. But he gives no rationale for why early Christians chose *any* Jude in the first place.

God's holy people." And verse 17 could sound like it is looking back on the apostolic age from a later time: "Dear friends, remember what the apostles of our Lord Jesus Christ foretold."[70] On the other hand, neither verse 3 nor any other verse in Jude defines the content of "the faith," and Paul already in the 50s can refer to "the word of the faith which we preach" (Rom 10:8, lit.) and call people to stand firm in "the faith" as their confession of the gospel (1 Cor 16:13). Verse 17 meanwhile could just as easily be a reference to what living apostles (since Jude apparently didn't think of himself as one) had already said earlier in their ministries (cf. the warnings against false teachers already in Galatians in the late 40s). Verses 6, 21, and 24, finally, show that Jude still held to a firm hope in Judgment Day, eternal life, and the glorious presence of Jesus that he would experience in the near future.[71]

More understandably, many scholars have questioned Jude's use of the Old Testament pseudepigrapha. In verse 9, Jude refers to an episode in the intertestamental work known as the Assumption of Moses. It has been lost, but we know about its contents from several other early Christian authors, and it formed part of the larger work of the Testament of Moses, much of which has been preserved.[72] We have no way of knowing if Jude thought Michael really did dispute with the devil over Moses's body or whether he used this illustration the way a contemporary preacher might cite a famous episode from Tolkien's *Lord of the Rings* to illustrate a point, without stopping to

---

[70] These exact references are what tip the scales toward pseudonymity for Lewis R. Donelson, *I and II Peter and Jude: A Commentary* (Louisville: Westminster John Knox, 2010), 162. Similarly, Burkett, *Introduction to the New Testament and the Origins of Christianity*, 446.

[71] "The letter pulses throughout with anticipation of the Lord's return, cares nothing for office or position, and deals with a dispute easily understood as possible in earliest Jewish Christianity."—William F. Brosend II, *James and Jude* (Cambridge: Cambridge University Press, 2004), 4.

[72] For details, see Bauckham, *Jude, 2 Peter*, 65–76.

make sure all in the audience understood the book was fiction, precisely because it was so well known.[73]

Slightly more complicated is Jude 1:14–15, which actually quotes 1 Enoch 1:9, when it declares, "See, the Lord is coming with thousands upon thousands of his holy ones to judge everyone, and to convict all of them of all the ungodly acts they have committed in their ungodliness, and of all the defiant words ungodly sinners have spoken against him." Does this mean Jude thinks 1 Enoch is inspired? No, Paul can quote pagan poets (Acts 17:28; Titus 1:12) without people drawing that conclusion. But here Jude says Enoch prophesied. Yes, just as John said Caiaphas prophesied (unwittingly) in John 11:51. In neither case is the source believed to be a *consistently* reliable mouthpiece for God. Still, Jude says, "Enoch, the seventh from Adam, prophesied." Surely that means he believed the historical Enoch actually spoke these words. No, the words, "Enoch, the seventh from Adam" come from the book of 1 Enoch itself (60:8) and can be taken as the name of the character in the book just as easily as the name of the ancient patriarch. In fact, in the ten Old Testament uses of his name, Enoch is never called "seventh from Adam," so this may be Jude's tip-off that he *is* referring to the character in 1 Enoch, not the figure in Genesis. All we know for sure is that Jude believed this one assertion in this famous intertestamental work of apocalyptic literature about God's coming with his angels to judge the ungodly was a true statement. It squares readily with canonical Scriptures like Zechariah 14:5, so that much should cause no problem.[74]

---

[73] Douglas J. Moo (*2 Peter, Jude* [Grand Rapids: Zondervan, 1996], 250) makes the identical point with the illustration of a contemporary preacher citing characters or episodes from *The Wizard of Oz* to illustrate a theological point. All listeners would recognize that no affirmation of historical reality was intended.

[74] Cf. Jobes, *Letters to the Church*, 257: "Jude does not have to think that *1 Enoch* is an inspired book or even a true book in general; he cites one small part of it that is in accord with biblical truth." Cf. Guthrie, *New Testament Introduction*,

Beyond these brief items, nothing in Jude significantly impinges on a study of the New Testament's historical reliability. One wonders how much of some scholars' efforts to marginalize Jude's contribution has been simply because it remains so out of sync with today's mindset of tolerating everything (except, of course, historic Christianity!). But those who "pervert the grace of our God into a license for immorality and deny Jesus Christ our only Sovereign and Lord" (v. 4) attack the center of everything good and decent in our universe to such an extent that the church must dissociate itself from those people when they continue to masquerade as true believers so the world will not confuse them with us. It may be counterproductive at times to use the more *ad hoc* and even *ad hominem* approaches that were a staple of the rhetoric of Jude's world, but for the sake of a credible witness, we should not continue to tolerate people in positions of Christian leadership whose practices and beliefs are so flagrantly, persistently, and unrepentantly anti-Christian.[75]

2 PETER

With 2 Peter we come to the most difficult of all the New Testament epistles to situate in its original context. Here for the first time appear not just modern questions about authorship but ancient ones, despite Peter's name firmly affixed in the manuscript tradition to the beginning of the text of the letter (1:1). Doubts about Petrine authorship were raised at least as early as Origen about the end of the second century (cited by Eusebius, *Hist. eccl.* 6.25.11; cf. also 3.3.1, 4;

914–16. Another option is that these intertestamental works were authoritative in some fashion for Jude's opponents so that he quotes their authorities against them. See Lee M. McDonald and Stanley E. Porter, *Early Christianity and Its Sacred Literature* (Peabody: Hendrickson, 2000), 544.

[75] "We can say that the message of judgment is especially relevant to people today, for our churches are prone to sentimentality, suffer from moral breakdown and too often fail to pronounce a definitive word of judgment because of an inadequate definition of love."—Schreiner, *1, 2 Peter, Jude*, 403.

3.25.3–4). Jerome in the late fourth century (*De vir. illust.* 1) likewise noted that many people rejected Petrine authorship.[76] Yet this did not keep Athanasius from declaring it canonical and acknowledging it to be widely held as canonical as early as in his Easter encyclical of 367. Ancient objections focused particularly on the lack of sufficient, early attestation of the letter, a dramatic difference in the style of the Greek from 1 Peter to 2 Peter (much more rugged and flowery simultaneously—i.e., touches of classical style combined with awkward Greek), and what seems to be a thoroughgoing Hellenistic theology, even to the point of claiming that Christians can share in the divine nature (2 Pet 1:4), just like various forms of Greco-Roman thought envisioned certain heroic individuals becoming deified after their deaths.[77]

In the modern era additional objections have been raised. The theology is supposedly too late for it to have come from Peter, inasmuch as he apparently died in the mid-60s (recall chap. 1). Much like the question of an apostolic Matthew's use of a nonapostolic Mark, why would a key apostolic leader like Peter have depended for almost a third of his work on Jude, the nonapostolic, comparatively obscure half brother of Jesus? If Jude wasn't necessarily early Catholic, surely 2

---

[76] Donald A. Hagner (*The New Testament: A Historical and Theological Introduction* [Grand Rapids: Baker, 2012], 722–23) observes that "no other book of the NT was accepted into the NT canon with more hesitance than 2 Peter, and no canonical book is so poorly attested in the early church."

[77] This was also the most influential text in the development of the Eastern Orthodox doctrine of deification, though unlike various pagan counterparts, it was never understood as humans sharing in God's or the gods' unique ontological nature. See Donald Fairbairn, *Eastern Orthodoxy Through Western Eyes* (Louisville and London: Westminster John Knox, 2002), 79–95; and Daniel B. Clendenin, *Eastern Orthodox Christianity: A Western Perspective* (Grand Rapids: Baker, 1994), 117–37. Other oft-cited features of Hellenism include its use of Tartarus for hell (2:4), the language of Greek moral philosophy (*aretē, eusebeia, enkratē*), and the destruction and renewal of the world (3:10–13).

Peter is.[78] After all, the delay of the Parousia appears centrally in this epistle. It is discussed explicitly in 3:3–10, but it is probably one of three main manifestations of an underlying "uniformitarian" world-view of the false teachers. If there is no supernatural intervention into the universe (3:4), then there is no prophecy or inspired Scripture, no final judgment at which God will hold people accountable for their immoral behavior, and no return of Christ—the three main theological topics addressed in the book's three chapters, in that order.[79]

In addition, 3:2 seems to look back on the apostolic age as part of the distant past: "I want you to recall the words spoken in the past by the holy prophets and the command given by our Lord and Savior through your apostles." Now, however, the "last days" have come when evil people arise and mock the prophecies while following a fully hedonistic lifestyle (v. 3).[80] What is more, enough time has elapsed that the author can identify a collection of Paul's writings as canonical Scripture (vv. 15–16).[81] But if Peter wrote 2 Peter, it would have had to be complete by the mid-60s, possibly even before Paul's last letters (or at least 2 Timothy) were even written. Indeed, when dates are selected for a pseudepigrapher to have penned 2 Peter, they often range well into the middle of the second century, making this

---

[78] Kelly, *Epistles of Peter and of Jude*, 235–36. Hagner (*New Testament*, 719–21) modifies this to "incipient early Catholicism."

[79] Bauckham, *Jude, 2 Peter*, 154–55, referring to the "eschatological skepticism" that has fueled "moral freedom." Edward Adams ("Where Is the Promise of His Coming? The Complaint of the Scoffers in 2 Peter 3:4," *New Testament Studies* 51 [2005]: 106–22) qualifies this so that the errorists might not have been denying Christ's return altogether, just not one accompanied by cataclysmic, divine intervention. Holladay (*Critical Introduction to the New Testament*, 510) thinks the delay of the Parousia itself is the underlying issue for the entire letter.

[80] Kelly, *Epistles of Peter and of Jude*, 235.

[81] Jonathan Knight, *2 Peter and Jude* (Sheffield: Sheffield Academic Press, 1995), 19–20.

the last of all the New Testament books to be written.[82] Perhaps most importantly, 2 Peter has the literary genre of a testament,[83] and other known testaments from Second Temple Judaism are all pseudepigraphical.

When there are early and not just modern objections to the apparently straightforward authorship claims of a biblical book, we should pay much more careful attention to their contents. Some conservative scholars, to be sure, have continued to maintain full Petrine authorship for 2 Peter, and they mount a respectable case. The external evidence in favor of Peter is still strong and much stronger than for any noncanonical Christian text that was occasionally put forward as a candidate for the canon.[84] If an amanuensis (whether or not Silas) *did* help put 1 Peter into the polished, finished form in which it appears, perhaps 2 Peter is the best Peter could do unaided.[85] Or perhaps Peter used two different scribes with different styles and writing abilities.[86] Alternately, Terrance Callan cites a "grand Asian" style of Greek that he believes 2 Peter has deliberately followed in this missive that explicitly calls itself its author's second letter to the same audience

---

[82] E.g., Terrance Callan, "Second Peter," in *First and Second Peter*, by Duane F. Watson and Terrance Callan (Grand Rapids: Baker, 2012), 136 (ca. AD 125); Donelson, *1 & 2 Peter and Jude*, 209 (between 120 and 150); Raymond E. Brown, *Introduction to the New Testament* (New York and London: Doubleday, 1997), 767 (130).

[83] Powell (*Introducing the New Testament*, 485) summarizes the four main elements of a testament as (1) "a heroic person offers a précis of his teaching or ideas"; (2) "the hero announces that his death is near"; (3) "the hero urges readers of the testament to remember his message after he is gone"; and (4) "the hero predicts what will happen after his death."

[84] For a complete collection of ancient canonical lists, see "Appendix D: Lists and Catalogues of New Testament Collections," in *The Canon Debate*, ed. Lee M. McDonald and James A. Sanders (Peabody: Hendrickson, 2002), 591–97.

[85] Dick Lucas and Christopher Green, *The Message of 2 Peter and Jude: The Promise of His Coming* (Leicester and Downers Grove: IVP, 1995), 240.

[86] Charles Bigg, *A Critical and Exegetical Commentary on the Epistles of St. Peter and St. Jude*, 2nd ed. (Edinburgh: T & T Clark, 1902), 247.

(3:1). While he still finds the letter pseudonymous, Ben Witherington uses the argument to make a closer connection with the apostle Peter.[87]

As for borrowing from Jude, if Peter thought the Lord's brother had found a compelling series of Old Testament and Jewish analogies for the false teachers Peter had to combat, and if as it appears their nature was similar to what Peter had to counter, why shouldn't he reuse a barrage of those analogies, especially if he knew that Jude's letter had been successful in its warnings? With respect to the delay of the Parousia, we have already seen that this was a theological dilemma in Thessalonica as early as about AD 50. With two thousands years' hindsight, we may chuckle at the thought of twenty years from the crucifixion seeming like a delay to early Christians, but two decades could easily have felt like a long time to those who heard their Lord intimate that he would return to them "soon" and who had no sense of the amount of time that might actually elapse. Second Peter 3:2 does indeed refer to the words of the holy prophets in the past, but these are most likely Old Testament prophets. The "ancestors" in verse 4 (literally, "fathers") are likewise most probably from pre-Christian Jewish days.[88] At the same time, "the command given by our Lord and Savior through your apostles" isn't even necessarily being referred to as in the past; if it is, many such commands would have already been given in the generation between Jesus' death (AD 30) and Peter's (ca. 65) so a later date for the letter is scarcely required.[89]

---

[87] Terrance Callan, "The Style of the Second Letter of Peter," *Biblica* 84 (2003): 202–24, following Demetrius, *On Style*, 38–124. Cf. also Witherington, *Letters and Homilies for Hellenized Christians*, vol. 2, 265–66, 273–74, who uses the term "Asiatic." It was a style designed to appeal to the emotions and impress on the listeners the importance of the topic.

[88] Norman R. Hillyer, *1 and 2 Peter, Jude* (Peabody: Hendrickson, 1992; Carlisle: Paternoster, 1995; Grand Rapids: Baker, 2011), 214.

[89] See further Michael Green, *The Second Epistle General of Peter and the General Epistle of Jude*, rev. ed. (Leicester: IVP; Grand Rapids: Eerdmans, 1987), 25–28, 127–29; Moo, *2 Peter, Jude*, 21–26.

Second Peter 3:15–16 does not say how many of Paul's letters were already known as Scripture. By 65, Galatians, 1 and 2 Thessalonians would have been circulating for fifteen years, while 1 and 2 Corinthians and Romans were eight to ten years old. Even Philemon, Colossians, Ephesians, and Philippians could have been known for three to five years. If Peter and Paul were both ministering in Rome, they could have seen each other repeatedly, and either one might have quickly recognized the inspired nature of the other's writings, well before their more widespread recognition in the church at large.[90] As for the testamentary genre of 2 Peter, it is not the case that all other Jewish testaments are pseudonymous, unless one by circular argumentation declares all other testaments in the Old and New Testaments to be the work of a pseudepigrapher. Plus, only 2 Peter 1:14–15 makes this letter explicitly testamentary; it is not dominated by themes of the supposed author's death and succession to the extent other full-fledged testaments are.[91]

Additional, positive reasons for supporting Petrine authorship for 2 Peter include the author's apparent eyewitness account of Jesus's transfiguration (cf. 1:16–18); the Gospels clarify that only Peter, James, and John visited that mountaintop with Jesus (Mark 9:2–8 pars.). At long last the time of fulfillment of the gospel was breaking into human history. The two different styles actually speak in favor of Petrine authorship because the would-be forger would have more likely done better in imitating Peter's style.[92] We think back to how one of the arguments against both 2 Thessalonians and Ephesians was just how *similar* their styles were to other pseudepigrapha especially

---

[90] Green, *Second Epistle General of Peter and the General Epistle of Jude*, 28–30.

[91] For other biblical testamentary works, see Mark D. Mathews, "The Genre of 2 Peter: A Comparison with Jewish and Early Christian Testaments," *Bulletin for Biblical Research* 21 (2011): 51–64. One could add in 1:3–13; 2:1–3; and 3:1–4, matching Powell's criteria (above).

[92] Schreiner, *1, 2 Peter, Jude*, 266 and n. 68.

when compared with 1 Thessalonians and Colossians, respectively. Furthermore, only here in the New Testament do we find the name *Sumeōn* attached to *Petros* (Simeon Peter—2 Pet 1:1), while in only one other passing reference (Acts 15:14) is *Sumeōn* used for this leader of the disciples at all. Yet it is the transliteration of the most Hebraic form of the name, more likely what Peter would himself use in a signature.[93] Despite numerous distinctives in vocabulary and syntax with 1 Peter, there are numerous parallels also.[94] Finally, plausible cases have been made for the false teachers that 2 Peter counters to be both Epicureans and Stoics,[95] despite those groups having held diametrically opposing perspectives on numerous topics. What these works actually demonstrate is how little we can know for sure about the letter's setting, but tellingly both groups of Greek philosophers had been around since at least the beginning of the third century BC, so no late date for 2 Peter is required if he was contesting either of them.

A mediating view has been suggested by Richard Bauckham. It takes 2 Peter to be pseudonymous but written by "an erstwhile colleague of Peter's [*sic*], who writes Peter's testament after his death, writing in his own way but able to be confident that he is being faithful to Peter's essential message."[96] Bauckham goes on to speculate that this might have been Linus, Peter's successor as the second overseer of the church

---

[93] Ibid., 260–1; Guthrie, *New Testament Introduction*, 820–21. In 1 Peter, perhaps due to the use of an amanuensis, the form of the name is simply *Petros* ("Peter")—1:1.

[94] For detailed lists comparing 2 Peter with 1 Peter and with several other early Christian writings, see J. B. Mayor, *The Epistle of S. Jude and the Second Epistle of S. Peter* (London and New York: Macmillan, 1907; Grand Rapids: Baker, 1979), lxviii–cxiv.

[95] See, respectively, Jerome H. Neyrey, *2 Peter, Jude* (New York and London: Doubleday, 1993); and J. Daryl Charles, *Virtue Amidst Vice: The Catalog of Virtues in 2 Peter 1* (Sheffield: Sheffield Academic Press, 1997).

[96] Bauckham, *Jude, 2 Peter*, 147.

at Rome.[97] We could modify this perspective and suggest that Peter had actually written some or all of the letter, but knowing his death was imminent, he prepared for someone else to finish it, polish it, write it up in his own hand, and/or publish it. This would make good sense of the puzzling 1:15: "And I will make every effort to see that after my departure you will always be able to remember these things." The word translated "departure" is *exodos*, which in various contexts can also refer to one's death. Verses 13–14 suggest that is precisely what it means here. If Peter realized his execution might occur before he was able to complete and/or publish this letter, then the role of his successor would not be to produce full-fledged pseudepigraphy but to put things in whatever order was still needed for posthumous publication.[98]

There would then be no deception, nor even "transparent fiction" in the letter's claim to be from an eyewitness of Jesus's transfiguration and to hear the heavenly voice (1:16–18). Peter, as we mentioned, *was* one of the inner three of Jesus's disciples permitted to experience that indescribable event. There would be no Hellenistic deification in 1:4, even if the language was chosen for contextualizing to a Greco-Roman audience. After all, the immediately subsequent context of verses 5–9 makes obvious that it is with respect to moral virtues only that Peter is envisaging Christians progressing in godlikeness.[99] The things that are hard to understand in Paul's letters that some people distort to their own destruction (3:16) would take on all the more poignancy in view

---

[97] Ibid., 160–61. Witherington (*Letters and Homilies for Hellenized Christians*, vol. 2, 282–83) also accepts this suggestion.

[98] Or perhaps Peter had not yet started to write but wanted to communicate his thoughts to the audiences troubled by these false teachers and made arrangements for his successor to do so. Witherington, *Letters and Homilies for Hellenized Christians*, vol. 2, 271–72, 279–85.

[99] See, in detail, James M. Starr, *Sharers in Divine Nature: 2 Peter 1:4 in Its Hellenistic Context* (Stockholm: Almqvist & Wiksell, 2000). Cf. also Scott Hafemann, "'Divine Nature' in 2 Pet 1,4 Within Its Eschatological Context," *Biblica* 94 (2013): 80–99.

of Peter's major gaffe in Syrian Antioch (Gal 2:11–14) but remedied already fifteen years earlier (Acts 15:7–11). And his repeated warnings against falling from a secure position would be all the more heartfelt as he recalled his own denials of Jesus during his earthly life (Mark 14:66–72). Yes, he believed the last days had arrived, but it appears that uniform, early Christian understanding saw Christ's death and resurrection as inaugurating the last days.[100]

Gene Green's judicious survey and balanced conclusions repay careful study. Apostolicity was the main issue that produced ancient doubts about 2 Peter. Widespread use, antiquity, and orthodoxy were not in question. But "ancient skepticism about the book did not have the final word," and it was accepted into the canon. Nevertheless, "one lesson from antiquity is that acceptance or rejection of the book as authentic should not be a test for orthodoxy."[101] In other words, what Marshall called "allonymity" in his study of the Pastorals may turn out to have even a stronger likelihood of applying to 2 Peter. If that should turn out to be true, and the jury is still out, it would affect neither the authority nor the truthfulness of the letter. No less a Christian luminary than John Calvin believed the language was not Peter's but one of his disciples who set forth Peter's thoughts in writing, "by his command, those things which the necessity of the times required."[102] Karen Jobes observes that even if the letter were not completed until after Peter died, *contra* Calvin, it could just as readily have been understood as proceeding from Peter.[103]

---

[100] See esp. throughout George E. Ladd, *A Theology of the New Testament*, rev. and ed. Donald A. Hagner (Grand Rapids: Eerdmans, 1993).

[101] Gene L. Green, *Jude and 2 Peter* (Grand Rapids: Baker, 2008), 144. Similarly Peter H. Davids, *The Letters of 2 Peter and Jude* (Grand Rapids: Eerdmans; Nottingham: Apollos, 2006), 129–30.

[102] John Calvin, *Commentaries on the Catholic Epistles*, trans. in 1855 by John Owen (Grand Rapids: Baker, repr. 1979), 363.

[103] Jobes, *Letters to the Church*, 362–67.

However one comes down on these precise nuances, 2 Peter certainly claims eyewitness support for the transfiguration and the words of the heavenly voice to Peter, James, and John in 1:16–18, lending additional credence to that miracle account. Wolfgang Grünstäudl believes a saying of Jesus lies behind 2 Peter 2:19 as well because something similar but not identical appears in four other early Christian texts of the first four centuries and is attributed to Jesus in the Pseudo-Clementine Recognitions.[104] Whether this is the case, it is a reminder that the way the biblical authors take earlier authoritative words and own them suggests that additional unmarked teachings of Jesus could appear scattered throughout the epistles. But because we don't necessarily have them attested anywhere else, we may never know their ultimate origin.

The Epistles of John

At first blush, it might seem that these three letters have the least of all to contribute to our topic of the New Testament's reliability. To begin with, no name or title appears anywhere within the text of what has come to be called 1 John. No name appears in what we have come to know as 2 John or 3 John either, though at least each of these short epistles begins with "the elder" as a title given to the writer. The style and themes of the three letters are extremely similar, suggesting to most scholars that all were composed by the same individual. Is anyone in the early church well enough known to be identified simply the title "the elder"? We saw in our study of the Gospel of John that either the apostle by that name or one of his disciples was called "John the elder."[105] Or, if the term refers more to age than to office here, we

---

[104] Wolfgang Grünstäudl, "On Slavery: A Possible *Herrenwort* in 2 Pet 2:19," *Novum Testamentum* 57 (2015): 57–71.

[105] Martin Hengel (*The Johannine Question* [London: SCM; Philadelphia: Trinity Press International, 1989], 24–73), therefore, postulates John the elder as the author of the letters as well.

also know that early church tradition believed the apostle John to have lived to a ripe old age to the time of Trajan (AD 98) as he ministered in and around Ephesus. We noted that John might have been only in his mid-teens when Jesus died, which means he could have been in his mid-eighties at the turn of the century.[106]

The external evidence of early church history is strong and unanimous in attributing these letters to John, normally understood to be the apostle. Does it matter for a study of historicity since the letters themselves make no such claim? The author of 1 John does include himself with a group of people whom he refers to in the first-person plural. He explains that Jesus Christ (1:3) is the one who "was from the beginning" (v. 1). He calls him "the Word of life," which "we have heard, which we have seen with our eyes, which we have looked at and our hands have touched." Then in verse 2 he adds, "We have seen it and testify to it." And "we proclaim to you the eternal life, which was with the Father and has appeared to us." Finally, in verse 3, he declares for a third time, "We proclaim to you what we have seen and heard." A more robust claim to have been physically present with Jesus during his earthly life could hardly be conceived. It would certainly seem that the author is stressing that he has been with Jesus and has known him intimately, all of which would fit the apostle John to a tee.[107]

Second John is addressed to an elect "lady" and "her children" whom the elder loves "in the truth" (v. 1). He expresses "great joy" to learn that some of this lady's children are walking in the truth (v. 4).

---

[106] The third most likely author of the Gospel of John, if not John the apostle or a separate John the elder, is Lazarus (recall chap. 4). Ben Witherington III, who has particularly championed this identification, thus postulates it for the authorship of the epistles also (*Letters and Homilies for Hellenized Christians*, vol. 1 [Downers Grove: IVP; Nottingham: Apollos, 2006], 394–99).

[107] D. A. Carson and Douglas J. Moo, *An Introduction to the New Testament*, 2nd ed. (Grand Rapids: Zondervan, 2005), 674–75; Guthrie, *New Testament Introduction*, 859–60.

He commands this "dear lady" that "we love one another" (v. 5). But he warns against those who come "to you" but don't bring sound teaching, not to take them "into your house or welcome them" (v. 10) because that would be to share "in their wicked work" (v. 11). He wants to communicate much more but hopes to do so in person (v. 12). The elder then closes the letter by sending greetings from "the children of your sister" (v. 13). Except for verses 1, 5, and 13, all of the references to "you" and "your" throughout this little epistle are plural. But why would John (or anyone else) write to an unidentified woman and her children? And why would the children of her sister (but not the sister herself) send greetings? What's wrong with welcoming someone into your house just because they believe in false doctrine? How would we ever show them Christ's love without hospitality?

Not surprisingly, from the earliest days on in church history, many have believed that these two women are separate (house) churches and their children are the members who worship there.[108] Not only do the greetings make better sense this way, but so do all the second-person plural forms. Not welcoming someone who doesn't bring the right teaching means not allowing false teachers to promulgate their beliefs within the congregation.[109] If the main problem is that these "deceivers" or little antichrists "do not acknowledge Jesus Christ as coming in the flesh" (v. 7), then we are looking at Docetism—the view that Christ only seemed to be human though he was fully God. Docetism was best known from ancient Gnostic thought. If these letters were written in the 90s, Gnosticism is indeed emerging in almost full-blown form, and all the pieces of the puzzle fit together. First John can

---

[108] Robert W. Yarbrough, *1–3 John* (Grand Rapids: Baker, 2008), 333–34, 359; Marianne Meye Thompson, *1–3 John* (Downers Grove and Leicester: IVP, 1992), 151, 157.

[109] Cf. Karen H. Jobes, *1, 2, & 3 John* (Grand Rapids: Zondervan, 2014), 271–72; Stephen S. Smalley, *1, 2, 3 John* (Waco: Word, 1984), 333.

then be seen as countering the same problems, especially in view of 1 John 4:1–3.[110]

Third John is less explicit about those the elder would warn against. He addresses a good friend and faithful believer named Gaius (vv. 1–3) and insists that nothing gives him "greater joy than to hear that my children are walking in the truth" (v. 4). Here the children almost have to be spiritual and not biological ones.[111] Throughout 1 John, the author frequently addressed everyone he was writing to as "dear children" (2:1, 12, 14, 18, 28; 3:7, 18; 4:4; 5:21), so the assumption that he is speaking of individual Christians in local house churches becomes a near certainty. Indeed, for the first time in these letters, 3 John refers to "the church" explicitly in verses 6, 9 and 10. Its author commends Demetrius to Gaius (v. 12) but warns him against Diotrephes, "who loves to be first" (v. 9). In this letter all the uses of "you" and "your" are singular, as one would expect with the elder writing to a private individual.

In short, there are just enough details in these three epistles to confirm a straightforward approach to authorship: someone who knew the historical Jesus stressed the need for specific congregations to believe not merely in the full deity of Christ but also in his full humanity. The elder could personally vouch for the fact that Jesus was

---

[110] Rudolf Schnackenburg (*The Johannine Epistles* [Tunbridge Wells: Burns & Oates; New York: Herder & Herder, 1993], 23) observes that the teaching countered is at least Docetist, probably one of the streams that produced full-fledged Gnosticism, and possibly even Cerinthian Gnosticism. Cf. also Colin G. Kruse, *The Letters of John* (Grand Rapids: Eerdmans; Leicester: Apollos, 2000), 26–27. For the most compelling challenge to this consensus, which views the secessionists as Jewish Christians returning to the synagogue after abandoning belief in Jesus as Messiah, see Daniel R. Streett, *They Went Out from Us: The Identity of the Opponents in First John* (Berlin and New York: de Gruyter, 2011).

[111] They could be those he has personally converted, but more likely they are any of those under his spiritual oversight. See John Christopher Thomas, *1 John, 2 John, 3 John* (Blandford Forum, UK: Deo, 2011), 24.

a real man, so no one should dare call this into question. The author writes with the authority one would expect from an apostle. He demonstrates an intimacy with his readers, especially with his epithet, "dear children," that one would envision John, the beloved disciple, who had ministered in and around Ephesus for 20 or 30 years by now to have had. And he can easily be seen as an elderly man (1 John 2:1, 28; 3:7; 2 John 1; 3 John 1).[112] Yet, not surprisingly by now, plenty of scholars call into question the tradition that John, the apostle, and son of Zebedee (or any other companion of Jesus during his earthly life) wrote these letters.

The style and emphases of the epistles of John closely approximate those of the Gospel of John.[113] So those who find the Gospel anonymous tend to remain agnostic about the authorship of the letters too. About the only thing they agree on is that they were not written by John the apostle. But even if one were to accept apostolic authorship of the Gospel, there are just enough differences in emphasis in the letters to ensure that some commentators would insist on interpreting them entirely separately from the Gospel.[114] A few have tried to parcel out the three epistles to two or three different authors, but the similarities among the three are too great for such hypotheses to convince even the majority of critical scholars.[115] Those who do treat

---

[112] Daniel L. Akin, *1, 2, 3 John* (Nashville: B&H, 2001), 27.

[113] See the select list of fifteen key similarities in Powell, *Introducing the New Testament*, 497: light and darkness, unity of Father and Son, "the truth," the Paraclete, hatred by the world, God's sending Christ to the world out of love, Jesus's coming in the flesh, Christ's laying down his life for others, being born of God, knowing God, abiding in God or Christ, new and old commandments, loving one another, water and blood, that joy may be complete.

[114] Classically C. H. Dodd, *The Johannine Epistles* (London: Hodder & Stoughton; New York: Harper and Row, 1946), xlvii–lvi. Cf. Georg Strecker, *The Johannine Letters* (Minneapolis: Fortress, 1996), xxxv–xlii; Holladay, *Critical Introduction to the New Testament*, 520–21.

[115] See Raymond E. Brown, *The Epistles of John* (Garden City: Doubleday, 1982), 13–19. For helpful tables of the most important linguistic similarities and

the epistles separately from the Gospel or one epistle separately from the other two do not advance additional arguments against Johannine authorship independently from those advanced against (at least the final form of) the Gospel (see above).

The question of the order of the Johannine writings has also been debated. Did the Gospel come before the Epistles or vice versa? Were the three letters written in their canonical order or in a different one? Were the three letters sent out at about the same time to the Ephesian community, with 1 John as a "general letter," 2 John as a "cover letter," and 3 John as a "personal letter"?[116] Sooner or later, just about every possible combination has been suggested, demonstrating how little we actually know.[117]

As good a case as any, and better than most, can be made for the chronology of the books ascribed traditionally to John to match their sequence in the New Testament. Raymond Brown, arguably the leading Johannine scholar of the past generation, defended an attractive though not demonstrable hypothesis that accounted for both the similarities and the differences among the various writings attributed to John. The Gospel of John played into the hands of some with Gnostic leanings who overemphasized features that 1 John then had to correct. By this time some were seceding from the community (1 John 2:19). But then they came back trying to get others to leave (2 John 9–10). Finally, in at least one house church, the secessionists have triumphed over the orthodox and are putting and keeping true believers out (3 John 10).[118]

---

differences among the epistles, see Judith Lieu, *The Second and Third Epistles of John: History and Background* (Edinburgh: T & T Clark, 1986), 217–22.

[116] Bruce G. Schuchard, *1–3 John* (St. Louis: Concordia, 2012), 19–23.

[117] Of the various proposals for a historical order differing from the canonical, perhaps most plausible is 2–3–1 John, as in I. Howard Marshall, *The Epistles of John* (Grand Rapids: Eerdmans, 1978).

[118] Raymond E. Brown, *The Community of the Beloved Disciple* (New York: Paulist, 1979), esp. 93–144.

Brown saw Johannine authorship, however, only at the beginning of a multiple-stage composition of the Gospel. The theory of a Johannine school—a group of John's followers—being responsible for the various stages of redaction and composition of the Johannine writings has been particularly popular especially since Brown first formulated his theories in the mid-1960s.[119] As we suggested in studying the Fourth Gospel, a limited form of this hypothesis may indeed be necessary to account for all of the internal evidence in these documents. But such theories can quickly become out of control and far outstrip what can actually be demonstrated with any significant degree of probability.[120] It is best to see John the apostle responsible for all three of these letters, at least to a substantial degree.[121]

Theology

The scope of this book does not permit a detailed comparison of the theologies of the New Testament authors. The focus is on historical reliability. But we saw in the last chapter that part of what leads to various critics imagining Paul to be the real founder of Christianity rather than Jesus is the perception that his letters are simply too different, theologically, from the Gospels and Acts to be seen as in substantial continuity with them. We suggested that perception was

---

[119] Raymond E. Brown, *The Gospel According to John I–XII* (Garden City: Doubleday, 1966), xxxiv–xxxix. Gary M. Burge (*The Letters of John* [Grand Rapids: Zondervan, 1996], 39) plausibly modifies this to three stages: an early draft of the Gospel by the apostle was misused by some; John penned the Christological corrections of the letters, the prologue of the Gospel, and possibly a few other minor points of editing; and after his death John's disciples gathered all his writings and possibly edited the Gospel a little bit more (especially by adding chap. 21).

[120] For an extreme example, see Urban C. von Wahlde, *The Gospel and Letters of John*, 3 vols. (Grand Rapids: Eerdmans, 2010).

[121] Helpful and thorough to this end is Donald W. Burdick, *The Letters of John the Apostle* (Chicago: Moody, 1985), 7–37.

unwarranted. But what about the distinctive theological emphases of the non-Pauline epistles? Are they in sync with the rest of the New Testament that we have surveyed thus far?

Obviously, Hebrews has enough in common with the letters explicitly attributed to Paul to have led many throughout church history to envision Paul writing it. Even if we disagree with this conclusion, the understanding that a new age has dawned with the Jesus event, in which the Hebrew Scriptures have been fulfilled, is a key link between Hebrews and Paul. So too are the Christologically interpreted quotations of the Old Testament and the pervasive theme of the supremacy of Jesus and his following over even the most respected rituals and figures of Jewish history, if they are venerated apart from the recognition of the arrival of Jeremiah's new covenant.

The priesthood of Christ, identified because he was a priest after the order of Melchizedek, is the most distinctive central theme of Hebrews, but it complements rather than contradicts the emphasis on propitiation in Romans 3:25. The definition of faith in Hebrews 11:1, illustrated by the heroes of the faith from Old Testament and intertestamental times, differs from Paul's emphasis on trust in Christ but fits well his conviction that we walk by faith and not by sight (2 Cor 5:7). The warnings against apostasy (esp. Heb 6:4–8) at first blush form the opposite end of the theological spectrum from John's promises about the security of the believer (in the letters, especially in 1 John 5:13), but on closer inspection the true believer in John must also remain in Christ (cf. 1 John 2:27), while Hebrews 6:9–10 immediately follows that writer's strongest warning with an affirmation of the belief in his audience's genuine Christianity.[122]

---

[122] On Hebrews' role compared with the other major NT witnesses, see further I. Howard Marshall, *New Testament Theology: Many Witnesses, One Gospel* (Downers Grove: IVP; Leicester: Apollos, 2004), 682–90.

James, as we already saw, can without forcing, be harmonized with Paul, once their differing definitions of key terms ("faith," "works," "justify") are recognized. Galatians 5:6 requires faith to be working through love, while Ephesians 2:10 follows immediately on the heels of salvation by grace through faith with the insistence that we are Christ's workmanship created for good works. The three key themes of James—trials and temptations, wisdom and speech, and riches and poverty—amplify and highlight teachings central to the Jesus of the Synoptics. We saw how James's teaching regularly echoed the ethical injunctions of the Sermon on the Mount/Plain and other Synoptic teaching of Jesus. Temptations proving Christ's character were central to and formed an inclusio around his public ministry—in the wilderness and in Gethsemane. Jesus's prophetic indictment of the abuse of material possessions and proclamation of God's special concern for the poor carry directly over to James.[123]

With 1 Peter we saw both parallels with a handful of key teachings of Jesus but also that a larger raft of passages saw Peter and Paul as imbibing of an identical theological milieu. Many commentators have seen two complementary themes dominating Peter's response to persecution—an inward-looking care for the needy within Christian circles ("a home for the homeless"[124]) balanced by an outward-looking winsome witness to society ("seeking the welfare of the city"[125]). John's Gospel and letters highlight the love command central to the first of these, while the domestic codes or *Haustafeln* crucial to the latter

---

[123] On the theology of James, see esp. Davids, *Epistle of James*, 34–57; and in light of the rest of the New Testament, Frank Thielman, *Theology of the New Testament: A Canonical and Synthetic Approach* (Grand Rapids: Zondervan, 2005), 496–511.

[124] John H. Elliott, *A Home for the Homeless: A Social-Scientific Criticism of 1 Peter, Its Situation and Strategy* (Philadelphia: Fortress; London: SCM, 1981; Eugene, OR: Wipf & Stock, 2005).

[125] Bruce W. Winter, *Seek the Welfare of the City: Christians as Benefactors and Citizens* (Grand Rapids: Eerdmans, 1994), 25–40.

emerge in several of Paul's letters as well, once we allow for there to be a close link between the deutero-Paulines and Paul himself.

The Epistles of John have regularly been seen as presenting three interrelated "tests of life"—belief in Jesus as the God-man, loving one another, and keeping Christ's commandments.[126] Interestingly, even if John did not intend these correlations consciously, Paul's emphases on faith and love and James's emphases on faith and works are brought together in John's triad of faith, love, and obedience. They also tie in closely with 2 Peter's and Jude's emphasis on standing fast against false teachers with the proto-Gnostics causing trouble for the Johannine community. Of course, false teachers were key problems behind Paul's writing Galatians, Philippians, 2 Corinthians 10–13, Colossians, 1 Timothy, and Titus, even if their precise heresies varied. And Jesus himself warned of those who would come in his name and deceive many. Even these brief remarks serve to show that we are not talking about separate religious movements in our various sources but a coherent body of thought with considerable unity in the midst of its diversity.

Conclusion

Most of the historical issues of greatest significance surrounding the non-Pauline epistles deal with questions about their authorship. Despite popular views to the contrary in critical circles, traditional ascriptions found in the early texts themselves can be sustained. This does not mean ascribing Pauline authorship to Hebrews since the early manuscripts made no such claim, but it does mean that most likely one of his close followers wrote it. Some posthumous composition was most likely needed to put 2 Peter into the form in which we

---

[126] See, classically, Robert Law, *The Tests of Life: A Study of the First Epistle of St. John* (Edinburgh: T & T Clark, 1909).

now have it, but it can still be viewed as Petrine in origin. No compelling reasons stand in the way of ascribing the letters of James, 1 Peter, 1, 2 and 3 John, and Jude to the ancient Christians who bore those names. Certainly in James, and probably in 1 Peter, we have reason to believe that the authors were aware of the Jesus tradition in oral form and that it had come down to them accurately. The most foundational themes central to each book, while not identical to one another, complement one another nicely and give no grounds for claims of outright contradiction.

Chapter 11

The Book of Revelation—Are Historical Matters Even Relevant?

O f all the documents to make an appearance in a book on the historical reliability of the New Testament, the book of Revelation seems like the oddest one out. For the average lay reader, sometimes overly influenced by the never-ending spate of popular-level prophecy books and novels penned by Christian authors without formal, advanced training in biblical scholarship, Revelation is filled with predictions about the last generation before Christ returns and depicts the end of human history as we know it.[1] Writers (and others) often assume this end is extremely near, perhaps even in our generation or lifetime. But this is only one of several major approaches that have been taken throughout the history of the church. Moreover, with

---

[1] See esp. Hal Lindsey, *The Late Great Planet Earth* (Grand Rapids: Zondervan, 1970), and his numerous subsequent works; Tim LaHaye and Jerry B. Jenkins, *Left Behind*, 16 vols. (Wheaton: Tyndale, 1995–2007); and Joel Rosenberg, *Epicenter 2.0: Why the Current Rumblings in the Middle East Will Change Your Future* (Wheaton: Tyndale, 2006), and his numerous subsequent works.

literally hundreds of predictions about the immediacy of the end made throughout church history, in every century and almost every decade, thus far every single one of them has proved false.[2] That alone should inspire some humility in the would-be interpreter of this final book of the Bible. We need to begin, therefore, with a brief survey of the various hermeneutical grids for making sense of this mysterious document.

Options for Interpretation

The approach that sees most of Revelation as yet unfulfilled (irrespective of how near one senses the end might be) is often called the *futurist* perspective on interpreting Revelation.[3] Hardly anything would be worth studying with respect to historical reliability of past events if this approach were all there were to say about how to understand this book. A second approach is called the *idealist* perspective. With this interpretive grid, all of the lessons that emerge from John's visions on the island of Patmos involve timeless issues, especially related to the conflict between good and evil, God and Satan, that play themselves out in varying ways over and over again throughout history. Once again a study of historical reliability would not have a lot to address,

---

[2] See the thorough survey in Francis X. Gumerlock, *The Day and the Hour: Christianity's Perennial Fascination with Predicting the End of the World* (Powder Springs, GA: American Vision, 2000). Cf. also Bernard McGinn, *Antichrist: Two Thousand Years of the Human Fascination with Evil* (San Francisco: HarperSanFrancisco, 1994; New York City: Columbia University Press, 1999).

[3] For all four perspectives italicized here, see esp. C. Marvin Pate, ed., *Four Views on the Book of Revelation* (Grand Rapids: Zondervan, 1998). For a synopsis format explaining each of the four approaches' interpretations to each passage of Revelation, see Steve Gregg, *Revelation: Four Views: A Parallel Commentary* (Nashville: Thomas Nelson, 1997); and C. Marvin Pate, *Reading Revelation: A Comparison of Four Interpretive Translations of the Apocalypse* (Grand Rapids: Kregel, 2009).

other than perhaps to demonstrate the repeated partial fulfillments of these prophecies off and on in the history of the church.[4]

A third approach is known as the *historicist* perspective. On this view an enormous amount of detail is worth scrutinizing. Historicists believe they can see the history of the church age unfold as one proceeds through Revelation, and the seven churches of chapters 2–3 form a microcosm of that history in chronological order. Thus the Laodicean church, the last of the seven John addresses (Rev 3:14–22), represents the church of today—lukewarm and in danger of being rejected by Christ altogether. But the penultimate era of church history is depicted by the Philadelphian church, one that receives no criticism, and for whom there is an open door (for evangelism?) that no one can close (3:7–13). Given the perennial human tendency, not limited to religious circles, to bemoan the present as a deterioration from a better era in the generation past, one can understand the timeless appeal of the historicist approach. But for it to work, it has to ignore all the weaknesses and failures of the previous generation and all of the strengths and successes of the present.

One can also see how the first two churches in Revelation 2–3 play into this scheme (at least from a Protestant perspective). First Ephesus, characterized as having lost its first love (2:1–7), nicely fits Christianity at the end of the first century, the close of the apostolic age, and the beginnings of the distinctively Roman Catholic aspects of the church. Smyrna appears second, the other church besides Philadelphia not to be criticized in any fashion, but unlike Philadelphia suffering persecution for its faith. Smyrna thus nicely corresponds with the second- to fourth-century Christians who were persecuted

---

[4] There are, of course, combinations of two or more of these approaches, just like the one we will adopt below. E.g., John Noë, "An Exegetical Basis for a Preterist-Idealist Understanding of the Book of Revelation," *Journal of the Evangelical Theological Society* 49 (2006): 767–96.

and even martyred before Rome's non-Christian hegemony over the church collapsed. The other three supposed eras, however, are not at all easy to see, unless of course one just ignores large strands of church history during those time periods. Neither Pergamum, nor Thyatira, nor Sardis are praised for much, which consigns almost the whole of church history to mediocrity or worse. But Protestants normally want to see the Reformation as an important, positive development, while Catholics would object to the characterization of the millennium of their hegemony as lackluster at best.

A fourth and final approach is called the *preterist* perspective, from a word meaning "past time."[5] It sees the wealth of detail in Revelation, and more specifically in John's visions, as depicting first-century realities, already complete by the time John put ink to papyrus. Sometimes it is taken as portraying what had occurred already by Nero's reign and pogrom, which ended in AD 68. In what is sometimes called the *fully preterist* view, even the text in Revelation 19:11–21 depicting Christ's return from heaven is viewed as having occurred already—usually understood as his invisible coming to earth to judge Israel in the war with Rome in AD 66–70, in which Jerusalem was virtually destroyed and perhaps as many as a million Jews slaughtered.[6] But this interpretation flies in the face of almost the entire history of Christian interpretation and, if taken to its logical conclusion, denies that there will be any kind of second coming or return of Christ in the future at all. This view becomes even more difficult to defend when one leaves the apocalyptic genre of Revelation for more straightforward historical and didactic books and passages in the New Testament that also refer

---

[5] For more on the various perspectives throughout church history, see esp. Arthur W. Wainwright, *Mysterious Apocalypse: Interpreting the Book of Revelation* (Nashville: Abingdon, 1993; Eugene, OR: Wipf & Stock, 2001).

[6] For another excellent anthology of contemporary approaches, including full preterism, see the various contributions to *Criswell Theological Review* 11.1 (2013).

to Jesus's return (esp. Acts 1:9–11; 1 Cor 15; 1 Thess 3:13; 4:13–5:11, 23; 2 Thess 2:1–12; Jas 5:7–8; 2 Peter 3:3–13; and 1 John 2:28).

The best approach, in my opinion, combines elements of both preterism and futurism.[7] When the angel tells John in Revelation 1:19 to "write, therefore, what you have seen, what is now and what will take place later," it is fair to envisage the first eighteen verses of the book as depicting what he has seen. Chapters 2–3 clearly fit "what is now."[8] The heavenly praise of chapters 4–5 could occur at any time after the resurrection of Christ, but with the depiction of Jesus's suddenly coming to solve the plight of who is worthy to open the seals of the scroll of coming judgment, we are probably meant to envisage a period still within John's lifetime.

Chapters 6–19 then proceed with events that must happen before the scroll of judgment can be unrolled and its contents disclosed. This suggests a series of prefatory punishments prior to the great tribulation that characterizes the time just before the end.[9] Not surprisingly, the first five seals, part of the first of three series of seven judgments each (Rev 6:1–11), all closely resemble events that occurred within the

---

[7] Of course, many of the events depicted have had multiple partial parallels throughout church history, even if the imagery was inspired by first-century events and institutions and even if there will one day be a climactic manifestation of many of them. To this extent one can speak also of an idealist element and, if one ignores all the contrary trends at any given time, a historicist element. The approach taken here is commonly associated with a historic premillennialist interpretation, on which see esp. Sung Wook Chung and Craig L. Blomberg, eds., *A Case for Historic Premillennialism* (Grand Rapids: Baker, 2009). Cf. also Eckhard J. Schnabel, *40 Questions About the End Times* (Grand Rapids: Kregel, 2011).

[8] Most commentators today see the expression "what you have seen" as then subdividing into two parts, "what is now" and "what will take place later." For the tripartite division into past, present, and future suggested here, see, e.g., John F. Walvoord, *The Revelation of Jesus Christ: A Commentary* (Chicago: Moody, 1966), 47–49.

[9] George E. Ladd, *A Commentary on the Revelation of John* (Grand Rapids: Eerdmans, 1972), 95–98; Gordon D. Fee, *Revelation* (Eugene, OR: Cascade, 2011), 91.

first century and have recurred many times throughout history ever since—imperialist expansionism, warfare, famine, death,[10] and a cry for vengeance on God's enemies. The sixth seal brings us to what can only be the end of human history as we know it, however metaphorically depicted it may be (6:12–17). Yet fourteen more judgments are to come! Perhaps the end of chapter 6 is a flash-forward to that end, almost like the person walking toward a cliff who arrives at its edge, looks over it, and recoils in horror at the prospect of falling off and retreats to a safe distance away.[11]

The second set of judgments is represented by a series of trumpets (8:1–9:21). Now we have devastations reminiscent of the plagues on Egypt in Moses's day (Exod 7:14–11:10), but on a much more awful scale. Over and over again John intones the fraction one-third. One-third of the earth was burned up, a third of the trees (Rev 8:7), a third of the creatures in the sea died, and a third of the ships were destroyed (v. 9). A fiery star falls on a third of the rivers and springs of water (v. 10); a third of the waters turned bitter (v. 11); a third of the sun, moon, and stars turned dark so that a third of the day and the night were

---

[10] Revelation 6:8 has at times been mistranslated or misread as if it said one-fourth of humanity would be killed, but the text actually says that Death and Hades were given power over a fourth of the earth to kill (an unspecified number of people) by sword, famine, plague, and wild beast. Cf. Ladd, *Commentary on the Revelation of John*, 101. Ian Boxall (*Revelation* [London: A & C Black, Peabody: Hendrickson, 2006] 112) notes the progression from one-fourth of the earth affected here, to one-third throughout the trumpet judgments, to no limitations in the bowl judgments. Each is depicted as worse than its predecessor(s).

[11] This is linked to what is sometimes called the telescopic approach to interpreting the relationship among the seals, trumpets, and bowls. It can be viewed as combining the best of the strictly chronological and strictly recapitulative approaches. See esp. H. Wayne House, *Chronological and Background Charts of the New Testament*, 2nd ed. (Grand Rapids: Zondervan, 2009), 146. Somewhat less precisely, but with the same combination of progress and recapitulation, see Stephen S. Smalley, *The Revelation to John: A Commentary on the Greek Text of the Apocalypse* (Downers Grove: IVP, 2005), 19–20.

without light (v. 12). Whatever other realities the elements in these visions are meant to symbolize, it appears clear that the magnitude of the judgments surpasses anything the world has previously known, even to this day in the twenty-first century.[12] With the fifth trumpet a distinction is made between God's people,[13] who are protected from harm, and everyone else, who experience torture of some unspecified nature. This unique separation of humanity also distinguishes this judgment from all those that have preceded it, at least throughout *Christian* history. Again, the sixth item in the series appears to bring us to the threshold of the end, only to have the visions continue.

The final heptad of judgments appears in 16:1–16. John sees them represented by seven bowls of God's wrath (v. 1). They are partly parallel to the trumpet judgments and hence again partly parallel to the plagues on Egypt. But this time there are no fractions restricting their effects to a minority of the world or the cosmos. Indeed, there are no restrictions at all. Not surprisingly there are no flash-forwards at the end of the seven or movement backward away from final judgment. After the six seals, we had to wait a full chapter before the seventh seal was explained (skipping all of Revelation 7), and then we learned only that there was silence in heaven for about a half an hour (8:1). After the six trumpets, we had to wait a chapter and a half before the seventh trumpet was blown (skipping all of Rev 10:1–11:14), and then

---

[12] Boxall (*Revelation*, 137–38) notes both that "the collapse of the created order is very much in view here" and that "even here the divine hand of restraint is in evidence: only a third is destroyed."

[13] Debates rage, of course, about whether *all* Christians alive at the beginning of the tribulation live through it or only certain select ones. See further below. But *some* do, on every interpretive scheme. The view popular in some circles, that all believers are raptured and that the only Christians alive during the tribulation are those who come to faith when they see other believers gone from the earth, makes a mockery of the picture here of Christ's followers being sealed so that they are spiritually protected before they begin to experience the physical horrors of these last days.

we heard only what Eugene Peterson has called "reversed thunder"[14]—lightning, thunder, hail, and an earthquake in heaven rather than on earth (11:15–19).

Because the seventh seal and seventh trumpet do not depict separate judgments on earth but introduce and set the stage for the next series, it has plausibly been suggested that the seventh seal *comprises* the first six trumpets, and the seventh trumpet *comprises* the first six bowls.[15] In this way we simultaneously reach the threshold of the end with the sixth seal and sixth trumpet, and yet there is still room for more to come. It is as if one put a magnifying glass to the seventh seal to see what it contained and only then saw the seven trumpets within it. Then, putting the magnifying glass on the seventh trumpet, one saw the seven bowls within it. After the first six bowls, however, there is no hiatus. One moves immediately to the seventh bowl, and now we do have imagery, even more complete and awful than that of the sixth seal and sixth trumpet, suggesting the dissolution of all things (16:17–21). Plus, all this is accompanied by the cry, "It is done!" (v. 17). The end which was still a way off in 5:11, and which would no longer be delayed in 10:6, has finally arrived.

This overview has not taken into account various interludes in the sequence of 21 judgments or chapters 17–22. But it suffices to establish the main principles with which we will move forward. All we have seen suggests that a *partly preterist, partly futurist* approach to interpreting Revelation is best. The events of chapters 1–5 can be seen as transpiring in the first century, in John's lifetime. The first five seals all occurred during the first century as well, though they have continued to occur throughout church history. From the sixth seal in 6:12

---

[14] Eugene Peterson, *Reversed Thunder: The Revelation of John and the Praying Imagination* (San Francisco: Harper & Row, 1988).

[15] J. Ramsey Michaels, *Interpreting the Book of Revelation* (Grand Rapids: Baker, 1992), 56–58; Ladd, *Commentary on the Revelation of John*, 122.

onwards, however, we should see Revelation as depicting, in highly symbolic garb, real events that will happen in the future but that have not yet occurred. Yet many of them had substantial precursors in the first century that gave impetus to God's disclosing the future to John with this specific imagery. One of the interludes has at least one significant flashback, when we return to the events surrounding the birth and ascension of Christ in 12:1–6. But the persecution against the woman who morphs into the Church in the rest of the chapter brings us back up to the last days or end times in chapter 13.[16] A similar flashback, despite amillennialist claims to the contrary,[17] should not be seen at 20:1 because the end of chapter 19 has just depicted the fate of two-thirds of the unholy trinity of Satan, Antichrist, and false prophet (the latter two introduced to us in chapter 13 as the beast from the sea and the beast from the earth, respectively). We naturally want to know the fate of Satan himself, and chapter 20 proceeds immediately to describe that. So the thousand-year or millennial period it depicts must be kept together with the events at the end of chapter 19 concerning the end of the age.[18]

The implications of this kind of preterist-futurist interpretation are that one must always seek to understand John's visions as John himself could be expected to have understood them. He would have communicated them as best as he could, no doubt often trying to describe the indescribable, with language he had reason to believe would make the most sense to the Christians in Asia Minor at the end of the first

---

[16] G. K. Beale, *The Book of Revelation* (Carlisle: Paternoster; Grand Rapids: Eerdmans, 1999), 624–43; Robert H. Mounce, *What Are We Waiting For? A Commentary on Revelation* (Grand Rapids: Eerdmans, 1992), 59–63.

[17] E.g., Vern S. Poythress, "Genre and Hermeneutics in Rev 20:1–6," *Journal of the Evangelical Theological Society* 36 (1993): 41–54; Beale, *Book of Revelation,* 974–83.

[18] Cf. further Craig S. Keener, *Revelation* (Grand Rapids: Zondervan, 2000), 463–65; Joseph L. Trafton, *Reading Revelation: A Literary and Theological Commentary* (Macon: Smyth & Helwys, 2005), 185.

century, when the work was most likely composed. Revelation is not a cryptogram intended to be mysterious to every generation until the last one, when suddenly for the first time the technology, politics, or culture of that day discloses the meaning of each image or symbol.[19] As Gordon Fee and Douglas Stuart have phrased it with admirable clarity, "The primary meaning of Revelation is what John intended it to mean, which in turn must also have been something his readers could have understood it to mean."[20] What was transparent then and there, unfortunately, has often become more opaque to many of us here and now.

To recover that originally intended meaning, when John does not himself spell it out, we must therefore rely on three main resources: (1) Old Testament allusions, especially when John reuses imagery from Old Testament prophetic and apocalyptic writings that had a standard or even specified meaning;[21] (2) intertestamental or Second Temple Jewish developments that would likely have been reasonably well known in Asia Minor;[22] and (3) more immediate Greco-Roman culture and history, especially related to John's depiction of the evil empire in the end times as akin to Rome.[23] The imagery of apocalypse

---

[19] The appropriate reply to those who cite Dan 12:9, with its command to Daniel not to worry about deciphering all that has been revealed to him "because the words are rolled up and sealed until the time of the end," is that Rev 22:10 explicitly commands John *not* to seal up the words of his prophecy.

[20] Gordon D. Fee and Douglas Stuart, *How to Read the Bible for All Its Worth*, 4th ed. (Grand Rapids: Zondervan, 2014), 263.

[21] On which, see esp. G. K. Beale, *John's Use of the Old Testament in Revelation* (London: Bloomsbury: T & T Clark, 2015).

[22] See esp. Paul R. Trebilco, *Jewish Communities in Asia Minor* (Cambridge: Cambridge University Press, 1991).

[23] On which, see esp. Steven J. Friesen, *Imperial Cults and the Apocalypse of John* (Oxford: Oxford University Press, 2001). For a survey of the most relevant literature, cf. Michael Naylor, "The Roman Imperial Cult and Revelation," *Currents in Biblical Research* 8 (2010): 207–39.

has been helpfully likened to that of a political cartoon.[24] Find a newspaper from the late 1980s and see an eagle holding an outstretched talon with an olive branch in it, even as a bear grasps its other end with its paw, and the person familiar with the American eagle, the Russian bear, and the olive branch as a sign of peace will recognize a picture of the increasingly positive relationship between the United States and the Soviet Union in its final years under Mikhail Gorbachev. Without that familiarity, the cartoon will be nonsensical or even mislead people into who knows what kind of outlandish interpretations.

These observations are reinforced by the combination of literary genres that Revelation comprises—*apocalypse, prophecy,* and *epistle.* The first word of the Greek text (*apokalupsis*—"revelation" in 1:1) announces the major genre for the book. It is an "apocalypse," a well-known Jewish, Greek, and Roman literary form by which past, present, and/or future events often leading up to the end of the world or some heavenly vision (or both) are depicted in highly symbolic garb.[25] Revelation is also prophetic (v. 3), so that it has direct ethical relevance to its first-century audience and describes real events that will transpire sometime in the future.[26] And it is epistolary, in that it has

---

[24] See, e.g., George R. Beasley-Murray, *The Book of Revelation* (London: Marshall, Morgan & Scott, 1978; Grand Rapids: Eerdmans, 1981), 16–17. Cf. Peterson, *Reversed Thunder,* 145–46.

[25] The classic, technical definition of *apocalyptic* appears in John J. Collins, "Introduction: Toward the Morphology of a Genre," *Semeia* 14 (1979): 9: "a genre of revelatory literature with a narrative framework, in which a revelation is mediated by an otherworldly being to a human recipient, disclosing a transcendent reality which is both temporal, insofar as it envisages eschatological salvation, and spatial insofar as it involves another, supernatural world." For an excellent book-length introduction, see John J. Collins, *The Apocalyptic Imagination: An Introduction to Jewish Apocalyptic Literature,* rev. ed. (Grand Rapids: Eerdmans; Livonia, MI: Dove Booksellers, 1998). For a succinct overview of approaches, see Scott M. Lewis, *What Are They Saying About New Testament Apocalyptic?* (Mahwah, NJ: Paulist, 2004).

[26] On Revelation as prophecy, see esp. Frederick D. Mazzaferri, *The Genre of the Book of Revelation from a Source-Critical Perspective* (Berlin and New York:

elements of a letter introduction in 1:4–6 and contains the seven letters to the seven churches in chapters 2–3.

So an interpretation of Revelation should be *futurist* in understanding the book to be a record of John's God-given visions about the
end of history, the return of Christ, the millennial kingdom, and the
eternal state. But they should be *preterist* in understanding those visions
to have begun with first-century events and, even when they shifted to
future events, to have used imagery that would have been meaningful to
first-century Christians in and around Ephesus based on their own historical-cultural backgrounds. The events from 6:12 onward, except for
chapter 12, did not happen in the first century, but John uses imagery
that first-century readers or hearers could have understood and often
partially related to events that had happened. A book on the historical
reliability of the New Testament, therefore, can discuss Revelation by
highlighting the major ways in which historical background information can make sense of the imagery of the book. The more we find
plausible interpretations of key elements and find them fitting together
coherently, the more our confidence should grow in the author's claims
that he had precisely these visions, and the more our confidence in the
truth of his predictions should grow as well. But if we find numerous anachronisms or inexplicable details, or inconsistencies in what is
taught by the imagery he uses, the more that confidence should wane.

Circumstances of Composition

We have spoken already of the author of Revelation as John. Of all
the writings traditionally ascribed to the apostle, the son of Zebedee,
this is the only one in which the name John actually appears within
the text itself (1:1, 4, 9; 22:8). From these passages we learn that this

---

de Gruyter, 1989). Cf. also Alan S. Bandy, *The Prophetic Lawsuit in the Book of
Revelation* (Sheffield: Sheffield Phoenix, 2010).

John considers himself a servant of Christ, detailing the revelations he has seen that represent "the word of God and the testimony of Jesus Christ" (v. 2).[27] He recounts them to seven churches representing the entire spectrum of Christianity, good and bad, in the province of Asia Minor (what we would call western Turkey).[28] John describes himself as a Christian brother from these churches and a "companion in the suffering and kingdom and patient endurance that are ours in Jesus" (v. 9). He declares that he is in exile on the island of Patmos because of the word of God and the testimony of Jesus, suggesting that he has been exiled from the mainland and the environs of Ephesus, as various individuals in the Roman Empire were punished with the ruling of *relegatio ad insulam* ("relegation to an island").[29] Verse 10 adds that he was in the Spirit "on the Lord's Day." In other words, when he began receiving these revelations, he was experiencing some kind of communion with God through the Holy Spirit on a Sunday, possibly having the same experience as Ezekiel, who uses the same language to describe his prophetic ministry (e.g., Ezek 2:2; 3:12; 11:1).[30]

Other passages do not use John's name but the first person singular, "I," "me," or "my" forms, most commonly in the contexts of what John saw or heard in his revelations, since he was largely a passive recipient

[27] Commentators debate whether these expressions contain objective ("the word about God," and "the testimony about Jesus Christ") or subjective genitives ("the word God gave," and "the testimony Jesus Christ gave"). They may contain elements of each (Beale, *Book of Revelation*, 184).

[28] Mounce (*What Are We Waiting For?*, 6) asserts that they reveal "the strengths and weaknesses of the church universal." Dennis E. Johnson (*Triumph of the Lamb: A Commentary on Revelation* [Phillipsburg, NJ: P & R, 2001], 93) speaks of them as "case studies in the conflict that confronts all churches in all the world at all times."

[29] Smalley, *Revelation to John*, 50–51, citing Tertullian, *De Praes. Haer.* 36, and noting also Victorinus's testimony in *Comm. In Apoc.* 10.3 that he was "condemned to the quarries" (i.e., forced to work at hard labor). For a full history of interpretation, see Ian Boxall, *Patmos in the Reception History of the Apocalypse* (Oxford: Oxford University Press, 2013).

[30] Beale, *Book of Revelation*, 203; Smalley, *Revelation to John*, 51.

of them. Occasionally, he has a short give-and-take with a heavenly messenger or angel, and on two occasions Jesus himself addresses him (1:10–20; 22:12–16). The one thing we never learn is which John is behind this apocalypse. Because of his experiences, he is sometimes called John the seer, but that doesn't answer more specific questions about his identity. The early church testimonies, with only one major exception, equate this John with the apostle by that name (Justin Martyr, *Dial.* 81.15; Irenaeus, *Adv. Haer.* 4.14.1, 5.26.1; Tertullian, *Contra Marc.* 3.14, 24; Clement of Alexandria, *Misc.* 6.106–7, *Tutor* 2.119).[31] The circumstances fit the ancient conviction that John lived to a ripe old age while ministering in and around Ephesus, the first of the seven cities addressed, and the major port from which one would travel to the island of Patmos. If John were the apostle, it would clearly explain why he would be a target of persecution.

The same swath of scholars that dispute apostolic authorship for the Gospel and/or the Epistles ascribed to John typically assert that an otherwise unknown John, an end-of-the-first-century Christian with close ties to the apostolic tradition but about whom we know nothing else, was the author of Revelation.[32] The similarities of vocabulary, themes, and style lead some to assume that this same John then was also the author of either the Fourth Gospel or the Epistles attributed to John or both.[33] But whereas the similarities of these ele-

---

[31] That exception was Dionysius of Alexandria in the third century who pointed out differences in language, concepts, and arrangement of Revelation, and noted that the author never called himself the beloved disciple. See further D. A. Carson and Douglas J. Moo, *An Introduction to the New Testament*, 2nd ed. (Grand Rapids: Zondervan, 2005), 701.

[32] E.g., Richard Bauckham, *The Theology of the Book of Revelation* (Cambridge: Cambridge University Press, 1993), 2; Brian K. Blount, *Revelation: A Commentary* (Louisville; Westminster John Knox, 2009), 7–8.

[33] Or a "Johannine school" of individuals, on which see esp. R. Alan Culpepper, *The Johannine School: An Evaluation of the Johannine-School Hypothesis Based on an Investigation of the Nature of Ancient Schools* (Missoula: Scholars, 1975).

ments between the Gospel and the Epistles are considerable, with comparatively few differences, there are enough distinctives in the Revelation to make other scholars unconvinced by the tradition that the John of Revelation authored any other New Testament books.[34] Still others find the ancient tradition of John the son of Zebedee as author persuasive.[35] Little of this matters, however, for a discussion of the trustworthiness of Revelation. Close associates of the twelve apostles were inspired to record accurate narratives in the Gospels of Mark and Luke and to write authoritative letters in the Epistles of James and Jude. If "John the seer" rather than "John the apostle" wrote the Revelation, nothing needs change about how the church trusts, interprets, or uses the book.

The date of the book is a little more important but only a little. Some who hold a mostly or fully preterist position lobby strongly for a date for Revelation in the 60s.[36] If someone's understanding of prophecy requires all of it to refer to future events predicted at one point and then fulfilled at a later time after the prophecy has been written down, and if someone is convinced that Christ's return in chapter 19 was completely fulfilled, without remainder, in the events of AD 70, then they would of course have to find a way to argue for its being earlier than that date. But this interpretation is so rare in church history and so improbable exegetically that it need not detain us here.[37] The standard preterist position may take all or most of the twenty-one

---

[34] E.g., Raymond E. Brown, *An Introduction to the New Testament* (New York and London: Doubleday, 1997), 774; Donald A. Hagner, *The New Testament: A Historical and Theological Introduction* (Grand Rapids: Baker, 2012), 766.

[35] E.g., Robert H. Mounce, *The Book of Revelation*, rev. ed. (Grand Rapids: Eerdmans, 1998), 8–15; Fee, *Revelation*, xviii–xix.

[36] See esp. Kenneth L. Gentry Jr., *Before Jerusalem Fell: Dating the Book of Revelation*, rev. ed. (Powder Springs, GA: American Vision, 1998).

[37] This is the full preterist position noted above, whereas Gentry represents the standard, partial preterist position and even argues against the full preterist view, while still holding for a date in the 60s.

judgments of Revelation as fulfilled metaphorically in the various horrors of the first century, or even before by 70, but still see the return of Christ as more literal, in the future, and still accept, with the early church, a date for the book during or just after the reign of Domitian and his persecution on churches in Asia Minor between 94 and 96.[38] Various details in the book make better sense if the book were written in the 90s rather than in the 60s: (1) Laodicea's recovery from the earthquake of 61; (2) tensions with local expressions of Judaism to such a degree that they can be called synagogues of Satan (2:9; 3:9); (3) full-blown expression of the *Nero redivivus* legend that appear behind the imagery of Revelation 12–13; (4) the decline of the prominence of the church in Ephesus (2:1–7); Gnosticism well on its way to becoming full-blown (cf. 2:24); and the famine of 92 as the background to 6:6.[39] But most of the evidence discussed here works equally well on a date in either of those two decades.

Other issues need not detain us. Some scholars have questioned whether Revelation was really written during a time of significant persecution or simply during a time of the perception of growing hostility from society and the fear of something more official and severe.[40] But the grounds on which these doubts have been proffered have been shown to be unstable.[41] Others place huge emphasis on whether Revelation best supports a dispensational, historic premillennial,

---

[38] E.g., George B. Caird, *The Revelation of St. John the Divine* (London: A & C Black; New York: Harper & Row, 1966; Peabody: Hendrickson, 1993), 6. While not defending preterism, Beale (*Revelation*, 44–46) similarly subdivides it into these two different approaches.

[39] See further Grant R. Osborne, *Revelation* (Grand Rapids: Baker, 2002), 6–9.

[40] See esp. Leonard L. Thompson, *The Book of Revelation: Apocalypse and Empire* (Oxford: Oxford University Press, 1990), 95–115.

[41] See, e.g., Ben Witherington III, *Revelation* (Cambridge: Cambridge University Press, 2003), 5–10.

amillennial, or postmillennial perspective.[42] I have elsewhere defended why I think the historic premillennial approach is best.[43] But for a survey of details in the book that make best sense when read in light of the historical background of readers in first-century Asia Minor, this debate proves largely irrelevant. It is time, therefore, to turn to the most important selection of details in the Apocalypse that dovetail with the history and culture of its original audience.

Reading Revelation in Light of Its Historical-Cultural Background

Setting the Stage: Chapter 1

The first expression that is less than transparent in the book of Revelation appears in 1:4. The straightforward translation of *apo tōn hepta pneumatōn* would be "from the seven spirits," but it is hard to envisage the monotheistic writer of this book placing seven spiritual entities in between his references to the eternal God ("him who is, and who was, and who is to come") and to Jesus Christ.[44] When we recognize that the expression could also be rendered "the sevenfold Spirit,"

---

[42] For a clear presentation of the main options, see Stanley J. Grenz, *The Millennial Maze: Sorting Out Evangelical Options* (Downers Grove: IVP, 1992); Millard J. Erickson, *A Basic Guide to Eschatology: Making Sense of the Millennium* (Grand Rapids: Baker, 1998); Darrell L. Bock, ed., *Three Views on the Millennium and Beyond* (Grand Rapids: Zondervan, 1999).

[43] Craig L. Blomberg, "Why I Am a Historic Premillennialist," *Criswell Theological Review*, n.s. 11.1 (2013): 71–87; cf. Craig L. Blomberg, "Historic Premillennialism in the Book of Revelation," in *Dragons, John, and Every Grain of Sand: Essays on the Book of Revelation in Honor of Dr. Robert Lowery*, ed. Shane J. Wood (Joplin, MO: College Press, 2011), 153–66; Craig L. Blomberg, "The Posttribulationism of the New Testament: Leaving *Left Behind* Behind," in *A Case for Historic Premillennialism*, 61–87.

[44] The other option is to see the seven spirits as the fullness of the angelic host. But this seems less likely in this theocentric and Christological context. See esp. Bauckham, *Theology of the Book of Revelation*, 110–15.

with seven as the classic Jewish number for completeness, going back to the creation account with its seven days, so that the sevenfold Spirit means God's perfect, complete Holy Spirit, then the verse makes good sense. We have here an early Trinitarian reference, not yet stylized into Father, Son, and Holy Spirit language or order but every bit as significant nevertheless.

Although Revelation is filled with allusions to the Old Testament, 1:7 forms a rare quotation. Zechariah 12:10 was used already by Matthew (24:30) and John (19:37) to refer to Jesus's return. Commentators debate whether these various uses of the passage in Zechariah are meant to refer to the peoples of the earth mourning in repentance or mourning because their judgment has been made certain, but most everyone recognizes that the New Testament writers understand the Old Testament text here as messianic.[45] In verse 8, alpha and omega are the first and last letters of the Greek alphabet, so that what is predicated of God matches exactly that which is said by Jesus about himself in verse 17.

The paragraph that comprises 1:12–18 forms a classic illustration of the kind of imagery found throughout Revelation. In it Christ appears as a human being walking among seven golden lampstands, with a golden sash, white hair, eyes like blazing fire, feet like glowing bronze, and his voice like the sound of rushing waters. In his right hand he holds seven stars and in his mouth a two-edged sword. His face meanwhile shines brilliantly. People who have taken this literally and drawn representations of it disclose how bizarre and even grotesque the portrait could appear.[46] Even if this is how Jesus appeared to John in this vision, it is not meant to describe what his literal appearance

---

[45] Marko Jauhiainen, *The Use of Zechariah in Revelation* (Tübingen: Mohr Siebeck, 2005).

[46] See, most famously, Albrecht Dürer's woodcut of this image, completed in 1498, accessed January 6, 2016, http://harpers.org/wp-content/uploads/duerer-7 -candlesticks.jpg.

in either heaven or on earth will necessarily be at any point in time. Rather it is the cumulative effect of all the detail that represents Jesus with imagery from his world as majestic, powerful, regal, and even militaristic.[47] Chapter 5:5–6 will refer to Christ as the Lion who is also a Lamb. Here we have in chapter 1 the same point as is communicated by the picture of Jesus as the king of the beasts.

Jesus himself explains that the lampstands are the seven churches addressed (v. 11) and that the stars are the angels (or messengers) of those churches (v. 20). Zechariah 4 had already used the picture of lampstands to represent God's Spirit among his people at worship, promising the rebuilding of the temple,[48] so we might have guessed at this meaning even had we not had a specific explanation. Stars often stood for angels in Second Temple Judaism, but the Greek word *angelos* can mean a human messenger as well. Probably, the idea is similar to that found in 1 Corinthians 11:10, in which angels watch over God's people at worship to guard them.[49] These overseers are directly addressed in Revelation 2:1, but the delivery of the letters to the seven churches of Asia Minor listed shows that this is also a real document meant to be read aloud in each congregation.

---

[47] Mounce, *What Are We Waiting For?*, 4. Cf. Boxall (*Revelation of Saint John*, 41), who adds the significance of all of the similes: John "is struggling to express what is ultimately inexpressible."

[48] See Paul L. Redditt, *Haggai, Zechariah and Malachi* (London: Marshall Pickering; Grand Rapids: Eerdmans, 1995), 67–71. Joyce G. Baldwin is even more specific: "The lampstand represents not the Lord but the witness of the temple and the Jewish community to Him" (*Haggai, Zechariah, Malachi* [Leicester and Downers Grove: IVP, 1972], 124. Substitute "church" for "temple" and "Christian" for "Jewish," and you have how Revelation is using the symbol.

[49] Cf. further Jürgen Roloff, *Revelation: A Continental Commentary* (Minneapolis: Fortress, 1993), 38–40. Cf. Johnson, *Triumph of the Lamb*, 62–63. Everett Ferguson ("Angels to the Churches in Revelation 1–3: Statis Quaestionis and Another Proposal," *Bulletin for Biblical Research* 21 [2011]: 371–86) surveys the scholarly landscape and proposes that the "angel" is the person who read the letter out to a given local church. This could easily have also been the messenger.

The Letters to the Seven Churches: Chapters 2–3

Entire, detailed tomes have been written on the possible links between distinctive features of each of the seven cities in which the Christians of Revelation 2–3 resided and the imagery used in the visions John was charged with communicating to them.[50] We can list only some of the most secure and important of them. From the rest of the New Testament, and especially Johannine, literature, the Ephesians clearly had a growing problem with false teachers, probably of a proto-Gnostic or at least docetic kind (recall chap. 9). Here we learn that the Ephesians have ultimately persevered against them (2:2–3) but their behavior has come at a cost. They have lost their first love, which in this context is less of an emotion than a will to obey all of Christ's commandments (cf. v. 4 with v. 5).[51] The threat of removing their lampstand from its place suggests the extinction of the church in Ephesus, which tragically did occur near the end of the second century.[52] The Nicolaitans (v. 6) are otherwise unknown, but presumably an element of the false teaching the Ephesians had to oppose. The tree of life recalls Genesis 2:9, especially in the context of God's paradise (Rev. 2:7) and is one of seven ways the promise of eternal life is depicted at the end of each of Revelation's letters. It is also possible that it is meant

---

[50] See esp. Colin J. Hemer, *The Letters to the Seven Churches of Asia in Their Local Setting* (Sheffield: JSOT, 1986; Grand Rapids: Eerdmans, 2001). Cf. also William M. Ramsay, *The Letters to the Seven Churches*, ed. Mark Wilson (Peabody: Hendrickson, 1994 [orig. 1904]); Roland H. Worth Jr., *The Seven Cities of the Apocalypse and Roman Culture* (New York: Paulist, 1998); and Roland H. Worth Jr., *The Seven Cities of the Apocalypse and Greco-Asian Culture* (New York: Paulist, 1999).

[51] Including loving the wayward church member. See Frederick J. Murphy, *Fallen Is Babylon: The Revelation of John* (Harrisburg: Trinity Press International, 1998), 115–16. Cf. Blount, *Revelation: A Commentary*, 51.

[52] Though see Osborne, *Revelation*, 108–9. It is not certain whether attempts to prevent the silting over of the Ephesian harbor that led to the city's decline were successful.

to contrast specifically with the Artemis cult oak-tree shrine in town and the asylum it claimed to offer the devotees of the goddess.[53]

Smyrna is the first of two churches in communities where "a synagogue of Satan" exists (2:9; cf. 3:9). These references should not be taken in anti-Semitic fashion, as if John were condemning all Jews or even all local synagogues. Rather it reflects the specific hostility of key Jewish leaders in Smyrna and Philadelphia and meshes with the frequent but not unbroken hostility seen in the book of Acts.[54] Stressing Jesus's deity and resurrection are also important (v. 8) for countering a strong imperial cult in Smyrna.[55] The city referred to itself as "first" among the cities of Asia Minor and viewed itself as having been resurrected in 290 BC after it was destroyed by the invading king of Lydia.[56] The ten-day persecution could reflect simply a round number for a short period of time, or it could be literal, given an inscription discovered in the city with identical syntax referring to a similar five-day period.[57] Overcomers, however, would receive a garland wreath; the garland crown was a well-known local emblem for the city's beauty.[58]

Pergamum was a center for Zeus worship, Asclepian healings, and the imperial cult, any or all of which could have been in mind with the reference to Satan having his throne where the people lived (2:13).[59]

---

[53] Hemer, *Letters to the Seven Churches of Asia in Their Local Setting*, 44–47; Osborne, *Revelation*, 124.

[54] See esp. Eduard Lohse ("Synagogue of Satan and Church of God: Jews and Christians in the Book of Revelation," *Svensk Exegetisk Årsbok* 58 [1993]: 606–24), who shows the ways in which Revelation elsewhere discloses Jews and Christians not having made a complete or formal break from one another. Cf. also Mark R. J. Bredin, "The Synagogue of Satan Accusation in Revelation 2:9," *Biblical Theology Bulletin* 28 (1998): 160–64.

[55] Smalley, *Revelation to John*, 65; Beale, *Book of Revelation*, 240.

[56] Osborne, *Revelation*, 128. Cf. Mounce, *Book of Revelation*, 270.

[57] Hemer, *Letters to the Seven Churches in Asia Minor in Their Local Setting*, 69–70.

[58] Mounce, *Book of Revelation*, 76–77; Osborne, *Revelation*, 135.

[59] Mounce, *Book of Revelation*, 79; Beale, *Book of Revelation*, 246.

The testimony and martyrdom of the local Christian named Antipas is otherwise unknown but certainly fits the Domitianic persecution. The teaching of Balaam (v. 14) is only slightly less mysterious than the sect of the Nicolaitans, which reappears in verse 15. The reference is to Numbers 22:1–25. Is it merely a coincidence that both *Balaam* (in Hebrew) and *Nikolaos* (in Greek) mean "conquer the people"? The expression describes what these false teachers were trying to accomplish; does it also suggest the two groups are one and the same, or at least each part of a larger entity? Hidden manna would have been understood to be the "bread of life" that many Jews believed would be restored in the end times and that Jesus spiritually provided in his own person and ministry (John 6:30–59). A white stone could be used as an admission ticket to a feast, a sign of initiation into a religious group, a vote of acquittal in a court, or a magical amulet offering permanent protection for its possessor.[60] Any or all of these could be "Christianized" to refer to its spiritual counterpart, demonstrating one to be part of God's true people. The new name probably refers to Jesus (or Christ, or Christian), reflective of the believer's new identity.

As with Pergamum, John addresses Thyatira with a picture of Jesus's coming in power and judgment because there is more condemnation than commendation. Jezebel, of course, was the evil queen and wife of King Ahab in Elijah's day (see esp. 1 Kings 21). The actual name of the prophet who was leading believers into sexual immorality and the eating of food sacrificed to idols in that context may have been something entirely different. But she functioned as a contemporary replica of Jezebel in her evil beliefs and practices (Rev 2:20). Because those who held to the teaching of Balaam in Pergamum also were accused of the same two sins, perhaps this "Jezebel" was the leader of those who followed "Balaam's" way. The sexual immorality

---

[60] David E. Aune, *Revelation 1–5* (Dallas: Word, 1997), 190–91. Cf. Blount, *Revelation: A Commentary*, 60.

committed explicitly with her could be literal, but it more likely refers to the idolatry she enticed her followers to pursue, just as the Israelites in the Old Testament were regularly likened to adulterers when they abandoned Yahweh for idols. Satan's so-called deep secrets (v. 24) could refer to some secret practice of this or another of the city's cults or even the belief in some branches of Gnosticism that one had to experience evil deeply in order to show that one was immune to its effects![61] Like someone smashing the beautiful pottery that Thyatira produced,[62] Christ would destroy those in the church who did not repent (v. 27). The morning star could refer to Venus as a key symbol of Roman sovereignty, implying that Christ would give the overcomer spiritual power greater even than what Rome offered.[63] Or it could be an oblique way of referring to his giving of himself (see 22:16 and cf. Num 24:17).

Sardis, the city, closely resembled its church. Both had been seen better times, and both refused to admit that those glory days were behind them (cf. 3:1b).[64] Coming like a thief (v. 3) is a probable allusion to the teaching of Jesus (in Luke). Soiling one's clothes was a common metaphor for committing wicked deeds, just as dressing in white denoted forgiveness, restoration, and renewal (v. 4). Blotting someone out of a book (v. 5) referred to removing someone from membership in a given community and makes its first metaphorical appearance in Scripture in Exodus 32:32–33. John uses the double negative, though, to stress that the overcomer will never have his or her name blotted out of God's book of the citizens of his kingdom. This contrasted strongly with the synagogues that were literally blotting Christians' names out of their books of members. Acknowledging someone before the angels

---

[61] Cf. further Osborne, *Revelation*, 162–63.

[62] Beale, *Book of Revelation*, 260. Cf. Smalley, *Revelation to John*, 72.

[63] Beale, *Book of Revelation*, 269. Cf. Boxall, *Revelation of Saint John*, 67.

[64] Mounce, *Book of Revelation*, 91. Cf. Fee, *Revelation*, 44–45.

in heaven recalls Christ's words in Luke 12:8 and Matthew 10:32. That Jesus could guarantee to preserve someone would have offered great comfort in a community with a seemingly impregnable hilltop fortress that had nevertheless twice fallen to enemies when its guards were too complacent to keep watch for people climbing up the steep cliffs atop which it sat.[65]

Philadelphians are helped by Christ in his role as holding "the key of David," which opens what no one can shut and vice versa (3:7). Old Testament background appears in Isaiah 22:22. Here the use suggests admission or denial into God's kingdom. The "hour of trial that is going to come on the whole world" (v. 10) has typically been linked with the great tribulation of 7:14, but if that association is correct, it is the only place in the seven letters where a reference occurs to the horrors of the end times just prior to Christ's return. Perhaps "world" here (Gk. *oikoumenē*), as it often did in the first century, means the Roman world or empire and refers to persecution in John's day or shortly afterwards.[66] Then Philadelphia would contrast even more directly with Smyrna. Both churches were faithful, but one was persecuted and the other not, showing that obedience to Christ's commands offers no guarantee of exemption from suffering. The pillar in the temple of God that no one will leave strikingly contrasts with the frequent earthquakes experienced in and around Philadelphia, which often caused people to flee from buildings that might crumble.[67] The new Jerusalem will reappear in chapter 21 as the community of all God's redeemed on the new earth in the eternal state.

---

[65] Osborne, *Revelation*, 174, 177.

[66] Is it merely a coincidence that the Philadelphian church lasted until 1392, long after the churches in the other six cities had been destroyed, several by the Islamic invasion already in the seventh century? See further Aune, *Revelation 1–5*, 240; Keener, *Revelation*, 154.

[67] Blount, *Revelation: A Commentary*, 66; Fee, *Revelation*, 45.

Maybe no letter to one of the seven churches receives as much illumination from historical-cultural background as does John's missive to Laodicea. Countless readers over the centuries have assumed that, when Christ declared that he wished the church would be either hot or cold, he was wanting it either to be clearly alive with passion for the things of God or clearly opposed, not in some in-between, wishy-washy state. Lukewarmness is what Christ rejects vehemently (3:15–16). But the testimony of ancient writers, confirmed by modern archaeology, demonstrates that Laodicea got its water supply via aqueducts either from the cool, invigorating mountain streams near neighboring Colossae or from the hot, therapeutic springs of neighboring Hierapolis. Unfortunately, by the time the water arrived at Laodicea, it was lukewarm and not as enjoyable to drink. Cold and hot are thus both metaphors for being good and godly.[68] After all, why would God ever want people to be implacably opposed to him when they might be on the verge of making a full and lasting commitment to Christ? Laodicea was also famous for its wealth as a banking center, its black wool industry, and a medical school that produced eye salve.[69] By contrast, verse 17 decries the poverty, blindness, and poorly clothed nature of the church there, spiritually speaking. Jesus offers them spiritual gold to become truly rich, pure spiritual clothing, and eye salve that would restore their spiritual sight (v. 18). His patient knocking at the doors of the church in hopes that it would allow him back into their

---

[68] See esp. M. J. S. Rudwick and E. M. B. Green, "The Laodicean Lukewarmness," *Expository Times* 69 (1957–58): 176–78; and Stanley E. Porter, "Why the Laodiceans Received Lukewarm Water (Revelation 3:15–18)," *Tyndale Bulletin* 38 (1987): 143–49. Craig R. Koester ("The Message to Laodicea and the Problem of Its Local Context: A Study of the Imagery in Rev 3:14–22," *New Testament Studies* 49 [2003]: 407–24) comes to the same conclusion based on ordinary dining practices in the ancient world rather than on the town's water supply. He also notes the wider familiarity than just in Laodicea of the imagery behind v. 17.

[69] Trafton, *Reading Revelation*, 52; Fee, *Revelation*, 57.

midst (v. 20) distinguishes itself dramatically from the forced entry by the Romans into the town despite its impressive triple gates.[70]

Heavenly Praise: Chapters 4–5

These two chapters do not need a lot of explanation with respect to historical-cultural background. To begin with, the scene unfolds in heaven rather than on earth. Moreover, much of the imagery is timeless and cross-cultural and needs little explanation—heavenly residents singing praises to the triune God, precious gems adding to the splendor and magnificence of the setting, and the accoutrements of universal adoration and worship. Nevertheless, we may note how first-century members of the churches in Asia Minor would have likely understood some of the other less unambiguous details.

A throne in heaven suggests the presence of God. That John saw merely "someone sitting on it" (4:2) not only reflects the reticence to speak of Yahweh too directly but the likelihood that John saw no face, no distinguishing appearance, merely a portion of a vague apparition of some kind, keeping God's full glory appropriately hidden for the time being. Even at that, what was disclosed was radiant and beautiful, like resplendent precious gems (v. 3). The four living creatures resemble the distinctives of the four faces of the flying creature in Ezekiel's vision (see especially Ezek 1:4–15), all of whom were viewed as strong and powerful animals. Nevertheless, like every other element of creation, they see and worship God ceaselessly (vv. 6–11). They declare his holiness in the language of Isaiah 6:3 (v. 8). Whatever glory or authority other heavenly beings or residents may have, they yield it to the Almighty—casting their crowns down before him (v. 10).[71]

---

[70] Hemer, *Letters to the Seven Churches in Asia Minor in Their Local Setting*, 204; Rudwick and Green, "Laodicean Lukewarmness," 178–79.

[71] I.e., "an act of vassalage or subordination," demonstrating "that homage belongs only to God. God alone is worthy of such obeisance." Even the Roman Emperor "will be forced to submit to God."—Osborne, *Revelation*, 239–40.

A scroll written on both sides and sealed with seven seals would have been extremely important, likely an imperial edict (5:1).[72] The Lion who is a Lamb sounds like a grotesque oxymoron until one realizes that both depict contrasting dimensions of Christ's ministry. The Warrior King is the one who first became the Suffering Servant and sacrificial victim for the sins of humanity (vv. 5–6).[73] The scroll, we will see, contains the coming judgments that God is going to pour out on the earth. Worthiness to disclose its contents depends on willingness to suffer for the eternal punishment merited by those who are about to experience temporal horrors (vv. 9–10). It is particularly striking when we realize that not even God in all his greatness and love can open the scroll, except to the extent that he is likewise the incarnate Messiah (vv. 3–5).

Seals, Trumpets, and Bowls (with Various Interludes): Chapters 6–19

Not only do the contents of the first five seals suggest events fulfilled in the first century and many times since, but also the imagery reinforces this suggestion. The scroll of judgment cannot be unrolled until the seals are removed, though of course one could look inside a small portion of it after most of the seals are taken off. Thus we should expect most or all of the seal judgments to be preludes or precursors to the period of great tribulation proper, introduced in 7:14.[74] We have

---

[72] Indeed, the entire chapter echoes Roman emperor worship but demonstrates that Christ not Caesar merits this tribute. See J. Daryl Charles, "Imperial Pretensions and the Throne Vision of the Lamb: Observations on the Function of Revelation 5," *Criswell Theological Review* 7 (1993): 85–97.

[73] Donald Guthrie, *The Relevance of John's Apocalypse* (Exeter: Paternoster; Grand Rapids: Eerdmans, 1987), 46–51; Bauckham, *Theology of the Book of Revelation*, 73–76.

[74] Osborne, *Revelation*, 250; Ladd, *Commentary on the Revelation of John*, 95–96, 98.

already mentioned the basic meaning of each seal, but we may add a few comments on accompanying imagery.

The rider on a white horse has often been identified as Jesus because of his role in 19:11. But this is an entirely different context, and there is no reason to make one and only one of the seals a reference to Christ's return to earth in triumph, when all of the others have to do with earlier events, solely involving judgment, and especially given the close parallelism of the paragraphs depicting each of the first seals.[75] The depiction of the third seal is one of the most compelling reasons for dating Revelation to the time of Domitian in the mid-90s. In AD 92, conditions were much like those described in 6:6. A significant drought killed much of the wheat and barley, making their prices skyrocket. But the olive trees and vines in the vineyards had deeper roots, enabling them to continue to grow.[76] These events would have been fresh in the minds of John's readers and all the more poignant as a result.

The sixth seal has led to all kinds of fanciful interpretations by those who have tried to interpret its imagery literally. Of course it is impossible for the heavens to recede like a scroll since they are not a solid substance that can be rolled up. And the use of simile throughout verses 12–14 reinforces this observation. Four times in verses 12–14, John uses the Greek *hōs* ("like" or "as") to compare what he saw to something that could be mentally imagined. He is obviously trying to find ways to describe what he has seen in his vision. Yet even when he is able to do so, that does not mean events will unfold exactly as

---

[75] The bow (v. 2) was an image of combat, especially among the Parthians to the northeast of the empire. The bow and arrow were also associated with the sun god, Apollo. Cf. further Murphy, *Fallen Is Babylon*, 205; Allen Kerkeslager, "Apollo, Greco-Roman Prophecy, and the Rider on the White Horse in Rev 6:2," *Journal of Biblical Literature* 112 (1993): 116–21.

[76] Justo L. González and Catherine G. González, *Revelation* (Louisville and London: Westminster John Knox, 1997), 48–49; Osborne, *Revelation*, 281.

he sees them; one has to understand what each element in his visions symbolizes. In other words, we don't need to anticipate four literal horses and riders with the colors given in chapter 6; we need to anticipate what they represent—militarism, warfare, famine, and death. But when John cannot describe a vision literally but repeatedly says x was "like" y, we know he is struggling even to put into words the ineffable. Thus we should not dissect verses 15–16 but recognize the cumulative effect of these details to mean something akin to our expressions, "All hell broke loose," or "The world was turned upside down." Verse 17 explains the meaning in sufficient detail: the great day of God's wrath upon the wicked has arrived.[77]

A hiatus occurs before the seventh seal is broken—the time at which we have suggested John steps back from the edge of the Abyss, so to speak, and which is comprised of the seven trumpet judgments. Here the key purpose is to introduce another kind of seal—the seal of the living God put on the foreheads of the servants of God (7:2–3). Some believers will live, no doubt, through the coming tribulation; the only question is, Who are they? The highly Jewish imagery of verses 4–8 has suggested to classic dispensationalists that only Jewish Christians (or *some* Jewish Christians) will remain on earth at this time, whereas everyone else will be raptured (cf. 7:14). Especially when we see the great contrast between 144,000 (12,000 from each of the twelve tribes of Israel) and a great multitude that cannot be counted from every people group standing before Christ's heavenly throne (v. 9), we can easily be tempted to adopt this perspective.[78] But just as in 5:5–6, John *heard* about a Lion but *looked* and saw a Lamb— with both being symbols for Jesus, here too John *hears* the number of

---

[77] Cf. Witherington, *Revelation*, 135–36; Philip E. Hughes, *The Book of Revelation* (Leicester: Apollos; Grand Rapids: Eerdmans, 1990), 92.

[78] E.g., Robert L. Thomas, *Revelation 1–7* (Chicago: Moody, 1992), 478; cf. also Walvoord, *Revelation of Jesus Christ*, 143.

those sealed (v. 4); but when he *looks*, he sees the numberless multitude (v. 9). It is better, therefore, to take both groups as pictures of the multiethnic church of Jesus Christ, embracing Jew and Gentile alike. On one hand it is the fulfillment of all the promises to Israel; on the other hand it is comprised of individuals "from every nation, tribe, people and language."[79] The language of 7:14 reads more naturally as a flash-forward, referring to those who were once *in* the great tribulation but now have come *out of* it.[80]

After the silence in heaven after the opening of the seventh seal, the fire, thunder, lightning, and earthquake emerge more like cosmic sound effects introducing the next series of judgments (8:1–5) than some independent event, separate from them.[81] The first four trumpets, as we have already noted, recall the plagues on Egypt in Pharaoh's day. The significance of those plagues was not that each carried some independent symbolism but rather the cumulative effect continually increased the suffering of the Egyptians so that their despot finally relented (at least temporarily) and let the Israelites leave. So, too, here we should not try to discern what fire and hail, turning waters bloody or bitter and striking the heavenly bodies, represent besides punishment and upheaval on a more widespread scale than the world has previously known.[82] Now the great tribulation has formally begun. Yet the repeated fraction of one-third throughout verses 6–12 reminds

---

[79] E.g., Roloff, *Revelation*, 98; Hughes, *Book of Revelation*, 94–95; Christopher R. Smith, "The Portrayal of the Church as the New Israel in the Names and Order of the Tribes in Revelation 7.5–8," *Journal for the Study of the New Testament* 39 (1990): 111–18; Richard Bauckham, "The List of the Tribes in Revelation 7 Again," *Journal for the Study of the New Testament* 42 (1991): 99–115.

[80] One would not normally introduce special guests from a foreign country, for example, by saying, "These people have come out of a terrible war zone" if they had never been in it in the first place. Cf. Ladd, *Commentary on the Revelation of John*, 117–18.

[81] Smalley, *Revelation to John*, 213–18; Trafton, *Reading Revelation*, 87–89.

[82] Smalley, *Revelation to John*, 218–19; Boxall, *Revelation of Saint John*, 137–38.

us that a majority of the world remains comparatively unaffected by these horrors; this is not yet the worst of what is to be unleashed on creation.[83]

Just as the fifth and sixth seals proved different from the first four, so likewise the fifth and sixth trumpets, also called the first and second of three woes (9:1–21), shift gears significantly. A star fallen from sky to earth sounds like a fallen angel (i.e., a demon). That he is given the key to the Abyss, believed to be a home of demons (v. 1), reinforces this perception. Despite Hal Lindsey's famous and creative notion that the locusts arising from the Abyss are armed helicopters,[84] their demonic origin (cf. also v. 11) suggests something more spiritual and supernatural (not to mention that no one in the first century could have ever been expected to imagine armed helicopters!).[85] Again, it is the gruesomeness and horror of their overall depiction (vv. 7–11) that is meant to strike us. If there was a first-century analogy intended, it would most likely have been the fierce Parthian cavalry to the northeast of the Roman Empire, whose riders often swung a mace-like weapon around behind them with one hand as they guided their horses into battle with their other hand.[86]

The sixth trumpet (or second woe) leads to the death of a third of humanity (vv. 15, 18). Is this physical or spiritual death? Huge armies of destroying angels appear twice in the Babylonian Talmud. In one instance, "180,000 angels of destruction go out every night," to wreak havoc with spiritual rather than physical force (*b. Pesahim* 112b; cf. also *b. Shabbat* 88a). If one takes the "two myriads of myriads" in verse

---

[83] Keener, *Revelation*, 272; Fee, *Revelation*, 124.

[84] Hal Lindsey, *There's a New World Coming: A Prophetic Odyssey* (Santa Ana, CA: Vision House Publishers, 1973), 138–39.

[85] Witherington, *Revelation*, 154. Cf. Paige Patterson, *Revelation* (Nashville: B&H, 2012), 221.

[86] Caird, *Revelation of St. John the Divine*, 122; Blount, *Revelation: A Commentary*, 179.

16 as an actual numeral ($2 \times 10,000 \times 10,000 = 200,000,000$) and then looks for ordinary human armies that could be amassed in such number, one can understand why Lindsey was led to suggest China (not to mention their political role at the height of the Cold War; otherwise India could almost as readily be conceived!).[87] But if the figure is simply the largest named number in the Greek language squared and multiplied by two and if the armies are demonic and supernatural, then such political demographics are irrelevant.[88]

The second interlude introduces us to another mighty angel and a little scroll (chap. 10). The angel's stride encompasses both land and sea (what it will take two separate demonic beasts to do later), as he represents God's universal sovereignty. John uses the diminutive form *bibliarion* for this scroll, distinguishing it from the one containing all of the judgments.[89] Just as in Ezekiel 2–3, the prophet is to eat it, discovering it to be bittersweet (v. 9). As in Ezekiel the sweetness comes from the salvation predicted for God's people; the bitterness from the judgment on unbelievers and the persecution of believers.[90] The seven thunders are mysterious because John is not allowed to write about them (vv. 3–4), but the message that is disclosed is sufficient: "There will be no more delay" (v. 6). That the mystery of God is accomplished with the seventh trumpet (v. 7) further reinforces our conviction that the seven bowls are simply an unpacking of what the seventh trumpet contains.

Most commentators acknowledge that chapter 11 contains some of the most difficult material to decipher in the entire Apocalypse. The

---

[87] Lindsey, *Late Great Planet Earth*, 86.

[88] David E. Aune, *Revelation 6–16* (Dallas: Word, 1998), 539. Cf. Smalley, *Revelation to John*, 240.

[89] Probably containing the contents of 11:1–13. See, e.g., Mounce, *Book of Revelation*, 202.

[90] Cf. Murphy, *Fallen Is Babylon*, 260; R. Dalrymple, "These Are the Ones . . . [Rev. 7]," *Biblica* 86 (2005): 396–406.

only solid hint we get concerning the measuring of the temple is that what is not measured is given over to outsiders for destruction (v. 2), which suggests that the part measured is somehow protected. There is both protection and destruction of the work of God's people during the tribulation. The two witnesses are described as having power similar to what Moses and Elijah exercised in Old Testament times (vv. 3–6). In keeping with the protection and destruction theme, they appear to have been killed, but then they are raised to life and taken to heaven (vv. 7–12). At least we can say that those who represent Christ during the tribulation may appear to have had their witness extinguished only to have it brought back to life again.[91] That this happens in a great city, metaphorically identified with the wicked towns and lands of Sodom and Egypt but is actually "where also their Lord was crucified" (v. 8) suggests Jerusalem. Perhaps we are meant to see the same occasion mentioned in Romans 11:25–26 when large numbers of Jewish people come to the Lord (cf. v. 13 here).[92]

Chapter 11:2–3 also introduces us to the first of several references in Revelation to a period of three and one-half years, alternately calculated as 42 months or 1,260 days (i.e., with thirty-day months). The most obvious symbolism of this time period is that it is half of seven, the number of completeness. In other words, three and one-half units of time and their numerical equivalents form a particularly incomplete and inadequate period.[93] One popular line of interpretation, since the rise of modern dispensationalism in the 1830s, has added the three-and-one-half-year period, variously described in chapter 11, to the three-and-one-half-year period mentioned several times in chapters

---

[91] Cf. David E. Holwerda, "The Church and the Little Scroll (Revelation 10, 11)," *Calvin Theological Journal* 34 (1999): 148.

[92] Ladd, *Commentary on the Book of Revelation*, 159–60. Many commentators, however, take the city to be Rome, given all the other allusions to Rome throughout the book.

[93] Roloff, *Revelation*, 130. Cf. Osborne, *Revelation*, 420.

12–13 to create the idea of the tribulation lasting seven years. But John nowhere adds any of these references together, nor does he ever refer to a seven-year period. One could imagine that if he had been shown that the tribulation lasted for seven years, God would be declaring it to be the last and most complete word on human history, a depressing and disturbing notion indeed. But if it is the consummately incomplete period, depicted as three and one-half years, then John holds out hope for something much better to come, as chapters 20–22 will disclose. After all, the literary unity of 11:1–14:5 suggests that we have only one period of time described variously and repeatedly in these chapters.[94]

That 12:1 forms the one flashback within chapters 6–19 reinforces this supposition. The chronology does not advance beyond where we left things in chapter 11 when additional references to three and one-half years appear in the next two chapters. The heavenly woman depicted in 12:1, who is ready to give birth to a male child in verse 2, seems not to represent Mary or any individual woman but the entire people of God, from whom the Messiah arises (v. 5, citing Ps 2:9).[95] Those people, who subsequently become not merely Jews and those who convert to Judaism but Christians of all ethnicities, are pursued and persecuted by Satan after he fails to thwart Jesus's birth, life, death, and exaltation (vv. 13, 15, 17). But Christians remain spiritually protected (vv. 6, 14, 16).[96] The time of Jesus's first coming is also the time at which Satan is cast out of heaven and hurled down to earth (vv. 7–9, 13; cf. Luke 10:18).

---

[94] Antoninus K. W. Siew, *The War Between the Two Beasts and the Two Witnesses: A Chiastic Reading of Revelation 11:1–14:5* (London and New York: T & T Clark, 2005).

[95] Mounce (*Book of Revelation*, 231) speaks of the entire "messianic community." Cf. Osborne, *Revelation*, 457–58.

[96] Beale, *Book of Revelation*, 679–80; Trafton, *Reading Revelation*, 124.

Chapter 13 introduces us to the other two members of the unholy trinity, each of whom is a parody of their holy counterparts.[97] The beast coming out of the sea has ten horns and seven heads, just like Satan, the dragon, did (12:3). The two are closely related yet not identical since the beast has its crowns on its horns rather than on its heads (13:1). Whereas Christ has godly names written on him (19:16), this Antichrist has blasphemous names on itself. It has body parts that resemble different animals (13:2), much akin to the visions of the beast in Daniel 7:1–8, which stood for various hostile empires, suggesting that again an evil empire is in view.[98] Rome provided the first-century model; the end-times empire will resemble ancient Rome on steroids! Just as God empowered Jesus, Satan empowered the Antichrist (13:2). Just as Christ was crucified and resurrected, this beast seemed to have a fatal wound on one of its heads that had been healed (v. 3). But the expression "seemed to have" (v. 3) suggests it was in some sense a fake—not a real death and resurrection as with Jesus.[99] All of the earth's inhabitants "whose names have not been written in the Lamb's book of life" will worship the beast (v. 8). In other words, ultimately there are only two kinds of people in the world—those who are Christ followers and those who are Satan followers, even if they may not realize it.

A second beast comes out of the earth (v. 11) as a parody of the Holy Spirit. It resembles a lamb (like Jesus) but speaks like Satan. It exercises the authority of the first beast, just as the Spirit exercises

---

[97] Mounce, *Book of Revelation*, 251; Fee, *Revelation*, 177.

[98] Smalley, *Revelation to John*, 336; Blount, *Revelation: A Commentary*, 246. See further Peter A. Abir, *The Cosmic Conflict of the Church: An Exegetico-Theological Study of Revelation 12, 7–12* (Frankfurt and New York: Peter Lang, 1995).

[99] A woodenly literal translation of v. 3a could read, "And one from its heads [was] like having been slain unto death, and its plague of death was healed." At any rate, the use of *hōs* ("like" or "as") makes the image a simile, not an actual description of what happened.

the authority of Jesus (v. 12). It works miraculous signs, including bringing fire from heaven, just as the Spirit produces miracles (vv. 13–14), including the tongues of fire at Pentecost. It empowered people to worship the first beast, just as the Spirit empowered people to worship Christ (v. 15). It singled out its followers with a mark on their foreheads just as God stamped his servants with a seal on theirs (v. 16; recall 7:3). The mysterious number 666 could be Hebrew *gematria* or numerology for Nero Caesar.[100] But perhaps more likely, in light of the way the rest of the book uses sevens as the complete number, 777 would be the complete triune number, making 666 the obvious parody. The three persons of the unholy triad of Satan, Antichrist, and false prophet try to imitate their counterparts in the Holy Trinity. They are convincing enough to fool many but always fall just short of the real thing, just as 666 falls just short of 777 in all three digits.[101]

The 144,000 of 7:5–8 make a reappearance in chapter 14. Only they could learn a new song accompanied by heavenly musicians resembling harpists (vv. 2–3). Now this elite cadre of witnesses who lived through the tribulation are said to have been redeemed from the earth (recall our comments on 7:14), furthering the support for our equation of the two diverse groups in chapter 7.[102] One should not read any misogyny into 14:4 or even any asceticism or promotion of celibacy. Purity from sexual intercourse is a recurring biblical metaphor, portraying the spiritual purity of not defiling oneself with idol

---

[100] This is the earliest known interpretation because already in the late second century Irenaeus knows of manuscripts that read 616 instead of 666. For 666, the consonants of Nero Caesar must have been, in Hebrew, NRWN QSR (50 + 200 + 6 + 50 + 100 + 60 + 200), spelling Nero with its alternate form as Neron. The more normal spelling, without the second *N*, would have reduced the total value of the letters by fifty, hence 616.

[101] Beasley-Murray, *Book of Revelation*, 219–21; Peterson, *Reversed Thunder*, 126.

[102] Beasley-Murray, *Book of Revelation*, 222; Smalley, *Revelation to John*, 355–56.

worship (see esp. throughout Hosea).[103] The imagery of firstfruits here is not identical to Paul's usage (Rom 8:23; 11:16; 1 Cor 15:20, 23), in which the initial fruit to appear on the tree represents the promise of more to come. Rather, this is the Old Testament use in which one offers the best of one's crops as a gift to God (Exod 23:16; 34:22; Lev 2:12; 23:17; etc.).[104] Out of all of humanity, believers become a living sacrifice for their Lord. Chapter 14:5 does not imply they are absolutely sinless, but they have not fallen prey to the one all-encompassing lie that the unholy trinity promoted—to abandon the one true God for a demonic counterfeit.[105]

A vision of three angels now balances out the dirty dealings of the three beasts. Together they preach the gospel, announce judgment on the evil end-times empire (now likened to Babylon—the most wicked and feared of the Israelites' Old Testament enemies), and promise eternal punishment for those who serve Satan rather than God (14:6–12). The chapter closes with two partially parallel visions—one of a harvest of the earth (like a farmer who reaped his grain with a sickle) in verses 14–17 and one of the winepress of God's wrath in verses 18–20. The latter clearly reuses Old Testament pictures of the judgment of the wicked. The former could be intended to be parallel, but more likely, especially in view of Jesus's seed parables,

---

[103] Elizabeth Schüssler Fiorenza, *Revelation: Vision of a Just World* (Minneapolis: Fortress, 1991), 88. More generally, cf. Raymond C. Ortlund Jr., *Whoredom: God's Unfaithful Wife in Biblical Theology* (Grand Rapids: Eerdmans; Leicester: Apollos, 1996) = *God's Unfaithful Wife: A Biblical Theology of Spiritual Adultery* (Downers Grove: IVP, 2003).

[104] Fee (*Revelation*, 193) thinks Jeremiah 2:2–3, referring back to the Exodus, is particularly in view. If the other meaning of "firstfruits" is pressed, believers alive during the tribulation could still be the firstfruits of all of God's people of all time, living and dead.

[105] Boxall (*Revelation of Saint John*, 204) summarizes: "The lie is that idolatry is harmless, that compromise is possible and even beneficial, that it does not destroy the soul."

may refer to the harvest of souls of people who come to Christ from throughout the world.[106]

Chapter 15 resembles the other heavenly visions, and visions of heavenly individuals, in which the details seem primarily to serve to create an overall impression of magnificence, brilliance, splendor, and purity.[107] Any single element may well not stand for anything specific on its own—the sea like glass (v. 2), the tabernacle of covenant law (v. 5), golden sashes (v. 6), or the smoke that came from the Lord's glory (v. 8). The worship offered by all the nations reinforces our conclusion that 14:14–16 depicted the conversion of people from all the world's ethnic groups.[108] The portrait also sets the stage for chapter 16 and the final series of seven judgments—the bowls of God's wrath (16:1). The first five bowls resemble though are not identical to the first five trumpet judgments and the plagues against Pharaoh in Exodus. Those who suffer because of them are those who "shed the blood of your holy people and your prophets" (v. 6). Directly or indirectly, they are responsible for many who have been martyred for their faith. As with both the seals and the trumpets, the sixth in this series of bowl judgments brings us to the edge of the precipice as the kings of the earth and their armies, empowered by the demonic trinity, gather together for a great battle (vv. 12–16).

This place in Hebrew is called Armageddon (a free Greek transliteration of the Hebrew *har Megiddo* or Mount Megiddo). Megiddo was a town at the western end of the Jezreel Valley—the breadbasket of ancient Galilee. It rose atop a hill some 40 to 60 meters (131–197

---

[106] See esp. Richard J. Bauckham, *The Climax of Prophecy: Studies on the Book of Revelation* (Edinburgh: T & T Clark, 1993), 238–337.

[107] Fee, *Revelation*, 211. Hughes (*Book of the Revelation*, 170) encapsulates it as "a preview, as it were, of the multitude of the redeemed rejoicing in the unclouded blessedness that is their destiny."

[108] Here appear the true "united nations" and perfect racial reconciliation (Osborne, *Revelation*, 573).

feet) above the valley floor below.[109] The area became proverbial as the site of great warfare due to the various battles that took place there in Israelite history, especially between the northern and southern kingdoms during the age of the divided monarchy (cf. Jdg 5:19; 2 Kgs 9:27; 2 Chr 35:22) and could refer to any great battlefield.[110] Once again with the seventh judgment in the series, all heaven and earth break loose so that we are on the verge of the dissolution of the universe (vv. 17–21). This time there is no retreat from the edge of the cliff, however. Instead, chapters 17–18 simply pause the action to describe in more detail this initially appealing but horrifically diabolical empire, now likened unambiguously to Rome—the city that sat on seven hills (17:9).[111] She is depicted as a prostitute (v. 1) who has fornicated with the kings of the earth—another use of sexual immorality to symbolize idolatrous behavior. The earth's people have become intoxicated with the wine of her adulteries (v. 2). Rome has conquered and/or made alliances with countless countries and added their pantheons of gods and goddesses to hers. She has become metaphorically drunk with the blood of martyrs, Christians killed for their faith (v. 6). Her emperors combine totalitarian political power with the religious arrogance and blasphemy of the imperial cult, claims to imperial deity and the requirement of worshipping Caesar. Rome, too, tries to parody Yahweh. But instead of being the ever-living one, the beast she rides

---

[109] "Tel Megiddo," *ShalomIl.com*, updated Oct. 29, 2011, accessed January 6, 2016, http://www.shalomil.com/places/tel-megiddo.

[110] Alan F. Johnson, "Revelation," in *Expositor's Bible Commentary, Revised,* ed. Tremper Longman III and David E. Garland, vol. 13 (Grand Rapids: Zondervan, 2006), 734. Hughes (*Book of the Revelation,* 178) explains, "Because of the literary character of the Apocalypse it is almost certainly a term of symbolical significance, denoting worldwide revolt rather than a particular territorial locality."

[111] David E. Aune (*Revelation 17–22* [Nashville: Thomas Nelson, 1998], 920–22) notes that a late first-century coin depicts the goddess Roma as a warrior, sitting on seven hills with her foot dipped into the Tiber River—all possible background imagery for this reference.

"once was, now is not, and yet will come" (v. 8), probably a reference to the belief by some that Nero, who committed suicide secretly, was really alive somewhere and amassing armies to come and march on Rome again.[112]

Verses 10–11 have provoked some of the most creative interpretations imaginable, but there is no natural place to start in creating a list of seven kings to end up with either Nero or Domitian. The republic became a monarchy with Augustus Caesar, after which came Tiberius, Caligula, Claudius, and Nero. If Nero is the fifth of the seven, or even sixth of eight (starting as early as Julius Caesar), the problem is that he was succeeded by three emperors in one year before Vespasian brought stability. If one skips over those three because they were so short-lived, one could make Vespasian the sixth, Titus the seventh, and Domitian the eight. But if "five have fallen, one is," and "the other has not yet come," that would make the book written during the time of Vespasian, corresponding to neither of the two most common suggestions, ancient or modern. It is better again to see seven as the complete number, meaning from God's perspective we are near the end but not there yet.[113] The ten horns representing ten kings (v. 12) also represent a common round number. Perhaps the number was inspired also by the ten provinces into which Rome was divided. The popular idea of a generation ago, again promulgated by Lindsey, that the (then) ten-member Common Market or European Union was in view[114] has been shown up for its foolishness by the ever-growing number of

---

[112] Gilles Quispel, *The Secret Book of Revelation* (New York: McGraw Hill, 1979), 96. Cf. Beale, *Book of Revelation*, 689–90, 872.

[113] Mounce, *Book of Revelation*, 316–18. For a table of the main proposals, trying to link with specific emperors, see Beale, *Book of Revelation*, 874. His discussion (pp. 872–75) shows the virtual impossibility of concluding for any one of them.

[114] See the presentation and sharp rebuttal of this perspective already 25 years ago by evangelical Christian statesman and member of the European Parliament, Sir Fred Catherwood, throughout his *Pro-Europe?* (Leicester: IVP, 1991).

members (28 as of mid-2015)! It is instructive to see how this political alliance turns in on itself, as evil and unholy alliances seem inevitably to do (vv. 16–18).[115]

If chapter 17 depicted the evil end-times empire as resembling Rome (and Babylon of old) in its political power and religious blasphemy, chapter 18 discloses that it was also the wealthiest realm imaginable in the first century. "The merchants of the earth will weep and mourn over her because no one buys their cargoes anymore" (v. 11)—cargoes that are then described as including some staples but primarily comprised of luxury goods, but also humans sold as slaves (vv. 12–13). The list is reminiscent of a bill of sale for the goods brought to the wealthy in Rome from every corner of the subjugated nations in far-flung portions of the empire.[116] Even ordinary sounds of happy, everyday life have vanished (vv. 22–23a). People looking for the closest modern-day equivalents should ask where one finds a nation (or a collection of multinational corporations?) that is the wealthiest superpower but also increasingly proves hostile to true Christianity.[117]

Chapter 19 brings us to the wedding feast of the Lamb (v. 7), the eschatological banquet of Isaiah 25:6–8, the great celebratory festival honoring Christ upon his return but for the benefit of all his people as well. Whether we are to envision literal food and drink, the intimacy of table fellowship in the ancient world is almost certainly the main point of this imagery.[118] But there is a second, macabre meal involving God's

[115] Mounce (*Book of Revelation*, 320) speaks of "the self-destroying power of evil," adding that "the wicked are not a happy band of brothers, but precisely because they are wicked they give way to jealousy and hatred."

[116] See further Bauckham, *Climax of Prophecy*, 338–83. Cf. throughout J. Nelson Kraybill, *Imperial Cult and Commerce in John's Apocalypse* (Sheffield: Sheffield Academic Press, 1996).

[117] Keener, *Revelation*, 442–43; Peterson, *Reversed Thunder*, 148.

[118] Aune, *Revelation 17–22*, 1063. Cf. throughout Craig L. Blomberg, *Contagious Holiness: Jesus' Meals with Sinners* (Leicester: Apollos; Downers Grove: IVP, 2005).

enemies, "the great supper of God" (Rev 19:17–18) in which the birds of prey feast on the carcasses of the soldiers in the armies slaughtered by Christ upon his return. Again this may not be a literal meal, or even a literal military slaughter, but the bottom line remains the destruction of all evil aligned against the Lord of the universe.[119] Chapter 19:19 picks up where 16:16 left off: the world's armies arrayed to do battle against the returning Christ. But the battle is over before it can begin; there will be no casualties among the redeemed (vv. 20–21).[120]

Millennium and a Re-created Universe: Chapters 20–22

We have already explained why it makes little sense to treat chapter 20 as a flashback, in which case only a (historic, not dispensational) premillennial understanding of Revelation accounts for all of the data presented. Because Christ has returned to earth, believers' reign with Christ also makes best sense as occurring on earth (v. 4), not spiritually and invisibly as in amillennialism.[121] At the end of the millennium, Satan is loosed to deceive the nations once more, if he can. After all, unbelievers alive when Christ returns apparently populate the planet during this phase of world history, too. Presumably they still reproduce, so that there are those at the end of this time who can still more explicitly serve Satan once he is freed (vv. 7–10). That any would still choose to do so after seeing the benevolence of Christ's reign so directly is a testimony of the depth of human depravity and the justice of eternal punishment. C. S. Lewis may well have been right when he postulated, in his classic novel *The Great Divorce*, that even if the inhabitants of hell were given a chance one day to be released and go to heaven they would refuse.[122]

---

[119] Smalley, *Revelation to John*, 496–97; Trafton, *Reading Revelation*, 182–83.

[120] Witherington, *Revelation*, 243; Peterson, *Reversed Thunder*, 165.

[121] Mounce, *Book of Revelation*, 366; Osborne, *Revelation*, 707.

[122] C. S. Lewis, *The Great Divorce* (London: G. Bles, 1946; New York and London: HarperCollins, 2001).

On any of the various interpretations of the millennium, the new heaven and new earth of Revelation 21–22 depict the eternal state. One can often plausibly speculate about the meaning of this or that detail, but again it is the overall impression of beauty, magnificence, perfect community among the redeemed, perfect joyful intimacy with God, and the absence of all suffering and sorrow that are meant to strike the reader the most. As with all of the imagery surveyed in this chapter, first-century meanings must be sought, even if the complete fulfillment lies still in the future. To take just one example, sea lovers may protest that a redeemed earth without any sea (21:1) could hardly be as enjoyable as one with various large bodies of salt water. But in the ancient Mediterranean world, the sea was often a place of great terror—storms leading to the loss of ships and their passengers or at least shipwreck, as well as the belief that they were prime territory for the habitations of demons.[123]

We could continue with further details of the new heavens and new earth that might have specific significance like this. For example, the kings of the earth bringing their glory into the eternal state (21:24) suggests some continuity between old and new creation as opposed to total dissolution and re-creation.[124] This in turn has massive significance for the ecological movement. We could go back and comb through the chapters already surveyed and pick up a few more minor items we have skipped over. But the quantity of data discussed should make the point with great clarity. The book of Revelation made best

---

[123] Cf. Aune, *Revelation 17–22*, 1,119; David Mathewson, "New Exodus as a Background for 'The Sea Was No More' in Revelation 21:10," *Trinity Journal* 24 (2003): 243–58; and Jonathan Moo, "The Sea That Is No More: Rev 21:1 and the Function of Sea Imagery in the Apocalypse of John," *Novum Testamentum* 51 (2009): 148–67.

[124] Among several important studies, see David Mathewson, "The Destiny of the Nations in Revelation 21:1–22:5: A Reconsideration," *Tyndale Bulletin* 53 (2002): 121–42.

sense of all to its original late first-century audience in Asia minor and must be interpreted via the requisite historical background information they simply knew intuitively.

Conclusion

Questions about historical reliability do not apply to apocalyptic literature in the same way they do to the other genres of the New Testament. One can argue for pre-Gospel tradition behind Matthew 23–24 and the book of Revelation;[125] but with the finished form of the Synoptics almost certainly available to John in the 90s, commonalities may also be due to John's more direct use of Synoptic tradition combined with whatever interpretive glosses his visionary experiences gave him. To the extent that John's Apocalypse depicts past or present events, from the perspective of the writer, however symbolically, one can confirm or disconfirm that they happened as alleged. But when one understands any significant portion of a given apocalypse to be referring to the future, even from the viewpoint of readers two millennia later, there is obviously no way yet to evaluate the accuracy of the prophecy. On the other hand, to the extent that such prophecies accurately summed up current or recent events from a first-century perspective, when one understands those prophecies to predict what will play itself out again sometime in the future on an ever grander but more awful scale, one can be confident that those scenarios will unfold in ways that will be discernible with the same levels of literal and metaphorical fulfillment.

The plausibility and popularity of the preterist position comes from the fact that the imagery of Revelation so consistently *does* match

---

[125] Paul T. Penley, *The Common Tradition Behind Synoptic Sayings of Judgment and John's Apocalypse: An Oral Interpretive Tradition of Old Testament Prophetic Material* (London: T & T Clark, 2010).

events and symbols of the late first-century Roman Empire. But, as we saw at the outset of this chapter, these matches are best understood as God's using the most understandable imagery for John and his audiences, with which they were intimately familiar, to portray, as it were, what the last days of the end times would be like. So we argued that a preterist-futurist approach to interpretation remains best. A good argument can still be made for John, the apostle and son of Zebedee, to have been the author of Revelation, but we also noted that little for our purposes depended on that conclusion. The date and circumstances seem likely to have been in the mid-90s under Domitian's short-lived but still intense persecution, but again not that much for interpretation depends on this conviction. The most prevalent and significant imagery in God's visions given to John was shown to be internally consistent, once the most likely meanings of the symbolism for late first-century inhabitants of Ephesus were uncovered. Given the amount of correlation between the letters to the seven churches in chapters 2–3 and the specific historical-cultural background of each of the seven communities, good reason also remains for believing that the future events prophesied will materialize as predicted.

Part Five

Canonicity and Transmission

Chapter 12

The Nag Hammadi Literature and New Testament Apocrypha

T hus far we have argued in detail for the reliability of the literature that forms the canonical New Testament. But what about
other ancient Christian literature? Can other documents compete
with the four New Testament Gospels, the Acts of the Apostles, the
thirteen letters of Paul, Hebrews, James, 1–2 Peter, 1–3 John and Jude,
or Revelation? To what extent can we speak of the historical trustworthiness of early noncanonical Christian literature? Should other
independent sources of information about Jesus and the early church
be added to our "database" of historical material?

This chapter will consider the two main bodies of literature from
the second through fifth centuries that to varying degrees came to be
deemed unorthodox and/or historically unreliable. The first is the collection of codices unearthed near Nag Hammadi in Egypt in late 1945.[1]

---

[1] The standard English edition is *The Nag Hammadi Library*, ed. James M.
Robinson, 2nd ed. (Leiden: Brill; New York: HarperCollins, 1988).

Most, though probably not all, of this collection is Gnostic in origin. Gnosticism was a branch of early Christianity that tended to be docetic in nature—believing in the full deity of Jesus but denying his full humanity. It combined ideas of Hellenistic philosophy and religion with emerging Christianity and occasionally sprinkled in small pinches of Judaism.[2] On the whole, though, it rejected the Old Testament in ways that apostolic Christianity never did, even at times embracing forms of anti-Semitism. Gnostic texts frequently focused on cosmology—questions surrounding the creation of the universe, the structure and role of unseen powers, and "aeons" or emanations from the now remote god of the Old Testament that mediates between humans and the heavenly beings. In Gnosticism, salvation generally comes by esoteric or elitist knowledge, especially the recognition that the spark of divinity lies inside each human being, which we have only to fan into flame to discover the power within. The material world was created by a rebellious emanation from the Godhead, so that matter is inherently evil. The faithful Gnostic, like many Greeks and Romans, looked as a result for the immortality of the soul but not the resurrection of the body, lest one be encumbered with something evil for all eternity.[3] Many of the Gnostic documents are called "Gospels," but not one is a narrative of even as much of Jesus's life as we find in the New Testament. Instead they tend to be collections of short sayings or dialogues supposedly of Jesus with one or more of his followers, which he spoke to them secretly after his resurrection.

---

[2] For the Jewish piece, see especially Carl B. Smith, *No Longer Jews: the Search for Gnostic Origins* (Peabody: Hendrickson, 2004). More generally, cf. also Birger A. Pearson, *Ancient Gnosticism: Traditions and Literature* (Minneapolis: Fortress, 2007).

[3] In addition to ibid., excellent, up-to-date introductions to ancient Gnosticism include Alastair H. B. Logan, *The Gnostics: Identifying an Early Christian Cult* (London and New York: T & T Clark, 2006); and Riemer Roukema, *Jesus, Gnosis and Dogma* (London and New York: T & T Clark, 2010).

The second body of literature to be surveyed is often called simply the New Testament Apocrypha.[4] It contains second- through fifth-century gospels, acts, epistles, and apocalypses. Again the gospels are not full-orbed narratives of Jesus's ministry but tend to fill in the gaps left by their canonical counterparts. What was Jesus like as a baby or a young boy? What did he do when he "descended to hell," to use the words officially added to the Apostles' Creed in the eighth century, half a millennium after the rest of the creed became standard in Christian usage? Because the canonical Acts of the Apostles really narrates significant numbers of episodes only from the ministries of Peter and Paul, the apocryphal acts fill in the gaps with stories about the travels and exploits of a number of the remaining apostles. One apocryphal letter purports to be the letter Paul wrote to the Corinthians in between what we call 1 and 2 Corinthians (see 2 Cor 2:4; 7:8). Others claim to preserve correspondence between Paul and Seneca, the Roman philosopher, or between Christ and Abgar, king of Syria.[5]

---

[4] The standard English edition is *New Testament Apocrypha*, ed. Wilhelm Schneemelcher, 2 vols., 2nd ed. (Cambridge: James Clarke; Louisville: Westminster John Knox, 1990–92).

[5] Some medieval and modern "apocrypha" have been created more duplicitously. For a treatment of a number of these, see Per Beskow, *Strange Tales About Jesus: A Survey of Unfamiliar Gospels* (Philadelphia: Fortress, 1983). The most celebrated medieval work in this vein has become the Gospel of Barnabas, a Muslim composition, which purports to be the original gospel that the canonical accounts have distorted. In it Judas replaces Jesus on the cross at the last minute, and no hint of Christ's divinity appears. For an English translation, see Lonsdale Ragg and Laura Ragg, *Gospel of Barnabas* (New York: Cosimo Classics, 2010). But the oldest known manuscript is a sixteenth-century Italian one, and there are no previous references to it anywhere in nearly a millennium of Islamic literature! The next oldest copy is an eighteenth-century Spanish version. The chances of its being truly ancient are nil. See Oddbjørn Leirvik, "History as a Literary Weapon: The Gospel of Barnabas in Muslim-Christian Polemics," *Studia Theologica* 54 (2001): 4–16; and Jan Joosten, "The Gospel of Barnabas and the Diatessaron," *Harvard Theological Review* 95 (2002): 73–96. For one of the most egregious modern examples of fictional apocrypha, see Drs. McIntosh and Twyman [*sic*], *The Archko Volume: Or, the*

Apocryphal apocalypses narrate the heavenly journeys of other early Christians besides John the seer and disclose Jewish and Christian counterparts to the "truths" disclosed through Gnostic cosmology.

Following these two surveys, we will look more briefly at some remaining documents that have been put forward for a "new *New Testament*," along with scattered sayings here and there that might qualify as authentic "agrapha"—sayings of Jesus not written in the canon. Finally, we will comment on how these additional sources stack up by several of the same criteria we used in assessing the reliability of the canonical texts. We do not have the space to examine every document that exists, but we will treat all of those that have been deemed by a significant slice of scholarship as relevant for studying New Testament reliability, and we will present representative examples of the remaining kinds of works that appear in these collections of ancient texts.

The Nag Hammadi Literature

The corpus of literature collected together into what has come to be called the Nag Hammadi Library contains forty-seven discrete documents. A few of these are clearly non-Gnostic or non-Christian. A brief fragment of Plato's *Republic* is one of them; another couple are Hermetic, a non-Christian Hellenistic philosophy akin to Gnosticism without any Christian elements. These include fragments of a work called Asclepius (21–29) and the Discourse on the Eighth and Ninth.[6]

Archeological Writings of the Sanhedrim and Talmuds of the Jews (New Canaan, CT: Keats, 1975 [orig. 1887]). This volume, purporting to contain records of the trials of Jesus, among other things, continues to be reprinted and pawned off as authentic despite the nineteenth-century conviction of its true author for forgery and plagiarism!

[6] Nicola Denzey Lewis, *Introduction to "Gnosticism": Ancient Voices, Christian Worlds* (Oxford: Oxford University Press, 2013), 207–17.

Some are not sufficiently distinctive in their ideology to be unambiguously associated merely with Gnostic Christianity (e.g., the Sentences of Sextus or the Acts of Peter and the Twelve Apostles).[7] The majority of them, however, contain clearly Gnostic ideas interwoven with Christian characters and concepts. Modern scholars have given the documents such esoteric names (based on their contents) as the Gospel of Truth, The Treatise on Resurrection, The Hypostasis of the Archons, the Exegesis of the Soul, the Book of Thomas the Contender, Eugnostos the Blessed, the Dialogue of the Savior, Thunder: Perfect Mind, The Concept of Our Great Power, The Second Treatise of the Great Seth, Zostrianos, The Thought of Norea, The Interpretation of Knowledge, and the Trimorphic Protennoia. Others are more conventionally labeled the Gospels of Thomas, Philip, Mary or the Egyptians; or the Apocryphon of James; the Acts of Peter and the Twelve Apostles; the Apocalypses of Paul, James, Adam, or Peter, and the Teachings of Silvanus.

Most of these books are preserved in Coptic, but portions of some have been discovered elsewhere in Greek or were discussed by the early church fathers in such a way as to suggest that they were first composed in Greek, making it likely that others were as well. Many, in their earliest form, may go back to the second and third centuries, even though their Coptic forms often date only from the fourth or fifth centuries.[8] Some may have existed, or even have first been written, in Syriac, inasmuch as Syria was home to a large number of Christian and quasi-Christian groups that produced Wisdom literature, often

---

[7] See especially Andrea J. Molinari, *The Acts of Peter and the Twelve Apostles (NHC 6.1): Allegory, Ascent, and Ministry in the Wake of the Decian Persecution* (Atlanta: SBL, 2000).

[8] For the extant fragments, see Andrew E. Bernhard, *Other Early Christian Gospels: A Critical Edition of the Surviving Greek Manuscripts* (London and New York: T & T Clark, 2006).

combining Hellenistic philosophies with Jewish or Christian concepts and creating at least partly heterodox literature.[9]

Representative Texts

The Apocryphon of James is perhaps best known for containing two parables attributed to Jesus not found in any other ancient documents. One calls on its listeners not to allow the kingdom of heaven to wither, comparing it to a palm shoot whose fruit fell on the ground, planting enough additional seeds around it that it used up the ground water and caused the original tree to wither (7, ll. 22–35). More positively, the other parable compares the Word to a grain of wheat, which someone sowed, had faith in, watched it sprout and produce many grains of seed, and loved (8, ll. 16–27). It is hard to be sure what these passages meant for their author; perhaps he was warning against Gnosticism proliferating so widely that it lost its elitist and distinctive nature but propagating enough so that it would continue to replenish itself with new adherents.[10] This same document, however, refers to a number of the passages in the canonical Gospels just by a title like "The Seed," "The Building," "The Lamps of the Virgins," "The Wage of the Workmen," and so on. This shows that this Apocryphon was composed, at least in part, at a later date than and written in knowledge of the New Testament Gospels, rather than forming an independent source of information about Jesus.

---

[9] See especially throughout Stevan L. Davies, *The Gospel of Thomas and Christian Wisdom* (New York: Seabury, 1983).

[10] Cf. David Brakke, "Parables and Plain Speech in the Fourth Gospel and the Apocryphon of James," *Journal of Early Christian Studies* 7 (1999): 215. Ron Cameron (*Sayings Traditions in the Apocryphon of James* [Cambridge, MA: Harvard University Press, 1984], 12–30) proposes a complex tradition-history for both passages, envisioning a core parable at the heart of each text as old and possibly going back to Jesus. A third passage can also be treated as a short parable or simile in 12, ll. 20–31 about the kingdom's being like a fruitful ear of corn.

The Gospel of Truth is important as a classic representation of second-century Gnosticism, most probably in its main, Valentinian form. An extended quotation from its opening paragraphs quickly discloses what a different world it represents than the canonical New Testament documents:

> The gospel of truth is a joy for those who have received from the Father of truth the gift of knowing him, through the power of the Word that came forth from the Pleroma—the one who is in the thought and the mind of the Father, that is, the one who is addressed as the Savior, [that] being the name of the work he is to perform for the redemption of those who were ignorant of the Father, while the name [of] the gospel is the proclamation of hope, being discovery for those who search for him.
>
> Indeed the all went about searching for the one from whom it (pl.) had come forth, and the all was inside of him, the incomprehensible, inconceivable one who is superior to every thought. Ignorance of the Father brought about anguish and terror. And the anguish grew solid like a fog so that no one was able to see. For this reason error became powerful; it fashioned its own matter foolishly, not having known the truth. It set about making a creature, with [all its] might preparing, in beauty, the substitute for the truth. (16, l. 31–17, l. 20)

Here we can see a few of the classic Gnostic themes. Salvation is all about correct knowledge as opposed to ignorance. Creation itself was an act of foolish error and a substitute for the truth, represented by pure mind. The Pleroma (Gk. for "fullness" [of the Godhead]) brought forth the Word. The "all" (another name for the totality of divine and angelic entities) sought for this gospel of redemption, only to find it inside those who became the true Gnostics. The Gospel of Truth likewise has a distinctive parable, one reminiscent of Jesus's parable of the lost sheep but with a clear Gnostic permutation: the Father is the shepherd who left the ninety-nine sheep to search for the one lost one. He rejoiced when he found it but not for its sake but because 100 is a complete number that was deficient when one was missing (31, l. 5–32, l. 17)![11]

The Treatise on the Resurrection illustrates some of the false teaching that may have already been taking shape in Corinth when Paul penned 1 Corinthians in the mid-50s. Scholars speak of an "overly realized eschatology," namely, the belief that the resurrection has already occurred spiritually and that there is no further bodily resurrection to which to look forward.[12] This document includes the following paragraph:

> Now if we are manifest in this world wearing him, we are that one's beams, and we are embraced by him until our setting, that is to say, our death in this life. We are drawn to heaven by him, like beams by the sun, not being restrained by anything. This is the spiritual resurrection which swallows up the psychic in the same way as the fleshly. (45, l. 9–46, l. 2)

Later the same author writes, "The *thought* of those who are saved shall not perish. The *mind* of those who have known him shall not perish" (46, ll. 22–24; emphasis added). Conversely, to those who ask if people leave their body behind, the author adds, "Let no one be given cause to doubt concerning this. . . . The visible members which

---

[11] For both the interpretation and application for the Gnostic, see Cullen I. K. Story, *The Nature of Truth in "The Gospel of Truth" and in the Writings of Justin Martyr: A Study of the Pattern of Orthodoxy in the Middle of the Second Christian Century* (Leiden: Brill, 1970), 22–23. Apart from this distinctive about the lost sheep, the parable resembles the form found in Matthew (usually held to be secondary to Luke's version) and is probably dependent on it. See Christopher M. Tuckett, "Synoptic Tradition in the Gospel of Truth and the Testimony of Truth," *Journal of Theological Studies* 35 (1984): 133–34.

[12] See especially Anthony C. Thiselton, "Realized Eschatology at Corinth," *New Testament Studies* 24 (1978): 510–26.

are dead shall not be saved" (47, l. 34–48, l.3). Again, "The world is an illusion, rather than the resurrection which has come into being through our Lord the Savior, Jesus Christ" (48, ll. 15–19). Finally, to clarify the nature of this resurrection, we read, "Therefore, do not . . . live in conformity with this flesh . . . but flee from the divisions and the fetters, and already you have the resurrection. For if he who will die knows about himself that he will die—even if he spends many years in this life he is brought to this—why not consider yourself as risen and (already) brought to this?" (49, ll. 9–24).[13]

The Gospel of Philip was little known until Dan Brown's novel *The Da Vinci Code* had one of its leading characters claim that Jesus was married to Mary Magdalene, based in part on a passage from this Gnostic text:

> And the companion of the [Savior is] Mary Magdalene. [But Christ loved] her more than [all] the disciples [and used to] kiss her [often] on her [mouth]. The rest of [the disciples were offended] by it [and expressed disapproval]. They said to him, "Why do you love her more than all of us?" The Savior answered and said to them, "Why do I not love you like her? When a blind man and one who sees are both together in darkness, they are no different from one another. When the light comes, then he who sees will see the light and he who is blind will remain in darkness." (63, l. 32–64, l. 9)

Brown's character alleged that in Aramaic the same word could mean both "companion" and "wife." That Jesus kissed Mary frequently on the mouth and loved her more than all of his male disciples combined with this allegation to lead to the charge that Jesus had married Mary.[14]

---

[13] For commentary on each of these passages, see esp. Bentley Layton, *The Gnostic Treatise on Resurrection from Nag Hammadi* (Missoula: Scholars, 1979).

[14] Dan Brown, *The Da Vinci Code* (New York: Doubleday, 2003), 323.

There are several fallacies with this argument, however. First, there is no obvious word in Aramaic that normally meant both "companion" and "wife."[15] Second, it is irrelevant what anything in Aramaic meant anyway; this Gospel was written in Greek and reflects no style or vocabulary to suggest an underlying Semitic source. Third, the Greek word for companion, *koinōnos,* has decidedly nonsexual overtones; it is the ordinary word used for sharing fellowship with another person.[16] Fourth, a brief kiss on the mouth in antiquity was not necessarily a sign of erotica; in several cultures it was a platonic greeting.[17] Fifth, the word "mouth" is not actually in the text of Philip. It has been restored by conjecture in a place where the manuscript is defective; hence, the brackets in the English translation. Sixth, Brown did not supply the full context for his quotation. In the second half of the excerpt above, Jesus implies that Mary has greater *spiritual* insight and perceptiveness. Jesus's love for her in this Gnostic context is therefore a spiritual and not a physical one. Earlier in this document Jesus had already explained that the heavenly person "begets" by spreading the word of knowledge from one person to another. And because words come from the mouth, the "perfect" (i.e., the fully initiated Gnostics) kiss one another on the mouth (58, l. 29–59, l. 6).[18] After all, the good Gnostics distance themselves from indulging the flesh. So the author of the Gospel of Philip would hardly introduce

---

[15] Richard S. Hess, the Earl S. Kalland Professor of Old Testament and Semitic Languages, Denver Seminary, in personal conversation, December 2003. Cf. also Tony Burke, *Secret Scriptures Revealed: A New Introduction to the Christian Apocrypha* (Grand Rapids: Eerdmans, 2013), 70.

[16] BDAG (553–54) lists as possible meanings, "one who takes part in someth. with someone, *companion, partner, sharer*" and "one who permits someone else to share in someth." The biblical and nonbiblical examples make clear that sexual sharing is not in view. BDAG has in mind the standard English usages of these words before they became sexualized (e.g., "partner") to refer to someone one has sex with outside of monogamous, heterosexual marriage.

[17] Burke, *Secret Scriptures Revealed,* 70.

[18] Cf. further Paul Foster, "The *Gospel of Philip,*" in *The Non-Canonical Gospels,* ed. Paul Foster (London and New York: T & T Clark, 2008), 74–76.

the otherwise unparalleled notion that Jesus, historically held to be celibate, had married a wife. Jesus's celibacy was good for the Gnostic, not something to be changed by asserting that he was married.[19]

The Dialogue of the Savior proves somewhat unique because it forms a collection of much shorter sayings of Jesus than most of the Gnostic literature. It also regularly features Matthew, Judas, and Mariam (Mary Magdalene?) interacting with Jesus but mentions none of his other followers. Much of Jesus's teaching here deals with the same cosmological topics that dominate those books that contain his longer discourses but occasionally passages parallel the Gospel of Thomas (on which, see pp. 570–79). Toward the end of the document, Judas says to Matthew, "We wish to know with what kind [of] garments we will be clothed, when we come forth from the corruption of the [flesh]." The Lord replies, "The archons [and] the governors have garments that are given to them for a time, which do not abide. As for you, [however], since you are sons of the truth, it is not with these temporary garments that you will clothe yourselves. Rather, I say to you that you will be blessed when you strip yourselves" (143, ll. 11–23). In other words, no bodily resurrection is anticipated, only a disembodied immortality. Shortly afterwards, Judas asks, "When we pray, how should we pray?" The Lord answers, "Pray in the place where there is no woman." Matthew then adds, first by quoting Jesus, "Destroy the works of womanhood," and then explains not because there is any other [manner of birth], but because "they will cease [giving birth]." Mariam protests, "They will never be obliterated." The Lord replies, however, "[Who] knows that they will [not] dissolve ... ?" (144, ll. 14–25). Women are valued primarily for their ability to bear children, which will no longer occur in the life to come.[20]

---

[19] Birger A. Pearson, "Did Jesus Marry?" *Bible Review* 21 (2005): 32–39.

[20] For a full-orbed anthology of perspectives about women in the Nag Hammadi Library, see Karen L. King, ed., *Images of the Feminine in Gnosticism* (Harrisburg: Trinity Press International, 2000).

The Apocalypse of Adam is representative of a minority of the Nag Hammadi documents that don't involve Jesus. Rather, this work purports to be the instruction of Adam to his son Seth (one of the Gnostic sects called itself Sethian). Again the topics that are treated largely involve heavenly powers, creation, error, secret revelation, and salvation by true knowledge. Somewhat unique is a poetic response, divided into thirteen stanzas, to the question of where error and deceptive words came from. The thirteen answers given are the heavens, a great prophet, a virgin womb, someone Solomon sought, a drop of water, an aeon which is below, a child, a cloud that enveloped a rock, muses, a cloud of desire, a father who desired his own daughter, two illuminators, and a word (77. 1. 27–82. 1. 20). This collection of answers forms a syncretistic combination of Jewish, Christian, and pagan notions![21]

The Gospel of Thomas

By far the most famous and significant find from Nag Hammadi was the Gospel of Thomas, sometimes called the Gnostic Gospel of Thomas to distinguish it from one of the New Testament Apocrypha often labeled the Infancy Gospel of Thomas. This is the only document from the entire library that consistently contains texts that resemble passages from the canonical Gospels, so it merits a section all its own.[22] Although the complete document exists only in a fourth-century Coptic manuscript, three fragments of it in Greek from the late second century were discovered at the end of the nineteenth and

---

[21] It may also have been an independent piece originally, incorporated somewhat awkwardly into this work. See Douglas M. Parrott, "The Thirteen Kingdoms of the Apocalypse of Adam: Origin, Meaning, and Significance," *Novum Testamentum* 37 (1989): 67–87.

[22] For an excellent readable introduction to this gospel, see Nicholas Perrin, *Thomas, the Other Gospel* (Louisville and London: Westminster John Knox, 2007); more technically, cf. Simon Gathercole, *The Composition of the Gospel of Thomas: Original Language and Influences* (Cambridge: Cambridge University Press, 2012).

beginning of the twentieth centuries. Like the other so-called gospels from Nag Hammadi, it is not a narrative of events from Jesus's life but a collection of "secret teachings which the living [i.e., resurrected] Jesus spoke," in this case 114 consecutive teachings often introduced with nothing more than "Jesus said."[23]

Roughly a third of the sayings have an identifiable parallel in the canonical Gospels. Sometimes the parallelism is close; sometimes it is more distant. Thomas 9, for example, contains a version of the parable of the sower much like its canonical counterparts, though in more abbreviated form and without any interpretation. Saying 20 explains that the kingdom of heaven "is like a mustard seed, the smallest of all seeds. But when it falls on tilled soil, it produces a great plant and becomes a shelter for birds of the sky."[24] Saying 26 closely matches Jesus's teaching from the Sermon on the Mount: "You see the mote in your brother's eye, but you do not see the beam in your own eye. When you cast the beam out of your own eye, then you will see clearly to cast the mote from your brother's eye." Numerous other examples could be given as well.

In many cases, sayings in Thomas that are paralleled in the Synoptics have one or two small twists that show the probable influence of Gnostic editing. Saying 8 is about a wise fisherman who casts

---

[23] Good recent commentaries, proceeding saying by saying throughout the text, include Simon Gathercole, *The Gospel of Thomas: Introduction and Commentary* (Leiden and Boston: Brill, 2014); Uwe-Karsten Plisch, *The Gospel of Thomas: Original Text with Commentary* (Stuttgart: Deutsche Bibelgesellschaft, 2008); and Petr Pokorný, *A Commentary on the Gospel of Thomas: From Interpretations to the Interpreted* (London and New York: T & T Clark, 2009).

[24] Unlike its Synoptic counterparts, however, this parable plants the seed in "tilled" soil, which could mean prepared for Gnostic revelation. Plisch (*Gospel of Thomas*, 79) calls this "certainly an interpretative addition that puts emphasis on human participation in the growing of the kingdom of God." Gathercole (*Gospel of Thomas: Introduction and Commentary*, 298) notes that even John Dominic Crossan, who so often prefers Thomas to the Synoptics, acknowledges Gnostic redaction here.

his net into the sea and draws it up full of fish. But instead of sorting numerous good fish from others that can't be salvaged, as in Matthew 13:47–50, here the fisherman finds one large fish and throws *all the others away*. Clearly the elitism of the Gnostic shines through.[25] Or in saying 16, which sounds much like Matthew 10:34 on bringing a sword rather than peace and dividing the members of a household, an additional concluding sentence declares that those who war against members of their own home because of their faith "will stand solitary," a recurring term throughout the Gnostic literature for the person with true insight into the nature of reality, including their own divine substance, and who thus stands out from the crowd of the ignorant.[26]

Between one-third and one-half of the sayings in Thomas show signs of a fully Gnostic origin. Some scholars have more stringent criteria than others for assigning something to Gnosticism, hence the variations in estimates. But there is little doubt about such texts as Thomas 29: "If the flesh came into being because of spirit, it is a wonder. But if spirit came into being because of the body, it is a wonder of wonders. Indeed, I am amazed at how this great wealth has made its home in this poverty."[27] When we remember that for the Gnostic the material world is inherently evil, this makes sense. It is amazing enough that something purely spiritual would create bodies;

---

[25] Gathercole (*Gospel of Thomas: Introduction and Commentary*, 237) thinks the large fish is knowledge or the kingdom (in Gnostic understanding); Plisch (*Gospel of Thomas*, 54) takes the big fish to be Christ (as understood in Gnosticism).

[26] Pokorný, *Gospel of Thomas*, 60. Cf. further Richard Valantasis, *The Gospel of Thomas* (London and New York: Routledge, 1997), 83–84.

[27] It is, of course, possible to reject the category Gnostic as unhelpful because all we have are individual sects, and then nothing in Thomas qualifies as Gnostic, as esp. with April D. DeConick, *Recovering the Original Gospel of Thomas: A History of the Gospel and Its Growth* (London and New York: T & T Clark, 2005); April D. DeConick, *The Original Gospel of Thomas in Translation: With a Commentary and New English Translation of the Complete Gospel* (London and New York: T & T Clark, 2006).

it is unimaginable that bodies should have created spirit. And it is amazing how spirits remain entrapped in bodies in this life. Saying 53 discloses some of the anti-Jewishness latent in much Gnostic thought: "His disciples said to Him, 'Is circumcision lawful or not?' He said to them, 'If it were beneficial, their father would beget them already circumcised from their mother. Rather, the true circumcision in spirit has become completely profitable.'" It is one thing for the New Testament to teach that circumcision is *no longer* necessary in Christ, but Thomas appears to promote the idea that it was *never* appropriate![28]

Particularly striking is the final passage, Thomas 114:

Simon Peter said to them, "Let Mary leave us, for women are not worthy of Life."

Jesus said, "I myself shall lead her in order to make her male, so that she too may become a living spirit resembling you males. For every woman who will make herself male will enter the Kingdom of Heaven."

We are not speaking of transgendered individuals here but of the belief that humanity was originally androgynous and must return to androgyny in the life to come.[29] And celibacy, in this life, can hasten this re-creation. This is not a document or movement truly compatible

---

[28] See especially Joshua W. Jipp and Michael J. Thate, "Dating Thomas: Logion 53 as a Test Case for Dating the Gospel of Thomas within an Early Christian Trajectory," *Bulletin for Biblical Research* 20 (2010): 237–55. On Thomas's wholesale rejection of Jewish ritual more generally, cf. Antti Marjanen, "Thomas in Jewish Religious Practices," in *Thomas at the Crossroads: Essays on the Gospel of Thomas*, ed. Risto Uro (Edinburgh: T & T Clark, 1998), 163–82.

[29] Cf. saying 22, in which the male becomes female and the female becomes male so that each person becomes a "single one" or "solitary." Cf. also Valantasis, *Gospel of Thomas*, 194–95. Pokorný (*Gospel of Thomas*, 154) thinks the imagery here is to return humanity to its state when only Adam existed. The masculine was considered to be spiritual; the feminine, material. If correct, this would leave Thomas's theology even less amenable to feminist commitments than the view that finds androgyny here.

with feminist objectives, as has often been claimed![30] As Michael Bird colorfully puts it, "The Jesus of the *Gospel of Thomas* is not a Jewish Messiah but more like a beatified beatnik dispensing amorphous aphorisms and even advocating salvation by androgyny."[31]

The remaining sayings of Thomas are neither demonstrably Gnostic nor obviously influenced by the canonical Gospels, though they *may* fall into one or both categories. Here is where scholars have often wondered if Thomas has preserved a few reasonably authentic teachings of the historical Jesus outside of the New Testament documents. Saying 98 announces, "The Kingdom of the Father is like a certain man who wanted to kill a powerful man. In his own house he drew his sword and stuck it into the wall in order to find out whether his hand could carry through. Then he slew the powerful man." The image is reminiscent of the little parable of binding the strong man in Mark 3:27, even though the specifics are different. One could easily imagine Jesus's having taught it, but it is hard to be sure.[32] The second half of saying 77 could have been originally an isolated piece of the Jesus tradition, similar in meaning to Matthew 18:20 on Christ's being everywhere: "Split a piece of wood, and I am there. Lift up the stone, and you will find me there." But, in context, it is combined with teachings about Christ being the "All," so perhaps it had a Gnostic interpretation from the outset.[33] Saying 82

---

[30] See esp. throughout Elaine Pagels, *The Gnostic Gospels* (New York: Random House, 1979); cf. also Elaine Pagels, *Beyond Belief: The Secret Gospel of Thomas* (New York: Random House, 2003).

[31] Michael F. Bird, *The Gospel of the Lord: How the Early Church Wrote the Story of Jesus* (Grand Rapids: Eerdmans, 2014), 296.

[32] The Jesus Seminar colored this entire parable pink, standing for something reasonably close to what Jesus actually said. See Robert W. Funk, Roy W. Hoover, and the Jesus Seminar, *The Five Gospels: The Search for the Authentic Words of Jesus* (New York: Macmillan, 1993), 524. See discussion on pp. 524–25.

[33] So also the Jesus Seminar (*The Five Gospels*, 515), which colors it all black and attributes it to pantheism. But Joachim Jeremias (*Unknown Sayings of Jesus*

reads, "Jesus said, 'He who is near me is near the fire, and he who is far from Me is far from the Kingdom.'" One can imagine both orthodox and Gnostic interpretations, but the poetry and imagery are reminiscent of the canonical Jesus.[34]

More avant-garde scholars have often imagined that, at least in places, Thomas preserves the most pristine form of the Jesus tradition.[35] A key reason for this is that nine out of the eleven parables Thomas and the Synoptics share are shorter in Thomas, and he never includes any interpretive commentary—certainly not the lengthy allegorical interpretations of the sower and the wheat and the weeds that appear in the canonical texts (Mark 4:14–20, 36–43). If one assumes that the Jesus tradition became progressively embellished and allegorized over time, this conclusion logically follows. But there is actually more evidence for abbreviation and "de-allegorization" of the Gospel tradition,[36] and enough signs of Gnostic redaction in Thomas's parables to make it more likely that they are later.[37] Indeed, numerous parallels can be found to every layer of Gospel tradition—sayings found

---

[London: SPCK, 1957; Eugene: Wipf & Stock, 2008], 95–98) suspects it is authentic.

[34] Edwin K. Broadhead, "An Authentic Saying of Jesus in the Gospel of Thomas," *New Testament Studies* 46 (2000): 132–49.

[35] The Jesus Seminar colors part or all of 33 of Thomas's 114 sayings pink or red, meaning that Jesus either said something similar to this or exactly this, respectively.

[36] For the classic form-critical "law" and its rebuttal, see Leslie R. Keylock, "Bultmann's Law of Increasing Distinctness," in *Current Issues in Biblical and Patristic Interpretation*, ed. Gerald F. Hawthorne (Grand Rapids: Eerdmans, 1975), 193–210. For a tendency toward *de*-allegorizing, esp. with parables, see Richard Bauckham, "Synoptic Parousia Parables and the Apocalypse," *New Testament Studies* 23 (1977): 165–69. Cf. also Richard Bauckham, "The Two Fig Tree Parables in the Apocalypse of Peter," *Journal of Biblical Literature* 104 (1985): 269–87.

[37] See esp. Craig L. Blomberg, "Tradition and Redaction in the Parables of the Gospel of Thomas," in *Gospel Perspectives*, vol. 5, ed. David Wenham (Sheffield: JSOT, 1985), 177–205; Craig L. Blomberg, "Orality and the Parables: With Special Reference to James D. G. Dunn's *Jesus Remembered*," in *Memories of Jesus: A Critical*

in all three Synoptics, in each of the three pairs of Synoptic Gospels, and in material unique to each of the four Gospels, including John. Even a parallel to the little parable of the seed growing secretly, a rare example of a teaching of Jesus found otherwise only in Mark (4:26–29), occurs in Thomas 21. All this makes it far more likely that Thomas knew, used, and modified the four canonical Gospels in their finished form than that every one of these layers or sources of the Gospel tradition independently knew and used Thomas.[38] When one recognizes that there is no actual evidence for dating this work earlier than the mid to late second century, this conclusion becomes almost certain.[39]

A further tipoff in this direction is the fact that Thomas contains parallels to uniquely Matthean and Lukan redaction of Mark. An excellent example appears in his version of the parable of the wicked tenants:

> He said, "There was a good man who owned a vineyard. He leased it to tenant farmers so that they might work it and he might collect the produce from them. He sent his servant so that the tenants might give him the produce of the vineyard. They seized his servant and beat him, all but killing him. The servant went back and told his master. The master said, 'Perhaps <they> did not recognize <him>.' He sent another

---

Appraisal of James D. G. Dunn's "Jesus Remembered," ed. Robert B. Stewart and Gary R. Habermas (Nashville: B&H, 2010), esp. 115–25.

[38] For a sustained argument for Thomas's dependence on the Synoptic tradition, see Mark Goodacre, *Thomas and the Gospels: The Case for Thomas's Familiarity with the Synoptic Gospels* (Grand Rapids: Eerdmans, 2012). Cf. also Gathercole, *Composition of the Gospel of Thomas,* 145–224.

[39] Gathercole (*Gospel of Thomas: Introduction and Commentary,* 112–24) argues persuasively for a date between AD 135 and 200. On Thomas's use of all layers of the canonical Gospel tradition, see also John H. Wood Jr., "The New Testament Gospels and the Gospel of Thomas: A New Direction," *New Testament Studies* 51 (2005): 575–95.

servant. The tenants beat this one as well. Then the owner sent his son and said, 'Perhaps they will show respect to my son.' Because the tenants knew that it was he who was the heir to the vineyard, they seized him and killed him. Let him who has ears hear." (Thomas 65)

There is little here that is undeniably Gnostic, though one wonders about the claim that the tenants may not have "recognized" the servant. The details in the Synoptics that allegorically point to Christ as the son of the vineyard owner are not as pronounced. But curiously, just as in Luke, the master qualifies his statements, saying only "perhaps" they will respect my son. After all, God was not caught by surprise when his Son was rejected. But this is a Lukan addition to his Markan source and not an indication of the earliest form of the parable. Telltale signs like this further reinforce our conclusion that Thomas is later than and dependent on the canonical tradition.[40]

The seemingly random order of the 114 sayings in Thomas continues to puzzle scholars and other readers. Occasionally, small groups of related teachings can be discerned. For example, immediately after the version of the wicked tenants just cited (Thos. 65) comes a parallel to the canonical conclusion of that parable (Mark 12:10–11 pars.): "Jesus said, 'Show me the stone which the builders have rejected. That one is the cornerstone'" (Thos. 66). There is no good reason these two passages should have been juxtaposed in either the Greek or Coptic of Thomas's text unless they already existed together in some form—exactly what the canonical Gospels show us.[41] On the other hand,

---

[40] Cf. Klyne R. Snodgrass, "The *Gospel of Thomas*: A Secondary Gospel," *Second Century* 7 (1989–90): esp. 28–31. More generally, see also Christopher M. Tuckett, "Thomas and the Synoptics," *Novum Testamentum* 30 (1988): 132–57.

[41] See especially Gathercole, *Composition of the Gospel of Thomas*, 188–94. Cf. also Goodacre, *Thomas and the Gospels*, 17, 151; Arland J. Hultgren, *The Parables of Jesus: A Commentary* (Grand Rapids: Eerdmans, 2000), 366.

there is a reason in Hebrew—the similarity between *bēn* ("son") and *eben* ("stone")—which makes it all the more likely that the juxtaposition of teachings goes back to Jesus.[42]

In a number of instances, a topical link between consecutive passages can be discerned. For example, in Thomas 96, a close parallel to the canonical parable of the leaven (Matt 13:33 par.) appears. Then comes the unparalleled parable of the woman carrying a jar of meal (Thos. 97). In this brief narrative she does not notice that the handle of her jar broke while she was walking a long distance home so that the meal spilled out. When she got home, she placed her jar down and found it empty. Whatever the meaning of this enigmatic story, one can see why the editor or composer of Thomas would have put it immediately after another parable about a woman with baking material.[43] Nicholas Perrin has argued that consistently additional links between consecutive sayings can be surmised if one translates the Coptic back into its most natural Syriac equivalents and looks for "catchwords"— terms or concepts that are repeated in juxtaposed passages, even if they don't always represent the main point of the teaching.[44] Simon Gathercole has analyzed these and doesn't find enough of them convincing to think they provide the key to breaking the code of Thomas's

---

[42] On the question of whether the wordplay would be recognized in Aramaic, see Klyne R. Snodgrass, *Stories with Intent: A Comprehensive Guide to the Parables of Jesus* (Grand Rapids: Eerdmans, 2008), 290. He notes that Josephus preserved the same wordplay in a different context even in Greek, so the slight difference between Aramaic and Hebrew would almost certainly not have blurred the pun.

[43] Richard Q. Ford, "Body Language: Jesus' Parables of the Woman with the Yeast, the Woman with the Jar, and the Man with the Sword," *Interpretation* 56 (2002): 295–306. DeConick (*Recovering the Original Gospel of Thomas*, 121) finds the topical grouping occurring in an earlier stratum of Thomas's tradition history, which she calls "an early Christian speech gospel, when one of Thomas' sources was composed."

[44] Nicholas Perrin, *Thomas and Tatian: The Relationship Between the Gospel of Thomas and the Diatessaron* (Atlanta: SBL, 2002).

order,[45] but they probably at least account for some of it (since about half of the catchwords are visible in the Coptic as well). And, of course, it is not necessary that juxtaposed teachings always did have a link with something nearby any more than one can always find reasons for the sequence of proverbs in the Hebrew Scriptures. But there is at least enough order to debunk the notion that Thomas presents a completely or nearly completely random collection of Jesus's teachings from the earliest stages of tradition, and that order was imposed on them only on later occasions. Most signs point to Thomas's being later than and dependent on the canonical Gospels. With the possible exception of a handful of unparalleled sayings that fit the portrait of the historical Jesus built up from the core of the Synoptic tradition, Thomas does not offer us additional reliable information about what Jesus taught.[46] If that is the case with the one document from Nag Hammadi with repeated, close parallels to the canonical tradition, it is all the more true when one generalizes about the entire corpus or library.[47]

The New Testament Apocrypha

The standard scholarly edition of this collection of ancient Christian and semi-Christian works also includes some of the most important Nag Hammadi texts, fragments of a few lines of otherwise unknown texts, and texts we know of only via quotations from early church

---

[45] Gathercole, *Composition of the Gospel of Thomas*, 24–104.

[46] For cautious, balanced treatments that neither rule out all possible new and independent sayings of the historical Jesus or refuse to acknowledge the amount that is secondary, see Hans-Josef Klauck, *Apocryphal Gospels: An Introduction* (London and New York: T & T Clark, 2003), 107–22; and Fred Lapham, *An Introduction to the New Testament Apocrypha* (London and New York: T & T Clark, 2003), 114–21.

[47] Cf. esp. Christopher M. Tuckett, *Nag Hammadi and the Gospel Tradition* (Edinburgh: T & T Clark, 1986); Gerard P. Luttikhuizen, *Gnostic Revisions of Genesis Stories and Early Jesus Traditions* (Leiden and Boston: Brill, 2006).

fathers.[48] Here we will focus just on those documents for which we actually have a fair amount of text and which have proved the most influential in the history of investigations of New Testament reliability.

Gospels

The Gospel of Peter most likely comes from the late second century.[49] The portion that exists focuses exclusively on the sequence of events that span the end of Jesus's trial before Pilate to his resurrection. Many of the details match canonical information; others offer plausible supplementary information that may or may not be based on any historical tradition. But all blame for Jesus's execution is shifted from being shared by the Roman and Jewish leaders to the Jews alone. The tomb is made far more secure than in the canonical accounts. The resurrection itself is actually depicted, rather than just Jesus's subsequent appearances. And several passages overly exalt Jesus beyond what is elsewhere attributed to one who was fully human, whether we label this explicitly docetic—the view that Christ only *seemed* (from Gk. *dokeō*) to be human.[50] The Gospel of Peter 4:10, for example, reads, "And they brought two malefactors and crucified the Lord in the midst between them. But he held his peace, as if he felt no pain." Even more dramatically, 9:34–37 expands on the resurrection by describing how the guards at the tomb "saw the heavens opened and two men came down from there in a great brightness and drew nigh to the sepulcher.

---

[48] See above, page 10 n. 12. There is also a second volume of non-Gospels material. We will not deal with the last of these two categories here for reasons of space and because they have yielded the fewest results for our purposes in past studies. See esp. James H. Charlesworth and Craig A. Evans, "Jesus in the Agrapha and Apocryphal Gospels," in *Studying the Historical Jesus: Evaluations of the State of Current Research*, ed. Bruce Chilton and Craig A. Evans (Leiden: Brill, 1994), 479–91.

[49] Paul Foster, "The *Gospel of Peter*," in *The Non-Canonical Gospels*, ed. Paul Foster (London and New York: T & T Clark, 2008), 41.

[50] Lapham, *Introduction to the New Testament Apocrypha*, 91–92.

That stone which had been laid against the entrance to the sepulcher started of itself to roll and gave way to the side, and the sepulcher was opened, and both the young men entered in." In the next section, after the soldiers awakened their centurion and the Jewish elders who were also keeping watch,

> They saw again three men come out from the sepulcher, and two of them sustaining the other, and a cross following them, and the heads of the two reaching to heaven, but that of him who was led of them by the hand overpassing the heavens. And they heard a voice out of the heavens crying "Hast thou preached to them that sleep?" and from the cross there was heard the answer, "Yea."[51]

The ideology behind these excerpts is obviously heterodox, whether or not it is formally Gnostic. Jesus is no longer human. He feels no pain despite the expected agony of crucifixion. He is taller than the clouds. And preaching to those who sleep could only have been introduced by someone who knew 1 Peter 3:18–22 and perhaps 4:6, anachronistically inserting information from a letter penned no earlier than the 60s into a gospel narrative purportedly describing something from the year 30. So when Dominic Crossan postulates a "Cross Gospel" that is based on parts of the Gospel of Peter, shorn of these legendary accretions, and which actually predated the Synoptic tradition,[52] it requires belief in early stages of composition of this document for which there is no actual evidence and which flies in the face

---

[51] Timothy P. Henderson (*The Gospel of Peter and Early Christian Apologetics* [Tübingen: Mohr Siebeck, 2011]) demonstrates that the entire document is best understood as a "rewritten Gospel" in response to criticism from outside the Christian movement about weaknesses in the canonical accounts.

[52] John Dominic Crossan, *The Cross That Spoke: The Origins of the Passion Narrative* (San Francisco: Harper & Row, 1988; Eugene: Wipf & Stock, 2008).1

of the actual evidence we have of a later date and of fanciful attempts to supplement the canonical documents.[53]

The Protevangelium of James is most likely a late second-century or early third-century work that purports to recount the birth of Mary, mother of Jesus, to a wealthy Jewish couple named Joachim and Anna.[54] Like John the Baptist's mother, Elizabeth, Anna has been barren and is miraculously allowed to conceive, and their daughter, Mary, was announced as someone special from birth onward and immensely popular within Israel. When she is sixteen, the angel tells her about her coming virginal conception, and the text expands on numerous details from Luke 1–2, along with Matthew 1–2. Mary even undergoes the bitter water test of Numbers 5:12–31 but is not affected, thus vindicating her purity. Joseph and Mary travel to Bethlehem and take refuge in a cave. Mary gives birth to Jesus and has a true virgin *birth*, not just a virginal conception. The attending midwife discovers that Mary's hymen remains unbroken even after the baby is born! More embellishments to the canonical birth narratives appear up through the encounter of Simeon with the Christ child.[55]

---

[53] Klauck (*Apocryphal Gospels*, 87) highlights numerous additional features characteristic of late, secondary Gospels: "The fact that Jesus is consistently called 'the Lord,' the lack of knowledge of Jewish customs, the transfer of responsibility for his death from Pilate to Herod and the Jews (a motif which is also dubious on theological grounds), the intensification of apologetic motifs to such a degree that alleged eyewitnesses of the resurrection are produced, and finally the emphasis on the miraculous elements in the narrative of the resurrection, with the descent into hell, huge angelic beings and a cross that speaks." Cf. also Peter M. Head, "On the Christology of the Gospel of Peter," *Vigiliae Christianae* 46 (1992): 209–24; Alan Kirk, "Examining Priorities: Another Look at the Gospel of Peter's Relationship to the New Testament Gospels," *New Testament Studies* 40 (1994): 572–95.

[54] Paul Foster, "The *Protevangelium of James*," in *the Non-Canonical Gospels*, ed. Paul Foster (London and New York: T & T Clark, 2008), 111–13.

[55] On the motives for the composition of this document, including esp. the exaltation of Mary, see Lily C. Vuong, "Purity, Piety, and the Purposes of the *Protevangelium of James*," in *"Non-Canonical" Religious Texts in Early Judaism and Early Christianity*, ed. Lee M. McDonald and James H. Charlesworth (London

The Infancy Story (or Gospel) of Thomas describes Jesus, the "boy wonder." According to this late second-century apocryphon, when Jesus was five he was playing at the ford of a brook and fashioned twelve sparrows from soft clay, violating Pharisaic traditions about work on the Sabbath. When Joseph confronted him, he clapped his hands and said to the sparrows, "Off with you!" (2:4), and they flew away chirping! Later when his playmate annoyed him, he was enraged and said to him, "See, now you also shall wither like a tree and shall bear neither leaves nor root nor fruit" (3:2). Immediately the child withered up. Then another child rammed Jesus in his shoulder, so that in his exasperation Jesus responded, "You shall not go further on your way," and the child at once died (4:1). When the parents of these children accosted Joseph to have him rebuke Jesus, Jesus made them blind.

On a more positive note, Jesus also raised a child who had fallen off a roof and died. Later he healed the foot of a young man who was bleeding to death after he accidentally split his sole chopping wood. When Joseph mistakenly made one beam shorter than its counterpart for a bed that a rich man had ordered, Jesus grabbed it and miraculously lengthened it to match the other one. Numerous other miracles of cursing and blessing dot this short document, including Jesus's confounding all his teachers who try to explain the alphabet to him by giving them elaborate allegorical interpretations of the meaning of each letter. Clearly the author is extrapolating from the canonical miracles and envisioning a superhuman child in all kinds of fanciful ways. This is not a Jesus who is compatible with the summary statement in Luke 2:52 that he *grew* "in wisdom and stature, and in favor

---

and New York: Bloomsbury T & T Clark, 2013), 205–21. For details of the emphasis on Mary's purity throughout, including ritual, sexual, and even menstrual purity, see Lily C. Vuong, *Gender and Purity in the Protevangelium of James* (Tübingen: Mohr Siebeck, 2013).

with God and man." This is a child who exhibits all divine powers from his earliest years onward.[56]

Extracts from the Gospel of Pseudo-Matthew expand these miraculous powers even further. Three days after his birth, while Jesus was resting in the manger, "an ox and an ass worshipped him. Then was fulfilled that which was said through the prophet Isaiah: 'The ox knows his owner and the ass his master's crib'" (14:1). Not only real animals, but even legendary animals behaved similarly. When the holy family was journeying in Egypt, accompanied by several other children, they stopped to rest in a cave and "suddenly many dragons came out of the cave." As the people cried out in terror, "Jesus got down from his mother's lap, and stood on his feet before the dragons; thereupon they worshipped Jesus, and then went back from them" (18:1). Jesus commanded the dragons not to harm anyone and they obeyed. Likewise, lions and leopards worshipped him in the wilderness. We have now come about as far from the historical Jesus as we can get in any ancient Christian text![57]

Acts

The same tendencies to embellish the exploits of the protagonists characterize the apocryphal acts of the various apostles.[58] The Acts of Andrew portrays Andrew working numerous miracles, especially

---

[56] A. G. van Aarde, "The Infancy Gospel of Thomas: Allegory or Myth—Gnostic or Ebionite?" *Verbum et Ecclesia* 26 (2005): 826–50.

[57] On the other hand this is not fantasy literature. Beasts regularly represented the violent world in which pre-Constantinian Christians lived, esp. when they were subject to imperial persecution. Several apocrypha show wild animals subject to Christ or the apostles, who always exercise power over them nonviolently, as a model for second- and third-century Christians. See esp. François Bovon, *New Testament and Christian Apocrypha* (Tübingen: Mohr Siebeck, 2009; Grand Rapids: Baker, 2011), 223–45.

[58] For an overall introduction, see Hans-Josef Klauck, *The Apocryphal Acts of the Apostles: An Introduction* (Waco: Baylor University Press, 2008).

physical healings and exorcisms, in Achaia, the southern half of the Greek peninsula. When a local leader trumps up charges against him to have him crucified, he goes willingly to the cross and addresses it as if it had been waiting for him to come and now he has arrived to satisfy its desires. He is affixed only loosely by his wrists and ankles, tied to the wooden beams with ropes, and he happily teaches those who stand by him for four days, by which time more than 2,000 of the townspeople besiege the local officials to release him. Finally, the order is given, but Andrew refuses to come down off the cross and struggle with this transient life any longer. So he gives up his spirit and dies. This third-century document reflects the desire for martyrdom that appeared already in early second-century Christianity in ways that contradict the New Testament's conviction that death is an enemy to be defeated rather than a destiny to be embraced or desired.[59]

The Acts of John appears to be a late third-century apocryphon. It depicts the apostle John working all manner of healings and resurrections. The most distinctive miracle involves a mass of bedbugs. When John and several traveling companions arrive at an inn, the bed on which John tries to sleep is full of bugs. So John commands them, "I tell you, you bugs, to behave yourselves, one and all; you must leave your home for tonight and be quiet in one place and keep your distance from the servants of God" (sec. 60). His companions laugh, continue talking quietly, while John falls asleep. The next morning they see by the door of the room a mass of bugs collected together and are amazed. John sits up in bed and looks at them and declares, "Since you have behaved yourselves and avoided my punishment go (back) to your own place." The bugs scurry back into the joints of the bed, and John moralizes that these creatures "listened to a man's voice" and

---

[59] A. Hilhorst, "The Apocryphal Acts as Martyrdom Texts: The Case of the Acts of Andrew," in *The Apocryphal Acts of John*, ed. Jan N. Bremmer (Kampen: Kok Pharos, 1995), 1–14.

obeyed, but those who hear God's voice "disobey his commandments and are irresponsible; how long will this go on?" (sec. 61).[60]

The Acts of Paul and Thecla is perhaps the best known of the apocryphal acts because it represents a widespread ascetic strain of postapostolic Christianity that portrays Paul as promoting celibacy as the Christian ideal. Thecla, a rich young woman engaged to be married, becomes enamored with Paul's teaching and refuses to see her fiancé or heed her parents' desires by going through with the marriage. Instead, she becomes an evangelist for this version of Paul's message, in keeping with the strand of second- through fifth-century Christianity that led to the Roman Catholic requirement of singleness and celibacy for priests and members of various monastic orders.[61] The document is legendary but may reflect the reality of a small group of early Christian women foregoing marriage for Christian service and, if it is not too anachronistic to put it this way, in that sense liberating themselves from conventional patriarchal structures of society.[62] But, like

---

[60] Animals at numerous junctures in the apocryphal acts, as in various other strands of Greek thought, recognize the presence of the divine and behave accordingly. See Christopher R. Matthews, "Articulate Animals: A Multivalent Motif in the Apocryphal Acts of the Apostles," in *The Apocryphal Acts of the Apostles*, ed. François Bovon, Ann Graham Brock, and Christopher R. Matthews (Cambridge, MA: Harvard University Press, 1999), 205–32. Janet E. Spittler (*Animals in the Apocryphal Acts of the Apostles* [Tübingen: Mohr Siebeck, 2008], 105–6) notes the potential play on words between "bugs" (*koreis*) and "girls" (*korai*), suspecting that John is actually banishing women from his bed in keeping with the ascetic ideals of this work.

[61] For a book-length introduction and commentary, see J. W. Barrier, *The Acts of Paul and Thecla: A Critical Commentary* (Tübingen: Mohr Siebeck, 2009). Exaggerated claims have often been made about the prominent role of women leaders in the earliest churches based on this document; for more sober conclusions, see Esther Y. L. Ng, "Acts of Paul and Thecla: Women's Stories and Precedent?" *Journal of Theological Studies* 55 (2004): 1–29. Tertullian (*De Baptismo* 17) does, however, describe what he views as the abuse of this apocryphal document by women appealing to it to justify their teaching and baptizing men.

[62] Virginia Burrus, *Chastity as Autonomy: Women in the Stories of Apocryphal Acts* (Lewiston and Queenston: Edwin Mellen, 1987). Cf. also Magda Misset-van de

other apocryphal accounts from this period, there is also the renunciation of riches for poverty so that the focus is not nearly so much on freedom *from* marriage (or wealth) as on freedom *to* serve.[63] The Acts of Paul and Thecla was also used for baptismal and other forms of catechetical instruction and to commend the overall piety represented by Thecla.[64]

Various apocryphal acts contain information that scholars suggest may well be historical, for example, Peter's crucifixion upside down under Nero, in the Acts of Peter 37–38, or the unflattering picture of Paul as short, bald, bowlegged, and with a crooked nose (though full of grace) in the Acts of Paul and Thecla 3. Information about locations to which certain apostles traveled may also be based on historical tradition, especially the accounts of Thomas evangelizing parts of the Indian subcontinent (Acts of Thomas, esp. secs. 1–29). But overall little in these documents sheds much light on the real exploits of the apostles. We can piece together scattered bits of other information from more orthodox early Christian sources, and various books present what is taught about the different apostles in the oldest documents, evaluating their relative merits. But reading straight through the Apocrypha adds little to our database of historical knowledge about these first Christian leaders.[65]

Weg, "Answers to the Plights of an Ascetic Woman Named Thecla," in *A Feminist Companion to the New Testament Apocrypha*, ed. Amy-Jill Levine with Maria Mayo Robbins (London: T & T Clark; Cleveland: Pilgrim, 2006), 146–62.

[63] See Andrew S. Jacobs, "'Her Own Proper Kinship': Marriage, Class and Women in the Apocryphal Acts of the Apostles," in *Feminist Companion to the New Testament Apocrypha*, ed. Levine with Robbins, 18–46. Cf. Susan A. Calef, "Thecla 'Tried and True' and the Inversion of Romance," in Levine, *Feminist*, 163–85.

[64] Glenn E. Snyder, *Acts of Paul: The Formation of a Pauline Corpus* (Tübingen: Mohr Siebeck, 2013), 258.

[65] Charlesworth and Evans, "Jesus in the Agrapha and Apocryphal Gospels," 491–533.

Epistles

The majority of postapostolic epistles appear in the Apostolic Fathers, a collection of largely orthodox second-century writings.[66] One or two are anonymous (The Epistle to Diognetus) or pseudonymous (The Epistle of Barnabas), while several were written by the people whose names are affixed to them (Clement, Ignatius, Polycarp). Invaluable for understanding the history of the forms of Christianity they represent, they shed little additional light on the contents of the New Testament letters, except on those occasions when they acknowledge that they do not speak with the same authority as the first generation of apostles (e.g., Ign. *Trall.* 3:3; 2 Clem. 2:4). The handful of epistles that appear in the New Testament Apocrypha were invented to fill in gaps in the biblical record (what *was* written in that lost letter to the Corinthians?), to account for some of the similarities between Paul and the Roman Stoic philosopher Seneca, or to imagine what Christ might have written to another royal figure. But they add nothing of historical value for understanding the lives of the true Paul or Jesus.[67]

Apocalypses

Apocryphal apocalypses supplement Old and New Testament teaching in various, largely legendary ways. The Ascension of Isaiah is probably best known for its belief that Isaiah was martyred by being sawn in two. The Apocalypse of Peter outlines various horrific tortures Peter supposedly saw in a visit to hell, among other things. Fifth

---

[66] The standard modern translation is Michael W. Holmes, *The Apostolic Fathers: Greek Texts and English Translations*, 3rd ed. (Grand Rapids: Baker, 2007).

[67] On 3 Corinthians, see esp. Vahan Hovhanessian, *Third Corinthians: Reclaiming Paul for Christian Orthodoxy* (New York: Peter Lang, 2000). Klauck's application to the apocryphal gospels of Walter Bauer's sentiments (*Apocryphal Gospels*, 223) applies equally well to the apocryphal epistles: they come from "a pious yearning to know more, a naïve curiosity, [and] delight in colourful pictures and folktales."

and Sixth Ezra purport to be prophecy from the time of that great fifth-century BC interpreter of the law, but they include such explicit references to New Testament events that they must be Christian in origin. For example, 5 Ezra 42–47 narrates Ezra's seeing on Mount Zion (in Jerusalem) a numberless multitude that praised the Lord in song. In their midst, taller than everyone else was a young man who set crowns upon the heads of everyone else present. As he did so, he grew even taller. Ezra asked his guide, an angel, who these people were and was told that they were "they who have laid aside their mortal clothing and put on the immortal and have confessed the name of God. Now are they crowned and receive palms." Then Ezra asked about the identity of the young man and was told, "This is the Son of God whom they have confessed in the world" (2:47). None of this is Old Testament language, but it all represents key imagery found in the New. Little wonder scholars consistently support its post-New Testament, Christian origin.[68]

Conclusions

We could continue with less well-known apocryphal literature, but we have given enough glimpses into them to make some generalizations. Many were designed to supplement the sparser parts of the New Testament with additional stories about Jesus and his first followers, satisfying people's curiosity with legendary embellishments to the canonical texts. They regularly heighten the miraculous element in these individuals' ministries. But unlike the miracles in the New Testament, which all serve to highlight the arrival of the kingdom of God and its Messiah (see chap. 14), these tend to be much more random, arbitrary, fanciful, capricious, and/or unnecessarily judgmental.[69]

---

[68] Theodore A. Bergren, "Gentile Christians, Exile, and Return in 5 Ezra 1:35–40," *Journal of Biblical Literature* 130 (2011): 593–612.

[69] Perhaps in the desire, at times, to have Jesus "outdo" his pagan rivals. See Ulricke Riemer, "Miracle Stories and Their Narrative Intent in the Context of the

There is little likelihood that they add new, independent, or accurate historical information about the first-century individuals they purport to depict.[70] On the other hand, they do provide important windows into key theological emphases of second- and third-century Christianity, whether with respect to celibacy or martyrdom, imperialism or wisdom, exalting Mary as more than merely human or exalting Jesus as no longer human.[71]

A New New Testament?

In 2013, Houghton Mifflin Harcourt Publishers released a volume edited by Hal Taussig entitled *A New New Testament*. It included the twenty-seven canonical books agreed on by all major branches of Christianity, but it added ten other documents and then grouped the resulting thirty-seven books somewhat differently than in the traditional canon. The books were collected into sections labeled "Gospels Featuring Jesus's Teachings," "Gospels, Poems, and Songs Between Heaven and Earth," "The Writings of Paul and an Introductory

---

Ruler Cult of Classical Antiquity," in *Wonders Never Cease: The Purpose of Narrating Miracle Stories in the New Testament and Its Religious Environment*, ed. Michael Labahn and Bert J. Lietaert Peerbolte (London and New York: T & T Clark, 2006), 32–47.

[70] See esp. John P. Meier, *A Marginal Jew: Rethinking the Historical Jesus*, vol. 1 (New York and London: Doubleday, 1991), 112–66.

[71] Burke (*Secret Scriptures Revealed*, 129–49) helpfully debunks nine myths about the apocrypha from both the left and the right wings of scholarship, which myths can be summarized as follows: (1) all of the apocrypha can be shown to be either after or before the canonical texts; (2) they were all forgeries intended to deceive; (3) they were all or primarily written by Gnostics; (4) they claim Jesus was not divine (if anything, their Jesus is not always human); (5) they are always bizarre and fanciful compared with their canonical counterparts; (6) they were written to undermine or compete with the canonical texts; (7) they were enormously popular prior to their suppression by a powerful minority within the Church; (8) they attempted to rewrite Christian history; and (9) reading them is harmful to one's faith. For our purposes, (6), (7), and (8) are the most important to debunk.

Prayer," "Literature in the Tradition of Paul with a Set of Introductory Prayers," "Diverse Letters, with a Set of Introductory Prayers," and "Literature in the Tradition of John, with an Introductory Set of Prayers." All of these segments were introduced with "An Ancient Prayer from the Early Christ Movements."[72]

Approximately twenty self-appointed scholars and/or church or synagogue leaders had gathered in New Orleans to discuss at length the notion of adding "recently discovered" documents to the canon. They represented some of the most liberal wings of Christianity and Judaism, and they limited themselves to considering books they believed were composed before about AD 170, believing that to be the period contemporaneous with the composition of the canonical texts.[73] It should be noted, however, that few New Testament scholars would date any of the canonical texts later than the earliest years of the second century and that the most responsible dates for the additional works chosen are in most instances late second and even third century. The ten resulting additions to the canon were the Prayer of Thanksgiving, the Gospel of Thomas, the Odes of Solomon, Thunder: Perfect Mind, the Gospel of Mary, the Gospel of Truth, the Prayer of the Apostle Paul, the Acts of Paul and Thecla, the Letter of Peter to Philip, and the Secret Revelation to John. We have already introduced the Gospel of Thomas, the Gospel of Truth, and the Acts of Paul and Thecla. Now we need to comment briefly on the other seven texts.

The Prayer of Thanksgiving is a short, thirteen-verse[74] blessing of God found in the Nag Hammadi Library with a few Gnostic

---

[72] *A New New Testament: A Bible for the 21st Century Combining Traditional and Newly Discovered Texts*, ed. Hal Taussig (Boston and New York: Houghton Mifflin Harcourt, 2013).

[73] Ibid., xxiv–xxv.

[74] Chapters and verses were added to the ten "newly discovered" books in ibid., for ease of referencing.

overtones. Much of it is beautiful, however, and orthodox in its thoughts. It begins:

> This is the prayer they said: We give thanks to you, every life and heart stretches toward you, O name untroubled, honored with the name of God, praised with the name of Father. To everyone and everything comes the kindness of the Father, and love and desire. And if there is a sweet and simple teaching, it gifts us mind, word, and knowledge: mind, that we may understand you; word, that we may interpret you; knowledge, that we may know you. (vv. 1–3)

The emphasis on knowledge, nevertheless, fits its Gnostic origin. The prayer next verges briefly into what could be interpreted in light of the unorthodox Gnostic belief that the spark of divinity is embedded in every person: "We rejoice that in the body you have made us divine through your knowledge" (v. 4a). This is a recurring theme that makes these books attractive to many in our world today who want to find their god within themselves apart from any external, objective standard of righteousness. The maternal imagery for God in this prayer also makes it popular with feminists: "O womb of all that grows, we have known you. O womb pregnant with the nature of the Father, we have known you. O never-ending endurance of the Father who gives birth, so we worship your goodness" (vv. 9–10).[75]

The Odes of Solomon are somewhat unique among early Christian literature in that they pseudonymously use the name of a famous Old Testament character for the putative author rather than someone from the New Testament. In many respects these odes resemble the poetry of the Hebrew Psalms, but they use references to Jesus such

---

[75] These two characteristics unify all the new documents chosen for inclusion in the *New New Testament*. So it is clear that there was a definite agenda beyond merely exposing Christians to a representative sampling of potentially edifying "newly discovered" documents.

as the Word, the Light, the Lord, and the Son of God in ways that indicate they emanated from some "Christian" movement.[76] Like a few similar documents, they are usually printed in collections of Old Testament pseudepigrapha but with introductions that comment on the Christian overlays they have received, whether or not they were entirely composed in Christian circles.[77] Again, the topics of saving knowledge inside of every person and of the feminine side of God appear throughout. For example, "The Father has the Lord appear to those who are his own, so that they might recognize the one who made them, so that they might not suppose that they exist of themselves. For he has set his way to knowledge, expanded her, lengthened her, brought her to all fullness, and set over her traces of light" (Book 1, Ode 7, vv. 12–14a).

Thunder: Perfect Mind is another short text from Nag Hammadi. Particularly noteworthy are its numerous antinomies, as this feminine emanation from the godhead describes herself:

> I am the first and the last. I am she who is honored and she who is mocked. I am the whore and the holy woman. I am the wife and the virgin. I am the mother and the daughter. I am the limbs of my mother. I am a sterile woman and she has many children. I am she whose wedding is extravagant and I didn't have a husband. I am the midwife and she who hasn't given birth. I am the comfort of my labor pains. I am the bride and the bridegroom. (1:5–9a)

---

[76] Michael Lattke (*The Odes of Solomon: A Commentary* [Minneapolis: Fortress, 2009], 6–10, 12–14) notes the influence of numerous New Testament books on the Odes. He acknowledges Jewish and Gnostic influence as well but places the work squarely within the Christian apocryphal tradition, at least in its final form, no earlier than the early second century.

[77] See esp. James H. Charlesworth, "The Odes of Solomon," in *The Old Testament Pseudepigrapha*, ed. James H. Charlesworth, vol. 2 (Garden City: Doubleday, 1985), 725–71.

And so it continues. The context is probably the Gnostic notion of uniting opposites (as in the hope for androgynous humanity in the life to come),[78] but one can see its appeal to postmodern people who like pondering paradoxes that appear to promise great power and an amazingly diverse identity for those who attain correct wisdom. Here Taussig, in his introduction to this work, maintains that "twentieth- and twenty-first century 'queer movements' have much to offer in understanding these ancient portraits of Thunder and Jesus."[79] Presumably, he is referring by extrapolation to the idea that one can embrace heterosexuality and homosexuality, just as Thunder's personification of Wisdom affirms so many other antinomies. Unfortunately, in light of Thunder's historical background, had it used such a combination, it would have done so in order to affirm the overcoming of both forms of sexual identity in an ascetic, celibate, gender-transcending form of existence,[80] which is quite different from what the LGBTQ movement normally demands!

The Gospel of Mary is another document from Nag Hammadi that few people knew anything about until Dan Brown popularized it, while misrepresenting it, in *The Da Vinci Code*.[81] Because this short set of dialogues between Mary (Magdalene?) and certain other apostles includes Peter saying to Mary, "Sister, we know that the Savior loved

---

[78] Pearson (*Ancient Gnosticism*, 236) cites Bentley Layton favorably in associating this literature with Classic Gnosticism, even as others try to dissociate it so that they can reinterpret these references more in keeping with their contemporary agendas. See, e.g., Lewis, *Introduction to "Gnosticism,"* 191–206. For a mediating position between these two, see David Brakke, *The Gnostics: Myth, Ritual, and Diversity in Early Christianity* (Cambridge, MA and London: Harvard University Press, 2010), 50–51.

[79] Hal Taussig, "An Introduction to 'The Thunder: Perfect Mind,'" in *A New New Testament*, ed. Taussig, 181.

[80] See especially Marvin W. Meyer, "Making Mary Male: The Categories 'Male' and 'Female' in the Gospel of Thomas," *New Testament Studies* 31 (1985): 554–70.

[81] Brown, *Da Vinci Code*, 324.

you more than the rest of the women" (6:1), people have speculated that Jesus had married Mary. This hardly follows. Indeed, this same document later has Levi explaining, "Surely the Savior's knowledge of her is trustworthy. That is why he loved her more than us" (10:10). Her keen insight into spiritual truths, rather than anything romantic or erotic, explains why Mary receives this praise. What makes the document attractive to the "New Orleans Council" that voted it into the *New New Testament*, however, is Jesus's saying, "There is no sin, but it is you who make sin when you do the things that are like the nature of adultery, which is called 'sin.' That is why the Good came into your midst, coming to the good which belongs to every nature, in order to restore it to its root" (3:3–6). But to affirm that sin is merely an illusion comes with a high cost—matter is inherently evil, as classically in Gnosticism. "Matter gives birth to a passion that has no likeness because it proceeds from what is contrary to nature" (3:10). Humans may have "the son of man" within them (4:5) but to avoid evil their souls must ascend leaving behind darkness, desire, ignorance, eagerness for death, the realm of the flesh, the "foolish wisdom of the flesh and wrathful wisdom" (9:18–24). This ascetic, disembodied immortality is not exactly the redemption most people long for.[82]

The Prayer of the Apostle Paul is another short (eleven-verse) prayer from the Nag Hammadi corpus. Little is unorthodox, but one can see the themes of wisdom and enlightenment, along with the revelation of mysteries, punctuating the text. It reads like a pastiche of words and phrases from the canonical epistles of Paul along with unparalleled prayers for authority and special knowledge. The opening lines read, "Grant me your mercy, my Redeemer; redeem me, for I am yours—the one who has come from you. You are my mind—birth me. You are my treasure—open for me. You are my fullness—receive me.

---

[82] For the theology of this book, along with text and commentary, see Christopher Tuckett, *The Gospel of Mary* (Oxford: Oxford University Press, 2007).

You are my rest—give me unrestrained maturity" (vv. 1–5). Halfway through, "Paul" prays, "Give me authority, I ask you. Give healing to my body when I ask you, through the one who brings good news, and redeem my soul, enlightened and eternal, and my spirit, and open my mind to the firstborn Child of the fullness of grace" (v. 8). The prayer's doxology closely resembles the later scribal addition to the Lord's Prayer (Matt 6:13): "For yours is the power and the glory, and the praise and the greatness, forever and ever. Amen" (v. 11).[83]

Still one more short Nag Hammadi document included in the *New New Testament* is the Letter of Peter to Philip. The Council was attracted to its clear mandate to preach the gospel even under threats of persecution, without any hint of longing for martyrdom as in some of the otherwise more orthodox second-century Christian literature.[84] Of course, "being courageous in the face of powers that harm people in our world"[85] for the Council often means promoting a feminist agenda, a gay agenda, or helping the marginalized and oppressed rather than repenting of sin and claiming the salvation available only through Christ's substitutionary atonement. In any case the Christ of this letter seems fairly docetic. Peter reminds the other apostles of Jesus's crucifixion but then adds that he "was a stranger to this suffering, but we are the ones who suffer because of the transgression of the Mother. Because of this, he did everything like us" (7:4).

The Secret Revelation of John first appeared on the antiquities market in Cairo in 1896. It is filled with names of powers and emanations known from much other Gnostic literature—Sophia, Pronoia, Barbelo, Yaldabaoth, Autogenes, and so on. Its main distinctive involves its take on the fall of Adam and Eve. As Taussig explains,

---

[83] On which see, e.g., Grant R. Osborne, *Matthew* (Grand Rapids: Zondervan, 2010), 231.

[84] Hal Taussig, "An Introduction to the Letter of Peter to Philip," in *A New New Testament*, ed. Taussig, 406.

[85] Ibid.

"Wisdom-Sophia's action makes her into a kind of Eve figure, but in this story the real Eve is not the cause of humankind's fall, but of its redemption. Here she is Adam's teacher, and the sexual intercourse of Adam and Eve marks not original sin, but a step toward salvation through Christ."[86] One can easily recognize from this description the book's attractiveness to those who like accounts of women holding the reins of spiritual power and who disapprove of sex being thought bad (even within monogamous, heterosexual marriage).[87] The fuller Gnostic worldview, of course, doesn't actually help to further either of these objectives since in it people actually become bodiless and therefore genderless in the eternal state.[88]

Although the *New New Testament* was released with a flurry of publicity and has been used in a smattering of liberal Protestant churches for special studies and conferences, it is unlikely to have a pronounced or long-lasting effect even in those circles. When people read the additional documents in their entirety, instead of focusing just on certain celebrated quotations, they will recognize the different worldview from orthodox Christianity and realize that these texts do not promote the values they think it does in certain places. Plus, the fascination with something ever new will lead the same people to a *New New New Testament* and then a *New New New New Testament*, ad infinitum. Two Bible passages come quickly to mind: "For the time

---

[86] Hal Taussig, "An Introduction to the Secret Revelation of John," in *A New New Testament*, ed. Taussig, 466.

[87] The Bible, of course, never equates Adam and Eve's sexual relationship with sin. This is a medieval Catholic notion.

[88] Not surprisingly, a movement has emerged to reread many of these documents apart from that fuller worldview and even to relativize the concept of Gnosticism. See especially Michael A. Williams, *Rethinking "Gnosticism": An Argument for Dismantling a Dubious Category* (Princeton: Princeton University Press, 1996). For an application of such a dismantling to the Secret Revelation of John, see Karen L. King, *The Secret Revelation of John* (Cambridge, MA: Harvard University Press, 2006).

will come when people will not put up with sound doctrine. Instead, to suit their own desires, they will gather around them a great number of teachers to say what their itching ears want them to hear. They will turn their ears away from the truth and turn aside to myths" (2 Tim 4:3–4). Instead of this behavior, we should heed the words of Jeremiah: "Stand at the crossroads and look; ask for the ancient paths, ask where the good way is, and walk in it, and you will find rest for your souls" (Jer 6:16).

Other Miscellaneous Documents and Agrapha

Still other noncanonical texts have emerged into either the scholarly or popular limelight in recent years as supposedly providing new insights into New Testament characters or events. In 2006, the Gospel of Judas, a document known from antiquity because of orthodox Christians who wrote against it, was published in English (after being discovered in the 1970s) and took the world by storm.[89] Yet another late second-century document, it purports to narrate a secret revelation Jesus gave to Judas Iscariot three days before the Passover celebration the night before the crucifixion. The two men discourse about cosmology with topics and characters common in Gnostic writings. Jesus predicts that Judas will betray him but discloses the docetic ideology of the document when he declares, "You will sacrifice the man that clothes me" (l. 137). The true Christ-spirit will be alive and well in heaven, divorced from the human individual Jesus has appeared to be during his earthly life. Meanwhile, although Judas's death will make it seem as though he was a traitor damned to hell, he will in fact be exalted in heaven above all the other apostles. This fits a theological perspective that would recur periodically throughout Christian history: since *someone* had to betray Jesus, the betrayer ought not to be condemned for doing so. What appears at

---

[89] *The Gospel of Judas*, ed. Rodolphe Kasser, Marvin Meyer, and Gregor Wurst (Washington, DC: National Geographic, 2006).

first like the greatest of treacheries actually turns into a profound spiritual accomplishment! The Gospel of Judas, like the rest of the Gnostic literature surveyed, gives us a fuller firsthand acquaintance with this syncretistic form of late second-century Christianity but offers no new or reliable insights into the historical characters named Jesus and Judas of the early first century.[90]

Sometimes works in which certain scholars become heavily invested turn out to be forgeries. In the fall of 2012, Harvard professor Karen King announced that an ancient Coptic gospel fragment had come into her possession, which contained a line that she translated as "Jesus said, 'my wife. . . .'" Immediately, online pundits proclaimed that Jesus really was married to Mary Magdalene, especially since the name Mary appeared elsewhere in the small fragment. King herself cautioned that all the document showed was an early Christian belief in Jesus having a wife, probably in heterodox circles and certainly not in the first century,[91] but many people paid no attention to her caveats. Other scholars noted that the same word in Coptic for "wife" is more commonly translated as "woman," and "my woman" was not an expression used for a spouse like we sometimes do but simply for someone a person was closely related to. For all we knew, the text could be referring to Mary, mother of Jesus.[92] Shortly afterwards, however, Durham

---

[90] An observation made throughout the works of scholars as otherwise diverse as Bart D. Ehrman, *The Lost Gospel of Judas Iscariot* (Oxford: Oxford University Press, 2006); N. T. Wright, *Judas and the Gospel of Jesus: Have We Missed the Truth About Christianity?* (Grand Rapids: Baker, 2006); and Stanley E. Porter and Gordon L. Heath, *The Lost Gospel of Judas: Separating Fact from Fiction* (Grand Rapids: Eerdmans, 2007). Subsequently discovered fragments of this document cast doubt on even this positive a portrait of Judas, however. See G. S. Robinson, "An Update on the Gospel of Judas (After Additional Fragments Resurfaced)," *Zeitschrift für die neutestamentliche Wissenschaft* 102 (2011): 110–29.

[91] "A New Gospel Revealed," *Harvard Magazine* (September 2012), accessed January 8, 2016, http://harvardmagazine.com/2012/09/new-gospel.

[92] Craig A. Evans, in personal conversation, September 2012.

New Testament scholar Frances Watson showed how virtually all of the words in this tiny fragment could be accounted for by someone "cutting and pasting" the letters and words of different parts of two sayings from the Gospel of Thomas (101 and 114), with the key word that could mean either "wife" or "woman" referring just to a woman.[93] Then Wuppertal professor Christian Askeland showed that the handwriting matched that of a manuscript of a portion of the Gospel of John in Coptic known to be forged, complete with seventeen consecutive identical line breaks after the same amount of text in both documents.[94] Although the *Harvard Theological Review* went on to publish articles already prepared for it by King and others on "The Gospel of Jesus' Wife,"[95] most other scholars who closely investigated matters agreed that the document was a modern forgery.[96] Of course, this conclusion received far less publicity than the initial sensationalist claims.

A longer-term puzzle involves something that has come to be known as the Secret Gospel of Mark. In 1958 Morton Smith reported his discovery in the library of the Mar Saba Monastery in the Judean wilderness of a two-and-a-half-page manuscript in the back of an edition of the genuine letters of Ignatius, the second-century bishop of Antioch, printed in 1646. The manuscript was said to have contained a letter from Clement of Alexandria written at about the beginning

---

[93] Francis Watson, "The Gospel of Jesus' Wife: How a Fake Gospel Fragment Was Composed," rev. ed. (September 26, 2012), accessed January 7, 2016, http://markgoodacre.org/Watson2.pdf.

[94] Christian Askeland, "A Fake Coptic John and Its Implications for the 'Gospel of Jesus's Wife,'" *Tyndale Bulletin* 65 (2014): 1–10.

[95] Karen L. King, "Jesus Said to Them, 'My Wife . . .'": A New Coptic Papyrus Fragment," *Harvard Theological Review* 107 (2014): 131–59. This article is followed by several other short ones detailing various scientific tests performed on the documents.

[96] The entire summer 2015 issue (61:3) of the prestigious, Cambridge-based journal *New Testament Studies*, is filled with studies decisively debunking the authentication of this scrap of papyrus. See esp. the articles by Simon Gathercole and Christian Askeland, and the editorial by Francis Watson.

of the third century, which denounced a variant form of the Gospel of Mark circulating among the hedonist sect of the Carpocratians. This fuller version of Mark contained secret teachings of Jesus intended only for initiates into the Lord's "great mysteries." For an example of the contents of "Secret Mark," Clement quoted an excerpt about Jesus's raising from death a young man who was so appreciative that he remained with Jesus one night to learn from him, wearing nothing but a linen cloth over his naked body as Jesus taught him the mysteries of the kingdom. Allegedly, the Carpocratians were using this document to support homosexual behavior, and Clement had to explain that this "Gospel" was *not* teaching that at all.[97]

From the outset one swath of scholarship was skeptical of Smith's claims, especially because his published study, complete with photographs, was not released for another fifteen years. Subsequently the manuscript was moved and the letter of Clement supposedly misplaced so that no one today can go back and examine it and make any decisions about its origin or contents. More recently, multiple scholarly studies have demonstrated reasonably convincingly that Morton Smith concocted all of this as a hoax.[98] The orthography of "Clement," especially with certain oddly shaped letters closely matches Smith's own handwriting when he reproduced ancient Greek. The basic plot of Smith's account of this document's discovery parallels a scene from Irving Wallace's novel *The Word*, published just before Smith's release

---

[97] See Morton Smith, *Clement of Alexandria and a Secret Gospel of Mark* (Cambridge, MA: Harvard University Press, 1973); Morton Smith, *The Secret Gospel: The Discovery and Interpretation of the Secret Gospel of Mark*, 3rd ed. (Clearlake, CA: Dawn Horse, 1998).

[98] See esp. Stephen C. Carlson, *The Gospel Hoax: Morton Smith's Invention of Secret Mark* (Waco: Baylor University Press, 2005); and Peter Jeffrey, *The Secret Gospel of Mark Unveiled: Imagined Rituals of Sex, Death, and Madness in a Biblical Forgery* (New Haven and London: Yale University Press, 2006).

of his book.[99] Smith himself had homosexual leanings and had been denied tenure at Columbia University, so he may have wanted to make a splash in the scholarly world and validate his sexual orientation at a time when there were far fewer ways of doing such things than there are today. Unfortunately, he passed away in 1991, so we cannot go back and ask him any more questions.[100] Francis Watson, however, has recently joined the conversation and believes he has established conclusively that Smith was the author of the document he claimed to have discovered, finding even closer parallels to Smith's story in the novel, *The Mystery of Mar Saba* by J. H. Hunter, which went through nine editions between 1940 and 1947.[101]

It might seem as if we have exhausted our search for historically helpful information about the formative events of first-century Christianity potentially to be found in heterodox sources from 150 years or more after the time of Christ. In fact, a series of individual sayings attributed to Jesus are scattered about a variety of ancient Christian writings, most of them orthodox, that sound much like the distinctive kinds of things Jesus taught, yet they are not paralleled in the canonical Gospels.[102] I have included the following list of eight of

[99] Robert M. Price, "Second Thoughts on the Secret Gospel," *Bulletin for Biblical Research* 14 (2004): 127–32.

[100] Still unconvinced that the document was a hoax is Stephen G. Brown, *Mark's Other Gospel: Rethinking Morton Smith's Controversial Discovery* (Waterloo, ON: Wilfrid Laurier University Press, 2005). But even he argues for it being a late and secondary document compared to canonical Mark, not a fragment of an earlier, more authentic one.

[101] Francis Watson, "Beyond Suspicion: On the Authorship of the Mar Saba Letter and the Secret Gospel of Mark," *Journal of Theological Studies* 61 (2010): 128–70.

[102] See, classically, Jeremias, *Unknown Sayings of Jesus*. He identifies 19 potentially authentic agrapha outside the New Testament. Five come from early church fathers, five from Oxyrhynchus's Greek gospel fragments (some of which are earlier versions of the Gnostic Gospels), three from Nag Hammadi, one from a textual variant inserted into Luke, and five from Jewish-Christian Gospels known only by those excerpts the church fathers quote.

the most probably authentic of these sayings elsewhere[103] but reproduce it here, minus the Gospel of Thomas 82 quoted already earlier in this chapter:

> On the same day Jesus saw a man working on the Sabbath, and said to him, "Man, if you know what you are doing, you are blessed, but if you do not know, you are cursed and an offender against the law."[104]

> No one will reach the kingdom of heaven without being tempted.[105]

> Ask for great things, and the little things will be added to you.[106]

> Be approved money-changers.[107]

> But the rich man began to scratch his head, and it pleased him not. And the Lord said to him: "How can you say, 'I have kept the law and the prophets?' For it is written in the law: 'You shall love your neighbor as yourself,' and lo, many of your brothers, sons of Abraham, are clad in filth, dying of hunger, and your house is full of many good things, and nothing of it goes out to them."[108]

> And never be joyful, save when you look upon your brother in love.[109]

---

[103] Craig L. Blomberg, *Jesus and the Gospels: An Introduction and Survey*, 2nd ed. (Nashville: B&H; Nottingham: Apollos, 2009), 439.

[104] An addition to Luke 6:5 in Codex Bezae, the prime exemplar of the Western manuscript text-type (on which, see below).

[105] Tertullian, *On Baptism*, 20.

[106] Clement of Alexandria, *Stromateis*, 1.24

[107] Origen, *Commentary on John*, 19.7 and several other Patristic sources.

[108] *Gospel of the Nazoreans* 16, as quoted by Origen, *Commentary on Matthew* 15.14.

[109] *Gospel of the Hebrews* 5, as quoted by Jerome, *Commentary on Ephesians* 3.

Woe to you blind who see not! You have washed yourself in water that is poured forth, in which dogs and swine lie night and day, and washed and scoured your outer skin, which harlots and flute girls also anoint, bathe, scour, and beautify to arouse desire in men, but inwardly they are filled with scorpions and with all manner of evil. But I and my disciples, of whom you say that we have not bathed, have bathed ourselves in the living and clean water, which comes down from the father in heaven.[110]

Some scholars would add considerably more *agrapha* (from the Greek for "unwritten" [in the canonical Gospels]); others would be dubious of even these few. But it is safe to say that responsible scholarship does not find outside the New Testament enough reliable historical material to shed any substantially different light on the Jesus of history and his first followers.

Historical Criteria

It is interesting to evaluate the noncanonical texts surveyed by the standard criteria for assessing the reliability of the canonical texts we have already discussed in various places.[111] In the next chapter we will observe the unprecedented thousands of hand-copied texts containing part or all of the New Testament. In comparison, most of the Gnostic texts from Nag Hammadi exist in exactly one document. Those that have been found in two separate texts typically vary considerably so that it is often difficult to know what the original exactly contained. In the case of the Gospel of Thomas, we are privileged to have one full Coptic text and three Greek fragments. The latter can actually be

---

[110] *pOxyrhynchus* 840.2.

[111] See further Craig L. Blomberg, "Canonical and Apocryphal Gospels: How Historically Reliable Are They?" *From Athens to Jerusalem* 6.3 (2006): 1–7.

dated to the late second century. The non-Gnostic New Testament Apocrypha occasionally circulated in much larger numbers, with the Protevangelium of James yielding as many as 140 copies.[112] But this is still a drop in the bucket compared to the New Testament texts (see below).

We have traced the debates concerning authorship and date for the canonical texts. But if the first-generation Christians to whom the New Testament books are attributed did not write them, almost certainly their close followers no more than a generation later did. In the case of the Apocrypha and the Gnostic texts, we are talking about anonymous or pseudonymous documents for which no hard evidence allows us to date them prior to the mid-second century. Nor can any reasons typically be discerned for selecting the first-century Christian leaders to whom they are attributed as if, for example, a school of a given person's followers had preserved over several generations distinctive traditions that were eventually written down. We have seen that the literary genres of the Gospels and Acts are best viewed as historical and biographical. But the apocryphal and Gnostic Gospels at best give consecutive episodes of only a brief stage of Jesus's life, and most are simply collections of his supposedly secret sayings or discourses. The apocryphal Acts does contain more narrative but still differs from canonical Acts in the theologies it promotes.

Precious little exists in any of these documents even to test against archaeological findings. Rarely are times or places or non-Christian figures even mentioned. Nor are there other documents to corroborate the kinds of things Jesus does and says or that the apostles teach or perform.[113] Unlike the canonical texts, there are rarely significant

---

[112] Foster, "*Protevangelium of James*," 111.

[113] Interestingly, the only miracle of Jesus mentioned in the Qur'an is the one from the Infancy Gospel of Thomas about the birds (Surah 5.110), confirming what we know from other sources, namely, that Muhammad's exposure to

portions of these later documents that cut against the theological grain they otherwise support. And the fact that many of them fill in perceived gaps in the canonical texts makes them almost certainly later writings designed specifically to satisfy people's curiosity about Jesus's hidden years or secret teachings and the exploits of the apostles not presented in the New Testament. Other apocalypses, narrating otherworldly journeys of the various apostles, perform the same function. Testimony from other Christian sources repeatedly rebuts the spurious claims of these texts. In our next chapter we will also sketch the processes involved in the formation of the New Testament canon and will see good reasons for the choices the early church made.

Conclusion

The literature from Nag Hammadi for the most part corroborates what the ancient heresiologists had already told us about Gnosticism. Now, however, we can read it firsthand from its proponents in the second through fifth centuries. Claims that any of these works go back to the first century or preserve independent tradition about Jesus or his first followers that is as reliable, if not even more reliable, than New Testament data are based on little more than wishful thinking. The Gospel of Thomas stands out among the Nag Hammadi literature as the only document with numerous close parallels to canonical teachings of Jesus at all. It is possible that a handful of its sayings represent authentic Jesus material not found in the canon, but a sizable majority can be seen as readily susceptible to Gnostic interpretation if not actually originated within Gnostic circles. Those that parallel New Testament passages frequently have additions or changes to them that move them in a more clearly Gnostic direction.

Christianity and biblical teaching was often via sectarian or heterodox branches of the Christian movement.

The remaining apocryphal gospels, Acts, epistles, and apocalypses add even less to our knowledge of the historical Jesus and his apostles, though again they offer invaluable insights into the later syncretistic groups that merged dimensions of Christianity with other popular schools of religious thought. Many of the Apocrypha are not unorthodox in their theology; they simply wanted to fill in the gaps in the canon with further undertakings and adventures of Jesus and his first followers. The *New New Testament* draws on both of these bodies of literature, but primarily the Gnostic works, to promote both feminism and looking within oneself to find divinity and a positive outlook on humanity. (Never mind the track record of appalling evil perpetrated by humans over the centuries and how poorly we function as our own gods.) Portions of some of these noncanonical documents seem to be more appreciative of women than certain passages in the New Testament. But pit Gnosticism as a whole against orthodox Christianity as a whole, and Gnosticism falls far short in its views of women, if only because its views of all of humanity embodied in this material world are so low.

A handful of isolated sayings from various ancient noncanonical documents may go back to Jesus, precisely because they resemble some of his distinctive style and themes. They certainly do not transform the historical Jesus into someone significantly different from the canonical Christ. When we see how virtually none of the standard historical criteria of authenticity enable us to place confidence in the reliability of these various sources, we are not surprised by this conclusion.

But what exactly was the process of forming the New Testament canon? Even if these additional books don't add to our historical database about first-century Christianity, are there other reasons they could or should have been included? What did set off the twenty-seven books we have in our standard New Testaments from the rest of ancient Christian literature? And even if we can give satisfying answers to these questions, how well were the texts copied over the centuries of handwritten scribal transmission before Gutenberg's invention of the printing press in the mid-1400s? Chapter 13 will examine these questions in more detail.

Chapter 13

Textual Transmission and the Formation of the Canon

Until a decade ago textual criticism was the least controversial subdiscipline of New Testament studies in which one could specialize. It was universally acknowledged by critics of all theological persuasions that the number and nature of ancient manuscripts available to us enabled scholars to reconstruct what the original writers of the New Testament first composed with an extraordinarily high degree of accuracy. All the discussions we have undertaken in previous chapters of this book were made possible precisely because the guild agreed that we had a secure foundation of stable texts of the twenty-seven books from Matthew to Revelation that we could analyze. Until recently, if a doctoral student wanted to write a thesis or dissertation on a topic where theological biases and presuppositions played the smallest role possible, one of the "safe" topics on which he or she could embark was an issue in the discipline of textual criticism.[1]

---

[1] Cf. Kenton L. Sparks, *God's Word in Human Words: An Evangelical Appropriation of Critical Biblical Scholarship* (Grand Rapids: Baker, 2008), 145.

Then Bart Ehrman's *Misquoting Jesus: The Story Behind Who Changed the Bible and Why* took the world by storm in 2005, spending the better part of the next year on the *New York Times* bestseller list.[2] Now it is commonplace for nonchurchgoers who have never studied the facts for themselves to believe and declare to others that the Bible (or even just the New Testament) was copied so many times and so poorly that we have little way of knowing any of its original contents. Even some scholars whose expertise does not lie in textual criticism have succumbed to the temptation to jump on the bandwagon Ehrman constructed.[3] If his views were in fact true, then the last twelve chapters would have been largely pointless because they all presuppose that we can know what the apostolic writers first announced and thus subject it to further analysis with respect to its historical reliability. Ironically, Ehrman's book and the changes in public perception are based on no new discoveries. Indeed, only a few of the statements in *Misquoting Jesus* are factually inaccurate, though there are a few key errors. Primarily, it is the spin Ehrman puts on the facts he recounts and the balancing evidence he does not supply that make it difficult for the nonspecialist to read and not come away doubting much of classic New Testament textual criticism.[4]

---

[2] Bart D. Ehrman, *Misquoting Jesus: The Story Behind Who Changed the Bible and Why* (San Francisco: HarperSanFrancisco, 2005).

[3] I have met students from around the country and overseas who tell me their religious studies professors in universities have taught them this and that Islamic apologists are particularly grateful for fodder to bolster their case that the Qur'an is superior to the Bible because it has been preserved more carefully. Of course, how carefully a work has been preserved has no necessary bearing on the truth of its contents. Moreover, it is a matter of historical record that the divergent copies of the Qur'an that existed during Muhammad's lifetime were all destroyed, save one, after Muhammad's death. Why destroy them unless they differed substantially and not in the small ways the New Testament manuscripts diverge?

[4] For excellent critiques of Ehrman's book, see Timothy P. Jones, *Misquoting Truth: A Guide to the Fallacies of Bart Ehrman's "Misquoting Jesus"* (Downers Grove: IVP, 2007); Bart D. Ehrman and Daniel B. Wallace, "The Textual Reliability of the

Since 2006, Ehrman has also written about "lost Christianities" and "suppressed books" that could or should have gone into the New Testament. Indeed, he has written even more on this topic than he has about textual criticism.[5] The fact I am writing about "the New Testament" in this book presupposes the Christian church's adoption of a canon, a collection of uniquely authoritative books it has believed to be God-inspired. But what if additional books were included, as in *A New New Testament* (see chap. 12)? What if some of the canonical New Testament texts were omitted? The picture of the church's teaching would clearly change in many cases. What was the process that led to the formation of the New Testament canon? Was it merely the winning party in fourth-century ecclesiastical battles who made the decisions as to what to include and exclude and who then rewrote the history of the process itself, as Ehrman and others have claimed?[6] Or are there good, independent reasons for privileging these twenty-seven books above all others that Christians have produced?

As also in this chapter, these two topics are often treated together because they are intertwined in several ways.[7] Without having a

---

New Testament: A Dialogue," in *The Reliability of the New Testament*, ed. Robert B. Stewart (Minneapolis: Fortress, 2011), esp. 27–46; and Stanley E. Porter, *How We Got the New Testament: Text, Transmission, Translation* (Grand Rapids: Baker, 2013), especially 65–72.

[5] See esp. Bart D. Ehrman, *Lost Scriptures: Books That Did Not Make It into the New Testament* (Oxford: Oxford University Press, 2003); Bart D. Ehrman, *Lost Christianities: The Battles for Scripture and the Faiths We Never Knew* (Oxford: Oxford University Press, 2003). Cf. also Bart D. Ehrman and Zlatko Plese, eds., *The Other Gospels: Accounts of Jesus from Outside the New Testament* (Oxford: Oxford University Press, 2014).

[6] See, e.g., Ehrman, *Lost Scriptures*, 2; David L. Dungan, *Constantine's Bible: Politics and the Making of the New Testament* (Minneapolis: Fortress, 2007), 120–21.

[7] E.g., Arthur G. Patzia, *The Making of the New Testament: Origin, Collection, Text and Canon* (Downers Grove: IVP, 1995); David L. Dungan, *The History of the Synoptic Problem: The Canon, the Text, the Composition and the Interpretation of the Gospels* (New York: Doubleday, 1999). For an Old Testament equivalent, see

612 | THE HISTORICAL RELIABILITY OF THE NEW TESTAMENT

high-level confidence in knowing what the original text of any book said, there is little point in debating its value, level of authority, and inclusion in the canon. Without having good reason to believe a certain book belonged in the New Testament, there is little reason to ask how much of its text we can accurately reconstruct as a foundation to assessing the historical reliability of Scripture. So we will treat both of these issues together in this chapter. Precisely because there are excellent reasons for believing we have accurate copies of what the biblical writers first wrote and that the church employed excellent criteria in determining its canon, we have not begun this book with these topics as some might have. But we need to include them here, before we sum up our findings, for the sake of completeness and because of the recent, widespread challenges to the historic consensus.

New Testament Textual Criticism

I have recently written on biblical textual criticism elsewhere,[8] so I will try not to duplicate too much of that material here. But some basics must be repeated. Ehrman speaks about scholars speculating as to the possibility of there being from 200,000 to 400,000 textual variants in all of the New Testament manuscripts of any size in any language produced before the invention of the printing press in about AD 1440.[9] By way of comparison, there are only about 138,000 words in the whole New Testament. Without further explanation, someone might imagine that every word was in doubt, with some of them having as many as three or four viable alternatives! Yet nothing could be further from the truth.

Shemaryahu Talmon, *Text and Canon of the Hebrew Bible: Collected Studies* (Winona Lake, IN: Eisenbrauns, 2010).

[8] Craig L. Blomberg, *Can We Still Believe the Bible? An Evangelical Engagement with Contemporary Questions* (Grand Rapids: Brazos, 2014), 13–41.

[9] Ehrman, *Misquoting Jesus*, 89.

As is well known, uninterpreted statistics can easily mislead. So can wrongly interpreted statistics. If there were only a small number of ancient manuscripts of the New Testament, with 200,000 variants, we would have cause for alarm. But we have to ask how many manuscripts these variants are actually spread among. Ed Komoszewski, James Sawyer, and Daniel Wallace provide an answer. There are well over 5,700 Greek manuscripts of anything from a small fragment of a few verses to entire New Testaments. There are approximately another 20,000 manuscripts, with the same spectrum of length and detail, of translations from the Greek into other ancient Middle Eastern and Eastern or Southern European languages.[10] Particularly common and among the oldest translations are Old Italic, Latin, Syriac (including both Old Syriac and Palestinian Syriac), Coptic (especially Sahidic and Bohairic), Armenian, Georgian, Ethiopic, and Old Slavonic.[11]

Suddenly Ehrman's statistics take on a different light. For the sake of ease of computation, we will round off the actual number and speak of 25,000 documents that those 200,000 variants are spread among. That means an average of eight *unique* variants per manuscript. Of course, one error may get repeated in dozens, hundreds, or even thousands of manuscripts, but that does not make a given manuscript any less reliable, that is, simply due to the frequency with which an error in it was duplicated elsewhere. If Ehrman's larger estimate of 400,000 variants should prove accurate, that would still mean only sixteen

---

[10] J. Ed Komoszewski, M. James Sawyer and Daniel B. Wallace, *Reinventing Jesus: What The Da Vinci Code and Other Novel Speculations Don't Tell You* (Grand Rapids: Kregel, 2006), 82. There are also more than a million quotations of New Testament texts in the church fathers, but many of these were not intended to be *exact* quotations, so it is hard to know when they reflect textual variants and when they simply represent free quotations.

[11] Barbara Aland, Kurt Aland, Johannes Karavidopoulos, Carlo M. Martini, and Bruce Metzger, eds., *The Greek New Testament*, 5th ed. (Stuttgart: Deutsche Bibelgesellschaft, 2014), 20*–26*.

unique variants per manuscript. Still, the numbers don't help much until we ask what kind of variants we are talking about.

Kinds of Textual Variants

A sizable majority of the differences among the manuscripts are differences of spelling, with the presence or absence of a movable *nu* being likely the most prevalent of all.[12] A *nu* is the Greek letter for the *n* sound, which often appears at the end of certain third-person plural verbs and certain dative plural nouns (and a handful of other word forms), while in other cases it is omitted. No difference of meaning exists between the two forms of a given word at all. Similarities in pronunciation between the Greek equivalents to a long *e*, to an *i*, and to the diphthongs *ei*, *ai*, and *oi* often led to further variant spellings of words. Occasionally letters would accidentally get copied twice, or else a scribe's eye might skip over a letter, especially when what resulted was also plausible Greek (or Latin or Syriac, etc.). Because Greek for centuries was written in all capital letters without spacing between words and without punctuation marks, these kinds of errors were easy to make.[13] Typists today make them when copying from other documents, even when those documents *do* include spacing and punctuation! Ehrman himself offers the delightful example of the ambiguity in the English illustration of ISAWABUNDANCEONTHETABLE.[14] Does this mean "I saw abundance on the table" or "I saw a bun dance on the table"? (If the latter, one is tempted to want to know which kind of bun, though that is not necessarily an issue for textual critics!)

---

[12] Komoszewski, Sawyer, and Wallace, *Reinventing Jesus*, 56.

[13] See further Kurt Aland and Barbara Aland, *The Text of the New Testament: An Introduction to the Critical Editions and to the Theory and Practice of Modern Textual Criticism* (Grand Rapids: Eerdmans; Leiden: Brill, 1987), 277–92.

[14] Ehrman, *Misquoting Jesus*, 48.

First Thessalonians 2:7b contains a famous example of the problems that words running together can cause.[15] Did Paul write ΑΛΛΕΓΕΝΗΘΗΜΕΝΝΗΠΙΟΙ or ΑΛΛΕΓΕΝΗΘΗΜΕΝΗΠΙΟΙ? The only difference comes about two-thirds of the way into the sequence of letters: should there be one or two *N*s? Separated into words and written in lowercase Greek, the options are ἀλλ' ἐγενήθημεν νήπιοι and ἀλλ' ἐγενήθημεν ἤπιοι, respectively. Transliterated, we have *all' egenēthēmen nēpioi* and *all' egenēthēmen ēpioi*. Translated, these two expressions yield, "but we became babies" and "but we became gentle."

This particular example also nicely illustrates how textual critics have to evaluate both external and internal evidence.[16] External evidence analyzes the nature and quality of the manuscripts that support a particular reading. How old are they? What track record of reliability do they have elsewhere? Can they be associated with "families" (groups) of similar manuscripts about which we know more? Do they fall into one of the four major "text types" of Greek manuscripts based on geographical origin, each of which tends to have recurring patterns of variants and fairly consistent patterns of transcription?[17] One can then usually rank the variants in a given passage according to the strength of the external evidence in their favor. The vast majority are too clear-cut to merit any further attention.

Internal evidence tries to identify the reading that best explains how all the other variants in a given verse or portion of a verse

---

[15] See, e.g., Michael W. Holmes, "New Testament Textual Criticism," in *Introducing New Testament Interpretation*, ed. Scot McKnight (Grand Rapids: Baker, 1989), 69–70.

[16] For a succinct introduction to both processes, see Daniel B. Wallace, "Laying a Foundation: *New Testament Textual Criticism*, in *Interpreting the New Testament Text: Introduction to the Art and Science of Exegesis*, ed. Darrell L. Bock and Buist M. Fanning (Wheaton: Crossway, 2006), 45–55.

[17] Aland and Aland, *Text of the New Testament*, 50–52; Wallace, "Laying a Foundation," 51–53.

derived from it. Internal evidence may be transcriptional or intrinsic.[18] Transcriptional analysis asks how scribes were most likely to have changed a particular text as they copied from a previous exemplar, whether that change was accidental or intentional. We have already mentioned several common phenomena that led to accidental changes. Others include skipping over one or more words because the same word or word ending appears multiple times in a line, so the scribe's eyes jumped from the place he actually left off copying to a nearby place that looks similar and thus omitted something. Deliberate changes include clarifying a grammatical or theological ambiguity. Deliberate changes were most commonly made because a scribe had reason to think (rightly or wrongly) that he was correcting a mistake in the manuscript from which he was copying.[19] Increasing the names or titles for Jesus out of reverence for him is another common change: "Jesus" might become "Jesus Christ" and then "Lord Jesus Christ."[20] The words for "we" and "you" (plural) were often confused, differing in Greek only by their initial vowel, and both often making sense in

[18] See also Craig L. Blomberg with Jennifer Foutz Markley, *A Handbook of New Testament Exegesis* (Grand Rapids: Baker, 2010), 21–24.

[19] Cf. Sylvie T. Raquel, "Authors or Preservers? Scribal Culture and the Theology of Scriptures," in *Reliability of the New Testament*, ed. Stewart, 173–85. D. C. Parker (*An Introduction to the New Testament Manuscripts and Their Texts* [Cambridge: Cambridge University Press, 2008], 151–54) even questions whether it is appropriate to speak of accidental vs. intentional changes rather than unconscious versus conscious alteration. He wonders if the concept of the Freudian slip might not be applicable to what have often been called intentional changes. In stressing the mechanical processes scribes typically followed, Parker leaves little room for "on-the-spot" conscious theological change. Instead, he envisions as possible the reliance on a second manuscript at points, the scribe's memory of other manuscripts, and a correction based on the careful study of a text ahead of the copying process.

[20] For this and numerous other minor changes to the text that arose to reinforce an exalted perspective on Jesus, see Bart D. Ehrman, *The Orthodox Corruption of Scripture: The Effect of Early Christological Controversies on the Text of the New Testament* (Oxford: Oxford University Press, 1993).

a given context. Intrinsic analysis, on the other hand, has to do with what the original author of a document would have most likely written, long before anyone began to copy his work. Is a certain word or word form more in keeping with the author's style or vocabulary but unusual enough that a scribe might have changed it to something more common or found elsewhere, especially in a parallel passage? Other principles could be discussed, but this much should give readers a flavor of the process.

In our example with 1 Thessalonians 2:7a above, the stronger external evidence supports the first reading: "we became babies" among you. But the evidence is not highly lopsided in favor of this one view; good early witnesses support "gentle" as well. Transcriptionally, it is slightly more likely that a scribe would have accidentally skipped over a letter that duplicated its immediate predecessor than that he would have copied the same letter twice by mistake. But again, the evidence is not overwhelmingly one-sided. Intrinsically, the problem comes when one looks at the immediate context. Paul has just talked about how he and his companions could have asserted their apostolic authority over the Thessalonians and burdened them with financial support (vv. 5–6). Instead they behaved in an opposite way. "Gentle" could fit this contrast nicely. Paul immediately proceeds to add that they were like a nursing mother caring for and nourishing her own children (v. 7b). "Gentle" could fit this simile nicely also. But textual critics work with the principle that the "harder reading" is usually the most original one. "Babies" (or "young children") is clearly the harder reading because Paul immediately shifts to likening himself to a mother caring for her small children rather than to being a small child himself. There is such a thing as a "too hard reading" that is just nonsensical. But this is not that extreme. In 1 Corinthians 3:9, Paul can call the church both God's "field" and God's "building" in back-to-back phrases within less than a half verse. All these lines of inquiry converge, therefore, to support the reading "babies" or "children" (cf. NIV, NET, NLT) as at least somewhat more probable than the reading "gentle" (so most English versions) as what Paul originally penned.[21]

How many New Testament variants are as significant and interesting as this one? Comparatively speaking, few are. The problem with Ehrman's presentation is not that he ever denies this. One can even deduce that this is the case if one reads his work carefully. It's just not what he emphasizes. What he does stress are the most dramatic and interesting of the textual variants, without helping the reader keep them in perspective. One comes away from his work wondering, *In how many other places in my Bible might there be a textual variant that we have never found that would represent the original wording of the text but would read quite differently from what we are used to reading?*[22] In the case of the New Testament, the answer is "probably nowhere." Think of it this way. Suppose an ancient manuscript were unearthed that had a new reading in one or more passages not attested in any of the more than 25,000 existing manuscripts. What would be the odds that it had preserved the original when all the others were in error? The answer is extremely miniscule. Probably the only context in which scholars would even countenance such an option is if such a manuscript were older than every known existing text of those passages.

---

[21] See further Jeffrey A. D. Weima, "'But We Became Infants Among You,'" *New Testament Studies* 46 (2000): 547–61. For the opposite perspective, cf. Charles A. Wanamaker, *The Epistle to the Thessalonians* (Grand Rapids: Eerdmans; Carlisle: Paternoster, 1990), 100. Astonishingly, the 1984 NIV had "gentle" without even an alternative in the margin. The TNIV then opted for "young children" with again no marginal note! Finally, the 2011 NIV gets the reading right but adds the footnote to the other option.

[22] Cf. Ehrman, *Misquoting Jesus*, 68: "The passages discussed above [Mark 16:9–20 and John 7:53–8:11] represent just two out of thousands of places in which the manuscripts of the New Testament came to be changed by scribes." He goes on to note that "although most of the changes are not of this magnitude, there are lots of significant changes" (68–69). Nothing in this conclusion to this chapter, or elsewhere, ever helps the reader realize there are *no* other changes of this magnitude, nor any other changes anywhere of even *one-sixth* of this magnitude!

That criterion alone would mean the discovery would have to be of a first- or second-century document. We have just over 100 second-century copies of small to substantial portions of numerous individual books, so if it were a second-century find, it would have to be of some portion of the New Testament not represented in any of them. Only a first-century find would unambiguously predate everything we have. But then one would have to come up with internal evidence, transcriptionally and intrinsically, to explain how a newly discovered reading was superior to everything else we have and yet disappeared without any subsequent trace of its existence. It is, of course, theoretically possible that the first scribe to copy an autograph (the original) made an intentional or unintentional change that made sense to all subsequent scribes and that no other scribe ever copied from the autograph itself, or that if some did, no one ever copied from them and the copies of the originals have been lost.

This scenario is extraordinary unlikely, however. Here is where Ehrman's three main actual errors enter in. He claims that the earliest scribes, copying books of the New Testament, at least up to the time of the legalizing of Christianity in the early fourth century, would have been nonprofessional scribes, much less skilled and more careless in their habits than the more professional ones that copied the text in later centuries.[23] We *do* know that nonbiblical documents were at times copied like this; the key giveaway is their sloppier, more scrawled form of handwriting. But not a single existing second- or third-century manuscript of any portion of the New Testament appears with that kind of handwriting.[24] In other words, the care used in reproducing

---

[23] Ehrman, *Misquoting Jesus*, 47–56, 71–72. Ehrman cites some Christian testimony to less careful scribal practice, but, if accurate, it must refer to manuscripts that were not preserved, a further sign of checks and balances in the early transmission of the text.

[24] Craig A. Evans, speaking at "The Word" conference at Grace Chapel, Englewood, CO, November 3, 2012, noted that he has personally examined originals or facsimiles of all the pre-Constantinian manuscripts of the Gospels, and not

the letters of the text shows that these were most likely skilled scribes rather than careless amateurs. Whether they were professionals (doing this part- or full-time for money) thus becomes irrelevant.

The second place where Ehrman joins company with most people who have tried to envisage the process of hand-copying ancient documents apart from the actual evidence is with the idea that, every decade or two, scrolls or codices would wear out and have to be recopied, even if they stayed in the same person's or community's possession. This model anachronistically imports modern practices of heavily using, reading, and marking cheaply produced paperback books, including Bibles, which have to be frequently replaced if a person wants a hard copy in good condition and with an attractive appearance. In the ancient world the average person did not own books. They were too costly, and most people were too poor to afford them. As long as cultures were largely oral, people memorized (either exactly or loosely) what they needed or wanted to remember. If they needed to consult a written exemplar, one per community, synagogue, church, trade guild, or government office was adequate. Only the handful of rich people had extensive personal libraries, though scholars, typically poorer, could acquire small ones.[25]

George Houston has studied the evidence from ancient public libraries as well.[26] Documents did circulate among the general populace but

---

one is written in the informal scrawls that often indicated sloppy copying by barely literate scribes. See also Andreas J. Köstenberger and Michael J. Kruger, *The Heresy of Orthodoxy: How Contemporary Culture's Fascination with Diversity Has Reshaped Our Understanding of Early Christianity* (Wheaton: Crossway, 2010), 186–90. *Contra* Ehrman, *Misquoting Jesus*, 38–41.

[25] Alan R. Millard, *Reading and Writing in the Time of Jesus* (Sheffield: Sheffield Academic Press, 2000), 17–18, 161.

[26] George W. Houston, "Papyrological Evidence for Book Collections and Libraries in the Roman Empire," in *Ancient Literacies: The Culture of Reading in Greece and Rome,* ed. William A. Johnson and Holt N. Parker (Oxford: Oxford University Press, 2009), 233–67. For a wide-ranging collection of essays on libraries in the ancient classical world, see *Ancient Libraries*, ed. Jason König, Katerina Oikonomopoulou, and Greg Woolf (Cambridge: Cambridge University Press, 2013).

nowhere nearly as commonly as with modern libraries. Far more important was the library's function as a place to preserve documents intact. When an important book was still in reasonably good condition, except that the ink of the letters was starting to fade, it was often reinked. Scribes carefully traced the letters with new ink on top of the original, rather than making a completely new book on costly new parchment or papyrus. Houston demonstrates that the average time of circulation for most handwritten or hand-copied library books in the ancient Mediterranean world was 150–200 years! Sometimes manuscripts remained available to be copied for up to 500 years! The existing complete New Testament from the fourth century known as Codex Vaticanus was even reinked after 600 years so that it could continue to be used.[27]

All this means is that we should not envision the autograph of a biblical book being recopied by dozens of independent scribes and then discarded. Nor would those copies of the autographs have remained in use just for a few decades. When Ehrman (or anyone else) says that what we have in even our oldest New Testament manuscripts are not even "copies of the copies of the copies of the original,"[28] he is going far beyond what the actual evidence allows anyone to demonstrate. Any second-century and most third-century manuscripts of books and collections of books could well have been copied directly from the autographs that Matthew, Mark, Luke, John, Paul, James, Peter, Jude, and the author of Hebrews themselves penned or dictated.[29] Of course, perhaps none of them was. Their appearance at diverse locations throughout the ancient Roman Empire means it may not have been possible for their scribes to have accessed the originals

---

[27] Craig A. Evans, *Jesus and His Word: The Archaeological Evidence* (Louisville: Westminster John Knox, 2012), 75.

[28] Ehrman, *Misquoting Jesus*, 10.

[29] And we have 102 such manuscripts from the second century alone. For this and other related statistics, see Larry W. Hurtado, *The Earliest Christian Artifacts: Manuscripts and Christian Origins* (Grand Rapids: Eerdmans, 2006), 20–21.

at all. But *somebody* at some point had to have transported a copy of the originals to a different portion of the empire, so it is entirely reasonable to imagine any or all of those documents being *copies* of copies of the originals.[30] In a context in which this literature was increasingly being viewed as sacred and where we can see for ourselves the care with which all the letters were formed, we should not imagine many errors creeping in after only two rounds of copying.

Ehrman is also wrong when he claims the existing manuscripts show copyists made more errors before Constantine's day in the early fourth century than afterwards.[31] There is a slightly greater percentage of differences among the existing texts as one moves from the older to the more recent texts during the years before 325 AD than when one does so after 325. But after that year the number of texts still in existence begins to grow exponentially so that the period of time between any two copies of a given book shrinks dramatically.[32] Of course, we would expect texts produced at about the identical time to show fewer differences than those which are a couple of decades apart. But there is no statistically significant difference in the nature or frequency of variants among texts *the same distance in time apart from one another* either before or after Constantine.[33]

---

[30] Cf. Evans, *Jesus and His Word*, 76.

[31] Ehrman, *Misquoting Jesus*, 47–56, 71–72.

[32] Daniel B. Wallace, "Lost in Transmission: How Badly Did the Scribes Corrupt the New Testament Text?" in *Revisiting the Corruption of the New Testament: Manuscript, Patristic, and Apocryphal Evidence* (Grand Rapids: Kregel, 2011), 51–52. Cf. also Daniel B. Wallace, in Ehrman and Wallace, "Textual Reliability of the New Testament," 30–41.

[33] See further Scott D. Charlesworth, "The Gospel Manuscript Tradition," in *The Content and Setting of the Gospel Tradition*, ed. Mark Harding and Alanna Nobbs (Grand Rapids: Eerdmans, 2010), 28–59. A major project underway, bound to last decades, will eventually collect all known textual evidence for all variants and enable scholars to make more accurate observations and generalizations. It is called the *Novum Testamentum Graecum, Editio Critica Maior* (Stuttgart: Deutsche Bibelgesellschaft, 2013).

As I write these words, the Internet has once again become flush with rumors about a forthcoming publication that will disclose fragments of a first-century Gospel of Mark. As with all such rumors, indeed, even after the publication of apparent findings, sober-minded people will await the process of peer review within the academy before forming strong opinions. What has been alleged as of this writing is that small pieces of papyrus were used inside mummy masks in Egypt in between the face of the corpse and the mask itself, just the way we might use pieces of old newspaper in wrapping and protecting boxed valuables today. These papyrus scraps are said to contain bits of various kinds of writings on them, including some from an early copy of Mark.[34] Should all this turn out to be true, there could well be slight variants from later copies of Mark, but it is unlikely that anything will be radically different. If it is, there would have to be a plausible explanation for how some difference could represent the original reading and, as just discussed, not have ever appeared anywhere else. Such a rationale would be difficult to come up with. The most logical conclusion would be that the new discovery was still not the autograph and that some error had crept in at an even earlier stage in the copying process.

In other words, echoing Dan Wallace, we can say with a high degree of confidence that we have the actual text of the autographs of the New Testament books in our modern critical editions of the Greek New Testaments—the fifth edition of the United Bible Societies' Greek New Testament and the twenty-eighth edition of the Nestlé-Aland *Novum Testamentum Graece*.[35] The only question at any given point

---

[34] E.g., Owen Jarus, "Mummy Mask May Reveal Oldest Known Gospel," *Live Science* (January 8, 2015), accessed January 7, 2016, http://www.livescience .com/49489-oldest-known-gospel-mummy-mask.html.

[35] Barbara Aland, Kurt Aland, Johannes Karavidopoulos, Carlo M. Martini, and Bruce Metzger, eds., *The Greek New Testament*, 5th rev. ed. (Stuttgart: Deutsche Bibelgesellschaft, 2014); Barbara Aland, Kurt Aland, Johannes Karavidopoulos, Carlo M. Martini, and Bruce Metzger, eds., *Nestle-Aland Novum Testamentum*

where the footnotes list the most important textual variants is whether that original reading is the one chosen by the committee for inclusion in the text itself or if from time to time it is actually one of the alternate readings in the footnotes.[36] This is a far cry from the claims of various skeptics that, because of all the textual variants, we really have no way of knowing what the original copies of the New Testament ever said!

Illustrations of Textual Variants

THE TWO MOST DRAMATIC NEW TESTAMENT EXAMPLES

What, then, is the full range of textual variants that does occur? Here again Ehrman starts his discussion with the most dramatic examples and never helps the reader put them in perspective.[37] Variants appear in two places that span what we now call a twelve-verse section of text. But there are only these two, we understand what happened with them, and there is no reason to suspect others are anywhere waiting to be discovered. One of these variants is the so-called longer ending of Mark (Mark 16:9–20); the other is the story of the woman caught in adultery (John 7:53–8:11). Neither is likely to be what the biblical authors first composed. But this should cause no consternation because we have so much evidence to help us recognize this, to enable us to make informed guesses as to what happened and why, and to be confident in what the original text said.

In the case of Mark 16:9–20, the vast majority of all late manuscripts do contain these verses. But neither Codex Sinaiticus nor Vaticanus, the two oldest, most complete New Testaments (from the fourth century) contain them, nor do a variety of Coptic, Armenian,

---

Graece (Stuttgart: Deutsche Bibelgesellschaft, 2012). Cf. also Michael W. Holmes, ed., *The Greek New Testament: SBL Edition* (Atlanta: SBL; Bellingham, WA: Logos Bible Software, 2010).

[36] Daniel B. Wallace, "Challenges in New Testament Textual Criticism for the Twenty-First Century," *Journal of the Evangelical Theological Society* 52 (2009): 95.

[37] Ehrman, *Misquoting Jesus*, 63–68.

and Georgian translations, and a number of early church fathers were also aware of manuscripts that did not contain them. Another cross-section of existing manuscripts contains these verses but with a critical note or a sign of some kind in the margin indicating doubt as to their authenticity.[38] An Old Italic manuscript and a marginal note in a Syriac manuscript have what has come to be called the shorter ending, which adds after verse 8, "Then they quickly reported all these instructions to those around Peter. After this, Jesus himself also sent out through them from east to west the sacred and imperishable proclamation of eternal salvation. Amen."[39] A larger group of manuscripts contains these sentences and then proceeds to include what we call verses 9–20. Codex Washingtonensis, from the late fourth or early fifth century, along with manuscripts the church father Jerome knew from that same era, inserts a long addition between verses 14 and 15, which reads:

> And those ones excused themselves, saying, "This age of law-lessness and unbelief is under Satan, who does not permit the truth and power of God to overcome the unclean things of the spirits. Therefore reveal your righteousness now." Thus they were speaking to Christ. And Christ was replying to them, "The term of the years of the authority of Satan has been fulfilled, but other terrible things draw near. And in behalf of those who sinned I was delivered over to death, that they might return to the truth and no longer sin, in order that they might inherit the spiritual and incorruptible glory of righteousness which is in heaven."[40]

---

[38] Aland, Aland, Karavidopoulos, Martini, and Metzger, eds., *Greek New Testament*, 187–88.

[39] New International Version (2011), marginal reading.

[40] Aland, Aland, Karavidopoulos, Martini, and Metzger, eds., *Novum Testamentum Graece*, 174–76. Cf. Craig A. Evans, *Mark 8:27–16:20* (Nashville: Thomas Nelson, 2001), 545.

Furthermore, the Greek style of verses 9–20, as also with these various other shorter or longer additions, differs dramatically from the rest of the Gospel of Mark.[41]

One can readily understand what would have motivated scribes to compose these various additional endings. Mark 16:8 concludes with the women fleeing from the tomb, trembling and bewildered, and saying nothing to anyone because they were afraid. Obviously, this is not the end of the story, for the other Gospels go on to narrate how the women overcame these initial reactions and did announce what they had seen to the apostles, and how Jesus subsequently appeared to a number of individuals and groups of his first followers. They probably believed the original ending of Mark was lost, imagining it perhaps to have been torn off, something that easily happened to the beginnings or endings of ancient scrolls or codices.[42] What verses 9–20 contain reads like a pastiche of excerpts from the other three Gospels, with a few bizarre additions on top of them. Probably the strangest is the promise, allegedly from Jesus, that those who believe in him "will pick up snakes with their hands; and when they drink deadly poison, it will not hurt them at all" (v. 18). Maybe this was inspired by Paul's experience on Malta in Acts 28:3–6, when he was bitten by a poisonous viper but survived unharmed and/or the experience of the seventy(-two) in Luke 10:19 when they returned from their mission and Jesus promised that they would "trample on snakes and scorpions" and not be harmed. But neither of these passages deliberately invites disaster by encouraging the handling of snakes or drinking their

---

[41] Travis B. Williams, "Bringing Method to the Madness: Examining the Style of the Longer Ending of Mark," *Bulletin for Biblical Research* 20 (2010): 397–417.

[42] See esp. James A. Kelhoffer, *Miracle and Mission: The Authentication of Missionaries and Their Message in the Longer Ending of Mark* (Tübingen: Mohr Siebeck, 2000). Commentators are divided between taking v. 8 as Mark's original ending or thinking his original ending has been lost, but few believe vv. 9–20 could be original.

venom! Christians should be relieved that what has come to be called Mark 16:18 was not something Jesus actually said or Mark originally wrote because snake-handling cults have always had fatalities.[43]

But why would Mark have wanted to end where he did in verse 8? His is the Gospel that most consistently depicts the fear and failure of the disciples.[44] Up to this point it has always been the male disciples who have blundered, whereas women have come across as exemplary. Now the women fear and fail him too, at least for a short time. All of Jesus's followers are on a level playing field again.[45] As we saw earlier, Mark was most likely writing to Rome in the 60s as persecution was increasing for the Christians there. No doubt many in the church were afraid and felt they had failed their Lord. Mark in essence is saying, "So did all of Jesus's first followers. And just as he went on to do great things through them, he can still use you powerfully as well."[46]

The story of the woman caught in adultery proves somewhat different. Whereas the vast majority of later manuscripts and even a few early ones contain Mark 16:9–20, a smaller percentage contain John 7:53–8:11. A much larger number of the oldest and typically most reliable texts lack it, even though a majority of late manuscripts

---

[43] Most recently, see Spencer Wilking and Lauren Effron, "Snake-Handling Pentecostal Pastor Dies from Snake Bite," *ABC News* (February 17, 2014), accessed January 7, 2016, http://abcnews.go.com/US/snake-handling-pentecostal-pastor-dies-snake-bite/story?id=22551754.

[44] See especially Douglas W. Geyer, *Fear, Anomaly, and Uncertainty in the Gospel of Mark* (Lanham, MD and London: Scarecrow Press, 2000).

[45] A. T. Lincoln, "The Promise and the Failure: Mark 16:7, 8," *Journal of Biblical Literature* 108 (1989): 288–90.

[46] Cf. further Craig L. Blomberg, *Jesus and the Gospels: An Introduction and Survey*, 2nd ed. (Nashville: B&H; Nottingham: IVP, 2009), 135–38, and the literature there cited. The work edited by David A. Black (*Perspectives on the Ending of Mark: Four Views* [Nashville: B & H, 2008]) is particularly misleading because it makes it appear as if about half of New Testament scholars believe vv. 9–20 actually are authentic (two of the four contributors take these verses as original), when in fact fewer than 1 percent of all the world's bona fide New Testament scholars do so.

do contain it. Several have asterisks or obeli in the margin, again acknowledging that copyists had questions about its authenticity. Some include only 8:2–11 or only 8:3–11, with or without asterisks. More intriguingly, the important early family of manuscripts known as family 13 place the story not in John at all but after Luke 21:38. One minuscule places it after John 7:36, another after John 21:25 (i.e., at the end of the Gospel), and one after Luke 24:53 (at the end of that Gospel)![47] Again, there are an inordinate number of textual variants within these verses as well.[48] Clearly this is a story looking for a home but not something John himself first penned.

Unlike the longer ending of Mark, there is nothing theologically unorthodox in this passage at all. Moreover, even liberal scholars often suggest it is something Jesus actually did.[49] No one else in his world that we know of would have been so gracious toward an indisputable adulteress while simultaneously putting the scribes and Pharisees in their place so deftly and cleverly. It has all the earmarks of a historical event. But it is almost certainly not something John included in his original Gospel.[50] John himself hyperbolically reminds his readers at the end of his narrative (John 21:25) just how much about Jesus is omitted in any work the length of one of the Gospels, so it should

---

[47] Aland, Aland, Karavidopoulos, Martini, and Metzger, eds., *Greek New Testament*, 338.

[48] Aland, Aland, Karavidopoulos, Martini, and Metzger, eds., *Novum Testamentum Graece*, 322–23. Cf. George R. Beasley-Murray, *John*, 2nd ed. (Nashville: Thomas Nelson, 1999), 143–45.

[49] Thus even Bart D. Ehrman, "Jesus and the Adulteress," *New Testament Studies* 34 (1988): 24–44.

[50] See esp. Gary M. Burge, "A Specific Problem in the New Testament Text and Canon: The Woman Caught in Adultery (John 7:53–8:11)," *Journal of the Evangelical Theological Society* 27 (1984): 141–48. Most recently, cf. Armin D. Baum, "Does the Pericopae Adulterae (John 7:53–8:11) Have Canonical Authority: An Interconfessional Approach," *Bulletin for Biblical Research* 24 (2014): 163–78.

occasion no surprise that a story like this was originally left out and that later scribes wanted to include it.[51]

But if two passages of such length were not originally in the New Testament books, yet were inserted later, might there not be numerous other similar places where something we now read wasn't there initially? As we have already seen, the chances of that being the case yet escaping all record in the voluminous textual tradition that we do have are virtually nil. And after these two long passages, the next longest textual variants affect only one or two verses. Almost all of these are later additions or subtractions intended to clarify the text, fill in perceived gaps, or harmonize one passage with another parallel or related text.

ONE- TO TWO-VERSE VARIANTS

One of the most well–known additions involves 1 John 5:7–8. Every Greek manuscript ever discovered all the way up through the fourteenth century lacks the words "there are three that testify," namely "in heaven: the Father, the word and the Holy Spirit, and these three are one. And there are three that testify on earth." But the Latin tradition represented by Jerome's Vulgate translation did contain them. When the Catholic Reformer, Erasmus, who was a contemporary of Luther in the early 1500s, left these words out of his Greek New Testament, based on an analysis of all the manuscripts he could amass, his superiors were irate. Insisting that he include them, they finally got Erasmus to vow that he would, if anyone could produce a *Greek* manuscript that contained them. Shortly thereafter, they produced one with all the signs of having been doctored, but Erasmus was true to his word, and the King James translators, who relied heavily on Erasmus's text,

---

[51] For a full overview of recent research, see Chris Keith, "Recent and Previous Research on the Pericope Adulterae (John 7.53–8.11)," *Currents in Biblical Research* 6 (2008): 377–404.

included the extra words as well.[52] Contemporary "King James Only" Christians often use this as a classic example of how "liberal" modern translations are, because they "delete" a text that makes a clear reference to the Trinity.[53] In fact, plenty of undisputed Trinitarian texts remain untouched, and modern translations are not deleting anything; they are including what they believe was most likely original without *adding* what later centuries' scribes added.

Proceeding in canonical order through the New Testament, the following verses that were added to the text over the centuries are omitted in the standard modern editions of the Greek New Testament.[54] (Note that these verses are taken from the footnotes in the 1984 edition of the NIV.) In each case there is insufficient external evidence to support the later addition but also internal evidence that explains why a scribe would have added it:

> Matthew 17:21: "But this kind does not go out except by prayer and fasting" (after the disciples' failed exorcism, added to harmonize the text with similar statements of Jesus elsewhere, at least within the Byzantine manuscript tradition; see especially Mark 9:29; cf. also Dan 9:3; Acts 14:23).

> Matthew 18:11: "The Son of Man came to save what was lost" (added to the parable of the lost sheep, with language similar to Luke 19:10).

> Matthew 23:14: "Woe to you, teachers of the law and Pharisees, you hypocrites! You devour widows' houses and for

---

[52] For full details, see Raymond E. Brown, *The Epistles of John* (Garden City: Doubleday, 1982), 775–87.

[53] Discussed and refuted in James R. White, *The King James Only Controversy: Can You Trust Modern Translations?*, 2nd ed. (Minneapolis: Bethany House, 2009), 99–104.

[54] Aland and Aland, *Text of the New Testament*, 292–300.

a show make lengthy prayers. Therefore you will be punished more severely" (added under the influence of Luke 11:52).

Mark 7:16: "If anyone has ears to hear, let him hear" (added under the influence of Mark 4:9 and 23).

Mark 9:44 and 46: "Where their worm does not die, and the fire is not quenched" (added to create a parallel with v. 48).

Mark 11:26: "But if you do not forgive, neither will your Father who is in heaven forgive your sins" (added under the influence of Matt 6:15).

Mark 15:28: "And the scripture was fulfilled which says, 'He was counted with the lawless ones'" (added under the influence of Luke 22:37).

Luke 17:36: "Two men will be in the field; one will be taken and the other left" (added to match Matt 24:40).

Luke 23:17: "Now he was obliged to release one man to them at the Feast" (added to harmonize with Mark 15:6 and Matt 27:15).

John 5:3b-4: "And they waited for the moving of the waters. From time to time an angel of the Lord would come down and stir up the waters. The first one into the pool after each such disturbance would be cured of whatever disease he had" (added to explain why the man was trying to get into the pool of Bethesda, possibly based on authentic tradition about what people believed would happen there).[55]

Acts 8:37: "Philip said, 'If you believe with all your heart, you may.' The eunuch answered, 'I believe that Jesus Christ is the

---

[55] Cf. Craig S. Keener, *The Gospel of John: A Commentary*, vol. 1 (Peabody: Hendrickson, 2003), 637–38.

632 | THE HISTORICAL RELIABILITY OF THE NEW TESTAMENT

Son of God'" (to compensate for the lack of any specific confession of faith on the part of the eunuch, probably based on
second-century confessional practice).[56]

Acts 15:34: "But Silas decided to remain there" (to make
explicit how Silas could be in Antioch when Paul left with
him in v. 40 (given that v. 33 could otherwise be understood as
meaning that Silas left as well). Of course, he could have left
only to return later).[57]

Acts 24:6–7: "And wanted to judge him according to our law.
But the commander, Lysias, came and with the use of much
force snatched him from our hands and ordered his accusers
to come before you" (making explicit what Acts has already
narrated, because otherwise Tertullus leaves unexplained how
a man the Jewish leaders seized has ended up in a Roman
prison).

Acts 28:29: "After he said this, the Jews left, arguing vigorously among themselves" (to create better closure for the
story, by narrating what would have been historically probable
anyway).

Romans 16:24: "May the grace of our Lord Jesus Christ be
with all of you. Amen" (because some manuscripts lack vv.
25–27, v. 24 was added to provide a "proper" letter ending for
those manuscripts).[58]

---

[56] Cf. Darrell L. Bock, *Acts* (Grand Rapids: Baker, 2007), 348, also citing
Barrett's and Bruce's commentaries.

[57] Ibid., 515, also citing Witherington's commentary.

[58] See further C. E. B. Cranfield, *A Critical and Exegetical Commentary on the
Epistle to the Romans*, vol. 2 (Edinburgh: T & T Clark, 1979), 803–5.

Among these more dramatic variants, there is a tendency for shorter passages to be expanded, but in the whole manuscript tradition of all the many trivial changes, it is far more common for passages to lose small words, another observation that guards against the assumption that scribes were wildly careless or theologically motivated in all but the smallest handful of variants.[59]

Shorter Variants

In addition to these fifteen examples of a spurious addition of at least one verse in length, there are numerous later additions of less than a verse. Arguably the four most significant and perhaps the best known are:

> Some manuscripts add "without cause" after "anyone who is angry with a brother or sister" in Matthew 5:22 to bring out the probable meaning of Jesus's statement.[60] Cf. Matthew 18:15 where some manuscripts add "against you" to "if your brother or sister sins."

> Some late manuscripts add "for yours is the kingdom and the power and the glory forever. Amen" in Matthew 6:13 to give the Lord's Prayer a proper doxology, probably inspired by some of the language in 1 Chronicles 29:10–11.[61]

> Most manuscripts have "in Ephesus" in Ephesians 1:1, but the three earliest and most reliable do not. Paul may well have penned this as a circular or encyclical letter with each

---

[59] See esp. James R. Royse, *Scribal Habits in Early Greek New Testament Papyri* (Leiden: Brill, 2008).

[60] Since elsewhere he himself models righteous indignation. See Craig L. Blomberg, *Matthew* (Nashville: Broadman, 1992), 106; cf. also David L. Turner, *Matthew* (Grand Rapids: Baker, 2008), 178.

[61] Donald A. Hagner, *Matthew 1–13* (Dallas: Word, 1993), 144–45; Grant R. Osborne, *Matthew* (Grand Rapids: Zondervan, 2010), 231.

church addressed copying it and inserting the name of its own community.[62]

Some early manuscripts add "coming on those who are disobedient" to Colossians 3:6 to clarify Paul's statement, "Because of these [vices listed in v. 5], the wrath of God is coming."

In other instances, some later manuscripts leave out wording that was probably original. Again, the external evidence tips the scales in that direction, and then internal evidence helps us understand why the wording was omitted. Perhaps the best known, most important, or most interesting examples are:

Matthew 16:2–3 is omitted by some early manuscripts, and it could be a later harmonizing insertion based on Luke 12:54–56. But it may also have been omitted by scribes in Egypt where red sky in the morning does not portend rain.[63]

Matthew 27:16 and 17 do not call Barabbas "Jesus Barabbas" in most manuscripts. Here external evidence would not suggest that "Jesus" was original. But internal evidence strongly suggests it was. What early Christian would add Jesus's name to that of the insurrectionist whom Pilate released instead of letting Jesus of Nazareth go free?[64]

Luke 22:19b–20 is missing in some manuscripts, starting with "given for you." Probably it was deleted because Luke has

[62] See the discussion of this and other alternatives in Peter T. O'Brien, *The Letter to the Ephesians* (Grand Rapids: Eerdmans; Leicester: Apollos, 1999), 84–87. O'Brien leans in this direction but recognizes problems with all the options.

[63] Bruce M. Metzger, *A Textual Commentary on the Greek New Testament*, 2nd ed. (Stuttgart: Deutsche Bibelgesellschaft; New York: UBS, 1994), 33.

[64] See further W. D. Davies and Dale C. Allison Jr., *A Critical and Exegetical Commentary on the Gospel According to Saint Matthew*, vol. 3 (Edinburgh: T & T Clark, 1997), 584–85 and especially n. 20.

already referred to both the cup (v. 17) and the bread (v. 19a). But the Passover meal involved four cups of wine, so Luke's fuller account makes sense at the historical level, which may have been lost sight of when the gospel proliferated outside of Jewish circles.[65]

Luke 22:43–44 are not present in many early manuscripts, about Jesus's sweat being like drops of blood after an angel appeared to him to strengthen him. It is hard to determine if they were original and were left out because they appeared to be overly sensational or incompatible with the divinity of Jesus, or if they were added to further stress Jesus's agony.[66]

Luke 23:34 is lacking in some early manuscripts, but one can understand why scribes would be reluctant to preserve Jesus's example of praying for forgiveness for his executioners. It is much harder to imagine anyone inventing this or adding it if Jesus did not say it and Luke did not originally include it.[67]

Romans 15–16 were omitted by the mid-second-century heretic, Marcion, at least in part probably because he would not have agreed with the theme of 15:1–13 on the strong who must bear with the failings of the weak and not please themselves (v. 1). As a result various existing manuscripts contain the doxology of 16:25–27 after chapter 14. Others place it after chapter 15. Some place it in one of these locations but then continue with the text as we have come to know it. Other

---

[65] Cf. esp. Bradly S. Billings, *Do This in Remembrance of Me: The Disputed Words in the Lukan Institution Narrative (Luke 22.19b–20): An Historico-Exegetical, Theological and Sociological Analysis* (London and New York: T & T Clark, 2006).

[66] Cf. the discussion in Darrell L. Bock, *Luke 9:51–24:53* (Grand Rapids: Baker, 1996), 1763–64.

[67] See esp. Joshua M. Strahan, *The Limits of a Text: Luke 23:34a as a Case Study in Theological Interpretation* (Winona Lake, IN: Eisenbrauns, 2012).

minor variations exist as well. The question is complex, but the doxology is probably original and belongs after 16:1–23.[68]

In still other cases, the textual options in a given verse involve two or more different readings. Some of the most important or interesting of these are:

> Should Mark 1:41 read that Jesus was "indignant" or "filled with compassion"? The external evidence strongly favors the latter, but the internal evidence even more strongly favors the former. What scribe would ever change Jesus's compassion to indignation in a context of a man's begging for physical healing, yet not presuming on Jesus's willingness?[69]

> Should John 10:29 read, "My Father, who has given them to me, is greater than all" or "What my Father has given me is greater than all"? It is much easier to envision scribes changing the former to the latter than vice versa. After all, the former reading could have suggested that Christ was not fully God, making scribes want to alter it, though in fact it need mean only that the Son was *functionally* subordinate rather than essentially or ontologically inferior (cf. 14:28; 1 Cor 15:28).[70]

> Did John originally write John 20:31 with the aorist or the present subjunctive—meaning, respectively, "that you may believe" or "that you may continue to believe"? The apparent evangelistic thrust of the Gospel suggests the former is

---

[68] See further Thomas R. Schreiner, *Romans* (Grand Rapids: Baker, 1998), 807–18.

[69] Cf. R. T. France, *The Gospel of Mark: A Commentary on the Greek Text* (Carlisle: Paternoster; Grand Rapids: Eerdmans, 2002), 115, 117.

[70] The classic study is C. K. Barrett, "The Father Is Greater Than I" (John 14:28): Subordinationist Christology in the New Testament," in *Essays on John*, ed. C. K. Barrett (London: SPCK, 1982), 19–36.

slightly more likely; the actual use of the Gospel, beginning in the Ephesian churches, could have led scribes to change to the latter.[71]

Did Paul write in Romans 5:1, "we have peace with God" or "let us have peace with God"? Five key early manuscripts have the hortatory, "let us" form. Yet this entire section (5:1–11) is about the theological truths that follow from God's having freely justified us through our faith in Christ, so a single exhortation would be the anomaly here. On the other hand, verse 2 contains a Greek word that is spelled identically (prior to the introduction of accent marks) in both indicative and subjunctive ("we boast" and "let us boast"). So a scribe familiar with the whole passage who interpreted verse 2 as containing a subjunctive could have then assumed that the short *o* in the verb "have" in verse 1 (the indicative *echomen*) was meant to be a long *o* (the subjunctive *echōmen*).[72]

Did Paul first pen "the testimony about God" or "God's mystery" in 1 Corinthians 2:1? The difference in Greek would be three letters (ΜΑΡΤΥΡΙΟΝ vs. ΜΥΣΤΗΡΙΟΝ). The external evidence is fairly evenly divided, both make good sense in the context, and one can envision scribes accidentally changing the wording based on the fact that Paul has already mentioned the testimony about Christ in 1:6 or on the fact that he will again mention a mystery in 2:7.[73]

---

[71] See esp. D. A. Carson, "The Purpose of the Fourth Gospel: John 20:31 Reconsidered," *Journal of Biblical Literature* 106 (1987): 639–51.

[72] Schreiner, *Romans*, 258.

[73] Here the UBSGNT's choice of "mystery" (likewise CEB, NAB, NJB, NLT, and NRSV) seems preferable to the KJV tradition of "testimony" (retained in ESV, HCSB, NASB, NET, and NIV). See Metzger, *Textual Commentary*, 480.

In 1 Corinthians 13:3, did Paul say, "If I . . . give over my body [to hardship] that I may boast" or "If I . . . give over my body to the flames?" Now the difference is only one letter (ΚΑΥΧΗΣΟΜΑΙ—"that I may boast") versus ΚΑΥΘΗΣΟΜΑΙ (lit., "that I may be burned"). The blander boast could easily have been perceived as a mistake for the more vivid burning, whereas it is unlikely scribes would have changed it in the other direction.[74]

Did Hebrews 4:2 originally read that the message the Israelites heard was of no value, "because they did not share the faith of those who obeyed" or "because they did not combine it with faith"? The external evidence supports the former; the internal evidence, the latter. English translations tend to mask the grammatical issues here so that they are not apparent without looking at the original Greek.[75]

Did James originally write that faith without deeds is "useless" or "dead" in James 2:20? He clearly said "dead" in verse 26, so scribes probably changed "useless" to "dead" to match that later verse.[76]

Did 2 Peter 3:10 originally say that the earth and everything done in it "will be laid bare" or "will be burned up"? Again, the reference to the elements' being destroyed by fire early in the verse could easily have suggested that "burned up" should

---

[74] Claude Perera, "Burn or Boast? A Text-Critical Analysis of 1 Cor 13:3," *Filología Neotestamentaria* 18 (2005): 111–28.

[75] See further Paul Ellingworth, *The Epistle to the Hebrews* (Carlisle: Paternoster; Grand Rapids: Eerdmans, 1993), 242–43.

[76] Craig L. Blomberg and Mariam J. Kamell, *James* (Grand Rapids: Zondervan, 2008), 136 n. 56.

be repeated, whereas it is hard to envision a scenario where a scribe would change "burned up" to "laid bare."[77]

A Unique Variant

A unique textual issue appears with 1 Corinthians 14:34–35, which contain famous verses silencing women in church. A few late manuscripts place these verses at the end of the chapter, after verse 40. A few other manuscripts, including some early ones, have signs in the margins suggesting that scribes had some kinds of questions about these verses but without indicating what those questions were. It is reasonable to assume they were aware of the issue of the competing locations for these verses, but we cannot know for sure. As a result, many liberal scholars and a few more conservative ones have argued that Paul did not first write these verses but that scribes later added them but did so in more than one place. On the other hand, unlike with the story of the woman caught in adultery or the longer ending of Mark, there are no manuscripts that lack these verses altogether. Where the vast majority of manuscripts position them, they appear to interrupt Paul's discussion of prophecy and tongues, to which he returns before the end of chapter 14. It would be most natural, therefore, for some scribes to put them after Paul had completed that topic.[78]

By themselves, however, all verses 34–35 do is raise more questions than they answer, so it is more likely that they originally belonged where they always appear in English translations and that the context of exercising and interpreting the so-called charismatic gifts creates a

---

[77] See esp. Jonathan Moo, "Continuity, Discontinuity, and Hope: The Contribution of New Testament Eschatology to a Distinctively Christian Environmental Ethos," *Tyndale Bulletin* 61 (2010): esp. 30–38.

[78] Cf. Elim Hiu, *Regulations Concerning Tongues and Prophecy in 1 Corinthians 14.26–40: Relevance Beyond the Corinthian Church* (London and New York: T & T Clark, 2010), 140–42; Anthony C. Thiselton, *The First Epistle to the Corinthians* (Grand Rapids: Eerdmans; Carlisle: Paternoster, 2000), 1150.

specific context that limits Paul's prohibitions to that context.[79] After all, he has just permitted women to pray and prophesy publicly in 11:5, so he is not likely contradicting himself in the span of so small a space. Gordon Fee, a leading evangelical textual critic, argues strongly that nowhere else in the New Testament manuscript tradition do we ever find a passage this long, which we have reason to believe was originally penned by the biblical author, to have been moved by scribes to another position in the text. So Fee contends vigorously for the perspective that Paul did not originally write it.[80] But neither do we ever find a passage this long which we have reason to believe was *not* originally penned by the biblical author to be present in all known manuscripts of the biblical book in which that passage appears. So either way, this is a unique example, and it seems easier to explain why scribes would have moved it than to explain why they would have invented or inserted it from elsewhere.

THE VAST MAJORITY OF VARIANTS

What, then, of all the less exciting textual variants that comprise the vast majority of the 1,438 variants chosen for inclusion in the United Bible Societies' Greek New Testament or the nearly 10,000 variants chosen for inclusion in the Nestlé-Aland edition? Most of the latter involve the presence or absence of a single word, often an article, conjunction, particle, or adverb. Or else they have to do with word order, with the meaning of the text remaining unaltered or extremely little altered. The former are at least a little more interesting. One way to get a feel for a representative cross-section of them is simply to describe all the variants included by the UBS[5] in a single text of some

---

[79] Craig L. Blomberg, "Women in Ministry: A Complementarian Perspective," in *Two Views on Women in Ministry,* rev. ed., ed. James R. Beck (Grand Rapids: Zondervan, 2005), 161–65.

[80] Gordon D. Fee, *The First Epistle to the Corinthians,* rev. ed. (Grand Rapids: Eerdmans, 2014), 780–92.

length. Take 1 Peter, for example. Here is a list of all the textual variants the UBS[5] presents.[81]

1:8—two different tenses for the participle that means "seeing"

1:9—"your" vs. "our" vs. no pronoun at all

1:22—"truth" vs. "truth through the Spirit" vs. "truth through the Holy Spirit" vs. "faith through the Spirit" vs. "love" (in the Latin tradition)

2:3—"if" vs. "since"

2:19—"grace" vs. "grace from God" vs. "grace of God"

2:19—"consciousness of God" vs. "consciousness of good" vs. "consciousness of a good God"

2:21—"suffered" vs. "died" vs. "suffered for us" vs. "died for us"

2:21—"for us" vs. "for you" and "to us" vs. "to you" in all four possible combinations (without changing word order)

2:25—"for you were going astray like sheep" vs. "for you were like sheep who were going astray"

3:7—"as with fellow heirs" vs. "as fellow heirs"

3:7—"the grace of life" (with "life" spelled two different ways) vs. "the grace of eternal life" vs. "the many-faceted grace of life"

3:8—"humble-minded" vs. "courteous" vs. "courteous, humble-minded"

3:14—"neither be troubled" vs. "in no way be troubled" vs. omitting the clause

3:15—"Christ" vs. "God" vs. "God himself" vs. "our God"

3:16—"you are slandered" vs. "they slander" vs. "they slander you as evildoers"

---

[81] Aland, Aland, Karavidopoulos, Martini, and Metzger, eds., *Greek New Testament*, 761–74.

3:18—"he suffered concerning sin" vs. "he suffered on behalf of sins" vs. "he died on behalf of you concerning sins" vs. "he died on behalf of us concerning sins" vs. "he died concerning our sins" vs. "he suffered on behalf of us concerning sins" vs. "he died on behalf of sinners"

3:21—"which" vs. "to whom" vs. omitting the pronoun

4:1—"having suffered" vs. "having suffered on our behalf" vs. "having suffered on your behalf" vs. "having died on your behalf"

4:14—"glory" vs. "glory and power" vs. "glory and his power"

4:14—"and the Spirit of God" vs. "the name of God and the Spirit" vs. "the Spirit of God"

4:14—"rests on" vs. "rests upon" vs. "has rested on" vs. "has rested upon"

4:14—no addition vs. the addition of "according to them, he is blasphemed, but according to you he is glorified"

4:16—"in this matter" vs. "in his name"

5:2—"overseeing not under compulsion but willingly according to God" vs. "overseeing not under compulsion but willingly" vs. "not under compulsion but willingly according to God" vs. "not under compulsion but willingly"

5:3—include the verse vs. omitting the verse

5:6—"in due time" vs. "in the time of visitation" vs. "in the time of your visitation"

5:8—"someone to devour" vs. "someone that he might devour" vs. "someone he will devour" vs. "to devour"

5:10—"you" (pl.) vs. "us"

5:10—"in Christ" vs. "in Christ Jesus"

5:10—"he will restore, confirm, strengthen, establish" vs. "he will restore you, confirm, strengthen, establish," vs. "to restore you, confirm, strengthen, establish" vs. "to restore, to confirm, to strengthen, to establish" vs. "he will restore, confirm, strengthen"

5:11—"the power" vs. "the glory" vs. "the glory, power" vs. "the glory and the power" vs. "the power and the glory" vs. "virtue and power" (Latin)

5:13—"Babylon" vs. "the church in Babylon" vs. "Rome"

5:14—"the kiss of love" vs. "a holy kiss" vs. "a holy kiss and of love"

5:14—"Christ" vs. "Christ Jesus" vs. "Christ Jesus, Amen."

When one realizes these are the most dramatic variants in all of 1 Peter in the entire manuscript tradition, one recognizes what a good shape the transmission of the tradition was in. Moreover, the committee that produced the fifth edition of the UBS assigned twenty of their decisions an {A} degree of confidence, their highest level. Nine were rated with a {B}, four with a {C}, and three as too close to call.

If one turns to Nestlé-Aland to see the kinds of additional variants they include that the UBS does not, the examples become even more trivial. In every case the external and/or internal evidence makes it so clear which reading was original that there is no serious dispute among scholars. From 1 Peter 1:1–7, we see the following:

1:1—"elect sojourners" vs. "elect and sojourners"

1:1—"Asia and Bithynia" vs. "both Asia and Bithynia" vs. "Asia" vs. "and Bithynia"

1:3—"given you new birth" vs. "given new birth"

1:3—"hope of life" vs. "living hope"

1:4—"undefiled and unfading" vs. "unfading and undefiled" vs. "undefiled"

1:4—"in heavens" vs. "in the heavens" vs. "in heaven"

1:4—"to you (pl.)" vs. "to us"

1:5—"in the power of God" vs. "in power"

1:6—"in whom you rejoice" vs. "whom you rejoice" vs. "you rejoice"

1:6—"in different kinds of trials" vs. "in many trials"

1:7—"the testing of your faith" vs. "the means of testing of your faith"

1:7—"but through fire" vs. "and through fire" vs. "but also through fire"

1:7—"glory and honor" vs. "honor and glory" vs. "honor and for glory"

A few more variants involve the presence or absence of an article or a change in word order that does not affect meaning or translation at all.[82] And remember that these are among the 10,000 or so most significant issues out of the 200,000–400,000 total variants.

Comparisons and Conclusions

The sheer quantity of manuscripts we have gives us a greater level of confidence in reconstructing the original autographs of the New Testament than for any other books in existence from the ancient Near East or Mediterranean World. In the Greco-Roman world Homer's *Iliad* and *Odyssey* formed the closest equivalent to a sacred Scripture, and we have only 2,500 copies of them, despite their having been composed no later than the eighth century BC. The collected works of the early second-century Roman historians exist in little more than 200 manuscripts. The works of the fifth-century BC Greek historian Herodotus still exist in about 75 copies, while we have 27 manuscripts of the Roman historian Livy whose life spanned the late first century BC through the early first century AD. We have about 20 manuscripts of Thucydides, the contemporary of Herodotus. And the oldest surviving manuscript for any of these authors dates from at least four

---

[82] Aland, Aland, Karavidopoulos, Martini, and Metzger, eds., *Novum Testamentum Graece*, 696.

centuries after the time it was first written. In some instances, the oldest manuscript we have comes from up to nine centuries after its original composition.[83]

In short, if the evidence for the New Testament books is not sufficient to reconstruct with a high degree of accuracy their entire contents, then let us not pretend to know what any ancient work of literature originally contained. But classical historians would laugh such a conclusion off as just plain silly. The wealth and nature of the evidence for the contents of the New Testament autographs remains overwhelming. We can know what the texts said, and where there are slight or even significant textual variants, it is crucial to stress, as Ehrman himself admits, that no orthodox doctrine or ethical practice of Christianity depends solely on some textually disputed reading or passage.[84]

The Formation of the New Testament Canon

But what about the choice of the 27 New Testament books? It makes little difference how carefully they were transmitted and preserved if we cannot be sure the early church made good decisions when they privileged these works as uniquely canonical. What about the commonly held conviction that the canon is simply the result of decisions made by the winners in ancient fourth-century religious and political infighting? Had those struggles turned out differently, would we have had a Gnostic canon? Would we have had the twenty-seven books but a number of others as well, as in *The New New Testament*? Were solid contenders for canonical status destroyed or suppressed so that subsequent generations would never be tempted to reconsider them?

---

[83] Komoszewski, Sawyer, and Wallace, *Reinventing Jesus*, 71.

[84] Cited by Daniel B. Wallace, "Has the New Testament Text Been Hopelessly Corrupted?" in *In Defense of the Bible: A Comprehensive Apologetic for the Authority of Scripture*, ed. Stephen B. Cowan and Terry L. Wilder (Nashville: B&H, 2013), 161.

All of these claims are commonplace in modern scholarship, but none of them is valid. We have already surveyed the Gnostic and apocryphal literature in the previous chapter, so we can be briefer here. But we need to say some things about the choices of the books we do have in our canon.

The story of the formation of the New Testament has been frequently retold.[85] We need sketch only some of the highlights here. The most important thing to say at the outset is that all of the first followers of Jesus were Jewish so that they already had a uniquely sacred Scripture, the Hebrew Bible, or what Christians would come to call the Old Testament. So the first question one should ask when thinking historically was why any Jews would consider any written documents as divine revelation on a par with a collection of documents they believed were God's eternal, immutable Word. Jews had already divided these Scriptures into three main categories—the Law, the Prophets, and the Writings (a catch-all category for everything not included in the first two sections).[86] This last category was called by a variety of expressions in pre-Christian days,[87] and the later rabbinic

---

[85] Standard works, with varying emphases, include Hans von Campenhausen, *The Formation of the Christian Bible* (Philadelphia: Fortress, 1972); F. F. Bruce, *The Canon of Scripture* (Leicester and Downers Grove: IVP, 1988); Harry Y. Gamble, *The New Testament Canon: Its Making and Meaning* (Philadelphia: Fortress, 1985; Eugene: Wipf & Stock, 2002); and Bruce M. Metzger, *The Canon of the New Testament: Its Origin, Development, and Significance* (Oxford: Clarendon, 1997).

[86] For a sketch of the probable development of these three parts of the Hebrew Bible, see Stephen G. Dempster, "Torah, Torah, Torah: The Emergence of the Tripartite Canon," in *Exploring the Origins of the Bible: Canon Formation in Historical, Literary, and Theological Perspective*, ed. Craig A. Evans and Emanuel Tov (Grand Rapids: Baker, 2008), 87–127.

[87] Ben Sira alone refers to this material as "the other Books of the Fathers," "the others that have followed in their steps," and "the rest of the Books." See Roger Beckwith, *The Old Testament Canon of the New Testament Church: And Its Background in Early Judaism* (London: SPCK; Grand Rapids: Eerdmans, 1985; Eugene: Wipf & Stock, 2008), 110.

literature suggests that a few debates were still going on about certain books, especially Esther (in which God never appears by name), Ecclesiastes (which can be viewed as being much more negative about this life than other Scriptures), and Song of Solomon (would God really view sexual pleasure so highly?).[88]

What is significant, however, is that despite the abundant amount of Jewish literature that proliferated after about 425 BC (the traditional date by which the canonical Old Testament books had all been written), we have no evidence to suggest any was seriously entertained as being added to the Hebrew Scriptures. Already in the first century, the Jewish historian Josephus, echoed by later rabbis, attributed this to the cessation of prophecy within Israel.[89] Although books of a prophetic or apocalyptic genre continued to appear, along with other works viewed in various Jewish circles as containing a derivative form of revelation, nothing before or after the rise of Christianity would ever supplant or supplement the 39 works (counting according to the English book divisions) of the Old Testament.

Nevertheless, those books that depict the chronologically latest events in Jewish history depicted in the Hebrew canon, for the most part are transparently open-ended. A majority of the writing prophets depict judgment for part or all of Israel in the short term but restoration and unprecedented blessings in the long term, as one comes to the close of their prophecies (see Isaiah, Ezekiel, Daniel, Hosea, Joel, Amos, Obadiah, Micah, Zephaniah, Haggai, and Zechariah). Hopes that some or all of these prophecies were being fulfilled by the successful Maccabean revolution in the second century BC were dashed when Rome invaded and occupied Israel in 63 BC and remained the

---

[88] For the rabbinic testimony, including the discussion of these books, see ibid., 274–337.

[89] On which, see esp. Benjamin D. Sommer, "Did Prophecy Cease? Evaluating a Reevaluation," *Journal of Biblical Literature* 115 (1996): 31–47.

dominant imperial force throughout the Mediterranean world for nearly half a millennium. The audacity of Jesus's ministry, as N. T. Wright has repeatedly demonstrated, was the claim, never expressed in so many words but displayed throughout his teachings and actions, that the Jewish exile was over.[90] Israelites could live as free people without one Roman soldier ever leaving his outpost!

Various New Testament writings build on this central conviction, even while contextualizing Jesus's message in a variety of ways for increasingly Gentile audiences. We don't know what first led Jesus's earliest followers to begin to think of a collection of Christian documents as on a par with God's uniquely authoritative Word in the Hebrew Scriptures, especially since Jesus himself left behind no writings of which anyone has ever been aware. The fact that he is the central character in them doubtless had much to do with the formation of a new canon. But Tertullian and Clement of Alexandria's opinions, expressed around the end of the second century, are as plausible as any. Jeremiah and Ezekiel had prophesied a coming new covenant (Jer 31:31–34; Ezek 37:22–28), and Christians believed Jesus, according to his own testimony, had inaugurated that new covenant (Luke 22:20; 1 Cor 11:25). But the Mosaic covenant produced inscripturated writings (the Torah), so surely a new and greater covenant should produce further Scriptures (Tert. *Contra Marc.* 4:1; Clem. *Strom.* 1:9; 3:11; 4:21; 5:13).[91] Nor would we expect that collection to grow over a long

---

[90] This is the main theme of N. T. Wright, *Jesus and the Victory of God* (London: SPCK; Minneapolis: Fortress, 1996). More briefly, cf. N. T. Wright, *The Challenge of Jesus: Rediscovering Who Jesus Was and Is* (Leicester and Downers Grove: IVP, 1999).

[91] Tertullian was thus the first to speak of these books as a New Testament (from the Latin *testamentum* for "will" or "testament," one of the two meanings of the Greek *diathēkē* along with "covenant"). See Bruce, *Canon of Scripture*, 180–83. For an expansion of this argument based on the covenantal nature of early Christianity, see Michael J. Kruger, *The Question of Canon: Challenging the Status Quo in the New Testament Debate* (Downers Grove: IVP, 2013), 57–67.

period of time or be open-ended like the Hebrew Scriptures were. Jesus, Christians believed, would fulfill all of the Hebrew Scriptures; what wasn't fulfilled in his first coming would be completed at his second, but the interim period of time would not be one of progressive revelation to be inscripturated as it was in the Old Testament. After all, everything that had to happen before his return had already occurred (Mark 13:30 pars.).

We can see glimpses of this "canon consciousness," not at all formally delimited, beginning to emerge even within the first century, within what would come to be called the New Testament documents themselves. Jesus, in John's Gospel, promises that the Spirit would enable his disciples to remember his teaching (John 14:26) and would testify about him (15:26), and would lead them into all truth (16:13). None of these passages clearly promises new *Scripture*; and none of them delimits what it would be, were it to appear; but the three texts are at least consistent with the later conviction that some had appeared.[92] First Timothy 5:18 cites Deuteronomy 25:4 as Scripture and then goes on to add a quotation from Luke 10:7. Of course, it is possible that Paul is referring only to the text of Deuteronomy as Scripture, but the more natural way of understanding the grammar is to take the two quotations as parallel references to Scripture. It is also possible that the Greek word *graphē* here simply means a "writing"; but because Paul, like almost all the New Testament authors, uses this term to mean the Hebrew Bible, it would appear that he intends to refer at the very least to some kind of uniquely authoritative document.[93] For those who find it impossible to believe that Paul in the mid-60s could have viewed the works of his beloved physician and

---

[92] Cf. D. Moody Smith, "When Did the Gospels Become Scripture?" *Journal of Biblical Literature* 119 (2000): 3–20.

[93] George W. Knight III, *The Pastoral Epistles* (Grand Rapids: Eerdmans; Carlisle: Paternoster, 1992), 234.

travel companion written just a few years earlier as inspired, this interpretation of 1 Timothy 5:18 becomes a major reason for their dating
this book much later and seeing it as pseudonymous (recall above).
But if Paul could recognize that the Thessalonians' maturity derived
from recognizing the spoken gospel message as the word of God (1
Thess 2:13), it seems hard to imagine him unable to recognize the
God-breathed nature of a work of his close colleague almost at once.[94]

More unambiguously, 2 Peter 3:16 refers to at least some of what
appears in Paul's letters as "other Scriptures." For many this is a key
reason for dating 2 Peter to the second century and not finding it
Petrine (again, see above). But if one refuses to argue in a circle and
countenances the possibility of Peter in the mid-60s recognizing even
just the earliest of Paul's letters from ten or more years previous as
uniquely inspired, then we have even clearer early evidence for a kind
of canon consciousness.[95] Whether any of these passages are admitted
as evidence, we have a plethora of quotations of and allusions to many
of the New Testament documents in that largely early second-century
body of literature known as the apostolic fathers. There is regularly a
sense that they are cited as authoritative, sometimes uniquely so (e.g.,
Ign. *Trall.* 3:3; 2 Clem. 2:4), occasionally called Scripture, and once in
a while put on a par with the Old Testament works.[96]

By the middle of the second century two challenges to orthodox
Christianity necessitated that believers think carefully about which
books they were treating as akin to the Hebrew Bible. The first was
the growth of full-fledged Gnosticism, especially as propounded by

---

[94] Cf. further Köstenberger and Kruger, *Heresy of Orthodoxy*, 129–32.

[95] On the authorship of 2 Peter, including a treatment of this issue, see esp.
Thomas R. Schreiner, *1, 2 Peter, Jude* (Nashville: B&H, 2003), 255–76. Cf. also
Köstenberger and Kruger, *Heresy of Orthodoxy*, 129–32.

[96] Clayton N. Jefford, *The Apostolic Fathers and the New Testament* (Peabody:
Hendrickson, 2006), 107–44; Köstenberger and Kruger, *Heresy of Orthodoxy*,
136–50.

Valentinus, which challenged various cardinal tenets of the faith head-on (recall above). The second was the anti-Jewishness of Marcion, bishop of Sinope, who created a minimal canon of parts of Luke and selections from the letters of Paul. Both movements to varying degrees rejected the most Jewish parts of Christianity and tended to pit a wrathful God of the Old Testament against a loving God whom Jesus incarnated. In rejecting both of these challenges as heretical, the sizable majority of early Christianity that remained faithful to its apostolic heritage had to begin reflecting more formally on which works it would accept as uniquely authoritative.[97] This is not, however, to say that we know of anyone besides Marcion proposing an alternate canon. Remarkably the Gnostics themselves did not, to our knowledge, put forward any of their literature as on a par with emerging New Testament Scripture, merely as worthy within their own communities to articulate their beliefs and practices.[98] Their debates with orthodoxy were not over canon but over hermeneutics.[99]

By the second half of the second century, the stakes became higher in the discussions about a New Testament canon. While still sporadic,

---

[97] For the influence of both of these movements, along with Montanism, see Everett Ferguson, "Factors Leading to the Selection and Closure of the New Testament Canon: A Survey of Some Recent Studies," in *The Canon Debate*, ed. Lee M. McDonald and James A. Sanders (Peabody: Hendrickson, 2002), 309–16.

[98] This literature "was neither persuasive nor popular and [the books] were never really serious contenders for inclusion within the canon." See Michael F. Bird, *The Gospel of the Lord: How the Early Church Wrote the Story of Jesus* (Grand Rapids: Eerdmans, 2014), 295.

[99] Nor were they interested, more generally, in building on any received canonical tradition like the Hebrew Scriptures. For all of these points, along with the nature of Gnostic appropriation of references from what would become New Testament documents, including authoritative appropriation, see Pheme Perkins, "Gnosticism and the Christian Bible," in ibid., 355–71. Cf. Pheme Perkins, *Gnosticism and the New Testament* (Minneapolis: Fortress, 1993), 194, on the Apocryphon of James' and the Gospel of Mary's use of the canonical Gospels' characters and contents: "The gospel canon and apostolic authority must be claimed for gnostic exegesis."

Roman persecution under those emperors who chose to inflict it was becoming ever more severe, including the potential for being executed simply for owning Christian literature. Those believers with enough means or in positions of leadership that allowed them to own Christian books had to determine which ones they were willing to die for rather than surrendering them to the authorities to be destroyed. And all these developments were unfolding 150–175 years before Christianity began to hold any base of political power in the empire. The idea that the selection of books to be included in a New Testament occurred solely or primarily as a response to a political debate when orthodox Christianity was legal and had a power base from which to operate founders on the rocks of chronology. Christianity had no political power in these second- and third-century days.[100]

Even more importantly, there is no significant dispute from the early centuries of Christianity over the unique value and origin of the Gospels of Matthew, Mark, Luke, and John, over the book of Acts, over the thirteen letters attributed to Paul, or over the epistles of 1 Peter and 1 John. Yet these works are most often challenged by today's revisionist historians. Radical scholars today wish to discredit or at least supplement the Gospels, the Acts, and the major epistles of the New Testament, as we saw with *A New New Testament* (chap. 12). In the ancient world the seven books that eventually were accepted in the New Testament, which at times received serious questioning, were Hebrews, James, 2 Peter, 2 and 3 John, Jude, and Revelation. The issues then were issues that are still sometimes raised—the lack of any confidence of knowing who the author of Hebrews was, apparent theological tensions between Paul and James, the strikingly different style and contents of 2 Peter compared with 1 Peter, the brief and personal nature of 2–3 John, the brevity along with the quotation of

---

[100] See esp. throughout William R. Farmer and Denis M. Farkasfalvy, *The Formation of the New Testament Canon* (New York: Paulist, 1983).

pseudepigraphical literature in Jude, and the puzzling genre and interpretation of Revelation as an apocalypse.[101]

Yet even with these questions, we can watch the number of documents accepted confidently into an emerging canon of the New Testament steadily grow as one moves from late second to the early fourth centuries. The Muratorian canon from the late second century[102] included the twenty undisputed books noted above plus Hebrews. Irenaeus from about the same period of time or just slightly later, added 2 John and acknowledged twenty-two books.[103] Tertullian, at the turn of the century, listed twenty-three, adding James and Revelation but excluding 2 John. In the early third century, Origen of Alexandria would distinguish three categories of books—those widely acknowledged, those doubted by some, and others that he rejected as teaching false doctrine. Listed as widely acknowledged were the four Gospels, Acts, the thirteen letters of Paul, 1 Peter, 1 John and Revelation. Listed as disputed were Hebrews, James, 2 Peter, 2–3 John and Jude, along

---

[101] See further Bruce, *Canon of Scripture*, 158–69.

[102] Attempts to redate it to the fourth century have not proved persuasive. See esp. the discussion and reaffirmation of the traditional date in Joseph Verheyden, "The Canon Muratori: A Matter of Dispute," in *The Biblical Canons*, ed. J.-M. Auwers and H. J. de Jonge (Leuven: Leuven University Press and Peeters, 2003), 487–556.

[103] Irenaeus's most famous statement was about the four Gospels—declaring that there had to be four just as there were four corners of the earth, four directions from which the wind blew, and four-faced cherubim who worshipped God (*Contra Her.* 3.11.9). But these would have been unpersuasive, even in the second century, unless there was already widespread agreement on the four. Irenaeus's argument makes sense as drawing analogies to what was already believed but not as trying to persuade the unbeliever. So the argument that Irenaeus was the first to delimit a canon fails—see Graham N. Stanton, "The Fourfold Gospel," *New Testament Studies* 43 (1997): 322. Cf. further Kruger (*Question of Canon*, 155–202), who also gives in rich detail the evidence of canon consciousness at the time of and prior to Irenaeus. For the four Gospels, cf. especially C. E. Hill, *Who Chose the Gospels? Probing the Great Gospel Conspiracy* (Oxford: Oxford University Press, 2010), 69–206.

with the *Didache*, the *Epistle of Barnabas*, the *Shepherd of Hermas*, the *Preaching of Peter*, and the *Acts of Paul and Thecla*.[104] Only one of these latter five documents was included in *A New New Testament*, the *Acts of Paul and Thecla*, which in turn was the most non-Gnostic-like work of the ten the New Orleans Council chose to add to the twenty-seven standard New Testament books.

The other four books on Origen's list of disputed works were largely orthodox documents in the general tradition of apostolic Christianity, even if with a little peculiar nuancing here and there. The main reason they were disputed was not their contents nearly so much as their date. As already noted, once second-century Christian documents started to be penned and collected, their own writers had the sense that they were neither inspired nor to be taken as authoritatively as the first-century canonical texts. Rejected altogether by Origen were a variety of heretical gospels and acts, especially various Gnostic works. The early fourth-century work of Eusebius of Caesarea closely mirrored Origen's lists. And all this took place before Constantine ever became the first Christian emperor, making Christianity a legal religion and giving it even the potential of suppressing what it believed to be deviant forms of the religion.

Growing up in a pre-Internet, pre-desktop-publishing world, I never dreamed that if I ever got to write real-live, peer-reviewed published books, some of the perspectives I would have to rebut would be those introduced in fictitious novels or by self-published authors. No one had conceived of the notion of a blog, much less imagined that some people would think that reading it was necessarily a means of gaining accurate information. Today, however, thanks to all these developments, countless people around the world, including some university professors, believe that Constantine's calling for the Council of Nicea in AD 325 led to the establishment of the canon of the New

---

[104] Bruce, *Canon of Scripture*, 192–95.

Testament. That was a piece of fiction Dan Brown made up in *The Da Vinci Code* and duped millions into believing.[105] The Council of Nicea was actually a gathering of Christian bishops to debate Trinitarian doctrine; its outgrowth, the Nicene Creed, is still recited regularly in Eastern Orthodox, Roman Catholic, and more liturgically minded Protestant churches, enunciating what the vast majority of all Christians through the centuries have believed about the roles of the Father, Son, and Holy Spirit.[106] Constantine did commission Eusebius to produce fifty new copies of the New Testament to be distributed around the empire, but that had nothing to do with any discussion about which books should be included. Eusebius, in fact, had already come to agree with the twenty-seven that have remained a part of the canon. The councils that formally ratified these twenty-seven were held in North Africa at Hippo (393) and Carthage (397) at the end of the fourth century. But Athanasius, bishop of Alexandria, in 367 in his Easter-time encyclical already compiled the same list of twenty-seven books, officially endorsing them as uniquely worthy of inclusion in the New Testament.[107]

Nor is it the case that the church, beginning in the fourth century, began suppressing other equally viable candidates for inclusion in the Christian canon. Most of the documents that were seriously considered but eventually not accepted were from the apostolic fathers, copies of which remained in some abundance. And the other works occasionally proposed for inclusion were still not the classic Gnostic works many are so enamored with today. Two appendices in James Sanders and Lee McDonald's wide-ranging anthology of studies on the biblical canon include references to all known primary sources

---

[105] Brown, *Da Vinci Code*, 231–35.

[106] For its evolution and various forms, see Philip Schaff, *The Creeds of Christendom*, rev. David S. Schaff (New York: Harper & Row, 1931), 24–29.

[107] Bruce M. Metzger, *The New Testament: Its Background, Growth, and Content*, 3rd ed. (Nashville: Abingdon, 2003), 316.

relevant to a study of the emergence of the New Testament canon and all thirty known lists and catalogues of books to form authoritative collections from the second through sixth centuries.[108] The book that appeared on the most lists that was not eventually selected was the mid-second-century orthodox writing known as the Shepherd of Hermas, a Jewish-Christian book of visions, mandates, and parables concerning key second-century theological debates. The Shepherd in fact appeared on five lists.[109] The Book of Wisdom (Old Testament apocryphal proverbs), the Epistle of Barnabas (which employed allegorical interpretation of the Hebrew Bible to show Christians as the true successors to Israel), and the Apocalypse of Peter (a Gnostic work presenting Jesus as a docetic redeemer) each appeared on three lists. First and 2 Clement (epistles from the apostolic fathers) are mentioned twice, and the Didache (teaching on ecclesiastical matters attributed to the Twelve), Sirach (another intertestamental work of Proverbs), the Psalms of Solomon (intertestamental Psalms) and the Acts of Paul and Thecla, the Apostolic Constitutions, the Two Ways, and the Preaching of Peter, once each. These works were largely orthodox in their theology (with the Acts of Paul and Thecla probably the least so) and not nearly as sectarian as the Gnostic literature.

The criteria that emerge from all of the early Christian conversations about the formation of a New Testament canon are never organized or systematized but may be inferred primarily to include apostolicity (authorship by an apostle or close associate of an apostle), catholicity (nearly universally accepted throughout the church in its

---

[108] Appendices B and D in *Canon Debate*, ed. McDonald and Sanders, 583–84, 591–97.

[109] Linking the two topics of this chapter together, K. Martin Heide ("Assessing the Stability of the Transmitted Texts of the New Testament and the *Shepherd of Hermas*," in *Reliability of the New Testament*, ed. Stewart, 125–59) shows that the care in the transmission of Hermas only rarely comes even close to the most careless copying of New Testament books.

various geographical locations), and orthodoxy (cohering with the apostolic tradition of the Christian faith in fulfillment of the Scriptures of Israel).[110] More subjective criteria like inspiration or self-attestation were also at times included.[111] Even after the ratification of the canon at the fourth-century councils, there was still some diversity in which books around the empire were considered normative.[112] This observation refutes the notion that the conciliar decisions were implemented in so heavy-handed a fashion that no one dared to speak out in favor of or against any other books.

While there are extremely isolated references to the destruction of noncanonical books at a particular location, the main reason most of this literature died out in usage was because it simply wasn't deemed to be as reliable, useful, or true by the vast majority of Christians.[113] Gnosticism likewise lost its appeal through attrition rather than suppression. Michael Bird correctly identifies three main criticisms of the noncanonical texts that led to their lack of acceptance:

> (1) the "Jesus" they set forth was not recognizable as the Jesus known in other sacred writings or congruent with apostolic tradition, (2) the "other" Gospels are often esoteric, elitist, and erroneous in what they affirm about God, creation, sin, holiness, ethics, and redemption, and (3) they do not properly have origins among Jesus' earliest followers and are late and tendentious.[114]

---

[110] For the strengths and weaknesses of appeals to these criteria, see Michael J. Kruger, *Canon Revisited: Establishing the Origins and Authority of the New Testament Books* (Wheaton: Crossway, 2012), 73–87.

[111] Ibid., 88–122. Cf. Metzger, *New Testament: Background, Growth and Content*, 318: "In the most basic sense neither individuals nor councils created the canon; instead they came to recognize and acknowledge the self-authenticating quality of these writings, which imposed themselves as canonical upon the church."

[112] Appendix D in *Canon Debate*, ed. McDonald and Sanders, 596–97.

[113] Köstenberger and Kruger, *Heresy of Orthodoxy*, 151–75.

[114] Michael F. Bird, *The Gospel of the Lord: How the Early Church Wrote the Story of Jesus* (Grand Rapids: Eerdmans, 2014), 293. Bird adds, "It was not the

As Darrell Bock likes to say, even when there are winners and losers in some kind of competition, sometimes winners actually deserve to win![115] It certainly appears that this was the case with the books of the New Testament canon. Furthermore, there is no actual evidence to date any of the noncanonical works to an earlier date than the canonical ones. Those who do so make their affirmations by sheer supposition and hypothesis. As Craig Evans puts it, "The only way someone can come up with a divergent 'Christianity' is to import a second-century writing or teacher into the middle of the first century." Ehrman and others who speak of lost Christianities "are talking about individuals and groups who moved away from the earlier, widely attested teaching of Jesus and the first generation of his followers."[116] The canonizers were thus ensuring that their Scriptures represented the roots of their faith, not some later mutant branches!

---

fault of Christian censors or a theological thought-police that the 'other' Gospels were criticized and rejected. The 'other' Gospels were not recognizable as 'gospel,' and they failed to capture the hearts, minds, and imaginations of Christians in the worldwide church. The proof of this is the limited number of extant manuscripts for many of these 'other' Gospels and the fact that many Jesus books were not known beyond their immediate circles" (p. 294).

[115] E.g., Darrell L. Bock, "Why the Gnostic Gospels Lost," *Belief.Net* (November 2006), accessed January 7, 2016, http://www.beliefnet.com/Faiths /Christianity/2006/11/Why-The-Gnostic-Gospels-Lost.aspx?p=1.

[116] Craig A. Evans, *Fabricating Jesus: How Modern Scholars Distort the Gospels* (Downers Grove: IVP, 2006), 202, 203. Or in the words of Jens Schröter, "The value of the extracanonical Jesus tradition therefore does not lie in changing a Jesus picture drawn from the writings of the first century. Rather, they [*sic*] bring before our eyes constellations and controversies of the second and third centuries in which different ways of referring to Jesus were demarcated from one another." See his *From Jesus to the New Testament: Early Christian Theology and the Origin of the New Testament Canon* (Tübingen: Mohr Siebeck; Waco: Baylor University Press, 2013), 254. Cf. also pp. 292–93: "The notion that the four-gospel collection was created at the end of the second century for ecclesiopolitical reasons and excluded other strands of tradition as 'heretical' neither does justice to the observations on the age of this collection nor to those on the relationship of the apocryphal Jesus tradition to the tradition preserved in this collection."

Conclusion

Despite frequent claims to the contrary, the books of the New Testament were copied with extraordinary care. Because of the sheer volume of manuscripts, both in Greek and in various other ancient languages into which the Scriptures were translated, there are an enormous number of textual variants. But the vast majority of these are extremely minor, and the size of the manuscript tradition also makes it possible to determine beyond any reasonable doubt what the original reading would have been in upwards of 99 percent of the text of the New Testament. Where there still is uncertainty, we can at least know that the original text is represented by *one* of the variant readings of a given passage. We do not have to worry that some new discovery could overthrow the testimony of so many thousands of manuscripts and their consistent usage throughout the history of the church. Certainly no theological doctrine or ethical practice of the Christian faith relies solely or even primarily on any textually disputed passage or passages.

The early church also made good choices in what it canonized. It might be better to speak of it as receiving or ratifying documents which from their composition were recognized as unique. Yes, there were some rough edges, including a minority of the texts, particularly some of the shortest, where debate continued for three centuries or so. Also a handful of texts supported by a multiplicity of sources for inclusion in the canon failed to make it. But a substantial gap remained in the amount of support that existed between the most poorly supported texts that made it into the canon and the most frequently supported ones that were rejected. As far as we can tell, the theologically most central texts of the New Testament were all acknowledged, virtually without question, from their inception. Meanwhile, the most intriguing documents propounding an alternate and heterodox form of Christianity were rarely if ever put forward for inclusion at all, even by their own adherents.

Part Six

The Problem of Miracles

Chapter 14

Miracles in the New Testament World and Today

I t is possible to be largely convinced of everything this book has maintained and still be skeptical of the reliability of the New Testament for one main reason we have yet to address. It is full of the miraculous. For twenty-first-century individuals steeped in the post-Enlightenment distrust of narratives about the supernatural, this one issue may trump all others. Of course, the fact that God is a central character throughout both Testaments is a defeater for the hard-core atheist. Yet many people today, whether they realize it or not, are more deistic than atheistic. They leave the door open for a "higher power," and "God" remains the most common name for that power. God may even interact with people, so they believe, through thoughts, circumstances, and gut feelings that the pure naturalist would attribute to mere biology. But introduce accounts of turning water into wine, walking on water, or raising the dead, and the walls go up. Everyone knows these things don't happen. In fact, they can't happen.

Of course, there are other ancient historical narratives with miracles in them, in which classical historians simply excise the miracle accounts and still derive much from the texts they believe really happened.[1] Wondrous signs often accompany predictions to reinforce their truthfulness, while omens portend evil events to come. The supernatural elements can be lifted from the accounts, and we still have coherent and credible narratives. Thomas Jefferson, as we noted in our first chapter, did something similar with the Gospels, literally cutting out of his Bible all of Jesus's miracles, but still admiring and trying to follow the teachings of Jesus, which he believed were enlightened and beneficial.[2] Nevertheless, as has often been pointed out, the miracles of the New Testament are not so easily detached from the overall story line of Scripture.[3] If Christ was not bodily raised from the dead, Paul insisted, then all our faith is futile (1 Cor 15:12–19).

---

[1] As we noted in chapter 1, a striking parallel to the issue of the four canonical Gospels appears in the four extant accounts of Caesar's crossing the Rubicon, one of the standard examples of a conclusively established fact from ancient history. Yet there are the same kinds of apparent discrepancies among the details that we often find in the New Testament, and one account even inserts a miracle in conjunction with it. See Paul Merkley, "The Gospels as Historical Testimony," *Evangelical Quarterly* 58 (1986): 328–36.

[2] Jefferson also distilled the Gospels down into the events and teachings by which he guided his life. Long after his death they were published in 1904. A facsimile edition is available today: Thomas Jefferson, *The Life and Morals of Jesus of Nazareth* (Washington: Smithsonian, 2011).

[3] Matthew 4:23 and 9:35 summarize how the teaching and miracles of Jesus were inextricably intertwined. See also Luke 4:18–21. Note, too, how Mark 8:17–18 and 4:11–12 link the disciples' misunderstanding of Jesus's miracles and his teachings together with reference to the same Old Testament passage (Isa 6:9). For an excellent survey of the place of the miracles in the Gospels as they now stand, see Colin Brown, *Miracles and the Critical Mind* (Grand Rapids: Eerdmans; Exeter; Paternoster, 1984), 293–325.

But if a God exists who could raise Christ, then none of the other scriptural miracles lies beyond his capability.[4]

Based on God's Existence

But does such a God exist? Historically, four classic arguments for his existence have dominated philosophical discussions. The cosmological argument begins with the existence of the universe and argues that it is more logical to believe in a cosmic Creator to account for what exists than to imagine that somehow it has always existed or that it came into existence at some point without any causal agent.[5] In colloquial language, "If there was a big bang, then there had to be a big banger!"[6] The teleological argument focuses on evidences of design in creation. One form of this that has become popular in recent years is the "intelligent design" movement, by no means limited to Christians, which points to a variety of "natural" phenomena that are "irreducibly complex." In other words, if a person postulates that they evolved one part at a time, there is no discernible use or function for each part and collection of parts until they reach a detailed level of complexity, making an evolutionary origin improbable. Examples include blood clotting, cilia, the human immune system, material

---

[4] Cf. Arthur Gibson, "Logic of the Resurrection," in *Resurrection*, ed. Stanley E. Porter, Michael A. Hayes, and David Tombs (Sheffield: Sheffield Academic Press, 1999), 166–94; and Terence L. Nichols, "Miracles in Science and Theology," *Zygon* 37 (2002): 703.

[5] See esp. William L. Craig, *The Kalām Cosmological Argument* (London: Macmillan; New York: Harper & Row, 1979; Eugene, OR: Wipf & Stock, 2000); William L. Craig, *The Cosmological Argument from Plato to Leibniz* (London: Macmillan, 1980; Eugene, OR: Wipf & Stock, 2001).

[6] I owe this summary to my daughter, Rachel K. Blomberg, when she came home from a Sunday school class at Mission Hills Church, Greenwood Village, Colorado, at approximately age eight, in the fall of 1998.

transportation within cells, and the synthesis of nucleotides (the building blocks of DNA).[7]

The third classic argument for God's existence is the moral one. This is sometimes mistakenly described as based on things all cultures that have ever existed have deemed right or wrong, so that it can then be debunked whenever one finds even one culture that did not agree with others on the morality or immorality of certain behavior. The actual argument, however, is based on the existence of concepts of morality among all *homo sapiens*, in ways we have no reason to believe exist in the rest of the animal kingdom. Sometimes this is combined with concepts like our ability to think reflectively, self-consciously, and religiously. We have the capacity for a relationship with God, if he exists, which we are not aware characterizes any other species.[8] Finally, there is the ontological argument, which begins with the premise that something that actually exists is necessarily greater than the mere concept of its existence. But God, by definition, is the greatest possible being. Therefore, since God's existence is greater than the mere concept of his existence, he must actually exist.[9] At least the first three of these arguments seem to be promoted by New Testament authors themselves, especially in Romans 1:19–20 and 32.

---

[7] See esp. Michael J. Behe, *Darwin's Black Box: The Biochemical Challenge to Evolution*, rev. ed. (New York: Free Press, 2006). Cf. also William A. Dembski, *The Design Inference: Eliminating Chance Through Small Probabilities* (Cambridge: Cambridge University Press, 1998); William A. Dembski, ed., *Signs of Intelligence: Understanding Intelligent Design* (Grand Rapids: Brazos, 2001).

[8] See esp. Douglas Groothuis, *Christian Apologetics: A Comprehensive Case for Biblical Faith* (Downers Grove: IVP; Nottingham: Apollos, 2011), 330–63, and the literature there cited. Cf. also Christian Smith, *Moral, Believing Animals: Human Personhood and Culture* (Oxford: Oxford University Press, 2003).

[9] See esp. Groothuis, *Christian Apologetics*, 185–206, and the literature there cited. Cf. also Yujin Nagasawa, "The Ontological Argument and the Devil," *Philosophical Quarterly* 60 (2010): 72–91; Yujin Nagasawa, "A New Defence of Anselmian Theism," *Philosophical Quarterly* 58 (2008): 577–96.

Philosophers continue to debate the nuances of each of these four arguments and whether any of them can be formally called "proofs" of God's existence. Probably it is better to think of them as pointers to God, phenomena that make faith reasonable even if not absolutely compelling. Others have argued that belief in God can be considered what philosophers call "properly basic"—something built into the fabric of reality that cannot be demonstrated but cannot be avoided—so that one simply postulates God and then shows how objections to the belief can be countered.[10] Some in this more presuppositionalist than evidentialist camp of philosophy go even further to argue that Christian faith hangs together as a coherent whole in ways other religions or worldviews do not, after one builds on their nonnegotiable foundations.[11]

Arguing for God in any greater detail, however, goes beyond the scope of this book. As has often been pointed out, attributing historical events to God's causation, directly or indirectly, is not itself a historical claim. On the other hand, that a person was unable to walk under his own power one moment, that someone laid hands on him and prayed for him in Jesus's name, that he felt a surge of warmth flow through an injured ankle, and that he was able to stand and walk unaided immediately afterwards are all historical claims that can be observed and confirmed or refuted. That it was indeed God in Christ who healed him is a theological claim that is a reasonable inference, but it is not itself subject to historical corroboration or mathematical

[10] Alvin Plantinga, "Is Belief in God 'Properly Basic'?" in Ed L. Miller, ed., *Believing in God: Readings on Faith and Reason* (Upper Saddle River, NJ: Prentice-Hall, 1996), 198–202. See now also Alvin Plantinga, *Knowledge and Christian Belief* (Grand Rapids: Eerdmans, 2015).

[11] The classic evangelical thinkers in this camp, who produced a flood of literature repeating and illustrating their methodology one to two generations ago, were Cornelius van Til and Gordon H. Clark. For a good introduction to the movement, see John S. Feinberg, *Can You Believe It's True? Christian Apologetics in a Modern and Postmodern Era* (Wheaton: Crossway, 2013), 249–96.

or scientific proof. Thus, one does not need to demonstrate God's existence to defend the reliability of Scripture's *historical* claims.[12]

Many scholars argue that miracles are in the same category as God's causal agency behind an event. That is to say, they transcend the ability of history to make any claims about them at all. This does not logically follow, however. Of course, if a miracle is defined only as something that happens when God supernaturally intervenes in a situation, then claiming that a miracle occurred would be a theological rather than a historical assertion. On the other hand, one could define a miracle more broadly as any event for which science has no known explanation, in which case determining whether a miracle occurred would not necessitate belief in God, merely investigating whether the event actually occurred and whether there are no known scientific explanations for it. As an intermediate option, a miracle could be an event that is more than just some random, isolated, and scientifically unexplainable action but that which transcends the natural laws of cause and effect and occurs in the context of a meaningful cluster of other events such that it is logical to postulate an intentional, personal agent behind it.[13]

Scientific and Philosophical Problems

Many historians would demur even then, however, and trot out the old arguments classically articulated by eighteenth-century Scottish

---

[12] Francis J. Beckwith, "History and Miracles," in *In Defense of Miracles: A Comprehensive Case for God's Action in History*, ed. R. Douglas Geivett and Gary R. Habermas (Downers Grove: IVP, 1997), 87–88.

[13] Richard L. Purtill has a similar though simpler definition ("Defining Miracles," in ibid., 62–63): "an event in which God temporarily makes an exception to the natural order of things, to show God is acting." I have deliberately broadened my definition to allow for other supernatural agents, such as angels and demons, or human agents God or other supernatural beings empower.

philosopher David Hume. In short, Hume made his personal experience the measure of what was and wasn't possible. If no one Hume knew and respected, including himself, had ever experienced a certain event, then he could not accept it as having actually happened. Hume bolstered this position with four arguments. (1) No alleged miracle has ever been supported by sufficient testimony that might not be mistaken. (2) People crave the miraculous, so they are less discerning in evaluating its genuineness. (3) Miracle reports tend to proliferate among the barbarous, not in the civilized parts of the world. (4) Miracle stories occur in all religions in support of mutually contradictory theological affirmations and therefore cancel one another out.[14]

None of these arguments is strong, however. Point (1) is itself a mere affirmation, not a demonstrable proposition. Item (2) simply means we need to apply more stringent criteria in examining claims about the miraculous. Claim (3) is directly tied to Hume's overall racism and disdain for the credibility of people in the majority of the eighteenth-century world.[15] Finally, (4) is too superficial a generalization to be helpful. In fact, no other religion besides Hinduism, Judaism, and Christianity have nearly as many claims for miracles, and nothing in Hinduism depends on the truthfulness of their miracle stories the way it does in Judaism and Christianity. Additionally, miraculous claims do not appear at all in the oldest Buddhist, Confucian, and Islamic traditions about the founding of those

---

[14] David Hume, *Enquiry Concerning Human Understanding*, rev. ed., ed. Tom L. Beauchamp (Oxford: Clarendon; New York: Oxford University Press, 2006). See esp. sec. 10.

[15] See esp. Charles Taliaferro and Anders Hendrickson, "Hume's Racism and His Case Against the Miraculous," *Philosophia Christi* 4 (2002): 219–26.

religions, though they do enter into later forms of Buddhism and Islam.[16] And non-Christian miracle claims "are also less analogous to those in the Gospels and Acts."[17]

Hume's outdated arguments often continue to be parroted by university professors and scholars even today without interaction or even seeming awareness of the devastating critiques they have received over the centuries.[18] I was a part of a panel discussion in the 2000s with Philip Sellew, a member of the Jesus Seminar, at the University of Minnesota, and I mentioned the frequency of credible testimony to the miraculous in the majority world today, and his response was just a glib, "Well, yes, that's what they think until they get education." Obviously, he assumed that either (a) all such testimony came from uneducated people, or (b) if it came from educated people, they hadn't had the right kind of education—namely, the Western naturalistic education that would debunk their belief in a supernatural realm.[19] Craig Keener cites testimony from parts of the world that regularly experienced miracles until Americans taught them not to interpret certain Bible texts literally![20]

More recently at Oregon State University, I have twice debated Carl Stecher, a thoughtful atheist who prefers to be called a nontheist because he does not consider himself opposed to belief in God. In fact,

---

[16] David K. Clark, "Miracles in the World Religions," in *In Defense of Miracles*, ed. Geivett and Habermas, 202–5. Cf. also Kenneth L. Woodward, *The Book of Miracles: The Meaning of the Miracle Stories in Christianity, Judaism, Buddhism, Hinduism, Islam* (New York: Simon & Schuster, 2000).

[17] Craig S. Keener, *Miracles: The Credibility of the New Testament Accounts*, vol. 1 (Grand Rapids: Baker, 2011), 249.

[18] See esp. Keener, *Miracles*, vol. 1, 107–210.

[19] Of course, today even in the Western world, among the so-called well-educated are large numbers of carefully documented miracles. See ibid., 426–507. For the percentages of Americans who have expressed belief in these kinds of miracles in recent polls, see ibid., 204.

[20] Ibid., 240–41.

he has written a stimulating article on how the *concept* of God can be helpful for society in certain contexts.[21] But as we engaged in considerable postdebate conversation, it became clear that the "bottom line" for why he does not believe in God is because he has never personally experienced anything he would consider miraculous, nor has anyone in the circle of his closest friends when he has asked them about it. It doesn't matter how credible or compelling anyone else's testimony is; if it doesn't come from someone he already knows and trusts, he won't believe it. Marcus Borg for years in public presentations would cite Van Harvey's classic defense of antisupernaturalism as his philosophical starting point, which amounts to the same thing.[22]

It is really rather remarkable, given the billion-dollar educational industry of the world of Western universities, which so frequently promotes atheism or agnosticism, while denigrating religious belief, or at least classic Christian belief, how the final fallback when all other lines of defense and argumentation have been removed is the simple protest by a given professor that "I haven't experienced miracles so I can't believe in them."[23] Yet if others were to use that argument to explain their rejection of the existence of outer space or the depths of the ocean, or the microscopic worlds of gene therapy or atom splitting, they would be laughed out of court. Just because someone hasn't personally experienced a phenomenon has little to do with its existence or nonexistence.

With nonscholars, far more times than I can remember, conversations about the existence of God have ended with, "I'd believe if only he'd reveal himself unambiguously to me." Of course, that's what the

---

[21] Carl Stecher, "God? No and Yes: A Skeptic's View," *Essays in the Philosophy of Humanism* 22 (2014): 93–108.

[22] Van A. Harvey, *The Historian and the Believer: The Morality of Historical Knowledge and Christian Belief*, rev. ed. (London and New York: Macmillan, 1996).

[23] Keener (*Miracles*, vol. 2, 688–704) documents in detail the "prejudice in the academy" on this issue.

rich man asked on behalf of his brothers in one of Jesus's parables, and Jesus replied that if they didn't believe the Scriptures they wouldn't believe if a man who rose from the dead and appeared to them (Luke 16:30–31). I have known professing Christians who have experienced miraculous healing, recognized the hand of God in it, and later rejected him altogether when he didn't orchestrate circumstances in their lives the way they wished he would. Human freedom to rebel against the obvious remains remarkably powerful. I know gifted evangelists who have had countless conversations with unbelievers throughout their ministries and who are convinced intellectual arguments never are the deepest issues for those who reject the existence of God. They may be the "presenting issues," to use the language of counseling, but they are not the ultimate ones. Instead, the bedrock issue eventually turns out to be whether people are willing to surrender their lives to Christ's leadership or want to remain in control of their lives for themselves, irrespective of the consequences. I don't know that I can agree that this is *always* the case because I have met people who became Christians almost immediately after their intellectual issues were resolved. But my experience has taught me that the issue of who is in control of a person's life is indeed the bottom-line issue for many, many people.[24]

Modern Miracles

Those who are willing to be truly intellectual, logical, and rational, instead of ruling out the supernatural *a priori* as always less likely than

---

[24] Esp. when one discovers, with Alvin Plantinga (*Where the Conflict Really Lies: Science, Religion and Naturalism* [Oxford: Oxford University Press, 2011]) the far deeper conflict between science and naturalism than between science and theism; and with David B. Hart (*Atheist Delusions: The Christian Revolution and Its Fashionable Enemies* [New Haven and London: Yale University Press, 2009]) how the transformations of society for the better throughout the history of Christianity have vastly outweighed any negative influences.

a naturalistic explanation of an unusual event, should instead weigh the credibility of the testimony to any event, however improbable it may seem. One may correctly observe that doctors regularly misdiagnose maladies on the one hand or struggle to explain the unusually rapid disappearance of signs and symptoms of illnesses and injuries on the other hand. Not all unexplained healings qualify as miracles. But when a tumor that has appeared on multiple MRIs suddenly vanishes, never to be seen again, and all its accompanying symptoms instantaneously stop after the concerted, public prayer of Christian believers in the context of a healing service,[25] skeptical explanations alleging a misdiagnosis ring hollow. That a supernatural being has responded to the prayer with an act of healing then becomes a reasonable explanation for the experience.[26] Rex Gardner, British medical doctor, after recording in the 1980s a collection of numerous miraculous healings in the contexts of Christian prayer verified by eyewitnesses and with medical documentation, concluded, "That God does heal in the late twentieth century should be accepted on the evidence of all these Case Records. If you do not accept those two statements, you may ask yourself what evidence you would be prepared to accept. If the answer proves to be 'None,' then you had better face the fact that you have abandoned logical enquiry."[27]

---

[25] An experience I have twice had, as an elder of a local church participating in the ritual of the anointing with oil of sick, fellow church members, following the procedure of James 5:13–18. I have also had dozens of friends and close relatives experience similar instantaneous healings or who have observed or participated in exorcisms. It is less rational to affirm by a kind of irreligious faith, in spite of the empirical evidence, that all of us were lying or deceived, than to acknowledge the reality of the miracles.

[26] The several hundred healings detailed in Keener (*Miracles*, 2 vols.) limit themselves to "cures in theologically or religiously pregnant contexts" (vol. 1, 258).

[27] Rex Gardner, *Healing Miracles: A Doctor Investigates* (London: Darton, Longman & Todd, 1986), 165. For the large percentage of doctors who believe they have seen miraculous healings, see Keener, *Miracles*, vol. 2, 721.

The same is true with miracles of spiritual deliverance. It can be difficult at times to distinguish outwardly between a person in the throes of a grand mal seizure and someone possessed by a violent demon. Responsible religious leaders should always summon medical help. But when an individual writhing on the floor of a church speaks to those who would help her in a deep, guttural bass voice, recoiling at the presence of a cross, and reacting with unusual hostility to the name of Jesus, one may suspect dark, spiritual forces at work. When such individuals suddenly become limp when demons are commanded to come out of them in Jesus's name, and when they within minutes are specimens of full health, including after medical examination, the rational conclusion to draw is that they were successfully exorcised, not that they merely suffered from some physical or mental illness.[28]

Miracles, if genuine, cannot occur too often or too predictably. If they did, we would stop calling them miracles and formulate new scientific laws or principles for how to reproduce them. Organizations or individuals have at times offered large sums of money for anyone who could accurately predict circumstances under which an event for which

---

[28] See the dozens of examples cataloged in ibid., vol. 2, 788–856. Cf. also M. Scott Peck, *Glimpses of the Devil: A Psychiatrist's Personal Accounts of Possession, Exorcism, and Redemption* (New York and London: Free Press, 2005); Anthony B. Finlay, *Demons: The Devil, Possession and Exorcism* (London: Blandford; New York: Sterling, 1999); and several of the chapters in Anthony N. S. Lane, ed., *The Unseen World: Christian Reflections on Angels, Demons and the Heavenly Realm* (Carlisle: Paternoster; Grand Rapids: Baker, 1996). For a global perspective, cf. A. Scott Moreau, Tokunboh Adeyemo, David G. Burnett, Bryant L. Myers, and Hwa Yung, eds., *Deliver Us from Evil: An Uneasy Frontier in Christian Mission* (Monrovia: CA: MARC, 2002). Of many possible additional examples, see the striking autobiography by my personal friend and former student Sharon Beekman, *Enticed by the Light: The Terrifying Story of One Woman's Encounter with the New Age* (Grand Rapids: Zondervan, 1997). For the nature of Jesus's exorcistic ministry, cf. esp. Graham H. Twelftree, *Jesus the Exorcist: A Contribution to the Study of the Historical Jesus* (Tübingen: Mohr; Peabody: Hendrickson, 1993; Eugene, OR: Wipf & Stock, 2011).

science has no explanation would occur, and they have never had to give that money away. Of course not. They have asked for something which by definition would disqualify it from being miraculous! Science studies the repeatable, namely, that which can be replicated and tested under laboratory conditions. A miracle, by definition, is unpredictable, and it may not even be repeatable at all. If it is, it will not necessarily be repeatable under the identical circumstances.[29] From a biblical perspective God never compels faith. Events that would be so public, so undeniable, and so frequent that a rational person would be compelled to attribute them only to God would then leave them little freedom to reject God. Our universe would be an entirely different kind than the one we currently know, populated by beings without the same kinds of freedom we currently enjoy.[30] And we know from both Scripture and experience that God never wanted to create that kind of universe. He always intended us to walk by faith and not by sight, to choose to love him apart from any coercion, including intellectual coercion.

On the other hand, Christian faith is not belief in the absurd. It is not a leap in the dark or a rejection of reason. Scripture and history offer enough examples of the miraculous, including in our contemporary world, to make Christian faith a reasonable commitment, even if those who wish to disbelieve can always find some angle from which to question things.[31] Craig Keener has recently compiled perhaps the

---

[29] Cf. Keener, *Miracles*, vol. 1, 125–26. For an insightful sociopolitical analysis, see Amanda Witmer, *Jesus, the Galilean Exorcist: The Exorcisms in Social and Political Context* (London and New York: T & T Clark, 2012). Witmer makes a good case for the authenticity of Jesus's exorcisms in the Gospels, though her analysis at the historical level seems to be somewhat reductionistic.

[30] On free will versus determinism, see, e.g., J. P. Moreland and William L. Craig, *Philosophical Foundations for a Christian Worldview* (Downers Grove: IVP, 2003), 267–84.

[31] See, e.g., Kenneth D. Boa and Robert M. Bowman Jr., *Faith Has Its Reasons: An Integrative Approach to Defending Christianity* (Colorado Springs: NavPress, 2001); Paul Copan and William L. Craig, *Contending with Christianity's Critics:*

most thorough and well-documented collection of the miraculous from every continent on the planet, especially within the present generation though scarcely limited to it. He has restricted his presentation to the most thoroughly researched, documented, and confirmed events and still has a catalog of literally hundreds of miraculous healings and exorcisms, a handful of resurrections, and even parallels to Jesus's nature miracles. By his own admission he has omitted hundreds more that probably did indeed occur, but he simply has not been able to amass enough documentation for them to make it through his strict filters.[32] It is one thing for a comparatively isolated Scottish philosopher in the 1700s to doubt word-of-mouth accounts of miracles from far-flung places; it is another in our technologically interconnected world to reject as fabricated the medical evidence of instantaneous healings, sometimes recorded by video cameras, in the context of concerted, public, Christian prayer. Such non-Christian dogmatism, not Christian belief, is what turns out to be unscientific.

But what are we to say about miracles in non-Christian contexts? First of all, strict criteria or filters must also be used before accepting *those* accounts also. But what if some accounts make it through our filters or satisfy our criteria? The Bible is replete with examples of God's working in nonsalvific ways through those who are not his people, so there is no theological reason and certainly no rational or logical reason Christians should not accept his choosing to work miracles for his sovereign purposes in various other contexts. In addition, the Scriptures demonstrate that certain kinds of unusual events can be due to either human manufacture or demonic in origin (the classic example involves Pharaoh's magicians—Exodus 7–9). We discredit

---

Answering New Atheists and Other Objectors (Nashville: B & H, 2009); and William A. Dembski and Michael R. Licona, *Evidence for God: 50 Arguments for Faith from the Bible, History, Philosophy, and Science* (Grand Rapids: Baker, 2010).

[32] Keener, *Miracles*, vol. 1, 255–60.

ourselves when we gullibly accept *all* miraculous claims made in Christian contexts but also when we accept *none* made anywhere else.[33] Indeed, we demonstrate the core truth behind Hume's second claim above on craving the miraculous, at least in our own theological contexts, even if Hume exaggerated its extent.

Today, though, antisupernaturalism in the larger scientific world, like its partial Christian equivalent, cessationism with respect to the charismatic gifts,[34] is not as entrenched as it was a generation ago. It certainly finds plenty of adherents, but natural scientists also often tend to dominate Christian student and faculty groups of major university campuses in the way specialists in the humanities did a generation ago. Today postmodernism may seem plausible if all one studies is literary interpretation, but mathematicians and physical scientists still know that certain procedures have one or a limited number of ways of being carried out, just as they know that one cannot simply will one's fallacious interpretations of data to become correct! They also increasingly recognize the limits of science in pontificating on what can or cannot ever happen.[35] Citing a Pew Forum study from

---

[33] Rightly ibid., vol. 1, 79–80. See also Harold Remus, *Pagan–Christian Conflict over Miracle in the Second Century* (Cambridge, MA: Philadelphia Patristic Foundation, 1983), who demonstrates that this was the standard approach of the earliest church also.

[34] One cessationist reviewer of my book, *Can We Still Believe the Bible? An Evangelical Engagement with Contemporary Questions* (Grand Rapids: Brazos, 2014), called my chapter on miracles the weakest one in the book because I cited contemporary miracles as evidence that miracles can happen. This seems to be a strange criticism, since it plays directly into Hume's skepticism. Even from a cessationist perspective, the more common interpretation of the contemporary phenomena is that they do reflect divine miracles, just not the specific "gift of miracles" exercised in the first century. This explanation may well prove to be a classic illustration of "a distinction without a difference."

[35] The standard work here is Peter Medawar, *The Limits of Science* (San Francisco: Harper & Row, 1984; Oxford: Oxford University Press, 1985), all the more significant because Medawar is an atheist but not on scientific grounds. Cf. also John C. Polkinghorne, *The Faith of a Physicist* (Princeton: Princeton University

2006 and extrapolating on the assumption of its representative status, Keener observes, "Those who are ready to dismiss all miracle claims should keep in mind that they are dismissing hundreds of millions of miracle claims—usually without having examined any of them."[36] Even if the statistic turns out to be too high, the point still stands. Summarily dismissing unexamined claims can scarcely be called rational, logical, or scientific.

Myths or Legends?

Indeed, today's most significant challenges to the credibility of the biblical miracles come from the discipline of comparative religions. Exaggerated or simply false claims in the media or blogosphere as to supposed parallels in antiquity to the miracles of Jesus and the apostles mislead those who are gullible and just looking for "reasons" to disbelieve. Countless websites catalog such parallels, but on closer inspection most of the closest, legitimate parallels are post-Christian; many of the alleged parallels are different from the biblical accounts; and quite a few claims are made up and not factually accurate at all. Particularly deceptive are instances where the figure listed is a pre-Christian person or god but the tradition of something miraculous that is asserted as a parallel is post-Christian in origin.[37]

Press, 1994); R. J. Berry, "Divine Action: Expected and Unexpected," *Zygon* 37 (2002): 72–90; Robert C. Koons, "Science and Theism: Concord, Not Conflict," in *The Rationality of Theism*, ed. Paul Copan and Paul K. Moser (London and New York: Routledge, 2003), 72–90; Stephen M. Barr, *Modern Physics and Ancient Faith* (Notre Dame, IN: University of Notre Dame Press, 2003); and Francis S. Collins, *The Language of God: A Scientist Presents Evidence for Belief* (New York: Free Press, 2006).

[36] Keener, *Miracles*, vol. 1, 237.

[37] Gareth McCaughan ("Alleged Pre-Christian Parallels to the Jesus Story" [April 14, 2009], accessed January 7, 2016, http://www.mccaughan.org.uk/g /essays/godmen.html) debunks one well-known list of sixteen supposed pre-Christian crucified and resurrected saviors. Cf. also J. Warner Wallace, "Those

I have elsewhere repeatedly discussed the handful of truly close parallels to Jesus's miracles, so will merely summarize my findings here.[38] We have already seen how the post-New Testament Christian miracles, primarily evidenced in the New Testament Apocrypha, fill in perceived gaps in the biblical accounts, satisfying people's curiosity about the exploits of Jesus and his first followers that are not recorded in the Gospels and Acts. A handful might also be based on authentic tradition, but in most cases the integral connection of the narratives to the overall gospel message about the person and work of Christ is missing. These miracles tend to be more trivial, more manipulative, more vengeful, or in support of later heterodox teaching.[39] Some may be designed to portray Jesus as a Greco-Roman god with powers superior to his Hellenistic rivals.[40]

Greek mythology contains accounts of gods and humans performing wonders similar to some of the New Testament miracle stories. The most common involve the dying and rising of nature gods according to the cycle of the seasons—death in winter and "resurrection" in

---

Pre-Christian Deities Aren't Much like Jesus After All," *Stand to Reason* (May 10, 2013), accessed January 7, 2016, http://www.str.org/blog/those-pre-christian -deities-aren%E2%80%99t-much-like-jesus-after-all#.VTlkR_A0NRo; and Mary Jo Sharp, "Is the Story of Jesus Borrowed from Pagan Myths?" in *In Defense of the Bible: A Comprehensive Apologetic for the Authority of Scripture*, ed. Steven B. Cowan and Terry L. Wilder (Nashville: B&H, 2013), 183–200.

[38] Craig L. Blomberg, *The Historical Reliability of the Gospels*, 2nd ed. (Nottingham: Apollos; Downers Grove: IVP, 2007), 112–27.

[39] Ulrike Riemer, "Miracle Stories and Their Narrative Intent in the Context of the Ruler Cult of Classical Antiquity," in *A Kind of Magic: Understanding Magic in the New Testament and Its Religious Environment*, ed. Michael Labahn and Bert Jan Lietaert Peerbolte (London and New York: T & T Clark, 2007), 32–47. Cf. also Hans-Josef Klauck, *Apocryphal Gospels: An Introduction* (London and New York: T & T Clark, 2003), 223.

[40] M. David Litwa, *Iesus Deus: The Early Christian Depiction of Jesus as a Mediterranean God* (Minneapolis: Fortress, 2014), 69–85.

spring (e.g., Isis and Osiris, with their son Horus[41]). But these do not involve human beings regaining bodily functions and full health after burial in a tomb. The reappearance of vegetation is simply likened to the rebirth of some otherwise invisible gods. Miraculous healings were also attributed to gods but not to people who had just recently been alive and demonstrably human. The largest cluster of parallels to the miracles of Jesus appears in the biography of the late first-century itinerant Greek philosopher, Apollonius of Tyana, by the third-century philosopher Philostratus.[42] But Apollonius ministered after the time of Christ (mid to late first century), and Philostratus wrote well after the completion of the Christian Gospels (early third century), so if anyone borrowed from anyone it would be the Greeks borrowing from the Christians. Most of the miracles in Greek and Roman religions, however, bear little resemblance to those of the New Testament: humans talking with animals and birds, transforming themselves into other creatures, charming rocks and trees with their music, appearing and disappearing at will, appearing at two places at the same time, traveling the world without eating, or sending their souls on journeys while their bodies remained at home.[43]

One also discovers the phenomenon of genuine, historical figures whose earliest biographers included few or no miraculous events being

---

[41] Horus was said to be a falcon, born of Isis after she had sex with her previously dead and dismembered husband, Osiris. Horus was never even alleged to be crucified and resurrected. Osiris was alleged to be resurrected—every year in conjunction with the fertility cycle as spring followed winter.

[42] Plutarch, *Moralia*, V, s.v. "Isis and Osiris."

[43] For a thorough survey that broadens out to include ancient Hellenistic fiction from the first through fourth centuries more generally, see Glen W. Bowersock, *Fiction as History: Nero to Julian* (Berkeley: University of California Press, 1994). Bowersock defends the thesis that where parallels are close enough to suggest borrowing, the Hellenistic world consistently depended on Christian tradition and attempted to trump it with its portrayal. The proliferation of partial parallels to the New Testament characters beginning in the mid to late first century is intriguing when they had been rare in previous eras in the ancient Mediterranean world.

overly glorified in later centuries. The life of Alexander the Great, for example, was embellished for more than a thousand years; earliest sources—themselves 500 years after his life—do not contain the miraculous events that those 500 years later do.[44] When we realize that the Gospels were written between thirty and sixty years after the death of Jesus, the likelihood of the miraculous encroaching in the Gospels where it didn't originally exist becomes slim. Sometimes figures from the distant past became quasi-deified, like Asclepius, god of healing, but the miracles that were believed to have happened at his healing shrines were not performed by living human beings, like Jesus of Nazareth, but by the god(s). Occasionally, Greco-Roman religious leaders went to elaborate lengths to make it appear as if a miracle had occurred, when in fact there were completely natural explanations,[45] but the age of using this argument to explain the *Gospel* miracles expired before the end of the nineteenth century!

Philostratus depicts Apollonius as showing great wisdom as a child, performing healings as an adult, correctly predicting the future, exorcising demons, appearing to his followers after he died, and ascending bodily into heaven. A particularly striking parallel to the account in Luke 7:11–17 of Jesus's raising the son of the widow in Nain appears when Apollonius, too, is said to touch the coffin of a newly deceased young woman during the funeral procession and bring her back to life. But Philostratus also casts doubt on whether the girl had in fact died or was what we would call comatose, and he suggests that Apollonius may have detected a spark of life still in her (*Life of Apollonius of Tyana*

---

[44] Robin L. Fox, *The Search for Alexander* (Boston: Little, Brown; London: Allen Lane, 1980), 33–46.

[45] A classic work debunking supposed parallels between Jesus and Dionysus, which includes the ancients' refutation of the apparently miraculous turning of water into wine in the temple of Dionysus is Heinz Noetzel, *Christus und Dionysos* (Stuttgart: Calwer Verlag, 1960).

4.45).[46] Moreover, as we have already seen, the events of his life, whatever actually happened, occurred and were recorded too late to have influenced the depiction of Christ in the Gospels.[47]

A popular alleged parallel to the birth of Christianity that was frequently touted a century or more ago during the "history of religions" era of scholarship has again been revived in some circles, most of them outside the discipline of New Testament studies itself. Mithraism, the religion that worshipped the Persian god, Mithras, was amalgamated with the Roman worship of *Sol Invictus* (the unconquerable sun), and a festival to Sol was celebrated every December 25. Mithras has been alleged to have been born of a virgin, died for our sins, resurrected from the dead, and worshipped during a ritual meal similar to the Christian Eucharist. Unfortunately for those who would try to derive Christianity from Mithraism, Mithras was actually depicted as having been born from a rock. As we noted earlier, the rock had not previously had sex, but that is stretching the definition of virgin beyond any useful boundaries. The bit about dying for our sins is just made up by modern supporters; what the ancient god Mithras was known for was slaughtering a fierce bull in preparation for the creation of humanity. The cultic meal in Mithraism bears little resemblance to the Eucharist, which was explicitly derived from the Jewish Passover ceremonies. Traditions about a resurrection did not spring up until the second or third centuries after Christ, and the reason Christians celebrated Jesus's birth on December 25 was precisely to take advantage of the Roman holiday and be left largely without harassment while

---

[46] For a plausible reconstruction of the historical Apollonius, see B. F. Harris, "Apollonius of Tyana: Fact and Fiction," *Journal of Religious History* 5 (1969): 189–99.

[47] If one dates Acts late, there may be helpful comparisons made with miracles in Acts, but even then differences stand out as much as similarities. See Andy Reimer, *Miracle and Magic: A Study in the Acts of the Apostles and the Life of Apollonius of Tyana* (London and New York: Sheffield Academic Press, 2002).

pagans were getting drunk to commemorate their sun god. Christians did not at this time claim this date as Jesus's actual birthday; that notion developed centuries later. Worse still, Mithraism was almost exclusively an all-male religion, militaristic in its imagery and practices, contrasting sharply with the pacifist and inclusivist religion of pre-Constantinian Christianity, which warmly welcomed women as well as men, putting them on virtually equal footing.[48]

One could look to the practice of deifying emperors or other individuals of renown after their deaths and occasionally attributing a stray miracle or two to some of them (e.g., Vespasian). But again, this is not what we find in the case of Jesus. His ministry was filled with miracles, and his resurrection vindicates claims made during his earthly life rather than according him postmortem honors for having been a great teacher or ruler. In fact, the previously common notion that there was a standard archetypal "divine man" figure used widely in pre-Christian Greco-Roman thought has been debunked for the myth that it is. Only by linking together largely disparate and divergent traditions from unrelated cultures and periods of time can even a plausible theory of such divinization be created; on close inspection it collapses altogether.[49]

Accounts of healings and exorcisms, especially in Second Temple Jewish literature, appear frequently, but no other body of literature portrays a human being consistently and immediately being able to perform these miracles without invoking a deity or without elaborate

---

[48] See further Jack Finegan, *Myth and Mystery: An Introduction to the Pagan Religions of the Biblical World* (Grand Rapids: Baker, 1989), 203–12; Antonia Tripolitis, *Religions of the Hellenistic-Roman Age* (Grand Rapids: Eerdmans, 2002), 47–57; and Ronald H. Nash, *The Gospel and the Greeks: Did the New Testament Borrow from Pagan Thought?*, rev. ed. (Phillipsburg, NJ: P & R, 2003), 133–38.

[49] See esp. Carl H. Holladay, *Theios Aner in Hellenistic Judaism: A Critique of the Use of This Category in New Testament Christology* (Missoula: Scholars, 1977); Barry L. Blackburn, *Theios Anēr and the Markan Miracle Traditions* (Tübingen: J. C. B. Mohr, 1991).

prayers, incantations, or the use of ritual paraphernalia.[50] The Gospels themselves refer to other Jewish exorcists so there is no need to doubt some miracle-working activity during intertestamental Judaism, just as God from time to time empowered completely mortal human beings in Old Testament texts for miraculous activities (see especially Moses, Elijah, and Elisha). The practice of looking at someone with an "evil eye" or a "good eye"—an intense stare designed to make something bad or good happen to that person *may* lie in the background to some of Jesus's miracles or, more probably, his teachings.[51] But it hardly plays a significant role as it does in the accounts of some ancient shamans. Jesus was certainly an exorcist, but attempts to compare him to a magician or practitioner of the occult have largely been abandoned due to lack of concrete evidence.[52]

The two most well-known healers in the Jewish literature depicting near contemporaries of Jesus are Honi the Rain-maker and Rabbi Hanina ben-Dosa. Honi was notorious for drawing a circle on the ground, standing in the middle of it, and praying to God for rain, insisting that he wouldn't leave the circle until God answered his prayers. Hanina has the following miracles attributed to him: surviving a poisonous snakebite unharmed, healing the sick from a distance by the fluency of his prayer, making bread appear in his family's oven

[50] See Graham H. Twelftree, "EI DE ... ΕΓΩ ΕΚΒΑΛΛΩ ΤΑ ΔΑΙΜΟΝΙΑ ...," in *Gospel Perspectives*, vol. 6, ed. David Wenham and Craig Blomberg (Sheffield: JSOT, 1986; Eugene, OR: Wipf & Stock, 2003), 383. Cf. Pieter J. Lalleman, "Healing by a Mere Touch as a Christian Concept," *Tyndale Bulletin* 48 (1997): 355–61.

[51] C. B. Bridges and R. E. Wheeler, "The Evil Eye in the Sermon on the Mount," *Stone-Campbell Journal* 4 (2001): 69–79; David A. Fiensy, "The Importance of New Testament Background Studies in Biblical Research: The 'Evil Eye' in Luke 11:34 as a Case Study," *Stone-Campbell Journal* 2 (1999): 75–88; John H. Elliott, "Matthew 20:1–15: A Parable of Invidious Comparison and Evil Eye Accusation," *Biblical Theology Bulletin* 22 (1992): 52–65.

[52] Particularly thorough in its canvassing the evidence is Edwin M. Yamauchi, "Magic or Miracle? Diseases, Demons and Exorcisms," in *Gospel Perspectives*, vol. 6, ed. Wenham and Blomberg, 89–183.

when they had run out, enabling a lamp to burn on vinegar rather than oil, and extending the beams on a neighbor's house when they were cut too short for adequate support.[53] But few of these miracles resemble those attributed to Jesus and his first followers, at least in the canonical texts. Neither do they dominate the accounts of these men's lives as they do in the New Testament stories of Jesus. Instead, the prayer and piety of the miracle workers rather than their immediate, divine authority is what is said to make them effective.[54]

Criteria of Authenticity

Thus far, our discussion has been largely ground clearing. There are no compelling scientific, philosophical, or "comparative religions" reasons for approaching the New Testament miracles skeptically. But can we say anything positive on their behalf? In our discussion of corroborating information for various Gospel details, we have commented on information that is relevant to individual miracle stories. But how do they stack up more globally? Many scholars who have their doubts about various details within the miracles of the Gospels or Acts, or who doubt some entire New Testament accounts, still believe there is good reason to see Jesus and his disciples as being bona fide miracle workers overall.[55]

---

[53] For complete details, see William S. Green, "Palestinian Holy Men: Charismatic Leadership and Rabbinic Tradition," in *Aufstieg und Niedergang der römischen Welt*, vol. 2, 19.2 (Berlin and New York: de Gruyter, 1979), 619–47. Cf. also A. J. Avery-Peck, "The Galilean Charismatic and Rabbinic Piety: The Holy Man in the Talmudic Literature," in *The Historical Jesus in Context*, ed. Amy-Jill Levine, Dale C. Allison Jr., and John Dominic Crossan (Princeton: Princeton University Press, 2006), 152–62.

[54] See esp. Eric Eve, *The Jewish Context of Jesus' Miracles* (London: Sheffield Academic Press, 2002), 272–95. Cf. also A. E. Harvey, *Jesus and the Constraints of History* (London: Duckworth; Philadelphia: Westminster, 1982), 107–13.

[55] Most significant is John P. Meier, *Marginal Jew*, vol. 2, 630: "Viewed globally, the tradition of Jesus' miracles is more firmly supported by the criteria of historicity

The classic criteria of authenticity, discussed above, all support the historicity of Jesus as a miracle worker. They are multiply attested, found in every Gospel, every one of the standard source-critical strata into which the Gospels are divided, Acts, the letters of Paul, Hebrews, and Revelation. Non-Christian evidence supports Jesus's miracle-working activity, given Josephus's reference to his wondrous deeds (*paradoxa*) and the Talmud's repeated insistence that Jesus was a sorcerer who led Israel astray.[56] Jesus's miracles were distinctively direct, without involving God in prayer, and did not play as dominant a part in his followers' post-Easter ministry, except perhaps for Paul, so the standard dissimilarity criterion is satisfied. Even when they did appear (especially in Acts), they were consistently performed "in Jesus's name."[57] The main message of the miracles is the arrival of the kingdom of God. And if the kingdom has come, then the King must be present, so the miracles likewise serve to authenticate Jesus's messianic identity. The criterion of coherence with the core authenticated teaching of Jesus is thereby also satisfied. The closest parallels are in Judaism, fitting the criterion of Palestinian environment.[58]

---

than are a number of other well-known and often readily accepted traditions about his life and ministry. . . . Put dramatically but with not too much exaggeration: if the miracle tradition from Jesus's public ministry were to be rejected *in toto* as unhistorical, so should every other Gospel tradition about him."

[56] On which, see esp. Graham N. Stanton, "Jesus of Nazareth: A Magician and a False Prophet Who Deceived God's People?" in *Jesus of Nazareth, Lord and Christ: Essays on the Historical Jesus and New Testament Christology*, ed. Joel B. Green and Max Turner (Grand Rapids: Eerdmans, 1994), 164–80.

[57] See esp. Graham H. Twelftree, *In the Name of Jesus: Exorcism Among Early Christians* (Grand Rapids: Baker, 2007).

[58] See further Craig L. Blomberg, "Healing," in *Dictionary of Jesus and the Gospels*, eds. Joel B. Green, Scot McKnight, and I. Howard Marshall (Downers Grove and Leicester: IVP, 1992), 304–5. The article on healing in the second edition of this otherwise excellent dictionary does not elaborate on the question of historicity, one of the outcomes of the editors' unfortunate policy of refusing to allow any of the original authors to revise and update their own articles.

If we reconfigure much of this information by means of the criterion of double similarity and double dissimilarity, the results remain equally positive. Jesus is not the only Jewish miracle worker, but he is sufficiently distinctive in his portraits from them not to have been readily invented by other Jewish writers or transmitters of the tradition. Jesus's disciples were empowered to replicate Jesus's ministry of healing and exorcism, even during his lifetime, and various followers, not just the twelve apostles, continue to work miracles after his death and resurrection. But they do not take front and center stage in Acts and the epistles to the same degree they do in the Gospels and, while continuing in the second and even third centuries, are largely absent from the institutionalized church, except in the hagiography composed about the Roman Catholic saints. Even here, most of these miracle accounts are of a different nature, not being integrally linked to the arrival of God's kingdom.[59]

Not surprisingly, then, many contemporary scholars, including a number of fairly liberal ones, will grant that Jesus worked miracles of healings and casting out of demons. They may decide that Jesus used his religious power and charisma in ways other special "spirit people" have throughout history so that none of this miracle-working activity demands that he be divine. They may suggest that he freed people to experience psychosomatic healings—the power of mind over the body in ways we do not yet fully understand. They may see him using language and methods his audiences would have understood as triggering physical healing and spiritual freedom from the powers that kept them enslaved, without necessarily imagining something truly supernatural occurring.

---

[59] See Claudia Rapp, "Saints and Holy Men," in *The Cambridge History of Christianity*, vol. 2, ed. Augustine Casiday and Frederick W. Norris (Cambridge: Cambridge University Press, 2007), 550. Rapp notes that OT and NT miracle workers, along with partial pagan analogs, became models for the legends attributed to the saints, sometimes explicitly for the saints to outdo, but that Christ himself was rarely the object of imitation.

Nature Miracles

When it comes to Jesus's so-called nature miracles, however, then the tide of scholarly opinion shifts back to an even more skeptical position.[60] But these accounts likewise mesh closely with Jesus's inauguration of the kingdom, at least when rightly understood. They also have a parabolic or symbolic dimension to them, making them cohere closely with that most distinctive and characteristic form of Jesus's teaching—the parable—widely agreed to form bedrock authentic Jesus tradition.[61] Take the unparalleled account of the turning of water into wine, for example. Both its significance and its historicity are easily questioned. Yet a fair consensus of scholars recognizes the wine at an ancient Jewish wedding as a key symbol of joy.[62] When we observe how John takes the time to specify that the liquid was contained in six stone jars used for Jewish purification rites (John 2:6), in a narrative otherwise so sparse as to lack even the mention of the time or manner of that liquid's transformation, we suspect that he understands the miracle to be representing the new joy of the new age Jesus is ushering in, in contrast to the old ways of Jewish ritual.[63] This perspective is reinforced when we discover the triple-tradition Synoptic parable, or extended simile, of new wine requiring new wineskins (Mark 2:22 pars.). The parable helps us interpret the miracle, as both illustrate a crucial dimension of God's kingdom.[64]

---

[60] See, e.g., John Dominic Crossan, *The Historical Jesus: The Life of a Mediterranean Jewish Peasant* (San Francisco: HarperSanFrancisco, 1991), 503–53; Gerd Theissen and Annette Merz, *The Historical Jesus: A Comprehensive Guide* (London: SCM; Minneapolis: Fortress, 1996), 281–325.

[61] Craig L. Blomberg, "The Miracles as Parables," in *Gospel Perspectives*, vol. 6, ed. Wenham and Blomberg, 327–59.

[62] Andreas Köstenberger (*John* [Grand Rapids: Baker, 2003], 93) cites *b. Pesah.* 109a: "There is no rejoicing save with wine."

[63] Moreover, "the running out of wine at the Cana wedding may be symbolic of the barrenness of Judaism" (ibid.).

[64] Cf. Craig L. Blomberg, *The Historical Reliability of John's Gospel: Issues and Commentary* (Downers Grove and Leicester, IVP, 2001), 85–86.

Or consider the one miracle in the canonical Gospels in which Jesus directly destroys a living organism. After approaching a fig tree at breakfast time but discovering only leaves on it rather than fruit (Mark 11:12–14 par.), Jesus curses it, and it withers up. Mark makes clear that it was unrealistic for Jesus to be looking for figs to eat, by saying it was not yet the season for them (v. 13b)! Attempts to salvage the story by assuming he was looking for some unripe predecessors to the edible fruit[65] reads into the passage something that appears in neither the text nor its context. Mark's classic sandwich structure, with the two parts of the miracle surrounding the temple clearing incident (Mark 11:12–14, 20–25), shows that Jesus's imagery was symbolic.[66] Fig trees with abundant fruit often characterized Israel in times of prosperity in Old Testament days (e.g., Mic 7:1–6; Jer 8:13); here the nation is threatened with destruction if it does not repent. Luke 13:6–9 contains a small parable about a barren fig tree that makes almost the identical point. At the very least Israel's current leadership is corrupt, and even if we cannot be sure Jesus meant to indict the entire country, the corrupt temple authorities stand condemned.[67]

The feedings of the 5,000 and 4,000 are only slightly less puzzling at first glance. Of course they provide life, not death, by means of nourishing the famished a long way from places where they could find or purchase adequate foodstuffs. The passages are not doublets of each other; a careful look at the geographical and ethnic details surrounding both passages in all the Gospels in which they appear

---

[65] E.g., James R. Edwards, *The Gospel According to Mark* (Grand Rapids: Eerdmans; Leicester: Apollos, 2002), 339–40.

[66] E.g., Robert H. Stein, *Mark* (Grand Rapids: Baker, 2008), 511–15. Cf. the full-length study by William R. Telford, *The Barren Temple and the Withered Tree* (Sheffield: JSOT, 1980; London: Bloomsbury T & T Clark, 2015).

[67] Cf. Darrell L. Bock, *Luke 9:51–24:53* (Grand Rapids: Baker, 1996), 1210–11, though this may be the beginning of Jesus's teaching about the temple's coming demise as well. See J. Bradley Chance, "The Cursing of the Temple and the Tearing of the Veil in the Gospel of Mark," *Biblical Interpretation* 15 (2007): 248–67.

demonstrates that the 5,000 were most likely a predominantly Jewish crowd; the 4,000, predominantly Gentile.[68] John appends Jesus's subsequent midrash or homily[69] in the Capernaum synagogue, in which he repeatedly refers to himself as the Bread of Life. But surely this is the point of the feeding miracles as well. Jesus is the source of spiritual nourishment for Jew and Gentile alike. No single parable stands out as clearly matching the miracle in meaning, as with our two previous examples, but the parable of the great supper (Luke 14:16–24) does depict outcasts, including possibly Gentiles, replacing the guests who were originally invited to the eschatological banquet, probably all Jews, without any concerns about ritual purity. The wilderness settings of the miraculous feedings meant that no one could have washed their hands for ritual or sanitary reasons prior to eating either.[70] Plus a key Jewish tradition looked for Messiah to replicate the miracle of the manna—bread from heaven (see esp. 2 Bar. 29:8). If Jesus is functioning like King Messiah, then the messianic age is arriving. Again the miracles cohere with Jesus's central and authentic announcement of the kingdom.

Jesus' storm-stilling miracle (Mark 4:35–41 pars.) is somewhat reminiscent of the parable of the two builders (Matt 7:24–27 par.), in which the homes built by the two men alternately survive or are destroyed by the storms that assail them. More directly relevant are Old Testament texts like Jonah or specific verses like Psalm 104:7 and

---

[68] Mark L. Strauss, *Mark* (Grand Rapids: Zondervan, 2014), 330–31. Cf. further Eric K. Wefald, "The Separate Gentile Mission in Mark: A Narrative Explanation of Markan Geography, the Two Feeding Accounts and Exorcisms," *Journal for the Study of the New Testament* 60 (1995): 3–26.

[69] See esp. Peder Borgen, *Bread from Heaven: An Exegetical Study of the Concept of Manna in the Gospel of John and the Writings of Philo* (Leiden: Brill, 1965). Cf. R. T. France, *The Gospel of Matthew* (Grand Rapids: Eerdmans, 2007), 600.

[70] Wilson C. K. Poon, "Superabundant Table Fellowship in the Kingdom: The Feeding of the Five Thousand and the Meal Motif in Luke," *Expository Times* 114 (2003): 226.

107:29, in which the waters fled at God's rebuke and God quieted the storm to a whisper (cf. also 65:7; 89:9). Jesus is again doing that which Jews previously attributed only to God, suggesting that he is not merely the Messiah but a divine Messiah.[71] When he walks on water (Mark 6:45–52 pars.), he similarly replicates what only Yahweh does in the Hebrew Scriptures. In Job 9:8, he "treads on the waves," while in Psalm 77:19 (MT v. 20), his "path led through the sea," his "way through the mighty waters," though his "footprints were not seen." This suggests that when Jesus declares to the disciples, "Take courage! It is I" (Mark 6:50), he may have been deliberately echoing God's words to Moses at the burning bush (LXX *egō eimi*) in Exodus 3:14 (literally, "I am"—the divine name).[72] Mark seems especially to be aware of this since he uniquely, among the Gospel accounts, contains the statement that Jesus "was about to pass by them" (6:48). The Greek verb is identical to the one in Exodus 34:6 when God passed by Moses and revealed a measure of his glory to him (*parerchomai*).[73] Both at Sinai and on the Sea of Galilee, we have theophanies, not random, self-serving miracles.

The miraculous fish catches of Luke 5:1–11 and John 21:1–14 remind the reader of the parable of the dragnet (Matt 13:47–50), although there the main point lies in the separation of the useful and the rotten fish. Form critically, the stories are "gift miracles," just like

---

[71] Cf. Joel Marcus, *Mark 1–8* (New York and London: Doubleday, 2000), 335–36; Robert L. Reymond, *Jesus, Divine Messiah: The New and Old Testament Witness* (Phillipsburg, NJ: Presbyterian & Reformed, 1990; Fearn, Ross-shire: Mentor Books, 2003), 114.

[72] Cf. further John P. Heil, *Jesus Walking on the Sea: Meaning and Gospel Functions of Matt. 14:22–33, Mark 6:45–52 and John 6:15b–21* (Rome: Biblical Institute Press, 1981); and Patrick J. Madden, *Jesus' Walking on the Sea: An Investigation of the Origin of the Narrative Account* (Berlin and New York: de Gruyter, 1997).

[73] Edwards, *The Gospel According to Mark*, 198–99; William L. Lane, *The Gospel According to Mark* (Grand Rapids: Eerdmans; 1974; London: Marshall, Morgan & Scott, 1975), 236.

the feedings of the 5,000 and 4,000, and they stress God's abundant provision for his people.[74] Once again Jesus supernaturally provides what one expects only God to be able to do. Once again as well, then, Jesus discloses himself to be not merely the Messiah but the divine Messiah.

Numerous didactic texts in the Gospels reinforce what we have seen with these nature miracles. Although there are all kinds of secondary reasons Jesus works miracles—showing compassion to those in need, instilling faith in those without it, responding to faith for certain other individuals, breaking down humanly erected barriers, and challenging distinctively Pharisaic laws (especially concerning the Sabbath[75])—the central reason for the miracles is to demonstrate the in-breaking of the kingdom, the arrival of the Messianic Age. But if the kingdom has arrived, then the King must have come; if the Messianic Age has been inaugurated, then the Messiah must be present. Thus we read most explicitly in Matthew 12:28 (par. Luke 11:20) Jesus's words, "But if it is by the Spirit of God that I drive out demons, then the kingdom of God has come upon you."[76]

But this is not the only Gospel text that points to this claim. In Matthew 11:3 (par. Luke 7:20), the imprisoned John the Baptist sends messengers to ask Jesus, "Are you the one who is to come, or should we expect someone else?" Jesus's reply, in essence, asks John to reflect on the significance of the miracles he has seen and heard about: "The blind receive sight, the lame walk, those who have leprosy are cleansed,

---

[74] Gerd Theissen, *The Miracle Stories in the Early Christian Tradition* (Edinburgh: T & T Clark; Philadelphia: Fortress, 1983), 105–6.

[75] On which, see esp. Michael H. Burer, *Divine Sabbath Work* (Winona Lake, IN: Eisenbrauns, 2012).

[76] See further Edward J. Woods, *The Finger of God and Pneumatology in Luke-Acts* (London: Sheffield Academic Press, 2001). More generally, cf. Craig A. Evans, "Inaugurating the Kingdom of God and Defeating the Kingdom of Satan," *Bulletin for Biblical Research* 15 (2005): 49–75.

the deaf hear, the dead are raised, and the good news is proclaimed to the poor" (v. 5). Isaiah 35:5–6 seems likely to be in the background of Jesus's choice of miracles to which to point.[77] In the eschatological age to come, the prophet promised, "Then will the eyes of the blind be opened and the ears of the deaf unstopped. Then will the lame leap like a deer, and the mute tongue shout for joy." In fact, the word for mute is *mogilalos* in the LXX, a term found elsewhere in the Greek Bible only in Mark 7:32 referring to a man who could "hardly talk." It appears that Jesus's miracles directly fulfilled Isaiah's prophecy, further reinforcing his claim to have inaugurated God's messianic kingdom.[78]

In Mark 2:10–11 and parallels, Jesus explains to the paralyzed man and his onlookers that the miraculous healing will demonstrate that he, the Son of man, has authority on earth to forgive sins. The logic of this passage is somewhat overly simplified by present-day interpreters. The way verse 7 is worded can easily lead the person unfamiliar with the relevant historical-cultural background to think that Jesus's mere declaration of the man's forgiveness of sins was blasphemous. Yet priests in the temple regularly announced the forgiveness of worshippers' sins after they offered their sacrifices. They were not usurping God's prerogatives in the least but making declaration that the proper procedures outlined in the law had been followed, and therefore they could assure the people their sins had been forgiven. Jesus's situation was unique because he was declaring that God had forgiven this paralyzed man's sins apart from any sacrifices and apart from priestly authority exercised in the temple precincts.[79] He

---

[77] Keener, *Miracles*, vol. 1, 60.

[78] Robert H. Gundry, *Mark: A Commentary on His Apology for the Cross* (Grand Rapids: Eerdmans, 1993), 388. More broadly, see esp. David P. Seccombe, *The King of God's Kingdom: A Solution to the Puzzle of Jesus* (Carlisle and Waynesboro, GA: Paternoster, 2002), 27–318.

[79] Nicholas Perrin, *Jesus the Temple* (London: SPCK; Grand Rapids: Baker, 2010), 140.

had no earthly priestly credentials, no formal rabbinic training, and he regularly contradicted popular legal interpretations of matters. Such a person could surely not be God's spokesman the way the authorized Jewish authorities were, or so those who accused him of blasphemy must have thought. Only one who was a divinely authorized *shaliach*—one sent from God—could overcome those obstacles.[80]

We could go into more detail on each of these nature miracles.[81] We could return to healings and exorcisms and look at them one by one also, applying a wide swath of the various criteria of authenticity. Several major works have undertaken precisely these tasks and consistently demonstrated reasons for believing, on historical grounds alone, in at least a core event behind virtually every miracle story that is authentic and, in many cases, reasons for believing the entire account is authentic.[82] We could follow Craig Keener's lead and discuss the best documented modern nature miracles, many of them

---

[80] On which, see esp. Simon Gathercole, *The Pre-existent Son: Recovering the Christologies of Matthew, Mark, and Luke* (Grand Rapids: Eerdmans, 2006), 177–89. Cf. also A. E. Harvey, "Christ as Agent," in *The Glory of Christ in the New Testament*, ed. Lincoln D. Hurst and N. T. Wright (Oxford: Clarendon, 1987), 239–50.

[81] Somewhat different is the so-called miracle of the coin in the fish's mouth (Matt 17:27). When one examines the literary form, one discovers this is not a narrative with declarations about what "happened" but merely a series of commands to the apostle Peter. Did he obey Jesus and go to the Sea of Galilee? Matthew never tells us. Sensationalizing website and blog posts about my denying a miracle story, most notably from Norman Geisler and F. David Farnell, contain radical distortions of the truth because (a) I have never said I don't believe Peter *could* have gone to the lake and caught just such a fish, and (b) there is no "story" to deny. The verse is not narrative in form—i.e., a series of past-tense, indicative mood statements declaring certain things to have happened. It is a series of commands. We simply do not know whether Peter obeyed them.

[82] H. van der Loos, *The Miracles of Jesus* (Leiden: Brill, 1965); Leopold Sabourin, *The Divine Miracles Discussed and Defended* (Rome: Catholic Book Agency, 1977); René Latourelle, *The Miracles of Jesus and the Theology of Miracles* (New York: Paulist, 1988); and Graham H. Twelftree, *Jesus, the Miracle Worker: A Historical and Theological Study* (Downers Grove: IVP, 1999).

related to weather or miraculous provision to meet basic needs.[83] We have now briefly discussed every major category of miracle except one—Jesus's resurrection and, by analogy, the revivifications of the people Jesus brought back to this worldly life. If the former were possible, the latter would follow as less difficult. But the resurrection has spawned a whole industry of scholarship itself, so we would do best to look at it in a discrete section of this chapter. To the resurrection, then, we turn next.

Resurrection

The apostle Paul declares straightforwardly what is at stake in this debate: "If Christ has not been raised, our preaching is useless and so is your faith. More than that, we are then found to be false witnesses about God, for we have testified about God that he raised Christ from the dead" (1 Cor 15:14–15). Again, he insists, "If Christ has not been raised, your faith is futile; you are still in your sins. Then those also who have fallen asleep in Christ are lost" (vv. 17–18). Moreover, "if only for this life we have hope in Christ, we are of all people most to be pitied" (v. 19). This stands in sharp contrast with those who have lived in comparative comfort in this world as believers and have declared that the benefits of being Christian *in this life alone* make it worthwhile, even should there turn out not to be a life to come![84]

---

[83] In addition to the examples distributed throughout his *Miracles*, see his chapter "The Historicity of the Nature Miracles" in a book on miracles, ed. Graham Twelftree (Eugene, OR: Wipf & Stock, forthcoming).

[84] As in the popular praise song by Andraé Crouch, "If Heaven Never Was Promised to Me," the chorus of which begins, "But if heaven never was promised to me . . . it's been worth just having the Lord in my life." See http://artists.letssingit. com/andrae-crouch-and-the-disciples-lyrics-if-heaven-was-never-promised-to-me-w8j4359#axzz3YGf975eb, accessed January 10, 2016. Given Paul's catalogues of sufferings throughout his Christian life vs. his prominence as a Jewish leader persecuting Christians, it is almost inconceivable that he could have thought this way!

But what kind of resurrection is Paul talking about? Many today would have us believe that it is something less than an objective bodily resurrection. Didn't Paul say "flesh and blood" could not inherit the kingdom of God (1 Cor 15:50)? Yes, but that was a stock idiom for fallen, mortal humanity.[85] Didn't he admit he experienced the risen Lord in a heavenly vision? Yes, yet he describes his experience in the same breath with the apostles' experiences with the resurrected Christ (1 Cor 15:8). So perhaps they too had a more subjective, visionary experience. After all, Paul himself said that his companions could not see Jesus like he could; all they heard was the sound of him speaking (Acts 9:7). Gerd Lüdemann argues forcefully along these lines.[86]

On the one hand, Lüdemann's historical reconstruction refutes those who would relegate resurrection belief to a late, slowly evolving legend that developed only when stories about Jesus, the simple Jewish rabbi, circulated long enough in Greco-Roman circles to take on fanciful dimensions of deity.[87] Lüdemann highlights Paul's earlier words in 1 Corinthians 15, in which he explains that what he received he passed on to the Corinthians "as of first importance" (v. 3) or perhaps "at the first" (or both). The language of receiving and passing on information in the context of a creedal declaration like verses 3–7 implies fixed, reliable oral tradition of a catechetical nature. Lüdemann explains that the heart of this creed must have been

---

[85] Anthony C. Thiselton, *The First Epistle to the Corinthians* (Carlisle: Paternoster; Grand Rapids: Eerdmans, 2000), 1291; David E. Garland, *1 Corinthians* (Grand Rapids: Baker, 2003), 742.

[86] Gerd Lüdemann with Alf Özen, *What Really Happened to Jesus: A Historical Approach to the Resurrection* (Louisville: Westminster John Knox, 1995), 82–130.

[87] As in Maurice Casey, *From Jewish Prophet to Gentile God: The Origins and Development of New Testament Christology* (Louisville and London: Westminster John Knox, 1991). For detailed demonstration of the revolutionary rather than evolutionary development of New Testament Christology, see Larry W. Hurtado, *Lord Jesus Christ: Devotion to Jesus in Earliest Christianity* (Grand Rapids: Eerdmans, 2003).

established by the time of Paul's own conversion, which had to have been within two or three years of Jesus's death, in light of the sum total of New Testament data. But that information was passed along to Paul in Damascus, a distance from Jerusalem, so a longer period of time would have been needed for the early Christian leaders to formulate the foundational, creedal elements of their fledgling faith and spread the word to places as far away as Syria that these were the truths to be taught to new converts. Lüdemann persuasively argues, therefore, that *belief* in Christ's bodily resurrection must have emerged in a Jewish context within *one to two years* after Jesus's death. This argument alone obliterates many theories of stories of Jesus's resurrection being modeled on Greco-Roman myths and emerging only after Christianity was well entrenched throughout the empire generations or more later.[88]

But Lüdemann also forthrightly explains that modern humans cannot believe in a true bodily resurrection.[89] What the disciples experienced must have been something more subjective or visionary. Although he dislikes the label, Lüdemann's view amounts to the old "mass hallucination" hypothesis. Indeed, various visionary experiences have been replicated by hundreds or thousands of onlookers throughout religious history—watching a statue of the virgin Mary appear to weep, for example. But detailed studies of accounts of mass hallucinations have shown that they always occur in conjunction with some fixed entity—a statue, a painting, a portion of the sky, or a landscape—something which under the "right" conditions can appear in a paranormal fashion.[90] Yet that is precisely what is never recorded

---

[88] Lüdemann with Özen, *What Really Happened to Jesus*, 9–16.

[89] Gerd Lüdemann, "Opening Statements," in *Jesus' Resurrection: Fact or Figment? A Debate Between William Lane Craig and Gerd Lüdemann*, ed. Paul Copan and Ronald K. Tacelli (Downers Grove: IVP, 2000), 45.

[90] See esp. John J. Johnson, "Were the Resurrection Appearances Hallucinations? Some Psychiatric and Psychological Considerations," *Churchman* 115 (2001):

inside or outside the Bible in the early Christian accounts of the resurrection. Multiple people, individually and in groups, saw Jesus in diverse locations, in distinct contexts, and when they were in different frames of mind. About the only consistent feature was that he was often not immediately recognized, exactly what we should expect with one whose disfigured, abused physical body had been remarkably healed, transformed, and glorified. On the other hand, in each instance there is the eventual moment of recognition, also what we should expect given Paul's teaching about the continuity as well as discontinuity in appearance between an earthly body and a resurrected body (1 Cor 15:35–58). Apart from his classic, old-line anti-supernaturalism, Lüdemann has provided solid reasons for believing in the historicity of Jesus's bodily resurrection.

Paul equates his experience of Jesus with that of the apostles before him. But that means he believed he saw Christ raised bodily from the dead just as the apostles had, even though he did not see the risen Lord close enough to the ground to touch him or watch him eat as they did (Acts 9:3–7). To argue that Paul is judging Jesus's appearances to others by his own experience is to reverse the chronological sequence narrated in Scripture.[91] The others' experiences came first. Paul the Jewish leader had already heard about them, which led him to persecute Christians as endangering the well-being of Judaism (Acts 8:1–3; 9:1–2). When he then met Jesus on the Damascus road and later likened his experience to those of the apostles before him, he was not depicting their testimony as akin to his; he was insisting that he had just as complete and legitimate an encounter with the resurrected

---

227–38. Cf. also Gary A. Sibcy, cited in Michael R. Licona, *The Resurrection of Jesus: A New Historiographical Approach* (Downers Grove: IVP, 2010), 484.

[91] For this point, along with a full treatment of Paul's beliefs about Jesus's resurrection, see Licona, *Resurrection of Jesus*, 349–55. On the physicality of the appearance of Jesus to Paul, see also Christopher Bryan, *The Resurrection of the Messiah* (Oxford: Oxford University Press, 2011), 217–20.

Jesus as anyone before him had. This becomes clear in those places where other believers are not ascribing Paul the same authority they give the Twelve, since Paul had not personally followed Jesus while he was alive (Gal 1:11–12; 1 Cor 9:1–2). It would not have helped Paul in the least to say, as it were, "Well, I had a subjective vision, and that's all the Twelve ever had either." No, he is claiming that his experience was every bit as objective and legitimating as theirs had been.[92]

But doesn't the term *resurrection* lend itself to metaphorical use? Maybe no one in the ancient world was talking about literally seeing or hearing anyone. Perhaps this was vivid, figurative language for affirming that the *cause* of Jesus lived on.[93] Living out his vision of the "brokerless kingdom," as John Dominic Crossan has called it, is what will save humanity.[94] Reject the imperial model, create small clusters of tight-knit, God-fearing communities that live by the nonviolent message of Jesus, love one another deeply, and attract others into your communities through that countercultural love, and you can transform the world, even though the man Jesus died and his body decayed.[95] It could be a compelling vision, but was it Jesus's vision? Was it Paul's or any other first-generation Christian's hope? It does not appear likely.

Had the gospel first emerged in Athens or Rome and after a generation of dissemination reached Jerusalem, this scenario might have

---

[92] William L. Craig, "The Bodily Resurrection of Jesus," in *Gospel Perspectives*, vol. 1, ed. R. T. France and David Wenham (Sheffield: JSOT, 1980; Eugene, OR: Wipf & Stock, 2003), 49–52; N. T. Wright, *The Resurrection of the Son of God* (London: SPCK; Minneapolis: Fortress, 2003), 318–19.

[93] E.g., John Dominic Crossan, in his various chapters in *The Resurrection of Jesus: John Dominic Crossan and N. T. Wright in Dialogue*, ed. Robert B. Stewart (Minneapolis: Fortress, 2006).

[94] Crossan, *Historical Jesus*, 225.

[95] Cf. also to varying degrees, Richard A. Horsley, *Jesus and Empire: The Kingdom of God and the New World Disorder* (Minneapolis: Fortress, 2003); and Marcus J. Borg, *Meeting Jesus Again for the First Time: The Historical Jesus and the Heart of Contemporary Faith* (New York and London: HarperCollins, 1994).

certain elements of plausibility to it. Bodily resurrection was rarely countenanced in the pre-Christian Greco-Roman world[96] whereas, except among the Sadducees, it was the norm for Jews.[97] One could then envision the story of a "spiritual" resurrection being retold repeatedly and over time morphing into the account of an increasingly bodily nature, as the gospel left Greek and Roman circles and took root in Jewish ones.[98] But, of course, that is exactly backwards from the actual sequence of events. All the first Christians were Jewish and only a generation later was Christianity more Gentile than Jewish. If anything, then, we would expect stories of bodily restoration to life to be at the core of the gospel tradition. And that is precisely what we find. James Ware examines the various approaches in the debate on the meaning of *egeirō* in the pre-Pauline formula in 1 Corinthians 15:4 and concludes that it "denotes the revivification of the crucified

---

[96] Wright, *Resurrection of the Son of God*, 32–84. For some apparent exceptions, see Stanley E. Porter, "Resurrection, the Greeks and the New Testament," in *Resurrection*, ed. Stanley E. Porter, Michael A. Hayes, and David Tombs (Sheffield: Sheffield Academic Press, 1999), 52–81. But see the response of Wright, *Resurrection of the Son of God*, 35.

[97] Wright, *Resurrection of the Son of God*, 85–206. Cf. also Jon D. Levenson, *Resurrection and the Restoration of Israel: The Ultimate Victory of the God of Life* (New Haven and London: Yale University Press, 2006).

[98] Cf. the hypothesis of Paul M. Fullmer, *Resurrection in Mark's Literary-Historical Perspective* (London and New York: T & T Clark, 2007). He, of course, recognizes that the direction of development was from Jewish to Greek. And most of what he refers to as resurrections are actually something short of the complete return to embodied life of someone who has definitely died. Dale C. Allison Jr. (*Resurrecting Jesus: The Earliest Christian Tradition and Its Interpreters* [London and New York: T & T Clark, 2005], 198–375) does not present an evolutionary hypothesis but would be content with a merely spiritual resurrection as the potential core of the visionary experiences he believes gave rise to the resurrection accounts, even while leaving the door open for the possibility of the empty tomb due to a bodily resurrection and admitting he would be pleased if they could be demonstrated. But he does not believe they can.

and entombed body of Jesus," and that "the language of the formula presupposes a narrative of the kind we see in the Synoptics and John."[99]

David Litwa has recently written a highly touted book canvassing a wide swath of ancient Greco-Roman literature, demonstrating various similarities between select early Christian depictions of Jesus and Hellenistic counterparts with other gods. With respect to Jesus's resurrection, Litwa highlights three specific examples of Greco-Roman "corporeal immortalization," a category that includes bodily resurrection but is much broader. Thus it encompasses becoming a star ("an astral body") or fine matter ("the aetherial Stoic soul").[100] It also subsumes "ascent, rapture, and disappearance," so individuals translated directly to heaven upon their deaths (or immediately before them), emperors who are deified after their deaths and appear in visions to someone still on earth, and heroes whose bodies can no longer be found are all included as significant parallels.[101] While Litwa rightly warns against emphasizing the differences between ancient Christian and pagan stories and while he stresses that he is not committing the genetic fallacy by arguing that Christians borrowed directly from identifiable pagan analogs, he appears to have gone somewhat too far in the opposite direction and not made nearly enough distinctions when he claims Christian deification of Jesus was birthed out of the same Hellenistic milieu as all these diverse phenomena.

Even granting his taxonomy, the examples to which Litwa appeals are Asclepius (translated to become a constellation of stars), Heracles (translated with or without his body, depending on the tradition), and Romulus (ascended, maybe after appearing to one person, and maybe without dying).[102] But not one of the clusters of stories about

---

[99] James Ware, "The Resurrection of Jesus in the Pre-Pauline Formula of 1 Cor. 15.3–5," *New Testament Studies* 60 (2014): 498.

[100] Litwa, *Iesus Deus*, 151 n. 34.

[101] Ibid., 153.

[102] Ibid., 156–68.

these figures depicts someone unambiguously known to have lived as a human being, said to have appeared after his death to a large number of people who lived during his lifetime (or any time until centuries later) by several of those people who agreed on affirming a tangible, bodily resurrection. More importantly, not one of these figures was the founder of a religion, the viability of which depended on reversing the unanimously agreed-on perception of that individual as accursed by God due to the nature of his death. Christianity most likely did use Hellenistic imagery to commend Jesus as superior to pagan gods, especially in post-New Testament literature.[103] But at its inception it was not trying to position Jesus atop the Greco-Roman pantheon of gods, or to present him as a great man worthy of deification, but to show that he was the Jewish Messiah, the fulfillment of the hopes of Israel, vindicated in the unusual but biblical interpretation of his mission as one who had to die for the sins of humanity before he could reign as Lord of the universe.[104] This is not a plotline found in any other literature of the ancient Mediterranean world despite made-up claims in nineteenth-century books reproduced uncritically on the Internet![105]

---

[103] Ibid., 69–109.

[104] Ibid., 16–18 (et passim) rightly stresses that Israel was significantly Hellenized, so that traditions of apotheosis would also have been known, but he does not deal with the actual categories and titles by which Jesus is predominantly presented in the New Testament, at least some of which (most notably, Messiah and Son of man) have no significant use in the Hellenized world and are strictly Hebraic and Jewish.

[105] Esp. Kersey Graves, *The World's Sixteen Crucified Saviors, or Christianity Before Christ*, repr. ed. (Bensenville, IL: Lusbena Books, 2014 [orig. 1875]). On April 30, 2015, thirteen separate editions of this volume were reprinted and for sale on amazon.com, showing to what great lengths some people will go to reproduce lies. To begin with, not one of these individuals was ever crucified! Contrast also the brief and superficial treatment in Bob Seidensticker, "Just One More Dying and Rising Savior," *Cross-examined: Clear Thinking About Christianity* (March 29, 2013), accessed January 10, 2016, http://www.patheos.com /blogs/crossexamined/2013/03/jesus-just-one-more-dying-and-rising-savior-2. A much higher-profile website to appear under the Google search "dying and

And, however implicitly or explicitly, it was an anti-imperial plot destined to get its proponents in trouble and even at times martyred by the empire, a problem affixed to none of the adherents to the classic Hellenistic mythologies.[106]

It is sometimes objected, however, that the earliest gospel account has no resurrection at all. When we recognize that the longer ending of Mark is not original (see chap. 13), we must admit that what we have of Mark that *is* original (Mark 16:1–8) does not contain the narrative of an actual resurrection appearance of Jesus to anyone. On the other hand, these eight verses closely resemble the beginnings of the resurrection narratives in Matthew and Luke that *do* go on to present actual appearances. They include the announcement by a young man in a white robe at the tomb that Jesus is no longer there but that he has risen (v. 6). They include his commissioning the women who encounter him to go tell his disciples that he is going ahead of them into Galilee and they will meet him there (v. 7), exactly as they do in the Gospel of Matthew (Matt 28:7). By this time in Mark's Gospel, especially in light of Peter's denial and Judas's betrayal, Jesus has shown himself to be an accurate predictor of the future, and he has predicted his death and resurrection three times (Mark 8:31–32 pars.; 9:31 pars.; and 10:33–34 pars.). All this should create the expectation on the part of Mark's readers that Jesus will in fact go before the Eleven to Galilee and appear to them there.[107] Tom Shepherd goes one step further and

---

resurrected gods," with more detailed and accurate analysis, is "Evidence for Jesus and Parallel Pagan 'Crucified Saviors' Examined," *Evangelical Catholic Apologetics* (December 2007), accessed January 10, 2016, http://www.philvaz.com/apologetics/JesusEvidenceCrucifiedSaviors.htm.

[106] Edward Pillar, "'Whom He Raised from the Dead': Exploring the Anti-Imperial Context of Paul's First Statement of Resurrection," in *Resurrection of the Dead: Biblical Traditions in Dialogue*, ed. Geert van Oyen and Tom Shepherd (Leuven and Walpole, MA: Peeters, 2012), 265–74.

[107] Gundry, *Mark*, 993. Cf. also Andrew T. Lincoln, "The Promise and the Failure—Mark 16:7, 8," *Journal of Biblical Literature* 108 (1989): 283–300.

argues that the abrupt ending creates the moral indignation for the reader that "this just is not right, someone must tell," propelling the reader to be the one to tell. In other words, just as the women's fear gave way to joyous proclamation in the other Gospels, even given the dynamics of Mark's narrative, "fear must give way to proclamation, love/devotion must overcome fright, [and] the resurrection of Jesus is the message the world must hear."[108]

Whether Mark deliberately wanted to catch his readers up short by ending with the women temporarily telling no one due to their fear or the original ending of Mark was lost and it did include one or more resurrection appearances, the fact that Mark wrote to a Christian community or collection of communities, probably in and around Rome, proves he knew they were already familiar with the resurrection story, or else they might never have become Christians.[109] As early as about 57, Paul had already written to the Roman Christians that belief in the bodily resurrection of Jesus was a nonnegotiable part of the faith (Rom 10:9–10). Mark, writing most likely in the early 60s, was not telling them the story for the first time, just creating an entire biography for the first time. The absence of a resurrection appearance from Mark 16:1–8 cannot indicate the absence of resurrection belief among the Roman Christians.

We have already addressed the related charge that the various Gospel accounts of the resurrection are irreconcilable in other respects. John Wenham's *Easter Enigma* remains an outstanding example of how to fit all of the information from all four Gospels into a plausible

---

[108] Tom Shepherd, "Promise and Power: A Narrative Analysis of the Resurrection Story in Mark 16 in Codex Vaticanus and Codex Washingtonianus," in *Resurrection of the Dead*, ed. van Oyen and Shepherd, 170.

[109] Cf. Sharyn Dowd, *Reading Mark: A Literary and Theological Commentary on the Second Gospel* (Macon, GA: Smyth & Helwys, 2000), 168–71; Darrell L. Bock, *Mark* (Cambridge: Cambridge University Press, 2015), 11–35.

and harmonious whole.[110] With some details there is even more than one way to fit the data together, and Wenham occasionally may not have opted for the most convincing way. But claims of the impossibility or at least the implausibility of existing harmonizations are greatly exaggerated! And the fact that the four writers each include enough unique material to their narratives, while overall clearly narrating the same event, suggests a greater degree of literary independence than is often the case among the Synoptics, decreasing the likelihood of collusion.[111]

Ever since Jesus lived, skeptics and critics have proposed certain completely naturalistic explanations for the resurrection narratives, which have been utterly debunked. Maybe Jesus's followers went to the wrong tomb, found it empty, and mistakenly believed Jesus was risen. But then all his detractors would have had to do was point them to the right one. Maybe Jesus never died; revived in the walk-in, cave-shaped tomb; escaped from an unsealed sarcophagus; rolled the sealed tomb stone door away; escaped the (sleeping?) guards; and convinced his followers he was alive again. But could one seriously imagine someone so weakened by crucifixion appearing in three days' time as the picture of health, looking better than he ever had before? Or perhaps the disciples stole and disposed of the body, inventing their story of Jesus's

---

[110] *Easter Enigma: Are the Resurrection Accounts in Conflict?* (Grand Rapids: Zondervan, 1984; Eugene, OR: Wipf & Stock, 2005). More briefly, cf. Murray J. Harris, *Raised Immortal: Resurrection and Immortality in the New Testament* (London: Marshall, Morgan Scott, 1983; Grand Rapids: Eerdmans, 1985), 69–71; and George E. Ladd, *I Believe in the Resurrection of Jesus* (Grand Rapids: Eerdmans; London: Hodder & Stoughton, 1975), 91–93.

[111] Cf. Hans E. Stier, cited approvingly in Hugo Staudinger, *The Jesus Family Tomb: Trustworthiness of the Gospels* (Edinburgh: T & T Clark, 1981), 77: "The sources for the resurrection of Jesus, with their relatively big contradictions over details, present for the historian for this very reason a criterion of extraordinary credibility. For if that were the fabrication of a congregation or similar group of people, then the tale would be consistently and obviously complete." Most of what Stier calls contradictions, however, refer simply to singly attested material.

resurrection. But then many of them, if early church tradition can be believed about their subsequent martyrdoms, died for a lie they knew they invented, a far cry from religious martyrs of other eras dying for what they believe in and believe not to be a lie![112] Although these and similar views have had surprising resurgence in recent popular writing and on the fringes of what might qualify as scholarship,[113] most bona fide researchers recognize how ludicrous each of these notions actually is. As for the claim in 2007 that Jesus's "family tomb" had been discovered in the Talpiot neighborhood of south Jerusalem, this has been thoroughly refuted from numerous perspectives.[114]

If we turn from responding to objections to the resurrection to offering positive evidence in its favor, strong arguments emerge. Given the superficial diversity in the canonical accounts, present to a greater degree than in most parts of a gospel synopsis, the remaining agreements stand out as all the more striking. One of those is the conviction in every one of the four Gospels that a group of women (even in John, Mary Magdalene speaks for a group of people she calls "we") arrived at the tomb first and heard the announcement of Christ's resurrection first. In all but Mark (excluding the longer ending), they are the first witnesses to the risen Jesus as well. In an environment in which women's testimony was regularly deemed less trustworthy than men's, in a climate in which only rarely could their testimony be accepted in a Jewish court of law, what individual or movement would ever invent

---

[112] On which, see Licona, *Resurrection of Jesus*, 366–71.

[113] See the thorough survey of the literature in Gary R. Habermas, "The Late Twentieth-Century Resurgence of Naturalistic Responses to Jesus' Resurrection," *Trinity Journal* 22 (2001): 179–96.

[114] For the original claims, see Simcha Jacobovici and Charles Pellegrino, *The Jesus Family Tomb: The Discovery, the Investigation, and the Evidence That Could Change History* (London and New York: HarperCollins, 2007). For the ongoing debate and helpful assessments of the evidence, see especially Charles L. Quarles, ed., *Buried Hope or Risen Savior? The Search for the Jesus Tomb* (Nashville: B&H, 2008).

MIRACLES IN THE NEW TESTAMENT WORLD AND TODAY | 707

accounts of women being the sole, initial witnesses tasked with the responsibility of passing on to the male disciples what they had seen and heard, including commands for those male disciples as to where they should go to see Jesus?[115]

A second argument in favor of the accuracy of the resurrection reports involves the significance of crucifixion. The Hebrew Scriptures clearly taught that anyone hanged on a tree was cursed by God (Deut 21:23). But the biblical cultures did not execute people with nooses as we think of them; Deuteronomy would have originally referred to the impalement of an already dead body on a piece of wood (hence, the NIV, "hung on a pole").[116] But Roman crucifixion had become so widespread that the rabbis had already decided the nature and posture of the execution sufficiently matched the intent and disgrace of impalement so that the same principle applied to a crucified victim.[117] No would-be Messiah could possibly be legitimate if crucified as a criminal by the Roman regime. How then did a group of all Jewish followers of Jesus come from earliest days onward to believe that Jesus was still the Messiah and a divine Messiah, no less? Only a supernatural return to life, like Christ's bodily resurrection, can explain that incongruity.[118]

---

[115] Cf. Licona, *Resurrection of Jesus*, 400–437; Wright, *Resurrection of the Son of God*, 607–8. That all the Gospel accounts of Jesus's resurrection appearances stress women as the first witnesses was a feature that embarrassed certain segments of the early church, and which they therefore tried to play down. See Claudia Setzer, "Excellent Women: Female Witness to the Resurrection," *Journal of Biblical Literature* 116 (1997): 259–72.

[116] Edward J. Woods, *Deuteronomy* (Nottingham and Downers Grove: IVP, 2014), 236. Cf. J. G. McConville, *Deuteronomy* (Nottingham: Apollos; Downers Grove: IVP, 2002), 332.

[117] See esp. David W. Chapman, *Ancient Jewish and Christian Perceptions of Crucifixion* (Tübingen: Mohr Siebeck, 2008; Grand Rapids: Baker, 2010), 117–77.

[118] The resurrection in turn "lays bare such an exalted disdain for things marked by death, by ensuring the future end of would-be powers and the divinely-wrought vindication of those who presently belong to the cross."—Matthew R. Malcolm,

So, too, the mere existence of the Christian church requires such an impetus. There were plenty of "bandits, prophets and messiahs"[119] in the first century, hoping to liberate Israel, usually by military violence. Every one of them was decisively squelched by Rome, usually accompanied by violent massacres of their followers. If a movement survived an initial slaughter, it was only because a family member or close followers of the would-be deliverer succeeded him as the new hope for messianic deliverance. In most cases the movement was done away with altogether.[120] There is no evidence from any ancient source that one of Jesus's followers was ever treated as the new Messiah, and yet his movement was not squelched. Instead, it quickly grew and flourished within the circles that knew about Jesus's execution. Indeed, they highlighted it as the center of their faith—a crucified Messiah who died not for his sins but for the sins of the world (see esp. Gal 3:13).[121] Only a miracle as dramatic as a resurrection could account for this striking paradox.

Even the boldness of the disciples to preach Jesus in the temple precincts in the presence of the Jewish leaders who executed Jesus shows such a turnabout from their cowering behind locked doors immediately after his crucifixion as to demand an explanation along the lines of a resurrection. As Wright puts it so eloquently:

"The Resurrection of the Dead in 1 Corinthians," in *Resurrection of the Dead*, ed. van Oyen and Shepherd, 286.

[119] Helpful labels to characterize the diverse, ragtag groups of rebels Josephus depicts. See Richard A. Horsley with John S. Hanson, *Bandits, Prophets, and Messiahs: Popular Movements at the Time of Jesus* (Minneapolis: Winston, 1985; London and New York: Continuum, 1999).

[120] N. T. Wright, "The Surprise of Resurrection," in *Jesus, the Final Days: What Really Happened*, ed. Troy A. Miller (Louisville: Westminster John Knox, 2009), 93–94. For an overview of the key individuals in these movements, see Craig A. Evans, *Jesus and His Contemporaries: Comparative Studies* (Boston and Leiden: Brill, 2001), 53–81.

[121] Cf. Thomas R. Schreiner, *Galatians* (Grand Rapids: Zondervan, 2010), 216–18.

The early Christians did not invent the empty tomb and the "meetings" or "sightings" of the risen Jesus in order to explain a faith they already had. They developed that faith because of the occurrence, and convergence, of these two phenomena. Nobody was expecting this kind of thing; no kind of conversion-experience would have generated such ideas; nobody would have invented it, no matter how guilty (or how forgiven) they felt, no matter how many hours they pored over the scriptures. To suggest otherwise is to stop doing history and to enter into a fantasy world of our own, a new cognitive dissonance in which the relentless modernist, desperately worried that the post-Enlightenment worldview seems in imminent danger of collapse, devises strategies for shoring it up nevertheless. In terms of the kind of proof which historians normally accept, the case we have presented that the tomb-plus-appearances combination is what generated early Christian belief, is as watertight as one is likely to find.[122]

One can, of course, question the authenticity of the details of the Gospel narratives that lead to the jarring juxtapositions we are discussing here. But the behavior of the disciples during and right after Jesus's passion and death is so disgraceful early Christians would scarcely have invented it. And the boldness and about-face of those same men in preaching Jesus, or something much like it, had to have occurred to explain the existence of the Church's emerging so immediately after his death.

Before the Jewish element in early Christianity became a negligible percentage of the movement, believers also began worshipping

---

[122] Wright, *The Resurrection of the Son of God*, 707. Cf. Russ Dudrey, "What the Writers Should Have Done Better: A Case for the Resurrection of Jesus Based on Ancient Criticism of the Resurrection Reports," *Stone-Campbell Journal* 3 (2000): 55–78.

on Sundays rather than Saturdays. The Sabbath (Saturday) was the divinely ordained day of the week for resting from work and formed one of the ten most central commandments in Jewish life (Exod 20:8–10; Deut 5:12–15). It would come to be their day of worship as well, precisely because they did not have to go to work. Most Jews had come to believe the Torah was immutable and would last forever (cf., e.g., Deut 29:29; Isa 40:8). Jesus, of course, claimed to fulfill the law (Matt 5:17) in ways that meant not all of the Levitical legislation would remain unchanged for his followers. Most notably, they gave up offering animal sacrifices as they recognized Christ to be the once-for-all sacrifice for sin. After Peter's vision of clean and unclean food and the command of the heavenly voice to eat it, Christians increasingly viewed the dietary laws as optional rather than mandatory (Mark 7:19b; Acts 10:9–16). After significant debates, circumcision was viewed similarly (Acts 15:1–21). But what do we say about the Ten Commandments? Jesus and Paul take up all of the other nine at one place or another and reaffirm them. One might imagine that they would treat the Sabbath law similarly.[123]

Three times in the New Testament, however, we read about believers worshipping on Sunday, the first day of the week (Acts 20:7; 1 Cor 16:2; Rev 1:10), rather than on the Sabbath. We know there was a Jewish element to the church in Corinth, so we cannot argue that Paul was envisioning only Gentiles gathering on a Sunday; Jew and Gentile Christians alike had chosen a different day for their most holy day than the one that was commanded in the Hebrew Scriptures.

---

[123] So strong has this assumption been in some circles that writers have performed exegetical cartwheels to try to support it. Best known is the Seventh-Day Adventist tradition, well represented by Samuele Bacchiocchi, *Divine Rest for Human Restlessness: A Theological Study of the Good News of the Sabbath for Today* (Rome: Pontifical Gregorian University Press, 1980). Cf. Samuele Bacchiocchi, *From Sabbath to Sunday: A Historical Investigation of the Rise of Sunday Observance in Early Christianity* (Rome: Pontifical Gregorian University Press, 1977).

Post-New Testament documents would demonstrate how quickly this became the norm.[124] We also know that Gentiles did not have one day in seven already established as a holiday on which they did not have to work. Greeks and Romans had several holidays every month, but it was according to an annual calendar of festival days scattered here and there rather than always on the same day of the week. Unless one of these special holidays happened to fall on a Sunday in a given year, Gentiles would have to work on Sundays, so that Sunday worship meant gathering either before dawn or after dusk, just before or after putting in a full day's work.[125] But that means there must have been some overwhelmingly compelling reason for them not to accommodate themselves to the best day for *Jewish* believers to worship, the Sabbath (Saturday), and for Jewish believers to begin celebrating their Christian faith on a different day from the day of worship prescribed in their Scriptures!

Only the objective bodily resurrection of Jesus datable to a specific Sunday morning, rather than a variety of subjective visionary experiences on a variety of days, can adequately account for this shift.[126] The resurrection then also explains how Paul can treat Sabbath observance as an *adiapharon*, a morally neutral matter, and allow for diverse practices among Christians as he calls on them not to judge one another with respect to that diversity (Rom 14:1–15:13). It explains how he can declare that Sabbaths are among the ceremonies that were a shadow of the things to come, whereas the reality is found in Christ

---

[124] See Richard J. Bauckham, "Sabbath and Sunday in the Post-Apostolic Church," in *From Sabbath to Lord's Day: A Biblical, Historical, and Theological Investigation,* ed. D. A. Carson (Grand Rapids: Zondervan, 1982; Eugene, OR: Wipf & Stock, 2000), 251–98.

[125] For these and related details, see Craig L. Blomberg, "The Sabbath as Fulfilled in Christ," in *Perspectives on the Sabbath: 4 Views,* ed. Christopher J. Donato (Nashville: B&H, 2011), 305–58.

[126] Murray J. Harris, *From Grave to Glory: Resurrection in the New Testament* (Grand Rapids: Zondervan, 1990), 151–52.

(Col 2:17). It explains, too, how the author of Hebrews can spiritual-ize and eschatologize the concept of Sabbath rest to include life in the Promised Land, becoming a Christian, and existence in the eternal state still to come (Heb 4:1–11).[127]

The issue of Sabbath worship brings to mind yet another argu-ment for a bodily resurrection. Christianity has never venerated a tomb claiming to have contained Jesus's body. Sages and philosophers, political and religious leaders alike almost uniformly throughout history have memorials of some kind erected in their honor at the locations where they are buried or are believed to have been buried. Centuries after Jesus's death, the Church of the Holy Sepulcher in Jerusalem was built to commemorate the place where he may have died, and his (temporary) burial may well have been close by. But it has never been accompanied by the claim that his body stayed there beyond the Sunday morning after his death. Other religions that have resurrection traditions do not have them beginning anywhere as early after the time of the death of the one honored, and many "resurrec-tion" traditions are not traditions of a bodily resurrection accompanied by an empty tomb.[128]

In recent decades some have tried to argue that Jesus's body would have been left on the cross to be eaten by dogs or other wild animals and that the remnants of his corpse would eventually have just been tossed into a shallow, makeshift grave, the location of which would not have been remembered. But Jews had much more respect for the corpses of their dead than this, even for those deemed to be criminals, if only for the sake of not defiling the land. Contrary to some claims, the Romans did in fact allow Jewish scruples to lead to appropriate

---

[127] See esp. Carson, ed., *From Sabbath to Lord's Day*. Cf. also Terence D. O'Hare, *The Sabbath Complete: And the Ascendancy of First-Day Worship* (Eugene, OR: Wipf & Stock, 2011).

[128] So also Peter G. Bolt, "Mark 16:1–8: The Empty Tomb of a Hero?" *Tyndale Bulletin* 47 (1996): 27–37.

burials in almost every instance of which we are aware.[129] The biblical account of Jesus's being buried in Joseph of Arimathea's borrowed tomb rings true to everything we know from history,[130] notwithstanding today's fashionable naysayers.

For those still trapped in the world of Ernst Troeltsch's definition of the historical-critical method, so that we can never believe anything happened in the past that does not have an observable, documented analogy in the present,[131] one final argument clamors for more attention than it usually has received. Even in the late twentieth and early twenty-first centuries, numerous people have been declared medically dead, ceased all vital signs, and yet come back to life. Some of these have occurred on operating tables or in other hospital contexts and therefore do not necessarily qualify as that which science cannot explain, except perhaps for the length of time they were lifeless before being revived or the fact that they had no lasting brain damage. Many of these people have reported having experiences of God or Jesus and a life to come during precisely the period of time when their brains registered no activity whatsoever. The literature on these experiences has become enormous; the common term for them is "near-death experiences." Sometimes those who were not previously believers have become Christians as a result.[132]

---

[129] Craig A. Evans, "The Silence of Burial," in *Jesus, the Final Days*, ed. Miller, 58–59, 62–69.

[130] See esp. William L. Craig, *Assessing the New Testament Evidence for the Historicity of the Resurrection of Jesus* (Lewiston and Lampeter: Edwin Mellen, 1989), 173–76; repeated in several of his other publications.

[131] Ernst Troeltsch, "Historical and Dogmatic Method in Theology," in *Religion in History* (Minneapolis: Fortress; Edinburgh: T & T Clark, 1991 [German original, 1898]), 13–14.

[132] The classic study remains Raymond A. Moody Jr., *Life After Life: The Investigation of a Phenomenon—Survival of Bodily Death*, 25th anniversary ed. (New York: HarperOne, 2001). Jeffrey Long with Paul Perry (*The Science of Near-Death Experiences* [New York: HarperOne, 2010]) has analyzed more than 3,000 near-death experiences and focuses on those in which patients with absolutely no

More astonishingly, there are a good smattering of documented cases where the only stimulus for resuscitation, after the disappearance of all perceptible signs of life, has been fervent, public Christian prayer. Usually these occur within minutes or at least hours of the perception of death; on rare occasions they have taken place up to two days afterwards.[133] Strictly speaking, these are not parallels to Jesus's resurrection to a transformed bodily existence believed to endure eternally but to the reanimations or revivifications that he (like Elijah and Elisha in Old Testament times and Peter and Paul in the book of Acts) performed on others. These people would one day die again. But the problem of science and medicine having no known way of explaining the phenomena that occurred remains the same in both categories of miracle.[134]

Conclusion

John Meier's verdict rings true: "If the miracle tradition from Jesus' public ministry were to be rejected *in toto* as unhistorical, so should every other Gospel tradition about him" (recall p. 685 n. 55). Of course, some skeptics would be happy to declare every other Gospel tradition about Jesus unhistorical, but the evidence is far too overwhelming that Jesus of Nazareth lived and ministered as an early first-century Jew in Israel to come to that conclusion. The two main reasons the miracles are often treated differently from the rest of the Jesus tradition are

---

brain waves over time were resuscitated and able accurately to describe events that occurred precisely during the time they had no scientifically detectable signs of life.

[133] See esp. Craig S. Keener, "'The Dead Are Raised' (Matthew 11:5 // Luke 7:22): Resuscitation Accounts in the Gospels and Eyewitness Testimony," *Bulletin for Biblical Research* 25 (2015): 55–79.

[134] The mysterious resurrection of select Old Testament saints in Matt 27:52–53 apparently refers to those who, like Jesus, would now live forever, and demonstrates the truth that Christ is the first fruits of those who will be resurrected from death (1 Cor 15:20, 23).

(1) the alleged lack of parallels in contemporary experience, and (2) the alleged parallels in ancient mythology. The evidence to refute (1) is now so plentiful and widespread that the only way to reject it is to charge millions of people worldwide with either lying or idiocy. This in turn requires an arrogance and prejudice of such a magnitude that it makes other forms of discrimination in our world seem mild in comparison. A response to (2) should be more nuanced. There *are* various partial parallels in the New Testament canon to a handful of ancient pagan miracle stories, but the differences outweigh the similarities in most instances and especially when they appear in pre-Christian contexts.

At first blush, the resurrection of Jesus seems to be a particularly difficult event to accept. On closer inspection the same two objections emerge here as with the other New Testament miracles, and the same lines of response must be offered. While not nearly as common as miraculous healings and exorcisms, or even nature miracles, documented revivifications to full health in this life have occurred, and upon closer inspection the alleged parallels to ancient myths are not nearly as substantial as they are often made to appear. Nor do they cohere in a pattern of demonstrating the arrival of the Messianic Age and therefore of the Messiah the way the New Testament miracles do. Neither the miracle stories in general nor the resurrection accounts in particular have to invalidate all of the lines of argument that our other chapters have been pulling together.

Conclusion

Presuppositions prove powerful in determining the perspectives one adopts with respect to the trustworthiness of the New Testament. If one is a committed naturalist or even a firm agnostic, the supernatural elements of the Scripture will prohibit one from accepting a large percentage of its claims. If one is closed to reasonable harmonizations of apparent discrepancies, one will conclude that the text is riddled with errors. If one is enamored with the slightest parallels with other ancient Mediterranean literature, one will relegate the Gospels and Acts to myth or legend, and at least half of the Epistles to pseudonymous authorship. Revelation will probably be discarded altogether as simply too outlandish to be of any use.

At the other end of the theological (or ideological) spectrum are those who are committed to the truth and accuracy of Scripture but too threatened by the questions raised by this volume to even consider any other options. Their faith may remain secure, but they will have little to say to the person who does not share their presuppositions. If they are Christian leaders or teachers, they may tell those who ask too many questions, "Just believe!" Unfortunately, this response almost never has its intended outcome; rather it convinces the questioners that their leaders have no answers and makes them even more skeptical. When certain scholars suggest that various sections of Scripture traditionally understood to be historical might have been intended to represent a different literary form or genre altogether, these leaders seek to exclude those scholars from their churches, schools, or academic societies. They seldom actually interact with the evidence proffered, sometimes they rather badly mispresent the perspective in question, but in any event not only is the new suggestion rejected, but the scholars who propose it are blacklisted.

I trust that the reader who has actually digested a large portion of my book recognizes that I take a conservative position on each of the issues addressed here. But I do not hold my views dogmatically, I do not seek to separate myself from others who take different perspectives, and I welcome dialog and debate about any or all of the issues I have discussed. Many (though by no means all) of the issues here can be matters for intra-evangelical debate as well as for discussion with scholars of all perspectives. With all of these caveats, I will now list what I believe are my most important conclusions. Fuller summaries appear at the end of each chapter.

A good case can still be made for Matthew, Mark, Luke, and John as the authors of the four Gospels that bear their names. A good case can still be made for dating the three Synoptic Gospels to the 60s of the first century and John to the 90s. But even if these conclusions are rejected, the Gospels are most likely only one person and ten to twenty years further removed from these individuals and dates. By ancient standards this is extraordinarily close in time and transmission to eyewitness testimony. With any other putatively historical sources from antiquity, we would consider ourselves highly fortunate and envision ourselves as having good access to accurate reports. This assumes, of course, that the literary genre of the Gospels is a historical or biographical one. After careful inspection of all the proposed options, it turns out that Jewish and Greco-Roman biographies are indeed the closest parallels. Of course we have to judge the Gospel writers by the standards of precision and excellence of their day and not anachronistically impose our modern ones upon them. Granted this caveat, they stand up to scrutiny remarkably well.

There are good reasons for believing that Mark's was the earliest complete Gospel but that other shorter written sources preceded his, including possibly an initial version of part or all of Matthew in Hebrew or Aramaic. It is likely that a collection of Jesus's most popular sayings had already been preserved, either in writing, orally, or some of each. We may refer to this, with scholarly convention, as Q, while recognizing that many of the superstructures erected upon the Q hypothesis can be flimsy. Oral traditions circulated before and after these various written sources were compiled. Three features give us reason to have confidence that they preserved the true gist of what Jesus said and did—the universal practice of memorization of sacred literature in ancient Mediterranean cultures, the oral custom of retelling epic stories with a certain degree of flexibility but within fixed limits, and the power of the community in fostering what is today most commonly called social memory.

Of course, each of the synoptists had his own theological agenda, but theological emphases do not inherently distort history; sometimes the nature of those emphases require telling it as accurately as possible. Redaction criticism and harmonization are not the antinomies so many on both the far right and the far left imagine them to be. The one can suggest some of *why* the Gospels differ in the ways they do; the other can show there are no necessary contradictions among those differing forms. A detailed survey of the most well-known and perplexing apparent contradictions in the Synoptic Gospels, occasionally with extrabiblical history and frequently internally as one compares parallels, demonstrates that none is without one or more reasonable

solutions. Another survey of the most significant examples of corroboration, usually via extrabiblical evidence, of key passages from
every chronological period covered in the Synoptic Gospels further
increases our confidence in their reliability.

The Gospel of John has typically been more suspect within critical scholarship, but the so-called new look on John is showing a much
larger number of John's distinctive features can be plausibly accepted
as historical. Because John is literarily independent of the Synoptics,
we should not be surprised that there is much greater diversity in
selection of material. John is nevertheless aware of the Synoptic content and has deliberately chosen not to repeat it at many junctures.
Without doubt Jesus's teaching is written in Johannine idiom, but a
careful comparison of large swaths of unparalleled material with the
Synoptics discloses a surprising number of verbal parallels and a large
amount of conceptual parallels. The subgenre of biography and historiography John represents differs a little from the Synoptics but
scarcely enough to locate this narrative in a different literary genre
altogether. A sequential walk through the Fourth Gospel again discloses, virtually in every chapter and major pericope, the kind of information that may be viewed as most probably historically accurate by a
variety of standard criteria of authenticity.

Luke's second volume, the Acts of the Apostles, provides us with
considerably more details that cohere with what we know from ancient
history outside the New Testament. We are not aware of any form of
fiction from antiquity that researched the setting, customs, places, and
lay of the land with so much care and without any necessary errors if
they were intending to compose fictitious narratives. Indeed, works of
fiction usually tipped their hand by blatantly inaccurate information
that most everyone would recognize. So much of what can be corroborated in Acts is fairly incidental to Luke's main points as well, so that it
is difficult to charge Luke with inventing this material due to theological motivation. Whereas the Gospels were first of all biographies and

secondarily historiography, with Acts the ranking is reversed, although with the genre of "collected biography" we come close to what we find in Acts.

We have no parallel Acts that covers the same territory as the canonical Acts to create any kind of "synoptic problem." But we have thirteen epistles ascribed to Paul, the protagonist in Acts 13–28. Especially when we notice that Luke never refers to these letters, it is remarkable that one can synthesize the information from both Acts and Paul and create a plausible, detailed chronology of the events during the years of Paul's public, recorded ministry. Only occasionally do apparent tensions surface; again these can be plausibly resolved. Far more often Acts provides background that illuminates Paul's letters, while Paul's letters supplement what we learn from Acts. Of course, given that Paul wrote almost all of his epistles before Acts, his testimony must be viewed as primary. But few verbal parallels would suggest Luke simply built up his narrative from material in the epistles, despite the recent claims of a radical few.

As we turn to considering Paul's letters on their own, how are we to respond to the vexed question of pseudonymity? Seven of the thirteen are virtually universally accepted as authentically Pauline: Romans, 1–2 Corinthians, Galatians, Philippians, 1 Thessalonians, and Philemon. Second Thessalonians and Colossians are semi-disputed, Ephesians is commonly doubted, and the Pastoral Epistles, outside of evangelical circles, are almost uniformly doubted. On the one hand, there is enough varied evidence from ancient Jewish and Christian circles, and enough unknowns about first-century attitudes, that we cannot dismiss all forms of pseudonymity as necessarily deceptive. Some may well have been an accepted literary device, even among first-century Christians, but it is hard to tell. On the other hand, strong cases can still be made for Pauline authorship of all thirteen letters attributed to him. The arguments against his having written the six doubted letters turn out to be not nearly as strong as many think.

Since Paul wrote so much, then, should he be credited with being the true founder of Christianity? Did his message so transform the teaching of the simple Galilean rabbi, Jesus, that we have to choose which portion of the New Testament to follow, the Gospels or the letters of Paul? Far from it! Although Paul only rarely quotes Jesus outright, he does allude to a surprising number of his teachings and is aware of a good cross-section of the events of his life. Some of Paul's major themes are different from those Jesus underlines, but Paul was a church planter and discipler of young Christians after Jesus's death and resurrection and the establishment of the church in a way Jesus could not have been during his earthly ministry. All of Paul's letters are written to churches or individuals who already know the gospel message that Christ taught and embodied. Views on certain topics like the role of the law or attitudes toward women turn out to be remarkably similar when one compares Jesus and Paul. Other themes that at first glance appear markedly different, such as the kingdom of God and justification by faith, on closer inspection turn out to be much more consonant with each other. Contextualizing the gospel message for non-Jewish audiences goes a long way to explain many of Paul's differences from Jesus's emphases.

At first blush the remaining New Testament epistles and the book of Revelation have little if anything to do with a treatment of the *historical* reliability of the New Testament. Issues of pseudonymity, however, have been raised to varying degrees with all of the letters of James, Peter, John, and Jude, along with John's Revelation. As it turns out, only the one letter that was also disputed in ancient times, 2 Peter, has a strong case against it. Even then there are plausible ways we can envision Peter's having written the letter, or at least the bulk of it, with possibly a posthumous editor. Hebrews remains the one originally anonymous letter. But all serious proposals for its authorship involved either Paul or one of his close followers. Revelation is worth including in a survey of this kind because to the extent that John's visions employed the historical meanings of their key imagery we can determine if they present a coherent and discernible message. To the extent they depict the fulfillment of certain past prophecies, we can gain in confidence concerning the fulfillment of those still to come.

Apocryphal Christian documents, including early Gnostic literature, used all four major literary genres of the New Testament books: gospels, acts, epistles, and apocalypses. Should they be consulted for historical information about Jesus and the first generation of Christianity as well? While a handful of sayings attributed to Jesus outside the canonical Gospels might just go back to him in one form or another, and while a handful of traditions about the lives and, more importantly, deaths of Jesus's first followers could reflect what they really did, in general the answer is no. These documents for the most part breathe the air of mid-second through mid-fourth century syncretistic Christian milieus, which are aware of, depend on, and supplement canonical texts or which treat topics, particularly cosmology, to which the New Testament documents pay little attention. They represent later theological interests or seek to plug the perceived gaps of the canonical texts, sometimes fancifully.

Broaching questions of the canon leads us to explore briefly how carefully the earliest manuscripts were copied by hand and how the documents that came to be uniquely authoritative for Christians were chosen for that distinction. In fact, the New Testament documents were extraordinarily carefully preserved, given the fact that no magisterium superintended their production and transmission, and given Christianity's strong commitment to spread the word rapidly, to translate the sacred texts into the languages of the people to whom they preached, and to disseminate them far and wide. A few noncanonical texts got a little support in the various discussions about a New Testament from the mid-second century to its ratification at the end of the fourth century. Conversely, six of the smaller, later letters and Revelation were occasionally questioned. But we have no evidence that any of the four Gospels, Acts, the letters of Paul, 1 Peter, or 1 John were ever in serious dispute, and we are not aware of any evidence that suggests the Gnostics ever tried to put their documents forward as candidates for inclusion in an emerging Christian canon. By the time Christianity finally had a power base in Rome in the fourth century, most of the books were securely in place. To argue that the selection of the canon was primarily a political power play is thus anachronistic in the extreme.

A final topic for consideration in this wide-ranging study is the miraculous dimension to the New Testament. Shouldn't this alone discredit its narrative works from consideration as serious history? Not in the least! Philosophical and scientific arguments against the supernatural have repeatedly been shown to make unwarranted claims. Carefully documented miracles on every continent in response to public, concerted Christian prayer have occurred in our world today by the hundreds and probably thousands, with parallels to virtually every form of New Testament miracle, especially with instantaneous physical healings and exorcisms. Supposed parallels with ancient myths or legends appear sparser than many claim. The closest ones are invariably post-Christian in origin, including post-Christian accretions attached to pre-Christian figures. By far the most common pattern in ancient Greco-Roman mythology are the stories of the gods and goddesses acting in conjunction with the annual cycle of the seasons. Their miracles, including "resurrections" (annually), do not involve historical human beings, much less figures from recent history at the times the myths proliferated. Surprisingly strong arguments for Jesus's miracles, including his resurrection, emerge even on historical grounds alone.

Some readers open to these conclusions might nevertheless ask how the historical reliability of the text proves its theological convictions or ethical instructions. The short answer is that it doesn't. It merely prepares the way or sets the stage for them. Speakers or writers who consistently make historical mistakes or deliberately falsify the kind of information that can be tested inspire no confidence that they should be heeded on any other topic or in any other kind of discourse. But those who demonstrate the painstaking care to get details right that the New Testament authors have shown at least deserve a thoughtful hearing on the kinds of topics that can't be assessed by historical criteria. My next major book is scheduled to be a New Testament theology, so I will try to help my readers make that transition in that volume.

It also does little good if someone reads this book, goes away convinced that the New Testament is historically trustworthy, but remains unfamiliar with the rest of its contents not discussed here. It does little good if someone does have a thorough grasp on the contents of Scripture but then refuses to become a Jesus follower, obeying his and the apostles' teachings, and applying the Bible to every area of life. But for those who are reluctant to take Scripture more seriously because they are unconvinced it is a historically valuable collection of documents, this book will hopefully remove some obstacles. For those who believe it and try to live by it but feel inadequate in explaining to others why it is trustworthy, hopefully this book will help. Of course, without the Spirit's work in a person's life, all historical conversation is in vain. But over the centuries the Spirit has shown that one of several key ways in which he has worked to bring people to Jesus and to grow them in their faith and walk with him is through historical evidences. It is my hope that he will continue to do so, in some small part at least, through this book as well.

NAME INDEX

SUBJECT INDEX

A

Abba, 140, 181, 428, 456
abomination that causes desolation,
    16, 425
Abyss, 539, 541
accommodationism, 66
Achaia, 9, 238, 329, 335, 337, 396,
    585
Acts of Andrew, 247, 584
Acts of John, 247, 585
Acts of Paul and Thecla, 247, 586,
    587, 591, 656
Acts of Peter, 247, 587
Acts of Peter and the Twelve
    Apostles, 563
Acts Seminar, 240, 294, 295
Advocate, 174
Aeneid, 243
allepigraphy, 406
allonymity, 406, 498
American eagle, 521
amillennialism, 552
Amphipolis, 278

ancient Greece, 18
ancient life spans, 19, 107
angel, 63, 77, 101, 102, 180, 262, 384,
    424, 434, 475, 476, 489, 515, 524,
    529, 533, 541, 542, 547, 582, 589,
    631, 635
Anointing at Bethany, 214
ante-Nicene Church Fathers, 437
Antichrist, 501, 519, 545, 546
antinomies, 187, 593, 594
Antiquities, 108, 143, 144, 290
anti-Semitism, 12, 285, 405, 560
Antonia Fortress, 136
Apocalypse, 520, 521, 524, 527, 542,
    554, 562, 563, 570, 588, 606, 607,
    653, 656, 723
Apocrypha, 428, 587, 605, 607
Apocryphon of James, 563, 564
Apollonia, 278
apologetics, xxv
Apostles' Creed, 437, 561
apostolic age, 488, 492, 513
Apostolic Constitutions, 656

Mysia, 278
Mystery of Mar Saba, The (Hunter), 602

N

Nablus, 197
Nag Hammadi, 559, 562, 570, 571, 579, 593, 594, 595, 596, 604, 606
Nag Hammadi Library, 562, 591
Nain, 126, 172, 213, 681
nature miracles, 676, 688, 692, 694, 715
Neapolis, 278, 327
neoorthodoxy, 66
Neoplatonism, 163
Nestlé-Aland *Novum Testamentum Graece*, 623
New New Testament, A (Taussig), 590, 591, 592, 594, 595, 596, 597, 607, 611, 645, 652, 654
New Orleans Council, 595, 654
New Testament Apocrypha, xxiii, 561, 570, 588, 605, 679
Nicanor Gate, 255
Nicolaitans, 530, 532

O

Odes of Solomon, 591, 592
Odyssey, 22, 38, 243, 644
Old Testament Apocrypha, 352
Old Testament prophecies, 61, 138
Olivet Discourse, 151, 181, 251
On History Writing (Lucian), 28
On the Reliability of the Old Testament (Kitchen), xxiv
oral tradition, 35, 37, 40, 42, 46, 48, 90, 155, 240, 295, 415, 417, 419, 428, 438, 696, 719
orthodoxy, 281, 352, 400, 498, 651, 657
Osiris, 680
overseers, 336, 337, 395, 402, 403, 529

P

Palestinian environment, 686
Palm Sunday, 215
Paneas, 129
Paphos, 270, 271
papyri, 286, 383
parable (defined), 122
parable of the wicked tenants, 88, 434, 576
Paraclete, 183
paraklētos, 174
parallelism, 15, 81, 164, 176, 364, 427, 428, 538, 571
parallels, 100, 119, 120, 142, 151, 166, 171, 175, 176, 177, 180, 186, 202, 207, 211, 215, 216, 218, 220, 221, 237, 238, 242, 243, 244, 247, 299, 323, 325, 330, 343, 344, 364, 387, 388, 393, 423, 424, 427, 435, 445, 455, 468, 482, 483, 496, 507, 575, 576, 579, 601, 602, 606, 676, 678, 679, 680, 686, 693, 701, 714, 715, 717, 719, 720, 721, 724
paroimiai, 170
Parousia, 183, 328, 406, 424, 469, 492, 494
paroxysm, 277
passion narrative, 140, 223, 227
Pastoral Epistles, 240, 302, 395, 400, 401, 408, 721
Patara, 287
Patmos, 512, 523, 524
patriarchs, 180, 352
Paul: Apostle of the Heart Set Free, 297
Paulinism, 411
Paul's arrest and imprisonments, 338–43
Paul's first missionary journey, 275, 320–25
Paul's second missionary journey, 320, 327–33, 337

SCRIPTURE INDEX

Joshua
7 *258*
18:6 *8, 10, 252*
20:6 *105*

Judges
5:19 *549*
5:24 *118*
20:9 *252*

Ruth
2:19 *118*

1 Samuel
8:22 *105*
21:1–6 *65*
28:3 *105*

2 Samuel
12:1–10 *122*
19:37 *105*

1 Kings
6:22 *476*
17:7–24 *213*
21 *532*

2 Kings
2:11 *190*
4:8–37 *213*
9:27 *549*
13:20–21 *213*

1 Chronicles
24:5 *31, 252*
29:10–11 *633*

2 Chronicles
24:20 *90*
24:21 *90*
35:22 *549*

Ezra
2:1 *105*

Nehemiah
7:6 *105*
9:15 *203*

Job
9:8 *181, 691*

Psalms
1:1 *118*
2:7 *454*
2:9 *544*
2:12 *118*
16:8–11 *253*
16:10 *323*
32:1 *118*
33:12 *118*
34:20 *227*
65:7 *691*
69:25 *252*
77:19 *181, 691*
78:24–25 *203*
89:9 *691*
104:7 *690*
104:15 *194*
107:29 *691*
109:8 *252*
110:1 *253*
118:22 *256, 434*

Isaiah
6:3 *536*
6:9 *664*
6:10 *215*
8:14 *434*
12:3 *204*
22 *131*
22:22 *534*
25:6–8 *551*
28:16 *434*
35:5–6 *693*
40:8 *710*
41:4 *178*
42:1 *454*
43:10 *13, 178, 207*

Mark